The
Mergers
and
Acquisitions
Handbook

The Mergers and Acquisitions Handbook

Milton L. Rock
Editor in Chief

Publisher, Mergers & Acquisitions
and
Former Chairman and Chief Executive Officer
Hay Group, Inc., Philadelphia, Pennsylvania

McGraw-Hill Book Company

New York   St. Louis   San Francisco   Auckland   Bogotá
Hamburg   London   Madrid   Milan
Mexico   Montreal   New Delhi   Panama
Paris   São Paulo   Singapore
Sydney   Tokyo   Toronto

Library of Congress Cataloging-in-Publication Data

The Mergers and acquisitions handbook.

    1. Consolidation and merger of corporations—
United States—Handbooks, manuals, etc. I. Rock,
Milton L.
HD2746.5.M465   1987   658.1'6   86-7358
ISBN 0-07-053350-4

    34567890 DOC/DOC 893210987

ISBN 0-07-053350-4

The editors for this book were Martha Jewett and Lynne Lackenbach,
the designer was Naomi Auerbach, and the production supervisor
was Sally Fliess. It was set in Melior by Saybrook Press.

Printed and bound by R.R. Donnelley & Sons Company.

To Shirl, the best deal I ever made!

Contents

Contributors

P. Michael Baldasaro   Partner, Arthur Andersen & Co., New York, New York (CHAPTER 24)

Douglass M. Barnes   Vice President—Marketing, Lind Brothers, Inc., New York, New York (CHAPTER 39)

Roger E. Birk,   Chairman, Retired, Merrill Lynch & Co., Inc., New York, New York (CHAPTER 7)

William Blumenthal,   Sutherland, Asbill & Brennan, Washington, D.C. (CHAPTER 36)

Geoffrey T. Boisi,   Partner, Goldman, Sachs & Co., New York, New York (CHAPTER 32)

Paul Broderick,   Partner, Deloitte Haskins & Sells, Richmond, Virginia (CHAPTER 19)

Robert F. Calman,   Vice Chairman, IU International Corp., Philadelphia, Pennsylvania (CHAPTER 33)

Richard E. Cheney,   Vice Chairman, Hill & Knowlton, Inc., New York, New York (CHAPTER 40)

Thomas L. Chrystie,   Adviser on Strategy, Merrill Lynch & Co., New York, New York (CHAPTER 46)

Charles R. Cory,   Associate, Morgan Stanley & Co., Incorporated, New York, New York (CHAPTER 16)

Michael R. Dabney,   Vice President and General Manager, General Electric Credit Corp., Stamford, Connecticut (CHAPTER 35)

James B. Dwyer III,   Senior Vice President, E.F. Hutton & Company, Inc., New York, New York (CHAPTER 12)

William J. Edwards,   Manager, Corporate Financial Counseling, Arthur D. Little, Inc., Cambridge, Massachusetts (CHAPTER 2)

Mark Feldman,   Principal, Hay Group, Walnut Creek, California (CHAPTER 28)

William S. Fishman,   Chairman of the Executive Committee, ARA Services, Inc., Philadelphia, Pennsylvania (CHAPTER 5)

James C. Freund,   Partner, Skadden, Arps, Slate, Meagher & Flom, New York, New York (CHAPTER 17)

Jeffrey Garner,   Associate, Donaldson, Lufkin & Jenrette, New York, New York (CHAPTER 12)

H. Richard Grafer,   Partner, Arthur Andersen & Co., New York, New York (CHAPTER 24)

J. Terrence Greve,   Operating Partner, Wallner & Co., San Diego, California (CHAPTER 31)

Gilbert W. Harrison,   Chairman, Financo, Inc., Philadelphia, Pennsylvania, and Managing Director, Shearson Lehman Brothers, New York, New York (CHAPTER 45)

John W. Herz,   Partner, Wolf Haldenstein Adler Freeman & Herz, New York, New York (CHAPTER 13)

John J. Horan, *Chairman and Chief Executive Officer, Merck & Co., Inc., Rahway, New Jersey* (CHAPTER 8)

Walter I. Jacobs, *President, U.S. Consulting, Hay Group, Inc., Philadelphia, Pennsylvania* (CHAPTER 27)

William B. Johnson, *Chairman and Chief Executive Officer, IC Industries, Inc., Chicago, Illinois* (CHAPTER 4)

Robert G. Kirk, *Saatchi & Saatchi Co. PLC, London, United Kingdom* (CHAPTER 34)

Eugene Kotlarchuk, *Senior Vice President, Shearson Lehman Brothers, New York, New York* (CHAPTER 1)

Joe B. Leonard, *Executive Vice President, International Association of Merger and Acquisition Consultants, Dallas, Texas* (APPENDIX A)

Peter Lorange, *Chairman, Department of Management, Wharton School, University of Pennsylvania, Philadelphia, Pennsylvania* (CHAPTER 1)

Ken Martin, *Senior Principal, Hay Group, Chicago, Illinois* (CHAPTER 28)

Alan H. Molod, *Partner, Wolf, Block, Schorr & Solis-Cohen, Philadelphia, Pennsylvania* (CHAPTER 23)

Ned Morse, *Senior Principal, Hay Group, Dallas, Texas* (CHAPTER 28)

Charles M. Nathan, *Managing Director, Merrill Lynch Capital Markets, New York, New York* (CHAPTER 42)

James M. Needham, *Partner, National Director of Mergers and Acquisitions, Arthur Young & Co., New York, New York* (CHAPTER 25)

Albert T. Olenzak, *Vice President, Corporate Planning and Public Policy, Sun Co., Inc., Radnor, Pennsylvania* (CHAPTER 10)

Terrence M. O'Toole, *Associate, Goldman, Sachs, & Co., New York, New York* (CHAPTER 32)

Arthur D. Perrone, Jr., *President, Geneva Business Services, Inc., Costa Mesa, California* (CHAPTER 9)

Alfred Rappaport, *Leonard Spacek Professor of Accounting and Information Systems, J. L. Kellogg Graduate School of Management, Northwestern University, Evanston, Illinois, and Chairman, The Alcar Group, Inc., Skokie, Illinois* (CHAPTER 15)

Judson P. Reis, *Managing Director, Morgan Stanley & Co., Incorporated, New York, New York* (CHAPTER 16)

Rory Riggs, *First Vice President, PaineWebber, Inc., Capital Markets, New York, New York* (CHAPTER 18)

Herald L. Ritch, *Vice President, Mergers & Acquisitions Department, Kidder, Peabody & Co., Inc., New York, New York* (CHAPTER 11)

Andrew D. Robertson, *Vice President, First National Bank of Chicago, Chicago, Illinois* (CHAPTER 20)

Christopher Roe, *Production Editor, Mergers & Acquisitions, Philadelphia, Pennsylvania* (CHAPTER 14)

Kenneth I. Rosenblum, *Dimensional Fund Advisors, Inc., Santa Monica, California* (CHAPTER 38)

Douglas E. Rosenthal, *Sutherland, Asbill & Brennan, Washington, D.C.* (CHAPTER 36)

Andrew M. Rouse, *Executive Vice President, CIGNA Corp., Philadelphia, Pennsylvania* (CHAPTER 26)

Malcolm I. Ruddock, *Director, Acquisitions and Divestments, Sun Co., Inc., Radnor, Pennsylvania* (CHAPTER 10)

Sam F. Segnar, *Chairman and Chief Executive Officer, Retired, HNG/InterNorth, Inc., Houston, Texas* (CHAPTER 6)

Kenneth P. Shapiro, *President, Hay/Huggins Co., Inc., Philadelphia, Pennsylvania* (CHAPTER 27)

Robert E. Shields, *Partner, Drinker Biddle & Reath, Philadelphia, Pennsylvania* (CHAPTER 22)

Martin Sikora, *Editor, Mergers & Acquisitions, Philadelphia, Pennsylvania* (CHAPTERS 37 and 43)

Harbir Singh, *Assistant Professor of Management, Wharton School, University of Pennsylvania, Philadelphia, Pennsylvania* (CHAPTER 1)

W. Peter Slusser, *Managing Director, PaineWebber, Inc., Capital Markets, New York, New York* (CHAPTER 18)

William St. John, *Executive Director, Association for Corporate Growth, Glenview, Illinois* (APPENDIX B)

Robert W. Taft, *Senior Vice President, Hill & Knowlton, Inc., New York, New York* (CHAPTER 40)

Donald C. Trauscht, *Vice President, Borg-Warner Corp., Chicago, Illinois* (CHAPTER 44)

Stephen M. Waters, *Managing Director, Shearson Lehman Brothers, New York, New York* (CHAPTER 41)

J. Fred Weston, *Cordner Professor of Money and Financial Markets, Graduate School of Management, University of California at Los Angeles, Los Angeles, California* (CHAPTER 3)

William L. White, *Principal, Towers Perrin Forster & Crosby, Los Angeles, California* (CHAPTER 30)

Michael Wise, *Associate Counsel, Midwest Stock Exchange, Inc., Chicago, Illinois* (CHAPTER 38)

Gary Wood, *Partner, Touche Ross & Co., Detroit, Michigan* (CHAPTER 29)

Guy P. Wyser-Pratte, *Executive Vice President, Prudential-Bache Securities, New York, New York* (CHAPTER 21)

Leonard Zweig, *Editor-in-Chief and Associate Publisher, Mergers & Acquisitions, Philadelphia, Pennsylvania* (CHAPTER 14)

Preface

Over the last several decades, mergers and acquisitions, and the related field of divestitures, have evolved into integral elements within the strategic plans of well-managed businesses. By the mid-1980s, the practice of mergers and acquisitions had become a fine business art, if not a science, a well-planned, deftly executed business maneuver that stands in marked contrast to the legendary but often haphazard approach to corporate buying and selling of bygone years. Recognition of the elevated status of mergers and acquisitions and the way in which they have expanded to touch virtually every corner of the modern business world have prompted the development of *The Mergers and Acquisitions Handbook*.

A compendium of state-of-the-art knowledge and practice in every facet of mergers and acquisitions, and divestitures, the *Handbook* delivers expert commentary on sound valuation of target companies, appropriate prices to pay, successful integration of merging concerns, corporate redeployment to increase shareholder value, and the global aspects of M&A, to name but a few of the areas covered. Each chapter has been prepared by a distinguished professional who has gained his or her expertise by practicing a relevant discipline on the M&A firing line.

The Mergers and Acquisitions Handbook is aimed at the practicing professional who, although skilled in one discipline, may need quick access to information about complementary talents and disciplines. But it also can be used by the professional or the business executive who needs merger and acquisition information only from time to time. The *Handbook* may be read from cover to cover by those who wish to steep themselves in the romance of M&A, or specific chapters may be isolated for easy reading by those whose needs are more focused.

Milton L. Rock

Introduction

If there is one unifying theme of *The Mergers and Acquisitions Handbook*, it is the maturation of the process by which American business buys and sells its operations. A basically unsystematic, opportunistic, even hit-or-miss proposition as recently as 20 years ago, merger, acquisition, and divestiture activity by the mid-1980s had evolved into a sophisticated, technologically oriented, and strategically established exercise employed by businesses of all sizes, configurations, industry characteristics, and ownership structures. It is a metamorphosis that I personally have tracked, not only as a close observer, but as a first-hand participant at virtually all levels.

I can attest to the "growing up" of M&A as an analyst-commentator, as a consultant to both buying and selling companies, as an acquirer, and most recently, as a seller of my own concern, The Hay Group, an international management consulting company, in one of the $100 million transactions of 1984. My experiences, moreover, have influenced heavily the structure, format, and contents of *The Mergers and Acquisitions Handbook*. From the very earliest points of its conception, we determined that the *Handbook* was not to be just another "how-to-do-it" book, a lecture in print, but a practical guide to every stage and facet of the M&A process, based on actual experiences, empirical evidence, and the realities of the modern demands of mergers, acquisitions, and divestitures.

But the *Handbook* introduces still another concept that is unique—so unexpected that it did not become clear until I was exploring the various alternatives for the future of The Hay Group before deciding to sell it: that is, the idea that the target or selling company may actually be an acquirer. Almost by definition, a book on mergers and acquisitions must focus primarily on the acquiring company. It is, after all, the acquirer that must justify the purchase and then make it work for the benefit of the company. But what I learned was that a target can also acquire much in a properly structured transaction; that it can play a large role in both its own future and that of the buyer; and, as I will detail later, that it has much to offer in return for what it "acquires" from the buyer. As a result, wherever possible, we have included extensive information directed primarily at the seller—its rights, responsibilities, negotiating strategies, what it should expect from a buyer, and other elements that can enhance its prospects under new ownership.

The Mergers and Acquisitions Handbook provides the framework for harnessing the techniques that have worked in the M&A marketplace and communicating them to the people who can use them to devise and implement profitable long-range strategies, promote business growth, and maximize shareholder value. Our authors represent a remarkably diverse array of professional disciplines, each of which is required at some phase of an M&A project. They have achieved singular eminence in their fields and have honed their skills in the M&A trenches. Each has concentrated directly on a field of expertise. With the serial presentation of the *Handbook*, a reader can cover the entire breadth of the M&A procedure—from strategic planning umbrella to the ticklish job of postmerger integration—or zero in on one or more specific facets without loss of continuity.

Part 1 covers strategic planning, use of models in planning, and potential payoffs in mergers and acquisitions.

Part 2 gives case histories of some recent mergers and acquisitions.

Part 3 discusses internal acquisition teams, pursuit of candidates, utilization of finders, and M&A software and data bases.

Part 4 covers valuation procedures, negotiating, forms of payment, tax planning, financing, and arbitrage.

Part 5 comments on closing services, paperwork, and due diligence.

Part 6 covers postmerger integration activities, including a case history of a successful blending of two brewing companies.

Part 7 discusses leveraged buy-outs, mergers of equals, divestitures, international acquisitions, and asset-based financing.

Part 8 includes antitrust guidelines, the regulatory climate, stock exchange reporting rules, proxy battles, public relations, takeover insurance, and defensive tactics.

Part 9 reports M&A experiences in the high-technology, retail, and banking industries.

The Appendixes describe three associations of M&A specialists.

EVOLUTION OF THE HAY GROUP

It is not an exaggeration to say that the seeds for *The Mergers and Acquisitions Handbook* were planted when I joined Hay as a freshly minted PhD out of the University of Rochester in 1949 and that they sprouted over the next three-and-a-half decades as Hay grew into one of the world's foremost consulting organizations. In the late 1940s, Hay, although it already had achieved considerable distinction in the then developing fields of personnel compensation and evaluation, was but a young firm with only three employees and a single office in my home city of Philadelphia. At our acquisition by Saatchi & Saatchi PLC, a UK-based, worldwide advertising organization, in December 1984, we operated 94 offices in 27 countries, employed more than 750 professional consultants and provided an enormous range of quality consulting services to corporations, government agencies, and institutions around the globe.

I became managing partner in 1958 and supervised a development strategy that involved a balanced blending of *de novo* expansion with selected acquisitions. In 1974, Hay acquired Huggins & Co., a firm founded in 1911 that provides pension, benefit, and actuarial evaluation services and was an excellent fit with our compensation consulting practice. Four years later, MSL Group International was acquired to give Hay capabilities in selection, recruitment, and placement of high-level corporate executives. Hay Career Counseling, added in 1980, provides outplacement services to management personnel. At the same time, a good-sized portion of Hay's basic consulting practice was related to merger and acquisition work. We have helped our clients select acquisition targets, assisted them in preacquisition analysis of suitable candidates, worked with them on negotiations, guided their development of strategic plans, and, as a logical extension of our management consulting specialties, developed programs for postmerger integration. Our Huggins Financial Services unit even has its own M&A department with the capability of providing complete intermediary services on a thoroughly professional and confidential basis.

Still another of my credentials in the M&A field is as publisher of *Mergers & Acquisitions*, the authoritative professional journal that details state-of-the-art technology and the most relevant, up-to-date information for practicing professionals in the M&A field. The editors of *Mergers & Acquisitions* were my primary associates in development and production of *The Mergers and Acquisitions Handbook*. In my role as publisher, I have commented extensively on key trends and issues in M&A, and maintained close communications with the heavyweights of the profession by chairing our quarterly roundtable discussions and through involvement in *Mergers & Acquisitions'* annual Advanced Issues Conference. As part of the terms of Saatchi & Saatchi's acquisition of Hay, I purchased *Mergers & Acquisitions* and now am the owner as well as publisher.

REACHING A CROSSROADS

But while I have literally seen the merger and acquisition business from every angle, my most significant adventure was the sale of Hay to Saatchi & Saatchi. The size of the deal is just one criterion. There were so many other important aspects of the deal—some unique, others exemplifications of what a typical aggressive, growth-minded business goes through in trying to provide for future expansion and continuity—that recounting our experiences forms a worthwhile gateway into the heart of *The Mergers and Acquisitions Handbook*. Among other things, our acquisition very well could become a prototype for valuing human resources businesses, and it underscored how a target could be an acquirer as well.

Despite careful monitoring and nurturing of our growth strategies and our fine internal financial management, we had by the mid-1980s determined that a bold new course was needed. Hay had become the foremost human resources organization in the world, and we had defined the areas—both within existing operations and in promising new ventures—that satisfied our aims for growth and profitability. The question was whether we had the financial and other resources to carry through and attract the skilled professionals we needed. We faced the traditional difficulties of a partnership in raising expansion capital, and our problems were compounded because retirement was imminent for several of our senior partners, threatening enormous drains on both finances and talent.

If much of this sounds familiar to any businessman or corporate executive trying to plan intelligently for the future, it should. But let me overlay the orthodox scenario with some complications that seldom bother the bakers of gingerbread, the builders of jet planes, the drillers for oil, the operators of electric utilities, the sellers of food and apparel, or the captains of railroads. Our physical assets were nil. Our primary assets, as with many service companies, were our human resources—Hay's people, expertise, contacts, reputation, clientele, and, to a lesser extent, the plethora of data gathered through more than four decades of consulting practice. These are hard to offer as collateral to a bank, harder to value in setting a price for a potential buyer, and often not too appealing to a seemingly compatible business that may be a suitable acquisition target but wants something with deeper pockets.

Thus, much of my time in the last few years has been consumed by exploring the options available to Hay in guaranteeing continuity and the financial resources for growth. Mergers and acquisitions—in either direction—were among many alternatives. We explored conversion to a corporate structure, a leveraged buy-out, and the securing of venture capital. A public offering was studied, although with full acknowledgment that stocks of service companies had not fared well. Joint ventures were scrutinized. And, of course, mergers and acquisitions were high on the list. We looked at consulting firms, insurance brokers, and other specialized service businesses that we might buy, as well as insurance companies, accounting firms, and consulting operations that might have purchased Hay, or joined forces with us in some type of business relationship.

As we continued to weigh the options, we developed alternative plans and criteria for use on whatever path we chose. For example, we determined that if Hay was acquired, the buyer would have to offer a culture match. It would have to be an entrepreneurial, dynamic, professional organization that was of large size, but not bureaucratic—obviously, not a buyer that falls out of the trees just by shaking the branches. This ruled out many prospective acquirers—and lots of opportunities on both sides came our way—including several large financial services organizations that were seeking to diversify into compatible nonfinancial services. One business that became more and more appealing the harder we studied it was advertising. Our independent conclusion proved to be quite prophetic.

THE MATCHING OF CULTURES

Saatchi & Saatchi came to us almost through the back door. Lehman Brothers, the prestigious investment banking firm, was aware of our interest in possible merger partners and also was representing Saatchi & Saatchi in its search for service businesses that would allow it to diversify. Saatchi & Saatchi is the largest advertising organization in the world, with agencies in more than 40 countries. Its U.S. agencies are Compton Advertising, McCaffrey & McCall, Backer & Spielvogel, and Ted Bates, long major factors in American advertising circles. An extremely well-managed business that has enjoyed immense growth just in advertising, Saatchi & Saatchi nonetheless was seriously interested in broadening its base of operations to provide other profitable and useful services to corporate clients. At about the same time that Saatchi & Saatchi acquired Hay, it also pressed its diversification strategy by purchasing a leading market and opinion research firm and a major mailing list organization. But when Lehman approached us, it did not have a direct Hay-Saatchi & Saatchi hookup in mind. Rather, it wanted our assistance in valuing and pricing a consulting business in the merger marketplace, which, as noted earlier, is no small feat considering the marked difference in the elements of worth that differentiate a human resources organization from a more orthodox business.

But having already identified a well-managed advertising firm—with its aggressiveness, creativity, entrepreneurial flair, and business and institutional clientele—as being compatible with Hay, we inquired whether talks with Saatchi might be useful. Our initial examination suggested a strong commonality of culture between the two organizations—including the extensive international experience and commitment of both. We could offer Saatchi not only a major diversification vehicle but also instant access to a high-quality business advisory services market on a global basis. Lehman arranged a meeting in London where Hay is well known, thanks to a large, active installation that has been providing quality consulting service to British businesses for many years.

Our initial purpose was to explore whether our cultures fit or clashed. I am convinced that this has to be a critical starting point for any M&A transaction. If two merger partners are not *simpatico* in style and approach to doing business, the transaction has two strikes against it from the start, and the prospects for a successful integration are dim. In fact, this theme is echoed in the chapters by Sam Segnar on InterNorth, Inc., and Bill Fishman on ARA Services, who describe compatibility as an essential ingredient in the earliest stages of merger talks. But while Bill and Sam are astutely attuned to the importance of people in running their businesses, I faced an even more extensive problem. People did more than just run Hay. They were Hay. Fortunately, I discovered that Saatchi & Saatchi was of like mind, not only about its own people but about the people who would come with the new businesses in different fields that they would acquire. This gave me the opportunity at this most preliminary of meetings to press two key points: Hay's need for assured continuity so that it could function as a viable growth business; and the reasons Hay would gain these advantages as part of another company. It was, in short, the way a target company actually could become an "acquirer."

Progress was remarkably swift. We confirmed the similarity of cultures and the mesh of strategies and agreed quickly that a price acceptable to both sides should be calculated. That was the easy part. Our next step, in concert with Lehman, was to develop a "blue book" that described Hay, stated its results for the last five years, and detailed its projections for the next three. Since a partnership does not represent traditional financial values in the merger market, it was necessary to reconstitute all relevant financial data—balance sheets, P&L statements, changes in position, etc.—as if Hay had operated as a corporation, and to shape the projections on a corporate basis as well. There also were some anxious moments over treatment of goodwill, but this issue faded quickly because English accounting rules then did not recognize goodwill.

But the most vexing problem by far was establishment of a price on human resources—on skills, talent, creativity, ingenuity, dedication, reputation, clientele, and a franchise that is firmly established in the bitterly competitive international marketplace. Further complicating the number crunching was that the problem had to be dealt with on a number of levels. One was the retention of qualified personnel, especially with several partners nearing retirement. The solution was to assign a substantial portion of the eventual purchase price—$25 million out of a total compensation of up to $125 million—to a contingency payment arrangement, pegged to the performance of key Hay personnel over a three-year period.

A VALUE ON HUMAN RESOURCES

Even the incentive plan, however, was a simple resolution compared with the broader problem of fixing a value on human resources. We were operating in virtually virgin territory. Consulting firms are not regularly bought and sold in the merger market, and rules of thumb are even rarer. It boiled down to a question of exactly what is an asset.

We literally had to write new rules in many cases. We could zero in initially on the signed contracts we had as well as on the small amount of physical assets that we owned. There was value in the Hay name, franchise, and international network. But above all, there were our people. We systematically inventoried our strengths, assigned values to them as best we could, and calculated what they could contribute to a combined Hay and Saatchi & Saatchi organization. Finally, we examined the value of linkage or synergy. At the very least, synergy would arise because our large base of clients could become prospects for other services offered by a combined organization. At the ultimate, we would be taking part in the formation of a truly global company with capabilities of offering an extraordinary wide range of business services, interchanging varied forms of expertise, and accessing every conceivable element of the corporate world in need of professional assistance.

When we put all these pieces together, we arrived at a basic purchase price of $100 million, plus $25 million incentive payments over a three-year period. Saatchi & Saatchi saw the same value in human resources that Hay did. Negotiations went smoothly and swiftly. It took just eight weeks from the signing of a letter of agreement to the closing of the deal on December 12, 1984. On a purely financial basis, the price was in effect modest. The price was roughly equal to Hay's fiscal 1984 revenues, only 10 times 1984 pretax earnings and six times projected 1985 pretax earnings. The stock market ratified our valuation computations and the concept of a global total service company. Saatchi & Saatchi raised the purchase money by selling $100 million worth of stock on the London Stock Exchange, increasing its number of outstanding shares by a third. The offer not only sold out in a matter of hours, but the share price actually rose by 15 percent.

Our reliance on people also demanded deft handling of postmerger integration. We had to recast Hay as a corporate subsidiary, assigning commensurate corporate titles and responsibilities to former partners and erecting an appropriate compensation schedule. My title, for example, changed from managing partner to chairman and chief executive officer. But the former Hay management team remains basically in place, and is free to run the company with complete autonomy. We also have created important linkages with other service arms of the Saatchi organization to pursue joint opportunities and exchange information and know-how. We were careful in planning the transition, mindful that the bang-bang pace at which the deal was consummated would force us to spring the announcement as a surprise to most Hay personnel. We set up immediate postannouncement meetings at every Hay office. A Hay senior official, fully briefed on every aspect of the sale, explained in detail exactly why the transaction took place, described Saatchi & Saatchi and its management style, delineated the effects on the future of Hay and its employees, affirmed Hay's continued management autonomy, and even examined Hay's financial picture. Probing questions were encouraged and answered frankly. Follow-up discussions were held when requested. At the same time, we prepared for the inevitable barrage of questions from the outside—from the press, the investment community, clients, suppliers, et al. Again, senior Hay people were available to deal with our interested constituencies.

Happily, life has gone on at Hay with an absolute minimum of disruption. Those people who planned to retire or leave before the merger have moved on to other endeavors, but the loss of personnel as a result of Hay's new status has been insignificant.

Our enthusiasm for the merger and the subsequent maintenance of spirit and morale at Hay are very much functions of the concept of the acquired company as an actual "acquirer." We have delivered much to Saatchi, for which it has paid a price considered fair by both sides. But Hay also has acquired much and stands to acquire even more in the future. For starters, the purchase price infused us with sufficient capital to "cash out" the senior partners as rewards for their role in making Hay a valuable target, without breaking the treasury. However, Hay's gain over the longer run is even more substantial. Hay has acquired continuity—the financial and other resources to recruit talented professionals, expand existing operations, extend our geographic scope, upgrade our technology, and push into profitable new areas of consulting services. We have acquired the corporate sponsorship and support of an organization with great prestige and eminence in its own field, and a strong but hands-off appreciation of Hay's abilities. We have acquired access to a range of other professional disciplines that can be useful to Hay and to the other parts of Saatchi.

The decision to sell is never easy. It wasn't for me or for the other partners at Hay. But selling doesn't have to mean selling out. Indeed, the concept of the target company as an acquirer may be one of the leading symbols of the maturity of the mergers and acquisitions process, which is what *The Mergers and Acquisitions Handbook* is all about. As one who has paid his dues in the M&A business, I wish you enjoyable reading and fervently hope that you can make profitable use of the vast lore of information that we have synthesized in the *Handbook*.

Milton L. Rock

ACKNOWLEDGMENTS

I express my deepest appreciation to the current and former personnel of *Mergers & Acquisitions*, the quarterly journal serving practicing professionals in the M&A field, whose talents and energies helped bring *The Mergers and Acquisitions Handbook* to fruition.

Alexandra Reed Lajoux, former editor of *Mergers & Acquisitions*, got the project off to a superb start by conceptualizing the *Handbook*, selecting the topics that required specific in-depth discussion, and enlisting the expert authors whose works appear in the following chapters.

Martin Sikora, current editor of *Mergers & Acquisitions*, tirelessly edited and refined each chapter to assure that it delivered the maximum in useful and practical information in the most readable fashion. He also contributed two chapters, supplied supplementary material, worked directly with the authors, and monitored the editing process to assure timely publication. He was assisted by Christopher M. Roe of the *Mergers & Acquisitions* staff and Andrew Elston, former managing editor of *Mergers & Acquisitions*.

Leonard Zweig, editor-in-chief of *Mergers & Acquisitions*, provided enormous supervisory support, further refining each chapter and often identifying information gaps that needed filling.

And of course, I thank each of the authors who willingly shared expertise and experience with us.

Part 1

Planning and Strategic Issues

Chapter 1

Corporate Acquisitions: A Strategic Perspective

Peter Lorange

Chairman, Department of Management, Wharton School,
University of Pennsylvania, Philadelphia, Pennsylvania

Eugene Kotlarchuk

Senior Vice President, Shearson Lehman Brothers,
New York, New York

Harbir Singh

Assistant Professor of Management, Wharton School,
University of Pennsylvania, Philadelphia, Pennsylvania

The diversified company that uses strategic planning to provide for its long-term survival constantly faces the choice of acquisition versus internal development to achieve growth. The decision should be geared to the basic strategy of the concern. Long-term survival of any corporation depends on its continued ability to develop strength relative to its competitors. Success in achieving this strength depends on the ability to shift resources from well-established, mature business activities to emerging business activities with growth potential. Within this ongoing process of self-renewal, the company must decide whether, given its basic strategy, it is better off shifting these resources through acquisitions or through redistribution among existing entities.

BUSINESS STRATEGIES

A diversified firm may have a hierarchy of business strategies. The strategic self-renewal process may take place at each level within the hierarchy. Acquisitions facilitate the strategic self-renewal at the portfolio level, the business family level, and the business element level.

The Portfolio Strategy. The philosophy at this level is to develop a set of interrelated businesses that provide reasonable balance and stability within the firm. The portfolio of businesses may be developed purely on financial bases and ignore relationships of technologies or markets among the businesses. Alternatively, the portfolio may be put together by joining businesses that are to some degree related in terms of technology, know-how, or product-market niches. The latter type of portfolio development will build an underlying theme for the interrelationships among the businesses, perhaps in the form of an essential or core skill. Planning for an acquisition in this context involves a search for business entities that will balance and strengthen the firm's overall portfolio theme.

The Business Family Strategy. The strategic challenge at this level is to formulate a set of closely related business activities that tend to build upon a common technology or know-how base as it applies to the acquirer's business practices. The acquisition is used to develop related new business activities. The business family strategy thus yields a group of interrelated businesses that allow the firm to exploit shared resources in technology, product markets, or distribution channels, and to build new businesses from the foundations of existing units. Acquisitions may be dictated by the need to enter new growth markets that permit the firm to apply its established base. Alternatively, acquisitions might be made to absorb an existing resource base and the know-how embodied in an already well-established business.

The Business Element Strategy. The strategic challenge at this level is to develop a competitive product/market strategy (vis-à-vis a given competitor) for capturing a particular customer. Success depends on developing competitive strength in a specific business segment. An acquisition under this strategy may be a means to a greater market share by takeover of a competitor. Such a move potentially can strengthen the firm's internal operations by broadening its product and/or service spectrum while simultaneously reducing competition.

ALTERNATIVE ACQUISITION APPROACHES

In strategic planning for acquisitions, a firm must decide which of these three strategies it is pursuing and then determine how an acquisition may, at a given strategic level, enhance its self-renewal. The essence of an acquisition, then, is to create a strategic advantage by paying for an existing business and integrating that entity with the firm's strategy at either the portfolio strategy, business family, or business element level.

The incentive to acquire exists when acquisition is more cost-effective than is internal development. For an acquisition to be viable, these conditions must apply:

- The price that is paid must be lower than the total resources necessary for internal development of a comparable strategic position.
- The anticipated benefits must reflect a generation of future values as part of the portfolio, business family, or business element strategy.

The intelligent acquirer must consider carefully what it is buying, and how the acquisition fits into its organization. What know-how is being bought? How productive is this know-how? Can meaningful synergy be developed between existing organizational entities and the acquired entity? It is impossible to calculate the benefit from the acquisition without assessing the synergistic value of the purchase, a process that goes far beyond a simple valuation of the assets and liabilities listed on the balance sheet.

Planning can expose the variety of reasons for making a corporate acquisition as well as the variations in anticipated benefits from the combinations of two firms. Acquisition of an ongoing business implies the purchase of a set of income-generating resources. But within that guideline, there are several different types of acquisitions, just as there are different strategy approaches. The types of acquisitions can be classified as horizontal, vertical, concentric, or unrelated (conglomerate) acquisitions.

Horizontal Acquisitions.   One firm acquires another firm in the same industry. The principal anticipated benefits from this type of acquisition are economies of scale in production and distribution, and possible increases in market power in a more concentrated industry. The primary impetus for strategic analysis of a horizontal acquisition would originate at the business element level. Benefits to the acquirer would be primarily in the form of a strengthened product-market strategic position.

Vertical Acquisitions.   The acquiring and target firms are in industries with strong supplier-buyer relationships. The acquired firm is either a supplier or a customer of the acquiring firm. Vertical acquisition usually is undertaken when the market for the intermediate product is imperfect, because of scarcity of resources, criticality of the purchased products, and control over production specifications of the intermediate product, among other reasons. Strategic analysis for making vertical acquisitions could reside at the business element level or at the business family level of the acquirer. At the business element level, vertical acquisitions that narrowly affect a specific product-market might be considered. At the business family level, acquisitions that benefit a group of business elements (and have transferable and broader resources) might be proposed.

Concentric Acquisitions. The acquirer and target firms are related through basic technologies, production processes, or markets. The acquired firm represents an extension of the product lines, market participations, or technologies of the acquiring firm. Concentric acquisitions represent an outward move by the acquiring firm from its current set of businesses into contiguous businesses. Benefits could be from economies of scope (exploitation of a shared resource) and, ideally, from entry into a related market having higher returns than the acquirer formerly enjoyed. The benefit potential to the acquirer is high, because these acquisitions offer opportunities to diversify around a common core of strategic resources. Concentric acquisitions could affect different business families in the acquiring firm. Thus, the primary planning and analysis might be at the corporate level, to promote a unifying theme among the firm's entities.

Unrelated or Conglomerate Acquisitions. These transactions are not aimed explicitly at shared resources, technologies, synergies, or product-market strategies. Rather, the focus is on how the acquired entity can enhance the overall stability and balance in the firm's total portfolio, in terms of better use and generation of resources. Strategic analysis for conglomerate acquisitions should be done at the corporate level and be incorporated in the portfolio strategy of the acquiring firm.

VALUATION OF AN ACQUISITION CANDIDATE

After the broad strategic criteria have been developed, the potential acquirer must affix values to specific acquisition candidates in line with the basic strategy that is being pursued. These questions must be addressed:

- *What is the strategic rationale for the acquisition?* The acquirer must determine which of the three basic strategies the transactions fits and then articulate the intended advantages the target will bring to the appropriate strategy.
- *Is it better to buy than develop internally?* The acquirer is forced into an assessment of the costs and benefits of reaching a particular business configuration through various types of mergers, internal development, or a combination of actions. The acquisition should be evaluated in relation to alternative modes of achieving a desired strategic position.
- *What resources does the acquisition bring beyond the financial statements?* The acquirer must assess the managerial quality of the target, the specific know-how of the target management, whether the target management will produce results after the acquisition, and whether the target management is likely to become unmotivated or leave. In addition, the acquirer should calculate its own expenditure of nonfinancial resources such as the cost of managerial time involved in making the acquisition work.
- *Are there discrepancies in the value that result from different viewpoints within the acquiring firm?* The acquirer must ask itself whether the acquisi-

tion is largely "political"—and based on the subjective judgments of some managers—or objective, and based on facts and firm criteria. If a large discrepancy between these two viewpoints exists, it is a warning that care must be taken and, if the discrepancies cannot be resolved, that the valuation procedure probably has not been sufficiently thorough.

Internal Development versus Acquisition

The choice between internal development and acquisition is determined largely by the costs and benefits, including important opportunity cost factors, which are often overlooked. These factors relate to the degree of "disturbance," or internal motivational dysfunction that might occur as a result of an acquisition.

Acquisition itself means that resources will have to be channeled from ongoing business activities to pay for the transaction. Since these resources could have been used for internal development, the existing organization might resist use of resources for outside purchases, and managements of existing businesses could lose motivation. Another potential source of loss of motivation is the disturbance that an acquisition unavoidably creates in the ongoing business activities of the organization. New people must be integrated into the functioning of the organization, new managerial assignments made, and new relationships developed. These integration activities take time, create human tension, and expend organizational energy.

The very fact that a firm is willing to pursue its strategies through acquisitions may have dysfunctional impact on its internal operations. Commitment to pursuing new business through internal means transmits an explicit message to the organization that top management has confidence in incumbent personnel. A strong negative motivational effect may be created by the firm that oscillates between internal development and acquisitions, because such a strategy may transmit mixed signals to the operating personnel. Commitment to internal excellence needs to be explicitly fostered in such an environment.

Because of these disruptions, and because strategic planning for acquisitions is highly judgmental, the relative success or advantage of an acquisition may be subject to controversy within an organization, depending on the points of view of its various elements. Management may find it advantageous to pursue an acquisition that adds know-how, develops competitive strength, or extends the scope of an existing business. These offer potential long-term payoffs, but they may create short-term problems in the form of the aforementioned internal disruptions. Therefore, members of the organization below top management might not share in the enthusiasm. Stockholders may like the acquisition if it offers long-term value to their holdings or maximization of profits. Again, however, organizational and political forces could impair the increase in value perceived by stockholders. Careful planning takes these disparate points of view into account.

Setting the Premium: Initial Considerations

A question often asked is: "What is the appropriate premium over market price to pay for a public company?" An acquirer that owns controlling interest in a company, sets profitability goals, and actively intervenes in strategy implementation expects to receive gains and often is willing to use part of them to pay a premium above the company's market value.

Many acquirers justify their acquisitions and acquisition prices on expected synergies. Examples include a new product line that fits the acquirer's present distribution channels, a raw product supplier that assures a manufacturer's uninterrupted needs at reasonable prices, and a seasonal business that buys a counterseasonal business to smooth the revenue stream.

Premiums paid for acquisitions recently have been significant, but it is questionable whether some of the high premiums will ever be recouped in adequate returns on investment. Perhaps some acquisitions are made for other than purely financial reasons. For example, some acquirers believe that they must pay a high premium for a target to assure their own survival, even if an adequate return on investment is never realized. The buyer may have decided that internal development is not feasible or that establishing a similar set of specialized resources on its own is more expensive. Such an acquirer would be willing to pay a significant premium. Even though the deal may be perceived as overpriced, the acquirer at least may regain part of its previous competitiveness, and assure its continued viability and growth.

An acquirer may buy another company to improve its financial position, in real terms or to convey a perception of a more secure financial position to the financial markets. For example, an acquirer with intensive research and development programs that is a heavy user of cash may acquire a heavy cash generator to fund its R&D needs. Acquisition of a cash generator might favorably affect the buyer's stock price and make it easier to raise money in the public marketplace through sale of securities. If the company is private, an improved cash flow position may reduce the cost of bank debt or enhance prospects of securing funds through a private placement.

Some acquisitions are secured at high premiums because of unrealistic assessments of future events. Most key methods for evaluating purchase price offers involve discounting of future income streams, which are based on assumptions of future performance of the company, future economic expectations, and future earnings increases through synergies. If the assumptions are too optimistic, overly generous premiums may never be recouped.

If survival or competition in a set of industries over the long term is the determining factor, an acquisition premium may be justifiable to the buying management. But before paying such premiums, management would be wise to study carefully (and seek opinions from third parties) whether internal development is the better course of action.

Determinants of the Premium

The extent of the premium to be paid is a key element in the decision to acquire a business. The purchase price usually is higher than the current value of a business, primarily because stockholders of the target company need an incentive to transfer control to another owner. The acquirer should start to calculate an offer by investigating the gap between the target's current market value and the value that the target will take on when it becomes part of the purchasing company. At the very least, these gains should exceed the amount paid over current value (on the premium).

The challenge in deciding the premium arises from the fact that the gains from an acquisition are contingent upon a set of actions by the acquiring firm. The buyer's problem is compounded by the lack of perfect information on the target firm before acquisition. Further, top management of the acquiring firm should not assume that a specific premium can be decided upon before negotiation (in the case of a merger) or bidding (in the case of a tender offer) is initiated, because a hostile reaction to a particular offer could force the acquirer to raise the bid. The acquirer should be prepared with an initial price offer and a reservation (exit) price. It also would be useful to have a series of intermediate points at which to make bids. Sophisticated buyers regard the final premium as the outcome of negotiation or bidding, not as a predetermined figure. The final premium may well equal a predetermined figure. However, this would happen only if the dynamics of the negotiation or competitive bidding process went entirely as the acquirer expected.

STEPS IN THE ACQUISITION PROCESS

The acquiring corporation should prepare for the acquisition event through these four steps: identifying the acquisition strategy and screening criteria, selecting the screening approach, making the acquisition, and planning the postacquisition integration process. The acquiring corporation must decide how it will screen attractive acquisition targets. A formal acquisition screen to identify attractive companies initially subordinates their availability as takeover candidates and emphasizes other criteria. An opportunistic approach reviews only companies that are known or rumored to be available. The choice of acquisition screen will depend, in part, on whether the acquisition will be based on a portfolio, business family, or business element strategy.

Understanding Your Own Strengths and Weaknesses

Before a firm's strategy or acquisition goals can be met, top management must identify its own internal strengths and weaknesses in such areas as availability of management time to accomplish the acquisition, finances, management quality, culture, organization, research and development, marketing, reputation in the marketplace, and long-term strategy. Although this step may seem obvious, many corporations treat it lightly and, based on inadequate knowledge of their own affairs, develop acquisition criteria that can lead to failure. These evaluations may be deemed unnecessary by an acquisition team if the acquisition search follows a strategic planning study or an ongoing planning effort. But practice has shown that even if the acquisition team is the same as the planning team, some important strengths and weaknesses are overlooked, especially those pertaining to the culture of the buying firm. Many strategic plans and analyses do not include an objective recognition of a company's culture. What is "culture"? Culture can be said to embody the beliefs and values of the company's management that influence the behavior of all the employees of the company. Culture includes management's perception of its image and identity, the company's work ethic, and its attitudes toward employees, customers, and the community.

If the acquirer does not explicitly identify its cultural match with the target firm, a tension-filled postacquisition period may ensue and result in the loss of management at both the acquirer and the acquired firm.

Developing Flexible Acquisition Criteria

After a firm understands its own strengths and weaknesses, and its strategic goals and alternatives, acquisition criteria can be developed. Criteria should be broad, yet specific enough to help the evaluating team recognize a potential fit. Specific criteria are especially important in reviewing opportunistic acquisition candidates. A realistic acquisition effort should not discard any leads on candidate companies. Many structured acquisition searches have become so rigid in scope that after a year or more of effort, no acquisition has resulted, or worse, a less attractive candidate is acquired because the opportunistic one was shunted aside very early.

Alternative Screening Approaches

The list of potentially attractive industries probably will be extensive even after obvious unsuitable candidates have been eliminated. To narrow the list further, the acquisition team should identify the industries with predicted favorable trends. Next, those industries that may prove synergistic to the acquirer's business should be highlighted. When a limited number of industries have been selected, companies in those industries should be examined to determine whether any are of the desired size that the buyer seeks.

The primary focus of this effort should be on the target's position in its industry segment, its perceived strengths and weaknesses compared to those of the acquirer, the target's potential financial results if it continues as an independent entity, and its positive or negative impact on the acquirer. The last factor is very important, because it will help in developing the price that realistically can be paid.

Opportunistic Approach

To reiterate, no leads on companies for sale should be discarded. One of those leads may fit the acquisition criteria better than any of the companies identified from any formal search. Thus, sufficiently specific criteria must exist so that an acquisition team readily can identify a potential fit, whether it comes in through the formal, structured acquisition program or through an outside broker network.

Analyzing Internal Development Alternatives

Before deciding on a specific acquisition, the acquirer should analyze on a case-by-case basis whether it is better off making the deal or pursuing the same ends through internal development. This step, often bypassed by acquirers, can help set the maximum price the buyer is willing to pay and give it one more chance to weigh the alternatives. Internal development studies often do not prod managements into action unless they are presented directly with viable alternatives such as acquisitions. But when there is a clear choice, based on adequate examination of the benefits and detriments of each route, management often has opted for internal development after a long period of dragging its feet.

Accordingly, an acquisition search should be viewed not as a *fait accompli*, but as a corporate development. The search may show that it is better for the company to proceed on an internal development course as soon as possible, so that it does not miss out on an emerging industry typified by a potential acquisition target. The acquisition search and the acquisition itself are but the culminations of the corporate goal and strategy. The search should be flexible enough to allow the corporation to decide on significant internal development in place of acquisition, if warranted.

Postacquisition Integration Plans

Preliminary postacquisition integration plans should be formulated even before negotiations take place. For example, if the target is very entrepreneurial and the acquirer is a large, structured company, it might be wise to state at the initial contact that the acquirer's intent is to have a hands-off policy after the merger if it wants to preserve the target's entrepreneurial flair. More important, however, the acquirer should anticipate some of the potential problems that may occur, particularly if relocation may be involved or if overlapping functions exist between merger partners. Integration plans should take into account personnel conflicts that may result from duplicate functions. Some recent methods used by corporations to ease the transition have included establishment of transition teams before the merger takes place, inviting management to social functions before and after the merger, and conducting attitude surveys on a confidential basis soon after the transaction is completed. In cases of conflicts, the acquirer should act swiftly even if the action is greeted unfavorably by some of the target company's management. Swift action may cause short-term losses, but it is better than a lingering conflict that will severely affect future performance of the company. The worst decision is to leave a conflict unresolved; this will lead to demoralized employees, lower productivity, and ultimately to lower stock values if news of such problems reaches the public.

Although a single generic strategy cannot be applied to all acquisitions, certain general tasks can be prescribed:

- Establishing which managers in the target company will be directly responsible for the target company or any of its activities after the acquisition.
- Planning for possible incentive compensation programs to motivate and assure retention of key managers of the target company.
- Developing probable reporting relationships and the degree of autonomy to be given the acquisition candidate.
- Analyzing which functions will probably be integrated and which will remain separate from the acquiring firm.
- Preparing for potential personnel conflicts, and identifying areas where such conflicts may occur. This will permit swift action in cases of irreconcilable differences and conflicts.
- Identifying cultural dissimilarities, deciding whether the functions that are not

integrated can or should retain their own cultures, and determining how cultural assimilation that is necessary can take place over time.

The exact recommendations for integration should depend on the type of acquisition that was consummated and on which of the three strategies the acquisition met. Table 1.1 shows some of the desirable integration approaches under the three strategies.

Integration of an acquired firm is an important factor in obtaining benefits from an acquisition. The acquired firm usually has some very desirable resources and some resources that are less desirable, and it is not easy to separate what the buyer wants to keep or emphasize and what it wants to divest or subordinate. This problem can be aggravated by cultural mismatches and the learning time the acquiring firm needs to determine how it will really increase the postacquisition revenues of the acquired firm. The main challenges after acquisition are the following:

- Setting a value on managerial know-how
- Determining whether to integrate the acquired firm or keep it independent
- Determining how to win commitment from the personnel of the acquired firm

An acquisition is based on the premise that some estimated gains (directly or implicitly) from the transaction will exceed the premium paid for the acquired firm. The postacquisition problems reside in the exploitation of these estimated

TABLE 1.1   Postacquisition Strategy Recommendations

Type of acquisition	Management integration	Functional integration	Long-term planning and control
Portfolio	Acquired firm should be autonomous.	Financial functions	Overall general plans
	Acquired firm should report to buyer's CEO or one level below CEO.		
Business family	Integrated organization and management.	Financial functions	Detailed operational plans and controls
	Reporting most appropriate at level below CEO (group vice president).	Marketing and distribution	
Business element	Integrated organization and management.	Financial functions	Most detailed operational plans and controls
	Reporting most appropriate at division level if kept unconsolidated. Most likely, target will be merged into acquirer's equivalent business.		

gains. Typically, this is a considerable challenge, because interaction between the acquirer and target company's management is very delicate. Winning commitment from the target management depends on the dynamics of the acquisition transaction (unfriendly takeover or merger) and the amount of cultural mismatch between the firms.

The integration of productive assets (physical facilities, production plants, distribution channels) is also an important dimension of the postacquisition challenge. A frequent reason for acquisition is the use of shared resources and the transferability of resources between firms. However, the cost of unbundling the target firm's resources may often exceed preacquisition estimates.

The management of corporate acquisitions is a complex and multidimensional process. We have shown how decision making for corporate acquisitions interacts with strategic planning in the large, diversified corporation. We note that the relationship between corporate strategy and acquisition analysis needs to be viewed in the larger context of the strategic planning process. We also note that this relationship does not translate into a simple set of decision rules that differentiate between successful and unsuccessful acquisitions. The emphasis on the diversification decision process enables managers to evaluate acquisition candidates against alternative modes of diversification, such as de novo entry or joint ventures. This emphasis also enables managers to address the important managerial challenges of the postacquisition period. Although not all problems associated with a given acquisition are fully foreseeable, this approach provides managers with an opportunity to deal with the more predictable postacquisition challenges.

Bibliography

Bradley, James, and Donald Korn, "The Changing Role of Corporate Acquisitions," *Journal of Business Strategy*, Spring 1982.

Lorange, Peter, *Corporate Planning: An Executive Viewpoint*, Prentice-Hall, Englewood Cliffs, N.J., 1980.

Rappaport, Alfred P., "Selecting Strategies That Create Shareholder Value," *Harvard Business Review*, May–June 1981.

Rumelt, Richard P., "Strategy, Structure and Economic Performance," Harvard University, Division of Research, Cambridge, Mass., 1974.

Salter, M. S., and W. Weinhold, *Diversification through Acquisition: Strategies for Creating Economic Value*, Free Press, New York, 1979.

Singh, Harbir, "Corporate Acquisitions and Economic Performance," University of Michigan, University Microfilms, Ann Arbor, 1984.

Steiner, Peter O., "Mergers: Motives, Effects and Policies," University of Michigan, Ann Arbor, 1975.

Yip, George S., *Barriers to Entry*, Lexington Books, Lexington, Mass., 1983.

Chapter 2

Planning Models for M&A Analysis

William J. Edwards

Manager, Corporate Financial Counseling,
Arthur D. Little, Inc., Cambridge, Massachusetts

"The more things change, the more they
remain the same."   ALPHONSE KARR, 1849

The use of models for analyzing and valuing acquisitions, mergers, and divestitures is neither a new nor a precise discipline. As a tool for decision making, modeling probably first appeared in the Stone Age, when people started to analyze and quantify the benefits to be derived from bartering for goods or services. Similarly, strategic analysis (the analysis of market demand, market share, competition, resource allocation, etc.) is not a recent phenomenon. The British and Dutch East India companies of the early 1600s were well versed in the economic advantages derived from market control.

The wave of merger, acquisition, and divestiture activity taking place during the 1980s has been attributed primarily to corporate America's rush to implement strategic plans. Many authoritative observers have characterized the strong activity as the era of strategy-driven mergers and acquisitions. Yet, to those who lived during the first quarter of this century or who have studied American business history, the 1980s wave of strategic merger and acquisition activity may not seem so new. Certainly, the motivations that underlie corporate America's recent tendency toward strategic consolidation are not new. They bear a striking resemblance to the economic principles embodied in the great basic-industry consolidations of the early twentieth century. The mergers and acquisitions that took place in the steel, railroad, oil, and automotive industries were implementations of ideas that focused on the objective of market control. The strategies formulated by Carnegie, Morgan, Gould, Rockefeller, Sloan, Ford, and other visionary magnates of that era were motivated by many of the same factors that drive the current wave of business consolidations.

The primary corporate objective of the industrial scions of the early twentieth century was not significantly different from that of their modern counterparts—namely, the maximization of stockholder wealth. There are, however, significant differences between the circumstances of the early twentieth century and those of the 1980s. The early corporations were controlled by the magnates themselves. Consequently, stockholder wealth was synonymous with personal wealth. Second, the lack of government regulations permitted these industrialists to base their strategy on a "monopolistic versus oligopolistic" view of the market. But despite these differences, there are many similarities in the business and economic principles that formed the basis for a corporate strategy of consolidation then and those that form the basis for such a strategy now. Although strategic consolidation is perhaps the primary force driving recent merger activity, a secondary force of importance is strategic diversification. The motivational forces that determine corporate America's diversification strategies also are not new. The era of business acquisitions and mergers that fell between World War II and the 1980s was characterized by American industry's emphasis on unrelated diversification. There were times during the heyday of the conglomerate merger, in the mid-1960s, when it was nearly impossible for the uninformed observer to understand the business rationale underlying the corporate plans being implemented. Yet the rush to build free-form conglomerates did have strategic underpinnings. The economic concept of amassing a portfolio of businesses that could minimize cyclicality embodied a method for reducing the risk of major fluctuations in earnings. The implementation of this strategy stabilized both earnings and dividends and was a financially motivated method for maximizing stockholders' wealth.

CREATION OF STOCKHOLDER VALUE

Strategic consolidation and strategic diversification are basically founded on the same corporate objective: the creation of stockholder value. To explain how these strategies have been used recently, it will be beneficial to describe them and differentiate between them from a historic perspective. Table 2.1 summarizes the key factors of the strategies of the early 1900s and the 1960s.

There are major differences between past strategies' factors and the factors driving the wave of acquisitions and mergers in the 1980s. First and foremost, the economic focus has broadened to include international markets. Historically, corporate strategy had a domestically focused, microeconomic perspective. With

TABLE 2.1   Historical Merger and Acquisition Strategies

Strategic consolidation in the early 1900s	Strategic diversification in the 1960s
Microeconomically focused—domestic	Macroeconomically focused—domestic
Market/industry control objective	Financial control objective
Operating line management perspective	Staff management perspective
Stockholder wealth created by control of competitive environment	Stockholder wealth created by reduction in earnings cyclicality and business risk across a broader portfolio of industries
Industry growth: critical element	Industry growth: noncritical element
Operationally oriented—reduction in cost of production and distribution is a key objective	Nonoperationally oriented—reduction in overhead and financing expenses is emphasized

the emergence of foreign competition as a significant factor in both U.S. and international markets, corporate management has been forced to broaden its analysis of the competitive environment to include worldwide markets and international competitors.

In addition, strategic consolidations in the 1980s increasingly have been driven by factors that are survival-oriented. The contraction of domestic demand for products caused by economic recessionary forces, the decrease in market shares of U.S. manufacturers caused by lower-priced foreign competition, and substitutions resulting from introductions of technologically superior products are factors that have dramatically affected the financial viability of many U.S. companies competing in basic industries. Whether it is because of the decrease in total market demand or the decline in percentage shares of markets, the financial performances of many historically successful industrial competitors have eroded to dangerously low levels. Management can take a limited number of tactical steps to improve financial performance. It can reduce the cost of producing goods by rationalizing capacity, improving labor productivity, or reducing or stabilizing wages and benefits; or it can cut selling, general, and administrative expenses by reducing its workforce, trimming discretionary expenses, closing sales and distribution locations, and taking other cost-cutting steps. Such tactical actions often are not sufficient to reverse the trends, however, if uncontrollable market forces are eroding the corporation's competitive position. Given the foregoing scenario, the strategic answer increasingly has been one of corporate divestiture.

The strategic diversification movement of the 1960s has turned into the strategic divestiture program of the 1980s. Regardless of the strategic or economic motivation, major corporate divestitures have grown enormously over the last decade. According to statistics extracted from the Mergers & Acquisitions Data Base, in 1979 there were 37 major divestitures, including 22 with announced prices totaling $2.1 billion. This trickle of activity reached torrential proportions by 1985. There were 977 major corporate divestitures with an estimated transaction value of nearly $41 billion. Corporate consolidations, like the stock market, are a two-way street. For every seller there has to be a buyer. Strategy-driven divestiture can have many motivations, but the common thread in the 1980s trend appears to be that the enterprise being divested does not or will not add value to stockholder wealth. Conversely, the acquiring company is appraising the enterprise as something that will enhance or preserve its stockholders' wealth. Both seller and buyer allegedly have the same information available to them, yet they make management decisions that can be characterized as diametrically opposite.

TECHNOLOGY BECOMES
PARAMOUNT ATTRACTION

Strategic diversification in the 1980s is motivated increasingly by corporate America's desire to participate in emerging, technologically focused industrial growth. It is a commonly held belief that technological innovation is the province of small, entrepreneurially driven business enterprises, and not the large, bureaucratic corporate institutions of the Fortune 500. Diversification, by definition, implies a broadening of operations and scope. But unlike the diversification of the 1960s, which was financially driven, the 1980s wave of activity is increasingly market/industry-driven. The large corporations with their huge financial resources sought to acquire positions in growth industries where competition is dictated not by financial or operational strength, but by technological factors. In many cases, the only rational entry strategy available to a corporation wishing to enter these markets or industries is acquisition or merger.

Table 2.2 summarizes the key factors that drove strategic consolidation and strategic divestitures in the 1980s. In many cases, they show a surprising similarity to the factors that motivated corporate management in earlier decades of the twentieth century, yet in many respects they differ. No longer is it sufficient to

TABLE 2.2 Merger and Acquisition Strategies of the 1980s

Strategic consolidation	Strategic diversification
Microeconomically focused—international	Macroeconomically focused—international
Market/industry cost and survival objectives	Market/industry participation objective
Marketing/production management perspective	Executive management perspective
Stockholder wealth protected by increased share of competitive environment	Stockholder wealth enhanced by participation in growth industries
Industry maturity: critical element	Industry maturity and basis of competition: critical elements
Operationally oriented—rationalization of industry capacity, sales and distribution economies	Technologically oriented—control of key factors that differentiate products

focus strategic decision making on domestic markets. The international market has become the competitive arena. Financial strength no longer assures participation in growth industries. Technological innovation and its management increasingly have become the keys to competitive position and future financial strength. Strategic management of the corporate enterprise increasingly has moved from a financially focused, portfolio-oriented perspective to a market-focused, operationally oriented perspective. As a result of these shifts in strategic perspective, the analytical task of financial professionals has become increasingly complex.

THE ANALYTICAL ENVIRONMENT

"Beauty is in the eye of the beholder."
    MARGARET W. HUNGERFORD, 1878

Like beauty, value is a very personal measure. Statistics compiled from the Mergers & Acquisitions Data Base indicate that the average premium paid, above market value, for acquiring publicly held companies during the late 1970s and early 1980s ranged from a high of 70 percent in 1979 to a low of 46 percent in 1984. This would imply that either professional analysts and their sophisticated investor clientele consistently have undervalued corporations or, alternatively, that strategic valuations by corporate management result in significantly higher value than traditional financial analysis would suggest.

The task of corporate executives and their staffs of financial analysts has not changed. Management must convince the board of directors, which represents the stockholders, that the corporation's proposed action will enhance or maintain stockholder wealth. Financial management's responsibility is to prove quantitatively that the sum of the parts in a proposed merger exceeds the combined value of either entity standing alone. Given that merger environment, how do financial executives convince boards of directors that

$$100 + 100 = 246 \rightarrow 270?$$

Determining the Premiums

The quantitative methodology for valuing corporations has not changed significantly over the last 20 years. Whether one operates from the perspective of the external independent financial analyst or the internal corporate financial executive, one must determine the present value of the corporation based on informed judgments of its expected future performance. Technical dissimilarities between individual, institutional, or corporate investors, such as tax considerations, do not account for the 46 to 70 percent range in premiums paid. Nor does valuation methodology account for these high premiums, because analysts tend to calculate value in an increasingly similar manner. Given that cash or cash equivalents are used to pay for investment, then the cash received while the investment is held, and the cash received from its sale or liquidation, become the principal ingredients in investment valuation.

On the surface, the analyst's tasks are simple: first determine how much cash will be received while the investment is held, then determine how much cash will be received when the investment is liquidated, and, finally, determine the minimum yield that stockholders will accept given both the business and financial risk inherent in such an investment. Knowing these three things (the cash flows, the residual value at the date of liquidation, and the required yield), an investor can determine an investment's present value by using the mathematical technique of discounting future cash receipts.

On a purely pragmatic basis, the premiums paid for publicly owned corporations are influenced by many noneconomic factors that may have greater impact on acquisition prices than the methods employed in the financial valuation process. An investment banker's advice on what it will take to close the deal, defensive competitive response (acting to prevent a financially strong corporation from acquiring a competitively, viable, but financially weak competitor), and other hard-to-quantify factors often have greater influence on acquisition pricing than either the analytical methods used or the discount (interest) rates selected. In the real world, acquisition pricing is more art than science, more driven by judgment than facts, more dependent on divergent views of markets and opportunities than differing techniques of valuation. If these observations were untrue, the market value of a corporation prior to acquisition would be more equal to the price paid by the acquiring company. There would be no white knights, Wall Street arbitrage specialists would not exist, and shark repellents and golden parachutes would not be needed by corporate managements to assure their continued incumbency.

Conforming to Strategic Plans

If conventional wisdom and pragmatic analysis confirm that neither the analytical framework and technical factors, nor valuation methodologies and Wall Street influences, account for the 46 to 70 percent premiums being paid in the market, then a key question remains. How do corporations quantitatively justify to themselves, and ultimately their stockholders, the prices paid for acquisitions? Strategic management of corporate resources, as enunciated in a corporation's strategic plan, is the key to answering the questions of why 46 to 70 percent premiums are being paid in the public marketplace for acquisitions and why there has been a 25-fold increase in corporate divestitures. Though strategic management has been around for more than 50 years, only recently has it been labeled a management style. The distinguishing feature of the 1980s is not strategic management, but rather the strategic plan.

The strategic plan integrates marketing into the financial planning process. As a result, the plan not only establishes the basis for operational budgets and internal resource allocations, but concurrently creates the analytical framework for acquisition and divestiture decision making. A strategic plan is based on detailed analysis of the competitive environment. The plan must delineate clearly the corporation's businesses in an analytical framework that quantifies industry demand, market share, product mix, selling prices, cost of goods, operating expenses, nonoperating costs, and financial resource requirements (e.g., operating-working capital, investment-capital assets, financial obligations debt repayment/stockholder dividends). This framework forms a solid foundation for analyzing the corporation's internal operations at both the business unit and consolidated levels, and concurrently permits the company to evaluate diversification and acquisition opportunities in a consistent manner. The strategic plan must be modeled in a knowledgeable manner in a computer-based environment that permits users to readily change their assumptions of the future. The strategic plan then becomes a dynamic framework for analyzing not only industry demand and industry capacity utilization, but also a structured framework for evaluating probable competitive responses to changes in forecast demand.

Interjecting the Strategic Model

Dynamic "what if" strategic models are communications tools that support executive management decisions, especially in the areas of resource allocation, divestitures, and acquisitions. The tool never should be so complex in its structure that only middle management can operate or explain it. Strategic models offer only a structure for consistent decision making. They never can become substitutes for management judgment, nor should they be constructed in a manner that attempts to quantify or integrate all possible factors that could affect operating performance. For example, knowledgeable management must appraise the competitive environment realistically when given a specific forecast of industry demand and formulate a competitive response in quantifiable terms. The strategic planning models of the 1980s should be used as a means of documenting assumptions that affect corporate performance and cash flows. An attempt to integrate fully the competitive environment (e.g., current and potential competitors), the technical environment (e.g., product obsolescence and product substitution), and the bargaining environment (material purchasing, international trade barriers, noncash bartering, etc.) in a single strategic model probably will never be justifiable on a cost/benefit basis.

A CONCEPTUAL FRAMEWORK FOR FINANCIAL MODELING

There is no universally applicable model capable of structuring the strategic plans of all corporations. Rather, the challenge to financial and planning practitioners is to construct a dynamic tool that is detailed enough to include all quantifiable variables having a material impact on either operating performance or corporate value, and at the same time simple enough so that decision makers will use it not only to evaluate alternatives but as the vehicle for communicating expected results.

Modeling in a strategic planning environment requires that corporate financial professionals must raise their sights. They no longer can focus strictly on earnings before taxes and noncash charges as the starting points for their analysis of cash flow and investment valuation. The process must begin at the level of international industry demand and proceed in an orderly manner through analyses of market shares, product mix, and product price. The foregoing variable components of revenue and the validity of the assumptions of what creates revenue have far greater impact on operating performance and corporate value than any other line item in a corporation's financial statement. The key to corporate performance and investment valuation lies not within the domain of financial theory, but within the microeconomic environment of both industry demand and competitive behavior. If the analysis of the factors that influence a corporation's market size and share is unsound, the resulting operating projection or investment valuation will be of little or no value. Financial management often has admonished its marketing and sales counterparts to remember that a sale is not a sale until a customer's check clears the bank. In the 1980s, strategic managers would be well advised to remind their financial counterparts that cash flow begins with revenue and not adjusted net income. The external economic and competitive forces that affect demand for a corporation's products are the most critical variables affecting operating cash flows. These factors are simultaneously the key influences on pricing strategy and the key determinants of productive capacity utilization. When the foregoing elements are known, it is a more or less mechanical task to determine a corporation's revenue, cost of goods, and standard gross margin.

Strategic and planning managers, on the other hand, actually must lower their sights and become more conversant with the realities of the internal environment. In the area of cost of goods, they must understand production capacity utilization issues. They must understand the impact that variations in cash flow caused by changing demand have on the fixed and variable costs of production. Similarly, they have to realize that the cost of an outside salesperson in the 1980s is about equal to the cost of borrowing $1 million for one year.

Managers from all functional disciplines must focus their sights on the increasing importance of financial resource allocation. The ability to analyze the cash flow impact of research and development and engineering expenditures in our increasingly technologically driven economy is critical to a well-developed strategic planning framework. These off-balance-sheet investments are beginning to surpass the historic capitalized asset investment as the primary determinants of long-term competitive advantage. Being a low-cost producer no longer assures that a corporation will remain in a competitively strong position.

Financial management has the responsibility of constructing models that are both technically sound and user-friendly. They must achieve this objective by reducing the number of financial variables and by increasing the number of strategic and operating variables that can be manipulated by users. There is always a danger that models of this nature may oversimplify the financial dimension of the analysis. But one should not forget that the objective is not accounting accuracy at the level of published financial statements. The objective is decision accuracy at the level of materiality.

DETERMINANTS OF CASH FLOW

Table 2.3 presents a schematic overview of the four primary components that, when integrated, constitute a strategic planning model. The first three components—gross margins, expenses, and resources—are the primary determinants of cash flow.

TABLE 2.3   Elements of a Strategic Analysis Model

Gross margin component:
  Market share
  Product mix
  Product price
  Standard product cost
Expense component:
  Manufacturing expense
  R&D and engineering expense
  Direct operating expense
  Indirect operating and nonoperating expense
Resource component:
  Operating requirements
  Investment requirements
  Financing requirements
Valuation component:
  Rate matrix
  Valuation matrix

Elements of Gross Margins

The gross margin component contains five matrix modules:

Industry demand—This is expressed in dollars or units, and requires a degree of detail sufficient to illustrate both historic and future trends relating to the product categories in which the operating unit competes.

Market share—The percentage share of industry demand accruing to the operating unit which is based on, and consistent with, the business strategies contained in the plan.

Product mix—The historic and projected products that will be sold by the operating unit in each forecast category of industry demand.

Product price—This details the pricing strategy on both a historic and projected basis for the operating units' products.

Product standard cost—In theory, this is a variable matrix when viewed in prospective terms, but in practice, it is normally a nonvariable component in strategic projections.

Factors in the Expense Component

The expense component contains four linear modules:

Manufacturing expense—The complexity and content of this module is dictated by the information available both historically and prospectively. At a minimum, noncash fixed expenses should be segregated.

R&D and engineering expense—A key dimension for assessing the off-balance-sheet investments in an operating unit's future competitive position.

Direct operating expense—These should be detailed at the levels of the market, sales, general, and administrative categories of direct expense (variable, semivariable and fixed cost elements).

Indirect operating and nonoperating expense—Included are noncash charges (amortization, depreciation, etc.), financing expense (interest, etc.), nonoperating expense (income), and provisions for taxes and dividends.

Composition of the Resource Component

The resource component contains three modules:

Operating requirements—This category tends to be revenue-and expense-dependent variables, unless changed by policy or other management intervention (e.g., terms and condition of sale). Normally included are balance sheet accounts, such as accounts receivable, inventories, prepaid expenses, accounts payable, accrued liabilities, and current and deferred taxes.

Investment requirements—These can be either dependent and/or independent variables, and include fixed assets, capitalized leases, amortizable noncurrent assets, and current and noncurrent contractual liabilities.

Financing requirements—These include both short-term and long-term debt obligations, which are independent variables; stockholders' equity, which is a dependent variable; and cash (surplus or shortfall), which is the slack variable.

Relating the Parts

There are 12 separate modules that can be assembled into the conventional statements of income, financial position, and cash flow. It should not surprise any reader that four of the 12 modules are used in determining revenue, the normal point of departure in traditional financial analysis, and that it takes six, or half the modules, to calculate the business unit's operating gross margin. The schematic framework for constructing strategic models focuses management's attention on those factors that can truly determine the value of an operating unit or acquisition. They are the external market for a corporation's goods and services, and the competitive environment that permits the corporation to share in that market at prices projected from the corporation's cost of making its products. The framework tends to emphasize the key ingredient of cash flow, which is revenue. Without revenue there can be no net income, no need for operating capital, nor any cash resources to repay the corporation's obligations to creditors, debtholders, or stockholders.

VALUATION PROCESS WITH A DISCOUNTED CASH FLOW APPROACH

One objective of strategic planning is to quantify the corporate/stockholder value derived from a given strategic operating plan and to be able to compare this expected value with that of alternative plans or operating scenarios. Quantification requires a forecast of operating cash flows, determination of a residual value, and selection of an appropriate discount rate. Finally, a method for testing alternative scenarios must exist if the process is to be efficient. This same structure of analysis also is required for valuation of either divestiture or merger opportunities.

In addition to the 12-module framework for determining operating cash flows, a forecasting model needs three major elements: the forecast's time horizon, the selection of an appropriate discount rate, and the selection of a residual value.

The Time Horizon

The easiest element to determine is the time horizon. The number of years to be forecast in a strategic plan, or for a divestiture or acquisition analysis, is strictly a function of what management is comfortable with. Most operating forecasts are in the 5- to 15-year range. The selection of the time horizon is based on the ability of planners to convince management and the board of directors that they can forecast industry demand, technological change, and international economic environments with sufficient accuracy to assure that the forecast results are materially valid for decision making.

The Discount Rate

As for the appropriate discount rate to be used for appraisal valuation of internal capital projects and for valuation of potential M&A opportunities, financial theorists have suggested the corporation's "cost of capital" as the proper rate. Financial theory is founded on the work of academicians who were working in the area of microeconomics in the mid- to late 1950s. The work of these academicians was based on research conducted by Gordon and Shapiro and their published papers relating to the required rates of profit in a corporate environment. It continued with the work of Harry Markowitz and James Tobin on the theory of portfolio selection, and was furthered by Franco Modigliani and H. M. Miller in their work on structure and valuation. The capital asset pricing model (CAPM) emerged from the pioneering work of Fisher, Fama, Jensen, Blume, and others during the 1960s. The CAPM established a framework for understanding a corporation's cost of equity capital and looked to the stock market as a key determinant in this process. Academicians have debated the concept of an efficient market, whether it be a weak, semistrong, or strong form, but perhaps one of the more relevant comments on the subject is a quote from C. W. J. Granger and O. Morgenstern in their 1970 publication, *Predictability of Stock Market Prices*: "The only valid statement," they said, "is that current price embodies all knowledge, all expectations and all discounts that infringe upon the market."[1]

Current Market Information.   The statement by Granger and Morgenstern is particularly appealing to the pragmatists among us. It suggests that we are rather safe in using current market information to establish the cost of a firm's equity capital. Textbooks have taught us that the cost of equity capital is equal to the risk-free rate plus a market return plus an individual corporate return. The formula is summarized in the mathematical equation:

$$K_e = R_f + B_j(R_m - R_f)$$

where K_e = cost of equity capital
R_f = risk-free rate
B_j = the beta coefficient
R_m = market return
$R_m - R_f$ = market return (premium)

Alternative Rates.   What are these various components, and how are they determined? First, the alleged risk-free rate is the rate on government bonds that is observed in the market at the date of analysis. It can be found by picking up a copy of *The Wall Street Journal* and turning to the section containing the prices and yields on U.S. government bonds, then selecting the yield (rate) that matches the time horizon of the forecast being made. Second, according to the work of R. G. Ibbotson and Rex A. Sinquefield, the forecast returns on a common stock will exceed those on long-term government debt by 5.4 percent (the observed range is 5.0 percent to 5.5 percent).[2] Finally, the risk-free premium for an individual public corporation security is the product of the market-risk premium times the individual security's systematic risk, or its beta coefficient. In actual practice, it is valuable to use not only the historic beta coefficient of the individual corporation, but the beta coefficient of the industry in which the corporation is competitively classified.

We will refrain from the necessarily long dissertation on determining the corporation's total cost of capital and whether current or future debt/equity ratios should be used to weight the various components. The mathematical procedures are well documented in many textbooks on corporate finance. From the practitioner's perspective, it is a far better technique to apply multiple discount rates to the cash flow forecasts resulting from the operating planning model. Table 2.4 outlines six primary determinants for alternative rates that can be used as the key components of the cost of capital.

Calculating Residual Value. The determination of residual value should depend on the objective of the evaluation. Seldom does one undertake analysis with the objective of liquidating the business entity being acquired. Similarly, it is highly unlikely that one plans to resell the enterprise as a stand-alone corporation. Therefore, in most evaluations, we are dealing with an ongoing business enterprise. For that reason, and because of the selection of the discounted cash flow (DCF) methodology for evaluation, perhaps the most intuitively appealing method of determining residual value is Alfred Rappaport's suggestion that the residual value is the present value of a perpetuity. In summary, Rappaport suggests that the present value of the residual is equal to earnings after taxes in the final year of the forecast, divided by the discount rate selected, times the discount factor at that time period. Stated mathematically:

$$\frac{EAT_N}{discount\ rate} \times discount\ factor_N = PV\ of\ residual_N$$

For practitioners of the free cash flow evaluation methodologies, a slight modification of Rappaport's models suggests substitution of net cash flow in the final time period of the analysis for the earnings aftertax component in the original form. This is stated mathematically as

$$\frac{NCF_N}{discount\ rate} \times discount\ factor_N = PV\ of\ residual_N$$

THE EVALUATION MATRIX

In the use of financial analytical models, whether for strategic planning, the evaluation of strategic plans, or the evaluation of merger and divestiture oppor-

TABLE 2.4   Important Elements Used by Strategic Models in Calculating Acquirer's Discount Rates

"Risk-free" rate, long-term government bonds
Industry market
Corporate market rate
Internal "hurdle rate"
Internal rate at 10% premium
Internal rate at 25% premium

tunities, it is extremely difficult for the analytical practitioner to assume the risk profile of executive management or boards of directors who are charged with decision making. For this reason, the use of a valuation matrix is recommended.

Figure 2.1 presents schematically the end product of the cash flow and residual valuation analysis. It combines three key pieces of information in a multidimensional matrix of information. The X axis is the time dimension, which runs from the initiation of the analysis through the time horizon selected by the analyst for presentation of the plan. The Y axis represents the present value at each point in time for which the discounted cash flows plus residual value are positive. Six separate rates are used to discount the expected cash flow. These rates are based on the cost of capital components outlined in Table 2.4. When coupled with the information and assumptions in the forecast relating to industry demand, market share, pricing, and cost of goods sold, and so on, that are contained explicitly in modules 1 to 12, the valuation matrix represents all expected present values, at varying discount rates, which are forecast in the strategic plan of operation presented. This matrix represents a framework in which the analyst does not have to select ahead of time either the appropriate discount rate or the time horizon, or interpret the motivational-risk bases of the executive managers charged with making the decision. Rather, the matrix presents management with an array of present values based on their own intuitive feelings about the strategic alternatives they are considering.

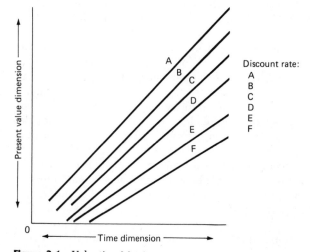

Figure 2.1   Valuation Matrix

MODELING IN A PERSONAL COMPUTER ENVIRONMENT

Anyone who has dealt with forecasts and with management's desire to test alternative marketing or operating scenarios knows that the emergence of the personal computer (PC) as an analytical tool and the development of spreadsheet software have been blessings. Sensitivity analysis, which alters variables to obtain alternative forecasts, is a critical part of the evaluation process. Modern PC spreadsheets have replaced pencils and paper, calculators, and mainframes as the tools of the analyst. The ability to conduct factor analysis on critical assumptions and the ability to analyze the impact of alternative scenarios in a timely manner are rather recent phenomena. Understanding the impact of various possible situations on the value of the operating entity, or on the strategic acquisition opportunity, is far more relevant than selecting a "correct discount rate." The PC is the modern slide rule/calculator that permits analysts to model dynamically that "what if" framework. Strategic models must contain all relevant or material variables, and must adhere to generally accepted accounting principles.

STRATEGY-DRIVEN ANALYSIS

Strategically oriented modeling, whether for planning, diversification, or divestiture valuation, is like the fundamentals of mathematics in that it requires mastery of the basics before the application of theory. Just as mathematics requires a mastery of addition and subtraction, the strategic modeling environment requires that analysts concentrate on the external factors that drive international market demand for the corporation's goods or services, and couple this knowledge with an understanding of the competitive environment. The competitive factor includes not only current international competitors, but any reasonable expectations of future competitive constraints resulting from technical advancements in products or product substitution. Multiplication and division are analogous to the need of strategic modelers to understand how both internal corporate policies and procedures, and external environments, determined by government regulation or industry practice, affect the current and the future economic viability of the acquiring corporation or its merger target.

Financial theory of the firm is similar to the mathematical concepts in calculus and statistics. The microeconomic and operational constraints that establish the competitive positions of the various industry players must be understood before the analyst can model the corporation. The infinite set of variables that could affect a corporation's financial performance must be condensed to the point where the variables having material impact on performance have been identified. Finally, numerical analysis for the mathematician is similar to the task of the person charged with strategic modeling in a financial environment, who must provide a framework that is flexible enough to permit quantification of alternative future scenarios, whether economic, political, technological, or societal.

Strategy-driven acquisition and merger analysis is based on the fundamental premises that:

- Businesses operate in a dynamic rather than a static environment.
- Strategic consolidations and diversifications are based on a strategic operating plan.
- External forces that influence industry demand and external factors that establish competitive position have greater impact on value than the methods used to determine that value.
- Cash flow starts with industry demand and not adjusted net income.
- Reality suggests that the prices paid in the market are often based on nonfinancial factors such as management's judgments and egos, the scarcity or overabundance of merger candidates, investment bankers' opinions of "what it will take to do the deal," and the personal biases of government regulators.

Strategic financial models are necessary for the quantification of expected value. But reality suggests that this determined value is only one element in a much more complex framework that establishes the amount paid for an acquisition, or the amount received for a divestiture.

NOTES

[1]C. W. J. Granger and O. Morgenstern, *Predictability of Stock Market Prices*, Heath Lexington Books, Lexington, Mass., 1970.

[2]R. G. Ibbotson and Rex A. Sinquefield, *Stock, Bonds, Bills and Inflation: The Past (1926–76) and the Future*, *Financial Analyst Research Foundation*, New York, 1977.

Chapter 3

The Payoff in Mergers and Acquisitions

J. Fred Weston

Cordner Professor of Money and Financial Markets,
Graduate School of Management,
University of California at Los Angeles,
Los Angeles, California

Growth is vital to the well-being of a business. Growth is the linchpin for programs to generate capital for financial health, upgrade technologies, strengthen market positions, enhance operating efficiencies, and recruit top-notch management talent by providing opportunities for promotions and broadened responsibilities. Without growth possibilities, most firms would lose their purposes for existing, stagnate, wither, and then die. For the soundly operated firm, restructuring and realignments frequently are necessary adjuncts of growth—either to expand the firm as a whole, or, in many cases, to cut back the overall size of the company so that emphasis can be placed on the business segments with the best growth prospects.

RESTRUCTURING OF BUSINESSES

Expanding, shrinking, or otherwise restructuring a company encompasses a broad range of practices, of which the most important and most frequently used are listed in Table 3.1. Although the groupings may be somewhat arbitrary, they serve to match specific restructuring mechanisms with the basic purposes that lead to their use.

Expansion

Mergers, tender offers, and joint ventures have played major roles in the expansion of many business firms. Mergers may be likened to a marriage in the romantic tradition. A period of courtship precedes the joining of two or more business entities into one firm, and the parties hope to live happily ever after. Tender offers may be equally harmonious and follow a courtship period, or they may be hostile devices for expansion-minded buyers to take over unwilling targets that have spurned their overtures. But they are principally distinguished from straight mergers in that one party takes the initiative in making a monetary offer, or its equivalent, for shares of the target. In joint ventures, two or more companies pool various types of resources to start a new business in which they share ownership. It is essentially a temporary partnership arrangement. The venture usually involves the intersection of only small parts of the creating companies' activities and often has a limited life, such as 10 to 15 years. The participants may invest cash and contribute other resources such as technology, brick-and-mortar, or marketing expertise.

Sell-offs

But corporate combinations, like marriages, may go sour, and the partners utilize several sell-off techniques to get a divorce. Divestitures involve selling off part of the assets of a company to another party—an individual, a group of investors, or another firm. In a pure voluntary corporate spin-off, a subsidiary is created and

TABLE 3.1   Forms of Business Restructuring

Buy-outs (expansion):
  Mergers
  Tender offers
  Joint ventures
Sell-offs:
  Divestitures
  Spin-offs
  Split-ups
  Split-offs
Corporate control:
  Premium buy-backs
  Standstill agreements
  Antitakeover amendments
  Proxy contests
Change in ownership:
  Share repurchase
  Going private
  Leveraged buy-outs

its shares are distributed, usually pro rata, to the existing equity holders of the parent company. That type of spin-off does not alter the shareholders' proportional ownership in both the parent and the new company. It creates an additional publicly held company whose stock is traded separately from the shares of the former parent. In a split-off, the stock of a subsidiary is distributed to only some of the parent firms' shareholders in exchange for their holdings in the parent. A split-off alters the ownership proportions in both the subsidiary and the parent. A split-off also may refer to a financing arrangement in which a parent sells part of the subsidiary's stock to the public. The partial public offering provides a cash inflow to the parent, which customarily maintains majority control of the subsidiary. In a split-up, a firm divides into two or more parts, distributing the stock of each new unit to its shareholders, and the parent ceases to exist.

Corporate Control

A third realignment grouping does not necessarily involve physical expansion or contraction of the firm but embraces steps designed to retain, strengthen, or change "corporate control."

The premium buy-back is an example of a maneuver ostensibly designed to rid incumbent management or controlling interests of a stockholder who is an actual or potential threat to the control position. The company will repurchase the shares of the unwanted stockholder and pay a premium over market price as an inducement. One of the most controversial such deals of recent years was the 1984 repurchase by Walt Disney Productions of an 11 percent interest held by investor Saul Steinberg at substantially more than prevailing market prices. The practice of taking a position with the intent of having management do a buy-back is known as "greenmailing." A buy-back often is accompanied by a standstill agreement in which the seller agrees not to buy into the company again for some period of time in the future. A standstill agreement does not always require a buy-back and simply may preclude a stockholder from increasing his or her holdings.

Antitakeover amendments to corporate charters and by-laws are designed to make companies more difficult and expensive to acquire and represent another mechanism for strengthening established control. Among the most popular of such provisions are the supermajority vote for mergers and other matters, staggered terms for election of directors, "fair price" rules that require uniform compensation for all stockholders, and "golden parachutes" to compensate managements ousted by changes in control.

In a proxy contest, a stockholder bloc opposed to the incumbent management and directors tries, through stockholder voting, to obtain, at minimum, representation on the board, and, at most, control of the board and the company.

Rearranged Ownership Structure

The final group of restructuring activities is called rearranged ownership structure. In a share repurchase, the corporation buys back some fraction of its outstanding common stock. The percentage of repurchased shares may be small, or it may be substantial and result in a change in the firm's control structure. For example, Teledyne, Inc., conducted an extensive share repurchase program in the 1980s, including an 8.7 million share buy-back in mid-1984, and increased the effective control position of Henry E. Singleton, chairman and chief executive officer. Singleton, who owned nearly 8 percent of Teledyne shares in early 1984, had an almost 9.5 percent interest by late in the year because he did not tender any of his stock to the company.

In a going-private transaction the entire equity interest in a public corporation is purchased by a small group of investors. The firm no longer is subject to the regulations of the Securities and Exchange Commission, whose purpose is to protect public investors. Going-private transactions typically include members of management who obtain a substantial proportion of the equity ownership of the private company. Usually, a small group of outside investors provides funds, secures representation on the private company's board, and arranges other financing from third-party investors. When financing from third parties involves substantial borrowing by the company, the transactions are termed leveraged buy-outs.

Issues Raised by Restructuring

Many of the restructuring forms have stirred controversy and debate. Are they good for the economic health of the nation, or are they bad? Do they divert the energies of managers from bona fide economic activity to financial manipulation? Do they use up financial resources that otherwise would be employed in "real" investment activities? Why has heightened merger activity been a phenomenon of the last 20 years?

In attempting to provide some explanations for these many activities, it will be useful to treat the expansion group of activities separately because it alone involves the combining and recombining of real assets. The remaining groups involve rearranging ownership and control structures in firms without necessarily altering asset positions.

THEORIES OF ASSET REDEPLOYMENT

Theories that underlie the efficacy of mergers, tender offers, and joint ventures can be grouped under five major headings:

- Efficiency
- Information
- Agency problems
- Market power
- Taxes

Efficiency Theory

The efficiency theory hypothesizes that a merger can either improve the performance of incumbent management or produce a more efficient company through achievement of some form of synergy. During the heyday of the conglomerate merger movement in the late 1960s, exaggerated claims for synergy were made under what came to be known as the "2 + 2 = 7" effect. The theory was that a merged firm would produce far better results than its constituent parts would if they remained independent entities. While the projected results from asset deployment were exaggerated, there is a solid basis for achieving positive net present value investments by recombining the activities of business operations. The synergies that produce these benefits generally fall into three classifications: operating synergy, financial synergy, and strategic realignment.

Operating Synergy. Operating synergy, or operating economies, may result from both horizontal and vertical mergers. For horizontal mergers, operating economies must stem from some form of economies of scale. These economies, in turn, may reflect indivisibilities and better utilization of capacity after the merger. Or important complementaries in organizational capabilities may be present to produce gains not attainable in the short run from internal investments.

In vertical integration, combining firms at different stages of an industry may achieve more efficient coordination of the different levels. The argument here is that costs of communication and various forms of bargaining, and opportunistic behavior can be avoided by vertical integration.[1]

Financial Synergy. Possible financial synergies involve some unsettled issues of finance theory. Nevertheless, empirical analysis of mergers may shed some light on the fundamental issues. Financial synergy proponents argue that the cost of capital function may be lowered for a number of reasons as a result of merger. If the cash flow streams of the two companies are not perfectly correlated, bankruptcy probabilities may be lowered. The prevailing view in finance theory is that if firms could fail and new ones formed to take their place without costs, bankruptcy would not matter. But the losses or costs from the failures of firms may be substantial. These losses include not only the direct costs of legal and other administrative fees but also the indirect costs of losing key managers and employees, as well as loss of customers (especially for makers of durable equipment, who may not be around to supply parts for maintenance in the future). Perhaps the largest indirect cost of bankruptcy is the loss of an effective, functioning organization that took years to develop. These direct and indirect losses can wipe out the value of shareholders' equity and reduce the value of creditors' claims as well. Thus, to the extent that bankruptcy and its attendant costs can be reduced by mergers that reduce the instability of company revenue streams, stockholders, creditors, and society as a whole benefit.

This debt-coinsurance effect benefits debtholders at the expense of shareholders.[2] However, this effect can be offset by increasing leverage after the merger, and the result will be increased tax savings on interest payments.[3] Indeed, Stapleton,[4] in the context of the option pricing theory, demonstrates that the increase in debt capacity does not require the existence of bankruptcy costs.

Another dimension, emphasized by Levy and Sarnat,[5] is economies of scale in flotation and transactions costs that may be realized by conglomerate firms. Arguments may be raised about the potential magnitude of these financial factors. Further questions could be raised as to why joint activities might not be taken by unmerged firms to achieve the same economies of scale in flotation and transaction costs. However, the heterogeneity of firms and the costs of contracting would seem to make such activities prohibitive, because such joint activities seldom take place in the real world.

Strategic Realignment to Changing Environments. The literature on long-range strategic planning has proliferated in recent years, specifically in the area of diversification through mergers. The emphasis of strategic planning research is on matters related to firms' environments and constituencies, as well as their operating decisions.[6] The strategic planning approach to mergers appears to imply either the possibilities of economies of scale or utilization of some unused capacity in the firm's present managerial capabilities. Another rationale is that by external diversification, the firm acquires management skills for needed augmentation of its present capabilities. This approach still leaves some questions unanswered. New capabilities and new markets could be developed internally. The less risky strategy may be to buy established organizations, but a competitive market for acquisitions implies that the net present value to acquirers from such investments is likely to be small. Nevertheless, if the changes in the environment call for a rapid adjustment, the combinations of existing firms may have significant positive benefits. Furthermore, if these investments can be used as a base for still additional investments with positive net present values, the strategy may succeed.

Information Theory

A second possible reason for mergers, tender offers, and joint ventures is the "information hypothesis." This refers to the revaluation of the ownership shares of firms because of new information that is generated during the merger negotiations, the tender offer process, or the joint venture planning. Alternative forms of the information hypothesis have been distinguished by Bradley, Desai, and Kim.[7] One is the "kick-in-the-pants" explanation. Management is stimulated to implement a higher-valued operating strategy. A second is the "sitting-on-a-gold-mine" hypothesis. The negotiations or tendering activity may result in dissemination of new information or lead the stock market to judge that the bidders have superior information. The market then may revalue previously "undervalued" shares.

A third aspect of information effects is a variant of the undervaluation hypothesis which suggests that firms have stepped up diversification efforts in recent years by expanding, or by entering new product or market areas on a bargain basis. The inflation of the 1970s had a double-barreled impact. Stock prices were depressed during the 1970s and did not recover until the latter part of 1982, after the rate of inflation declined and business prospects improved. The second impact of inflation was to raise current replacement costs of assets substantially above their recorded historical book values. These twin effects resulted in a decline of the q-ratio, defined as the ratio of the market value of a company's shares to the replacement costs of the assets represented by those shares.

In the annual volumes of the *Economic Report of the President* (produced by the Council of Economic Advisers), the q-ratio was calculated for a period of years for all nonfinancial corporations as a group. The data were included in a table entitled "Determinants of Business Fixed Investment." From this and other sources, the q-ratio in the 1980s was running between 0.5 and 0.6. This means that the market value of a firm's securities were little more than one-half the value of the brick-and-mortar behind them.

Thus, if a company seeks capacity to produce a particular product, it is cheaper to buy a firm that manufactures the product than to build brick-and-mortar from scratch. If Firm A seeks to add capacity, this activity implies that its marginal q-ratio is greater than 1. If other firms in its industry have average q-ratios of less than 1, it is efficient for Firm A to add capacity by purchase. For example, if the q-ratio is 0.6 and the premium paid over market value to make an acquisition is 50 percent, the resulting purchase price is 0.6 times 1.5, or 0.9. In that scenario, the average purchase price still would be 10 percent below the current replacement cost of the acquired assets. This potential advantage provided a broad basis for the implementation of the undervaluation theory in recent years, as q-ratios declined.

For companies in natural resource industries, q-ratios have been as low as 0.2 because of high estimated values of reserves in the ground that have been used in the denominator. Such a low q-ratio provided a basis for paying very large premiums when natural resource firms were acquired. For example, the cash and securities offered by U.S. Steel in November 1981 for Marathon Oil represented about $106 per share—about a 75 percent premium over the $60 price of Marathon in early September. However, some Marathon shareholders initiated lawsuits because they stated that earlier outside appraisals had estimated the value of Marathon's reserves in the ground and other assets at more than double the price paid by U.S. Steel. Of course, these appraisals were subject to considerable uncertainty. As it turned out, the sharp decline in oil prices that began in early 1983 impaired the values of oil and other natural resource reserves.

Agency Problems Theory

Jensen and Meckling[8] formulated the implications of agency problems. An agency problem arises when managers own only a fraction of a company's shares. Partial ownership may cause managers to work less vigorously than otherwise and/or consume more perquisites (such as luxurious offices, company cars, memberships in clubs), because the majority owners bear most of the cost. The argument can be made that in large corporations with widely dispersed ownership, individual owners do not have sufficient incentive to expend the substantial resources required to monitor the behavior of managers. A number of compensation arrangements and the market for managers may mitigate the agency problem.[9]

Another market mechanism is the threat of takeover, which may substitute for individual shareholders' efforts to monitor the managers. The agency explanation of mergers extends the previous work by Manne.[10] Manne emphasized the market for corporate control and viewed a merger as a threat of takeover if a firm's management lagged in performance either because of inefficiency or agency problems.

A variant of the agency problem is the managerialism theory of conglomerate mergers that was developed by Mueller.[11] Mueller hypothesized that managers are motivated continually to increase the sizes of their firms. He assumed that the compensation to managers is a function of the size of the firm, and also argued that managers adopt an unduly low investment hurdle rate in their analyses of merger opportunities. But in a study critical of earlier evidence, Lewellen and Huntsman[12] presented findings that managers' compensation is significantly correlated with the firm's profit rate, not its level of sales. The basic premise of the managerialism theory, therefore, is doubtful.

Agency theory suggests that when the market for managers does not solve the agency problem, the market for firms, or merger activity, will come into play. This theory suggests, therefore, that merger activity is a method of dealing with the agency problem. The managerialism theory argues that the agency problem cannot be solved, and that merger activity manifests the agency problems of inefficient, external investments by managers. Empirical evidence presented later will enable us to test these competing theories.

Market Power Theory

An objection sometimes raised against permitting a firm to increase its market share by merger is that the result will be undue concentration in the industry. Indeed, traditional public policy in the United States held that when four or fewer firms accounted for 40 percent or more of the sales in a given market or line of business, an undesirable market structure, or "undue concentration," existed. The argument, in brief, was that if four or fewer firms account for a substantial percentage of an industry's sales, these firms recognized the impact of their actions and policies on one another. This recognized interdependence, the argument continued, leads to a consideration of actions, as well as reactions to changes in policy, that tend toward "tacit collusion." As a result, the prices and profits of the firms contain monopoly elements. Thus, if economies from mergers cannot be established, it was argued that the resulting increases in concentration were motivated by monopoly gains. If economies of scale can be demonstrated, then a comparison of efficiencies versus the effects of increased concentration must be made.

In 1982, and again in 1984, the Department of Justice announced new merger guidelines to supersede those issued in 1968. The new merger guidelines adopted the Herfindahl-Hirschman index (HHI), which takes into consideration the market shares of all of the firms in the industry. The theory behind the HHI is that if one or more firms have relatively high market shares, this is of greater concern than the combined share of the largest four firms. If, in market A, four firms each hold a 15 percent market share and the remaining 40 percent is held by 40 firms, each with a 1 percent market share, the HHI is

$$HHI = 4(15)^2 + 40(1)^2 = 940$$

In market B, however, one firm has a 57 percent market share and the remaining 43 percent is held by 43 firms, each with a 1 percent market share. As with market A, the four-firm concentration ratio is 60 percent. However, the HHI is

$$HHI = (57)^2 + 43(1)^2 = 3,292$$

Thus, market A would be considered unconcentrated while market B, with its very high HHI level, would be considered highly concentrated. However, the key difference from the old four-firm ratio is that HHI registers a concern about inequality as well as degree of concentration. Yet the economic basis for either concern has not been well established. Whereas some economists hold that high concentration, however measured, causes some degree of monopoly, other economists hold that increased concentration is generally the *result* of active and intense competition. They argue further that the intense competition continues among large firms in concentrated industries because the dimensions of decision making over prices, outputs, types of products, quality of products, service, and so on, are so numerous and of so many gradations that collusion simply is not feasible.

But there is a possibility that the value gains from restructuring result from increases in monopoly power rather than increases in efficiency. Several studies are relevant to this issue.

James Ellert examined the monopoly-efficiency conflict at great length.[13] He analyzed the data for 205 defendants in antimerger complaints from 1950 to 1972 and found that, for periods beginning four years before the complaints were brought, the residual performances were positive and statistically significant for the defendants. As expected, a residual became negative upon the filing of a complaint. However, the negative residuals were relatively small. Ellert observed that the record of effective management of assets by acquiring firms in the years preceding merger activity may be the real causes of complaints by their rivals to antitrust authorities. Ellert terms this a "harassment" hypothesis. He indicates that there are incentives for complaining rivals to follow this course. Government agencies bear the costs of prosecution and, if successful, their actions will handicap the defendants to the advantage of their rivals. The harassment hypothesis is clearly the opposite of a monopoly explanation of merger activity. If the monopoly theory is valid, both parties should gain from the merger.

The monopoly theory was weakened even further in studies by Robert Stillman and Epsen Eckbo, who looked at how mergers affected the rivals of acquiring firms.[14] Their studies appear to support the efficiency basis for mergers. Ellert emphasized that acquiring firms had positive residuals before their mergers and acquired firms had negative residuals before being taken over. Stillman's evidence was that rival firms did not benefit from the announcement of proposed mergers, which is inconsistent with the concentration-collusion hypothesis. Eckbo found positive residuals at the merger announcement, but no negative effects on rivals when it appeared that the merger would be blocked by the antitrust authorities. This pattern of relationships, he said, indicates that the main effect of a merger is to signal the possibility that the merging firms will achieve economies, thus providing information to rivals that such economies also may be available to them.

Tax Considerations Theory

A key tax benefit available in mergers can be the substitution of capital gains taxes for ordinary income taxes. A judicious acquirer can reap the advantage by purchasing a growth company that has paid little or no dividends, hanging on to it during its lushest expansion period, and selling it after the growth has peaked to realize capital gains. When growth of the property has slowed to the point that earnings retention cannot be justified to the Internal Revenue Service, the incentive for sale is created. Rather than pay out future earnings as dividends subject to ordinary personal income taxes, a seller can capitalize future earnings by divesting the business.

Another tax factor arises from the credits enjoyed by firms with accumulated tax losses. Although a business purpose other than the capture of tax credits must be demonstrated, a firm with tax losses can shelter the profits of another firm with which it merges. The Economic Recovery Tax Act of 1981 provided for the sale of tax credits from accelerated depreciation (without selling an entire business), and such transactions often were executed through sale-leaseback arrangements on physical properties. The popularity of this tactic suggested that tax inducements to mergers may lose appeal if there are alternative methods for securing equivalent tax benefits.

Tax considerations also are in play when the prospect of achieving stepped-up depreciable assets is a strong incentive to acquire. This motivation points up a way of trying to avoid the penalty of depreciation on lower historical costs during periods of high inflation.

Still other tax effects are associated with inheritance taxes. A closely held firm may be sold when the owners grow older, because they face uncertainty about the value placed on the firm for estate tax purposes. A sale also may provide greater liquidity for the payment of estate taxes.

A study of mergers in the newspaper industry illustrates the interlocked effects of stepped-up depreciation and inheritance tax influences.[15] The stepped-up basis for depreciable assets leads to competition among bidding firms, resulting in payment of substantial premiums to acquire newspaper properties. These high, demonstrated market values then are used by the IRS in setting values on newspaper companies for estate tax purposes. But the realization of the tax benefits of the higher depreciable values requires an actual transaction. This is a fact of life that has stimulated the purchase of individual newspaper companies by newspaper chains.

THEORIES OF RESTRUCTURING

Whereas the expansion activities involve the combining of assets, the remaining groups of restructuring methods center on the uncombining of assets, or what some authorities have termed "reverse mergers." Even though shrinkage or contraction may characterize reverse mergers, a synergy argument also has been advanced on their behalf. Unlike expansions, in which proponents of synergy claim that the total is greater than the sum of its parts—the aforementioned $2 + 2 = 7$ effect—reverse mergers supposedly improve total results by subtraction, or an implied "5 − 1 = 7" effect. Obviously, there is no logical basis in mathematics for this approach, but some analysts believe that it works in the corporate context. For example, various forms of divestiture can be rationalized on the grounds that they transfer assets to a higher-valued use or to a more efficient user. Or a divestiture may enhance a firm's value by slicing off a business that was a poor fit with the remaining operations. If these theories are valid, good divestiture programs may increase market values of both the divesting and purchasing firms.

EMPIRICAL STUDIES
OF CORPORATE CONTROL

In recent years most studies of merger performance have drawn on new developments in financial economics, in particular an approach called residual analysis. On average, securities will yield returns that are related to their underlying risks. However, unusually favorable or unfavorable events will cause security prices to be reassessed. New favorable information will cause security prices to rise so that returns are higher than predicted by the normal ("security market-line") relationships between returns and risk, as measured by the beta coefficient. Unfavorable information will have the opposite effect. These shifts in returns are called "security market-line residuals," or "abnormal returns." In empirical studies of postmerger return, the relevant events are announcements and completions of mergers. The analysis involves a comparison between the actual returns of the merging firms and the returns that are predicted from the market-line or beta relationships between return and risk. The research results measure the cumulative average residuals for various periods before and after a key event, usually an announcement date. The results of a considerable number of studies on all types of merger and corporate control situations are summarized in Table 3.2.

In mergers, the acquired firms, on average, experienced a 20 percent excess or abnormal return. For acquiring firms the residuals as percentage returns appear to be positive on average, but small. When expressed in absolute dollar amounts, the gains in mergers are about evenly divided between acquiring and acquired firms. But because acquiring firms on average are much larger, their percentage positive returns are small. In tender offers, the excess returns for acquired firms run about 35 percent. On average, acquiring firms appear to have a small positive return that is statistically significant.

For joint ventures, the participating firms averaged only a 2 to 3 percent positive return that is significant. However, when expressed as a percentage of the dollar investment involved, the returns appear to be 23 percent. Similarly, in sell-offs of various types, such as divestitures and spin-offs, there is a positive return to the selling firm of 2 to 3 percent. But when related to the value of the assets spun off, the investment return is about 50 percent.

On share repurchases there is a positive return of about 16 percent associated with the announcement of such programs. On average, when proxy contests are announced there is a plus 10 percent excess return. Announcements of going-

TABLE 3.2   Empirical Results of Stockholder Returns in Studies of Mergers and Corporate Control

Studies	Excess stockholder returns
Mergers	
1. Acquired firms	20%
2. Acquiring firms	1−2%
Tender offers	
1. Acquired firms	35%
2. Acquiring firms	3−5%
Joint ventures	
1. Absolute[a]	2.2%
2. As percent of investment	23%
Sell-offs	
1. Absolute[b]	1.5%
2. As percent of value of unit sold	50%
Premium buy-backs	
1. Single blocks from outsiders	−2%
2. From insiders or small shareholdings	1.2%
3. Sellers of single blocks	1.5%
Standstill agreements (nonparticipating stockholders)	−4%
Antitakeover amendments	1.5%
Proxy contests	10%
Share repurchases	16%
Going private	20%
Leveraged buy-outs	50%

[a]To shareholders of all firms participating in the joint ventures.
[b]To shareholders of selling firms.

private deals result in a plus 20 percent positive residual. Premium buy-backs result in a small negative effect on the residuals. There is about a 2.0 negative return, which is statistically significant, associated with buying off a corporate raider. The standstill agreement in which a potential buyer group agrees not to make further investments to achieve control is associated with a negative 4 percent excess return. The announcement of antitakeover amendments to make acquisition of a given company more difficult appears to result in a small positive excess return of about 2 percent. This positive return is statistically significant. Finally, leveraged buy-outs result in a large positive return of about 50 percent upon the announcement of such a program.

In summary, most of the event studies associated with mergers, tender offers, and other aspects of corporate control show positive gains to shareholders. Only the premium purchase and standstill agreements, used to buy off potential raiders, result in negative returns. In connection with mergers, tender offers, and joint ventures, it appears that real value may be added as a basis for the increase in valuation. The source of the increases in value represents some combination of efficiency, information effects or signaling, reduction of agency problems, and tax advantages. The empirical studies have been unable to separate the relative importance of these four major factors in pro-rating the benefits of buy-outs and sell-offs.

The basis for increases in value associated with the other elements of corporate control relate largely to organizational aspects of running large business firms. These gains relate to more clearly identifying responsibility for results and to the more direct linking of managerial rewards with stock price and performance. But, on average, various aspects of mergers, tender offers, and rearranging corporate ownership and control relationships seem to represent expected positive net present value activities. It would appear that they supplement other types of investment activity in improving business performance.

DRUCKER REVISED: RULES FOR SUCCESSFUL MERGERS

In his classic op-ed piece in *The Wall Street Journal* of October 15, 1981, Peter Drucker sets forth "five rules of successful acquisition." Noting that the current merger movement in the United States paralleled the tremendous wave of acquisitions in Germany in 1920–1922, a period of chronic inflation, Drucker saw a general principle at work: During severe inflation, fixed assets become available at prices below book value and even further below replacement costs. The low stock market valuations of companies, he noted, are due in substantial degree to sustained underdepreciation because of tax regulations. Thus, the basic cause of the increased merger activity under inflation represents a flight out of money and into assets.

Despite this financial rationale for M&A activity, Drucker said that for a merger to make business sense, it must follow five rules:

- Acquirer must contribute something to the acquired company.
- Acquirer and target must share a common core of unity.
- Acquirer must respect the business of the acquired company.
- Within a year or so, the acquiring company must be able to provide top management to the acquired company.
- Within the first years of merger, managements in both companies should receive promotions.

Drucker supports his prescriptions by selected examples of successes and failures. But does the mass of empirical research bear Drucker out? My survey of M&A studies since the mid-1970s would answer in the affirmative.

Buy and Build Correlations

The dollar value of merger and acquisition activity in the United States on average has been related to the dollar value of plant and equipment expenditures as shown in Table 3.3. It will be observed that generally when plant and equipment expenditures rise or fall, M&A activity similarly increases or decreases. The year 1983 was an exception, but data indicate that they were tracking in 1984. When a statistical regression relationship is calculated, M&A activity in dollars increases by about one-fifth the increase in P&E expenditures. Thus in a year when P&E expenditures increase by $20 billion, M&A activity will increase

TABLE 3.3 Merger and Acquisition Activity in Relation to Plant and Equipment Expenditures

Year (1)	Dollar amount of M&As (in billions) (2)	Plant and equipment expenditures (in billions) (3)
1967	$18.0	$ 83.4
1968	43.0	88.5
1969	23.7	99.5
1970	16.4	105.6
1971	12.6	108.5
1972	16.7	120.3
1973	16.7	137.7
1974	12.5	157.0
1975	11.8	157.8
1976	20.0	171.5
1977	21.9	198.1
1978	34.2	231.2
1979	43.5	270.5
1980	44.3	295.6
1981	82.6	321.5
1982	53.8	316.4
1983	73.1	302.5

SOURCE: Col. (2) W. T. Grimm.
Col. (3) U.S. Department of Commerce.

on average by about $4 billion. While numerous factors affect M&A activity, a strong influence is the level of investment activity. This suggests that similar types of economic forces influence both types of investment activity and that there is a similar economic rationale for both types of activity.

Furthermore, the timing of annual merger activity is empirically influenced by the ratio of the market value of firms to their replacement costs. This q-ratio, as defined earlier, is a measure of investment opportunities in plant and equipment, either directly or through mergers. This factor can be split into two variables: the growth rate of GNP (positive), and the level of the realized real interest rates (negative). Statistically, these factors are significantly related to the level of merger activity. In addition, the studies indicate that financial variables are particularly important for pure conglomerate mergers.

Creation of Value

As detailed above, most studies of mergers in recent years have used residual analysis of stock performance. These studies compare the returns realized by investors in merger stocks when merger and tender offers are announced to the returns realized in the general market. The difference represents abnormal returns on residuals from predicted market returns. The positive findings permit some generalizations.

The value of the merged firms appears to be greater than the sum of the components. This implies that value is created and increased by mergers, reflecting underlying economics and efficiencies of corporate fusion. Other findings include:

- Shareholders of acquired firms during the period just before the announcement date of a merger or tender offer gain by about 15 percent in mergers and about 30 percent in tender offers. However, in earlier periods, the abnormal returns of acquired firms are negative, indicating that their managements were not performing up to their potentials.
- Shareholders of acquiring firms for the period before the announcement dates realize modest positive returns, but these are not always statistically significant. In earlier periods, however, their shareholders' abnormal returns are positive, indicating that acquiring firms previously had a record of successfully managing asset growth.
- Target residuals do not decline after the merger. This further indicates that the mergers, on average, are based on valid economic or business reasons.

The studies summarized above generally include all types of mergers— horizontal, vertical, and conglomerate. Studies of conglomerate mergers produced approximately the same pattern of results. Pure conglomerate mergers appear to violate the Drucker imperative of relatedness. But because of antitrust constraints against horizontal and vertical mergers, more than 75 percent of the mergers and acquisitions since the early 1950s have been classified as "conglomerate" by the Federal Trade Commission. Furthermore, studies of conglomerate mergers have found that their financial market performances for their shareholders have not been statistically different from the general market averages, or other broad composites such as the returns from mutual funds.

Closer analysis suggests that the so-called conglomerate mergers that were studied did not violate the Drucker rules. In each case, acquiring and acquired firms shared some relatedness. For some it was the ability to share sophisticated financial planning and control systems or some generic managerial capabilities; for others it was the ability to adjust effectively to changing economic environments. In most cases, the acquiring firms had available managerial capabilities and cash flows, but faced product markets whose growth prospects were below average.

Guidelines for the 1980s

Despite this analysis, examination of the systematic evidence suggests that the Drucker rules may be unduly restrictive if interpreted too literally. In essence the Drucker rules can be boiled down to these guidelines:

- The companies must have activities that are related in some way.
- The merger parties should not be overly restrictive in defining the scope of potential relatedness.
- Because combining two companies involves substantial trauma and readjustment, a strong emphasis on maintaining and enhancing managerial rewards and incentives is required in the postmerger period.
- Even with a strong management compensation program, the acquirer must be prepared to cover for the departure of key management of the target.

- If the price isn't right, someone is going to get hurt, regardless of how well a merger is planned to minimize mistakes and overcome wishful thinking.

RATIONAL BEHAVIOR AND MAXIMIZED VALUE

The preponderance of empirical evidence supports the judgment that corporate restructuring activity is rational, value-maximizing behavior. On average, the total gains measured as rates of return or in absolute amounts associated with restructuring events are positive. Thus the evidence does not support the managerialism theory which holds that managements resort to restructuring simply to increase the size of firms, to increase their own compensation, or to achieve the prestige of controlling large corporate enterprises.

The major studies of the monopoly-versus-efficiency issue obtain somewhat complex empirical patterns. However, all interpret their results as supporting the efficiency theory. Thus, the wide range of corporate restructuring activities that we observe appears to represent a response to the characteristics of the economic environment, and facilitates resource reallocations within that economy.

NOTES

[1]O. E. Williamson, "The Vertical Integration of Production: Market Failure Considerations," *The American Economic Review*, May 1971, pp. 112–123; K. J. Arrow, "Vertical Integration and Communications," *Bell Journal of Economics*, Spring 1975, pp. 173–183; Benajmin Klein, Robert G. Crawford, and Armen A. Alchian, "Vertical Integration, Appropriable Rents, and the Competitive Contracting Process," *Journal of Law and Economics*, October 1978, pp. 297–325.

[2]Robert C. Higgins, and Lawrence D. Schall, "Corporate Bankruptcy and Conglomerate Merger," *Journal of Finance*, 30 (March 1975), pp. 93–113.

[3]D. Galai, and R. W. Masulis, "The Option Pricing Model and the Risk Factor of Stock," *Journal of Financial Economics*, January/March 1976, pp. 53–82.

[4]R. C. Stapleton, "Mergers, Debt Capacity, and the Valuation of Corporate Loans," in M. Keenan and L. J. White, eds., *Mergers and Acquisitions*, D. C. Heath, Lexington, Mass., 1982, chap. 2.

[5]H. Levy, and M. Sarnat, "Diversification, Portfolio Analysis and the Uneasy Case for Conglomerate Mergers," *Journal of Finance*, September 1970, pp. 795–802.

[6]C. Summer, *Strategic Behavior in Business and Government*, Little, Brown, Boston, 1980.

[7]M. Bradley, Anand Desai, and E. Han Kim, "The Rationale behind Interfirm Tender Offers: Information or Syngery?" *Journal of Financial Economics*, April 1983, pp. 183–206.

[8]M. Jensen, and W. Meckling, "Theory of the Firm: Managerial Behavior, Agency Costs and Ownership Structure," *Journal of Financial Economics*, October 1976, pp. 305–360.

[9]E. Fama, "Agency Problems and the Theory of the Firm," *Journal of Political Economy*, April 1980, pp. 288–307.

[10]H. G. Manne, "Mergers and the Market for Corporate Control," *Journal of Political Economy*, April 1965, pp. 110–120.

[11]D. C. Mueller, "A Theory of Conglomerate Mergers," *Quarterly Journal of Economics*, November 1969, pp. 643–659.

[12]Wilbur G. Lewellen, and B. Huntsman, "Managerial Pay and Corporate Performance," *American Economic Review*, September 1970, pp. 710–722.

[13]James C. Ellert, "Mergers, Antitrust Law Enforcement, and Stockholder Returns," *Journal of Finance*, May 1976, pp. 715–732.

[14]Robert S. Stillman, "Examining Antitrust Policy towards Horizontal Mergers," *Journal of Financial Economics*, April 1983, pp. 225–240; B. E. Eckbo, "Horizontal Mergers, Collusion, and Stockholder Wealth," *Journal of Financial Economics*, April 1983, pp. 241–273.

[15]James N. Dertouzos, and Kenneth E. Thorpe, "Newspaper Groups: Economies of Scale, Tax Laws, and Merger Incentives," Rand Corp. R-2878-SBA, Santa Monica, Calif., June 1982.

Part 2

Cases of Growth and Diversification

Chapter 4

IC Industries: Acquiring to Diversify

William B. Johnson

Chairman and Chief Executive Officer, IC Industries, Inc.,
Chicago, Illinois

In 1985, IC Industries was a diversified company with $5 billion in assets, $4 billion in revenues, and operations in specialty foods, consumer services, commercial products, and rail transportation. That structure resulted from a far-reaching diversification and asset redeployment that began in 1968 from a base that consisted of a $300 million regional railroad, the Illinois Central. Moreover, IC Industries planned on becoming an even more focused growth company by disposing of the railroad and concentrating on areas of the economy that showed promise for long-term growth.

The mid-1980s structure resulted from implementation of three stages of strategic planning. Each stage established goals to be achieved by a combination of acquisitions, dispositions, joint ventures, and selective expansion of facilities. We identified our core businesses and supported their growth. We disposed of marginal operations. Throughout the process we provided for the reordering of priorities when it became advantageous. We have emerged as a "young company" that nonetheless has a long history.

The company originated as the Illinois Central Railroad, which was chartered in 1851. Running from Chicago to New Orleans, the Illinois Central was instrumental in stimulating the emergence of Chicago as a major rail center, and, indeed, the industrial and agricultural development of much of middle America. Many of the towns in its service region were, in fact, named by the railroad's engineers. The company's history fills a massive volume studded with famous names that date to before the Civil War. Abraham Lincoln, who provided legal services to the railroad, is only the best-known example.

With about 6,500 route miles in 12 states, the railroad, now known as the Illinois Central Gulf (ICG), is the seventh largest in the United States. It remains highly visible, as most large railroads are. In fact, some securities analysts in the mid-1980s still tended to think of IC Industries as primarily a railroad company, although we had not been so for more than 15 years.

The process by which the company ceased being "only a railroad" began in the early 1960s. The decision to diversify was not then, and was not subsequently, based on any lack of faith in the essential nature of the railroads. Rather, the objective was to enter businesses that would be less capital-intensive, less labor-intensive, less cyclical, and less government-regulated than the railroad, and that would have better growth prospects.

Because the Interstate Commerce Commission prohibits railroads from owning unrelated businesses, management organized Illinois Central Industries as a holding company and incorporated it in Delaware in August 1962. The change of the corporate name to IC Industries, Inc., came in 1975. The Illinois Central Railroad provided the capital, balance sheet, and people for the new holding company. Little significant diversification was accomplished during the first few years, but the basic groundwork had been laid.

STAGE I: SETTING STRATEGIC OBJECTIVES

In 1966, the year I joined the company, IC Industries developed its first strategic plan, later called Stage I. As announced to the company's shareholders during the annual meeting that year, the plan had four objectives:

1. Modernization of the Illinois Central, which was a profitable business but in need of extensive improvements
2. Accomplishment of a sound rail merger that would make the railroad more efficient and expand its service in the growing industrial areas of the South
3. Development of the company's extensive real estate holdings, valuable land that was no longer needed for railroad operations on Chicago's lakefront, in New Orleans, and elsewhere along the rail system's main line
4. Diversification, the most important, ambitious, and challenging objective

Within two years, we had made significant progress toward all of these goals. First, the railroad launched an accelerated program of rehabilitation. Second, after much careful searching for an appropriate merger partner railroad, the Illinois Central identified the Gulf, Mobile & Ohio (G.M. & O), a connecting system that provided entry to a number of additional markets. An agreement with the G.M. & O. was reached in 1967; after five years of review by the Interstate

Commerce Commission and the courts, the merger was consummated in August 1972, and the ICG was formed.

In the third area, real estate, the company by 1968 had initiated a program of land sales, property management, and joint ventures, including partnership interest in Illinois Center Corp. This project eventually led to the development of Illinois Center, an 83-acre residential and commercial "city within a city" on what had been unsightly railroad yards in downtown Chicago.

Most important, by late 1968, we had made significant progress toward our fourth objective, diversification. We had explored significant positions in industries outside the railroad business where the company could find increased freedom to control its own destiny. We started by acquiring two small companies: Chandeysson Electric Co., St. Louis (1965), a rebuilder of heavy electrical equipment, and Waukesha Foundry Co., Inc., Waukesha, Wisconsin (1968), a manufacturer of precision castings and corrosion-resistant pumps and pumping systems. In 1968, we took a giant step by acquiring Abex Corp., a $275 million manufacturer of automotive products, specialty castings, hydraulic equipment, and rail products.

After the acquisition of Abex, we were no longer "just a railroad." Abex, in fact, was just as large as the railroad. With this one major nonrailroad acquisition, our overall size was nearly doubled. Moreover, because of Abex's extensive foreign operations, IC Industries was transformed from a Midwestern railroad into a truly multinational company.

With its strengthened railroad and competitive industrial companies, IC Industries had created a strong base for future growth.

SEARCH FOR EARNINGS STABILITY

Nonetheless, many of the markets served by all of these components of the corporation were highly cyclical. It was clear that IC Industries needed to continue its program of diversification to achieve stability of earnings in good times or bad. All conglomerates diversify to achieve size and growth. We decided to diversify not only for growth, but for stability and strength.

One industry that offered both of these qualities was soft drink bottling. The most logical candidate for a major acquisition in this industry was Pepsi-Cola General Bottlers, Inc., headquartered in Chicago. With a six-state distribution franchise, Pepsi General would give us the strongest possible entry into the growing soft drink industry. We purchased this $100 million company in February 1970, and built on that base by acquiring Dad's Root Beer, another fine old Chicago company, in 1971; the assets of Bubble Up Co., Inc., in 1973; and several other successful Pepsi franchise operations in the Midwest during the 1970s and 1980s. With a solid line-up of complementary soft drink products, Pepsi General has been a significant and steady contributor to our overall earnings.

After acquiring Pepsi General, we continued pressing for additional balance to our portfolio by seeking additional acquisitions in consumer products and services. One that soon attracted our attention was Midas International Corp., a Chicago-based franchisor of automotive service shops. Midas and Pepsi General both derived their strength from stable consumer markets that counterbalanced the commercial focus of the railroad and Abex. Midas' unique merchandising concept emphasized specialty exhaust system service by marketing mufflers and related exhaust components directly to motorists through a far-flung chain of franchised retail outlets.

In January 1972, we acquired this $100 million company. We quickly recognized that its greatest strength lay in its unique merchandising concept, and a few years later we began work toward the eventual divestiture of its relatively cyclical recreational vehicle manufacturing operations. As a result of this divestiture, which was concluded in August 1982, Midas was freed to focus entirely on its "under-the-car" service specialty, which it has extended into the areas of brake service, shock absorber replacement, and front-end alignment.

The Pepsi General and Midas acquisitions represented deliberate steps in the transformation of IC Industries into a large consumer-oriented company. This has continued to be evolutionary, because each major acquisition has, in a sense, created a "new" IC Industries with new products and services, new markets and marketing strategies, and new financial cycles. Each subsequent acquisition or divestiture has, therefore, been made in response to the practical experience of this "new" IC Industries, not the one that preceded it.

The working out of this evolutionary process has necessitated a high degree of flexibility. Companies such as Pepsi General and Midas, which have produced consistent contributions to corporate goals, have been not only retained, but nurtured. However, if an acquisition or line of business falls persistently short of performance targets, we analyze it intensively and frequently mark it for divestment.

An example of the latter was IC's former Financial Services Group, which we began building in the early 1970s with the acquisition of Lincoln Financial, Inc., Houston, and Midwest Life Insurance Co., Lincoln, Nebraska. The life insurance and other services provided by this group offered the advantages of being low in both capital and labor requirements in comparison with some of our other industries. However, the subsequent revolution in the financial services industry convinced us that in order to compete effectively, a vastly larger company was of the essence. Because we determined there were more rewarding opportunities in other industries, we chose not to expand in this direction, and by 1979 we had divested all of our financial services companies.

STAGE II: CONSUMER PRODUCTS THRUST

On the basis of largely successful experiences in diversification, we adopted in 1976 a new set of goals, referred to as Stage II of our long-range plans. These goals were to acquire a large, free-standing consumer products company, to expand or dispose of our Financial Services Group, and to merge or sell the railroad. As noted earlier, divestiture of financial services was completed in 1979. We deferred disposition of the railroad, first until major main-line rehabilitation had been completed and, later, to take advantage of $341 million in tax benefits offered by the Economic Recovery Tax Act, approved in 1981.

By 1978, IC Industries was ready to approach the goal of acquiring a large consumer products concern. Our balance sheet was in good order. We were in a position to seek a large, free-standing company that would offer additional protection from cyclicality through potential for consistent earnings in both good times and bad. After eliminating financial services from consideration, the food business, in which we had already gained experience with Pepsi General, seemed the logical place to look. We targeted Pet, Inc., a nearly $1 billion company with an excellent record as a marketer of packaged foods and a producer of food store equipment under the Hussmann name. With a stable of leading consumer brands already to its credit, Pet offered earnings stability and growth that was largely recession-proof—the largest counterbalance until then to our commercial businesses—as well as a host of possible future synergies.

Considering how well Pet has fared in the IC fold, it is rather remarkable that initial contacts between the two companies were stressful. Pet resisted the first overtures and was planning to acquire the Hardees fast food chain, which we did not want. But after follow-up talks and an increase in our offer, Pet dropped the Hardees deal and agreed to be acquired in a cash tender offer that cost IC $406 million. Some analysts suggested that we overpaid. But since the acquisition, the compound growth rates of 16 percent for Pet and 21 percent for Hussmann have provided a powerful anticyclical boost to total corporate earnings.

The purchase of Pet serves well to illustrate our approach to acquisitions that can be described as aggressive prudence. When we decided to enter the food business, careful research pointed to Pet as a clear choice. It was a free-standing company marketing highly respected brands. It had strength and depth of management. Its balance sheet was in good order. Prospects for growth were exceptional, particularly in meeting new lifestyle demands for packaged convenience foods.

We made known our interest and intentions, entered into negotiations, and rather quickly arrived at a price acceptable to both parties. Our criteria and procedure in acquiring Pet typify our philosophy. We have avoided bidding wars and protracted resistance. We much prefer to welcome a new company to the IC Industries family rather than drag it into the corporate fold, kicking and screaming.

After acquiring successful companies such as Pet, IC Industries consistently has demonstrated a willingness to rely primarily upon such companies' operational know-how, giving them increased assistance, when justified, but also allowing them "room to run." All of our major subsidiaries have their own boards, most of them with outside directors. Corporate headquarters has moved very deliberately, learning as much as possible about the products and markets in acquired companies before making decisions about their future directions. However, once corporate headquarters has acquired sufficient knowledge of a company's business, we have offered carefully considered counsel designed to maximize its strengths, and encouraged the management to develop and implement its own asset redeployment and selective investment programs. Since its acquisition, for example, Pet has been made even stronger through a planned program of acquisition and divestiture. Between 1978 and 1984, Pet divested 14 low-potential businesses, including Musselman Fruit Products, Laura Scudder

Snack Foods, the 9-0-5 and Vendome stores units, and most of its Merchants Refrigeration warehouses; acquired three high-potential companies in baking and specialty foods; reorganized; and strengthened its worldwide position in specialty packaged foods. With a stable of well-known brands such as Pet, Pet-Ritz, Old El Paso, Whitman's, and Underwood, 80 percent of Pet's key product lines hold the number one or number two position in their markets.

STAGE III: TECHNOLOGY AND MARKET PENETRATION

We announced Stage III of our strategic plan in 1981. Among our stated goals were to expand the technological base for commercial products and increase penetration in markets outside the United States.

William A. Underwood, Co., a maker of meat spreads and baked beans, was a particularly successful acquisition for Pet in 1982. Prior to the acquisition of Pet, there would have been little, if any, logical relationship between Underwood and the rest of IC Industries. With Pet already assimilated, however, Underwood was not only a logical fit, but one that provided excellent synergies with Pet's existing brands and manufacturing facilities. Underwood also brought a strong foothold in foreign markets, a strength that since has been applied to overseas introductions of other Pet brands.

Hussman Corp., acquired as part of Pet, subsequently became an IC Industries subsidiary in its own right. The company, which was the first supermarket fixture manufacturer to enter the refrigeration business, now is a leading supplier of refrigerated display and merchandising equipment for the food store industry. Hussmann's continuing growth has been powered, in part, by acquisitions of operations in Mexico, Canada, and the United Kingdom. It now serves markets in 70 countries.

We took a quantum step toward our goal of technology enhancement with the acquisition of Pneumo Corp. in October 1984. The $1.3 billion company is a leading producer of aircraft landing gear and sophisticated flight control systems. The pooling of Pneumo and Abex aerospace capabilities presents opportunities for expanded involvement in the next generation of military and commercial aircraft and space vehicles. Pneumo's other operations, a food chain and a drugstore group, were divested in 1985. We are convinced that Pneumo will prove to be as important to IC Industries as Pet and Hussmann have been.

IC Industries has achieved most of its strategic goals. Our planning has paid off. Thanks to our diversified structure, the consumer companies—Pet, Pepsi General, and Midas—maintained strong sales and earnings that provided a safety net for unavoidable cyclical setbacks at Abex and the railroad during periods of recession, including 1981 and 1982. As the economy improved later in the 1980s, the latter two companies, cylical but still strong, have shown the leverage to rebound with economic up-cycles and thus to serve as "charge vehicles" for the company as a whole.

THREE-LEGGED BALANCE

The strength and balance that has been achieved through IC Industries' diversification will continue to form the basis for its future growth. IC Industries' long-range plan focuses on development of the company through solid investments in three basic areas: specialty foods, consumer services, and commercial products. In the mid-1980s, we also reactivated planning for disposition of the railroad, now that we have taken full advantage of the available tax benefits of this operation.

This unique diversity not only provides protection against the ups and downs of the economic cycle and gives the company optimal opportunities for long-term profit and growth, but also provides investors with the kind of diversity, protection, and growth potential they seek in their own portfolio.

By dividing IC Industries into these three areas, one can see more clearly the distinct types of potential represented by each. Food and soft drink industries continue to grow at a steady pace. Consumer services of the kind represented by Midas have a strong potential for growth. Commercial products provide opportunities for highly leveraged earnings, particularly in times of economic recovery.

This kind of balance is the ultimate justification for our deliberate process of diversification. It is the result of the program we began in the early 1960s. And it has increased the value of our shareholders' investment. That is what American capitalism is all about—and it negates the criticisms of those who call for one "standard model" for corporate structures, whether based on synergism, "pure play," or centralized or decentralized management control.

There is no standard formula for success through diversification, but there is no arguing with it when it works. IC Industries now is substantially protected against the violent swings in the economy. We intend to maintain this strength by making the most productive use of assets, relying heavily on a leadership in each subsidiary that is monitored closely, supported financially, and provided with liberal incentives through parent company programs that reward performance. Future acquisitions, to expand existing lines of business or to enter new ones, will remain high on our list of goals for asset deployment.

Chapter 5

ARA Services: Seeking a Common Thread

William S. Fishman

Chairman of the Executive Committee,
ARA Services, Inc., Philadelphia, Pennsylvania

Services represent the fastest-growing sector of our national economy. In the mid-1950s, the United States became the first country in the world to have its workforce shift from predominantly blue-collar (manufacturing) to white-collar (services). Some 57 percent of gross national product already comes from the service sector; in the 1980s we expect that more than 70 percent of the nation's workers will be employed in the service sector. ARA Services, Inc., identified the service sector as an area of tremendous opportunity about 40 years ago, and its primary strategy in the intervening years has been to concentrate on providing services.

Mergers and acquisitions have played major roles in both the growth and diversification of ARA that have resulted from our basic strategy. We have completed more than 300 acquisitions, which, coupled with internal expansion, have turned ARA into the largest and most diversified services concern in the United States. The company manages food and refreshment facilities, periodicals distribution, health and family care services, textile rental and maintenance, and transportation services. In the 1984 fiscal year, ARA revenues in the United States and in eight foreign countries exceeded $3.4 billion. We employed

115,000 people worldwide and served more than 10 million people each day at more than 400,000 locations.

Key operating areas include:

Food service—We manage food and refreshment services for people on the job, students at schools and colleges, hospital patients and staff, senior citizens at community centers, air travelers, and people enjoying their leisure hours in parks, stadiums, resorts, and fine restaurants.

Distribution—We manage the delivery of 380 million magazines and books a year to 25,000 retail outlets—more than any other company.

Health care—Health care services are provided through institutional long-term care facilities for the chronically ill and the aged; Spectrum Emergency Care, which manages emergency department staffing and business systems for nearly 300 client hospitals; and Correctional Medical Systems, which provides medical services for inmates in 16 correctional facilities in more than five states. In a related area, National Child Care manages 100 child care centers in 10 states.

Business services—Aratex Services, which rents, maintains, and delivers personalized work apparel and environmental control items to clients throughout the United States is the largest garment and textile rental company in the world. ARA Maintenance Services manages building maintenance and infection control programs for institutions and industry, and provides ground services at 15 major airports.

Transportation—Smith's Transfer division specializes in less-than-truckload shipments and warehousing for 50,000 clients in 37 states. ARA Fleet Services manages fleet maintenance for local governments and operates a remanufacturing center for ARA and client vehicles.

EXTENDING PROFESSIONAL SERVICE TECHNIQUES

To understand how we got here, we must turn the clock back to 1936 and change the location to California, where Davidson Automatic Merchandising Co. was founded by Davre and Henry Davidson. Their first major account was with Douglas Aircraft; the first week's receipts from Douglas totaled $7.56. The primary product was peanuts. In 1941, I joined Automatic Merchandising Co., a vending firm that was providing a variety of services in Chicago and Detroit. Davre, Henry, and I became friends. We shared some clients. They served plants on the West Coast and I served their facilities in the Midwest. We exchanged ideas and shared the same business philosophies. By the time we merged in 1959 to form ARA, it was clear to us that we were in the service industry and could expand from our base in vending operations.

The Food Service Industry

Our success to that point was based on development of a system for professionally providing a direct service to people. In seeking expansion, we wanted to apply those techniques to other services that enjoyed constant demand and could not be postponed, inventoried, or imported. We also sought to meet needs that were basic—such as the need for food and beverages—and that could provide the company with stability. We determined that the logical extension of our operation would be into personal food service. Many of our clients operated cafeterias for their employees, but vending almost always was separate, and considered a competitor. We felt that these services should be complementary and that they had the ingredients for a perfect match. This is how we came to acquire Slater Co. in Philadelphia for $15 million in July 1961.

Slater was founded on the campus of the University of Pennsylvania in 1926 as a food service manager for fraternity houses. In the early 1930s, Slater gained its first industrial account; in the 1940s, its first college; and in 1952, its first hospital client. It was a well-run, efficient operation that managed food service for a wide range of clients and employed thousands of persons throughout the eastern half of the United States. It was an excellent Eastern counterpart for our Midwest and Western bases of operations. Slater represented a golden opportunity for us to both expand into personal food services and to acquire a host of highly qualified top management people. This since has become a basic consideration in major acquisitions. Many Slater people are still with us—including some senior officers of our company. This gave us for the first time a very important ingredient in the ARA service management system: corporate staff support. Slater had assembled in its Philadelphia headquarters a staff of top management personnel with a wide range of skills who could supply expert support for the operators in the field.

With the acquisition of Slater, we divided our operations into three markets—business and industry, schools and colleges, and hospitals—and then concentrated on developing specialized expertise for each. This quickly led to two basic conclusions about our industry:

- Expertise is transferable. What proves to be very effective in one account quite often can be used in another.
- Each account, no matter how large or small, represents a unique challenge. No two are really identical. Each demands specialized solutions. Each demands a personalized service, frequently serving two masters: the contracting client and the ultimate consumer.

Often, the aims of these two masters are different. A university might desire good, well-balanced meals, whereas the students may want an all-night Rathskeller offering beer and sandwiches. It is our job to make both happy.

Leisure and Recreation Markets

We realized the importance of flexibility in making the necessary adjustments to minimize the valleys and maximize the peaks of the economic cycles in our markets, while always being on the alert for new opportunities and new markets. This was primarily the function of the top management, which must anticipate changes in economic conditions, identify market trends, and hopefully, plan in advance to adjust accordingly.

One of the changes that was noted in the mid-1960s was the trend to a shorter workweek and longer vacations. This meant more leisure time and more time away from the job—which would mean lower revenues for us. Therefore, in 1966 we decided that where our ultimate consumers went we would follow. We moved into the leisure and recreation market through the formation of what is now known as ARA Leisure Services, Inc. This unit now provides food services at major stadiums, arenas, convention centers, race tracks, and even state and national parks, where we also handle lodging. The operation of the motel and lodging facilities gave us an added dimension in our range of services that could be employed elsewhere. Travel, a natural adjunct to the leisure and recreation market, was such a field.

In 1967 we acquired Air LaCarte, which prepares meals for in-flight dining and serves 59 airlines from six flight kitchens. Air LaCarte was sold in 1983 because it no longer conformed to our expectations for future growth potential. Through another acquisition, Aero Enterprises, we expanded into operation of concessionnaire services at airports, including newsstands, gift and jewelry shops, novelty stores, cafeterias, restaurants, and cocktail lounges. From there we moved onto the runways with Ground Services, Inc., which provides complete passenger, baggage, and cargo handling. This segment in turn was expanded to include specialty services—screening of passengers and baggage before boarding as well as ticketing and aircraft turnaround operations.

Our object has been constantly to improve and expand the range of services we provide at airports so that we can offer a broader base and wider expertise than our competitors. We are able to make a proposal to manage, under contract to a city, the complete operation of its municipal airport. This covers the administration, development of a master plan, arranging financing for needed expansion, and overseeing the necessary construction, as well as concurrently providing the full range of services that airlines and travelers require.

Distribution of Periodicals

The transfer of expertise probably was never more evident than when we entered the field of periodicals distribution. The first time our management people saw a warehouse for the distribution of newspapers, magazines, and books, they recognized it immediately as a vending products warehouse. The basic functions essentially were ones we already had mastered: inventory control, packing for shipment, routing trucks, distribution, strict accounting, and fleet maintenance. To take full advantage of this interchangeability, we acquired District News Co. of Washington, D.C., in 1968, which became the forerunner of our Distributive Services Group. ARA's Magazine and Book Division, expanded heavily by other acquisitions, is the leader in the distributive field.

Oil-Drilling Rig Services

In keeping with our basic concepts of flexibility and probing for new markets, we moved into providing food management and housekeeping services on offshore oil rigs in the Gulf of Mexico in 1968. This division has expanded to other locales such as Alaska, Newfoundland, Trinidad, and the West Coast. We provided food and housekeeping service for the first rig in the Baltimore Canyon off the Atlantic Coast. In the United Kingdom we manage such services for rigs in the North Sea, and are extending this business to exploration rigs in North Atlantic waters off the Canadian coast. These are 24-hour-a-day, seven-day-a-week operations.

Services for the Elderly and the Young

During the 1960s, our planning process signaled that there was a large and growing need to provide care for the elderly. ARA was a pioneer in providing hot, nutritional meals to the elderly, but there were many more areas in which our wide range of skills could be applied. As a result of an intensive market study begun in 1970, we decided to focus on the nursing home management market. We sought out one of the top-quality nursing home companies and in September 1973 acquired National Living Centers, which then operated 41 health care facilities with 4,100 beds. Ten years later, ARA was operating 266 nursing and special care facilities and four retirement centers with more than 31,000 beds in the Midwest, South, Southwest, and West.

Moving to the other end of the age spectrum, we had been serving young people in schools since 1950. But in the late 1960s, we identified expanding demand for school bus service as a growing problem for districts throughout the country. Educators knew little about the service but were being forced into it at great expense and consumption of time. Because we had worked with children and had experience in buying and maintaining rolling stock, routing, controls, recruiting, and training, school bus service appeared to be a natural expansion of our service base. In the early 1970s, we formed the ARA School Bus Transportation Group and soon became the leading school bus contractor in the country. We subsequently sold the school bus operations but remain in the business by providing management for clients who own buses and pay us a fee for our services. We disposed of our "rolling stock" business because we found that the system for awarding school bus contracts frequently does not allow for superior service where the criteria are based strictly on the lowest bid.

Environmental Services

Another example of understanding the client's problems and designing a service to help was the formation of our Environmental Services Group. We provide specialized, professionally managed housekeeping operations for hospitals to improve efficiency, lower costs, reduce turnover, and relieve the hospital administrator of a major burden. Utilizing our talents for working with the skilled and semiskilled employee, this group now offers environmental services to clients in 17 states.

We entered the textile rental service business with the acquisition of Aratex Services, Inc., in 1977 and expanded it tremendously by acquiring Means Services in 1982. We are the largest textile service company in the country, providing regular pickup and delivery service for more than 200,000 client organizations in 36 states. More than 1 million American workers wear Aratex uniforms on the job. Many are protected by Aratex workgloves and other safety apparel, or use our industrial convenience items, such as shop towels or walk-off mats.

We also are continuing to expand Aratex's Araclean division, which processes particulate-free and sterilized garments for hospitals, pharmaceutical firms, and high-technology industries.

Although the expansion into environmental services may seem, at first glance, to be uncharacteristic of our company's expertise in the food service business, it actually has an inner logic that we followed very carefully. Consider, for example, a hospital where we provide the food service. Through the provision of that service, we become, in effect, not just experts in the food service of that hospital but experts in the overall traffic of the institution. We come to know all the people and all the divisions, be they surgical, convalescence, or other. Consequently, we are prepared to sell other diversified services to the same market and the same people. Our knowledge of the total care system and the people within a given client institution is a tremendous advantage to us, and a move into environmental services is thus a logical extension of our expertise.

Encore Services, Inc., became a part of ARA's Environmental Services Group in 1979. It provides computer-controlled maintenance of air conditioning, electrical, and plumbing systems; major appliances for individual condominium owners in Florida and Arizona; and grounds maintenance, janitorial, pest control, and accounting services for large condominium complexes. Again, there was an inner logic to this acquisition. We found that many of the characteristics of Encore's business systems were the same as ours. We shared a common understanding of such matters as scheduling of repairs, recording of service, and maintenance of equipment and machinery. In fact, Encore brought to us some new maintenance and servicing techniques that could be shared with our other lines of business.

Trucking and Shipping

Smith's Transfer Corp., which merged into ARA in early 1980, specializes in less-than-truckload shipments of general commodities, such as machinery, textiles, chemicals, and various consumer goods, to customers in 36 Eastern and Midwestern states, California, and Toronto. Its 7,700 tractors, trailers, and trucks operate from more than 140 terminal and warehousing facilities and haul more than 2.5 million tons of cargo each year. Although at first glance the acquisition of Smith's may appear to be outside our normal lines of service business, in reality it was not. There were many similarities between our ongoing operations and the operations of Smith's. There were similarities in terminal operations and bulk breakpoints. We shared common know-how in warehousing and distribution and in the operation and maintenance of vehicles. In addition, Smith's and our other operations employed many of the same types of people. It takes a special kind of person to be either a route driver or a trucker, and we shared this type of people knowledge.

The People Care Business

Late in 1980 we expanded into the people care business with the acquisition of National Child Care Centers, Inc., which operated 117 child care centers in 10 states, with a licensed capacity for over 20,000 children. The company provides preschool and school-age children with an away-from-home environment where they can continue their education and social development under programmed professional supervision while their parents are at work.

Again, there was a rationale. We already had been very heavily into the training and education of people. It followed logically that we ultimately would get into the education business at some level and, in my view, National Child Care is evolving into a genuine preschool experience, a part of the overall education of young people. Child care has gone beyond the babysitting phase, and National Child Care is in the forefront of efforts to expand and enhance child care programs.

ESTABLISHING PERSONAL RELATIONSHIPS

From my participation in some 300 acquisitions, several lessons have emerged from my experience. Initially, I have learned that there must always be sound and logical business reasons for entertaining any acquisition in the first place. But I have also learned that there are no magic formulas. There may be a pattern, or an internal consistency, as I have tried to point out, but every situation is different and there's no point in trying to boil this down to a set formula. The most important facet of any transaction is to establish a personal relationship between the seller and the buyer—not as companies but as individuals. Until the seller has faith and believes in the buyer, the transaction is a very cold and probably unsuccessful one. If any lesson is to be learned, it is this: Acquisitions are not simply a financial game. If you are going to train people to become experts in acquisitions, train them as if they were being groomed as salespeople.

I once worked for the better part of three years on acquiring a company in Chicago that we wanted very much, and I wasn't getting anywhere. The target company was a competitor, so there was a natural skepticism and hostility between us. One day I took the owner to a restaurant in Chicago. When the waiter arrived, my guest broke into tears. It turned out that years earlier the waiter had served his father, who had recently died. This fellow had a tough, hard shell, but he wasn't hard inside. When I understood what he was crying about, he and I began to relate. Those are the kinds of things that get into an acquisition that finance people don't always understand.

THE SEARCH FOR
COMPATIBLE ACQUISITIONS

We're always looking for acquisition candidates, but that doesn't mean we always acquire firms that become available to us. Some people characterize ARA as being an acquisition-growth company, but that is not completely true. About two-thirds of our growth since 1959 has been by internal growth and about one-third by acquisitions. Acquisitions offer just one type of marketing, one type of growth, one type of planning and implementation.

Most of our acquisitions are what many people call "add-ons"—to expand an existing service by acquiring a similar operation in an adjacent geographic area or within the same region. An example is Aratex, our workwear company. We acquired one company and have helped expand it with six additional acquisitions. The core acquisition was doing about $80 million, but it has grown to $300 million by acquisition, plus marketing and sales programs.

The first step in our acquisition process is to decide whether we would like to be in a certain industry and if that industry provides a "fit" with the overall character of our company. Then we identify the best candidate in that industry. When we decided to go into the motor freight carrier business, we did a complete industry study. Another executive and I visited 15 different motor carriers before we selected Smith's Transfer as our logical candidate for acquisition.

In evaluating target candidates, we select the candidate firms very carefully on the basis of their records of growth, performance and earnings, reputation for integrity and good business practices, and, very important, the quality of management. We determine whether the personalities of the acquired company and ours will mesh. All marriages are not created in heaven, and neither are all acquisitions. We've walked away from many acquisitions because we felt that the management of the company was not likely to be a good partner for us. We don't want any surprises after the acquisition. And we want happy management. We have maintained more than 80 percent of the acquired management through the years.

Retaining Management Is Vital

I credit the application of people-management skills for our success at retaining management. We treat the acquired management as though it is part of our team and always has been.

For example, we count tenure at ARA Services to include service with the acquired company. We can't buy people. We can buy assets, we can buy cash, and we can buy property, but we don't buy people. If we tried to, they wouldn't be at ARA very long. We do our best to motivate people to come with the acquired companies and join our team. There have been fewer than 10 transactions in which we acquired the company with the intent of replacing management. We want to acquire an ongoing successful management base to which we can add.

It is critically important, of course, to get to know the management of a company you are interested in acquiring. If they are in a business related to ours, or one we have occasion to observe, we learn from contact with them. If they are in a business we have been in we go by their trade reputation and we spend a lot of time with them. We live with the management of a prospective acquisition until we really feel we know these people and their problems—and what the people problems might be if they joined ARA.

One of the big differences between a service company and an industrial company in an acquisition is that we are not acquiring a product, but adding people who know how to deliver a service. If you deliver an inferior product, you can fix that product or replace it. If you perform bad service, it's difficult to fix it after the fact. People remember the mistakes you make in the service business more than they remember the good performance. We can serve meals, as we do, twice a day for 364 days in a college dining service, but if we serve a bad meal, or in some other way make the client/customer dissatisfied on the last day of the year, they remember that very well.

Mistakes and Divestitures Are Rare

Certainly not every acquisition has panned out. We've made some mistakes but not many. I'd say fewer than 10 turned out to be bad deals. These were mistakes in judgment. In a few instances, we ignored our own instincts and didn't pay enough attention to our intuition. We forced our answers.

This happened when we acquired the Morse organization in the construction management business. Afterward, we found that it was not the kind of business that fit our background and experience. It was a good business, but not under our management. It continues to succeed under the original owner-management, which bought it back from us. We also learned a lesson when we bought the Fry management consulting firm. The consulting business is highly dependent on individual people within the organization, and was not a good fit for a company like ours, which is built on systems and controls. It was not a business we belonged in, and it took us about four years to find that out.

Evaluating Target Companies

Our corporate staff at headquarters does the research on proposed acquisitions. There are several staffs that work on them. Our finance department, for example, has people assigned to analyze track records, financials, balance sheets, and P&Ls on the proposed acquirees. With a public company that's fairly simple. If it's a private company, we have to start negotiations before we see the material and get down to negotiating price. We also use our own security department to verify the reputation and integrity of a company. Our auditing department audits their books and records. Our marketing department reports to us on the target's marketing techniques. We conduct surveys of their clients to determine customer/client satisfaction and to let us know whether this acquiree has been able to satisfy the marketplace.

In the past, we've been helped by the board and its development committee when we were searching for good acquisition candidates, and we've been voted down by the board or the development committee when a member may know something that causes him not to like a particular transaction. The board once voted us down on a proposal for a food and vending operation in a foreign country because it believed our interests would be better served if we did not go into that country.

A Form of Selling

Making an acquisition is really another form of selling. The principal job in the beginning of the acquisition process is to persuade or demonstrate to the acquiree that we're the kind of company it should become part of, and to explain the benefits that would accrue from a combination. When we go out to sell, we're actually trying to find out what the prospective client thinks it wants, what it really wants, how much it is willing to pay, and how much we can provide the service for. It's the same in an acquisition.

Essentially, we have grown by concentrating on what we do best: providing basic services where the need is constant and can't be postponed, and realizing that we are part of, and growing with, the service sector of the economy. ARA has proven to be a sound, predictable company. Rarely have we had to go outside the company to finance growth. Our total capitalization usually has been about 35 percent long-term debt and 65 percent equity. ARA has never turned down a growth opportunity because of a lack of financial capability.

ARA'S OWN LBO AND THE FUTURE

In fact, our financial predictability was a major factor in gaining the confidence of the financial institutions that responded so readily in providing the funds for ARA's $882 million leveraged buy-out in 1984. Now that the company has gone private, I am confident that its growth and success will continue and will be enhanced under the current management. That is principally because what we have to sell is our professional management expertise, and the leveraged buy-out has given some of the best managers in the service industry in America a long-term stake in the future of the company. Nothing could better guarantee the continuity and high levels of performance that have become so characteristic of ARA over the past 25 years.

There is great promise for the service management industry. More and more firms and institutions forced to cope with increasing economic pressures are reexamining some of the services they provide to determine what can be contracted to professional managers. Service is a labor-intensive industry that presents many problems, but there is one large consolation: No technological development can seriously harm us.

Chapter 6

InterNorth: The Energy Connection

Sam F. Segnar

Chairman and Chief Executive Officer, Retired,
HNG/InterNorth, Inc., Houston, Texas

Acquisition can be a quick and efficient means of participating in a new market or expanding an existing one. As a result, an acquisition can be a tool to enhance a long-term strategy, and it has a particular attraction to a company whose traditional businesses have limited potential for growth. This was a situation that our company faced at the start of the 1980s.

Our problems were compounded, moreover, because we were an energy company operating in an era when energy markets are changing radically. Prices for all forms of energy lack stability. And energy consumption, to say the least, will not experience rapid expansion.

Nevertheless, we had profited from our expertise in the energy business. Fundamentally, we did not intend to disregard or dilute our strength. Energy was a market that we knew, that we had studied, and, best of all, that we had made money in. All of our initial acquisition efforts were centered on companies related to the energy business, such as those that provide energy-related equipment, like Crouse-Hinds Co. and Bucyrus-Erie Co., or those that produce energy directly, like Belco Petroleum Corp.

We decided on the acquisition tool because we determined that our traditional energy businesses had limited growth potential, particularly in the United States.

PLANNING FOR CHANGE

In 1980 we celebrated our fiftieth anniversary and changed our name from Northern Natural Gas to InterNorth. The name change was significant: It proclaimed our intent to restructure, retained a bridge to the past, and, at the same time, indicated our interest in the future—particularly international markets.

We reported record net income of $186 million and operating revenues exceeding $2.5 billion for 1980. But we realized that our objective of increasing earnings 3 to 4 percent annually after inflation was unrealistic unless we changed the company. Our natural gas business was heading toward the transition of decontrol. Market forces would determine profitability rather than investment. We realized that the price of natural gas would reach parity with the prices of competing fuels. This would not be the ideal climate for rapid growth and high returns. At the same time, our petrochemical and natural gas liquids interests were centered in commodity businesses, where the markets were highly competitive and subject to rapid swings in the general economy.

Our conservative perception of the domestic energy industry was confirmed by our energy forecasts. For the rest of this century, growth in the oil and gas business would be slower than general economic growth. In particular, oil demand would fall, and natural gas demand would be essentially flat. However, our look at the future did suggest two areas that would do better: electricity and coal. Demand for both is expected to be high, and both compete against natural gas. Electricity, particularly, competes in the residential market, whereas coal is an alternative fuel in the industrial and electric utility markets. It became obvious that we should be involved in the use of coal and in the generation, transmission, or application of electrical energy.

SHAPING AN ACQUISITION STRATEGY

Conceptually, this view of the energy business helped to shape our long-term strategy. When we thought about our company in the year 1990, we realized that:

- Our natural gas interests, which made up about 50 percent of our earnings in 1980, would account for about 25 percent in 1990.
- The liquid fuels business would drop to about 20 percent of earnings from 31 percent.
- Petrochemicals, which supplied about 9 percent, would expand to about 15 percent.

- The exploration and production share would increase to 15 percent from 6.5 percent.

When we totaled the numbers, they added up to less than 100 percent. There was a gap between our earnings objectives and the potential of our existing businesses. Notably, our natural gas pipeline company would not be able to meet its objectives. Thus, an earnings gap of about 25 percent would have to be filled by new activities.

History provided some perspective for the decisions we would have to make. Anyone who looks at the list of the top 25 corporations in 1925 and compares it to the list of the top 25 in 1975 will notice that there were very few survivors and that those that did remain had changed significantly. In examining the comparisons we also noticed that it was dangerous to count on a single activity. So although our strength had been in natural gas, we appreciated the need to change. Yet there was no need for radical change. We could maintain our involvement in energy. Obviously, there would be opportunities in the electricity market—a market that InterNorth understood. Electricity has been and will continue to be a strong competitor of natural gas. In order to operate our natural gas business successfully, we had to examine the electricity industry so we could understand the competition. We were, as a result, well versed in electricity pricing and growth patterns.

To participate in the electricity market, we decided, it was not necessary to produce that energy form. We could avoid the long-term capital commitments and myriad utility-related problems by being involved in markets that are on either side of the generating plant. We could provide feedstock for producing electricity, the equipment used to provide this feed, and distribution equipment. This would be an activity that could even complement our existing businesses. If either oil or gas was used for generating electricity, we could participate. We could even be instrumental in satisfying electricity demand by pursuing cogeneration possibilities. The electricity market also would involve coal. Coal is the other energy source that should experience real growth, partially as a prime feed for electrical generation. It was another business in which our company should be an active player, we determined.

With these factors in mind, a strategy was defined. As a company, we would:

- Redeploy our assets
- Expand our base to meet our earnings objectives
- Make use of our knowledge and experience in energy-related businesses
- Concentrate on electricity-related ventures.

These general goals were refined even further. The preparation of our corporate energy forecasts exposed us to the difficulty of pinpointing energy prices. Anyone in the energy business since the early 1970s has felt the effects of price volatility. To limit price effects, we decided to position InterNorth in businesses where the price of fuel was not an overwhelmingly important factor. These types of businesses could provide a stabilizing influence in uncertain times.

There were other criteria. Time and capital were important factors. In three to seven years we would not be able to meet our financial goals with just our existing businesses. Obviously, there wasn't time to develop new businesses from scratch. Also, the market had been very unpredictable. Flexibility was important. The ability to redirect assets quickly would be essential in the future. But InterNorth's existing businesses were extremely capital-intensive, and this type of structure is not very adaptable to change. It was a structure we wished to avoid in the future.

With these factors in mind, we decided to acquire companies as a solution to our timing problem, and we decided to supplement full acquisitions by acquiring minority positions in a number of firms. Acquisition would enable us to expand while developing new businesses of our own. Acquiring minority positions would permit maximum flexibility. If, over a period of time, these companies grew as we anticipated, and it was beneficial for everyone involved, we could increase our holdings. Should the arrangement prove to be unsuitable, we could keep the minority stake or sell it and move our investment elsewhere.

While formulating our program, we also realized that we might have to complement our overall acquisition strategy by divesting businesses that would not be able to contribute to our future, yet that had real current value to another owner. Besides ridding ourselves of operations that didn't meet our financial goals, or were situated in areas where we didn't plan to expand, the divestitures could generate cash for retiring or restructuring debt and provide funds for reinvestment in promising new ventures.

ESTABLISHING TIME FRAMES

In any plan, timing is a significant factor. To enhance the value of our company optimally, we had to consider three distinct time frames: the short term, or up to three years out; the midterm, or three to seven years out; and the long term, or seven to 15 years out.

Shareholders and investment analysts want a company to pay attention to today's problems. Our three-year budget, operating plans, capital requirements, and earnings goals emphasized our existing businesses. The short-term plan was well focused and set to meet shareholder and analysts' demands for current performance.

Midterm emphasis was on the investment decision. New businesses were nurtured to pick up the slack caused by the leveling off of mature activities such as the natural gas businesses. The crude and condensate interests and the International Division, which were fairly young, were expected to grow appreciably in the midterm. And the 1983 acquisition of Belco Petroleum resulted in the immediate expansion of existing exploration and production activities.

For the long term, we had to be positioned to operate profitably in a different world. It was this time frame that forced us to consider expansion into new areas. Our thrust to participate in electricity and coal—including cogeneration activities, an investment in Bucyrus-Erie, and a joint-venture coal pipeline—fit into this category.

AN INITIAL MOVE, A SOBERING LESSON

In September 1980, InterNorth offered to purchase 6.7 million shares of Crouse-Hinds Co., Syracuse, New York, for approximately $40 per share. This was the first attempt at implementing our strategy. Crouse-Hinds was a manufacturer of electrical products with domestic and international facilities. At the time, Crouse-Hinds, which had revenues of more than $372 million in 1979, was attempting to acquire Belden Corp., a producer of wire and cable. As part of our offer, we required that Crouse-Hinds drop its interest in Belden.

Initially, we tried to purchase about 55 percent of Crouse-Hinds with cash. We planned to acquire the rest of the company with preferred stock. But less than a week after we made the bid, Crouse-Hind's directors advised their stockholders to reject the offer. Belden and Crouse-Hinds then filed a number of lawsuits to impede our takeover attempt. In November, InterNorth amended its offer to include Belden and reduced the proposed price to $37 a share for Crouse-Hinds common stock. But that same month Crouse-Hinds announced a merger agreement with Cooper Industries, Inc., and the deal was completed the following month, after we had dropped out.

Crouse-Hinds was a very attractive target. In the 1970s, the company's income grew to an annual rate of 23 percent, and it typically earned better than an 18 percent return on equity. In addition, Crouse-Hinds was able to maintain its superior performance despite poor general economic conditions. Basically, the business was balanced by its various markets so that its earnings were not very cyclical—a particular attraction to us because InterNorth must weather the storms of the petrochemical and liquid markets. Crouse-Hinds's prospects for the future seemed to be excellent. The company made electrical construction materials, load centers, circuit breakers, lighting equipment, industrial controls, and electrical distribution equipment. It expected above-average growth in sales related to marine oil exploration and production, synfuel projects, airport lighting, and pipeline construction. International sales also would be boosted by demands from overseas companies in the liquids production, petrochemical, and oil-refining areas.

In almost every way, Crouse-Hinds fit our strategic goals. Its activities were energy-related, its business served the electrical market, and its business was not cyclical. There was also an important financial advantage. Crouse-Hinds had little debt. This would have helped us maintain our creditworthiness even after the acquisition. Because we were committed to a diversification in investments, we wished to control our own cost of capital.

Eventually, our decision was based on price. When we made our initial offer, Crouse-Hinds common was selling for $37 to $38 a share. After we made the offer, the market price of the stock went to $41.25 a share. Our decision not to pursue the deal was difficult. Our initial offer was for more than three and one-half times the book value of Crouse-Hinds. We found it difficult to justify spending much more, and we did not wish to participate in a senseless bidding war. Although we were not successful in acquiring Crouse-Hinds, our ambition and our goals became more widely known in the financial community. As a result, an increased number of opportunities was presented to us.

THE MINORITY POSITION, AN ALTERNATIVE STRATEGY

The next year we pursued another aspect of our strategy—to obtain a minority position in a firm involved in the energy business. In January 1982, we bought 8.8 percent of the common stock of Bucyrus-Erie, acquiring 1.8 million shares at $17 to $20 a share.

Based in Milwaukee, Bucyrus-Erie is a major manufacturer of heavy duty equipment used in the mining of coal, uranium and other minerals. Here, we sought to improve our position in the coal industry. Our own coal operations had suffered from market factors and technical problems. Our participation in this business was too specific—concentrated in Western coal operations. We believed that in the long term the market for coal would be quite good. However, there was always the potential for market fluctuations, particularly in the early 1980s. Bucyrus-Erie's position in the coal industry is more broad-based. Its equipment is used not only in the United States, but also in Europe, Africa, India, Australia, and the Soviet Union. The company also produces equipment used in oil production and refining. In 1982, InterNorth entered a five-year "standstill" agreement with Bucyrus-Erie, under which InterNorth would limit its holdings to 20 percent of Bucyrus-Erie's outstanding stock. Our total stake subsequently was increased to 4.1 million shares. The agreement also stipulated that I would become a member of the Bucyrus-Erie board.

Again, we achieved our objectives. We became more involved in the coal business, and we attained maximum flexibility in terms of our investment. We also managed to get a good deal. We acquired this stock at the market price, which at the time was below book value. In an outright takeover, we might have been forced to pay a substantial premium.

THE FIRST BIG DEAL

On April 12, 1983, InterNorth agreed to acquire Belco Petroleum Corp., headquartered in New York. We paid $31.50 a share for 10.2 million shares of Belco common stock and exchanged InterNorth preferred stock for the remainder of Belco's outstanding common. The total value of the deal was $750 million, and it represented our first large complete acquisition.

Belco Petroleum, which had more than $344 million in revenues in 1982, was an oil and gas exploration company with interests in the United States, Canada, and Peru. At the end of 1982 the company had oil reserves of 77.1 million barrels and natural gas reserves of 829 billion cubic feet. In acquiring Belco we considered our midterm goals. We had projected that our exploration and production activities would contribute more to earnings by the 1990s, and by purchasing Belco we moved to fulfill this prediction. The acquisition immediately extended and improved our exploration and production activities. After the acquisition, InterNorth's total cost of finding oil dropped significantly below industry average.

Financially, Belco was sound. Its long-term debt was only 8.6 percent of equity.

In addition, it was able to contribute immediately to earnings. In 1982, Belco earned $104 million, or $4.35 a share.

SOPHISTICATION GROWS WITH EXPERIENCE

We have managed to change the face of our company. Not only did we acquire new interests, but we divested one business, Northern Propane Gas; decided to participate in a joint venture, Energy Transportation Systems Inc. (ETSI); and started some new ventures, notably crude and condensate trading and international petrochemical trading.

We established the International Division in 1982, the same year we significantly expanded our crude oil and petroleum product trading activities. In January 1983 we increased our commitment to the coal market by obtaining a 29.5 percent interest in the ETSI joint venture. We entered into partnership with three other companies to construct a coal slurry pipeline that will transport coal from the Powder River Basin in Wyoming to electricity generating plants in the south central United States. The 1,400-mile pipeline was to be completed by 1986. This was a midterm move to increase our participation in coal.

The retail propane division, Northern Propane Gas, was sold to Penn Central Corp. for about $100 million in November 1983. Northern Propane served about 330,000 customers in 25 states east of the Rocky Mountains. Our decision to sell was based on our financial outlook for that business. We had no intention of abandoning the natural gas liquids industry, but we felt that while Northern Propane was healthy, we could obtain a reasonable value for it. In the future, we surmised, its value would diminish. Basically, we planned to use the funds to refinance high-cost debt.

We also disposed of our interest in Bucyrus-Erie after determining that the company's new strategic directions would take it away from our primary energy interests.

All of this activity involving acquisition, divestiture, and new businesses was directed by the strategy that was established in 1980. We were concerned with our ability to compete in the marketplace and to cope with the conditions of the energy markets in the future. It was satisfying to be successful.

EPILOGUE

In 1985, InterNorth acquired Houston Natural Gas Corp., an integrated natural gas organization, to create a company that, by the end of that year, had revenues of nearly $10.3 billion and operating profits of nearly $204 million. The transaction was valued at $2.5 billion. The company, which later changed its name to Enron Corp., now has pipeline, natural gas production facilities and reserves, petrochemical plants, and other operations throughout the Midwest, Southwest, and West. Headquarters was moved to Houston after the transaction was completed.

Chapter 7

Merrill Lynch: Branching out in Financial Services

Roger E. Birk

Chairman, Retired, Merrill Lynch & Co., Inc.,
New York, New York

Essential to a company's healthy growth is a set of clearly defined strategies. These strategies must provide workable guidelines on where the company wants to go and how it can best get there. They also must offer sufficient flexibility and room for regular reevaluation, so that the plans can be adjusted as the company's own needs and the general economic and investment environment change. That's what we counsel our investment banking clients, and that's also how we seek to direct our own development.

Naturally, our basic strategy at Merrill Lynch has undergone a series of evolutions and refinements to keep up with changing times. However, we have made these adjustments without essentially changing our direction or the principal objectives we long have pursued. Merrill Lynch's fundamental strategy can best be defined as being aimed at enhancing its role as the premier investment-based company within the overall financial services industry.

In pursuit of this strategy, the company judiciously has used acquisitions both to round out its capacities in certain established areas and to move into some related fields. Its major growth, however, has come from within, and we expect that trend to continue.

More specific objectives of our long-term strategy are to widen the spectrum of investment and investment-related services we offer, and to strengthen our ability to service the upscale end of our business.

From the standpoint of an acquirer's objectives, acquisitions can be classified as:

- Operating acquisitions that become part of the ongoing business of an operating unit. These are a means of accomplishing an approved operating plan—through a decision to buy rather than create added facilities and services.
- Building-block acquisitions to acquire expertise in a desired area. These can open windows for subsequent internal growth.
- Diversification mergers or acquisitions, intended to provide an extension into a new line of business.

Then there are certain more specialized variations. Particularly pertinent to our experience, we might list:

- Networking, which can be accomplished through joint ventures—or, sometimes, simply through operating agreements—that combine the capabilities of two or more partners to provide new or more comprehensive services.
- R&D-type investments—or taking a financial interest in a company engaged in a field such as information processing. The investment is viewed primarily as a convenient, limited-risk way to examine and keep abreast of advanced technology at an early stage, before the applications are ready for the market.

EVOLUTION OF MERRILL LYNCH

In reviewing Merrill Lynch's acquisition record, one should remember that the modern firm itself was formed through the historic merger in 1940 of Merrill Lynch with E. A. Pierce and also Cassatt & Co. This was followed the next year by the merger with Fenner & Beane to form Merrill Lynch, Pierce, Fenner & Beane. Merrill Lynch thus became by far the largest securities and commodities brokerage firm in the nation. More important, however, this merger-created firm established new patterns in scope of service, investor education, accessibility, and disclosure. Merrill Lynch added a handful of other securities houses during the 1940s; all fit into what we would define as the operating category. They augmented our geographic spread. Overwhelmingly, however, our main growth came from internal expansion, as the number of branch offices increased from 87 in 1942 to 137 in 1960, while gross operating income grew from $9 million to $130 million.

Government Securities

A significant shift in the acquisition pattern occurred in 1964, when Merrill Lynch acquired the business of C. J. Devine, a leading government securities dealer. That was clearly a building-block acquisition. It brought the company into a new sector of the securities field, with expertise on which major expansion could be based. It also guided our subsequent expansion into a huge variety of debt and money market instruments. Many of these instruments were still undeveloped—often, not even imagined—in 1964. In addition, C. J. Devine provided the base for what were to prove important synergistic relationships.

Lease Financing

In 1968, we acquired Hubbard, Westervelt & Mottelay in what was truly a landmark step for us. At the time, it was an operating acquisition for our investment banking group. Hubbard was a specialist in net-lease financing, a capability we wanted to develop. But while Hubbard had engaged almost exclusively in credit net leasing of real estate, it also turned into a suitable stepping stone toward general real estate financing. From there we eventually expanded into other aspects of real estate. Thus, Hubbard evolved into a building block for what is now a major area of Merrill Lynch operations—an area that by 1984 contributed nearly a half billion dollars to our annual revenue.

Hubbard itself became the source of many internally developed units, some of which subsequently made acquisitions of their own. Hubbard and the capabilities that evolved from it now serve as a kind of pivot, bringing our real estate and securities-based activities into a logical synergistic whole within our "stick-to-our-knitting," investment-anchored strategy.

The basic Hubbard operation also was expanded significantly. In its 40 years before acquisition, Hubbard never had produced more than $1 million in revenues, but in the first five years under our ownership, we had developed it into a $30 million-a-year business.

Real Estate Finance and Services

Subsequently, Hubbard expertise promoted internal development of many real estate activities, such as leasing and mortgage banking (which we supplemented with an acquisition). Hubbard has also brought to market the largest public syndications of income-producing equity real estate partnerships.

In the mid-1970s we began a serious study of the residential real estate field and determined that a full-fledged presence would make sense for us. We also decided that this area would best be approached through experts already in the business.

As a first and slightly indirect step (though a very logical one for our strategic purposes), in 1977 we acquired TICOR's relocation service company and renamed it Merrill Lynch Relocation Management. This was a good example of the building-block acquisition technique. The relocation company contracts with corporations to assist employees who are being transferred. That is a good business in itself. But even more important to our long-range efforts, the relocation company provided a solid base for establishing our own residential real estate brokerage network. It supplied us with executive talent and know-how to get started on this operation, and, because relocating work entails dealings with leading real estate brokers throughout the country, it was in a good position to evaluate and lead us to quality establishments.

To build this brokerage network, we established Merrill Lynch Realty Associates in the fall of 1978 as the subsidiary for administering the operating units, which we began acquiring in 1979. By 1986, we were established in more than 40 major markets. Although the actual brokerage units have sprung primarily from operating acquisitions, they have been strengthened by subsequent internal efforts, as well as by supplementary operating acquisitions.

Proper timing is obviously an important issue in acquisitions, but there are multiple considerations. For instance, by the time we were ready to roll in retail real estate, the country was headed into the worst housing depression in a generation. That led to a period of greater initial losses than had been contemplated for our operation. But, by the same token, we were able to buy up quality brokerage companies at more reasonable prices, and thus were able to establish a substantial network with a relatively moderate investment.

We have also become increasingly active in commercial real estate brokerage. Some commercial operations came to us along with residential acquisitions. In addition, some types of commercial and industrial brokerage endeavors were derived from Hubbard. In most cases, however, we have started our own discrete commercial units in major markets.

In another sector of real estate, Hubbard diversified its financing capabilities with the 1978 addition of Huntoon Paige, a specialist in mortgage banking, particularly in the servicing of mortgages for others—a fee-based activity that is attractive for its stability. We also have developed a strong capability as a mortgage originator.

To summarize our real estate efforts, we have made various strategic acquisitions that were used as jumping-off points for further expansion. Even more important, many of the activities acquired and initiated have been used to build increasing interrelation among the various real estate units—and with various units on the securities and investment banking sides of Merrill Lynch—to weave a strong fabric of investment and real-estate-related services.

Although the details certainly could not have been foreseen, the basic strategy that was laid out in the mid-1970s largely has been carried out.

Specialty Insurance Ventures

Between the Hubbard acquisition and our subsequent rounds of external real estate expansion, we entered the specialty insurance field when we acquired Seattle-based Family Life Insurance Co. in 1974. Family Life offers primarily mortgage-protection insurance to homeowners. It was regarded at the time as a modest diversification into another sector of financial services—one that promised steady if less spectacular growth than the volatile securities business. That was an especially appealing prospect in view of the unsettled state of Wall Street as it headed toward deregulation and intensified competition.

Family Life fulfilled the primary objective. Since its acquisition, its earnings have grown at an annual rate of nearly 20 percent. But perhaps more significant for Merrill Lynch's long-term program, Family Life, with its service to homeowners, also provided another logical relationship with the real estate interests we were to develop. Furthermore, Family Life, while distinctly a specialist, secured for us a valuable base for acquiring an in-depth understanding of the life insurance business.

An axiom of strategic planning, of course, is that decisions on what not to do can be as important as decisions for positive action. For instance, we concluded that full-scale insurance underwriting would not fit our plans, at least under prevailing circumstances, though some selected insurance underwriting activities could prove attractive. We also recognized additional opportunities for Family

Life in relation with Merrill Lynch. After careful study, Family Life began in 1983 to develop some insurance programs that could be offered through the Merrill Lynch, Pierce, Fenner & Smith branch network.

The insurance-real estate relationship also led us to what seemed another logical acquisition: the purchase of AMIC in 1979. AMIC insures mortgage lenders against default by the homeowner. AMIC turned out to be an example of another requirement of a sound, comprehensive merger and acquisition policy: Be ready to divest when a program doesn't work out or conditions change.

AMIC was continually profitable under Merrill Lynch, but the environment changed radically soon after its acquisition. Interest rates soared to record-high levels, drastically slowing housing and mortgage activity and changing the consumer's savings patterns to put severe liquidity pressures on the savings and loan industry. Many savings and loans felt especially threatened by the tremendous growth of money market funds that Merrill Lynch and other securities firms sponsored. And these savings and loan's were AMIC's chief insurance customers. It became evident that under these circumstances the Merrill Lynch affiliation was not helpful to AMIC's pursuit of business, so in late 1981 we sold the company.

Building on the Core

AMIC actually was our second divestiture because of changed circumstances. In 1969 we had expanded the scope of our investment services by acquiring the financial management and economic consulting firm of Lionel D. Edie. In 1976, because of the expected impact of new federal pension legislation, we divested ourselves of the Edie company and its pension advisory business, along with the Edie name. However, we retained a number of businesses stemming from the Edie operation, which we developed into major Merrill Lynch endeavors. Among them are what is now Merrill Lynch Asset Management, the leading sponsor and advisor of mutual funds; the nation's largest family of money market funds, led by the Merrill Lynch Ready Assets Trust; and Merrill Lynch Economics, which provides in-house economic analysis support in addition to its external consulting business.

Thus, even though divested, Edie furnished the core for important activities that we proceeded to develop and expand. This building-up process also has been applied in acquisitions closer to the basic securities business.

In 1969, the acquisition of Royal Securities greatly enlarged our presence in Canada, including wider geographic coverage. Since then, we have substantially broadened our coverage of products and services through the subsidiary now known as Merrill Lynch Canada.

Our history also contains one example of a securities acquisition we neither planned nor sought. In late 1970, at the strong urging of the New York Stock Exchange (NYSE), we took over the failing brokerage house of Goodbody & Co. Even though the NYSE membership provided some reimbursement, it was a costly undertaking. However, we also realized some fruitful results. We acquired a great many talented people, and we gained early expertise in unit trusts and options trading, both of which we developed into major activities during the 1970s.

A more clear-cut enhancement of our strategic plan was made possible by our acquisition in 1978 of White, Weld & Co., a prominent securities firm that was particularly strong in investment banking while its retail business catered to customers with relatively large accounts. Thus, White Weld enhanced the operating plans of both our capital markets and individual investor sectors, as it expanded our investment banking capabilities and moved us toward a more upscale retail market mix. Similarly, the 1984 acquisition of the long-established Wall Street firm of Becker Paribas augmented Merrill Lynch's strong money market capabilities and added key professionals in other capital markets areas.

THE ROLE OF NETWORKING

There can be attractive alternatives to the acquisition route for expanding the scope of operations. One option is "networking," where two or more companies each furnish certain services or products that can be combined to provide new, broader services, packages, or operating procedures. The concept itself is not new, and there are plenty of long-established examples—such as when a securities firm with substantial operating capacity provides clearing services for other brokers.

Merrill Lynch began to offer its securities-processing services to other firms in 1976. We since have become increasingly active in this area of leveraging our operating facilities and expertise, especially after these "wholesaling" operations were placed in a separate subsidiary, Broadcort Capital Corp., in 1983. Through Broadcort, which has its own New York Stock Exchange membership, we now provide order execution, clearance, financing, custodial, and other functions to more than 100 broker-dealers. We also offer these client firms access to such investment vehicles as mutual and money market funds and tax investments. We extended our reach through Securities Options Corp., acquired in 1983, which provides clearing and financing services for over-the-counter and options market makers. More recently, we have arranged to provide clearing services for specialists on the New York and other exchanges. Through a subsidiary, we also have become a specialist on the Pacific Stock Exchange. All these actions extend our relations with others in the investment industry.

The whole networking concept has gained rapidly in popularity in recent years throughout the financial services industry. For example, networking procedures have been developed to provide additional liquidity for banks and thrift institutions by having their certificates of deposit retailed through securities firms to individual investors. Similarly, both securities firms and banks now market various insurance products. And more and more banks have networking arrangements with discount securities brokers.

Merrill Lynch utilized networking in establishing in 1977 what is probably its best-known invention—the Cash Management Account or CMA financial service—aimed at keeping the investor's funds constantly at work. Immediate access to funds and borrowing power was made possible through a networking arrangement with Bank One of Columbus, Ohio, which furnished the bank-related services, including check and VISA debit card processing.

Joint Ventures

Going beyond mere organizational (i.e., noninvestment) cooperation are joint ventures that draw on the different capabilities of the participants. For instance, in 1984 Merrill Lynch and IBM formed International MarketNet to offer an information distribution and office automation system that combines market data services, enhanced communications, software, minicomputers, and desktop computers. We had taken the lead in developing the system for our own use, but the partnership also will market it to other financial institutions.

Through another joint venture and in conjunction with the Port Authority of New York and New Jersey, we are developing a teleport on Staten Island, New York, and a related fiber optics network to provide ground connections in the New York-New Jersey metropolitan area. This will give businesses in the area high-quality access to communications satellites. We expect to be both a major user of the service and a beneficiary of its business success.

Together with some other investment, insurance, and finance firms, we helped establish FGIC Corp., whose subsidiary, Financial Guaranty Insurance Co., guarantees prompt payment of interest and principal of municipal bonds. The insured bonds can get top-quality ratings from the rating agencies and this usually results in lower interest rates and greater marketability.

Within the investment industry, we opted for a joint venture for increased access to the Southeast Asia market. In 1982, we acquired a minority interest in Sun Hung Kai, a major securities and financial services firm based in Hong Kong. In view of the subsequent turmoil in the Hong Kong markets caused by uncertainties over the Crown Colony's political future, timing of the investment could have been more propitious. But we believe that the long-term objectives of access to East Asia and the People's Republic of China remain valid. This experience serves to emphasize a prime requisite for a sound acquisition and investment policy: Each project must be judged for its long-term merits.

In another move to strengthen our capabilities beyond U.S. borders, Merrill Lynch Canada in 1984 took a position in Great Lakes Group, Inc., of Toronto, which, along with utility interests, owns a Canadian securities company equipped for major merchant banking roles in private placements, mergers and acquisitions, financial consulting, and direct investments. Merrill Lynch Canada, as a registered broker-dealer, can complement these strengths by bringing underwritings public and dealing with the investing public. Great Lakes is a member of the diversified Brascan, Ltd., family of companies, and thus provides a tie to major Canadian industrial interests.

R&D INVESTMENTS

We at Merrill Lynch are always conscious that we are engaged in an industry whose successful operations depend heavily on high technology and state-of-the-art skills, especially in information distribution and processing. Consequently, we find it useful to supplement our extensive direct efforts with what can be called R&D investments. This means taking a minority interest in some companies that explore promising concepts. Our primary investment purpose in these cases is not a direct financial return but contribution of seed money for exploring potentially worthwhile concepts and reaping, at relatively modest cost, the knowledge to be gained from close association with these projects. For instance, we acquired an interest in Institutional Networks (InstiNet), which operates a direct securities trading market with automated order execution that we have already started to utilize for making markets in 100 over-the-counter stocks; in Financial News Network, which offers a stream of financial information via cable TV systems; in Comp-U-Card, a computerized buying service; and in RanData, a small Australian company that has developed a data encryption system.

AN ORDERLY STRATEGIC PATTERN

Our merger, acquisition, and investment moves take many forms and are undertaken for a variety of purposes. But in all projects, regardless of size or type, we seek to follow an orderly pattern, weighing the risks, rewards, and costs (both in cash and involvement).

Relying on our in-house investment banking know-how, we have mapped a series of formal procedures. Proposed acquisitions are studied in detail by a project team with members from the financial, legal, and strategic development areas and from the operating units directly involved. Appropriate approvals are required at four major stages of consideration: to pursue the project, negotiate, sign contracts, and, finally, close the deal. It is understood that any acquisition—indeed, any business decision—entails risks, but we depend on our careful procedures and management skills to raise the odds in our favor.

Although there is obviously room for many different approaches, every company needs a plan or strategy to deal with mergers and acquisitions. The plan should take account of the company's specific aims, condition, and style, and must allow for ample flexibility. In the fast-moving world of the 1980s, the planner wants a running suit, not a straitjacket.

At Merrill Lynch, our strategy—based on the expertise we bring to the table as a leading investment banker, as well as on our particular needs and corporate culture—is to use acquisitions as the seeds from which fruitful internal growth can sprout.

Chapter 8

Merck & Co.: Study in Internal Growth

John J. Horan

Chairman and Chief Executive Officer, Merck & Co., Inc., Rahway, New Jersey

Merck & Co. Inc., is the largest company in the U.S. ethical (prescription) pharmaceutical market, and one of the largest in the world. In 1985, its total sales were $3.55 billion, predominantly in human health products. Since the early 1970s, the company deliberately has pursued a strategy of achieving growth primarily through investment in its existing areas of interest: human and animal health and specialty chemicals.

MERCK'S 300-YEAR HISTORY

The company had its roots in Germany, where the Merck family, starting in 1668, first operated an apothecary, and later a fine chemicals business. In 1889, a family member, George Merck, was sent to the United States to establish a branch in New York. At first, this business was limited to importing drugs and fine chemicals, but soon it began its own manufacturing operations. During World War I, all German ownership interests in the American company were eliminated, and thereafter Merck & Co., Inc., became a publicly owned U.S. company headed by George Merck, who had become an American citizen in 1895. The original German company continues in Darmstadt, Germany, under the name E. Merck, but has no connection with the U.S.-based Merck & Co., Inc.

The company continued to grow and in 1933 George W. Merck, who succeeded his father in 1925, took a bold initiative that set the tone of the company to this day. He established a research laboratory in which scientists would carry out work of a caliber comparable to that of the best universities in the world. Prior to that time, academic scientists had looked down on industrial research, and it was very difficult to attract top-quality scientists to staff industrial laboratories. In what was then a radical departure from the typical industrial pattern of secrecy, Merck encouraged company scientists to publish their basic research findings in scientific journals and at professional meetings, to pursue promising basic research leads regardless of the likelihood of immediate practical return, and to undertake close collaboration with scientists in university and government laboratories in the United States and Europe. This effort met with early success and, in 1935, made a major contribution in the development of thiamine (vitamin B_1). This was followed in rapid succession by the development of other vitamins such as riboflavin (vitamin B_2) and calcium pantothenate.In addition, the Merck research groups discovered calcium pantothenate (vitamin B_6),

In the ensuing years, the Merck research laboratories played a key role in developing many breakthrough drugs, including cortisone, vitamin B_{12}, and streptomycin. Research and development was established as a cornerstone of the company and a key element in its growth strategy.

A number of early leads in research proved to be ineffective in human diseases, but turned out to have application as drugs for poultry and livestock. This led the company into the animal and plant health area, where it continues to be a significant factor in world markets.

The company's marketing structure also underwent a profound evolution in earlier decades. Merck's principal business until the mid 1940s was the manufacture of bulk pharmaceutical and specialty chemicals. It sold its medicinal chemicals to other drug companies, which converted them into final dosage forms (e.g., tablets, capsules, liquid solutions) and marketed them under their own brand names. After World War II, these companies increasingly began to manufacture their own basic raw materials, thereby reducing their dependence on outside bulk suppliers. Merck then began to market its own products. In the late 1940s, it established a force of representatives to promote and sell finished pharmaceuticals, but found itself unable to compete effectively against the professional sales forces of the established pharmaceutical companies such as Lilly, Upjohn, and Parke Davis.

Faced with a lack of success in its effort to maintain a leading position in this changing market on its own, Merck looked to the outside to augment its capabilities. In 1953 it merged with Sharp & Dohme, Inc., a Philadelphia pharmaceutical company with a long history and a fine reputation in the medical community, a well-established distribution network, an extensive product line, and its own research program. It was an excellent fit, bringing together all of the elements of a fully integrated, research-oriented health products company.

THE NATURE OF THE ETHICAL PHARMACEUTICAL BUSINESS

The prescription pharmaceutical business is truly worldwide in scope. Multinational companies based in the United States and in Europe compete with each other and with local companies in almost every national market. The industry is highly competitive and has a low level of concentration. Market shares of the leading companies are less than 10 percent in the United States and less than 5 percent in international markets.

The innovative, or research-intensive, pharmaceutical industry is a relatively recent phenomenon, having emerged as late as the 1930s. Prior to that, there was relatively little development of new drugs. Indeed, before the 1930s, the physician's drug armamentarium was severely limited and not very effective against many diseases. Most of the significant medicines in use today were discovered after 1940.

During the 1940s and 1950s, scientists did not have the understanding to predict, on a theoretical basis, what substances would or would not be effective. Therefore, new compounds were tested by trial and error, through screening processes, to determine which ones produced therapeutic responses in living organisms. In recent decades, medical science has made dramatic strides in its comprehension of the workings of the human body, down to the cellular and molecular levels.

By the 1980s, it was becoming possible for scientists to design a new chemical molecule on paper for a particular therapeutic purpose, and to synthesize that molecule in the laboratory for actual testing. Moreover, they sometimes can "design out" the undesirable characteristics of a drug molecule that might cause unwanted side effects in some patients. The value of these new capabilities already has been demonstrated, and many scientists believe that the flow of new and better drugs soon will accelerate dramatically.

Despite this greater scientific understanding and the availability of instrumentation that is many, many times faster and more accurate than that available only a decade ago, the cost and time necessary to develop a new drug continue to increase dramatically. In 1962, it took two years and an investment of approximately $4 million to discover, develop, and gain regulatory approval for a new drug in the United States. Today, the time frame has increased to seven to 10 years, and the cost is about $75 million. That has two major ramifications:

First, sustaining a business strategy based on innovation in the pharmaceutical industry requires a long-term commitment to develop a research organization of world-class caliber. It must operate at the leading edge of discovery in order to bring forth a sufficient stream of new products to fuel the company's continuing growth. The financial investment for research must be higher than in most other industries. Merck's plans for 1986 included $450 million for R&D, most of it in the health area.

Second, it is essential that a company operate worldwide in order to spread this cost of research over many markets. It would not be feasible to recoup the cost of a broad-based research program, no matter how successful, from sales in only one national market, even one as large as the United States.

STRATEGIC DECISIONS AT MERCK

Merck looks at the future of its business through a systematic strategic planning process—a function that has been well established in the company for more than 20 years. Each year, management carefully reviews the company's strengths and weaknesses, the businesses it is in, and others it may want to be in. Out of this assessment emerge the corporate strategic objectives.

The company has put mechanisms in place to assure that, in pursuing these established objectives, all feasible options are considered: internal investment, licensing of technology developed by others, and outside acquisitions.

Strategic opportunities for internal investment have generally been in the three pillars of Merck's existing businesses: research, manufacturing, and marketing.

A corporate licensing group searches for opportunities to license new products or new technology developed in other laboratories—particularly pharmaceutical products—to complement the company's internal R&D program. It is not possible for one company, even one with a research program the size of Merck's, to cover adequately all areas of therapeutic interest. Licensing offers one way to fill some gaps.

A corporate development group actively seeks out acquisition opportunities consistent with the corporate strategy. These have ranged from major multibillion-dollar companies to smaller entities intended to augment parts of Merck's existing businesses.

The program has produced steady, incremental expansion, even though no single transaction has been of a magnitude to alter the fundamental structure of the company. Merck has extended its presence in overseas markets by the acquisition of important local pharmaceutical companies such as Thomas Morson & Son, Ltd., in the United Kingdom; Laboratoires Chibret S.A. in France; Charles E. Frosst & Co. in Canada; and Erik Lindblom & Co. in Sweden.

In the animal health area, Merck acquired Hubbard Farms, Inc., a leader in poultry genetics; SPAFAS, Inc., a producer of eggs and poultry free of specific pathogens; and British United Turkeys, Ltd., a leading supplier of breeding stock to the turkey industry in Europe.

In specialty chemicals, which has historically been an important part of Merck's business, the market is highly segmented. Different marketing skills are needed for each area. In those sectors where Merck did not have internal expertise, it has sought to expand by acquisition. It acquired Kelco (alginates from seaweed and biosynthetic xanthan gums) and Calgon Corp. (activated carbon and chemicals for treatment of industrial cooling water). The acquisition of Baltimore Aircoil Co. (cooling systems for commercial and industrial facilities) further expanded Merck's presence in the cooling water systems business. However, in 1985, Merck divested Baltimore Aircoil after determining that the business no longer fit its basic long-range strategy.

The strategic review process also identifies businesses or product lines that should be divested or terminated. For example, the Calgon acquisition included an established line of consumer products in the soap and detergent field. Merck later decided that it did not have the sales volume in the field necessary to compete effectively, and so divested this product line, while retaining the

Calgon specialty chemical and environmental products businesses. A number of other product lines not consistent with Merck objectives also have been divested in recent years.

Any strategic investment decision—whether it be internal investment, licensing, or acquisition—must be compatible with the growth rates and return on investment that Merck has set as its targets, consistent with the objective of providing its shareholders with a superior rate of return on their investment.

STRATEGY DURING THE 1970s AND 1980s

In recent times, Merck has found that investment to expand its own position in the health and specialty chemical fields has offered the most attractive potential returns. This is not surprising, because during the same period, the health field also has attracted major new commitments of resources from companies throughout the world seeking entry into these markets. In the United States these include such corporate giants as DuPont, Dow, Monsanto, and Procter & Gamble. The result is a continuing overall increase in investment in the health field and an increase in present and potential competition.

Merck's basic strategy is to maintain its leadership position in human and animal health in the face of the intensified competition. Human health, in this context, is defined by the company to include not only its primary pharmaceutical business, but other areas where its skills in research, its knowledge of health care delivery systems worldwide, and its other assets would be relevant.

Emphasis on R&D

A central part of that strategy has been to establish and maintain a superiority in R&D effectiveness. To accomplish that the company has increased significantly the rate of investment in research and development. Annual expenditures for R&D have been increased an average of 15 percent per year for the past 10 years and 17 percent per year for the last five.

Although Merck had been preeminent in research for decades, it recognized in the mid-1970s that it had to accelerate its efforts if it was to take advantage of the truly breakthrough scientific progress taking place in the life sciences and to keep pace with the rapid development of new research equipment and instrumentation. The company undertook a major program of capital investment, totaling $375 million, to modernize and expand its R&D facilities. Through 1984, that program included commitments for 14 major new laboratory buildings at six sites in four countries around the world, of which 11 were completed.

The physical assets are, of course, secondary to the caliber of scientists in the laboratories. There, too, the company has worked hard to build on an already strong base. Since 1975, the professional R&D staff has been increased by 60 percent. Merck has attracted a new generation of established, world-class scientists to augment the already strong leadership that has existed in its laboratories. In addition, the company has continued to be successful in attracting some of the best young researchers coming from the leading graduate schools.

Payoff in an Accelerating Growth Rate

This expansion has already yielded promising results. By 1984, Merck's R&D "pipeline" contained more promising new products under development than ever before in its history. Those products are expected to increase the company's growth rate in the mid-1980s and beyond.

At the same time, Merck has moved aggressively to license many promising products.

In a major transaction, Merck, in 1982, concluded a long-term, joint-venture agreement with AB Astra, a research-based Swedish pharmaceutical company. Under its terms, Merck received the rights to develop and market in the United States new products discovered by Astra for approximately 10 years, after which a totally separate joint-venture company will handle these and subsequent new products of Astra research in the United States. This approach capitalized on Merck's production and marketing skills.

Strengthening Marketing Capabilities

The full potential of Merck's current flow of new products would not be realized unless its marketing capabilities also were strengthened. The company has done this in two ways: by expanding its staff of professional representatives (those who visit physicians and hospitals to bring them information on drug products) and by acquisitions in countries where its marketing presence was not well established.

Merck's U.S. pharmaceutical division, Merck Sharp & Dohme (which is the market leader in this country), increased its force of professional representatives by more than two-thirds. Similar steps have been taken elsewhere. For example, the company's subsidiary in Germany, the third largest market in the world, has increased its professional representatives by nearly 50 percent during the past three years.

Acquisitions were made in selected countries to improve Merck's market position. In Spain, its subsidiary ranked number 20 in the market, but in 1983, the company acquired Laboratories Abello, the seventh largest Spanish pharmaceutical company. The combined business placed Merck in the number one position in that country.

In 1983 Merck also took a historic step in Japan. It agreed to purchase a majority interest in Banyu Pharmaceutical Co., Ltd., a major Japanese pharmaceutical company. It is believed that this was the first time that a majority interest in an established Japanese company in the first section of the Tokyo stock exchange had been acquired by a non-Japanese corporation. At the same time, Merck purchased a majority interest in another, smaller Japanese company, Torii & Co., Ltd. Those two, together with a long-established joint-venture company already owned by Merck and Banyu, gave Merck a presence in Japan comparable to that of the leading Japanese companies in the world's second largest pharmaceutical market.

In the specialty chemical field, Merck added Alginate Industries, Ltd. (British producer of algins from seaweed), in 1979, and Rotary Drilling Services, Inc. (oil field specialty chemicals), in 1981. The company now has a broad line of high-value-added chemical products for important industries, ranging from food processing to water management to oil field recovery. In this business, too, there has been strong investment in research and development, aimed at accelerated growth through new products and entry into new markets.

Improvements in Productivity

In its manufacturing area, the company undertook an accelerated program to modernize and automate its production facilities. In a research-based company such as Merck, the manufacture of active ingredients for pharmaceuticals frequently involves very complex chemical processes. Many of its new products are completely new molecules, developed in its laboratories, which were not known to science before. New processes must be designed for their large-scale production. The nature of the product also requires stricter standards of quality and purity than exist in most other industries. Merck's modernization has added flexibility to accommodate the coming new products, improved the quality and reliability of the operations, and introduced new efficiencies. One of the company's primary objectives is to be the low-cost producer wherever it competes.

OUTLOOK FOR THE FUTURE

For the present, Merck's strategy has worked well. The internal investments and selected outside acquisitions have positioned the company favorably for the next five to 10 years in each of its fields of interest. However, the company's strategy must remain flexible because of several factors that may change the structure of the health industry, in particular, in the coming decades.

International competition will increase. The large European companies will continue to be strong, as they have been in the past. Major new entrants will merge in the United States and elsewhere in the world. The Japanese drug industry, which has been developing considerable capabilities in research and development and marketing in its domestic markets, is expected to move effectively into world markets.

On the research side, biotechnology has spawned entrepreneurial companies financed by venture capital. Some of these will be successful. In the meantime, they add to the overall investment in research in human and animal health.

Throughout the world the pressures for lower health costs have been growing. Prescription drugs, which in the United States constitute only about 10 percent of the total health care bill, can, in most instances, reduce overall costs by shortening hospital stays and eliminating the need for surgery. New pharmaceutical products today and in the future must increasingly demonstrate cost-effectiveness, as well as superior therapeutic effect, in order to succeed in the marketplace. These considerations must be built into the management of the company's research and development program.

It is likely that not all companies will be successful in this changing environment. Merck believes that its significant investments in research, production, and marketing, along with the high caliber of the people it has recruited and developed, have positioned it to remain in the forefront in its key business areas.

Chapter 9

The Entrepreneur's Choices for Growth

Arthur D. Perrone, Jr.

President, Geneva Business Services, Inc.,
Costa Mesa, California

Since the mid-1970s, the United States has been experiencing a virtual second Industrial Revolution that has been accomplished on the backs of small and medium-sized private businesses. More familiarly, the far-reaching trend has been called the renaissance of entrepreneurship. Although the entrepreneurial movement has been nourished by a multiplicity of contributing factors, the basic denominator appears to be a realization that the general economy and scores of individuals derive the greatest benefits when manufacture, service, and distribution in certain products and markets are controlled by smaller, closely held companies.

Manifestations of the trend abound. Venture capital organizations, increasingly professional and able to gather funds from an ever-widening universe of contributing sources, have nurtured scores of start-up companies. Large companies have divested unwanted components to managements of the units or to small concerns that seem better able to manage them optimally. Publicly held companies that haven't been able to make it to their satisfaction in the stock market have gone private. And smaller, closely held companies themselves have sought expansion by buying firms of similar configurations.

All of this activity has created enormous opportunity for mergers and acquisitions in the so-called middle market, which is composed largely of the smaller and medium-sized companies that are basically privately held and entrepreneurial. Indeed, M&A activity has been remarkably brisk in this segment of American business. But while the trend is recognized and the visible trappings generally apparent, precious little detail is known about the middle market.

Quantitatively, there is an information gap because privately held companies are essentially that—private. Compulsion to report financial and other information publicly does not exist, and the information problem is compounded by special circumstances. For example, many owners of private businesses will do everything possible to minimize profits so that taxes also can be minimized. As a result, the fact of life in the private marketplace is that the integrity of most information reflecting the performance of private companies is open to question. Qualitatively, the information void may be even wider. Most people outside the middle market—including large companies that may fix on private companies as logical acquisition targets—know little about the realities of owning and operating a private company, the personality characteristics required to make it successful, the needs and objectives of the entrepreneur, and the way in which the owner is tied directly to the business.

As a specialist in mergers and acquisitions in the middle market, Geneva has evaluated well over 1,400 privately owned businesses totaling more than $2.5 billion in purchase prices. Our M&A organization has grown to be one of the largest in the country in terms of closings of initiated transactions, and we continue to expand our financial services to meet the growing needs of this marketplace. We have, through our experience, developed considerable insight and information on the middle market, and a good jumping-off point for understanding its M&A mechanisms would be the sharing of part of the profile that we developed on the entrepreneur as a potential acquisition target.

SOME CHARACTERISTICS OF THE ENTREPRENEUR

Generally an individual of high net worth, the typical owner of a mid-sized business nonetheless has problems of illiquidity, and the desire to convert this wealth into a more liquid form is often the driving force behind a decision to sell. The owner has high retained earnings and significant undeclared dividends. But tax laws create a fiscal dilemma in which the entrepreneur neither can keep nor draw out the profits in a prudent manner. Moreover, the owner almost solely bears personal responsibility for losses, even though profits are likely to be widely shared through employee-management incentives, bonuses, pension and profit-sharing plans, and accelerated tax rates. Many owners therefore find they can make more money through juidicious sales than by continuing to operate their businesses. In some cases, good business sense demands that a private company owner sell out.

In a study of some 1,000 Geneva clients, we learned that primary reasons for selling tend to be subjective. To be sure, finances represent a major factor. But some owners believe they might want to sell and retire for other reasons. Subjectively, the owner often recognizes the loss of desire to continue personally guaranteeing the business debts and to provide the operating capital necessary to make the company grow. But in the majority of the cases, the major reason that entrepreneurs want to sell is that they are bored and burned out. They have built their businesses and lived through the early building years as part of their evolutionary process. Then the "builder" reaches an evolutionary plateau and asks, "What's next?"

Statistically, the sellers are, on average, 58 to 63 years of age and enjoy six-figure incomes. In addition to their direct compensation, they are drawing an average of $27,000 a year in perks, and have been in business 19 years. They have paid for their homes, have put the kids through school, and have begun to ask themselves whether the business is all there is to life. The risk-taking dimension of the entrepreneur has diminished because of age, experience, and accumulated wealth. They are not necessarily in the mood to bet their businesses, to explore new directions, or to bet more of themselves in standing up to the rigors of yet another business cycle. The "prudent man rule," that no more than 20 percent of one's net worth should be tied up in any one asset, intuitively is understood when the realization dawns that as much as 80 percent of an owner's total estate is tied to the illiquid business equity. There is a desire to "take some chips off the table."

Our experience in dealing with mid-size acquisition candidates has taught us that in most cases they are successful businessmen who understand their business and their product or service. But although they are conversant with cash flow, they usually are not financial- or sales-oriented. This lack of financial expertise affects them when they attempt to develop alternative financing plans for themselves and their businesses. It often carries through into their personal and estate affairs.

Toward the Sell Decision

One recurring element or characteristic of the typical owner of a closely held company is a phobia about parting with even a small portion of the equity in the business. To keep good people on the payroll, the owner would much rather pay princely salaries along with some cleverly conceived indirect forms of compensation than surrender any equity in the business. The entrepreneurial aversion to surrendering equity becomes a real problem when the entrepreneur encounters a venture capitalist or a small business investment corporation (SBIC) for the first time. Remember, the expert business manager may have little or no financial experience. The firm's accountant or bookkeeper is just slightly more sophisticated. Suddenly, the owner is confronted by strangers who want to see a business plan or desire a piece of the business, all in exchange for a loan.

In the owner's mind, this is not much different than dealing with a loan shark in a dark alley. The entrepreneur has worked 10 years or more to develop product and market acceptance, has fought and solved the major problems of developing the business, and, now with a growth opportunity just ahead, strangers expect to get 25 to 40 percent of the business. Where were they when the owner awoke at three o'clock some morning worrying about meeting the payroll the next Friday?

The entrepreneur searches for alternatives and a friend advises: "Go public, you'll make millions." This leads to another "foreign" territory—the investment banking community. In paneled conference rooms, well-dressed, well-educated corporate finance experts talk about the costs, the length of time the owner will have to stay with the company, the public reports, and the new organization that must be developed over the next 12 months, especially the new marketing expert, controller, and, very likely, a new CEO. They comment on the "road show" for investors and financial analysts and all the time that must be spent away from the business. And, of course, they inject that the market for public offerings is not as "hot" as it was last year at this time. Often, the vanity of bragging around the club about the company's initial public offering price is outweighed by the owner's reluctance for the fishbowl life of a public company chief executive. The difference between running one's own show and facing a new board of directors or a room full of angry shareholders at an annual meeting becomes vivid.

The demands of taking in partners, through either venture capital or an initial public offering, are confusing and frightening to many entrepreneurs. Life was easier when the main worry was a competitor's price cut. To complicate matters, the owner learns, when the future looks most glum, that his children hate the business and want to move to other parts of the country. "Maybe I should sell," the entrepreneur muses, "but who would want this lousy business?" In truth, the business may not be lousy at all, and there may be plenty of takers willing to pay a fair price. Certainly, the available and estimated statistics suggest a greatly viable market in which selling out can be anything but a last resort or a shotgun affair.

A HANDLE ON THE MIDDLE MARKET

There are approximately 4.4 million corporations on file with the Internal Revenue Service, and new ventures are added to the list daily. All but 11,000 of these businesses are private. Another 12 million or more businesses are operated as sole proprietorships or partnerships.

Eighty-three percent of the 4.4 million target corporations (or 3.6 million firms) have annual sales of less than $1 million. There are, at the other extreme, 13,000 firms, or 0.4 percent, with sales above $50 million. By definition, the middle market consists of approximately 730,000 firms with sales ranging from $1 million to $50 million, the great majority of which are privately owned (see Table 9.1).

We estimate that total merger and acquisition activity in the middle market will be slightly above 1 percent, or that about 10,000 businesses will change hands every year; in only 2,500 of these transactions will a public company be a buyer or seller. The lion's share of the sellers in the mid-sized market consists of entrepreneurs who are owners of closely held businesses. Most have started the business from scratch and never have owned or sold another business.

Another way to look at the middle marketplace is through employment. If we consider total people employed (excluding government and self-employed), 55 percent of the workforce is employed by firms that have 99 or fewer employees. A vivid example of how the American economic base is built on small and medium-size businesses is that 95 percent of the businesses in the United States have 49 or fewer employees but employ 43 percent of the workforce (see Table 9.2).

One of the fascinating elements of the middle market is that within several industry classifications, private companies actually outperformed their public counterparts, according to a recent Geneva study. When we compared the return on sales of private versus public companies, we found that privately held companies in metal manufacturing, diversified service, electronics and appliances, transportation equipment, and measuring, scientific, and photographic equipment outperformed their public counterparts. In fairness, the opposite was true of companies in pharmaceuticals, mining and crude oil production, soaps and cosmetics, publishing and printing, and office equipment.

FINANCING SOURCES IN THE PRIVATE MARKETPLACE

In the December 1984 issue of *Inc.*, James W. Morrison wrote, "America's big companies, even those in declining industries, already have plenty of options for obtaining capital. They can sell long-term bonds that carry lower interest rates than most small businesses ever see. They have access to huge pools of capital controlled by such institutional investors as pension funds and insurance companies. They can issue new stock or negotiate new credit lines with major financial institutions and they can take advantage of tax breaks written by Congress to their specifications. Given these choices, one could conclude that a big, estab-

TABLE 9.1   Businesses by Revenue Size

Revenue	Approximate number[a]	Percent of total
0–$500,000	3,000,000	69.0
$500,000–$1,000,000	600,000	14.0
$1,000,000–$5,000,000	600,000	14.0
$5,000,000–$10,000,000	70,000	1.4
$10,000,000–$50,000,000	60,000	1.4
$50,000,000–$100,000,000	6,000	0.2
$100,000,000–$1 billion	6,000	0.2
$1 billion+	600	—

[a]Excludes sole proprietorships and partnerships.

TABLE 9.2   Employees[a]

Number of employees	Percent of businesses	Percent of workforce
1–9	74.0	16
10–49	21.0	27
50–99	4.0	12
100–999	0.9	31
Over 1,000	0.1	14

[a]Excluding government and self-employed.

lished company that can't raise capital in the existing market probably isn't such a hot investment.''

The owner of the small to mid-sized business, however, does not enjoy the same choices as the bigger, publicly held companies. Again, subjective elements are involved. A financing decision should be based on the market and the business opportunity. But what may be right for the business may not be in concert with the owner's personal goals and objectives. Growth opportunities require not only capital but organization and more energy. "Why earn more if I just pay more taxes?" is an often-heard complaint. Also, the owner knows that because of the limited sources of funding, a major portion of personal equity may have to be put on the line as security to obtain necessary financing. Therefore, the business decision regarding financing is greatly influenced by the owner's personal attitudes.

The commercial banks, which have been traditional sources of funding for the private owner, are interested in historical results and performances. The owner's personal and business assets are keys to protecting the loan. A growth opportunity usually has no history. A new market opportunity always presents a risk. No matter how persuasive the owner is about the opportunity, the money will be loaned only on the basis of the net worth and personal guarantees of the business and its owner.

Obviously, a longstanding relationship with the bank is helpful. It ensures some knowledge of the business person and the track record of the company, its history, times of struggle and survival, and accomplishments—all of the elements that don't appear on a financial statement but can be the prime determinants in the lending decision. But tradition doesn't guarantee that a loan will be made. Lenders are influenced by "what's hot and what's not" in the marketplace, and if the proposed opportunity is in an area that is currently out of favor, the loan request can run into trouble. Moreover, personnel changes at banks are frequent, and the entrepreneur may be pitching the loan request to lending officers who are, in effect, unfamiliar with the company's achievements.

Where the average mid-sized business owner comes up short, to reiterate, is in the lack of experience in finance. The entrepreneur often is not only unaware of the alternative sources of funds that are available, but probably lacks a business plan that can be utilized when a promising funding source is found. The entrepreneur probably is too busy to develop a plan, even if able to produce one, and the chances are that the costs of preparing the plan are low on the priority list of expenses. The whole idea of business and financial planning is foreign to the middle-market business owner. Planning, particularly long-range and strategic planning, seldom occurs in the private marketplace. The companies generally have short-term views. The financial focus is on cash flow and projecting cash. Peter Drucker says that smaller business is not opportunistic but rather problematical. It lives from one problem to another. The question, "What is our business and what should it be?" is seldom asked. Strategic, marketing, financial, and operational plans seldom are formalized and committed to paper.

From a merger and acquisition standpoint, as a result of inexperience in the planning area, mid-sized companies find it difficult to present plans and relate to the potential corporate buyer. As an example, asset-based financing has been around since the earliest days of finance, but it is still a source that makes the average small-to-mid-sized business owner uncomfortable. Frankly, the thought of using and tying up the company's resources, such as accounts receivable, inventory, real estate, machinery, and equipment, as security for a relatively small, growth-oriented capital loan is bothersome. An additional turnoff is that rates for asset-based financing can be high for the mid-sized business owner because of the high costs to originate and service the loan. Businesses expect to pay from two to six points over prime in most commercial finance transactions. The lender generally will monitor levels and quality of accounts receivable and inventory on a weekly basis. That process is costly, as are appraisals when plant and equipment make up the security for the loan, and it is an accounting nuisance. And although lenders often will lend up to 80 percent of the value of good receivables, the percentage a borrower can receive on the value of inventory can vary greatly, based on what the lender believes can be realized from liquidation of the inventory in case of default.

Increased competition in the financial community has seen several new players enter the corporate finance game in the middle market. Commercial banks no longer are the sole sources of funds for the business owner. Savings and loans, mutual savings banks, and other thrift institutions now can lend up to 10 percent of their assets in commercial transactions. The commercial finance subsidiaries of equipment suppliers are aggressive competitors in the commercial finance arena. However, the financing problem for the middle-market business owner is that many of these lenders are not interested in doing a deal of less than $2 million. If the small to mid-sized entrepreneur does not go to a banker for the business loan, the chances are good that a premium will be charged by whatever new lender does supply the money. Again, business owners will be asked to personally guarantee the loan. It is for this recurring reason that many profitable mid-sized businesses go to market. The owner gets fed up with having to mortgage hearth and home for a new piece of machinery.

The Small Business Administration, once structured and committed as a source of funding for the small, private owner, now presents other types of difficulties for the borrowing entrepreneur. Endless amounts of paperwork, innumerable delays, and a great degree of impersonalization in processing and deciding on the loan application have triggered serious questions as to whether the SBA is an effective source of financing. An interesting by-product of the SBA is the creation of a service industry populated by firms that, for a fee, will help the applicant go through the process. The SBA's future is being debated in Washington, and some legislative and executive branch authorities, claiming that it no longer meets its original objectives, have argued that it should be eliminated.

PROBLEMS IN GOING TO MARKET AS A SELLER

The problems of taking a small to mid-sized private company to the M&A market are legion. Perhaps the most subjective element is the lack of sophistication on the part of the seller compared to the sophistication found in the average buyer. The seller probably will sell one business in a lifetime, whereas the average active corporate buyer will acquire five to seven companies in two years and the average private buyer will acquire three to five companies. It is difficult to communicate the objective quality of earnings to the buyer. A lack of faith in private company earnings typically requires the seller to share risk in the way the deal is structured, whereas larger acquisitions stand on their own merits. Normally, a public company will have audited financial statements so that the credibility of earnings is better. However, only 10 to 15 percent of small to medium-sized private companies have audited financials.

The financial statements must be recast because the typical private company owner's goal has been to minimize earnings to ease the tax burden. This, of course, is the direct opposite of the driving force in public companies, where the normal objective is to maximize earnings to increase per-share value and better reward the shareholders. The basic goal in recasting is to represent more accurately the true earning power of a company and the related value of its assets. Recasting the balance sheet may include removing excess cash after consideration of the cyclical working capital needs of the business. Inventory also is an area that may need recasting. Inventories in a private company typically are understated for tax purposes. Fixed assets are appraised at replacement value, as well as at orderly liquidation value, as opposed to book value. A review must be made to consider off-balance-sheet assets such as patents or firm contract rights.

Recasting the income statement is perhaps most critical in the area of compensation. The basic goal in recasting a company's owner-related compensation expenditures is to present a view of the business as if it were managed by professional, nonowner managers. Total compensation, both direct and indirect, bonuses, pension plans, condominiums, club membership, cars, excess travel, and many other items frequently must be removed. Adequate compensation and related fringe benefits for professional managers are substituted for these owner-related items. A less expensive auto often replaces a Mercedes, for example, with the company treated as if it were a profit center of a larger corporation rather than the source of support for an owner's lifestyle. The costing of inventories and the proper matching of such cost with revenue is still another important area to review. When completed, the recasting process will result in a new set of financials for the company's latest three-year period that will more closely approximate the real earnings stream.

But the most critical aspect of preparing the small company for sale is an assessment of the potential growth of the business. Documenting the market and its growth, profiling customers and competitors, and determining the prospects given adequate financing and a synergistic organization are integral elements of the exercise. Invariably, the private business owner has a void in estimating the true parameters of growth because of a variety of limitations. If the owner is from an engineering background, the company may have stressed product quality yet never really exploited the total market opportunities. Staffing and financing constraints may have dictated stress on local customers rather than on broader national or international markets. Inability to swing a working capital loan a few years ago may have precluded the planned hiring of a few more salespeople who might have made the difference between a truly outstanding profit year and a merely good one. Yet these limitations can be turned to advantages when the time to sell arrives. With demonstrably unexploited opportunities, the small company is ripe for an acquisition.

This scenario is more common than uncommon, and it is a principal reason that the middle marketplace is fertile ground for corporate acquirers. But determining a market value for smaller, private companies is as much an art as a science. As beauty is in the eyes of a beholder, value is in the eyes of a synergistic buyer. The key to deriving fair value for a business is finding the buyer who understands and appreciates where the business has been, how it is currently positioned, and what growth potential it enjoys. A buyer's willingness to look beyond historical financials, determine what the real earnings flow has been, appreciate the company's position in the marketplace and its growth potential, and understand the owner's needs is what makes a deal.

STRUCTURING THE SMALLER DEAL

Once a proper buyer is identified and the buyer and seller have developed a positive chemistry between themselves, we have the makings of a deal. But closing may depend on a full understanding of what drives the owner of a private business. Money or price alone many times won't do the deal. The business is the owner's "baby," and there must be assurances that it is being passed on to someone who will take care of it properly and make it bigger and better. Money was not the primary motivation during the entrepreneurial period. The major objective was having the biggest and/or the best product or organization. Excellence, quality, pride of doing, making it go when others said it wouldn't are why the owner may have given up part of a stomach and, possibly, a family or two. The seller wants to be sure that the new owner knows, understands, and appreciates all of this, but the seller's personal and financial objectives also must be met. They may be a future earnings stream to maintain a lifestyle. They may be an estate plan for the grandchildren. A sufficient tax shelter may be available to handle ordinary income, or the seller may be in need of estate and tax planning.

All of these elements are part of deal structuring—an entirely different animal in the middle market than in the public arena. If there is a primary caveat in the negotiating stage, it is not to talk price until needs are understood—the needs of the buyer as well as the seller. The buyer may have very legitimate concerns that the seller must understand. The buyer may have excess cash; or conversely, the buyer's lenders may have placed limits on the capacity for incurring future debt. The buyer may have stock it considers undervalued, or may enjoy tax shelters or tax credits that may play a part in reaching the eventual terms. There is always the possibility of a goodwill accounting problem because of low net worth on the seller's books. The recommended order of the negotiations, then, is first talk needs, then talk deal structure, then determine price.

Ultimately, creative deal structuring is the key to closing. Geneva's growth in terms of being one of the largest firms in this marketplace is our ability to understand needs and to provide innovative techniques in deal making.

The closely held business offers opportunities for deal structuring that are not available in dealing with the public acquisition. Most often, the selling entrepreneur is going to be driven by security as opposed to immediate cash. Thus, installment notes, secured by annuities, can allow the buyer to provide funds to the seller without paying 100 percent of the price in cash. A 20-year installment payment enables the buyer to purchase the face amount of the 20-year annuity at a discount of approximately 65 percent. A $1 million installment becomes a $350,000 cash outlay if the first installment commences 60 months from the date the annuity is purchased and the annuity runs over 20 years. If the selling entrepreneur fears cost-of-living increases, a buyer might consider issuing tax-free, zero-based bonds. Zero-based bonds bear deep discounts that provide the buyer with an innovative financing tool. And a continuation of perks, often overlooked when negotiating with the private business owner, may be a satisfactory compensation element.

Proper tax planning on the part of the seller may allow a large portion of the purchase price to be taken in ordinary income, reducing the buyer's goodwill problem and increasing overall the total purchase price. Consulting and no-compete agreements are frequently used. The use of earn-outs allows the seller to capture part of the future earnings of the company in the purchase price and reduces some of the buyer risks. Properly structured, earn-outs can have favorable tax treatments to both parties.

Partial acquisitions offer still another innovative deal-making variation. This can be used when one partner or a younger member of the family wants to remain with the selling business. The buyer may purchase part of the company's equity and take an option to acquire the rest at some future date and price. The future price can be based on a number of interesting scenarios covering achievement of specified goals or performance levels. As part of the arrangement, the buyer may make credit lines or other resources available to the company.

The use of real estate provides another vehicle for creative deal structuring and tax planning through the allocation of purchase price and the use of leases, especially if multiple retail outlets are involved. The allocation of the purchase price is a key element of deal structuring. The review and evaluation of off-balance-sheet assets is an important step that too frequently is overlooked or not given proper consideration. Careful review can result in allocations of purchase prices that obtain capital gain treatment for sellers and amortization of purchase prices for buyers.

The average acquisition in the middle market involves a combination of elements—cash, stock, notes, agreements requiring the sellers not to compete with their old companies, consulting agreements, royalty agreements, earn-outs based on future performance, release agreements of certain assets, and a variety of financial instruments designed to increase the seller's comfort level and meet the needs and objectives of both parties to the transaction.

Intermediaries such as Geneva that work to bring middle-market buyers and sellers together are distinguished by their abilities to capture the flexibilities and innovations that are possible in this distinct marketplace. The competent intermediary first should understand the market value of the business in the hands of a synergistic buyer, the needs and the motivations of the entrepreneur, and the objectives of the buyer, and then be cognizant of the best available deal structuring techniques that can mesh these elements. The intermediary should be in contact with competent professional service firms such as financing sources, legal, tax, and accounting experts, and organizations that are knowledgeable of the vast selection of creative financial instruments available today, all of whom may have to be interfaced with selectively to get a particular deal done. Lastly, the intermediary must be able to pull all those resources together, communicate effectively, negotiate intelligently, and shepherd the process to a successful close.

With the entrepreneur's star again on the ascendancy, M&A opportunities in the middle market are vast, but the most successful players—practitioners, buyers, and sellers—will be those who know the rules of the road.

Part 3

Organizing to Merge and Acquire

Chapter 10

The Internal Acquisition Team

Albert T. Olenzak

Vice President, Corporate Planning and Public Policy, Sun Co., Inc., Radnor, Pennsylvania

Malcolm I. Ruddock

Director, Acquisitions and Divestments, Sun Co., Inc., Radnor Pennsylvania

The acquisition of another company is an inherently risky proposition. The corporate landscape is littered with poorly conceived, planned, or implemented acquisitions that led directly to the acquirer's loss of shareholder value, and, in some cases, to corporate failure. However, there are also notable examples of corporations that have used acquisitions as a powerful long-term corporate development tool.

There is no absolute guarantee of success in the acquisition process, but the acquisition that is planned and implemented by a carefully chosen team of internal and external professional specialists, working with line management, has the best odds of improving shareholder value. The acquisition team consists of three distinct subgroups of individuals with overlapping responsibilities. They cover the following functional activities of the acquisition process:

- Planning
- Transaction analysis
- Implementation

The composition and size of the team is dependent on numerous factors, the most important of which are

- Complexity of transaction
- Type of transaction: related business or diversification
- Size of acquisition versus size of acquirer
- Size and experience of acquirer's staff

The team always should be under the control of line management, and line management should participate actively in *all* stages of the process. Decision making for every stage should be controlled internally and not abdicated to external professionals, such as investment bankers and lawyers. There can be a tendency to permit external professionals to make important decisions because of the complexities of transactions and difficulties with time constraints. At the same time, however, the team should heed the advice of those highly skilled professionals, who are retained at great cost.

If a proposed acquisition represents a diversification, the composition of the acquisition team should include outside expertise. This is especially important in the planning and evaluation stage. When Sun Co. diversified into wholesale distribution, for example, it retained as a member of the team a former chief executive officer of a large participant in the wholesale distribution industry. For planning and implementation of diversification into the general freight trucking industry, Sun retained one of the most experienced transportation consulting groups in the country to assist in planning, selection of criteria, and implementation. The consulting firm performed operating audits of acquisition candidates prior to closing that proved to be invaluable. In both of these major diversification moves, Sun was very successful. Without these outside groups, major mistakes could have been made by moves into unrelated businesses.

With these general comments on the overall process, the composition and activities of the subgroups involved in the acquisition process now can be explored in detail.

THE PLANNING PHASE

Successful mergers and acquisitions are the result of combining keen conceptual preparation with incisive and timely implementation. One without the other is an invitation to disaster. And there is a lot at stake: In few other activities can management significantly change the basic character of a company and affect the welfare of the shareholders in so short a time.

Academic analyses of case histories over many years confirm what most managers know intuitively. First, the target company's shareholders, who can pay taxes and reinvest immediately in a portfolio of similar companies, receive an instantaneous transfer of wealth. Second, although there may be big winners and big losers over time, the data show over and over again that, on *average*, the acquirer can expect to break even.

The general objective of all merger-acquisition activity is to increase shareholder value—a difficult task. Therefore, planners must be on the team and must be intimately involved—not only in the initial search phase, but in the final decision as well. The final purchase price must not be a function only of the heated give and take of negotiation, but must be constrained by estimates of strategic value.

Selection for Strategic Fit

The initial selection of acquisition targets is a function of the strategic needs and preferences of the company and its management. Strategy should be stated explicitly. The most important consideration is whether the target is in a related or unrelated business.

The "related" merger is essentially a growth or expansion thrust aimed at increasing market share, expanding product lines, acquiring necessary resources, or fully utilizing an existing capability. It aims at synergy and is easily understood by management, but may trigger antitrust difficulties. Relatedness may vary from acquiring a company in the same business to building on a specific division's expertise—sometimes called "linked" relatedness.

Unrelated acquisitions are sought to diversify the ongoing earnings of the company; although antitrust problems are minimized, synergy is difficult to achieve, and companies run the risk of misunderstanding and mismanaging the new business. A number of theorists frown on conglomerate mergers because, critics claim, they accomplish little that shareholders cannot do for themselves.

Acquisitions also may be thought of as offensive or defensive. An offensive move is simply the best way among various alternatives to carry out a corporate strategy. Most related acquisitions and some diversifications fall in this class. Defensive acquisitions, on the other hand, are responses to the inability of management to create enough investment opportunities internally or to the threat of the firm itself being acquired. Defensive actions often are somewhat unfocused or opportunistic. However, most top managers feel a strong obligation to ensure the survival of the corporation and its employees by being certain that the firm has future investment opportunities. Often, this entails considerable risk and may take the form of venture or new technology company acquisitions.

In addition, managers will often set additional preferences or constraints such as size, geography, or financial parameters, the list being as long as the number of mergers done. Whatever the final selection screen, it is important to realize that consideration of strategic fit is but a rough measuring tool, and explicit valuation of those companies that pass muster will provide much finer ranking criteria.

Valuation Work by the Team

Having established a list of target candidates on the basis of strategy, management must consider if the acquiring company can win. In other words, will its shareholder value be increased? The best estimate of fair value for large public firms trading in efficient markets is the current stock price. But a premium must be paid to get the company. Thus, the basic question is: Can the company get its premium back? This requires a trial-and-error solution, because the premium will be determined by subsequent negotiation. The planning team members can estimate the potential added value of the combination by considering three components:

Static values—The stock currently may be undervalued because of hidden assets, recent bad news, or a less-than-free information policy. If it is a private company, the owners may have a low estimate of its true value or be willing to accept a low value to achieve liquidity. Tax benefits and operating efficiencies achievable immediately after the combination also figure in the valuation process.

Dynamic values—These may be passive or proactive. Passive values are present when an acquirer forecasts a more favorable future than that implied by the stock market valuation of the target. This is a future bet. Proactive values are achieved by all those changes the new management intends to effect to achieve synergy or financial efficiencies (discounted at the proper rate). Obviously, companies that are currently mismanaged or underleveraged may furnish large gains.

Costs—All costs and expenses of combining the two companies must be subtracted.

The consideration of strategic fit is used mainly in the target selection phase. Consideration of valuation, however, is a continuous process. It is used first to sharpen the target selection process; its more important use, however, is to control a fast-moving process involving many transaction variations and alternatives that are suggested by people with different vested interests. It is not necessary for planners to be part of the negotiating team, but constant communication is necessary between them and the negotiators.

Whether the deal turns out to be a good one in five to 10 years will depend on the price paid, the structure of the transaction, and other specifics of the deal. But it is the planner's job to argue value as the deal is being molded into final form.

THE TRANSACTION ANALYSIS PHASE

The planning process has identified the acquisition candidate and the initial valuation of the target on the basis of an economic forecast. Transaction analysis takes this information and uses it to evaluate legal, tax accounting, and financing considerations of alternative approaches to generate preferred acquisition structures, currency mode, and trade-off value. This analysis also provides information for formulating the acquisition strategies to be pursued. The principal functional disciplines to be included in this part of the team are legal, taxation, finance, accounting, and investment banking.

Legal Considerations

The degree of legal involvement at this stage depends on whether the target is a public or private company. If the target is a public company, it is advisable to retain outside legal counsel, because few corporations have lawyers experienced in public takeovers, especially if hostile, or the necessary legal manpower to deal with the serious time constraints.

At this stage, the legal involvement will concentrate on the following areas:

- Review of appropriate federal securities law
- Review of applicable state takeover statutes
- Antitrust review and the necessity for a Hart-Scott-Rodino (HSR) filing
- Approval processes required for both companies depending on deal structure or currency utilized
- Legal ramifications of alternative acquisition strategies

If a company has a lawyer with experience in acquisitions, and the target is not a public company, there is no reason why the internal legal staff should not represent the company and save significant legal fees. If the transaction appears complicated or time will be extremely important, it may be advisable to retain outside counsel. The ability of a large law firm to provide, on short notice, the significant experienced manpower required in complicated large transactions, including armies of secretaries who will work all night, can be more than worth the extra cost.

Sun very successfully has done most of its acquisition and divestment legal work inside and saved a considerable amount of money. However, an acquirer should recognize that it also makes good business sense to retain outside attorneys for the team when the job is just too big for inside counsel. The outside firms should not replace one's own lawyers; they should supplement staff counsel.

During this stage of the analysis, internal counsel should review the requirements for retaining local, state, or foreign counsel and/or special counsel (regulatory, labor, etc.) and then get outside counsel involved early in the planning process. This is especially true for foreign acquisitions or a domestic acquisition involving significant foreign assets. Some countries, such as Canada, have laws restricting transfer of control of their corporations. This restriction affects the transfer of control of a Canadian subsidiary's U.S. parent corporation. It is a mistake to wait until the implementation phase to attempt to retain foreign counsel, and to familiarize them with the transaction. There are many situations in which advice from special outside counsel can change the structure of the transaction or the overall strategy.

If the antitrust review indicates that there may be difficulty in avoiding a challenge during the HSR filing process, this is the time for lawyers to prepare the necessary documents, recommend changes in the transaction, or supervise the collection and assembly of operational data to support the HSR filing.

The lawyers' involvement in this stage also can prevent serious problems later in the HSR filing process by reviewing all presentation material that is prepared by the teams and given to line decision makers. Any material of this nature relating to markets and competition must be submitted with the HSR filing.

Tax Ramifications

The involvement of tax specialists during the transaction analysis process is extremely important in effecting the most tax-efficient transaction. An in-house tax attorney and tax accountant experienced in mergers and acquisitions should be involved. If external counsel must be consulted, internal tax accountants should work closely with them.

The tax specialists will review the different tax structures available and have the economic analysts run case studies based on the tax considerations. With this exercise, a recommended tax strategy, and alternatives with trade-off values, can be calculated. Although it may not be possible to use the most tax-efficient structure, this analysis will suggest the costs of selecting the alternatives and the resulting reduction in purchase price that will be required to obtain a desired financial return.

A determination should be made as to the necessity of an IRS tax ruling for each of the possible deal structures. If the seller is expected to require a tax ruling, the timing and risk of the transaction will be affected. If the transaction is a public takeover, the tax impact on the various types of shareholders—individual, corporate, and trust—should be thoroughly analyzed.

Bringing in the Finance People

Without an ample quantity of acquisition currency, whether cash, notes, or equity securities, most of the team's efforts are purely academic. If the proposed acquisition will require raising cash externally, the early involvement of financial people in assessing credit sources, terms, limitations, and the effect on the corporation's remaining financial capacity is imperative. The financing aspects of the team's activities could well be the critical path.

A member of the corporate finance department and/or an investment banker should participate in the financial planning of the transaction. If the acquirer is large and the acquisition a small cash purchase, the involvement of finance at this stage may not be needed except for the appropriate budgeting of required cash. If the transaction is large and taps significant financial resources of the company, the top financial officer of the company should participate directly.

When notes, preferred stock, a convertible security, or warrants are utilized, the finance members of the team should bring in an investment banker to assist in determining the satisfactory range of terms and conditions for the different currencies to obtain the required valuation, subsequent market acceptance, tax efficiency, income and balance sheet impact.

Accounting Examinations

At Sun, a senior member of the accounting staff is on the acquisition team. For a larger transaction, the controller of the company actively participates. There are many occasions when representatives of Sun's public accounting firm are asked to participate indirectly and to comment on how they would treat certain aspects of a transaction. Pooling accounting is a good example, because it is difficult, at best, to accomplish and has a dramatic effect on the accounting characterization of the transaction.

At the stage where the transaction has been narrowed to several alternative structures, the accountant should calculate the effect of the transaction on the balance sheet and income statement. Through use of pooling or purchase accounting methodology, the new balance sheet should be approximated. The economic forecast should be recalculated by utilization of the accounting, financing, and tax input generated by other members of the team. The result should be a long-range forecast, five years or more, of the impact of the deal on the overall combined balance sheet and income statement. The effects on earnings per share, performance ratios, financial capacity, bond rating, and probable impact on stock value should be estimated.

Investment Banker Relationships

Investment bankers are regular members of Sun's acquisition team for large transactions and for all transactions involving the acquisition of a public corporation, no matter how small. The banker brings to the corporate team professional expertise gained from assisting in hundreds of M&A transactions and financings, and should be brought into the process as early as possible.

An acquiring company that has never used an investment banker should have its people meet with the principal employees of the banker who are being assigned to the deal. The company insiders should assess the bankers' suitability for the specific type of corporate development activity being pursued and their familiarity with the appropriate industry. The outside banking people selected for the team should be identified and acknowledged in an engagement letter.

The investment banker should be thoroughly involved in all aspects of the acquisition. Advice and service are expensive and should be used. Aside from advice on acquisition strategy selection and on tactics during implementation, the investment banker can provide a high-level approach to target management, fairness opinions, deal structuring, dealer/manager services in tender offers, and financial advice.

THE IMPLEMENTATION PHASE

Once the candidate has been selected and valued and the acquisition strategy has been determined, the action begins. The participants in this last phase include those in the transaction analysis phase plus some additional participants. There are two functional groups working closely together: those involved in negotiating, and those involved in due diligence.

Negotiating the Deal

Most transactions require negotiation of the final terms of the agreement between the parties. Even tender offers, except for the most hostile, involve negotiations. The person selected as lead negotiator should be an individual with good negotiating skills, an excellent familiarity with the subject matter, and experience in negotiating transactions. At Sun, all but the largest acquisitions are negotiated by individuals within the appropriate subsidiary and not by the parent company. Others involved are lawyers, tax counsel, accountants, investment bankers, and operational and financial experts.

Due Diligence

If the acquisition is friendly and not a tender offer, there will be ample time to complete a full due diligence review of the company to be acquired before the deal is consummated. This activity is extremely important, because it is designed to eliminate surprises after the purchase. A buyer cannot rely solely on representations and warranties by the target to protect against the unforeseen. Prior to making final commitment to purchase, the following should be considered:

Financial Audit. Either an internal or public accounting group should perform an audit before closing on the purchase of any private corporation that does not have recent audited financials.

Risk Management Review. Risk management review has become more important with the heightened levels of interest in alleged carcinogenic agents and the impact of industrial activity on the environment. Sun has, on occasion, retained occupational health consultants to review the potential health risks of a target company's products or workplace.

Other Audits. Depending on the nature of the business being acquired and judgment as to the likely areas of risk, an assortment of specialists can be fielded. When Sun made early investments in diverse industries, outside consultants familiar with an industry were retained to complete extensive operational audits as part of the due diligence procedures. These reviews were not only helpful in determining if the acquisition candidate was worth buying, but useful in determining operational problems and identifying weak management that should be replaced after the acquisition. Tax audits, legal audits, and human resource audits also should be considered.

In one acquisition, both the operational audit and the accounting audit uncovered a weakness in a target's new automated billing system that could have resulted in $1 million of lost receivables. The sellers did not agree with the findings and, therefore, were willing to set aside escrow funds from the sale proceeds. Within a year, Sun has collected a significant amount from the escrow for the receivables actually lost.

The largest due diligence team fielded by Sun had to validate real estate records for a multibillion-dollar asset purchase of oil and gas properties. Almost 400 professionals were involved.

Even tender offers, if friendly, can and should be subject to due diligence review. In one friendly takeover of a public company by Sun, the agreement was struck on a Friday night, after the close of the market. A preselected team of internal and external specialists came onto the premises within an hour of the agreement and worked around the clock until Sunday afternoon, but found nothing negative. The final commitments were made and the press release issued before the opening of the market on Monday. Although highly unlikely, financial statements filed with the SEC can be fraudulently prepared, and even a limited due diligence effort might avoid a potentially serious mistake in such cases.

For public takeovers, the acquirer in the implementation phase also must deal with printers, special legal counsel, public relations firms, proxy solicitors, information agents, and transfer agents.

From start to finish, acquisitions involve the active participation and coordination of numerous skilled professionals from inside and outside the company to complete successfully an acquisition that, in the final analysis, will increase shareholder value.

Chapter 11

Pursuing Acquisition Candidates

Herald L. Ritch

Vice President, Mergers & Acquisitions Department,
Kidder, Peabody & Co., Inc., New York, New York

The U.S. merger and acquisition environment has been extremely competitive for the last several years, which makes it advantageous for would-be acquirers to be both well prepared and opportunistic if they are to make the most of attractive acquisition possibilities that come their way. My experience as a merger and acquisition professional suggests to me that would-be acquirers can dramatically enhance their abilities to identify and pursue acquisition candidates by, first, understanding key trends in the merger market and their causes, and, second, being well prepared in all major phases of the acquisition process in order to be able to move intelligently on short notice.

THE MODERN MERGER AND ACQUISITION MARKET

There are several trends in the merger environment of the 1980s that are worth describing and analyzing. Competition is, indeed, frenzied, with multiple bidders frequently slugging it out for the same property. Prices, too, seem high in reference to many common pricing indices. Quality companies have entered the acquisition arena with a vengeance as both buyers and sellers. In contrast to the late 1960s and early 1970s, the sheer pace of transactions is blistering, with thousands of M&A transactions—including thousands of divestitures, hundreds of leveraged buy-outs, and hundreds of transactions in excess of $100 million in size—being consummated within the 1983-1985 period alone. As a result, the time frame in which acquirers' decisions are being made has been greatly compressed via these competitive pressures.

The two basic causes of this energy-charged merger environment are economic factors and the revolution over the last decade in takeover techniques and tactics, or the "technology" of the merger business.

Economic Factors. One of the important economic factors that has sparked takeover fever is the much-discussed and well-documented idea that across a wide swath of American industries it is cheaper to buy existing companies than to attempt to replicate them *de novo*. Another key economic factor has been the availability of enormous amounts of credit for acquisition financing from the commercial banking sector, with such credit available not only to blue chip borrowers, but to companies with lesser credit ratings and to leveraged buy-out groups. A final driving force behind the recent acquisition boom has been the enormous liquidity in many sectors of the economy, caused in no small measure by corporate tax law changes.

Takeover Techniques and Tactics. Many modern takeover techniques and tactics came about as the result of the influence of unnegotiated takeovers, particularly throughout the period beginning in the mid-1970s. Unnegotiated takeovers include any unilateral attempt by a would-be acquirer to gain control of a company without the approval of the company's present management or board of directors. They may take the form of tender offers, exchange offers, or proxy contests. Unnegotiated takeover attempts by corporations had their serious beginnings in the conglomerate acquisition wave of the 1960s, with companies such as LTV Corp. offering their securities as considerations, usually at modest premiums over the current trading prices of target company stocks.

STRATEGIES FOR UNNEGOTIATED MERGERS

Saturday Night Special. By the early to mid-1970s, the "Saturday night special" had arrived with great force. The Saturday night special is a seven-day cash tender offer for all of the stock of a target, usually beginning on a Saturday, both to gain a timing advantage and to prevent the defense from being able to round up key advisers easily. In subsequent years, numerous other tender offer-related developments have occurred, including new Securities and Exchange Commission (SEC) regulations that dramatically changed the tender offer process, two-tier bids with multiple pro-ration pools, defensive self-tenders, and Pac-Man tenders.

Bear Hug.   Another major development from the unnegotiated arena is the "bear hug." The bear hug is a unilateral offer to acquire a company made directly to its board of directors in letter form, and disclosing enough specifics regarding price and terms that an announcement of the offer must be made by the target, if it has not been made already by the would-be acquirer. A bear hug letter typically contains a tight time frame for a formal response to the offer and may threaten a follow-up tender offer, or unstated other actions, if a favorable reply is not received in the allotted period of time.

Nibble Strategy.   Perhaps the most common unnegotiated M&A technique is the "nibble strategy." This involves acquiring a minority stake of from just under 5 percent to, say, 30 percent of the stock of a public company in the open market. Legally, any purchaser of 5 percent of a company's stock must file a 13D form with the SEC indicating how much stock has been acquired, some background about the purchaser, and a statement of the purchaser's intentions regarding the target. In the classic case, where a nibbler takes a position and then makes a tender offer for the rest of the company's stock, the nibbler is in the closest thing to a no-lose position in the takeover arena. The nibbler either takes control of the company, having lowered its purchase price to the extent that no control premium was paid on the up-front stock it acquired, or the nibbler sells its stock position at a profit to a "white knight" bidder that does offer a premium in a rescue bid for the target. Because of its elegant simplicity and effectiveness, the nibble strategy will continue to be employed until legislative or regulatory measures are taken to stop it.

Swipe.   A further unnegotiated technique is the "swipe." A swipe occurs when a company's board of directors signs a definitive agreement to sell the firm, only to have an opportunistic bidder pounce on the seller with a higher offer. These are always powerful offers, because the target's board previously has indicated both a willingness to sell and to do so at a lower price. But swipes are especially powerful in thwarting management-led leveraged buy-outs, where independent directors are under greater-than-normal pressure, due to the compounding effect of the usual concerns about management's conflicts of interest and the sensitivity caused by having agreed to sell to insiders at a lower price.

All of these unnegotiated techniques, as well as numerous other tactical tricks of the trade emanating from the unnegotiated takeover area, have had a pronounced impact on negotiated transactions. In sharp contrast to the leisurely manner in which many companies historically approached acquisition transactions by drafting an agreement in principle and issuing a corresponding press release first, and getting down to brass tacks later, buyers of the 1980s typically run very scared. If at all possible, no smart buyer should announce a transaction without a definitive agreement, all necessary financing, and appropriate features to ensure the probability of ultimately consummating the transaction (so-called lock-ups) already in place.

PREPARING FOR A
COMPETITIVE ENVIRONMENT

As the discussion of trends in the merger market and their causes demonstrates, would-be buyers of companies must be well prepared and ready to move in order to compete effectively in the current acquisition environment. To be in the right place at the right time, many successful acquirers expend great management time and effort in most, if not all, of the following six phases of the acquisition process: strategic planning, homework, opportunity identification, evaluation, approach, and execution. By designing an acquisition program to direct sufficient attention to each of these phases, an acquirer can bring a great deal of discipline to bear on the acquisition process and, therefore, do a better job of completing those acquisitions that it should do on reasonable terms, and avoiding those transactions that do not make sense for it.

Strategic Planning Phase

Strategic planning is the first step in successfully implementing an acquisition program. Able acquirers know what their organizations are all about and why. Thus, before embarking on a corporate acquisition program and committing to the big stakes associated with it, most good acquirers spend considerable time going through a period of corporate introspection and self-analysis. Early in this process it is critical to determine whether growth via acquisition is desirable and, if so, why. If acquisitions are worth pursuing, what type of transaction is best? Should it be a related business, or is complete diversification the aim of the effort?

At the outset of this strategic planning phase, it is important to insert a consideration of the time commitment involved in an acquisition program. Even with fairly broad business objectives and acquisition criteria, the corporate acquisition process is very time-consuming, with no certainty of success in achieving stated objectives. Much time and money can be spent exploring situations, only to result in disappointment for any of a number of reasons. Therefore, a major acquisition program should not be started by a company that cannot devote sufficient top management time to the effort.

If it is clear early in the strategic planning review that acquisitions make strategic sense, it is a good idea to compile a list of desired acquisition objectives, whether they be of the financial, business, managerial, or other type. Moreover, it is usually enlightening to make an assessment of the strengths and weaknesses of both the would-be purchaser and one or two potential acquisition candidates. These exercises, taken together, help to develop a good understanding within an entity's top management as to what qualitative issues are critical to it as a buyer.

After considering those factors, it is necessary to establish a framework for evaluating acquisition opportunities. Are the corporation's acquisition interests served only where a good business fit exists, or alternatively, does the corporation have a portfolio mentality? Is sheer opportunism the lifeblood and tradition of the enterprise? Will the corporation only do negotiated transactions? It is very important to answer these questions honestly so that much wheel-spinning and embarrassment is avoided. For example, if a particular company's board of directors is relatively indecisive and does not have the stomach for a fight, it should acknowledge that hostile takeovers are probably not its cup of tea.

Finally, after all of the above issues have been carefully considered and fully debated internally, it is important that a would-be acquirer's top management team establish fairly formal strategic acquisition criteria. In doing so, they should be careful not to either manufacture a "wish list" so stringent that no realistic acquisition could ever pass muster, or to be so general in their acquisition criteria that they provide no real guidance as to what is, or is not, a desirable acquisition candidate. Furthermore, top management should be conscious of the trade-offs they are making as they set up these criteria. For example, executives should be aware that the more rigorous and selective the strategic acquisition criteria become, the greater the odds of not consummating an acquisition in the desired time frame.

Homework Phase

The homework phase involves general preparatory work, including the organization of an entity's acquisition team and the education of that same group about the basic mechanics of corporate acquisitions. The internal composition of an acquisition team varies significantly from one company to another. Indeed, internal acquisition team members can vary significantly within the same company from one transaction to the next, depending on a particular acquisition candidate's size, the key personalities involved, and myriad other factors. However, two worthwhile observations regarding the rational structuring of an internal acquisition team can be made. First, as transactions get larger, more public, and more complex, the greater is the need for chief executive officer involvement on the team. Second, able acquirers generally include on their internal team the senior line officer who will have direct profit-center responsibility for a business after it is acquired.

In addition to internal team members, external advisers, including legal and financial advisers, management consultants, and other appropriate advisers, usually are assembled when a major acquisition program is established. Interestingly, many accomplished acquirers espouse the view that it is useful for key internal and external team members to get to know each other in advance of an actual transaction. Intuitively, this seems to make sense, because the people dynamics of a potential acquisition are so crucial to its ultimate outcome.

The second major aspect of the homework phase involves exposure to the basic mechanics of corporate acquisition transactions. Frequently, informal primers are given by the external team members to internal team members on a variety of topics, including the differences between a corporate merger and a cash tender offer; legal issues regarding acquisitions, including SEC matters and the rights and responsibilities of corporate directors in the acquisition area; accounting and tax matters; regulatory issues of likely interest; antitrust issues, including the practical implications of the Hart-Scott-Rodino Act of 1976; and stock market workings, in particular those involving risk arbitrage. Being conversant in these areas is definitely desirable, but this knowledge should be tempered with the old adage that a little bit of knowledge is dangerous. For example, the rigid application of an acquisition approach that worked well in one context may prove a terrible technique in another, somewhat similar situation, because of a very slight difference in circumstance such as enactment of a new tax, a different regulatory context, or a different state of incorporation of the target company.

Opportunity Identification Phase

The first stage of the opportunity identification phase generally involves the top management of a company. After reflecting on its strategic acquisition criteria, management should determine whether it makes business sense to put industries that meet these criteria under the microscope and ascertain if these industries are really as attractive as they appear superficially and whether they are indeed congruent with the company's strategic interests. At this time, management consultants, research analysts, financial advisers, and other advisers may be called upon to provide perspective on the target industries from their respective disciplines. Ultimately, these inputs lead to the decision that a given industry is or is not strategically attractive to the corporation.

Once it has been determined that a particular industry is strategically attractive, the next step is to identify specific companies that make good acquisition candidates within the target industry. Sometimes this is a simple process, especially if the entire industry is composed of two or three public companies. However, an industry more often is fragmented and includes important private companies and divisions of public companies as competitors. Many industries have large numbers of players. Therefore, it is frequently very important to tap a variety of sources for ideas on specific companies. These sources generally include both internal and external team members, the business press, analysts, and investment bankers, as well as other business and personal acquaintances.

Two final, very important sources of specific-company ideas involve looking at targets in strategically attractive industries that are either current takeover targets or have announced transactions involving their sales in the last few years, only to have such deals fall through. These are two categories of acquisition candidates that have the single most important attribute—availability. As a result, it is especially important to focus on those companies in strategically attractive industries that recently have been, or currently are, the targets of unilateral takeover attempts, that are the subjects of takeover rumors, that have been parties to broker acquisition transactions, that have undergone recent substantial top management changes, or that might be in a transaction mode for other reasons.

As specific companies in target industries become better identified, and more information about them is accumulated, it is important for the acquisition team members to create a list of prime acquisition candidates as well as a list of other companies of possible interest. All of these companies will be studied carefully in the next phase.

A final key aspect of the opportunity identification phase involves a would-be acquirer's communication of its distilled acquisition interests to the business community. By identifying publicly those industries that it finds strategically attractive as targets of opportunity for acquisitions, an acquirer should experience an increase in the flow of acquisition ideas brought to it, as well as better overall quality in the ideas it receives. Moreover, this communication better prepares the marketplace for any changes in the acquiring entity's strategic direction.

Evaluation Phase

In the evaluation phase, acquirers carefully review those companies on their list of prime acquisition candidates as well as other companies that are of secondary interest to them. In this review, the first cut is once again to compare each candidate with the acquirer's strategic acquisition criteria. This has the effect of keeping the acquiring entity's eye on the ball.

The next portion of the evaluation phase includes a traditional business review of each company, including a risk analysis and financial review. Understanding each target company's markets, market shares, competitors, customers, and market dynamics is critical. A qualitative feel for the target's management team and an assessment of any hidden assets and liabilities are also important at this stage of the process. Examples of hidden assets might include assets such as appreciated real estate or natural resources with fair market values substantially in excess of their stated book value, whereas hidden liabilities might include substantial litigation risks, an unfunded pension liability, or an uneconomic contract. Not surprisingly, it is also necessary to make a practical assessment of the target's availability, not just in a vacuum, but in light of the acquiring entity's world view. For example, if the target company is available only via a hostile transaction and that is contrary to the would-be acquirer's policy, it should be regarded as not presently available.

In evaluating key acquisition candidates, it is important ultimately to make preliminary judgments about the economic values of these enterprises. Investment bankers and consultants frequently can play a valuable role in providing independent assessments of the reasonableness of management's assumptions, and conveying knowledge of specific industries and companies. These valuations should be viewed as being subject to change when more information is gathered, particularly if direct access to the target, its financial projections, and other confidential information become possible at a later time.

Another portion of the evaluation phase is a legal assessment of each key acquisition candidate. The paramount issue here is whether there are any show-stoppers that would legally prevent the would-be acquirer from consummating an acquisition of a particular candidate. Specifically, are there any antitrust, regulatory, contractual, or other legal impediments that would present an obstacle to completion of a transaction? If these barriers are present, this is the time to determine if there are ways of overcoming them.

Approach Phase

If, after completing all of the analysis in the evaluation phase, a particular acquisition candidate continues to look attractive, the next step is to consider what approach strategy makes sense for that company. At this stage of the process, most able acquirers consult with their internal and external acquisition team members, and review the results of their evaluation of the candidate, together with an analysis of the motivations of the key players involved with the acquisition target. Do its owners want to sell? Is there a management-succession problem within the company? Have the directors of the company openly split with one another? How much stock do insiders own? What is the cost basis of their stock? Have they been increasing or reducing their positions recently?

The motivational assessment of the acquisition candidates has to be overlaid on the financial structuring of a business combination. Tax, accounting, and pricing issues have to be considered in designing an offer that will appeal to these key individuals and yet remain attractive from the acquiring entity's viewpoint. Other factors impinging on the financial engineering of a transaction include a detailed analysis of the shareholder groups of both the acquirer and candidate, the likely level of competition in the marketplace for the given company, and general market considerations.

After a would-be buyer considers the motivations of the key people within an acquisition candidate and the financial engineering constraints and trade-offs present in a particular situation, it is time to develop customized approach tactics with respect to the acquisition candidate. Although each approach is unique, there are three general categories: the friendly persuasion approach, the opportunistic approach, and the completely unnegotiated approach described earlier. Most transactions begin with a friendly persuasion approach, in which the potential acquirer attempts to convince another company to negotiate its sale. The obvious advantages of a friendly transaction are that it is likely to be the least costly form of transaction, management of the desired company is more apt to remain, the acquirer will have more and better information for making a judgment as to the attractiveness of the target, the acquirer frequently has more time to evaluate the acquisition's merits, and lock-ups are more likely to be available.

The success of the friendly persuasion approach tends to be a function of three key factors. The first is the independence quotient of the target, that is, the degree to which the target's management and board of directors value their independence. The second is the ability of the acquirer's primary executive to relate well to his or her counterpart at the target. It is critically important in designing an approach to remember that most public company chief executives on the receiving end of a friendly approach initially are inclined to have two thoughts running through their minds. They are not interested in selling to anyone; and they are concerned about keeping the overture absolutely confidential to avoid leakage of information that could unleash market forces that eventually could force their companies to be sold. The third key factor in the success of a friendly approach is the price the acquirer is willing to pay.

Opportunistic approaches to acquisitions occupy the middle of the approach spectrum and may lead to negotiated or unnegotiated transactions. These approaches include overtures to a target company that has been hit with an unnegotiated takeover attempt, has telegraphed its salability through a broad solicitation being managed by an intermediary on its behalf, or already has agreed to sell itself to another potential buyer. (An approach in this latter case would use the previously described swipe technique.) If the target already is subject to a hostile takeover attempt, it is very important for a friendly would-be buyer to place an early call to the target to indicate any potential interest in acting as a white knight. This will maximize the probability of gaining direct access to the target's key people and advisers as the situation develops. If it is impossible to play the white knight role for reasons beyond the buyer's control, it may be possible for the acquirer to be a "gray knight," a bidder who enters the fray after the shooting has started but before it has reached an acquisition agreement with the target.

A buyer employing the opportunistic approach in response to a target's broad buyer solicitation effort, even when the campaign involves an actual auction, can seek a competitive edge by trying to preempt the solicitation/auction process and transform it into a one-to-one negotiation. This sometimes can be done purely via conventional means—being very responsive to the seller's price and nonprice objectives, exhibiting a willingness to work virtually around the clock on the project, retaining able advisers for the project, and otherwise demonstrating a can-do mentality. If this "we try harder" approach does not work, consideration should be given to either making a preemptive bid with a short time fuse, or attempting to split the target from its advisers, usually by convincing the selling principal that the potential acquirer qualitatively is the best buyer, and that it would be aggressive on price and other terms if the process were not akin to a big poker game.

Lastly, with respect to completely unnegotiated offer approaches, it is important to be alert to the fact that it is unwise to launch a hostile offer without first battening down the hatches. The fate of Bendix Corp. in its attempted 1982 takeover of Martin Marietta Corp. demonstrates the importance of having one's own defenses set before getting into a fight. Bendix exposed its flanks to a Pac Man attack by Martin Marietta Corp. and ultimately extricated itself only by being acquired by Allied Corp. A final bit of advice in the case of unnegotiated offers is to set your maximum price in advance of launching a hostile bid and stick to that decision unless compelling new information surfaces to change your view.

Execution Phase

The execution stage is exactly what it sounds like: getting the job done. The roles of special legal and financial advisers are very important, because critical decisions frequently have to be made under fighter-pilot-like conditions and time constraints. In addition to being very knowledgeable about a host of acquisition-related subject areas and understanding idiomatic solutions to common issues that crop up in negotiations, these advisers frequently have special negotiating skills honed through sheer practice. This is clearly the area where the relative contributions of legal and financial advisers are greatest, and it is the area where most able acquirers will seek out and listen to advice.

Perhaps the most critical facet of the acquisition process for a would-be acquirer is the importance of its remaining focused on its strategic acquisition criteria in the exciting execution phase. In the heat of a hostile takeover or in the fervor of pursuing a friendly acquisition, acquirers have been known to make major mistakes, such as dramatically overpaying for target companies, or effecting business combinations that do not achieve stated strategic objectives. However, the truly successful acquirer retains its concentration on desired objectives during this crucial phase, and only goes through with the deal if its strategic objectives can be achieved.

TIME IS COMPRESSED

The M&A arena has been extremely competitive the last several years because of both economic reasons and the influence of increasingly sophisticated techniques and strategies that developed in the area of unnegotiated takeovers but have heavily influenced market psychology and business practices in the area of negotiated transactions as well. The resultant compression in time available to would-be acquirers has forced successful buyers to undertake a substantial amount of advance preparation in various phases of the acquisition process in order to be ready to compete when they believe it is in their interests to do so. Corporations can enhance their ability to identify and pursue acquisitions successfully by understanding the dynamics at work in the current acquisition marketplace and preparing themselves accordingly to do business in this environment.

Chapter 12

Finding More Than a Finder

James B. Dwyer III

Senior Vice President, E. F. Hutton & Company, Inc., New York, New York

Jeffrey Garner

Donaldson, Lufkin & Jenrette, New York, New York

The first step in choosing someone to assist you in buying or selling a business is to define your objectives. The purchase or sale of a business is a fundamental strategic action. The alternatives must be carefully considered and the broad implications of external change weighed before proceeding with definitive steps. Decide firmly what you plan to accomplish with a purchase or sale. In the case of acquisition, the specific question could be: Do you wish to complement your product line or extend your geographic reach? If it's a sale, the key question could be: Do you wish to leave the business and retire, or remain and manage the business as part of an entity with greater financial resources?

As a fundamental goal in a purchase, you want to acquire the highest-quality business for the lowest cost: in a sale, you want to sell your business to the highest-quality buyer at the highest price. As an acquirer you may have investible funds at infrequent intervals and need the purchased business to propel your overall corporate growth. As a seller, your opportunity to sell occurs only once and the inherent value built up over the years must be protected and recognized in the transaction.

WHAT DO YOU NEED?

As you undoubtedly have done throughout the course of successfully managing your business, you will seek expert assistance from someone whose success has been in the profession of handling corporate mergers and acquisitions. Your associate should be an expert in the merger and acquisition field who also possesses a familiarity and sensitivity to your personal and business goals and objectives.

WHAT IS AVAILABLE?

The ideal consultant for you is the one who can provide the most value added. In the M&A area, three broad types of individuals are available: the finder, the business broker, and the financial adviser. Each provides a different level of service, and the choice of which to use should depend on your individual situation.

The Finder

You probably have met a finder, or potential finder, in your business. Usually, the finder is an individual who acts as a matchmaker in the business community, and who frequently maintains a full-time career as an attorney, commercial banker, accountant, or other service-sector professional. Finders rely primarily on their personal contacts and, if engaged by you, they will introduce the subject of your buying or selling a business to their acquaintances. Before coming to an explicit arrangement with a finder to represent your interests, it would be prudent to inquire into and confirm the person's track record. Ask for references from previous clients and spend time talking to the finder. Generally, the finder is not a specialist in buying or selling a business, and qualifications among finders can vary greatly.

Once you are satisfied as to the character and skills of the individual finder, it is necessary to elaborate exactly what you expect of him or her and to what degree the finder may represent you. Generally, a finder acts only to introduce you to parties with whom a transaction might be arranged. Confidential operating information and transaction terms, especially those involving price valuations, are best not discussed with finders. The use of finders will, by the nature of their activity, tell the marketplace of your intentions to buy or sell, and leaks of sensitive information or negotiating posture would jeopardize your position in any meeting the finder arranged. The most efficient use of a finder is in transactions involving small companies with relatively straightforward businesses. In these situations, the acquisition or sale often can be evaluated quickly after the finder's introduction of the two principal parties.

The Business Broker

An array of services that is broader than those offered by finders can be provided by business brokers in your community. They are usually principals in local firms with contacts throughout the area and visibility as clearinghouses of information on regional businesses. Business brokers can identify companies in your industry and your preferred locations and, with their firm's credibility behind them, can make a cold introduction on your behalf to the principal of a potential seller or acquirer. Unlike finders, business brokers try to participate in any negotiations arising from their introduction. Anyone retaining a broker must establish at an early point the degree to which he or she will act on a client's behalf. A broker may be useful in suggesting a broad range of values in which your transaction may fall, particularly if your business, or desired new business, is a relatively straightforward operation.

The Financial Adviser

The broadest spectrum of services available when buying or selling a business may be found in an investment bank and, more recently, at certain large accounting firms and commercial banks. Professionals in these national or regional firms can act as full-service financial advisers in the specialized area of corporate mergers and acquisitions. They offer a host of services unavailable elsewhere. One of the most valuable, and least known, is prepurchase or presale assistance. The financial adviser may suggest a strategy involving a minor capital restructuring, the disposal of nonessential assets, and/or the modification of operations to place your business in the best possible posture prior to an acquisition or sale.

Financial advisers have extensive experience in valuing companies in proposed mergers. Determining the proper and acceptable valuation of a company is of paramount importance to owners and management, and frequently is best accomplished by means of a professional third party. The availability of a realistic appraisal of a company's value, based on constant contact with the merger market together with knowledge of valuation techniques and what companies generally are paying for control of businesses, can help determine an achievable price.

The process of identifying the proper potential targets or acquirers is a key element in a successful transaction. In this process, a financial adviser can search across the entire nation, and perhaps abroad, to locate as complete a list of potential candidates as possible. These may include companies outside the industry of buyer or seller. With a constant involvement in merger and acquisition transactions of all types and in all industries, the financial adviser maintains current criteria on a comprehensive list of potential buyers and also may represent or be aware of certain companies quietly seeking new capital from an upstream merger partner. Knowledge of this type is derived from constant participation in the M&A environment and is specifically developed to allow financial advisers to offer realistic advice.

An adviser will, for an acquisition, provide strategic advice to guide the most efficient search for an acquisition candidate, and, for a sale, outline steps to help a seller receive the highest price from the best buyer. The adviser is aware that its own professional reputation is linked with its assessment of and suggestions for your business. The professionalism of the financial adviser coupled with a transaction-oriented compensation schedule, under which fees are paid based on deal success, encourages the adviser to tailor your acquisition or sale strategy to the reality of the marketplace.

After bringing the parties together, the financial adviser will continue full involvement in the transaction. In the case of a sale, for example, the adviser will prepare a confidential memorandum that provides a detailed analysis of the selling company to a prospective buyer. Particular emphasis is placed on negotiating the financial aspects and the structuring of the proposed transaction. Other important services could include advice on legal, tax, and accounting matters; management transition; and the arrangement of financing with institutions. The adviser plays many roles during the negotiating period. In addition to guiding the discussions so that they proceed in an orderly and timely manner, the adviser's actions as a buffer between principals can aid both buyer and seller in avoiding pitfalls that could endanger future relationships within the merged enterprise.

Financial advisers can provide assistance to almost any type of business. Large, computerized data resources complement the expertise of individual advisers and facilitate the valuation process as well as the identification of potential merger partners. The adviser also is equipped to communicate effectively any special characteristics about the client company—such as good future prospects despite an erratic past performance, or a maturing business that is nonetheless cash-rich. By having the capability to supplement qualitative descriptions of the client concern with quantitative comparisons with similar companies, the adviser can help you focus on the outstanding aspects of your business that may, in the case of a sale, command a premium in the price.

As a practical matter, however, financial advisers generally do not work with smaller companies. Their province consists of larger firms with annual aftertax net income of more than $2 million.

WHAT WILL YOU GET?

A series of examples may help clarify the role of each type of transaction consultant and suggest the value performed in return for their fee.

The Finder

For an executive making small acquisitions, the services of a finder may suffice and complement the work of the in-house professional staff. A pleasure boat manufacturer wishing to expand into new coastal markets, for example, initially may tell finders in these localities of its intent and general criteria, and then encourage the finders to "beat the bushes" for specific candidates. When lists of small, privately owned boat builders and maintenance shops are presented by the finders, the acquirer can be introduced to the owners selected as the most likely targets. These matchmaking activities are of great assistance to a large national firm that has internal expertise in evaluation, negotiation, and closing, but that lacks ability to identify a broad range of small-scale candidates.

The Business Broker

A moderate-sized business choosing to expand via acquisition may turn to a business broker for assistance in locating a potential target and in launching negotiations on the proper basis. A Texas company wishing to add a Florida operation to better serve the Gulf area, for instance, may call upon a Florida business broker to identify local companies in its industry, both private and public, and to offer guidelines on the valuation of these candidates. Factors that are peculiar to the Florida market, and not present in Texas, may be reflected in the value that the Florida proprietor expects and requires from the bidder. The business broker can make the acquirer a more informed buyer and thereby improve the chances for a successful transaction. In addition, some business brokers have specialties that can greatly improve the "do-ability" of acquisitions or sales, such as expertise in particular industries or certain types of transactions, including leveraged and management buy-outs, employee stock-option-plan buy-outs, and sale-leaseback arrangements. As with finders, it is necessary to inquire into the record of brokers and to ascertain their levels of professionalism.

The Financial Adviser

The wide array of services that a financial adviser can provide is illustrated by an actual case history of a sale. An entrepreneur who had built a profitable service business in a Western state considered selling out because of estate considerations. He contacted an investment banking firm that, he had noted, was mentioned prominently in a number of recent M&A transactions. The first thing that caught the adviser's eye was that the service business enjoyed a special, but generally unrecognized niche in its industry—one of those aforementioned unique characteristics that can command a premium. Thus, the financial adviser's initial analysis was oriented toward uncovering data to confirm the size and profitability of the niche and the company's market position. This information was incorporated in a confidential selling memorandum, a bound, 55-page, in-depth description of the business and its future prospects. The document was designed to answer 90 percent of a potential buyer's questions, a device that in effect helps prequalify the most serious contenders and generate prompt consideration by such bidders.

While the memorandum was being prepared, the adviser identified a select list of potential buyers. An initial valuation of the business was made to establish an asking price, set negotiating strategy, and spotlight which bidders would be able to afford the business. Several computerized data bases allowed rapid screening of thousands of public and private companies. Financial strength of the buyer was chosen as a prime criterion, and certain industry and geographic criteria were used to further screen the large comprehensive list of potential buyers.

Some additions and many deletions resulted from further investigation of these companies and conversations with other professionals at the investment banking firm. Because of their personal contacts with senior managements and their knowledge of individual companies' corporate strategies and acquisition preferences, the investment banker's professional advisers form a unique and valuable resource.

When the confidential memorandum and the select list of potential acquirers were completed, the process of introducing the client's business to the chief executive officers of the primary potential bidders was begun. After several rounds of discussion, one CEO developed a serious interest. Because the selling memorandum's information had answered most buyer's questions, the next step was to have that CEO meet the selling entrepreneur. At this first meeting, and in all negotiations through closing, the financial adviser participated fully, acting both as a negotiator on its client's behalf, and as a buffer between two strong and successful personalities. The financial adviser facilitated progress by asking its client's toughest questions and fielding the buyer's most sensitive inquiries. When the discussions turned to price and terms, the adviser also set the strategy. The initial asking price was determined after the adviser had provided a detailed study of valuations of companies that recently had been sold in the same industry. The adviser also prepared a detailed analysis of the tax implications to the shareholders with respect to the proposed form of consideration.

In general, the financial adviser acted as the catalytic agent throughout the transaction, until a successful closing was executed. In this case, the owner received a price reflecting a substantial premium over the company's net book value and an above-average multiple of net income.

WHAT TO PAY?

The varying degrees of service provided by the three types of associates can result in slightly different fee structures. Finders are generally paid a "5-4-3-2-1" fee (5 percent of the first $1 million of a purchase price, 4 percent of the second million, 3 percent of the third million, 2 percent of the fourth million, and 1 percent of any additional consideration) for a completed transaction that they, as nonexclusive agents, initiated. Business brokers are generally paid similarly if a transaction that they initiated is consummated. Finders and business brokers may accept consideration in lieu of cash, such as stock in the new enterprise. Many, though, prefer to be paid in cash at or soon after a closing to limit their continuing exposure. They believe that the matchmaker's job is completed once a transaction has been agreed to and closed. Financial advisers typically are paid contingent upon completion of a transaction. Fees sometimes take the form of inverted percentages, with a smaller percentage paid on a consideration received up to a certain benchmark and a larger percentage on a consideration received above such a level. For example, in a sale for which the seller wants at least $10 million, the fee may be 2 percent on the first $10 million and 5 percent on any additional consideration received.

Given the considerable time involved in a six- to nine-month team effort, an initial retainer often is paid the adviser and is then credited against any subsequent contingent fee. A financial adviser generally requires an exclusive sales arrangement, and perhaps an exclusive purchase arrangement for acquisition searches, for a six- to nine-month period. The fees charged may approximate the 5-4-3-2-1 formula for small transactions and a fixed or inverted percentage for larger transactions. Out-of-pocket expenses, primarily travel costs and computer time, typically are reimbursed by the clients.

HOW TO PROCEED

Once you have made the decision to buy or sell a business, and have studied the benefits and costs of the available consultants needed to assist you, the next step is to examine the context of your business and your needs for assistance. The size, location, performance record, current capitalization, and future prospects of the business define the complexity of the situation. The importance of the contemplated transaction to the business and the depth of advice that is required also help determine the type of intermediary that should be retained. With the exception of business size, which figures in the willingness of financial advisers to accept assignments, any intermediary can be engaged. In practice, CEOs will endeavor to engage the most professional intermediary their circumstances will allow.

HOW TO FIND INTERMEDIARIES

Finding the appropriate intermediary can be a time-consuming process. But the fact that a change in corporate ownership is possibly the most important event in the life of a business underscores that this time is well spent. Finders most often are found through personal referrals of business associates. Attorneys, commercial bankers, and accountants may be able to suggest a number of individuals. Referrals should not be considered carte blanche recommendations. Check with a finder's previous clients after he or she has been interviewed. Business brokers may, in addition to personal referrals, be found through the local Chamber of Commerce and in the telephone book, under "Business Broker." Again, it is necessary to check into the services they have performed in the past.

Financial advisers may be found through referrals, from the Chamber of Commerce, in the telephone book under "Investment Banks," and through a number of professional publications. Sources containing articles by and for advisers, advertising by advisers of their services, and rankings of advisers by transaction activity and financial strength include: *Mergers and Acquisitions; Directory of Intermediaries for Mergers, Buyouts and Acquisitions; National Review of Corporate Acquisitions; Acquisitions/Divestitures; Yearbook on Corporate Mergers, Joint Ventures and Corporate Policy; Association for Corporate Growth Membership Directory; Institutional Investor;* and newspapers, particularly *The Wall Street Journal* and *Barron's.* Libraries probably will have many, if not all, of these sources.

Once you have identified and interviewed a likely firm or individual practitioner, do not hesitate to ask for a referral. In the end you should be comfortable not only with the intermediary firm that will assist you, but, of utmost importance, with the individuals who will be actively involved in and responsible for the success of your buying and selling negotiations.

Chapter 13

Broker and Finder Agreements*

John W. Herz**

*Partner, Wolf Haldenstein Adler Freeman & Herz,
New York, New York*

This chapter is directed primarily to the persons who need it the most: the sellers of small and medium-sized businesses who need the services of an intermediary to find or deal with a potential buyer.

Early in the life of most acquisition plans, the time comes to engage the services of a broker, finder, or other intermediary for that best of all possible deals. The type of intermediary selected will vary according to the size of the prospective deal, the type of involvement desired from the intermediary, and the value of the business to be sold. For a large acquisition demanding heavy

*This chapter was adapted (with updating) from a chapter in J. Herz, C. Baller, and P. Gaynor, eds., *Business Acquisitions,* Practicing Law Institute, New York, 1981, Suppl. 1983, 3 vols. This publication may be obtained from the Practicing Law Institute, 810 Seventh Avenue, New York, New York, 10019.

**Mr. Herz is a partner in the law firm of Wolf Haldenstein Adler Freeman & Herz. The assistance of Robert L. Davidson, a partner, and Mark C. Silverstein, an associate of the same firm, is gratefully acknowledged.

intermediary involvement and a high degree of sophistication, the services of an established investment banking firm are needed. At the other extreme, the seller and buyer may need only a finder's introduction.

For each of these intermediary types, and for all the shades in between, there are different standards and sources for selection.

BROKERS AND FINDERS

Distinctions between Brokers and Finders

Brokers and finders are the two main types of intermediaries. A broker is involved in every stage of the transaction. For example, a broker may study the business, prepare a write-up of the business to distribute to prospective buyers or sellers, educate the seller in methods of finding a potential buyer, develop a list of likely candidates, and assist in negotiating the transaction and in designing it so that it will result in the optimum benefit to the client. A finder has the sole function of introducing the parties. Because there are many shades between true brokers and true finders, with the same persons and firms filling all the possible roles, either in different transactions or throughout a single transaction, the terms are often used interchangeably to refer to any intermediary.[1]

Must Brokers or Finders Be Licensed?

Unlike real estate brokers, few states require business brokers or other intermediaries to be licensed. However, where a transaction involves a transfer of real estate, the laws requiring real estate broker licensing may apply. Also, where a transaction involves a sale of stock instead of assets, federal securities laws may require that the intermediary be a registered securities broker.

Are Brokers or Finders Necessary?

Many people have begun to question the necessity for intermediaries, and they wonder whether they would be better off trying to arrange a sale or merger without an intermediary. The main complaint is that, from the buyer's point of view, the businesses listed with many intermediaries are not suitable, and time is needlessly wasted on these prospects.[2] Of course, any complaints by buyers affect sellers, because the sellers rely on the intermediary to find prospective buyers. However, this complaint should be viewed more as a warning in choosing an intermediary than as a reason not to use one.

The proper intermediary will be of great assistance in many areas. An intermediary will be helpful in valuing the business in question.[3] A broker will aid in the negotiation of the deal. Using the broker as a buffer may encourage more open discussions than those possible between the buyer and seller alone.[4] As a negotiator, a good broker can be invaluable. A broker will analyze the management structure of each party and establish a means of approach, anticipating and adjusting for the reactions of the other side.[5]

Overall, intermediaries serve many useful functions. However, be aware that an intermediary will not often do more than is asked. Business objectives should, therefore, be stated broadly in the first instance, so as not to foreclose any opportunities.[6]

Types of Brokers and Finders in Small Deals and Large Deals

The typical small or intermediate-sized business is interested in entering into a single purchase or sale transaction. The seller generally hires and arranges to pay the intermediary. The intermediary agrees to aid the seller in the search for a suitable buyer. The intermediary might accomplish this by approaching potential buyers, unsolicited, or by working with buyers who are actively seeking acquisitions. However, even in those instances where the buyer approaches the intermediary, it is generally the seller who pays the intermediary's fee.

The large corporations who are looking for acquisitions may have their own specialized staffs or may continuously use the services of intermediaries, often keeping them on retainers. Corporations seeking to expand and diversify are always looking for acquisition prospects, while diversified corporations seeking to concentrate in a single industry may need to dispose of several divisions or subsidiaries.

For small transactions, the names of brokers or finders active for sales of businesses in a particular trade are often known to persons in that trade. Many smaller brokers or finders firms are listed in the Yellow Pages. Sellers can also speak to their bankers, accountants, or attorneys, who may either act as intermediaries or recommend intermediaries.

Deals involving hundreds of millions or billions of dollars, which frequently occur in today's business world, utilize different types of intermediaries than do the smaller deals:

- Large investment banking firms will often act as intermediaries in addition to arranging financing.
- Large corporations hire their own staffs and bring their business acquisition work "in-house."
- Large corporate buyers retain brokers and finders on a regular basis.

BROKERS' AND FINDERS' FEES

The Basic Types of Fee Arrangements

An intermediary's fee is often negotiable. The seller should know that though the intermediary may quote a fee as the standard rate, it "ain't necessarily so"—and may well be negotiable.

Generally, the intermediary's fee is contingent on the closing of the sale of the business and is based on some percentage of the sale price. The most usual fee scale, other than for a small deal, is what is known as the Lehman formula, or the 5-4-3-2-1 formula. Under that formula, 5 percent is paid on the first $1 million of sale price, 4 percent on the next $1 million, 3 percent on the next $1 million, 2 percent on the next $1 million, and 1 percent on the amount in excess of $4 million.

Several courts have accepted the Lehman formula as an appropriate method for determining damages in actions brought by intermediaries to recover the reasonable value of services rendered.[7] Of late, however, this formula has come under attack by smaller brokers, who find that inflation has rendered it penurious. In a small transaction, the intermediary's fee may range between 5 and 10 percent of the sales price. A fixed percentage, rather than a declining percentage, is frequently used in transactions of all sizes.

Appropriately, when the intermediary has special knowledge and expertise about the business involved, a premium above and beyond the formula compensation may be awarded.[8] On the other hand, the Lehman fee would be excessive in the case of a finder who merely introduces the parties and does not perform many of the functions ordinarily performed by a broker.[9] A formula should be, at most, a guideline. An intermediary's compensation should depend not only on the size of the deal but also on the nature and extent of the services rendered.

A purely contingent fee, though the general rule, may be inappropriate in some cases. A broker who performs services beyond finding the eventual buyer or seller may be unwilling to operate on a purely contingent basis. This is even more likely to be the case where the broker is retained by the buyer to find an appropriate business to acquire. Such a broker may want to be compensated, and the client may agree to compensate the broker, on a time basis with a contingent fee if a sale is consummated within a specified period. The time charges would be credited against the amount payable under the contingent fee.

A broker retained on that basis may be granted an "exclusive" for a fixed period of time. This means that the specified percentage commission will be paid if the client strikes a deal with anyone the client met during this time, regardless of whether the broker was the introducing party and even though the sale is consummated after the expiration of that period. The broker may also want to serve as a nonexclusive broker after the period of exclusivity expires.

While a contingent fee offers the seeming advantage of not being payable if the deal falls through, that is also its disadvantage. If a broker is being relied upon to negotiate the transaction, consider whose interests will be of paramount concern. The broker cannot be relied upon to be totally objective as long as the fee is contingent upon, or greatly increased by, the closing of the transaction.[10] This does not mean that the client should not rely upon the broker or that the client should guarantee a fee to the broker; it means only that the client should view more critically the recommendations of the broker.

How the Structure of the Sale Affects the Fee

The intermediary's compensation is normally defined in terms of a percentage of the price of the sale. But in this context, sale price depends on what has been sold—stock or assets.

The sale price in an assets transaction is completely different from the sale price in a stock transaction, though the net economic effect to the buyer and the seller may be exactly the same in both cases. Assume that a corporation has $5 million in assets and $2 million in liabilities, and that the purchaser is to pay $4 million cash for the business. If the transaction is a stock sale, the purchase price is $4 million. If the transaction is a sale of assets, with the usual assumption of liabilities, the purchase price consists of cash paid ($4 million), plus the liabilities assumed by the buyer ($2 million), for an aggregate of $6 million. Nonetheless, the intermediary's compensation should be the same in both cases: The services rendered are the same, and the resulting purchase price is the same to the parties. Thus, in the ordinary case, the fee should be measured by the cash price of $4 million. (Note that when a corporation has little net worth, and loans that have been made to the corporation were personally guaranteed by the stockholders, the assumption of those liabilities by the buyer may be a key factor in the transaction, and provision for the intermediary's compensation should be made accordingly.)

The problem of defining the purchase price is particularly difficult in the sale of a closely held corporation, because the true consideration paid by the buyer often takes some form other than direct payment of the purchase price. Thus, for tax or even business reasons, the buyer may pay the selling stockholders for their covenants not to compete. Similarly, a generous long-term employment contract may be a key part of the transaction. An intermediary might be justified in arguing that in such cases compensation should be measured by the payment for the covenant and in some part by the generous employment compensation.

When the sale is of only a part interest in a corporation, there may be benefits to the continuing stockholders apart from the payment of the purchase price. Thus, in addition to buying a portion of the stock, the buyer may agree to make a substantial loan to the corporation to provide it with necessary working capital. If a mortgage broker had arranged for such a loan, there is no doubt that there would have been a fee to pay for placing the loan. When a loan to the business is an integral part of the transaction, the intermediary should receive compensation for it.

It is impossible for the intermediary to anticipate all benefits to the seller at the time the agreement is initially made. Some forms of agreements have tried to cover such contingencies by providing that the intermediary's compensation be measured by the sale price and "any other economic benefits" inuring to the seller corporation or its shareholders. Within the confines of the usual one-page or two-page broker's or finder's agreement, only such a catch-all phrase can seek to protect the intermediary from the myriad ingenious methods that have been devised for paying the seller for the business. As the deal takes shape, the parties should clarify in writing the measure of the intermediary's fee, if their original agreement has not clearly covered this phase of the transaction.

Fees in Stock Deals

The method of payment of the intermediary's compensation becomes more difficult when the sale price is paid in stock. Frequently, the parties will expect the intermediary to accept the fee in the form of stock. This may create a tax problem for the intermediary, who must pay an income tax determined by the fair market value of the stock received even though it is not a taxable transaction for the seller.

If the transaction is a stock-for-stock deal and the intermediary's fee is payable by the selling stockholders, they will not want the fee to be paid in cash, particularly if the stock cannot be sold immediately, for such payment would have to come out of their own cash resources. In such a case, the intermediary might accede to the seller's request during the negotiations that the intermediary accept the fee in the form of stock, or at least mostly in stock. If the fee is paid in stock, the selling stockholders will have ample stock to make the payment. Even in a stock-for-assets or a merger deal, the parties may want the intermediary to take the fee in the form of stock to preserve the cash in the business. When the intermediary receives the fee in the form of stock, the amount of stock that is received will be an agreed percentage of the number of shares transferred to the seller. If the sale price consists in part of a contingent stock pay-out, the intermediary will receive the agreed percentage of shares out of each contingent stock payment as and when it is made.

If the seller receives stock and the intermediary is to be paid in cash, the stock received by the seller must be valued in order to compute the fee. The same valuation question arises when the intermediary is paid in shares at a percentage that varies depending on the total value of the shares received by the seller, as under the Lehman formula. Generally, the traded price of the stock will be used for this purpose, despite the fact that an appraisal of the value of the stock would show a lesser value, as is the case when the seller receives investment stock.

WHO PAYS THE FEE?

Generally, it is the seller who retains and is obligated to pay the intermediary. Where the seller has the responsibility for the fee, it should not be assumed that this is fully allowed for by the parties in fixing the price with the result that the final economic effect is that the fee is borne by the buyer. There are many factors that are involved in computing the sale price, and it is rare that a premium to cover the intermediary's fee would be included.

The seller's obligation to the intermediary does not, except in a merger, pass to the buyer unless expressly assumed. This is true not only in a stock purchase but also in an asset purchase. Though in the typical asset purchase the buyer assumes all disclosed obligations of the seller to date of closing,[11] this provision usually excludes intermediary's fees of the seller.[12] Some buyers add a specific provision negating the assumption of any of the seller's expenses in connection with the sale.

There are instances, however, where the intermediary's fee is the obligation of the buyer. The buyer may be the one who initially retained the intermediary to find a business available to be acquired in a specific field, or, during the course of the negotiation, the buyer may assume the seller's obligation to pay the intermediary's fee. If the buyer has retained the intermediary, their agreement may provide that the intermediary will look to the seller for payment of the fee. Generally, in such a case, the buyer will assure the payment of the intermediary if full payment cannot be obtained from the seller.

When the seller has the initial responsibility for the fee and the buyer is a large corporation, it is not unusual for the buyer to wind up paying the fee. The buyer will also bear the economic cost of the intermediary's fee in the case of an asset purchase or merger where the fee is paid out of the seller's assets being purchased after a fixed sale price has been negotiated. For a buyer to avoid this result, the sale agreement would either have to provide for a reduction in the sale price or require that the seller pay the intermediary's fee out of the sale's proceeds.

The Importance of Written Agreements

In any event, the intermediary should not only have a written agreement with the party who is expected to pay the fee, but there should be a specific paragraph in the contract of sale setting forth this obligation. If a buyer and seller are each to pay a portion of the fee, there should be a disclosure of that fact to each of them by the intermediary and a written acknowledgment of the arrangement by each of the parties.

When the seller's business is listed with an intermediary and the seller agrees to pay a full commission to the intermediary, the seller may want a written assurance that the intermediary will not seek to obtain any compensation from the buyer. The seller may desire this not only for whatever impact the commission would have on the price the buyer is willing to pay, but also for the seller's satisfaction in knowing that the intermediary will not be doubly compensated. This is particularly important where the intermediary is a finder, who can legally be paid by both parties, whereas a broker is the agent for only one party.

When the transaction takes the form of a sale of stock, the seller's obligation to pay the intermediary rests upon the selling stockholders. When the transaction takes the form of a sale of assets, the selling corporation is obligated to pay the intermediary. When the transaction takes the form of a merger, the obligation to the intermediary becomes, as a matter of statutory law, the obligation of the surviving corporation.[13] The impact of this obligation can, of course, be varied by specific agreement of the parties.

Occasionally, an employee, officer, or director of a selling company may be offered a finder's fee. Be aware, however, that the selling company's employees, officers, or directors may be required to relinquish any such fee because of their fiduciary duty to the selling company shareholders. In order to be able to accept or retain such a fee, the proposed recipient must receive the approval of either the selling company's board of directors or its shareholders. The manner in which this approval must be granted varies from state to state based on statutory rules and common law.[14]

Must More Than One Fee Ever Be Paid?

The seller should make certain that there will not be more than one commission owed. In the agreement with the intermediary, the seller should include a provision for the intermediary to indemnify the seller against the claims of any other person who came into the deal through the intermediary and who seeks compensation for services. This will make it clear that any commitment the intermediary makes to a cobroker or cofinder or other party is between them and is not binding upon the client.

In the agreement with the buyer, the seller should include a provision for the buyer to indemnify the seller against claims for compensation by any other person founded upon the act of the buyer. The buyer may then want a reciprocal covenant from the seller.

When and How Is the Fee Paid?

If the sale price is payable in a lump sum, the intermediary gets the commission in full at the time of the closing.

When the purchase price is payable in installments, the full intermediary commission usually comes out of the down payment. This may work a hardship on the seller, particularly when the down payment is small. If the seller anticipates an installment sale when the agreement with the intermediary is made, provision for the payment of the intermediary out of each installment may be made. If the transaction takes the form of an installment sale during the negotiations, the intermediary may agree at that time to accept the fee out of each installment rather than in full at the closing. On the other hand, if payment of the purchase price is certain but is payable in installments primarily for the seller's tax purposes, then there is no reason why the intermediary's fee should be deferred.

Escrows and Earn-outs

When a portion of the sale price is determined on an earn-out basis, that is, the amount of the payments are contingent upon operations after the closing, the intermediary must be paid out of those payments as they are made to the seller, for the parties will have no way of knowing at the closing what the earn-out will be. The intermediary's compensation will be measured by the actual payments that are made by the buyer under the earn-out provision.

When a small portion of the sale price is placed in escrow in order to assure the fulfillment of the usual seller's warranties, the intermediary will often be paid in the same manner as if there had been no escrow, without deferral of a portion of the fee. When, however, the escrow is a substantial portion of the sale price or covers more than the usual seller's warranties (for example, when the buyer and seller use an escrow as a device for handling an earn-out or other future contingency), the intermediary's fee on the escrowed portion is generally payable only when and to the extent that delivery is made out of escrow to the seller.

CAN THE FEE AFFECT THE TAX NATURE OF THE SALE?

If the seller receives cash on the sale, the intermediary's fee can be paid out of the cash received.

However, many sales of businesses are structured, primarily for tax reasons, so that the seller receives no cash on the sale but receives only shares of the buying corporation (or shares of the buying corporation's parent company).

Despite the fact that the seller has not received cash, the intermediary will usually desire that the fee be paid in cash. If the fee were paid in stock, the stock received by the intermediary usually would be subject to resale restrictions under the securities laws.[15] Furthermore, though the shares may not be readily convertible to cash, the intermediary upon receipt of the shares has taxable income equal to the value of the shares received. When the shares are subject to securities laws restrictions on resale, the value of the shares to be shown as taxable income is measured without taking the restrictions into account.[16] The issue, then, is how to pay the intermediary in cash without affecting the "tax-free" aspect for the seller.

In a merger transaction, the obligation to pay the intermediary can be fulfilled by the surviving corporation without affecting the tax-free nature of the merger.

When the transaction is a stock-for-assets exchange and the selling corporation is obligated to pay the intermediary, there are at least two methods that can be used to pay the intermediary's fee in cash without affecting the tax-free nature of the exchange. First, the selling corporation can pay the fee prior to the exchange and, thereby, exchange only its remaining assets, or the selling corporation can generally hold back sufficient cash to pay the fee out of the cash retained after the exchange. If the seller's cash is insufficient, it can hold back accounts receivable or other liquid assets sufficient to enable it to realize the cash required to pay the intermediary. The holding back of assets is usable only when, as is usually the case, the assets required to be withheld to pay the intermediary are of a small magnitude so that the assets exchanged will be "substantially all" of the seller's assets.[17] Second, the buyer can assume the seller's obligation to pay the intermediary's fee.[18] Under this method, the intermediary's fee must be paid directly by the buyer. The buyer cannot transfer assets to the selling corporation for the seller to use to pay the fee.

When the transaction is a stock-for-stock exchange, the sellers are the shareholders, and it is the shareholders who will be obligated to pay the intermediary's fee. In these transactions, there are also at least two methods that can be used to pay the intermediary's fee in cash without affecting the tax-free nature of the exchange. First, the buyer can assume the obligation of the selling shareholders to pay the intermediary's fee.[19] Again, the buyer must then pay the intermediary directly and not transfer assets to the selling shareholders. Second, the selling shareholders can pay the intermediary's fee out of their own liquid assets, or they can sell some of the shares, subject to resale restrictions under the securities laws[20] and the incurring of a tax on the sale, and pay the intermediary's fee out of the sale proceeds.

BROKER AND FINDER AGREEMENTS

Must There Be a Written Agreement?

An intermediary's right to compensation depends on a contract, written or oral. Many states have a statute of frauds provision which specifies that an intermediary has a right to compensation only if there is a written agreement signed by the party from whom compensation is sought.[21] In the absence of such statute, however, the contract can be express or implied in fact and, if express, it can be written or oral.[22] In those states that do not require an agreement in writing, a contract may be implied solely from the fact that the seller accepted an introduction to a prospective buyer knowing that the person who made the introduction expected to receive compensation for doing so.[23]

In large public deals transacted by investment bankers, it is not unusual to proceed on faith alone. In smaller transactions, a written agreement is usual. But in all cases, an understanding should be reached at the start, and a written agreement is highly advisable to avoid further disagreements.

When the introducing party's usual business does not consist of acting as an intermediary, then the seller should ascertain whether or not compensation is expected before accepting the introduction. This applies when a banker, lawyer, accountant, or business acquaintance is the introducing party, as frequently happens.

The written contract gives all parties certain protections. It protects the seller by putting down in black and white the fact that the compensation is payable only if the deal closes, and that this applies even though the failure to close is the fault of the seller. Where an intermediary's sole function is to find a buyer or seller that fits the client's specifications, the seller will not want to pay any compensation unless the sale has been consummated, regardless of how far the transaction has progressed—even through contract and almost to closing—and regardless of whether the seller or buyer has been the one who caused the transaction not to close.

In the absence of a written agreement, a client might be tempted to bypass an intermediary after learning of a prospective match. Therefore, an intermediary should endeavor not to disclose the names of prospective buyers until there is a written, signed contract. Sometimes, however, a client might insist on learning the identity of a proposed buyer or seller before signing an agreement. This creates a problem in a state that has a statute-of-frauds provision governing intermediaries. The intermediary may seek to enlist the cooperation of the prospective buyer, though the typical buyer will be reluctant to become involved in any dispute between the seller and intermediary. A supportive buyer, however, may be willing to insist that the seller sign a written agreement with the intermediary before the buyer will proceed with the deal, or even better, that the buyer will agree to compensate the finder and allow for this in negotiating the purchase price. In the last analysis, the only real protection for the intermediary in a statute-of-frauds state is to obtain a written agreement before starting work.

What Is in the Agreement?

The initial agreement must set forth the contemplated transaction in the *broadest possible terms*, because often the final form of the contemplated transaction is not known when the initial agreement with the intermediary is executed, or may change during negotiations. Thus, the agreement should state that the intermediary shall receive a commission when the seller sells all or a substantial part of the assets, or all or a controlling stock interest in the company, or merges with a party introduced to the seller by the intermediary.

It is important to describe the exact parties to the transaction. Normally, a selling corporation executes the agreement with the broker or finder. But if the transaction takes the form of a sale of stock, the proper parties are the shareholders of the selling corporation rather than the corporation itself. If the agreement with the intermediary is executed by the selling corporation, but the transaction takes the form of a stock sale, the courts may nevertheless impose responsibility for the intermediary's fee upon the selling stockholders. A court may be reluctant to do this, however, where the statute of frauds applies, and the writing must be signed by the party to be charged. In order to avoid this problem, the intermediary facing a possible stock sale should have the principal shareholders sign "agreed to" at the foot of the contract with the corporation.

On occasion, an intermediary may assist the parties in bringing about a transaction that was not contemplated when the retainer agreement was signed and is not covered by the agreement. Where the statute of frauds applies, an intermediary will generally not be able to overcome the requirement for a writing by claiming that the original agreement was modified orally to cover the eventual transaction.[24] In such a case, an intermediary who does not wish to risk losing his commission should obtain a new contract or amendment that accurately reflects the proposed transaction.

The contract should also set forth whether the intermediary is retained on an exclusive or nonexclusive basis. The normal arrangement will be nonexclusive, so that the seller is free to deal with any prospective purchaser not introduced to him by the intermediary. From the intermediary's viewpoint, the contract should specify a right to compensation if the eventual buyer is a party introduced to the seller by the intermediary even where the closing takes place after the termination of the intermediary's agreement. This eliminates any question of initiation that might otherwise arise when the purchaser or seller sought shows no initial interest or when there is a termination of negotiations and a recommencement of them at a later date.[25]

If there is initially no sale and the client later hires another intermediary, the client should be wary of owing a double commission if the new intermediary presents the same prospective buyer and a sale is then made. If that situation is likely to arise, the seller should include a clause in the agreement negating the fee of an intermediary where there has been a prior introduction to the same prospective buyer. It then becomes a question of fact as to who made the first introduction, but only one commission will be payable. Some finders, therefore, establish their position by confirming each introduction by letter.

A broker's services normally consist of more than an introduction of the parties to each other, and thus, the definition of services to be rendered may include the intermediary's assistance in the negotiations. The agreement should, for the broker's protection, state that the intermediary will assist when requested to do so by the seller. In this case, the seller cannot defeat the broker's rights to a full commission on the ground that the broker performed no services in the negotiations when in fact the seller did not call upon the broker to do so, or when the broker has been prevented from doing so by the parties.[26]

The intermediary's right to compensation should apply to an introduction brought about directly or indirectly. This would help establish a claim if the intermediary introduces the seller to a prospective buyer who in turn introduces the seller to someone else who buys the business.

How Can Confidential Information Be Protected?

The seller of a closely held corporation may not be eager to disclose basic financial information. However, such a seller must give considerable detailed information during the negotiation. Highly secret matters, such as customer lists and manufacturing processes, may be saved for the last.

The client must find an intermediary whose judgment can be trusted. Even so, the seller should consider stating in the agreement that no information about the seller's business or the fact that it is available for sale will be disclosed by the intermediary unless the name of the person to whom it is to be disclosed is first submitted to and approved by the seller. The seller may then take protective steps directly with the potential buyer.

If the buyer or seller is a publicly held company, the intermediary must treat the transaction as confidential and must neither trade in the stock of the publicly held buyer or seller before a public announcement of the transaction has been made by them nor tip off others who may trade in the stock.

What Kinds of Special Agreements Can Be Reached?

There are several types of special intermediary agreements.

Sometimes an intermediary will advise the seller that the intermediary has a specific potential buyer in mind and wants to fix the terms of compensation before the introduction is made. As in any agreement, the intermediary should make sure the terms are sufficiently broad.

Sometimes a broker may insist on an exclusive agreement. There are, in general, two types of exclusive agreements. In one case, sometimes referred to as an exclusive sales agreement, the broker is entitled to a commission in the event of any sale of the business, no matter how it is brought about. In the other case, sometimes referred to as an exclusive agency agreement, the broker is entitled to a commission on any sale except one made directly by the seller without the intervention of any intermediary. But the agreement should not rely on any such terminology. It should set forth whether the broker is entitled to a commission on all sales, and if not, classes of excluded sales should be specifically set forth. Finders generally do not receive exclusive agreements.

An exclusive agreement should have a fixed duration or be terminable by either party after a specific date, or after a specific notice period. The broker may expend substantial time and effort seeking to find a buyer and, therefore, the exclusive agreement should be of sufficient duration so that the broker will have a reasonable opportunity to earn a commission.

When Does the Agreement Terminate?

Normally, the agreement with an intermediary is terminable at will by either party, and there should be a provision for written notice of termination. Making the duration clear is only one of several important steps, however. The intermediary should include in the agreement a provision specifying that should a sale be consummated after the termination of the agreement to a party introduced to the seller by the intermediary (or if there is an exclusive, introduced by anyone during the terms of the exclusive), the intermediary shall be entitled to a commission. Because a broker may be required to assist in the negotiations, the proposed provision as applied to a broker should state that the obligation to assist will survive the termination of the agreement. The broker must, of course, then be available to assist in any negotiations that take place after termination of the brokerage agreement.

NOTES

[1]In this chapter the term "intermediary" will be used as the generic for all intermediaries, and the terms "broker" and "finder" will be used consistent with the definitions set forth.

[2]See, e.g., Jensen, "Seeking a Candidate for Merger or Acquisition," *Business Horizons,* May–June 1982, p. 80; Kierulff, "Finding the Best Candidate," *Harvard Business Review,* January–February 1981, p. 66; Howell, "Lessons from an Acquisition Specialist," *Management Review,* November 1979, p. 37.

[3]See J. Herz, C. Baller, and P. Gaynor, eds., *Business Acquisitions,* 2d ed., Practising Law Institute, New York, 1981, Suppl. 1983, chap. 1.

[4]Jensen, op. cit., p. 80.

[5]Strickland, "How an Investment Banker Prepares a Company for a Tender Offer," *Management Accounting,* February 1980, p. 26.

[6]See Balgove, "Planning for Successful Acquisitions," *The Director,* June 1980, p. 21.

[7]*Ehrman v. Cooke Elec. Co.,* 630 F.2d 529 (7th Cir. 1980); *Havenfield Corp. v. H&R Block, Inc.,* 509 F. 2d 1263 (8th Cir.), *cert. denied,* 421 U.S. 999 (1975); *Flammia v. Mite Corp.,* 401 F.Supp. 121 (E.D.N.Y. 1975), 553 F.2d 93 (2d Cir. 1977); *Schaller v. Litton Ind., Inc.,* 307 F.Supp.126 (E.D. Wis. 1969).

[8]*Flammia v. Mite Corp., supra,* note 7.

[9]*Havenfield Corp. v. H&R Block, Inc., supra,* note 7.

[10]See, e.g., Michael Webb, *How to Acquire a Company,* Gower Press, Epping, Essex, U.K., 1974, app. 4, "How to Use Merger Brokers or other Acquisition Advisors."

[11]See Herz et al., op. cit., chaps. 5 and 12 and 1983, Supplement thereto.

[12]It might be argued that if the seller fails to pay, and if the bulk sales law is applicable but has not been complied with, the intermediary may have the right to reach the assets sold in the hands of the buyer. UCC §6-104(1). Nonetheless, a question arises whether the intermediary is a creditor at the time notice is required under the code. See UCC §6-109(1).

[13]See, e.g., N.Y. Bus. Corp. Law §906 (b) (3) (McKinney, 1979); Del. Code Ann. tit. 8, §259 (a) (rev. ed., 1974).

[14]See, e.g., N.Y. Bus. Corp. Law §716, Del. Gen. Corp. Law, §144.

[15]See Herz et al., op. cit., chap. 15, and 1983, Supplement thereto.

[16]IRC §83.

[17]The statutory test is set forth in Internal Revenue Code §368 (a)(1)(C). The present ruling position of the Internal Revenue Service is that the "substantially all" requirement is complied with if the acquired corporation transfers assets constituting of at least 90 percent of the market value of its net assets and at least 70 percent of the market value of its gross assets. Rev. Proc. 77–37, 1977-2 C.B. 568.

[18]Rev. Rul. 73-54, 1973-1 C.B. 187.

[19]Ibid.

[20]See Herz et al., op. cit., chap. 15, and 1983, Supplement thereto.

[21]The written obligation to pay an intermediary need not be in a contract between seller and broker, but may be set forth in the contract between buyer and seller and may arise even though the seller never expressly retained the broker. See *Ficor, Inc., v. National Kinney Corp.,* 67 App. Div.2d 659, 412 N.Y.S.2d 621 (1979); See also *William B. May Co., Inc., v. Monaco Associates,* 80 A.D. 2d 798, 437 N.Y.S.2d 91 (1981) (Real estate brokers).

[22]See, e.g., *John Flemming, Inc. v. Beutel,* 395 F.2d 21 (7th Cir. 1968).

[23]*Consolidated Oil & Gas, Inc., v. Roberts*, 162 Colo. 149, 425 P.2d 282 (1967).

[24]*Intercontinental Planning, Ltd., v. Daystrom, Inc.*, 24 N.Y. 2d 372, 248 N.E.2d 576, 300 N.Y.S. 2d 817 (1969); *Roberts v. Champion Int'l Inc.*, 52 App. Div. 2d 773, 382 N.Y.S.2d 790, *appeal dismissed*, 40 N.Y. 2d 805, 389 N.Y.S. 2d 1025 (1976). But see *Peters v. Sigma Data Computing Corp.*, 397 F.Supp. 1098 (E.D.N.Y. 1975).

[25]See *Simon v. Electrospace Corp.*, 28 N.Y.2d 136, 269 N.E.2d 21, 320 N.Y.S.2d 225 (1971).

[26]Ibid.

Appendix
Form*
Brokerage Agreement

Comments: This was a brokerage agreement for the sale of the assets or shares of a financially successful, closely held corporation with two stockholders. Because it was not anticipated that any part of the sale price would be paid in the form of a covenant not to compete or other indirect method, as might otherwise be the case in the sale of a close corporation, the broker required no protective clauses for such possibilities.

The seller had confidence in the brokerage firm and thus did not require the broker to submit to the seller in advance the names of prospective purchasers. But the seller did retain the right to control the information to be submitted to prospective purchasers and the persons to whom it would be submitted.

In this case, the broker was to be paid in cash regardless of the form of the consideration received by seller.

The form does not provide for a merger or consolidation of the selling corporation (or the reverse merger of another company into it), because the possibility of such a transaction was remote.

May 30, 1984

Mr. John Doe
XYZ Corporation
Number Street
City, State ZIP Code

Dear Mr. Doe:

This letter confirms the terms upon which you have retained us to serve as brokers in the sale of XYZ CORPORATION (the "Company") or its shares:

(1) If and when a sale of the Company or its shares to a party introduced to the Company or its shareholders, directly or indirectly, by us has been consummated, we shall be paid a commission by the Company or its shareholders, computed on the basis of the following percentages of the consideration, or the value thereof if not paid in cash, received by the Company or its shareholders:

Five percent (5%) of the consideration up to $1 million, plus

Four percent (4%) of the consideration from $1 to $2 million, plus

---

*This form is a modified version of that appearing in Herz et al., *Business Acquisitions*, vol. III, part III, as cited in Note 3 of the text.

Three percent (3%) of the consideration from $2 to $3 million, plus
Two percent (2%) of the consideration from $3 to $4 million, plus
One percent (1%) of the consideration in excess of $4 million.
The commission shall be payable in cash.

No commission shall be payable if a sale is not consummated, regardless of whether or not the failure to consummate is due to the fault of the Company or its shareholders.

A sale of the Company or its shares shall be deemed to include a sale of all or part of the assets of the Company or a sale of all or a majority of the outstanding common shares of the Company.

In determining the consideration received by the Company or its shareholders:

(a) The consideration shall be deemed to include both cash and any securities or other property received by the Company or its shareholders in the transaction. Assumption of the Company's debts in the transaction shall not be deemed consideration.

(b) Securities that are listed on a national exchange shall be valued at the average closing price on the twenty trading days before the date the sale is closed.

(c) Securities that are traded over the counter shall be valued at the average closing bid price on the twenty trading days before the date the sale is closed.

(2) If any part of the consideration shall be payable in installments or shall be contingent upon future earnings, our commission shall be payable in the same proportionate amounts and at the same times as such installments or contingent payments are made. In all other cases, payment shall be made at the closing of the sale.

(3) We shall assist the Company or its shareholders in its or their negotiations with any party introduced, directly or indirectly, by us to the extent that the Company or its shareholders request us to do so.

We shall not disclose any information regarding the Company, including financial information, that the Company or its shareholders direct us not to disclose or to anyone to whom the Company or its shareholders directs us not to disclose.

(4) We may, in our sole discretion, engage the services of any persons (including other brokers) without additional cost to you. In such event, all the commissions payable pursuant to paragraph (1) shall be paid to us and, upon such payment, we shall indemnify the Company and its shareholders against any liability for brokerage fees or other compensation claimed by such other persons. We shall not seek or accept a commission from any party to the sale other than the Company or its shareholders.

(5) This agreement may be terminated by the Company and its shareholders or by us at any time on thirty (30) days' notice, provided that such termination shall not affect our right to commissions on the consummation of a sale subsequent to such termination to a party introduced to the Company or its shareholders, directly or indirectly, by us prior to such termination, and our obligation to assist in the negotiations with such a party on the request of the Company or its shareholders shall survive such termination.

If the foregoing correctly reflects our understanding, please so indicate on the duplicate copy of this letter, whereupon this letter shall constitute a binding Brokerage Agreement between us.

Very truly yours,

_____

AGREED AND ACCEPTED:
XYZ CORPORATION

By: _____
John Doe, President

_____
John Doe

_____
Jane Doe

Chapter 14

Computer Products: Implements of the Craft

Leonard Zweig

Editor-in-Chief and Associate Publisher,
Mergers & Acquisitions, Philadelphia, Pennsylvania

Christopher Roe

Production Editor, Mergers & Acquisitions,
Philadelphia, Pennsylvania

Computer data base and software companies have created a number of informational and analytical tools for the mergers and acquistions specialist. The sheer amount of information that must be analyzed to make a sound aquisition or divestiture decision, and the speed, accuracy, and security essential to make it successful, have made the computer an important implement of the M&A craft.

Computer assistance allows the M&A analyst to screen hundreds of potential acquisition candidates quickly and accurately, to take into account a wide range of financial statistics and ever-changing values (such as stock prices), to construct multiple deal structures and payment packages, and to estimate the impact of a particular merger on the future financials of the acquirer, the target, or the combined company. In addition, because the professional can work the numbers with minimal support staff, the secrecy essential to successful acquisitions is less likely to be breached, and those who make the decisions have direct access to the information they need.

The available software ranges from products designed to perform specific functions with a minimum of input by the user, to more flexible systems that the sophisticated user can mold to perform special tasks. Data bases can be sources of basic company financials, industry data, or the specifics of particular transactions and can allow the professional to make relevant comparisons in searching for possible acquirers or targets, or in constructing or pricing a deal.

In this guide to representative M&A products and the companies that produce them, the descriptions are provided by the companies and the list serves as a compilation of information on software packages and data bases, rather than as an evaluation or recommendation of particular products. Addresses and phone numbers are provided for readers who seek more information.

ALCAR: THE VALUE PLANNER, THE MERGER PLANNER

Alcar is a leader in providing microcomputer software to enhance the business capabilities of banks, corporations, and accounting firms. Alcar software is designed around the shareholder value approach to strategic planning and M&A analysis. This approach is based on discounted cash flow analysis with a long-term perspective.

The Value Planner is Alcar's flagship product. It gives users the power to generate historical and forecasted financial statements, including income statements, balance sheets, cash flow statements, and ratios. Simultaneously, the Value Planner evaluates these forecasts in terms of their contribution to shareholder value. The Value Planner is used in mergers and acquisitions to generate projected financials for buyer and seller, to determine values for buyer and seller, and to provide a consistent approach for evaluating acquisition or divestiture candidates.

The Merger Planner is another Alcar software tool of special value to M&A executives and analysts. The Merger Planner enhances the Value Planner's capabilities by giving users the ability to analyze mergers, acquisitions, and divestitures. Users can combine buyer and seller into a new entity by specifying deal structure, taxable or nontaxable methods of combination, and purchase or pooling accounting treatment.

The analytical power of the Merger Planner makes it an especially valuable tool for determining:

- The impact of a merger, acquisition, or divestiture on the value of company stock
- Combined buyer/seller financials
- Net present value and internal rate of return of the deal
- Sensitivity of a deal to changes in key factors

For more information about Alcar products and services, phone or write:

Alcar Group, Inc.
5215 Old Orchard Road
Skokie, IL 60076
(312) 967-4200

APPLIED DATA RESEARCH: ADR/EMPIRE

Applied Data Research, Inc., offers the software product ADR/EMPIRE, a comprehensive decision support system that provides a leading modeling language, interactive analysis, and graphics for financial management. EMPIRE also includes a flexible report writer, statistics, forecasting, and Monte Carlo simulation (for uncertainty analysis). Interactive analysis tools include "what if," target value, and sensitivity analyses. A unique graphics feature allows users to do "what if" and target value analyses on a graph through simple cursor positioning.

EMPIRE also interfaces on ADR'S DATACOM/DB data base management system and ADR's eMAIL electronic mail system. Users can load current corporate data into EMPIRE models, process the information, create reports and graphs, and then distribute them throughout the organization using ADR/eMAIL.

EMPIRE's PC component, ADR/PC EMPIRE, allows users to convert Lotus 1-2-3 and VisiCalc spreadsheets into EMPIRE models for use on the mainframe. This allows users who have outgrown their spreadsheet environment or need power graphics and forecasting to convert spreadsheets quickly into a mainframe environment.

For more information on EMPIRE, phone or write:

Applied Data Research, Inc.
Route 206 and Orchard Road, CN-8
Princeton, NJ 08540
(201) 874-9000

DATA RESOURCES: FINANCIAL AND ECONOMIC STATISTICS

The Financial Institutions Group of Data Resources, Inc., is a leading provider of data and software to decision makers in merger and acquisition analysis. Supported by the world's largest collection of computer-accessible financial and economic data bases, the staff works daily with M&A clients to:

- Screen candidates based on client-defined criteria by company, industry, and geographic definitions
- Rank M&A candidates by key financial indicators
- Perform competitive and pro forma analysis
- Forecast national and regional economies, industry performance, and company-specific concepts
- Display analysis with high-resolution multidimensional graphics

Primary data bases provided to support M&A analysis include: COMPUSTAT, with detailed balance sheet and income statement items for all publicly traded companies; Banktrak, with selected balance sheet and income statement items including lead bank data for more than 35,000 privately held companies and subsidiaries of publicly traded companies; DRIBAS, with FDIC call reports and income information on commercial bank holding companies, commercial banks, and savings and loans. Data bases for market and transaction data include DRICOM, commodities; DRISEC, equity and corporate debt; and DRIFACS, government agency issues, interest and exchange rates, and bank credit statistics. Data Resources also provides industrial data and forecasts and in-depth analysis of all major U.S. industries.

Data Resources' computerized information is available for client access through timesharing, personal computers, and in-house mainframes.

For more information on DRI's products and services, phone or write:

Data Resources, Inc.
25 Broadway
New York, NY 10004
(212) 208-1200

DISCLOSURE, INC.: MICRODISCLOSURE

Disclosure markets microDISCLOSURE, a software package that accesses the Disclosure data base on the Dialog Information Services host computer. Components in this software package are a system disk, used for accessing Dialog, a data base disk for downloading financial items, and a reports disk for the manipulation of downloaded data. This user-friendly software gives business and financial information on over 10,000 public companies. The data are extracted from annual and periodic reports filed with the Securities and Exchange Commission and cover all NYSE, AMEX, and over-the-counter companies.

The menu-driven software allows searches for companies by 85 different categories including types of business; company name; asset, liability, and income statement information; and ticker symbol and share information. The user can download the financial information retrieved on microDISCLOSURE. Once downloaded, the research and analysis disk can be used to create report formats and financial ratios. Downloaded files can also be converted to DIF files to be used with VisiCalc, Lotus 1-2-3, and other spreadsheet programs.

Merger and acquisition applications include determination of the financial strength of a possible acquisition through the review of income statements and balance sheets, examination of stock ownership to judge the feasibility of a successful takeover, and finally, the search for companies by subject area or SIC code to find compatible merger candidates.

For more information on microDISCLOSURE or the Disclosure data base, phone or write:

Disclosure, Inc.
5161 River Road
Bethesda, MD 20816
(301) 951-1300

FEROX MICROSYSTEMS: ENCORE!

The main product of Ferox Microsystems, Inc., ENCORE!, is a powerful financial modeling and graphics system well suited for doing the financial analysis associated with mergers and acquisitions. Pro forma projections of the combined entity are done easily with ENCORE!'s simple-to-use consolidation feature.

ENCORE!'s flexible reporting along with screen or plotter graphics aid in presenting the case for acquisition to directors, lenders, and investors. Built-in tax and depreciation tables come in handy for the "hands-on" analyst, while the ability to customize menus puts power in the hands of those who need it most. Ferox backs ENCORE! with a strong user-support team.

For more information on ENCORE!, write or phone:

Ferox Microsystems, Inc.
1701 N. Fort Myer Drive
Suite 611
Arlington, VA 22209
(703) 841-0800

INTERACTIVE DATA: PC ORIENTATION

Interactive Data Corp., a subsidiary of Chase Manhattan Bank, provides a number of products and data bases to the financial professional working in mergers and acquisitions. All of Interactive Data's M&A analysis tools are accessible on IBM and IBM-compatible personal computers, with a minimum of 320K RAM (random access memory).

PC SCREEN is a microcomputer screening product that accesses COMPU-STAT and Interactive's financial data bases for company and pricing information, and screens a universe of over 6,000 companies. Users may screen based on daily updates of market information, e.g., prices and dividends; financial statement items and ratios, updated weekly; three- and five-year growth rates; earnings estimates; historical annual and quarterly data; and a variety of business-line and geographic segment data. Graphics, on-line help, and downloading to the Lotus spreadsheet package are all part of PC SCREEN.

DataSheet is a software product providing an easy-to-use, fast way to get information on publicly traded securities into a personal computer. DataSheet resembles an electronic spreadsheet by employing the commonly used row-and-column format. DataSheet's microcomputer/mainframe link makes 20 years of financial statement data, 16 years of pricing information, and over 400 items of information on each firm immediately available. It accesses COMPUSTAT, Value Line, I/B/E/S, as well as Interactive's data bases. On the international side, DataSheet provides access to fundamental and market data including special data bases for evaluating securities in the Eurobond market.

PC FORMA is a microcomputer-based tool for projecting company fundamentals that allows the user to make assumptions about forecast methods for each balance sheet and income statement line item, and to display all historical and forecast data in either tabular-report or graphic format. PC FORMA is excellent for cash flow or earnings analysis and allows the user to choose either an earnings-driven or sales-driven model. All functions are selected through a menu, and historical data can be loaded from a file saved by PC FORMA's companion product, DataSheet.

In-depth quantitative analysis capabilities, customized to user needs, are available on a timesharing basis from Interactive Data.

For more information, phone or write:

Interactive Data Corp.
303 Wyman Street
Waltham, MA 02254
(617) 895-4602

MERGERS & ACQUISITIONS: M&A DATA BASE

Mergers & Acquisitions magazine produces the M&A Data Base, a source of information on more than 20,000 transactions valued at $1 million or more involving both public and private companies from 1979 to the present. The M&A Data Base covers mergers, acquisitions, divestitures, leveraged buy-outs, tender offers, and partial acquisitions. In addition to transactions within the United States, the data base includes acquisitions abroad by U.S. companies and foreign company acquisitions in the United States. Regular updates provide new information on pending, completed, and unsuccessful deals.

The M&A Data Base may be used to price companies, identify potential buyers, monitor the competition, negotiate a better deal, compute stock premiums, price stock blocks, structure a deal, and perform other tasks.

The user can access the data base by SIC codes, type of deal, company name, sales volume, deal value, company location, transaction date, and many other criteria. The data base also can generate reports that include terms of the deal, premium paid, sales and earnings, P/E ratios, company descriptions, status of transactions, financial advisers, and additional information.

The M&A Data Base is available on-line and allows the user to search quickly through thousands of mergers and acquisitions to locate the ones relevant to particular information requirements. Alternatively, the data base staff can prepare and send out a customized, hard-copy report within 24 hours.

For more information on the M&A Data Base, phone or write:

M&A Data Base
229 South 18th Street
Rittenhouse Square
Philadelphia, PA 19103
1 (800) MERGING or (215) 875-2631

SECURITIES DATA CO.: MERGERS AND TENDERS

Securities Data Co. maintains a data base with information on mergers, tender offers, and self-tender offers in the United States and certain transactions abroad.

The data base includes information on 6,000 transactions since January 1981.
The data base includes information on both the target's and the acquirer's financial positions, managers and fees, specifics of each transaction, price tracking, and geographic locations of both the target and the acquirer.

The service is used to produce reports for firms considering whether to make or accept tender or merger offers. The statistics may be used for market research purposes. Information provides comparative data, helpful in structuring new mergers.

For more information on the Securities Data data base, phone or write:

Securities Data Co.
62 William Street
New York, NY 10005
(212) 668-0940

SIMKIN ASSOCIATES:
MICROCOMPUTER SOFTWARE

Simkin Associates specializes in merger and acquisition software for microcomputers. Current product offerings include:

VP FINANCE—A corporate financial planning and valuation model for analyzing strategic plans or an acquisition candidate

VP MERGERS & ACQUISITIONS—A merger deal simulation model fully compatible with VP FINANCE, for analyzing the impact of a merger on a buying company.

Both models are written in Lotus 1-2-3 and run on an IBM PC. They combine the best features of propriety M&A modeling systems running on timeshared computers with the power of Lotus 1-2-3. The models feature a custom command menu, which allows the user to enter input data directly into the spreadsheet, save data, load data from a file, calculate the model, and display reports and graphics.

VP FINANCE allows the user to simulate different strategies and their impact on financial variables. For example, it can determine easily the impact of a change in sales growth, margins, or leverage on earnings per share, cash flow, or DCF valuation. The model produces seven standard reports and 10 standard graphics exhibits. VP MERGERS & ACQUISITIONS allows the user to simulate the impact of different accounting methods (i.e., purchase versus pooling), merger currencies (i.e., cash, debt, and/or stock), and tax treatments (i.e., taxable versus tax-free reorganizations) on the buyer's financials. The model generates eight standard reports and 10 standard graphics exhibits.

For more information on Simkin software, phone or write:

Simkin Associates
5519 Balboa Drive
Oakland, CA 94611
(415) 889-5457

STANDARD & POOR'S: COMPUSTAT

Standard & Poor's Compustat Services, Inc., produces COMPUSTAT, a data base containing financial, statistical, market, and business information on over 6,500 publicly owned industrial, banking, and utility companies. COMPUSTAT financial data provide a full range of fundamental data, including income statements, balance sheets, and sources and uses of funds. Annual and quarterly information, updated weekly, is available for up to 20 years. Primary data base applications include merger and acquisition analysis, competitive analysis, and financial analysis.

COMPUSTAT can help management:

- Define financial characteristics desirable in an acquisition candidate and search the data base with predetermined financial and operating criteria to identify candidates whose consolidated or line-of-business results meet these requirements.
- Perform reliable forecasts, sensitivity studies, and valuation analyses, and evaluate the capital structure of the new entity and the increase in shareholder wealth.
- Divest operations or businesses by comparing financial characteristics with others in the industry and with companies that have defended successfully against acquisitions. COMPUSTAT also can help identify more desirable merger targets and develop contingency plans for competitive bids.

COMPUSTAT services are available through lease of tapes, hard-disk cartridges, and floppy diskettes from Standard & Poor's Compustat Services, or through various on-line service companies.

For more information on COMPUSTAT, phone or write:

Standard & Poor's Compustat Services, Inc.
7400 S. Alton Court
Englewood, CO 80112
(800) 525-8640 or (303) 771-6510

VALUE LINE DATA SERVICES: COMPANY FINANCIALS

Value Line Data Services has several electronic products of interest to business people working in the area of mergers and acquisitions. These include the Value Line financial data bases and DataWindow.

Value Line's financial data bases will provide hunting grounds for merger and acquisition searches. These financial data bases are accessible via personal computer, magnetic tape, or timesharing. The core data base includes data on 1,700 of the most actively traded public companies. The file for each of those companies contains over 400 items of information for each of 30 years. Value Line also provides information on approximately 200 emerging companies whose market capitalization is under $500 million.

There are two additional data base files. One is Value Line's Small Company File, which covers 800 companies whose market capitalization and annual sales are typically under $100 million. The other is the Estimates and Projections File, which includes Value Line's proprietary investment measures such as Timeliness and Safety Ranks as well as a comprehensive variety of estimated data over the next three to five years.

With an IBM personal computer, a subset of the Value Line data base can be accessed using DataWindow, an investment software system that provides, instantaneously, lists of companies that have specific characteristics.

For more information on Value Lines products, phone or write:

Value Line Data Services
711 Third Avenue
New York, NY 10017
(212) 687-3965

Part 4

Pricing, Negotiating, and Deal Structuring

Chapter 15

Discounted Cash Flow Valuation*

Alfred Rappaport

*Leonard Spacek Professor of Accounting and
Information Systems, J. L. Kellogg Graduate School
of Management, Northwestern University,
Evanston, Illinois, and Chairman, The Alcar Group, Inc.,
Skokie, Illinois*

Since the mid-1970s we have been in the midst of a major wave of corporate acquisitions. In contrast to the 1960s, when acquirers were mainly free-wheeling conglomerates, the merger movement of the late 1970s and early to mid-1980s includes such long-established giants of U.S. industry as Du Pont, General Electric, and U.S. Steel. Because of the greater political stability of the United States, foreign companies also have become increasingly active buyers of U.S. companies.

Most acquisitions of recent years were accomplished with cash, rather than with packages of securities, as was common in the 1960s. Finally, the recent merger movement involves the frequent use of tender offers that often lead to contested bids, and to the payment of substantial premiums above the premerger market value of the target company.

The popular explanation for the recent merger rage is that the market is "undervaluing" many solid companies, thus making it substantially cheaper to buy rather than to build. Couple this belief with the fact that many corporations are enjoying relatively strong debt capacity positions and the widely held view that government regulation and uncertainty about the economy make internal

---

*Revised and updated version of an article originally published in July–August 1979 issue of *Harvard Business Review*.

growth strategies relatively unattractive, and we see why mergers and acquisitions have become increasingly important parts of corporate growth strategy.

Despite all of the foregoing rationale, more than a few of the recent acquisitions will fail to create value for the acquirer's shareholders. After all, shareholder value depends not on premerger market valuation of the target company but on the actual acquisition price the acquiring company pays compared with the selling company's cash flow contribution to the combined company.

Only a limited supply of acquisition candidates is available at the price that enables the acquirer to earn an acceptable economic return on investment. A well-conceived financial evaluation program that minimizes the risk of buying an economically unattractive company or paying too much for an attractive one is particularly important in today's seller's market. The dramatic increase in premiums that must be paid by a successful bidder calls for more careful analysis by buyers than ever before.

Because of the competitive nature of the acquisition market, companies not only need to respond wisely but often must respond quickly as well. The growing independence of corporate boards and their demand for better information to support strategic decisions such as acquisitions have raised the general standard for acquisition analysis. Finally, sound analysis, convincingly communicated, can yield substantial benefits in negotiating with the target company's management or, in the case of tender offers, its stockholders.

This chapter shows how management can estimate how much value a prospective acquisition will, in fact, create. In brief, we present a comprehensive framework for acquisition analysis based on contemporary financial theory—an approach that has been profitably employed in practice. The analysis provides management and the board of the acquiring company with information both for making a decision on the candidate and for formulating an effective negotiating strategy for the acquisition.

STEPS IN THE ACQUISITION ANALYSIS

The process of analyzing acquisitions falls broadly into three stages: planning, search and screen, and financial evaluation.

The acquisition planning process begins with a review of corporate objectives and product-market strategies for various strategic business units. The acquiring company should define its potential directions for corporate growth and diversification in terms of corporate strengths and weaknesses and an assessment of the company's social, economic, political, and technological environment. This analysis produces a set of acquisition objectives and criteria.

Specified criteria often include statements about industry parameters, such as projected market growth rate, degree of regulation, ease of entry, and capital-versus-labor intensity. Company criteria for quality of management, share of market, profitability, size, and capital structure also commonly appear on acquisition criteria lists.

The search-and-screen process is a systematic approach to compiling a list of good acquisition prospects. The search focuses on how and where to look for candidates, and the screening process selects a few of the best candidates from literally thousands of possibilities, according to objectives and criteria developed in the planning phase.

Finally comes the financial evaluation process, which is the focus of this chapter. A good analysis should enable management to answer such questions as:

- What is the maximum price that should be paid for the target company?
- What are the principal areas of risk?
- What are the earnings, cash flow, and balance sheet implications of the acquisition?
- What is the best way to finance the acquisition?

Corporate Self-evaluation

The financial evaluation process involves both a self-evaluation by the acquiring company and the evaluation of the candidate for acquisition. The scope and detail of corporate self-evaluation will necessarily vary according to the needs of each company.[1]

The fundamental questions posed by a self-evaluation are: (1) How much is my company worth? (2) How would its value be affected by each of several scenarios? The first question involves generation of a "most likely" estimate of the company's value based on management's detailed assessment of its objectives, strategies, and plans. The second question calls for an assessment of value based on a range of plausible scenarios that enable management to test the joint effect of hypothesized combinations of product-market strategies and environmental forces.

Corporate self-evaluation, when conducted as an economic assessment of the value created for shareholders by various strategic planning options, promises potential benefits for all companies. In the context of the acquisition market, self-evaluation takes on special significance.

First, while a company might view itself as an acquirer, few companies are totally exempt from a possible takeover. From 1979 to 1985, 79 acquisitions exceeding $1 billion were completed. The roster of acquired companies includes such names as Cities Service, Conoco, Getty Oil, Gulf Corp., Heublein, Kennecott, Marathon Oil, General Foods, Nabisco Brands, American Broadcasting, and Carnation. Self-evaluation provides management and the board with a continuing basis for responding to tender offers or acquisition inquiries responsibly and quickly. Second, the self-evaluation process might well call attention to strategic divestment opportunities. Finally, self-evaluation offers acquisition-minded companies a basis for assessing the comparative advantages of a cash versus an exchange-of-shares offer.

Acquiring companies commonly value the purchase price for an acquisition at the market value of the shares exchanged. This practice is not economically sound and could be misleading and costly to the acquiring company. A well-conceived analysis for an exchange-of-shares acquisition requires sound valuations of both buying and selling companies. If the acquirer's management believes the market is undervaluing its shares, then valuing the purchase price at market might well induce the company to overpay for the acquisition or to earn less than the minimum acceptable rate of return. Conversely, if management believes the market is overvaluing its shares, then valuing the purchase price at market obscures the opportunity to offer the seller's shareholders additional shares while still achieving the minimum acceptable return.

Valuation of Acquisitions

It has been estimated that as many as half of the major acquisition-minded companies rely extensively on the discounted cash flow (DCF) technique to analyze acquisitions.[2] While mergers and acquisitions involve a considerably more complex set of managerial problems than the purchase of an ordinary asset such as a machine or a plant, the economic substance of these transactions is the same. In each case, there is a current outlay made in anticipation of a stream of future cash flows.

Thus the DCF criterion applies not only to internal growth investments, such as additions to existing capacity, but equally to external growth investments, such as acquisitions. An essential feature of the DCF technique is that it explicitly takes into account that a dollar of cash received today is worth more than a dollar received a year from now, because today's dollar can be invested to earn a return during the intervening time.

To establish the maximum acceptable acquisition price under the DCF approach, estimates are needed for (1) the incremental cash flows expected to be generated because of the acquisition and (2) the "discount rate" or "cost of capital," that is, the minimum acceptable rate of return required by the market for new investments by the company.

In projecting the cash flow stream of a prospective acquisition, what should be taken into account is the cash flow contribution the candidate is expected to make to the acquiring company. The results of this projection may well differ from a projection of the candidate's cash flow as an independent company. This is because the acquirer may be able to achieve operating economies not available to the selling company alone. Furthermore, acquisitions generally provide new postacquisition investment opportunities whose initial outlays and subsequent benefits also need to be incorporated in the cash flow schedule. Cash flow is defined as:

Cash flow = (operating profit)(1 − income tax rate) + depreciation and
other noncash charges − (incremental working capital
investments + capital expenditures)

The Forecast Period. In developing the cash flow schedule, two additional issues need to be considered:

- What is the basis for setting the length of the forecast period—that is, the period beyond which the cash flows associated with the acquisition are not specifically projected?
- How is the residual value of the acquisition established at the end of the forecast period?

A common practice is to forecast cash flows period by period until the level of uncertainty makes management too "uncomfortable" to go any further. Although practice varies with industry setting, management policy, and the special circumstances of the acquisition, five or 10 years appears to be an arbitrarily set forecasting duration that is used in many situations. A better approach suggests that the forecast duration for cash flows should continue only as long as the expected rate of return on incremental investment required to support forecasted sales growth exceeds the cost-of-capital rate.

If for subsequent periods one assumes that the company's return on incremental investment equals the cost-of-capital rate, then the market would be indifferent to whether management invests in expansion projects or pays cash dividends that shareholders can in turn invest in identically risky opportunities yielding an identical rate of return. In other words, the value of the company is unaffected by growth when the company is investng in projects earning at the cost of capital, or at the minimum acceptable risk-adjusted rate of return required by the market.

Thus, for purposes of simplification, we can assume a 100 percent payout of earnings after the end of the forecast period or, equivalently, a zero growth rate without affecting the valuation of the company. (An implied assumption of this model is that the depreciation amount can be invested to maintain the company's productive capacity.) The residual value is then the present value of the resulting cash flow perpetuity beginning one year after the horizon date. Of course, if after the end of the forecast period the return on investment is expected to decline below the cost-of-capital rate, this factor can be incorporated in the calculation.

The Cost of Capital. When the acquisition candidate's risk is judged to be the same as the acquirer's overall risk, the appropriate rate for discounting the candidate's cash flow stream is the acquirer's cost of capital. The cost of capital or the minimum acceptable rate of return on new investments is based on the rate investors can expect to earn by investing in alternative, identically risky securities.

The cost of capital is calculated as the weighted average of the costs of debt and equity capital. For example, suppose that a company's aftertax cost of debt is 5 percent and it estimates its cost of equity to be 15 percent. Further, it plans to raise future capital in the following proportions: 20 percent by way of debt and 80 percent by equity. Table 15.1 shows how to compute the company's cost of capital (the risk-adjusted, weighted-average cost of debt and equity).

It is important to emphasize that the acquiring company's use of its own cost of capital to discount the target's projected cash flows is appropriate only when it can be safely assumed that the acquisition will not affect the riskiness of the acquirer. The specific riskiness of each prospective candidate should be taken into account in setting the discount rate, with higher rates used for more risky investments.

If a single discount rate is used for all acquisitions, then those with the highest risk will seem most attractive. Because the weighted-average risk of its component segments determines the company's cost of capital, these high-risk acquisitions will increase a company's cost of capital and thereby decrease the value of its stock.

TABLE 15.1 One Company's Weighted-Average Cost of Capital

	Weight	Cost	Weighted cost
Debt	0.20	0.05	0.01
Equity	0.80	0.15	0.12
Weighted-average cost of capital			0.13

MITNOR CORP.:
HYPOTHETICAL RUNTHROUGH

As an illustration of the recommended approach to acquisition analysis, consider the hypothetical case of Mitnor Corp.'s interest in acquiring Rano Products. Mitnor is a leading manufacturer and distributor in the industrial packaging and materials handling market. Sales for the most recent year totaled $600 million. Mitnor's acquisition strategy is geared toward buying companies with either similar marketing and distribution characteristics, similar production technologies, or a similar research and development orientation. Rano Products, a $50 million sales organization with an impressive new-product development record in industrial packaging, fits Mitnor's general acquisition criteria particularly well. Premerger financial statements for Mitnor and Rano are shown in Table 15.2.

TABLE 15.2 Premerger Financial Statements for Mitnor and Rano (in millions of dollars)

	Mitnor	Rano
Statement of Income (year ended December 31)		
Sales	$600.00	$50.00
Operating expenses	522.00	42.50
Operating profit	$ 78.00	$ 7.50
Interest on debt	4.50	.40
Earnings before taxes	$ 73.50	$ 7.10
Provision for income taxes	36.00	3.55
Net income	$ 37.50	$ 3.55
Number of common shares outstanding (in millions)	$ 10.00	$ 1.11
Earnings per share	3.75	3.20
Dividends per share	1.30	.64
Statement of Financial Position (at year-end)		
Net working capital	$180.00	$ 7.50
Marketable securities	25.00	1.00
Other assets	2.00	1.60
Gross property, plant, and equipment	216.00	20.00
Less accumulated depreciation	(95.00)	(8.00)
	$328.00	$22.10
Interest-bearing debt	$ 56.00	$ 5.10
Shareholders' equity	$272.00	17.00
	$328.00	$22.10

Acquisition for Cash

The Value Planner and The Merger Planner microcomputer models developed by The Alcar Group, Inc., generate a comprehensive analysis for acquisitions financed by cash, stock, or any combination of cash, debt, preferred stock, and common stock. The analysis to follow will concern only the cash and exchange-of-shares cases. In the cash acquisition case, the analysis follows six essential steps:

- Develop estimates needed to project Rano's cash flow contribution for various growth and profitability scenarios.
- Estimate the minimum acceptable rate of return for acquisition of Rano.
- Compute the maximum acceptable cash price to be paid for Rano under various scenarios and minimum acceptable rates of return.
- Compute the rate of return that Mitnor will earn for a range of price offers and for various growth and profitability scenarios.
- Analyze the feasibility of a cash purchase in light of Mitnor's current liquidity and target debt/equity ratio.
- Evaluate the impact of the acquisition on the earnings per share and capital structure of Mitnor.

Step 1: Develop Cash Flow Projections.   The cash flow formula presented earlier may be restated in equivalent form as

$$CF_t = S_{t-1}(1 + g_t)(p_t)(1 - T_t) - (S_t - S_{t-1})(f_t + w_t)$$

where CF = cash flow
S = sales
g = annual growth rate in sales
p = operating profit margin as a percentage of sales
T = income tax rate
f = incremental fixed capital investment required (i.e., total capital investment net of replacement of existing capacity estimated by depreciation) per dollar of sales increase
w = incremental working capital investment required per dollar of sales increase

Once estimates are provided for five variables, g, p, T, f, and w, it is possible to project cash flow.

Table 15.3 shows Mitnor management's "most likely" estimates for Rano's operations, assuming Mitnor control; Table 15.4 shows a complete projected 10-year cash flow statement for Rano.

Before developing additional scenarios for Rano, I should make some brief comments on how to estimate some of the cash flow variables. First, the income tax rate is the cash rate rather than a book rate based on the accountant's income tax expense, which often includes a portion that is deferred.

Second, for some companies, a direct projection of capital investment requirements per dollar of sales increase will prove a difficult task. To gain an estimate of the recent value of this coefficient, simply take the sum of all capital investments less depreciation over the past five or 10 years and divide this total by the increase in sales from the beginning to the end of the period. With this approach,

TABLE 15.3 Most Likely Estimates for Rano's Operations under Mitnor Control

	Years		
	1-5	6-7	8-10
Sales growth rate (g)	0.15	0.12	0.12
Operations profit margin as a percentage of sale (p)	0.18	0.15	0.12
Income tax rate (T)	0.46	0.46	0.46
Incremental fixed capital investment (f)	0.20	0.20	0.20
Incremental working capital investment (w)	0.15	0.15	0.15

Employing the cash flow formula for year 1:

$$CF_1 = 50(1 + 0.15)(0.18)(1 - 0.46) - (57.5 - 50)(0.20 + 0.15) = 2.96$$

the resulting coefficient not only represents the capital investment historically required per dollar of sales increase, but also impounds any cost increases for replacement of existing capacity.

One should estimate changes in incremental working capital investment with care. Actual year-to-year balance sheet changes in working capital investment required for operations may not provide a good measure of the rise or decline in funds required. There are two main reasons for this: (1) The year-end balance sheet figures may not reflect the average or normal needs of the business during the year; and (2) the inventory accounts may overstate the magnitude of the funds committed by the company.

To estimate the additional cash requirements, the increased inventory investment should be measured by the variable costs for any additional units of inventory required.

In addition to its most likely estimate for Rano, Mitnor's management developed two additional (conservative and optimistic) scenarios for sales growth and operating profit margins. Table 15.5 gives a summary of all three scenarios. Mitnor's management also may wish to examine additional cases to test the effect of alternative assumptions about the cash income tax rate and both the fixed capital investment and working capital investment per dollar of sales increase.

Recall that cash flows should be forecast only for the period when the expected rate of return on incremental investment exceeds the minimum acceptable rate of return for the acquisition. It is possible to determine this in a simple yet analytical, nonarbitrary, fashion. To do so, we compute the minimum incremental pretax return on sales or incremental threshold margin (ITM) needed to earn the minimum acceptable rate of return on the acquisition (k). Necessary components include the investment requirements for working capital (w) and fixed assets (f) for each additional dollar of sales and a given projected tax rate (T). The formula for ITM is:

$$\text{Incremental threshold margin} = \frac{(f + w)k}{(1 - T)(1 + k)}$$

Mitnor's management believes that when Rano's growth begins to slow down, its working capital requirements per dollar of additional sales will increase from

TABLE 15.4 Projected 10-Year Cash Flow Statement for Rano (in millions of dollars)

	Year									
	1	2	3	4	5	6	7	8	9	10
Sales	$57.50	$66.12	$76.04	$87.45	$100.57	$112.64	$126.15	$141.29	$158.25	$177.23
Operating expenses	47.15	54.22	62.34	71.71	82.47	95.74	107.23	124.34	139.26	155.96
Operating profit	$10.35	$11.90	$13.70	$15.74	$18.10	$16.90	$18.92	$16.95	$18.99	$21.27
Cash income taxes	4.76	5.48	6.30	7.24	8.33	7.78	8.70	7.79	8.74	9.78
Operating profit after taxes	$5.59	$6.42	$7.40	$8.50	$9.78	$9.12	$10.22	$9.16	$10.25	$11.49
Depreciation	1.60	1.85	2.13	2.46	2.84	3.28	3.74	4.25	4.83	5.49
Less incremental fixed capital investment	(3.10)	(3.57)	(4.12)	(4.74)	(5.47)	(5.69)	(6.44)	(7.28)	(8.22)	(9.29)
Less incremental working capital investment	(1.13)	(1.29)	(1.49)	(1.71)	(1.97)	(1.81)	(2.03)	(2.27)	(2.54)	(2.85)
Cash flow from operations	$2.96	$3.41	$3.92	$4.51	$5.18	$4.90	$5.49	$3.86	$4.32	$4.84

TABLE 15.5 Additional Scenarios for Sales Growth and Operating Profit Margins

Scenario	Sales growth (g)			Operating profit margins (p)		
	Years			Years		
	1−5	6−7	8−10	1−5	6−7	8−10
1. Conservative	0.14	0.12	0.10	0.17	0.14	0.11
2. Most likely	0.15	0.12	0.12	0.18	0.15	0.12
3. Optimistic	0.18	0.15	0.12	0.20	0.16	0.12

15 cents to about 20 cents and its tax rate will increase from 46 percent to 50 percent. As will be shown in the next section, the minimum acceptable rate of return on the Rano acquisition is 13 percent Thus:

$$\text{Incremental threshold margin} = \frac{(0.20 + 0.20)(0.13)}{(1 - 0.50)(1 + 0.13)}$$

$$\text{ITM} = \underline{\underline{0.092}}$$

Mitnor's management has enough confidence to forecast pretax sales returns above 9.2 percent for only the next 10 years, and thus the forecast duration for the Rano acquisition is limited to that period.

Step 2: Estimate Minimum Acceptable Rate of Return for Acquisition. In developing a company's cost of capital, measuring the aftertax cost of debt is relatively straightforward. The cost of equity capital, however, is more difficult to estimate.

Rational, risk-averse investors expect to earn a rate of return that will compensate them for accepting greater investment risk. Thus, in assessing the company's cost of equity capital, or the minimum expected return that will induce investors to buy the company's shares, it is reasonable to assume that they will demand the risk-free rate as reflected in the current yields available in government bonds, plus a premium for accepting equity risk.

Assume that the risk-free rate on government bonds has been in the neighborhood of 8.8 percent. By investing in a portfolio broadly representative of the overall equity market, it is possible to diversify away substantially all of the unsystematic risk—that is, risk specific to individual companies. Therefore, securities are likely to be priced at levels that reward investors only for the nondiversifiable market risk—that is, the systematic risk in movements in the overall market.

The risk premium for the overall market is the excess of the expected return on a representative market index such as the Standard & Poor's 500 stock index over the risk-free return. Empirical studies have estimated this market risk premium (representative market index minus risk-free rate) to average historically about 5 to 5.5 percent.[3] We will use a 5.2 percent premium in subsequent calculations.

Investing in an individual security generally involves more or less risk than investing in a broad market portfolio. Thus one must adjust the market risk premium appropriately in estimating the cost of equity for an individual security. The risk premium for a security is the product of the market risk premium times the individual security's systematic risk, as measured by its beta coefficient.

The rate of return from dividends and capital appreciation on a market portfolio will, by definition, fluctuate identically with the market, and, therefore, its beta is equal to 1.0. A beta for an individual security is an index of its risk expressed as its volatility of return in relation to that of a market portfolio. Securities with betas greater than 1.0 are more volatile than the market, and thus would be expected to have a risk premium greater than the overall market risk premium, or the average-risk stock with a beta of 1.0.

For example, if a stock moves 1.5 percent when the market moves 1 percent the stock would have a beta of 1.5. Securities with betas of less than 1.0 are less volatile than the market and thus would command risk premiums that are less than the market risk premium. In summary, the cost of equity capital may be calculated by the following equation:

$$k_e = Rf + Bj(R_M - R_F)$$

where k_e = cost of equity capital
R_F = risk-free rate
B_j = beta coefficient
R_M = representative market index

The acquiring company, Mitnor, with a beta of 1.0, estimated its cost of equity as 14 percent with the foregoing equation:

$$k_e = 0.088 + 1.0(0.052)$$
$$= \underline{0.140}$$

Since interest on debt is tax-deductible, the rate of return that must be earned on the debt portion of the company's capital structure to maintain the earnings available to common shareholders is the aftertax cost of debt. The aftertax cost of borrowed capital is Mitnor's current before-tax interest rate (9.5 percent) times 1 minus its tax rate of 46 percent, which is equal to 5.1 percent. Mitnor's target debt/equity ratio is 0.30; or, equivalently, debt is targeted at 23 percent and equity at 77 percent of its overall capitalization, as Table 15.6 shows in estimating Mitnor's weighted average cost of capital. The appropriate rate for discounting Mitnor cash flows to establish its estimated value then is 12 percent.

For new capital projects, including acquisitions, that are deemed to have about the same risk as the overall company, Mitnor can use its 12 percent cost-of-capital rate as the appropriate discount rate. Because the company's cost of capital is determined by the weighted-average risk of its component segments,

TABLE 15.6.   Mitnor's Cost of Capital

	Weight	Cost	Weighted cost
Debt	0.23	0.051	0.012
Equity	0.77	0.140	0.108
Cost of capital			0.120

the specific risk of each prospective acquisition should be estimated in order to arrive at the discount rate to apply to the candidate's cash flows.

Rano, with a beta coefficient of 1.25, is more risky than Mitnor. The formula for cost of equity capital for Rano is:

$$k_e = 0.088 + 1.25(0.052)$$
$$= \underline{\underline{0.153}}$$

On this basis, the risk-adjusted cost of capital for the Rano acquisition is as shown in Table 15.7.

Step 3: Compute Maximum Acceptable Cash Price. This step involves taking the cash flow projections developed in step 1 and discounting them at the rate developed in step 2. Table 15.8 shows the computation of the maximum acceptable cash price for the most likely scenario. The maximum price of $44.51 million, or $40.10 per share, for Rano compares with a $25 current market price for Rano shares. Thus, for the most likely case, Mitnor can pay up to $15 per share over current market or a 60 percent premium, and still achieve its minimum acceptable 13 percent return on the acquisition.

Table 15.9 shows the maximum acceptable cash price for each of the three scenarios for a range of discount rates. To earn a 13 percent rate of return, Mitnor can pay at maximum $38 million ($34.25 per share) assuming the conservative scenario, and up to $53 million ($47.80 per share) assuming the optimistic scenario. Note that as Mitnor demands a greater return on its investment, there is a drop in the maximum price it can pay. For example, in the most likely scenario, the maximum price falls from $44.52 million to $39.67 million as the return requirement goes from 13 to 14 percent.

Step 4: Compute Rate of Return for Various Offering Prices and Scenarios. Mitnor management believes that the absolute minimum successful bid for Rano would be $35 million, or $31.50 per share. Mitnor's investment bankers estimated that it may take a bid of as high as $45 million, or $40.50 per share, to gain control of Rano shares. Table 15.10 presents the rates of return that will be earned for four different offering prices, ranging from $35 million to $45 million for each of the three scenarios.

Under the optimistic scenario, Mitnor could expect a return of 14.4 percent if it were to pay $45 million. For the most likely case, an offer of $45 million would yield a 12.9 percent return, or just under the minimum acceptable rate of 13 percent. This is as expected, because the maximum acceptable cash price as

TABLE 15.7   Cost of Capital for Rano Acquisition

	Weight	Cost	Weighted cost
Debt	0.23	0.054[a]	0.012
Common equity	0.77	0.153	0.118
Cost of capital			0.130

[a]Before-tax debt rate of 10 percent times 1 minus the estimated tax rate of 46 percent.

TABLE 15.8   Maximum Acceptable Cash Price for Rano—Most Likely Scenario, with a Discount Rate of 13 Percent (in millions of dollars)

Year	Cash flow from operations	Present value	Cumulative present value
1	$ 2.96	$ 2.62	$ 2.62
2	3.41	2.67	5.29
3	3.92	2.72	8.01
4	4.51	2.76	10.77
5	5.13	2.81	13.59
6	4.90	2.35	15.94
7	5.49	2.33	18.27
8	3.86	1.45	19.72
9	4.32	1.44	21.16
10	4.84	1.43	22.59
Residual value	11.48	26.02[a]	48.61
Plus marketable securities not required for current operations			1.00
Corporate value			49.61
Less debt assumed			5.10
Maximum acceptable cash price (shareholder value)			$44.51
Maximum acceptable cash price per share (shareholder value per share)			$40.10

[a] $\dfrac{\text{Year 10 operating profit after taxes}}{\text{Discount rate}} \times \text{year 10 discount factor} = \dfrac{11.48}{0.13} \times 0.2946 = 26.02$

TABLE 15.9   Maximum Acceptable Cash Price for Three Scenarios and a Range of Discount Rates

Scenario	Discount rate				
	0.11	0.12	0.13	0.14	0.15
1. Conservative:					
Total price ($ millions)	$48.84	$42.91	$38.02	$33.93	$30.47
Per-share price	44.00	38.66	34.25	30.57	27.45
2. Most likely:					
Total price ($ millions)	57.35	50.31	44.51	39.67	35.58
Per-share price	51.67	45.33	40.10	35.74	32.05
3. Optimistic:					
Total price ($ millions)	68.37	59.97	53.05	47.28	42.41
Per-share price	61.59	54.03	47.80	42.59	38.21

TABLE 15.10   Rate of Return for Various Offering Prices and Scenarios

Scenario	Offering price				
	Total ($ millions)	$35.00	$38.00	$40.00	$45.00
	Per share	$31.53	$34.23	$36.04	$40.54
1. Conservative		0.137	0.130	0.126	0.116
2. Most likely		0.152	0.144	0.139	0.129
3. Optimistic		0.169	0.161	0.156	0.144

calculated in Table 15.8 is $44.51 million, or just under the $45 million offer. If Mitnor attaches a relatively high probability to the conservative scenario, the risk associated with offers exceeding $38 million becomes apparent.

Step 5: Analyze Feasibility of Cash Purchase. While Mitnor management views the relevant purchase price range for Rano as somewhere between $35 million and $45 million, it also must establish whether an all-cash deal is feasible in light of Mitnor's current liquidity and target debt/equity ratio. The maximum funds available for the purchase of Rano equal the postmerger debt capacity of the combined company less the combined premerger debt of the two companies plus the combined premerger marketable securities of the two companies. (Funds beyond the minimum cash required for everyday operations of the business are excluded from working capital and classified as "marketable securities.")

In an all-cash transaction governed by purchase accounting, the shareholders equity of the acquirer is unchanged. The postmerger debt capacity then is Mitnor's shareholders equity of $272 million times the targeted debt/equity ratio of 0.30, or $81.6 million. Mitnor and Rano have premerger debt balances of $56 million and $5.1 million, respectively, for a total of $61.1 million.

The unused debt capacity is thus $81.6 million minus $61.1 million, or $20.5 million. Add to this the combined marketable securities of Mitnor and Rano of $26 million, and the maximum funds available for the cash purchase of Rano will be $46.5 million. A cash purchase is therefore feasible within the tentative price range of $35 to $45 million.

Step 6: Evaluate Impact of Acquisition on Mitnor's EPS and Capital Structure. Because reported earnings per share (EPS) continue to be of great interest to the financial community, a complete acquisition analysis should include a comparison of projected EPS both with and without the acquisition. Table 15.11 contains this comparative projection. The EPS stream with the acquisition of Rano is systematically greater than the stream without acquisition. The EPS standard, and particularly a short-term EPS standard, is not, however, a reliable basis for assessing whether the acquisition will in fact create value for shareholders.[4]

Several problems arise when EPS is used as a standard for evaluating acquisitions. First, because of accounting measurement problems, the EPS figure can be determined by alternative, equally acceptable methods—for example, LIFO versus FIFO. Second, the EPS standard ignores the time value of money. Third, it does not take risk into account. Risk is conditioned not only by the nature of the investment projects a company undertakes, but by the relative proportions of debt and equity used to finance those investments.

A company can increase EPS by increasing leverage as long as the marginal return on investment is greater than the interest rate on the new debt. However, if the marginal return on investment is less than the risk-adjusted cost of capital or if the increased leverage leads to an increased cost of capital, then the value of the company could decline despite increasing earnings per share.

Primarily because the acquisition of Rano requires that Mitnor partially fi-

TABLE 15.11   Mitnor's Projected EPS, Debt/Equity Ratio, and Unused Debt Capacity—without and with Rano Acquisition

Year	EPS		Debt/equity		Unused debt capacity (in millions of dollars)	
	Without	With	Without	With	Without	With
0	$ 3.75	$ 4.10	0.21	0.26	$ 25.60	$ 20.50
1	4.53	4.89	0.19	0.27	34.44	9.42
2	5.09	5.51	0.17	0.28	44.22	7.00
3	5.71	6.20	0.19	0.29	40.26	4.20
4	6.38	6.99	0.21	0.30	35.45	.98
5	7.14	7.87	0.24	0.31	29.67	−2.71
6	7.62	8.29	0.26	0.31	22.69	−7.77
7	8.49	9.27	0.27	0.32	14.49	−13.64
8	9.46	10.14	0.29	0.33	4.91	−22.34
9	10.55	11.33	0.31	0.34	−6.23	−32.36
10	11.76	12.66	0.32	0.35	−19.16	−43.88

Note: Assumed cash purchase price for Rano is $35 million.

nance the purchase price with bank borrowing, the debt/equity ratios with the acquisition are greater than those without the acquisition (see Table 15.11). Note that even without the Rano acquisition, Mitnor is in danger of violating its target debt/equity ratio of 0.30 by the ninth year. The acquisition of Rano accelerates the problem to the fifth year. Whether Mitnor purchases Rano or not, management now must be alert to the financing problem, which may force it to issue additional shares or reevaluate its present capital structure policy.

Acquisition for Stock

The first two steps in the acquisition-for-stock analysis, projecting Rano operating cash flows and setting the discount rate, already have been completed in connection with the acquisition-for-cash analysis developed in the previous section. The remaining steps of the acquisition-for-stock analysis are:

- Estimate the value of Mitnor shares.
- Compute the maximum number of shares that Mitnor can exchange to acquire Rano under various scenarios and minimum acceptable rates of return.
- Evaluate the impact of the acquisition on the earnings per share and capital structure of Mitnor.

Step 1: Estimate Value of Mitnor Shares.   Mitnor conducted a comprehensive corporate self-evaluation that included an assessment of its estimated present value based on a range of scenarios. In the interest of brevity, we consider here only its most likely scenario.

Management made most likely projections for its operations, as shown in Table 15.12. Again using the equation for the cost of equity capital, the incremental threshold margin (the minimum profit margin as a percentage of sales increase needed to earn Mitnor's 12 percent cost of capital) is 10.9 percent.

TABLE 15.12 Most Likely Estimates for Mitnor Operations without Acquisition

	Years		
	1−5	6−7	8−10
Sales growth rate (g)	0.125	0.120	0.120
Operating profit margin as a percentage of sales (p)	0.130	0.125	0.125
Income tax rate (T)	0.460	0.460	0.460
Incremental fixed capital investment (f)	0.250	0.250	0.250
Incremental working capital investment (w)	0.300	0.300	0.300

$$\text{Incremental threshold margin} = \frac{(f + w)(k)}{(1 - T)(1 + k)}$$

$$= \frac{(0.25 + 0.30)(0.12)}{(1 - 0.46)(1.12)}$$

$$= 10.9 \text{ percent}$$

Since management can confidently forecast pretax return on sales returns above 10.9 percent for only the next 10 years, the cash flow projections will be limited to that period.

Table 15.13 presents the computation of the value of Mitnor's equity. Its estimated value of $36.80 per share contrasts with its current market value of $22 per share. Because Mitnor management believes its shares to be undervalued by the market, in the absence of other compelling factors it will be reluctant to acquire Rano by means of an exchange of shares.

TABLE 15.13 Estimated Present Value of Mitnor Equity—Most Likely Scenario, with a Discount Rate of 12 Percent (in millions of dollars)

Year	Cash flow from operations	Present value	Cumulative present value
1	$ 6.13	$ 5.48	$ 5.48
2	6.90	5.50	10.98
3	7.76	5.53	16.51
4	8.74	5.55	22.06
5	9.83	5.58	27.63
6	10.38	5.26	32.89
7	11.63	5.26	38.15
8	13.02	5.26	43.41
9	14.58	5.26	48.67
10	16.33	5.26	53.93
Residual value	128.62	345.10[a]	399.03
Plus marketable securities not required for current operations			25.00
Mitnor's corporate value			$424.03
Less debt outstanding			56.00
Mitnor's shareholder value			$368.03
Mitnor's shareholder per share			$ 36.80

[a] $\dfrac{\text{Year 10 operating profit after taxes}}{\text{Discount rate}} \times \text{year 10 discount factor} = \dfrac{128.62}{0.12} \times 0.32197 = 345.10$

To illustrate, suppose that Mitnor were to offer $35 million in cash for Rano. Assume the most likely case, that the maximum acceptable cash price is $44.51 million (see Table 15.8); thus the acquisition would create about $9.5 million in value for Mitnor shareholders. Now assume that, instead, Mitnor agrees to exchange $35 million in market value of its shares in order to acquire Rano. In contrast with the cash transaction, in the exchange-of-shares case, Mitnor shareholders can expect to be worse off by $12.1 million.

With Mitnor shares selling at $22, the company must exchange 1.59 million shares to meet the $35 million offer for Rano. There are currently 10 million Mitnor shares outstanding. After the merger, the combined company will be owned 86.27 percent by current Mitnor shareholders and 13.73 percent by Rano shareholders. The $12.1 million loss by Mitnor shareholders can then be calculated as shown in Table 15.14.

Step 2: Compute Maximum Number of Shares Mitnor Can Exchange.   The maximum acceptable number of shares to exchange for each of the three scenarios and for a range of discount rates appears in Table 15.15. To earn a 13 percent rate of return, Mitnor can exchange no more than 1.033, 1.210, and 1.442 million shares, assuming the conservative, most likely, and optimistic scenarios, respectively. Consider, for a moment, the most likely case. At a market value per share of $22, the 1.21 million Mitnor shares exchanged would have a total value of $26.62 million, which is less than Rano's current market value of $27.75 million—that is, 1.11 million shares at $25 per share. Because of the market's apparent undervaluation of Mitnor's shares, an exchange ratio likely to be acceptable to Rano clearly will be unattractive to Mitnor.

Step 3: Evaluate Impact of Acquisition on Mitnor's EPS and Capital Structure.   The $35 million purchase price is just under 10 times Rano's most recent year's earnings of $3.55 million. At its current market price per share of $22, Mitnor is selling at about six times its most recent earnings. The acquiring company always will suffer immediate EPS dilution whenever the price/

TABLE 15.14   Calculation of Loss by Mitnor Shareholders (in millions of dollars)

Mitnor receives 86.27% of Rano's present value of $44.51 million (see Table 15.8)	$38.4
Mitnor gives up 13.73% of its present value of $368.03 million (see Table 15.13)	(50.5)
Dilution of Mitnor's shareholder value	$12.1

TABLE 15.15   Maximum Acceptable Shares to Exchange for Three Scenarios and a Range of Discount Rates (in millions)

	Discount rate				
Scenario	0.11	0.12	0.13	0.14	0.15
1. Conservative	1.327	1.166	1.033	0.922	0.828
2. Most likely	1.558	1.367	1.210	1.078	0.967
3. Optimistic	1.858	1.630	1.442	1.285	1.152

earnings ratio paid for the selling company is greater than its own. Mitnor would suffer immediate dilution from $3.75 a share to $3.54 a share in the current year. A comparison of EPS for cash versus an exchange-of-shares transaction appears as part of Table 15.16. As expected, the EPS projections for a cash deal are consistently higher than those for an exchange of shares.

However, the acquisition of Rano for shares rather than cash would remove, at least for now, Mitnor's projected financing problem. In contrast to cash acquisition, an exchange of shares enables Mitnor to have unused debt capacity at its disposal throughout the 10-year forecast period. Despite the relative attractiveness of this financing flexibility, Mitnor management recognized that it could not expect a reasonable rate of return by offering an exchange of shares to Rano.

TWOFOLD RESULTS

The experience of companies that have implemented the foregoing approach to acquisition analysis indicates that it is not only an effective way of evaluating a prospective acquisition candidate, but serves as a catalyst for reevaluating a company's overall strategic plans. The results also enable management to justify acquisition recommendations to the board of directors in an economically sound, convincing fashion.

Various companies have used this shareholder value approach for evaluation of serious candidates as well as for initial screening of potential candidates. In the latter case, initial input estimates are quickly generated to establish whether the range of maximum acceptable prices is greater than the current value of the target companies. With the aid of a recently developed microcomputer model, this can be accomplished quickly and at relatively low cost.

Whether companies are seeking acquisitions or are acquisition targets, it is increasingly clear that they must provide better information to enable top man-

TABLE 15.16 Mitnor's Projected EPS, Debt/Equity Ratio, and Unused Debt Capacity—Cash versus Exchange of Shares

	EPS		Debt/equity		Unused debt capacity (in millions of dollars)	
Year	Cash	Stock	Cash	Stock	Cash	Stock
0	$ 4.10	$ 3.54	0.26	0.21	$ 20.50	$ 25.60
1	4.89	4.37	0.27	0.19	9.42	35.46
2	5.51	4.93	0.28	0.17	7.00	46.62
3	6.20	5.55	0.29	0.18	4.20	48.04
4	6.99	6.23	0.30	0.20	0.98	46.37
5	7.87	7.00	0.31	0.21	−2.71	44.29
6	8.29	7.37	0.31	0.23	−7.77	40.90
7	9.27	8.22	0.32	0.24	−13.64	36.78
8	10.14	8.98	0.33	0.26	−22.34	29.90
9	11.33	10.01	0.34	0.27	−32.36	−21.79
10	12.66	11.17	0.35	0.29	−43.88	−12.29

Note: Assumed purchase price for Rano is $35 million.

agements and boards to make well-conceived, timely decisions. Use of the approach outlined here should improve the prospects of creating value for shareholders by acquisitions.

NOTES

[1]For a more detailed description on how to conduct a corporate self-evaluation, see Alfred Rappaport, "Do You Know the Value of Your Company?" *Mergers and Acquisitions,* Spring 1979.

[2]"The Cash-Flow Takeover Formula," *Business Week,* December 18, 1978, p. 86.

[3]For example, see Roger G. Ibbotson and Rex A. Sinquefield, *Stock, Bonds, Bills, and Inflation: The Past (1926–1976) and the Future (1977–2000),* Financial Analysts Research Foundation, New York, 1977, p. 57. In the more recent 1982 edition, the historical market risk premium is estimated at 6.1 percent.

[4]For a more detailed discussion of the shortcomings of earnings as a financial standard for corporate performance see Alfred Rappaport, "Corporate Performance Standards and Shareholder Value," *The Journal of Business Strategy,* Spring 1983.

Chapter 16

The Fine Art of Valuation

Judson P. Reis

Managing Director, Morgan Stanley & Co., Incorporated,
New York, New York

Charles R. Cory

Associate, Morgan Stanley & Co., Incorporated,
New York, New York

Value, like beauty, is often in the eye of the beholder. Like beauty, it also can be ephemeral or it can be enduring. The process of determining, in a rational way, what a certain asset, group of assets, or company is worth is the foundation of the investment banker's role in any merger or acquisition assignment. Although most valuation work is done within the framework of a specific transaction and for a specific client, an investment banker also must be knowledgeable about how others will perceive the value of the property in question and how market forces or the business needs of others can affect the price at which an asset or company will clear the market.

A well-executed valuation of the company under study enables the investment banker to:

- Determine the appropriate range of acquisition values for the company, and advise the client as either a seller or a buyer
- Advise the client regarding the feasibility of a proposed transaction (either acquisition or divestiture) using the valuation as a frame of reference and the client's own views about value as guidelines

- Prepare for negotiation with the principal and the advisers on the other side of a transaction
- Opine on the fairness of the transaction to the shareholders of the client

The advice that stems from a thorough valuation, in short, is precisely the advice for which a client turns to his banker.

APPROACHES TO ACQUISITION ANALYSIS

Because valuation is the foundation for so many facets of advice, it is not surprising that "valuation" may encompass several distinct but closely interrelated concepts. None of these valuation tools is inherently better than the others, and each method is used in different circumstances. The two primary valuation concepts used by investment bankers are intrinsic financial value and acquisition value.

Intrinsic Value

Intrinsic financial value captures the discounted present value of the free cash flows generated by the assets of a business as a going concern plus a terminal value of the business, also discounted to the present at an appropriate discount rate. Thus, intrinsic valuation looks at a time series of financial flows over a certain period and attempts to estimate what a purchaser would pay for these cash flows from a purely financial point of view. The discounted cash flow (DCF) methodology used to arrive at this value is necessarily predicated on a series of assumptions about the nature of the cash flows and a judgment as to the appropriate rate at which to discount these flows. The intrinsic value of the company, therefore, *changes* as the assumptions from which the forecasts are generated or discounted are changed. As is true in most analyses, a DCF valuation is only as good as the assumptions or projections on which it is based.

The investment banker will assume a leading role in testing the credibility of any forecasts used for the DCF analysis and even may be called upon to develop a forecast in consultation with the client. Whether supplied by the seller or the buyer, or developed by the banker, the projections always must be subjected to a test of reasonableness. One of the most exacting tests of reasonableness is to compare the historical performance of the company on certain key financial measures (e.g., rate of sales growth, profit margins, capital intensity) to the forecasted performance. A forecast that, for example, projects dramatic improvements in margins (as is often the case in sellers' projections) must be investigated further before it is accepted at face value. As a cross-check, the investment banker often will prepare an analysis that compares the historical and projected financial performance of the specific company being valued to the performance of comparable companies. Moreover, by analyzing the forecast and using his or her knowledge of industry economics, the banker can give closer scrutiny to the line items that are most crucial to the free cash flow generation of the target.

Acquisition Value

The acquisition value of a company, which may differ significantly from its intrinsic financial value, seeks to estimate the price at which the company would "trade in the market for corporate control." Acquisition value thus is the price an acquirer would pay to control the target's assets and the free cash flows (FCFs) they generate. Two other observations about acquisition value are appropriate. First, a market for corporate control undoubtedly exists. Transactions occur almost daily at prices significantly above current secondary trading levels. Investment bankers continually are conducting public and private auctions which attract a number of bidders. Experience shows that these contests in the market for corporate control can be very competitive and therefore should accurately reflect value.

The second observation about acquisition value is that the value of a company as an independent entity often will be different than the value of the company when it is combined with another firm. The acquisition value will reflect the incremental cash flows generated by consolidated tax savings, cost savings due to the elimination of redundant operations, distribution economies, or other such synergies. Synergy is a controversial topic, and the actual realization of synergies is infinitely more difficult to achieve than the recognition that they should exist in certain situations. But if synergy is reduced to this limited definition—incremental increases in free cash flow that come about *because* of the combination—it is clear that valuation should take into account the synergistic elements of any proposed business combination.

Liquidation and Replacement Value

There are other valuation concepts that an investment banker may consider. In transactions in which assets are important factors, both liquidation value and replacement value can be quite useful. Liquidation value is an estimate of the net proceeds (after expenses) of selling the assets of the company at their fair market values and satisfying all liabilities and paying taxes. Some estimate of the time horizon over which the liquidation will take place must be developed also, so that the present value of the liquidation can be estimated. Liquidation value will often represent a floor or minimum value for a transaction. An estimate of the replacement value of the company—duplicating at current costs all of a company's assets—also may be a relevant measure, especially if a potential buyer is viewing an acquisition as an alternative to entering the business *de novo* or completely by internal expansion.

In addition to intrinsic and acquisition value, investment bankers typically attempt to estimate, on a pro forma basis, the market valuation of a publicly traded acquirer after a contemplated acquisition transaction is completed. To perform this task, the pro forma financial and business effects of the merger on the acquirer are calculated (especially the pro forma earnings pickup or dilution and key credit statistics), and a judgment is made as to how the combined entity will trade in the marketplace, both in the near term and over time. Pro forma financial analysis can be especially critical when the contemplated transaction is large in relation to the size of the acquirer. It is usually desirable to evaluate the pro forma impact *prior* to initiating a transaction, because it helps to clarify the relative attractiveness of the transaction over a range of values and because it may help to set limits on the value the buyer will (or should) pay.

PRACTICAL VALUATION CONCEPTS

Having laid out various types of valuation analyses that investment bankers perform and some of the rationale for their use, we can present a more detailed discussion of these concepts and the attendent methodologies. One should realize that in many real-world situations all of these valuation processes will proceed simultaneously, waxing and waning in importance according to the client's state of mind and the competitive dynamics of the transaction. Most important, valuation analysis often must be performed in a compressed time period and based on remarkably incomplete information.

Intrinsic Financial or DCF Valuation

To state the premise again, DCF valuation posits that the buyer purchases a time series (into infinity) of free cash flows that are generated by the assets he or she is buying. DCF does not value the *total* cash flow of the business. Rather, it values only the *free* cash flow. In so doing, this analysis separates and ascribes value only to the cash flows that can be taken out of the business. Cash that is generated but used to sustain the business (such as increases in working capital and capital expenditures) does not count in the DCF value. Cash flow that must be retained in the business creates no incremental value for the buyer.

Another methodological nuance should be noted before free cash flow can be fully defined. As explained in detail below, DCF valuation uses a discount rate that reflects the firm's weighted-average cost of capital or the price it must pay to suppliers of both debt and equity. Accordingly, the free cash flows to be discounted should be developed independent of financing costs. In valuing a going concern with existing liabilities, therefore, the aftertax cost of interest is added back to the cash flow to create an unlevered free cash flow. It is this series of free cash flows that, when discounted to the present and combined with a terminal value (also discounted to the present), represents the economic value of the firm on a stand-alone basis. Thus, free cash flow in any given year of operation is defined as:

	Net income (after taxes)
plus:	noncash charges
plus:	aftertax interest cost (interest expense)$(1 - \text{tax rate})$
less:	capital expenditures
less:	net investment in working capital
equals:	free cash flow (unlevered)

Terminal Value

As noted earlier, DCF valuation seeks to value the company as a going concern into infinity. As a practical matter, however, no banker or businessperson is comfortable with projections going out 20 years, let alone 100 years or infinity. So DCF valuation is separated into two components: a forecast of FCFs for some term of years, and a terminal value that is a surrogate for the present value of the FCFs that occur in the years after the end of the forecast period. Typically, we construct five to 10 years of pro forma financial statements, derive the FCFs for the forecasted years, and then estimate a terminal value for the company.

Terminal value at the end of the period of cash flow forecasts may be arrived at in different ways, such as estimating book value, applying a price/earnings multiple to forecasted earnings, or employing a cash flow multiple. Terminal book value is estimated by projecting the balance sheet forward to the last year of the forecast horizon and arriving at the book value of the common equity account at that time. It is assumed, under this scenario, that the interim free cash flow has been paid out. A terminal price/earnings multiple essentially values the firm at the end of the horizon in the same way that the stock market would value it—by capitalizing the then current earnings. The choice of the proper price/earnings (P/E) multiple will, obviously, have a large effect on the terminal value, and care therefore should be taken to choose a multiple consistent with the characteristics of both the industry and company at that time. It would be nonsensical, for example, to use a very high P/E at the end of the horizon for a company that was forecasted to have stable margins and relatively low growth rates.

The third means to estimate a terminal value, using a multiple of FCF, is slightly more complicated but methodologically more consistent with the premises of DCF valuation. In essence, this technique multiplies the FCF in the last forecast year by a multiplier that attempts to estimate the value of the cash flows in perpetuity. The multiplier is derived by the formula

$$\frac{(1 + g)}{(k - g)}$$

where g is the assumed rate of growth of the cash flow stream into the future and k is the weighted-average cost of capital. This formula capitalizes a stream that is growing at g percent into the future but being discounted to the present at k percent. In practice, the banker may use all three of these terminal value estimation techniques in an attempt to cross-check each method and instill greater confidence in the terminal value estimate.

Present Value Calculations

Once the series of free cash flows and terminal value are estimated, the present value of these two components must be calculated. An acquirer is paying *today* for access to the cash flows generated by the assets in the future; therefore, these flows must be discounted to the present. The proper discount rate can be estimated by calculating the marginal weighted-average cost of capital (k):

$$\bar{k} = k_e \ (\% \ \text{equity}) + k_d(1 - t)(\% \ \text{debt})$$

where k_e = cost of equity
$\qquad k_d$ = pretax cost of debt
$\qquad t$ = marginal tax rate
$\quad \%$ debt = percentage of debt/total capitalization
$\% $ equity = percentage of equity/total capitalization

The cost of debt can be calculated fairly easily by looking at new-issue, medium-term debt rates for similar credits. The cost of equity, however, is calculated using the capital asset pricing model; that is,

$$k_e = r_f + B(r_m - r_f)$$

This equation shows that the return to equity holders, and so its cost to the issuer, depends on the level of return of a riskless investment (r_f) plus an additional return determined by taking on the level of risk associated with this company (B) and the long-term market return in excess of the risk-free rate $(r_m - r_f)$. Investment bankers hew pretty closely to modern financial theory here, going so far as to unlever the beta (a measure of the risk of shares of publicly held companies) and releveraging it to the targeted or optimum balance of debt and equity. Bankers also will construct "surrogate" betas for calculating the cost of equity for nontraded subsidiaries or private companies. As a practical matter, however, the weighted-average cost of capital never is used as a point estimate of the "right" discount rate. Instead, this calculation defines the center of a range of discount rates (usually one to two percentage points on either side of the estimate) that will be used to discount the cash flows.

Cost of Capital

Another DCF methodological point needs to be made. The proper weighted-average cost of capital to be estimated is that of the *acquiree*, not that of the acquirer. This strikes some clients as counterintuitive: Why not use the buyer's weighted-average cost of capital? The acquiree's cost of capital, to give the shortest answer, captures the inherent risk associated with its assets and, thus, the uncertainty regarding the timing and the magnitude of the cash flows generated by those assets. (Stated another way: The target's cost of capital is the price it must pay to the suppliers of capital to motivate them to invest in that company.) When this approach is utilized, it becomes clear that use of the acquirer's cost of capital focuses on the wrong bundle of risks in constructing a discount rate.

Investment bankers spend a goodly portion of their time performing sensitivity analysis on a DCF valuation. A DCF is only as accurate as the assumptions underlying it, and the most direct way to delineate the margin of error is by varying the assumptions—in effect, designing different operating or financial scenarios for the company—and noting the results. Sensitivity analysis always focuses on the key line items that most affect the valuation. Throughout these financial gymnastics, the range of discount rates is held constant. (Remember that the discount rate captures the risk associated with these assets; that is, it accounts for the variability in the timing and magnitude of the cash flows.) The result of the sensitivity phase of analysis is a range of values for the company or assets in question at a given discount rate.

Acquisition Valuation Methods

Acquisition valuation is perhaps less theoretical and more concerned with the real world than DCF valuation. It is an attempt to estimate where a company will "trade" in the market for corporate control. An obvious starting point in determining acquisition value is current stock market trading levels, or for a private company, an estimate of where it would trade in the public market if it were publicly traded. Such estimates usually can be made easily, and within reasonably tight parameters, by comparison with similar public companies and by analyzing the financial and business characteristics of the property in question. The value of a company in the market for corporate control usually is higher (and often very much higher) than its value in the secondary trading market. This result is news to some financial reporters and baffles some academics, but in the end redounds to the benefit of the shareholders.

Why is this? Part of the answer is found in the word "control." If nothing else, control of assets and the ability to direct all of the free cash flow generated by assets are worth more to a business manager than participation in a small percentage of a business, without control, is worth to the individual stockholder.

Although in some instances acquisition values will be very similar to DCF values, in other instances they may be quite different. In arriving at acquisition values, an investment banker must go beyond DCF analyses and use accumulated knowledge and judgment. A thorough knowledge of comparable precedent transactions, and an up-to-date and accurate assessment of the wishes, corporate strategies, business economics, peculiarities, and points of view of the known and potential participants in any given merger or acquisition transaction, are all essential to this valuation.

Multiples in Acquisition Prices

Analysis of acquisition precedent—or the record of comparable transactions— is a fairly straightforward means to begin to establish acquisition value. The investment banker is looking at price as a multiple of _____, and the "blank" can be filled in with any number of financial measures. The most commonly used measures are earnings, book value, and cash flow.

These multiples will vary in the acquisition market for the same reason they will vary in the secondary trading markets made on the floor of the New York Stock Exchange. Companies with characteristics such as superior sales and earnings growth records, better financial returns and prospects, sustained consistent performance, and strong brand franchises will be *acquired* for higher multiples—just as companies with these characteristics will *trade* at higher multiples on the Exchange. A fundamental assumption of this analysis is that companies in the same industry share common characteristics that should be reflected in their acquisition valuation. In fact, the evidence shows that multiples paid in acquisitions in a given industry will cluster around a certain norm. The variations around these benchmarks can be significant, however, and it is the investment banker's job to understand thoroughly the reasons for the variability.

The investment banker also must be wary of any distortion in the financial statistics used in such calculations. These figures always should be calculated on a consistent basis—free from distortion because of accounting conventions, for example. Two very common sources of distortion are cyclicality and leverage. For a company whose margins and earnings fluctuate markedly throughout the business cycle, the point in the cycle at which the business was sold will affect the P/E paid. Cyclicality can be corrected for quickly, however, by using an average operating margin over a full business cycle and restating the target's income statement in the period prior to acquisition, thus using a "normalized" margin rather than the actual or reported margin. Normalization—and this point should not be lost in the elegance of the solution—necessarily assumes that the margin pressure is cyclical and not due to some long-term, secular alteration in the margin structure of the industry. Additionally, an investment banker may find that normalization is not an adequate solution because a buyer always will ascribe less value to the company when the target is on the downward leg of the cycle (where the cash flow picture is weakening and improvement is well in the future) than on the upward leg (where cash flows are improving over the near term). A second major area for scrutiny is the effect of interest expense on earnings. The solution to this problem is to restate the P/E paid on a gross un-levered basis, that is, total price paid (the purchase price of equity and the market value of the debt on the acquiree's books) divided by earnings before interest and taxes. This adjustment may be particularly important when dealing with a subsidiary of a company that carries debt only at the parent level.

The multiple of book value paid is, for certain types of companies, also a useful pricing mechanism in the market for corporate control. Again, one must ensure that different accounting conventions are adequately taken into account. A book value multiple is a better predictor in industries that employ stable technology and are relatively capital-intensive. Book value multiples also are used widely in the financial services industry, where they function partially as surrogates for net liquidation value because the assets and liabilities are carried at values (theoretically at least) close to market. The multiple of cash flow, intuitively attractive because of the potential relationship to DCF valuation, also can be very useful.

Many other specialized multiples are employed in the valuation process in situations where the denominator of the fraction bears particular business significance for the industry. Oil companies, for example, can be valued on the basis of dollars paid per net equivalent barrel of reserves to recognize the underlying asset value of the hydrocarbon assets. Cable TV operations, to cite another example, often are valued by looking at multiples associated with their subscriber base. Examination of comparable transactions, using either traditional or industry-specific multiples, is not a mechanical process but an exercise of judgment. As with DCF valuation, the process does not produce one "correct" value but a range of defensible values. In examining this range of values, assuming they are based on comparable statistics, an investment banker also must be aware of environmental factors such as the level of interest rates, or the general expectation of the direction of certain commodity prices, such as the price of oil, at the time specific transactions were negotiated.

The Art and the Judgment

In the end, even when armed with the results of various analyses such as DCF values, secondary market trading levels, a history of comparable transactions, and estimates of liquidation or replacement values, the evaluator moves from the arena of seeming precision and science to the realm of judgment and art. What seems dear to one professional may be cheap to another. Factors such as market knowledge, negotiating ability, and even good luck all can cause changes in the perception of value. A company with tax loss carryforwards, excess distribution capacity, a strong business imperative to round out or add a specific product line, and an unhappy history of building new businesses from scratch can look at exactly the same analyses as a similar company without these characteristics and find much more value in a specific acquisition candidate. Likewise, a company with a certain culture or way of doing business may find more value in a company whose culture is similar than will another would-be acquirer whose approach to managing its business is very different. The knowledge of these intangible factors, the ability to use this knowledge, imagination, and creativity enable a good investment banker to elevate valuation from a science to an art. Ultimately, the ability either to affect "the eyes of the beholder" and what these eyes perceive as value, or to find the right "eyes," is a skill that is based on the results of analysis but goes beyond the pure mechanics of analysis.

One final word on "market premium," a concept that commands much attention in the press and in certain scholarly journals. It has been our experience in practically all major control transactions that the premium paid over the market trading level of the stock of the company is a derived figure rather than an analytical tool or concept in its own right. When the various types of analysis outlined in this chapter justify values over current secondary market trading levels, an acquirer may enter into a transaction at a premium over these market levels. But the decision to pay a premium to current market value rests on the *conclusion* of the analysis and is not a valuation exercise in its own right. DCF values and comparable transaction multiples, adjusted for specific transaction or environmental factors, offer a much more consistent explanation of the values paid in control transactions than a history of premiums paid over market trading levels. However, market premium is a useful concept in assessing how a seller or its shareholders may react to a specific proposal. There are examples of control transactions being completed at very low or negative premiums (discounts) to market. But as a practical matter, if no premium is offered, many transactions will have small likelihood of success, regardless of the validity of the valuation analysis supporting the buyer's position. The major exception to this observation is the relatively rare "merger of equals" transaction, where little or no premium is offered or received by either party to the transaction.

Fairness Opinions

Performing the analysis and arriving at a value view puts the investment banker in a position to play many roles for the client. Bankers often are engaged primarily to form objective, third-party views on the value of the business to be bought or sold. The valuation exercise also can be a part of a more comprehensive involvement, in which the banker comes to a value judgment and articulates and defends that position in a negotiating context.

If negotiations lead to a transaction, the banker also may be asked to render a "fairness opinion" on the deal. A fairness opinion, which is addressed to a board of directors, expresses the investment banker's opinion that the price paid in the transaction is "fair from a financial point of view" to the shareholders of the company. The import of the opinion varies depending on the context in which it is rendered. When the banker represents the seller, the opinion gives comfort to the seller's board that the target's shareholders are receiving a fair price for their shares. When the banker represents the buyer, on the other hand, the opinion gives the board comfort that the price to be paid for the target is not so unreasonable that it is unfair to the shareholders of the acquiring company.

Chapter 17

Merger Negotiations

James C. Freund

**Partner, Skadden, Arps, Slate, Meagher & Flom,
New York, New York**

When you cut through all the financial and legal hocus-pocus—the accounting treatment, the tax aspects, the corporate and securities considerations—an acquisition is basically a deal between two parties. If they can't agree, the deal doesn't get done. The way they reach agreement is by negotiating.

FRAME OF REFERENCE

Talking about merger negotiations requires a frame of reference—a sense of where you are. Otherwise, it's like blind men feeling parts of an elephant.

There are three principal elements of the framework:

- The characteristics of the deal (including the nature of the companies, the form of purchase price, and the kind of transaction)
- The point you're at in the acquisition chronology
- Whether you're the seller or the purchaser

Seller or Purchaser

Take the last point. It's not just the purchaser wanting to buy cheap and the seller wanting to sell dear. It's two totally different points of view. The seller knows what's being sold, but the buyer isn't quite sure what's being bought. So the buyer's efforts are directed at finding out as much as possible about the seller, both to judge whether the deal makes sense and to create protections in case the seller proves to possess less than meets the eye.

By contrast, the seller is ducking and weaving—walking a thin line between disclosing enough of the bad stuff so that the buyer won't have future recourse, but not so much as to cause the buyer to walk away from the deal.

Characteristics of the Deal

Public or Private Seller. The first significant characteristic of the deal is whether the seller is publicly or privately owned. With a private seller, the purchaser works hard at unearthing the basic facts about the acquired company and seeks two types of contractual protection: the ability to walk away prior to closing if important aspects of the company turn out to be mirages[5] (what lawyers call "conditions"), and the opportunity to be made whole if negative facts turn up after the closing (what lawyers call "indemnification"). With a public seller, the purchaser is buying less of a pig in a poke (since the seller has been subjected to the rigors of public reporting and Securities and Exchange Commission scrutiny), so less digging may be needed. On the other hand, indemnification is usually not available—so the moment of truth arrives at the closing. Obviously, this can affect the negotiating.

Form of Purchase Price. Next is the type of consideration being offered, which bears on what offensive negotiations the seller has to initiate. Cash is the cleanest; all the seller has to worry about is whether it will be there at the closing. If the purchaser is issuing notes or debentures, then the seller has to be concerned with the purchaser's credit down the road. And if the price is paid in the purchaser's common stock, then the seller isn't just selling a company, but also making a significant equity investment in the purchaser, which calls for a lot more knowledge and a judgment on the paper being received. (Today, of course, many deals—particularly those in the public area—involve part cash and part paper.)

Type of Deal. The third characteristic is the type of acquisition. For example, when a private company is being acquired, the issue may be whether the purchaser is acquiring the seller's assets (subject to certain agreed-upon disclosed liabilities) or the seller's stock. In buying stock, the purchaser will be stuck with all the seller's liabilities, known or unknown. This requires the buyer to ferret out the seller's contingent liabilities, tax exposures, and other possible problems, and to negotiate for provisions under which the seller's stockholders will indemnify and hold the buyer harmless from any losses or expenses incurred through contractual misrepresentations. The buyer of assets has fewer concerns along these lines.

If the seller is public, the difference is often between whether the acquisition is done in one piece, as with a merger-type transaction, or in several steps—combining, for example, block purchases of shares, a tender offer to all shareholders, and a back-end merger. The complexities here can be elegant—particularly when the multistep deal also involves part cash and part stock. Such intricacies obviously have an impact on the negotiating.

Chronology of the Deal

Finally, the point that's been reached in the chronology of the deal can affect many of the strategic and tactical decisions the buyer and seller are called upon to make.

In most acquisitions, there's an initial period of preliminary negotiations prior to any meeting of the minds. If these negotiations are successful, the parties agree in principle on the basic points (such as price); this is often memorialized in a letter of intent. A press release may be issued concurrently. While not a binding contractual obligation, the letter of intent evidences a serious mutual intent to go forward, and—as a brief, straightforward document—is particularly useful in getting a private seller over the hump of parting with the business. This method may be preferable to risking a potential negative reaction by presenting the seller initially with an 80-page "insurance policy" (the acquisition agreement), with him as the "insurer."

The parties then enter into detailed negotiations that cluster around a formal, legally binding acquisition agreement that contains all the terms and conditions of the deal. Typically, most significant acquisition transactions are not closed simultaneously with the signing of the agreement, but rather several weeks or months down the road. The extra time provides for actions that can occur only subsequent to signing or that take time to accomplish, such as soliciting the approval of public stockholders.

So, for purposes of evaluating various issues that may arise, or deciding whether to introduce other issues that haven't yet been on the table, the negotiator must ask what point has been reached in the acquisition process: Have the parties' minds met? Are they legally bound? Is this the best time, from your perspective as buyer or seller, to negotiate particular issues?

For example, as a general rule, it's in the best interests of a seller of substance (who isn't teetering on the verge of bankruptcy and seeking any port in the storm) to negotiate as many significant points as possible before agreement in principle is reached and the transaction announced. In this preliminary stage—when the purchaser is smacking lips over the prospects of bringing the seller into the fold, but the seller hasn't agreed to the price—the seller possesses the maximum leverage to extract real concessions from the purchaser. The seller's edge lies in such areas as the terms of his employment with the purchaser, seats on the buyer's board of directors, registration rights for stock issued in the deal, the terms of any notes to be received, and permitted dividends prior to closing.

Conversely, announcement of the proposed deal usually constitutes a big change in position for a seller. Once suppliers, customers, employees, and competitors know about the acquisition, the seller's business is viewed in quite a different light. If, for any reason, the deal does not go through—no matter what the ostensible reason disclosed to the public—everyone will assume that the purchaser discovered some serious negatives about the seller's business that can have obvious ill effects on the seller's future prospects. The seller's strong interest in seeing that nothing goes wrong, once the transaction has been announced, weakens the seller's bargaining position in the later rounds. The purchaser, realizing what the seller now has at stake, often takes the tack that the parties should just agree on the price and leave everything else for a later date. ("We'll let the lawyers worry about that other stuff" is a typical remark at this point.)

That, at least, is the conventional wisdom. The fact is that, in this present age of hot competition for desirable acquisition candidates, many purchasers prefer not to announce an agreement in principle without having the seller locked up—the fear being that other bidders will promptly get on the telephone and try to snatch the prize away.

Another issue underscoring the negotiating significance of the time frame is the valuation of the purchaser's stock that will be issued to the seller. The agreement on the purchase price may call for $10 million worth of the purchaser's shares, but what value should be assigned? Presumably, it will relate to the market price of the purchaser's stock, but as of when? Should the value be premised on the time the agreement in principle is reached; or when a binding agreement is signed; or at the closing, when the seller actually gets the shares; or on an average price over a specified period? This can be important, because prices can change dramatically over the course of a long-winded acquisition transaction. This same negotiating issue also can arise in the much more complex context of a part-cash, part-stock, tender offer/merger combined transaction, involving such esoteric items as "collars" (placing limits on the number of shares issuable should the stock price change dramatically in the course of a deal) and "cramdowns" (requiring someone who opts for cash to take stock, or vice versa, in order to ensure the required relative percentage selection of cash and stock).

NEGOTIATING THE PURCHASE PRICE

Let's talk about purchase price. As a lawyer, I'd never presume to advise a buyer how much to pay for an acquisition or counsel a seller on how much to accept for a company. But if I know what they really have in mind—which isn't always the case, because many clients (in effect) negotiate with their lawyers—I can offer some helpful advice on how to get there. Here are my personal 10 guidelines in this area:

So Long, Buddy. At the point in the deal when you're negotiating price, neither party is committed. So, if you take an unreasonable position—which might have some appeal under the rubric of playing hardball—you have to realize that the negotiators on the other side may just get up and walk away. It's not like a labor negotiation, for instance, where the two sides ultimately have to do business. Nor is it like settling litigation, where you're paying a price to remove uncertainty. There's usually somebody else waiting in the wings to buy the seller, and another target of opportunity for the buyer.

Don't Win Big. Moreover, I've always felt that, at least from a psychological point of view, if you *really* win, you lose. For example, a purchaser offers $6 million; the seller asks $10 million; the purchaser sticks at $6 million. The seller says "it's a deal." Now, the purchaser whirls around to his advisers and cries: "Hey, wait a minute—what's going on here? What does this seller know about his business that I don't know?" That purchaser would be much happier paying something more than $6 million and feeling that some hard-fought negotiations had been endured. Tight is better.

Don't Let It All Hang Out. In this day and age, it's simply foolish to start out with your best offer as a purchaser, or express your minimum acceptable price as a seller—even if you label it as such, and ooze sincerity. The other side just won't believe you. In addition, they want to have the satisfaction of seeing you move in their direction.

No Unilateral Bidding. Try not to get in the position of bidding against yourself. For example, a purchaser offers $6 million; the seller says, "That's way too low; I won't even consider it; you'll have to do better." The purchaser bids $6.5 million. Not wise. Why go up in price without knowing what the seller is looking for? The buyer is better off holding fire and trying to persuade the seller to name a price. An exception is where you have reason to believe that the seller will put forth an absurdly high price—much above the actual goal—and thereby dig a hole from which it will be difficult to escape. You should use other means to ascertain the seller's level of interest and keep the bidding unilateral for the moment.

A Pox on Small Gradations. If the bid is $6 million and the asking price is $10 million, and the buyer inches up to $6.1 million, $6.15 million, and so forth, it's possible a deal may be reached in a few years. But in the real world, the likelihood that negotiations will be aborted along the way is just too great. Also, constant changing of the price proposal—even with small changes—encourages the other side to wait for next week's version; there's no credibility, no finality, to any particular offer. I recommend a limited number of bolder moves.

The Real Key. Stated affirmatively, the most important ingredient for successful acquisition negotiations is taking responsible positions and making meaningful concessions at appropriate junctures.

Here's Why. Always develop and express to the other side a rationale for your initial price proposal and any subsequent moves. It helps, of course, if the rationale makes good sense. But even if it doesn't make sense—even if it's something as subjective as a seller saying, "I just want to walk away from this deal netting $5 million for myself after taxes; that's been my long-term personal goal"—the other side has to give it some credibility. A reasoned approach puts some backbone into your position. By contrast, numbers that appear to have been plucked out of the air carry little weight in your adversary's assessment.

Stick for a Day. If you come into a meeting and offer a price, together with good rationale to back it up, then no matter what cries of inadequacy it provokes from the other side, you shouldn't retreat from it at that session. If you do, it will undermine the force of your proposal. By all means, keep talking. Find out as much as you can about the other party's needs, discuss other issues, even suggest (if necessary) that you ultimately might have some price flexibility. But don't waffle that day.

No Bluffs. Never state definitively that a certain price is as far as you're willing to go if that's not your actual walkaway price. You run too great a risk that the other side will either believe you, find the price unacceptable, and terminate the negotiations; or will not believe you, call your bluff, and place you in the embarrassing position of having to back down. There are other ways to get across the relative solidity of your position without getting yourself in this uncomfortable position.

Slow Down on Splitting. When the bidding starts to get close—let's say the range has been narrowed to $7.6 million and $8 million—don't rush prematurely into the middle, offering to split the difference. Assume the purchaser does offer to split at $7.8 million. That becomes the purchaser's new position, while the seller is still at $8 million. The deal probably will end up closer to $7.9 million. There are more subtle means of ensuring that both sides move toward the midpoint.

ISSUES BEYOND PRICE

Once beyond price, most of the issues to be negotiated involve the acquisition agreement. The representations and warranties, the covenants, the conditions to closing, and the indemnification provisions generate quite a bit of heat (and not just among lawyers, although they tend to lead the charge). Pitched battles are fought over such seemingly innocuous concepts as materiality and such reasonable-sounding phrases as "to the best of seller's knowledge."

I suggest the negotiators keep these important ABCs in mind:

A—for gaining Advantages, where appropriate;
B—for never forgetting there are Businessmen involved; and
C—for solving problems and achieving Compromises.

The key for any negotiator is achieving a functional balance between getting a leg up on the adversary and working out satisfactory compromises, while not losing sight of the human elements involved. You win some, you lose some (not the really crucial ones, however), you compromise some, and, above all, you keep communicating.

Gaining Advantages

Let's start out on the offensive. After all, there are gamelike aspects to the acquisition business, and attaining your goals not only makes good business sense but induces a heady sense of satisfaction.

The biggest advantage in negotiating most agreements, including those in an acquisition, is drafting the document. The other side can kick and scream over the contents, but in my experience, it never gets all the way back to an evenhanded contract. Typically, drafting the document is the purchaser's prerogative, which definitely should be asserted; but if you're a seller, at least you can volunteer to draft those portions inserted into the agreement at your insistence. But remember, the most egregious provisions rarely go unnoticed. They're inevitably contravened, which leads to hard negotiations and often unsatisfactory compromises. The real value lies in subtlety—the ability to inflict legal results on your adversaries without their knowing they've been had.

You need persistence to prevail in this trade. Never show up for an out-of-town bargaining session with your suitcases packed, having checked out of the hotel. Instead, convey the impression that you have all the time in the world to hold fast on basic points. But remember, you also need perspective. You must know when to press and when to yield—and you can't hang tough on all the little issues.

Labeling your position on each issue as nonnegotiable is not calculated to make a deal; and banging your fist on the table, whether out of frustration or to show toughness, is out of place in these sorts of transactions. But remember, there are times when it's important to take a stand on a real deal breaker (not a sideshow). Sometimes a momentary flare-up of emotion is needed—for example, when your adversary tries to retract what has already been conceded—as a warning of a dangerous road ahead.

The gut issue is whether to give up points that you can afford to cede, or hold them back as trading bait for other matters that may arise later. This is part of the broader issue of timing, which comes up at so many points in the acquisition context. If there's little ostensible justification for your position, it's probably better to yield on the spot, because you'll undoubtedly need your adversary's cooperation on different issues later on. If your position has merit, the key aspect to weigh is what's still ahead. If you suspect there's much yet to come, there's probably no rush to reach an accommodation.

When you have negotiated more than one acquisition, you'll find yourself picking up some of the tricks of the trade. One is to use a really absurd example to illustrate the crazy result your adversary's overbroad draftmanship could produce. Another is to listen carefully to what your adversary says in one context, and then throw these words back in another. Don't be ashamed to indulge in such tactics. They work, and you need all the help you can get.

The Businessmen

It's easy to lose sight of the people involved in one of these deals, but a good negotiator never does. I've seen acquisitions negotiated over a period of several months, to the point where all problems appear to have been solved and both sides are on the verge of signing an agreement. Suddenly, the seller walks away. The seller hasn't been properly stroked, or fears unwelcome changes will occur as part of the purchaser's corporate bureaucracy.

When negotiating, make sure to determine who the real decision maker is on the other side. It may not be the person who's doing all the talking. But the decision maker is the one to make your pitch to—and if that person is not in the room, then save your breath. Above all, don't get caught in a situation where you are authorized to make concessions, but the person sitting on the other side of the table lacks the same discretion.

I find that I need to spend more time in an acquisition discussing matters—negotiating, if you will—with my clients than with the adversaries. Energizing a corporate team to move in a constructive direction is not an easy task for businessmen or lawyers because there are lots of bases to touch. Those furthest from the negotiations tend to take the toughest line. And whoever plays the role of the moving force (since most movement is toward the center) has to risk being perceived as "giving away the store." But I'm convinced that this is the only way deals get done, and you must allow time for the process.

A word about lawyers. Many businessmen subscribe to the view that lawyers not only don't make deals, they break them. Much of this attitude stems from the timing of the situation. Often, after the parties' minds have met on the subject of price, the lawyers are called in and they proceed to ask hard questions on which the negotiators have neglected to focus. These questions involve such touchy matters as escrows and noncompetition covenants. As disagreements inevitably surface, the attorneys shape up as the handiest scapegoats. Nevertheless, there is some truth to the observation, because many lawyers—trained to view propositions with a cynical eye, searching for what could go wrong, ferreting out the problems ignored by others—have a tendency to overdo this negativism, often at the expense of the deal. You should be able to distinguish between a lawyer who acts constructively, pointing out a problem and suggesting possible alternative solutions, and one who simply nitpicks. It takes large doses of flexibility and improvisation to see an acquisition through to fruition, and you ought to feel comfortable that your lawyer is working effectively toward achieving your goals.

Compromise

I start with the proposition that almost all situations of seeming impasse are ultimately soluble. It may, however, take a little imagination. So many issues that masquerade under other colors really just involve money. By moving that commodity around a little—sometimes dressed up in acceptable costumes to save face—buyer and seller can work most things out.

It often takes some real creativity to discover the common ground on which both sides can agree. They have to distinguish between the positions that each is taking, and their respective real interests, which may be considerably narrower. The key often lies in splitting into segments what had appeared to be an indivisible issue.

Finally, as you get down to the short strokes at the end of a deal, little issues tend to become magnified out of all proportion to their actual importance. Try to put things in perspective. Keep cool, keep communicating, and keep your eye on the ball, which—when it gets down to the wire—is getting the deal done.

Chapter 18

Payment Modes and Acquisition Currencies

W. Peter Slusser

Managing Director, PaineWebber, Inc., Capital Markets,
New York, New York

Rory Riggs

First Vice President, PaineWebber, Inc., Capital
Markets, New York, New York

The means of payment used to effect a merger or acquisition is a critical element of the transaction. It may well determine both the ability to complete the acquisition and the success of the business after the transaction has been accomplished.

In the following discussion, we will describe the advantages and disadvantages of different forms of payment from the perspective of both the buyer and seller, and demonstrate how transactions may be structured to the benefit of both parties. The value that can be gained by structuring a transaction that is mutually beneficial to both parties is a primary reason why friendly, negotiated transactions generally are favored over hostile means of gaining control. It is through friendly negotiations and mutual determination of payment structure that many transactions are made workable and practical financial arrangements can be reached.

THE NEED FOR FLEXIBILITY

The flexibility available through different means of payment and the ability to balance the requirements of both buyer and seller typically are the key ingredients of negotiated settlements. Both elements can be brought into play with significant value for both buyer and seller when the transaction matches cash requirements of both sides. If the payment terms are stretched over a considerable length of time, for example, the seller's desire to reduce current tax exposure can be matched with the buyer's desire to minimize current cash costs.

Similarly, flexibility can help if there is a large gap between bid and asked prices. One solution is to structure the transaction by paying a portion of the purchase price up front and making the rest contingent on the target's future earnings performance. Through this technique, commonly known as an earn-out, the owners of the acquired company get a chance to prove their assertions about the value of the business. At the same time the buyer is afforded a framework for justifying a premium price and protecting itself against potential downside risks.

In late 1984, First Interstate Bancorp acquired Commercial Alliance Corp., a leading equipment leasing company with an outstanding record. A substantial premium was justified—provided that Commercial Alliance could maintain its record. First Interstate initially paid $18 a share, or a total of $184.3 million, and earmarked another $4 a share for disbursement if Commercial Alliance met specific earnings targets through 1986. In a similar situation, General Motors Corp. paid a full price for Electronic Data Systems Corp.—a 1984 transaction valued at $2.5 billion—but tailored the terms to let EDS shareholders take part of their payment in a special class of common stock whose value was tied entirely to the performance of EDS. This contingent value was estimated at approximately 20 percent of the total transaction price, based on the value differential offered EDS stockholders.

While both First Interstate and General Motors structured offers with contingent payments based on continued earnings of the acquired companies, the acquisition of Seafirst Corp., Seattle, by BankAmerica Corp. in 1983 offered a converse situation. BankAmerica acquired an ailing institution that was near bankruptcy. It structured the offer with a preferred stock that based the final principal payment on the future performance of Seafirst's loan portfolio. In this case, BankAmerica used the contingent payment technique both to protect itself from continued losses on Seafirst's portfolio and to reward Seafirst's shareholders if conditions improved.

In essence, these cases outline the reasons contingent payments can be effective. If there is a significant difference between the best case and the worst case that a reasonable businessman can expect, the fairest solution is often a contingent payment based on actual results. The flexibility provided through techniques such as earn-outs demonstrates why the means of payment are vital to a transaction.

SPECIFIC SECURITIES IN ACQUISITIONS

The forms of payments in mergers and acquisitions run the gamut from cash to stock to debt to mixtures of securities that combine many features. The issuance of securities to target shareholders in public transactions is very common. In all cases, the basis for evaluating specific M&A currencies is the value received by the sellers. In many transactions, securities issued in a merger may sell for less than their stated value in public markets. For example, when Occidental Petroleum acquired Cities Service for $4.2 billion in 1982, it issued five series of notes with an aggregate principal equal to a value of $25.32 per share, which sold for approximately 50 percent of the stated value after the securities were issued. Occidental also issued preferred stock with a stated value of $100 per share, which later traded at approximately 60 percent of the stated value. There are many reasons why the public market values the securities below the so-called merger price. But the fact that the market value of securities issued in a merger may not equal their stated value typically is not the critical issue in the transaction. Generally, both the buyer and the seller know the value of securities issued, and that value is fully considered in the offer. The important considerations from the seller's point of view are that it (1) receives a value greater than that offered by any other bidder and (2) receives the compensation more quickly than if it waited for another acquirer to raise the money. From the buyer's viewpoint, the most important consideration is that it was able to issue securities cost-effectively and in the denomination necessary to close the transaction.

Although selected securities require a great deal of study, the most common medium of exchange in mergers and acquisitions during the 1980s was cash. It is the quickest and easiest payment form to evaluate, and it provides both parties with maximum flexibility after the closing. Table 18.1 shows a summary of the forms of payment used in more than 1,200 mergers and acquisitions that were closed from 1980 to 1984 and are included in PaineWebber's merger and acquisition data base. Nearly 60 percent of the transactions recorded in the data base were straight cash transactions.

The value offered in a transaction also may depend on the type of currency being offered. For example, if more than 50 percent of the transaction value is in the form of equity securities, the transaction usually is structured as a tax-free exchange insofar as the equity portion is concerned. The equity securities received by the target shareholders would not be taxable until the securities are sold. This structure, although advantageous to target shareholders, may not be to the acquirer's advantage, because it prevents the buyer from realizing certain postacquisition tax benefits.

TABLE 18.1 Forms of Payment, Selected Merger and Acquisition Transactions, 1980–1984

	Number of transactions	Percent of total
100% cash	691	57%
Debt, or debt and cash	69	6
100% common stock	217	18
100% equity, not all common	31	3
Equity plus cash and/or debt	196	16
	1,204	100

SOURCE: PaineWebber, Inc., merger and acquisition data base.

Table 18.2 summarizes premiums paid in the acquisitions that are included in Table 18.1. The data show that in transactions in which more than 50 percent of the consideration is in the form of equity securities, the premium over the target's market value prior to the bid is, on average, less than the premium received in fully taxable transactions. The data support the critical fact that value received by one party is typically matched by value received by the other side of the transaction. In considering the attributes of taxable versus tax-free transactions, it is not uncommon for an acquirer to place one price on a tax-free transaction and another price on a transaction that is fully taxable to target shareholders.

Seller Financing

In analyzing data such as those contained in Table 18.2, it is important to consider the value of securities issued in acquisitions in general, and, more specifically, the matter of seller financing. A transaction in which the target receives considerable amounts of debt securities is effectively seller-financed. Seller financing thus becomes important because the selling shareholders, in essence, are financing the acquisition by taking fixed obligations of the surviving company. Conceptually, seller financing is similar to a contingent payout, except that in seller financing, the payment is a binding, fixed obligation of the surviving company that is not tied to future performance. Like contingent payments, seller financing is used as a means by which the seller ultimately can receive the price it was asking. But the selling shareholder needs to be thoroughly apprised as to the real value of the paper he or she is getting.

There are several areas in which seller financing may be used. For example, in the sale of a division, seller financing may allow the selling corporation to receive the book value of the assets being sold. An extreme example is the sale of Atari by Warner Communications to Jack Tramiel in 1984. Tramiel, former president of Commodore International, acquired a money-losing computer busi-

TABLE 18.2   Premiums by Form of Payment in Selected Merger and Acquisition Transactions, 1980–1984

	Premium over		Premium over	
	Price 2 months prior to announcement	Price 1 day prior to announcement	Tangible book value	Last 12 months earnings per share
Mean for transactions using:				
100% cash	71%	56%	2.04x	17.09x
Debt, or debt and cash	70	49	2.25	17.40
100% common stock	57	39	2.95	20.62
100% equity; not all common	64	53	1.79	18.08
Equity plus cash and/or debt	67	44	2.02	15.16
Mean for all transactions	67%	50%	2.21	17.44

SOURCE: PaineWebber, Inc., merger and acquisition data base.

ness, which, given both its recent performance and its projected capital expenditures, would have been extremely difficult to finance for cash or ordinary securities. But by providing Warner with debt securities and warrants to purchase Atari stock, Tramiel effectively was able to finance the acquisition entirely through the future earnings of the operations under his management. Several leveraged buy-outs (LBOs) of public companies provide other examples. Seller financing in the form of subordinated securities sometimes provided the layer of equity financing that allowed the buyer group to finance the purchase. This is different from asking shareholders to take securities of an acquiring company. In the LBO case, the securities offered to the sellers are backed only by the operations of the business being sold. Contrast that with having sellers take securities from Mobil or General Motors.

With that background, we can describe the principal forms of payments as well as their strategic aspects, financial considerations, and accounting issues.

PAYING WITH CASH

Strategic Issues

Table 18.1 affirms that full-cash transactions have been the most common in the 1980s. Cash is clean. All parties know the value. A cash deal generally can be transacted faster than with any other currency, and if the transaction takes the form of a cash tender offer, it does not require extensive proxy registration with the Securities and Exchange Commission. Noncash payment modes typically require some form of registration, which can complicate and lengthen the timing of the transaction. In addition, securities that otherwise might be issued in an acquisition often can be issued after the deal is closed to refinance the cash paid out in the transaction.

Financial Considerations

There are a number of important considerations in paying cash for an acquisition. A primary reason that cash is most frequently used and generates the highest premiums is that the all-cash transaction allows the purchaser the greatest flexibility from a tax standpoint, although the transaction is clearly a taxable event to selling shareholders. The purchaser has certain posttransaction tax elections that may produce significantly greater cash flow than the target enjoyed before the acquisition. Much of the tax benefit comes from writing up the tax basis of the assets in order to create larger noncash depreciation or amortization expenses that reduce taxable earnings and increase cash flow through resultant tax savings.

But on the pure economics of the deal, the advantages or the disadvantages of using cash versus securities are less clear-cut, and the buyer virtually must determine the appropriate payment mode via a case-by-case analysis. The issue to be determined is which structure will provide the best postacquisition returns.

Accounting Matters

The acquisition of a company for cash also is clean from an accounting standpoint. Whether cash is used to purchase stock or to purchase assets, purchase accounting methods are required under generally accepted accounting principles (GAAP), and all acquired assets and liabilities must be carried at their market values. Because the purchase price may reflect that the target valued its assets below the market, this may require the buyer to write up the assets to comply with the GAAP. Thus, GAAP also recognizes that when assets are written up for tax purposes, they indeed do have greater value because of the increase in cash flow.

It should be noted that in order to increase the tax basis for the assets, the government may require the repayment of certain tax credits or deductions taken since the original purchase of the assets. Unless the benefits gained from writing up the assets are greater than the "recapture" tax expense, a buyer typically will not write up the assets. This choice, however, is not available according to GAAP purchase accounting rules, which require a buyer to write up the book value of an acquired company's assets to at least the purchase price.

COMMON STOCK TRANSACTIONS

Strategic Issues

On the surface, the issuance of common stock as payment in an acquisition may seem to be as simple and as straightforward as paying in cash. From a strategic viewpoint, however, an exchange-of-shares deal has diverse implications, perhaps the most diverse of any form of payment. Beyond the payment stage, the framers of the deal must consider such elements as the shareholder base and stock market performance of the acquiring company, the buyer's future financial performance, and various long-range tax consequences. Thus, many aspects of a common stock transaction that may appear to be tactical considerations in the execution of the deal may well turn out to be strategic.

Perhaps the most common appeal of paying in common stock is that it substitutes paper—albeit paper that presumably can be easily converted to cash by recipients—for a large outlay of cash or a heavy accumulation of debt. It might be advantageous for both parties—especially if the seller intends to remain a stockholder for a considerable length of time into the future—to produce a combined company that is not encumbered by heavy debt or a liquidity squeeze.

Second, the exchange of shares is tax-free under federal laws. The recipients pay no tax on the stock received but do have to pay taxes when and if they sell the stock. Moreover, in a stock transaction, many of the complicated purchase accounting requirements of a cash deal can be avoided if the transaction can be accounted for on a pooling-of-interest basis—or combining the earnings and other financial data of the two firms—which is permitted under an exchange of shares.

Despite these advantages, there are several potentially negative consequences. A paramount concern is that the issuance of additional shares could threaten to dilute the buyer's earnings per share, a key element that is factored into the stock price.

The entire matter of stock market performance and the seller's relationship to the combined company as a shareholder offers a host of ramifications. In a straight-cash deal, it is axiomatic that the seller simply can walk away and not worry about future performance. Not so with a stock deal. While the seller may benefit if the shares of the combined company rise, its compensation always is at risk and constantly threatened by loss of value should the shares decline. The seller's stockholder relationship also can have varied consequences. Substantial stock ownership in the acquirer could induce the seller's management to remain with the company, work hard to increase the value of their investment, and even serve as a defensive strong point should the acquiring company itself become a takeover target. The trade-off is the continual threat that the stock may be sold after the completion of the acquisition. If the block received by the selling company is large relative to the total outstanding shares of the acquirer, sale of these shares can create considerable pressure on the postacquisition price of the buyer. In the long run, the economics of the transaction will outweigh specific technical factors. But investment bankers and other intermediaries who help structure transactions will try to avoid any major overhangs on the buyer's stock price.

Financial Considerations

In making the decision on whether to use common stock or an alternate currency, the two parties must determine:

- The perceived value of the buyer's stock from the viewpoint of both the acquirer and the target
- Whether the fixed charges involved in the financing of the acquisition with debt or securities are so great that common stock is desirable

Value depends on the specifics of each transaction. As market prices fluctuate up and down, so do buyers' and sellers' perceived value of the securities. The most important issues are that the acquirer, who best knows the prospects of its business, believes that its stock is fairly priced and that the seller is secure in the belief that the securities received will not deteriorate in value after completion of the acquisition.

The matter of whether the fixed charges incurred in an acquisition are too great is a risk/return determination. In reality, management of public companies generally must approach any acquisition with the risk/return profile of its common shareholder firmly in mind.

Accounting Matters

The key accounting consideration is the trade-off between pooling-of-interest and purchasing accounting. Pooling, to reiterate, is available when an acquisition is financed primarily with common stock and both the acquirer and seller must meet specific guidelines. When the consideration paid in an acquisition is significantly greater than the target's net asset value, the acquisition may work better from an accounting standpoint under a pooling of interests, because the fixed charges to income associated with purchase accounting adjustments can be avoided. This is the singular case where value given and value received may be identical but where the choice of accounting methods may yield materially different results. Thus, this is the key type of transaction in which accounting procedure well may be a strategic issue.

ACQUIRING FOR DEBT OR PREFERRED STOCK

Strategic Issues

The issuance of debt or preferred stock in a merger or acquisition is generally a financing decision. It becomes a strategic decision when the acquisition is difficult to finance without issuing securities, or the securities can be structured to provide target shareholders with certain tax benefits.

Acquisitions that are difficult to finance without debt or preferred securities typically fall into two categories:

- Transactions that are so large that the size of the required financing is hard to get in timely or cost-effective fashion
- Acquisitions of businesses whose earning power precludes sufficient financing by alternative modes

There are two important implications for this type of financing. If the target is a sound business, the relative size of the transaction should not be an obstacle. Further, because debt or preferred instruments generally are issued in friendly, negotiated transactions, the structure can be arranged to match the objectives of the shareholders and the merging companies.

The previously cited acquisition of Cities Service by Occidental Petroleum is a good example of a transaction that allowed an acquirer to issue denominations of securities that it would not have been able to issue cost-effectively prior to the acquisition. The Atari sale is a classic example of an acquisition that could not have been financed without acquisition paper. However, because Warner Communications, Atari's parent, believed that there was a sound business reason behind Tramiel's plan, it was willing to take notes of the acquired company. Specifically, they were notes that did not require principal payments for several years, so the pressures on Atari's cash would be relieved in the early years of the new ownership. Many leveraged buy-outs of corporate subsidiaries have resulted in the issuance of acquisition securities to the selling parent in order to complete the transaction. If there is a sound business plan behind an acquisition and it will justify the proposed price, it often is possible to have the seller accept acquisition securities.

The tax position of the target shareholders also may be cause for paying debt or preferred securities. A common method of deferring the tax liability of the selling shareholders is the installment note. Under the tax code it is possible to structure a note so that the sellers will not be taxed until the principal payments are made. Through this method, people who sell a business can defer their tax liability over several years while earning interest on the pretax amount of the note until the principal is paid. Installment notes are difficult to structure in transactions with public companies that have large, diverse shareholder groups. However, they are frequently used in the sales of closely held companies.

Financial Considerations

The issuance of debt or preferred stock in a merger or acquisition is generally a financing decision. Certain questions should be examined, such as:

- What would it cost to issue the security in the acquisition versus raising the money through other means?
- Are there ways of structuring the instrument so that the target shareholders may get certain tax benefits and, in return, accept a lower coupon rate?
- Is it better for the buyer, from a cost or a balance sheet standpoint, to issue debt or preferred stock than another type of acquisition currency?

Accounting Matters

With the issuance of debt or preferred stock, an acquisition will be treated as a purchase. The balance sheet for book purposes will reflect the value paid, according to purchase accounting. The value of the securities issues is booked in the same manner as if they had been issued prior to the acquisition, except that they become a cost of the acquisition. The only possible exception is the case where the principal payment is based contingently on the future earnings of the company. In this case, only that value of the initial payment typically is accounted for. The remaining value is booked when the payment of the balance is considered likely.

CONVERTIBLE SECURITIES AS COMPENSATION

Strategic Issues

Securities convertible into common stock offer an excellent means of issuing common stock in an acquisition without immediate share dilution. A company issues either debt or preferred stock with the stated value equal to the purchase price, but specifies that the security is convertible into its common stock at some future point at a price greater than its current market value. This effectively allows the acquirer to issue fewer shares than if the acquisition been financed entirely with common stock. It requires payment of fixed interest yields or preferred dividends for a period of time.

In practice, the use of convertible securities focuses almost entirely on convert-ible preferred stock. Because of tax laws related to acquisition indebtedness, it sometimes is very difficult to deduct for tax purposes the interest payments on convertible debt utilized in consummating a deal. But if a preferred equity security is issued, it is possible to structure the transaction so that target shareholders receive the new securities tax-free, until the securities are sold.

Financial Considerations

The principal financial considerations in issuing convertible securities are the value of the acquirer's underlying common stock, and the current dividend yield of both the target's stock and the stock of the acquirer.

It is not uncommon for target shareholders to be receptive to convertible securities because they provide a dividend stream superior to the yields the target paid. At the same time, if stock makes sense, convertible securities represent a way for the acquirer to lessen the dilution.

Accounting Matters

Convertible securities have implications for both the balance sheet and earnings per share.

As long as any security other than common stock is used in a transaction, the acquisition is accounted for as a purchase for book purposes. The treatment for tax purposes will depend on many factors.

The effect on earnings per share depends on the relative amount of securities issued and on the terms. Generally, convertible securities are treated in the calculation of primary earnings per share as if they were a straight debt or preferred instrument. The only exception is when the interest rate on the security is less than three-quarters of the rate on bonds of AA caliber. In this instance, for book accounting purposes, primary earnings per share is calculated on the assumption that the security had been converted. As a normal procedure, however, most companies calculate a fully diluted earnings per share, which treats all convertible securities as if they were converted into common. It is important to note that if there is a material conversion premium, fully diluted earnings per share always will be greater if, for the same dollar amount of acquisition value transacted, convertible securities are used rather than underlying common stock.

CONTINGENT PAYMENTS

Strategic Issues

Contingent payments usually are structured so that part of a purchase price is contingent on the target's postacquisition achievement of certain performance goals. For example, the buyer may agree to pay the seller a prearranged amount if the seller achieves 10 percent earnings growth for each of the two years after the acquisition. The use of the contingent payment has two important strategic considerations. It helps bridge the gap when there is a large difference between the bid price and the asking price for a business, and contingent payments provide an excellent means to keep and motivate former owners of a business during the years immediately following an acquisition.

Financial Considerations

The most important financial consideration in a contingent payment is the fair evaluation of the cost and benefits of the structure. Because contingent payments are structured to bridge a gap between bid and ask prices, the buyer should consider the overall cost relative to what might be paid up front.

Accounting Matters

Accounting for contingent payments has two levels. The first is the treatment of the payments as they are made. The second involves the accounting rules followed in determining the formula.

From an accounting viewpoint, one of the most difficult aspects of contingent payments is that all payments generally accrue to goodwill. Because this results in an aftertax payment for which there is no tax benefit, a cost/benefit analysis is necessary. Another important aspect of accounting for contingent payments is that their existence eliminates the use of pooling-of-interest accounting.

The most important accounting issues in arriving at a contingent formula are:

- Basing the earnings on the same operating standards used to develop the buyer's historic earnings
- Setting guidelines to minimize possibilities of one-time aberrations that may unduly inflate or reduce the contingent payments

Two common methods used in contingency arrangements are utilization of pretax earnings as a base to eliminate inconsistencies in accounting, and paying the earn-out on either a cumulative earnings basis or on a basis that generates pro rata payments based on a consistent earnings record.

Hybrid Currencies

Although we have addressed the major issues in structuring acquisition currency, some topics, such as warrants, have not been discussed because, in essence, they fall into other categories. In the case of warrants, it is very difficult to separate them from convertible securities as far as implications and strategies are concerned. However, it should be noted that in certain specific cases, there may well be accounting or tax considerations that make hybrid currencies advantageous. A key role of the acquisition professional is understanding the interplay between different forms of payment and structuring the payment form that is acceptable to all parties. It is through careful analysis of the needs of the parties and the matching of these needs with appropriate acquisition currencies that value can be created.

Chapter 19

Tax Planning Options*

Paul Broderick

Deloitte Haskins & Sells, Richmond, Virginia

To structure the right kind of nontaxable merger and acquisition transaction, a planner must be familiar with all types of tax-free arrangements and their many variations. Just one oversight can deny desired tax effects, while triggering adverse tax consequences for all parties.

One essential ingredient for any properly structured transaction is a well-defined plan to provide maximum tax benefits to the corporation and its shareholders. Before deciding to structure a nontaxable transaction, a deal maker must ask:

- Do we really want nontaxable reorganization status or should we liquidate?
- Should we consider structuring a taxable transaction?
- Do we qualify for nontaxable status, and if so, what?

The corporate reorganization provisions of Section 368 of the Internal Revenue Code are exceptions to the general rule of federal taxation that gains or losses must be recognized on dispositions of property. In enacting the tax-free reorganization provisions, Congress recognized that the new enterprise or new corporate

---

*Editor's note: This chapter was prepared prior to any changes in tax laws enacted by Congress in 1986. In view of that and continual changes in regulations and interpretations, it is suggested that anyone contemplating an acquisition assess carefully the latest application of the tax laws.

structure is a continuation of the old investment. Under the continuity-of-investment theory, gain or loss, although realized, is not recognized.

Thus, according to the rule, a corporation recognizes neither gain nor loss on the transfer of its property for stock or securities in another corporation. Because the business enterprise of the acquired corporation itself "carries over," its tax attributes—net operating losses, earnings, accounting methods—carry over as well. The shareholders and security holders of the acquired corporation also are permitted to exchange their stock or securities for other stock or securities of the continuing corporation without recognizing gain or loss.

THE LAW GOVERNING
TAX-FREE REORGANIZATIONS

Here is the general statutory scheme of a tax-free acquisitive reorganization described in Section 368:

- The acquired corporation recognizes no gain or loss when it transfers its assets to the acquirer or when its liabilities are assumed.
- The acquiring corporation recognizes no gain or loss when it issues its stock in exchange for a target's property. The acquirer uses the same tax basis as the target for the acquired assets.
- The acquirer uses the same holding period as the seller (for capital gains purposes) for the acquired assets.
- The acquirer inherits the tax attributes of the target, or transferor (net operating loss carryovers, etc.).
- The acquired corporation's shareholders recognize no gain or loss on the exchange of their stock for shares of stock of the acquirer. Other forms of payment (known as boot) received in addition to stock or securities are taxable.
- The tax basis of the stock received by the selling shareholders is the same as the tax basis of the shares they surrendered.
- The holding period (for capital gains purposes) of the stock received by the target's shareholders includes the holding period of the stock that was surrendered.

Section 1.368-1 of the Income Tax Regulations contains three general requirements that must be met for the transaction to qualify as a tax-free reorganization.

Business Purpose. A reorganization transaction must be undertaken for corporate business reasons. Personal motivations of the shareholders, however, will not disqualify a transaction undertaken for significant corporate business reasons.

Continuity of Shareholder Interest. The shareholders of the acquired or reorganized corporation must have a continuing interest in the business enterprise of their old firm, which is represented by stock they own in the acquiring or continuing concern. If the property received for their stock of the acquired corporation includes cash or securities, the transaction can remain tax-free if the value of the stock received by selling stockholders equals at least 50 percent of the value of their former firm's outstanding shares. Notes, debentures, stock purchase rights, or warrants will not satisfy the continuity-of-interest test unless a sufficient amount of stock also is issued. There must not be a prearranged plan for disposing of the stock received in a reorganization if the transaction is to meet the continuity-of-interest test.

Continuity of Business Enterprise.   Current regulations provide that the continuity-of-business enterprise test will be satisfied only if (1) the acquired corporation's historic business is continued by the buyer, or (2) the acquiring corporation uses a significant portion of the seller's historic business assets in its operations. The regulations were revised in 1980 to deny tax-free treatment to the so-called cash merger transaction, in which a corporation sells its operating assets for cash before being acquired itself by an investment company in a tax-free merger. Although the selling corporation recognized gain and recapture on the sale of its assets, the shareholders were able to diversify their investment tax-free prior to 1980. After initially approving such transactions, and despite much contrary case law, the IRS now considers cash mergers to be taxable.

The continuity-of-shareholder interest and continuity-of-business-enterprise requirements apply only to an acquired business. Thus, an acquirer is free to discontinue any part of its own historic business operations without affecting the tax-free nature of the reorganization.

TYPES OF CORPORATE REORGANIZATIONS

Type A: The Versatile Merger

The most commonly known type of reorganization is the consolidation or statutory merger. It occurs when one or more corporations "merge" into another firm under the laws of their respective states of incorporation. The transferor, or acquired corporation, ceases to exist legally, while the transferee, or acquiring corporation, continues as an operating concern. In consolidations, two or more corporations combine to form a third, newly created corporate entity, and the transferors go out of existence.

A strong appeal in a Type A reorganization is that it offers a great deal of flexibility in structuring the transaction, as well as in the type of consideration that the stockholders and security holders of the target may receive. The Code also permits all or part of the target's assets to be transferred to a subsidiary of the acquiring company. It is even permissible for all or part of the assets to be transferred directly to one or more of the acquirer's subsidiaries.

The type of payment received by the target's stockholders for their stock can determine the taxability of the transaction. For example, if the shareholders of joint-owned corporations receive stock and debt securities in a merger or consolidation of the two concerns, the debt instruments may be treated as a taxable dividend. Similarly, if two companies owned by the same interests combine through a stock or asset acquisition of one by the other, the deal may throw off a taxable dividend if the acquiring firm uses anything but its stock. In both cases, a pure stock-for-stock acquisition causes no problems.

The reorganization provisions of the Code often overlap. Thus, a merger of a subsidiary that is at least 80 percent owned into its parent corporation usually will be treated as a tax-free liquidation of the subsidiary. In the case of a downstream merger of a parent into a subsidiary, the reorganization rules will apply even if all of the stock of the subsidiary was purchased just before the merger.

Triangular Reorganizations. A Type A reorganization also includes so-called subsidiary merger or "triangular merger" transactions. This technique is a variation on the transaction in which assets of the acquired corporation are dropped into a subsidiary of the acquirer. In a subsidiary reorganization, the acquired company merges into a subsidiary of the acquirer, and the shareholders of the acquired corporation receive stock of the corporation that controls the surviving company.

Triangular reorganizations are used principally by corporations that want to avoid obtaining shareholder approval for the acquisition of assets. The "reverse triangular" reorganization occurs when the acquiring corporation merges its subsidiary into the target. The merging subsidiary (usually a newly formed corporation) goes out of existence, and the target corporation becomes a wholly owned subsidiary of the acquiring parent. In addition to the standard continuity-of-interest, continuity-of-business-enterprise, and business purpose requirements, triangular reorganizations have strict stock and asset rules that must be satisfied in order for a transaction to qualify as a Type A reorganization. In some cases, a Type A reorganization is the last move in a series of steps designed to effect the acquisition of the target's assets after its stock has been purchased. The tax effect of these so-called creeping mergers is dependent largely on the independence of the steps. If all of the target's stock is acquired for cash or other nonstock consideration, a subsequent merger of the acquired corporation into a company other than the acquirer may not quality as a tax-free reorganization. If at least 50 percent of the target's stock is exchanged for the acquirer's stock, however, the transaction will qualify.

Importance of Timing. The timing of a transaction can make the difference between a taxable sale and a nontaxable reorganization. For example, if the stock of the target corporation was not purchased recently, its present shareholders generally will be deemed to be the historic shareholders for purposes of meeting the continuity-of-interest requirement. The shorter the period between the purchase of stock and the reorganization, however, the more likely the IRS will challenge the assertion that the continuity-of-shareholder-interest requirement has been met.

Other appealing features of a Type A reorganization include its many acceptable variations and the wide variety of payment modes that may be used. This versatility can preserve tax-free treatment for a deal that does not qualify under other reorganization categories, even though the steps of the deal may fit statutory requirements. For example, a Type B reorganization (to be discussed below) allows only voting stock to be used in gaining control. The buyer has control when it owns at least 80 percent of the target's shares. Thus, if something is paid in addition to voting stock, the deal still may qualify as a reverse triangular reorganization if the stock allowed the buyer to achieve 80 percent control in the transaction and the other forms of consideration were merely incidental to the acquisition of control.

Type B: A Stock Swap Stressing Control

A Type B reorganization is an example of a tax-free transaction in which the selling corporation does not have to be terminated. The target stays alive as a controlled subsidiary—conforming to the aforementioned 80 percent control requirement—and retains its assets and tax attributes. The only change is that the target's stockholders become stockholders of the buyer, or a parent company that controls the actual buyer, through receipt of voting shares.

A Type B reorganization leaves no leeway for paying anything but voting stock—it may be common or preferred—to acquire the target's stock. Any other consideration, including warrants, kills tax-free treatment. In addition, while the buyer may issue either its stock or stock of its parent to acquire the target, it may not issue a combination of the two equities without destroying tax-free status for the transaction. Even if the seller wins a sale-contract concession that forces the acquirer to redeem its stock at some future point, the deal can continue to qualify for tax relief if a sufficient waiting period is provided.

Despite the voting-stock requirement, there is still some flexibility in achieving a Type B reorganization. The most critical transaction—the key step in which voting stock is required exclusively—is the one that puts the buyer at or over the 80 percent threshold. Thus, a buyer that expanded an interest in the target in steps, by paying cash, notes, or something other than voting stock prior to the step that actually resulted in control, still may receive tax-free treatment. For example, a buyer with a 1 percent stake acquired for cash in an unrelated transaction can take control by acquiring another 79 percent for stock in one swoop. However, buyers could be required to prove that the precontrol purchases were unrelated to the final effort to acquire control in a tax-free reorganization.

Other variations may be used in given cases. A Type B transaction may be jeopardized because a 5 percent shareholder of the target refuses to accept the acquirer's voting stock. The buyer does not want a minority partner in its proposed subsidiary. To get tax-free status, the acquiring corporation can create a wholly owned subsidiary to hold stock equal to the fair market value of 95 percent of the target's outstanding stock. This is followed by a statutory merger in which a newly formed subsidiary is merged into the target. The target's shareholders receive solely voting stock of the acquiring corporation. Shareholders who refuse to accept voting stock of the acquiring corporation are entitled to receive (from the acquired corporation only) cash for their stock upon the exercise of their dissenters' rights. In the transaction, the corporate existence of the new subsidiary terminates and the target becomes a wholly owned subsidiary of the acquirer. The acquisition of all of the stock of a corporation, followed by the prearranged liquidation of the target into the acquiring company, will qualify as neither a Type A nor a Type B reorganization, but may qualify as a tax-free Type C reorganization.

Type C: "Substantially All" Assets for Voting Common

A transaction in which one corporation acquires substantially all of the properties of another corporation in exchange solely for all or a part of its voting stock generally will qualify as a Type C reorganization.

As is the case with Type B reorganizations, it is permissible to issue either stock of the acquiring corporation, or stock of a corporation in control of the acquirer, but not stock of both. The key requirement of a Type C reorganization is that substantially all (but not all) of the assets must be acquired solely for voting stock. Thus, a limited amount of money or other property may be used to acquire the assets of the target corporation. Assumption of liabilities in the transaction generally is ignored.

If all of the assets are acquired, as is normally the case, establishing the existence of a Type C reorganization is not difficult. A problem arises, however, when less than all of the assets of the target are acquired. In that case it is necessary to establish that "substantially all" of the assets have been acquired solely for voting stock. For advance-ruling purposes, the IRS considers the term "substantially all" to mean at least 90 percent of the fair market value of the net assets and at least 70 percent of the fair market value of the gross assets of the transferor corporation. The more practical approach considers the nature and amount of properties retained by the seller and the purpose for their retention, rather than the transfer of a set percentage of assets.

Distribution of Proceeds. Prior to the 1984 Tax Act changes, the Type C reorganization permitted the transferor corporation to continue in existence and to retain assets, either for continuing in business with the retained assets or functioning as a holding company. Under the new rules, all of the retained assets and consideration received from the acquiring corporation (stock and other property) must be distributed pursuant to the plan of reorganization. There is no strict requirement in the new law that the transferor corporation be dissolved, however. The Tax Act authorizes the Treasury Department to issue regulations imposing conditions for waiving the distribution requirement if the transferor corporation and its shareholders are treated as if the distribution had occurred, and any retained property is contributed to the capital of a new corporation. Treasury also has authority to issue regulations allocating the earnings and profits of the transferor corporation between the transferor and the buyer, as well as an 80 percent parent of the transferor corporation.

Because the "continuity-of-shareholder-interest" requirement is directed toward the acquiring corporation, there is no apparent prohibition upon the disposition of the stock of the nonliquidated transferor corporation by its shareholders.

Thus, it still may be possible to sell the corporate charter of an assetless "shell," through the sale of its stock, without affecting the tax-free reorganization in which its assets were sold. There also is no apparent prohibition upon the reactivation of the transferor corporation with newly contributed assets or borrowed funds. Although assumption of liabilities by the acquirer may be disregarded generally in determining whether a transaction qualifies as a Type C reorganization, the assumption of an abnormal amount of liabilities may cause the transaction to fail as a tax-free reorganization.

"Substantially All" Assets Must Be Acquired.   The definition of a Type C reorganization requires that "substantially all" of the properties of a company be acquired solely in exchange for voting stock of the acquiring corporation. On its face, this means that up to 20 percent of the assets can be acquired for cash or other property. If cash or other property is used, however, the acquiring corporation must obtain at least 80 percent of the fair market value of all of the property of the target solely for voting stock.

In determining whether 80 percent has been acquired solely for voting stock, the total of any liabilities assumed by the acquiring corporation, and the amount of any liabilities to which the acquired property is subject, are treated as money paid for the property. For example, Corporation Y has property valued at $100,000 that is subject to a liability of $17,000. Corporation X proposes to acquire all of the assets of Corporation Y for a combination of Corporation X voting stock and cash. Because Corporation X will take the Corporation Y assets subject to the liabilities, the liabilities will be treated as cash or other property. Therefore, at least 80 percent of the assets of Corporation Y ($80,000) must be acquired for Corporation X stock. The maximum amount of cash that can be paid is $3,000, because the liabilities of $17,000 are treated as cash or other property even though Corporation X does not assume those liabilities.

As in most other types of acquisitive reorganizations, the tax-free nature of the transaction is not defeated if all or part of the assets of the acquired corporation are transferred to one or more subsidiaries of the acquirer.

Type D: Transfer to Controlled Corporation

A Type D reorganization is a transfer of all or part of corporate assets to a corporation controlled by the transferor business, its shareholders, or both. However, the requirement is that stock or securities of the controlled entity be distributed in a transaction that qualifies under Section 354, 355, or 356 of the Code. To qualify under Section 354, the transferor or acquired corporation must transfer "substantially all" of its assets to the receiving company. Although the IRS's definition of "substantially all" is the same for both Type C and Type D reorganizations, the judicial interpretation of "substantially all" is much more liberal than the IRS's advance-ruling requirement. For example, the IRS advance-ruling guidelines call for the transfer of at least 90 percent of the fair market value of net assets; whereas a number of courts have held that a transfer of necessary business assets satisfied the "substantially all" test. The IRS is free to invoke a stricter standard for advance-ruling purposes (to prevent tax-free reorganization treatment) than it uses for litigation purposes. The issue arises most often when the IRS tries to recharacterize a liquidation that is followed by a transfer to a corporation as a Type D reorganization with a dividend. A Type D reorganization usually will occur when the transferred assets are sufficient to constitute an active trade or business, even though the amount does not meet the IRS's definition of "substantially all."

Section 368(a)(1(D)) of the Code provides for the transfer by a corporation of "all or a part" of its assets to another corporation. The use of such language was intended to cover the two types of situations that occur in Type D reorganizations. The first is the Section 354 transaction, in which at least substantially all of the assets are transferred. The second is the Section 355 transaction, in which a valid Type D reorganization occurs when only a part of the assets are transferred. However, in order to qualify as a Type D reorganization pursuant to Section 355 of the Code, the requirements of the latter section must be met.

Dealing with an Overlap.   An overlap between a Type C and Type D reorganization can cause problems. First, a transaction that fully qualifies as a Type C reorganization may be declared taxable in whole or in part simply because it also is described as a Type D reorganization and all of the requirements of a Type D reorganization have not been met. Specifically, in order to qualify as either a Type C or a Type D reorganization, the deal must meet Code requirements that the transferor corporation distribute to its shareholders the stock of the acquiring company that it receives plus any remaining property pursuant to the plan. However, because future regulations may outline instances under which a transaction may qualify as a Type C reorganization even though assets are not distributed, Type C reorganizations still may be vulnerable to attack as nonqualifying Type D reorganizations.

Avoiding Tax Imposition.   The second problem created in a Type C–Type D overlap is that transactions that qualify as Type D reorganizations are subject to the requirements of Section 357(c) of the Code. That Section covers a Type D reorganization transfer in which assumed liabilities, plus the liabilities to which the transferred assets are subject, exceed the total of the adjusted tax basis of the property. The excess will be recognized as income by the transferor or target, according to the Section.

One way of avoiding an unhappy postscript is to ensure that the transaction cannot also be described as a Type D reorganization. To accomplish this, the buying corporation could acquire assets by using stock of a controlling parent company. This will prevent an unintended overlap, because Type C reorganizations permit the use of a parent corporation's stock whereas the Type D reorganization rules do not.

Section 355 provides an exception from dividend treatment for divisive-type transactions in which stock of a controlled corporation is distributed (spun off) to some or all of the shareholders of the distributing company. The normal rule requiring a transfer of substantially all of the transferor's assets in a Type D reorganization is inapplicable if the stock of the transferee corporation is distributed pursuant to Section 355. Through this exception, a Type D reorganization facilitates the division of corporate business enterprises into separate corporations. Section 355 divisions are subject to strict business activity, corporate business purpose, and nondevice rules, and require great care to avoid dividend treatment.

Type E (Recapitalization): Restructuring a Single Firm

A recapitalization is the readjustment of the financial structure of a single corporation in which an acquisition is not involved. Recapitalization exchanges are exempt from the continuity-of-business and continuity-of-shareholder-interest rules. Recapitalizations also are exempt from the rules on reduction of net operating loss carryover that apply when shareholders of a money-losing corporation do not maintain a continuing interest through stock ownership in the acquiring concern. The only potential tax effect of a recapitalization is on the shareholders of the recapitalized corporation.

There are three principal types of recapitalization transactions. The first and most common is the stock-for-stock exchange. Typically, shareholders exchange existing common stock for new preferred stock. This has the effect of providing the exchanging shareholder with guaranteed income and the nonexchanging shareholders with future capital growth. Type E also can be used to squeeze out minority shareholders. The second is the bond-for-stock exchange, in which a bondholder exchanges his or her senior interest (bonds) for a junior interest (stock) in the corporation. This is normally done to improve the balance sheet by eliminating debt. Under the 1984 Tax Act changes, the exchange will not produce debt-forgiveness income to the corporation if it is in Chapter 11 or is insolvent. The third type of exchange is the bond-for-bond exchange, which usually occurs in the wake of changes in interest rates, profitability, or creditworthiness of the debtor corporation.

One of the pitfalls of a Type E recapitalization is the classification of newly issued preferred stock as "Section 306 stock." The sale or exchange of Section 306 stock can result in ordinary income to the shareholder no matter how long held or in what manner disposed of. Section 306 stock arises most often in a recapitalization when the exchanging shareholder winds up with both common and preferred stock of the same corporation. Fortunately, there are a number of ways of eliminating the Section 306 stock taint.

Type F: A Mere Change in Form

A Type F reorganization is defined in the Internal Revenue Code as "a mere change in identity, form, or place of organization, however effected." The principal differences between Type F reorganizations and other types are in the way the tax attribute carryover rules apply to them. Section 381(a) of the Code provides for the carryover of various tax attributes to the acquiring corporation. In each instance, the taxable year of the transferor corporation ends and the buyer is not permitted to carry back a net operating loss to a taxable year of the transferor. The exception is the Type F reorganization. The taxable year of the corporation that has undergone a Type F reorganization remains the same, and the company is free to carry back net operating losses to its prior taxable years. The reason for the exception is a congressional recognition that the reorganized corporation is, in substance, identical to the old company.

Type G (Bankruptcy): Insolvency Reorganization

The most recent addition to the reorganization provisions is the Type G reorganization enacted by Congress as part of the Bankruptcy Tax Act of 1980. The Type G reorganization is similar to a Type D and other reorganizations in form. However, in the case of overlaps, Type G has exclusive jurisdiction. Thus, a transfer of assets in exchange for stock or securities pursuant to a court-approved insolvency reorganization plan will constitute a tax-free Type G reorganization. No gain or loss will be recognized for the transferor corporation or the exchanging shareholders and security holders. In addition, the tax attributes of the debtor corporation carry over to the acquirer. The Type G reorganization permits triangular reorganizations as well as the postreorganization transfers of assets to subsidiary corporations.

ADDITIONAL TAX CONCERNS

Net Operating Losses

A key ingredient in any tax-free acquisition is the continued availability of any net operating loss carryforwards (NOLs) of the acquired corporation. Generally, Section 382(b) limits the availability of the NOLs of either the acquired or the acquiring corporation if the shareholders of the money-losing company do not have a sufficient stock interest in the acquiring corporation. Thus, even the NOLs of the acquirer can be reduced if the acquired corporation is larger or more valuable than the buyer.

Apart from the requirement of a corporate business reason for any reorganization, a business purpose also is required to avoid the loss of the acquired corporation's NOLs. Section 269 gives the IRS broad discretion to disallow NOLs if the acquisition was undertaken "for tax avoidance purposes." However, continuing a historic business of the acquired corporation usually may be sufficient to preserve the NOLs in the face of an IRS challenge.

Party Taxable Transactions

No acquisition plan should overlook the benefits of a taxable or a partly taxable stock or asset acquisition. Under Section 338 of the Code, corporations may be able to acquire both the assets and the tax attributes (including NOLs) of a target corporation without issuing stock. If the target has no desirable tax attributes, the acquiring corporation has the option of acquiring the target's assets on a "stepped-up" or stock-cost basis. The purchaser of stock can acquire the target corporation with its tax attributes (NOLs) intact, or it can acquire assets on a tax basis equal to the total amount paid for the target stock. But it cannot do both. It is no longer necessary to liquidate the target corporation to trigger the increase in the tax basis of its assets. On the other hand, liquidating a target corporation to acquire its NOLs can enable an acquiring corporation to avoid the difficult consolidated return limits on the use of the NOLs of a newly acquired company.

The tax treatment of a purchase of at least 80 percent of a corporation's stock by another corporation is dependent entirely on whether a "Section 338 election" is made. Certainly, the election should not be made until all options have been considered.

Tax planning for acquisitions acquired a new measure of certainty when the IRS decided to respect the integrity of a Section 351 transfer even though the transaction also may constitute a defective reorganization.

Weighing the Alternatives

In determining which types of nontaxable corporate reorganization—A through G—a transaction may qualify under, an acquirer should consider the overlaps and differences among various types to ensure that the transaction is not inadvertently disqualified. It could be that a taxable transaction is the best alternative.

The guidelines for choosing the proper reorganization form provide an acquirer with the materials it needs for plotting preliminary tax strategy. Given the complexity of the reorganization rules, however, as well as the far-reaching impact of a poorly designed transaction, a visit to a qualified tax expert is well worth the trip.

Chapter 20

Golden Rules of M&A Financing

Andrew D. Robertson

Vice President, First National Bank of Chicago,
Chicago, Illinois

Lenders aggressively seek acquisition financing because they like the business. Interest rates tend to be higher than on other loans, fees are attractive, and acquisition lending can be a means of "up-tiering" relationships, or securing other profitable lending transactions or service arrangements with the borrowing customer. Nonetheless, lenders will scrutinize requests for acquisition financing very carefully, because substantial risks are often involved.

No two acquisition financing transactions are exactly the same. Differences may stem from the complexity, structure, size, and mode of the transaction; the borrower's size and credit rating; or whether the deal is a leveraged buy-out. In addition, lenders usually are more responsive to regular customers than to noncustomers. However, many similar or common principles may be applied regardless of what the transaction entails.

In the ensuing discussion, we will focus on the common aspects of the various methods for financing acquisitions, starting with the role of the agent bank in commercial bank-financed transactions and continuing with such alternative techniques and instruments as convertible securities, warrants, exchanges of stock, private placements, junk bonds, employee stock ownership plans

(ESOPs), and nonbank financing. The agent bank was selected as the focal point for the bank financing analysis because its role, functions, and services are far broader and more comprehensive than that of the bank that merely participates in providing financing. The agent bank's process involves two key stages—the initiation phase and the follow-up, due diligence phase that leads to either a lending commitment or a rejection of the deal.

INITIATION STAGE IN BANK FINANCING

Bank financing in an acquisition generally begins when a client approaches the bank and wants a quick response as to the institution's interest in supplying funds to swing the purchase. Major policy and credit issues must be addressed immediately by the bank, including, if applicable, its positions on hostile take-overs, conflicts of interest, greenmail, and leveraged buy-outs (LBOs). The bank also must consider the appropriateness of the loan in the context of legal strictures on its lending limits and diversification of its loan portfolio.

In the policy area, for example, banks traditionally have been reluctant to participate in hostile takeovers if the target is a bank customer. Since 1984, however, some large banks have altered their policies and have appeared willing to supply financing for hostile takeovers, irrespective of whether the target is a customer. Similarly, the mid-1980s brought some change in policy toward leveraged buyouts. A favorable posture was redirected toward a more cautious approach because of a shift in bankers' risk appetites, economic, money market, and banking industry conditions, and warnings from regulators about overinvolvement in debt-heavy transactions. Another go-slow sign on LBOs was flashed by the evolving legal issue of "fraudulent conveyance," under which other creditors can attack the bank's right to repayment of its loan if the target goes bankrupt under new ownership. The rationale is that the banks, by providing the financing, have facilitated a transaction in which the target shareholders—the sellers—are paid before the company's existing creditors. As a result, the creditors may claim that they were put at risk because the target's cash flow and assets were encumbered by the transaction. The banks have countered by trying to make sure in advance that sufficient funds can be generated to satisfy all creditors, including themselves. They have demanded that the target have a strong "break-up" valuation so they can determine if all debts can be paid through asset sales should the company falter. And the bank's specific policies must be juxtaposed with legal lending and diversification limits that affect how much can be loaned in certain types of transactions, to individual customers, and to specific industries.

Credit issues are determined by the structure of the proposed transaction, amortization period, degrees of leverage and interest coverage, form and content of the loan covenants, pricing of the deal, collateral, and sources of payment. In addition, credit screens include an assessment of the future prospects of the industry, the strength of the company to be acquired, the quality of its management, and sensitivity analyses based on differing assumptions about the future of the company and its industry.

In preparation for its loan request, the borrower should select experienced financial and legal advisers and seek funds from a bank that has acted as agent on similar transactions. This is especially important if the agent must form a syndicate of banks to participate in the financing. Equity financing should be arranged early in the process, because the banks require evidence of equity commitments before making their decisions.

The Engagement Letter

This entire process might be handled very quickly—perhaps in as little as a day or two—if the borrower is well known to the bank and the transaction is "routine." Otherwise, the procedure could be much more time-consuming. But whether short or long, the initiation stage results only in an indication of interest by the bank, not the firm commitment that must await completion of due diligence. If the borrower seeks a large loan in which the bank must act as the agent in putting a syndicate of funding banks together, a 'go-ahead" decision will result in an engagement letter that advances the initiation stage to a new and more in-depth phase. In this section of the process, corollary business matters, such as divestitures, private placements, and swaps, may be discussed, and a timetable is established for completion of financing arrangements. The engagement letter summarizes the key terms of the transaction that will be reviewed and resolved prior to a commitment, and it may indicate the amount that the agent bank is considering for its own participation.

Overall fees charged by the bank usually range between 0.5 and 1 percent of the total borrowing but can go higher. These charges may include an engagement fee, financial advisory fees, syndication fees for the agent, commitment fees, closing and ongoing servicing fees, and a broken-deal fee if the transaction collapses after a certain point. Interest rates on the loan depend on a number of factors, including general money market conditions, availability of funds, equity investments, and safety or riskiness of the loan. In the mid-1980s rates on large LBO loans were about 1.5 percentage points over prime, with an eight-year amortization.

THE DUE DILIGENCE STAGE

The due diligence stage covers an in-depth analysis of the proposed transaction to generate information for a bank's decision on whether to actually commit a specific amount of funds within a specific financing structure. Proper execution of this stage requires regular meetings between the bank and the borrower. Specific tasks include reviews of all financial and other information, valuation of business units to be sold, and plant tours for the agent and other key banks. Among the critical calculations and conclusions reached by these exercises are achievability of financial forecasts in light of historical performance, initial leverage and interest coverage ratios, verification of facts and assumptions contained in the prospectus or offering circular, security for the transaction, and continuity of existing management.

Information Requirements

The bank reviews detailed information for each operating company or division of the target. These data typically include five years of historical financial statements, forecasts and assumptions covering the term of the proposed loan, disclosure of contingent liabilities, detailed descriptions of products, market share by product, competitive analysis by product or product group, customer and supplier analysis, description of manufacturing processes and technologies, labor status, and biographies of key managers. Pro forma consolidated financial forecasts should show anticipated seasonal working capital requirements, the impact of business cycles, the capital expenditure budget, and key financial ratios (debt/equity, debt/cash flow, coverage of interest, etc.). A range of forecasts based on differing economic, market, and other assumptions should be presented, including, most important, a "pessimistic" outlook based on the poorest conceivable conditions. This helps determine if interest costs can be covered in a worst-case situation.

Other information sought by the bank in this phase might include legal and supporting documents relating to the acquisition or merger, identities of the equity participants and their records, research reports by analysts or investment bankers, and copies of long-term debt and indenture agreements.

Analysis of Key Data

The bank analyzes cash flows and balance sheets for changes in volumes, margins, interest rates, capital expenditures, and receivable/inventory turnovers. It compares the historical changes with the forecast and reviews market conditions and trends. The bank's primary concern is interest coverage, that is, whether the business can safely pay off the loan. Most banks want a beginning coverage of about 1.5 to 1 that will improve steadily thereafter. The debt/equity ratio normally should begin at no more than 5 to 1 (see Table 20.1 for a projected capitalization). Admittedly, some leveraged buy-outs that have not met these criteria nevertheless have received financing. But they usually had other favorable characteristics such as the potential for realization of excess values through divestitures.

Assessment of Management's Ability

Lenders can be expected to look closely at management's ability, reputation, and standing in its industry. Management's track record and its actual performance against business plans are assessed, along with its historical ability to manage during adverse market conditions. Lenders want to be assured that management has a clear sense of direction and is capable of achieving its goals. This evaluation is done by the agent bank during plant visits, meetings where key managers make formal presentations, and informal meetings. If the transaction is a leveraged buy-out, the amount of personal equity being put into the deal by management and the organizers will be an important consideration.

TABLE 20.1   Projected Capitalization of an Acquired Company (dollars in millions)

	At closing	1985	1986	1987	1988	1989	1990
Long-term debt:							
Bank debt	$ 295	$ 289	$ 157	$ 155	$ 120	$ 84	$ 53
Senior notes	135	135	135	135	135	135	135
Existing debt	170	165	160	155	150	145	140
Senior subordinated debentures	115	115	115	115	115	115	115
Subordinated debentures	85	85	85	85	85	85	85
Total long-term debt	$ 800	789	652	645	605	564	528
Preferred stock:							
Existing	$ 20	14	0	0	0	0	0
14.0% exchangeable	105	115	132	141	167	184	183
Variable rate	15	15	15	15	15	15	15
13.5% cumulative	40	43	48	55	62	71	77
Common stock	20	20	20	20	20	20	20
Retained earnings	0	(6)	1	5	10	20	45
Total equity	$ 200	201	216	236	274	310	340
Total capitalization	$ 1,000	$ 990	$ 868	$ 881	$ 879	$ 874	$868
Debt equity ratio	4.00X	3.93X	3.02X	2.73X	2.21X	1.82X	1.55X

Note: This displays the debt/equity structure of a moderately leveraged acquisition. The improvement in the debt/equity ratio is a favorable trend and is probably within most banks' requirements.

Covenants in the Loan Agreement

Typical affirmative and negative covenants require the submission of quarterly financial information; limitations on further borrowing, payment of dividends, acquisitions, and capital expenditures; specifications requiring minimum net worth, working capital, and interest coverage ratios; and, possibly, limits on management remuneration and employment contracts.

The time frame from initiation to commitment usually varies and depends on the complexity of the previously described factors. If the borrower does its homework and is an important bank customer, the entire period could be compressed into a few weeks. However, in large, complex acquisitions where detailed information is not readily available, several months may be required. Generally, the more complex the transaction, the longer the bank takes to respond. Other factors affecting the timing include the size and financial health of the target company; the nature of the transaction; the resolution of legal, regulatory, and structural issues; and negotiations with other interested parties such as existing lenders, subordinated debt holders, equity participants, and mezzanine lenders.

Innovative Techniques in Bank Financing

The perimeters of the banks' basic approach to acquisition financing have been stretched significantly by numerous creative variations designed to accommodate the increasing complexities of modern deal structuring and keep the banks competitive with alternative credit sources. In one hostile takeover attempt, for example, the bank pegged a part of its fee to the change in the target's stock price. Thus, if the price went up and the client that was pursuing the target was outbid, yet benefited by tendering its shares at a profit to the successful acquirer, the bank was to get a portion of the profit. In other cases, banks have been willing to tie their fees to earn-out formulas based on future profits that result from the acquisition.

In other cases, the banks have been able to become inventive by sharing financing with nonbank affiliates in their parent holding companies. Many banks have been willing take "equity kickers," either stock in the client company or rights to purchase stock at a later date, to help supply financing. In a particularly complex transaction, the bank put together a package by supplying a commercial loan, getting its own venture capital fund to make an investment, and arranging for additional financing through an insurance company. The structure of bank financing has become so flexible that banks and borrowers can center on any alternative that makes business sense in a particular deal.

ALTERNATIVES TO BANK FINANCING

Various types of equity instruments and private debt placements have served as traditional means of nonbank financing. By the mid-1980s, the historically prevalent techniques had been joined by such increasingly important financing creations as junk bonds and employee stock ownership plans.

Equity and Private Placements

The main advantages of using equity are that the transaction can be tax-free to the seller and handled on a pooling-of-interest basis by the buyer. But common stock most often is used when the acquirer's price/earnings ratio is higher than that of the target and initial dilution of earnings per share can be avoided. The use of stock in acquisitions historically has trended with the cycles of the stock market. When prices and multiples are high, buyers can issue fewer shares and avoid or minimize dilution. Conversely, share exchanges are less popular in down markets. Convertible preferred stock, which sells at a premium to common, may be advantageous in minimizing dilution because fewer shares ultimately are issued. Numerous considerations are involved in deciding whether to use convertible preferred in an acquisition. For example, it requires the calculation and reporting of fully diluted earnings per share, which affects the buyer's price/earnings ratio and cash flow. Straight preferred stock is normally the most expensive way of financing acquisitions through equity. Thus, preferred is used less frequently than common or convertible shares, except in large leveraged buy-outs where it may be within a range of securities that are issued. Stock purchase warrants often are used because they initially reduce common equity dilution, do not require dividend or interest payments, and may provide additional funds when exercised.

The market for private placement of corporate debt and equity has grown considerably in recent years and by the mid-1980s exceeded $200 billion in principal amount outstanding. Annual private-issue volume was in excess of $50 billion in 1984 alone. The majority of privately placed offerings are debt securities, although equity and quasi-equity financings have gained popularity among larger private lenders. Transactions involving so-called equity kickers, or provisions that allow lenders to take or buy some equity in the borrower, have been a relatively small but growing portion of the overall market.

The traditional core of the private market consists of intermediate to long-term, fixed-rate loans to corporate borrowers of medium credit quality (companies with debt securities rated A/A or BBB/Baa). Large insurance companies dominate this part of the private market, with unsecured loans evidenced by a loan agreement or bond purchase agreement. Higher-quality credits (companies rated AA/Aa or above) also borrow in the private market for a number of reasons, including the private market's significantly reduced disclosure requirements and the flexibility a borrower enjoys by dealing with a small number of sophisticated investors. Principal lenders to these high-quality credits include savings banks, life insurance companies, fire and casualty insurers, pension and retirement funds, and certain trust funds. These organizations tend to be conservative in their buying habits because of particular investment objectives, or statutory and other mandated fiduciary obligations. On the low-quality side of the private market (companies rated low Baa and below), lenders to riskier credits include commercial finance companies, which provide both fixed- and floating-rate loans on a secured basis, and large insurance companies which seek lower-quality credits to stimulate higher yields.

A wide variety of financial instruments can be sold privately, including senior and subordinated debt, secured debt, lease finance debt and equity, tax-exempt debt, and government-guaranteed notes and bonds. Because the buying group tends to be quite sophisticated, private placements permit financings that are structurally complex or require ongoing investor action (such as repricing, remarketing, puts, and calls) to be accomplished quickly and at the lowest possible cost.

Junk Bonds

Junk bonds, so called because of their low investment ratings (usually less than BBB) and relatively high risks, became important sources of acquisition financing in the mid-1980s and were especially popular with corporate "raiders" and hostile acquirers. These instruments (which actually may include notes, debentures, and preferred stock as well as bonds) are subordinate to senior bank debt, but pay high yields to offset their increased risk of default. Junk bonds figured as financing vehicles of the mid-1980s in the Farley Industries acquisition of Northwest Industries, Inc., T. Boone Pickens's takeover bid for Unocal, Inc., financier Carl Icahn's bid for Uniroyal, Inc., and Sir James Goldsmith's bid for Crown Zellerbach Corp. One of the most publicized junk bond bids was Atlanta broadcaster Ted Turner's 1985 proposal to take over CBS, Inc. Turner's own company, Turner Broadcasting System, Inc., had a net worth of only about $200 million, yet it made a run at giant CBS with a package of securities, mostly junk bonds, carrying a face value of about $5 billion.

Employee Stock Ownership Plans

Employee stock ownership plans (ESOPs) provide a source of acquisition financing with tax advantages for buyers, sellers, and lenders. Essentially, the ESOP provides a vehicle for employees to gain stock ownership in their companies. However, management participants in ESOP leveraged buy-outs often have wound up with disproportionate shares of the acquiring companies and stirred serious criticisms as to the fairness of the plans as a practical matter.

ESOP transactions are complicated, but basically work in a similar manner. A new corporation (Newco) is formed to acquire all the outstanding stock of the target corporation. The ESOP, established about the same time, then borrows from a bank to finance its acquisition of employer stock. The loan is guaranteed by Newco and is secured by the Newco stock that the ESOP has bought. This loan is treated as a liability of Newco. Newco terminates the old pension plan, recovers excess assets, and uses these funds to help finance the remaining, non-ESOP portion of the acquisition. Newco makes an annual tax-deductible contribution to the ESOP of up to 25 percent of employee compensation, and the plan uses this money to pay off its loan. Both principal and interest are tax-deductible for Newco. The bank pays taxes on only 50 percent of the interest income, which reduces the interest rate charged on the loan to the ESOP. As the loan is repaid, stock is allocated to each employee's ESOP account. When employees retire or quit, they withdraw their stock or often sell it back to the ESOP.

ESOPs have been used both to execute acquisitions and as part of defensive strategies. Dan River, Inc., Dentsply International, Inc., Blue Bell, Inc., Parsons Corp., and the Weirton Steel division of National Steel Corp. were among the businesses purchased through ESOP involvement in the mid-1980s. Defensively, the ESOP approach was proposed most notably in 1985 by Phillips Petroleum Corp. as part of its plan to fight off a hostile offer from T. Boone Pickens. On the defensive side, the company typically sells a portion of its stock to the ESOP to create a large interest that will be in hands presumably friendly to management.

Despite their advantages, ESOPs are not suitable for all transactions and may be of dubious value for companies with small workforces, poor profits, or low tax bases.

THE FINANCING CHOICES

Commercial banks, which represent the largest sources of the most orthodox acquisition financings, like the business and try to be as responsive as possible to borrowers. If necessary, billions of dollars can be mobilized and committed in days. But although the acquirer might find the bank generally willing to lend, it also must be prepared to face a rigorous and demanding due diligence process to prove that the transaction and the loan are viable. However, in the merger and acquisition environment of the 1980s, the borrower has an enormously broad range of alternatives, including private placements with institutional buyers, stock swaps, convertible securities, warrants, junk bonds, ESOPs, and commercial finance companies. The choice may well go to the heart of the success of the transaction, but the buyer-borrower must remember that financing is only part of the transaction, not the transaction itself. The most ingenious or creative financing is secondary to the critical issue of whether the acquisition makes sense strategically. That is the first question the prudent lender asks. If the answer is positive, there's a strong likelihood that the other elements of financing will fall into place.

Chapter 21

Merger Arbitrage*

Guy P. Wyser-Pratte

Executive Vice President, Prudential-Bache Securities,
New York, New York

Arbitrageurs are not investors in the formal sense of the word; that is, they are not normally buying or selling securities because of their investment value. Arbitrageurs do, however, commit capital to the "deal"—the merger, tender offer, recapitalization, etc.—rather than to the particular security. They must take positions in the deal in such a way that they are at the risk of the deal, and not at the risk of the market. They accomplish this by taking a short position in the securities being offered, as part of the deal, in exchange for the securities they purchase. So, in a merger of Company X into Company Y, the arbitrageur's investment is one of X long and Y short, or the merger of X into Y. Once they have taken this hedged position, arbitrageurs are no longer concerned with the vagaries of the marketplace—so long as the deal goes through.

There is a definite and fairly common sequence to arbitrageurs' financial analysis that allows them to arrive at investment decisions. They (1) gather information about the particular deal, (2) calculate the value of the securities offered, (3) determine the length of the time that capital should be tied up in the deal, (4) calculate the expected per-annum return on invested capital, (5) determine and weigh all the possible risks and problem areas that might preclude

---

*This chapter is excerpted from Guy P. Wyser-Pratte's monograph, "Risk Arbitrage II," published by the Salomon Brothers Center for the Study of Financial Institutions at the Graduate School of Business Administration, New York University.

consummation of the transaction, (6) assess the various tax implications and establish a tax strategy, (7) determine the amount of stock available for borrowing in order to be able to sell short, and (8) determine the amount of capital to be committed to the deal based on a careful balancing of (1) through (7) above.

GATHERING INFORMATION

The arbitrageur's task begins with the announcement of a proposed merger, which will appear in the financial press, usually *The Wall Street Journal*, or perhaps the Dow Jones or Western Union *Newswire*. The arbitrageur's first question will be: "Is this a good deal?" The question pertains not so much to the potential profitability for the arbitrageur's firm, but rather to the business logic of the merger, the quality of the two partners proposing the marriage, their record of successful marriages, the fairness of the financial terms of the merger to the shareholders of the "bride," and a postmerger pro forma evaluation of the "groom." The essential question here is: Will the deal go through?"

The answers to many of the above questions may be obtained by an analysis of the annual reports of the companies, plus the write-ups in either Moody's or Standard and Poor's Stock Records. The business logic of the merger may require deeper analysis, particularly an assessment of industry trends together with an evaluation of the financial and competitive postures of both companies within their respective industries. It is often best to hear from the companies themselves the purported reasons for their proposed merger. It is at this point that the curtain rises on one of the great comic operas of Wall Street: obtaining information from the involved companies about their proposed merger. It is indeed comic because the companies will always present a rosy prognosis for the successful consummation of their proposed marriage, while the arbitrage community, always suspicious, will, in their conversations with the companies, try to draw out the hard and cold facts about the real state of affairs: the actual stage of the negotiations as well as the matter of business logic. Because of Securities and Exchange Commission (SEC) police actions in the securities industry during the 1970s, getting answers from the companies, much less straight ones, is becoming extremely difficult. Yet, even when companies do answer, the arbitrageur must carefully read between the lines, as the companies are aware that their answers may influence an arbitrageur to buy or sell their respective securities, and managements are extremely sensitive to market price fluctuations.

Approaching companies to gather information is thus ticklish for the arbitrageurs. They must tailor their approach depending on whether they are interrogating the bride or the groom. The bride is normally totally cooperative, realizing that the arbitrageur can, by purchasing her stock, accumulate votes which will naturally be cast in favor of the merger. So, to the bride, the arbitrageur can candidly state his or her business. The groom is an entirely different matter. He will not be pleased that his stock may become the subject of constant short selling by arbitrageurs; he is thus often elusive in his responses. To counteract this, the arbitrageur must often become the "wolf in sheep's clothing," by assuming the role of the investment banker who seems to be desirous of assisting the groom with his acquisition program—both the present proposed merger and future plans. In this manner arbitrageurs ingratiate themselves with the host in order to ask those delicate questions about the pending merger negotiations. The arbitrageur may also don the garb of the institutional salesperson who is attempting to place with institutional investors the new securities that may be offered to the bride. If the salesperson is to sell those securities effectively, he or she must know the details of the merger, particularly the date when these securities will be issued, which will coincide roughly with the closing of the merger transaction. Not surprisingly, most grooms with active acquisition programs are well aware of the guises of the arbitrageur. Some cooperate, others don't. Those whose stocks will least be affected by short selling seem to cooperate most.

The information that is sought from the companies is hardly of an "inside" nature—a fact most companies do not realize—but rather has to do with the information set and related decisions that will have to be made to consummate the merger, and the current status of the information. The arbitrageur's questions, therefore, deal basically with the following:

1. The accounting treatment (purchase versus pooling)
2. The type of reorganization under the Internal Revenue Code: statutory merger, sale of assets, etc.
3. Whether a preliminary agreement has been reached, or whether the negotiations consist only of a handshake
4. If a definitive agreement has been reached, and if not, when it will be
5. Conditions under which the definitive agreement may be terminated by either party
6. Whether a formal tax ruling will be required from the IRS, or whether parties will proceed on advice of counsel
7. The approximate date the application will be made for the tax ruling
8. The approximate date that the proxy material will be filed with the SEC
9. The date the proxy material is expected to clear the SEC and be mailed to the shareholders
10. The dates for the respective shareholder meetings
11. Where the major blocks of the companies' stock are held
12. The other rulings that may be required—FCC, CAB, Maritime Board, Federal Reserve Board, ICC, Justice Department, Federal Trade Commission
13. The probable closing date

Once the arbitrageur has established the answers to some or all of the above, he or she will continuously check to verify what the companies are selling. The arbitrageur will, for example, check with the SEC to determine that the proxy material has really been filed, with the IRS to ascertain that the tax ruling application has been filed, and so forth. As the seriousness of the companies' intent to merge is corroborated by activities meeting the various requirements, the arbitrageur will become increasingly interested in either taking a position or adding to it. That the companies are serious is evidenced by the extent of the paperwork carried out.

But further evidence of the merits of the merger proposal is required. It is necessary to analyze the financial terms from both parties' points of view, to see, first, if the terms are likely to be favorably voted upon. For the bride, this entails among other things a comparison of its market price with the market value of the securities to be received; the current dividend rate with the rate to be received on the package of the groom's securities; the current earnings with the earnings represented by the securities offered by the groom; and a comparison of the growth of those earnings. Brides often find these days that they are giving up future earnings for current market value.

The groom requires a pro forma evaluation. Whether or not the groom will experience dilution now or in the future depends on the respective earnings growth rates translated through the proposed payment to be made for the bride. Too much initial dilution is something that would cause immediate concern to the arbitrageur, as would the danger of this in the future. For example, the proposed merger of C.I.T. Financial Corporation and Xerox never reached the altar due to the drag that C.I.T. was expected to cause on Xerox's future earnings.

FIGURING OF PARITIES

Hardly a day passes without the announcement of at least one or two new merger or exchange offers. As each particular deal is promulgated, an arbitrageur may or may not immediately decide to take a position. In any case, the arbitrageur must be able, with relative agility, to figure out what each package of securities is worth, for he or she is in the precarious position of having to commit the firm's capital to a high-risk situation. The total, or "work-out," value of a particular package is commonly referred to as the parity.

Packages of securities offered in all types of reorganizations are becoming increasingly difficult to calculate because of the use of warrants, debentures, sliding ratios, and so on. The moral of the story is that a deal, more often than not, is worth neither what the newspapers nor what the merger parties say it is worth. It is generally worth less. So investor beware!

DETERMINATION OF THE TIME ELEMENT

An accurate determination of how long it will take to consummate a particular arbitrage transaction is of the utmost importance to the arbitrageur, for it represents one of the key elements determining the potential return on invested capital. Determination of the probable period of time the funds will be tied up is by no means an easy task, for there are many variables involved in each of the requisite steps to complete a merger, any one of which may involve incalculable delays postponing the legal closing of the deal.

RETURN ON INVESTMENT

With the calculation of the expected dollar profit, plus an estimate of the amount of time that capital will be employed in the particular transaction, an arbitrageur can estimate the (annualized) return on investment.

THE RISKS

Prior to establishing a position in an arbitrage situation, the arbitrageur must carefully weigh the various potential risks involved. Any one of a number of elements can result in an enormous loss if the deal is not consummated, or may sharply reduce the return on investment if it is not completed according to schedule. The following are considered to be the normal risks involved during the course of merger negotiations.

Double Price Risk

Premiums ranging generally from 10 percent to even 50 percent—exceptionally even 100 percent—may be offered for acquisition targets. An arbitrageur, when taking a long position, is thereby assuming a great part of this premium in the price he or she pays. Should the deal be sabotaged for some reason, the downside price slide can be rather large. So one must carefully calculate the downside risk.[1] In addition, there is a price risk in the stock of the groom, which has been sold short. If there is a lack of liquidity in this stock there may be an equally large loss on covering the short sale. When a merger proposal is terminated, all arbitrageurs try to cover their short sales at the same time, causing an artificially higher price for the groom.[2] (If the short sales had artificially depressed the price of the groom during the period the groom was subject to arbitraging, one can assume that upon the short covering the groom will return whence it came, pari passu). In any case, the arbitrage position is a double-edged sword if the merger breaks.

Alteration of the Terms

If the exchange ratio is changed after a position has been taken, the change is likely to alter the projected profit. For example, if there was an exchange of Y common for X common, and more Y common was subsequently offered for X, it would mean greater profit. However, if in place of Y common it was decided to give Y debentures plus Y warrants, then the arbitrageur would be short Y common, which would have to be covered, possibly eliminating the profit. Naturally, less Y common for X would also result in the arbitrageur being short Y common (or short X), with an accompanying reduction in projected profit.

A Sharp Increase in the Market Price of the Groom

This will often cause the groom to feel he is perhaps paying too much for the bride, and if he tries to renegotiate a cheaper price for her, she may decide not to accept the lower offer. In any case, a sharp run-up in the groom's price causes great discomfiture to the arbitrageur, who is forced to pay a greater premium for the bride—over her investment value—as the parity, which corresponds to the price of the groom, increases. If the arbitrageur has taken a full hedge position before this run-up, then the threat of a broken deal looms ever more ominous.

A Sharp Decrease in the Groom's Market Price

The reverse situation has the bride becoming disenchanted over the diminishing value (parity) of the offer, with an eventual attempt at renegotiation.

Competing Bids

It is a nice feeling to be long on a stock that is the subject of a bidding contest. However, when one has taken the full arbitrage position, long and short, the necessity to cover the short in the face of another's bid may prove disastrous.

Shareholder Dissent

Certain shareholders of the bride may feel they are selling out too cheaply, or those of the groom may feel that they are paying too much. These feelings may lead to what are termed "nuisance suits," usually resulting in delays in the timetable.

Shareholder dissent may present a real threat when, by state law, shareholders are accorded appraisal rights on their securities. Managements of both companies will normally have set a limit on the number of shareholders who can request appraisal and payment of cash for their shares in lieu of the securities of the groom. If the limit is substantially surpassed, there is a high probability of termination of the merger agreement. This sometimes stems from the fact that the tax-free status of the merger may be endangered by the payment of too much cash.

Substantiation of Financial Warranties

The financial warranties promulgated in the definitive agreement are subject to auditing reviews. One of the usual termination clauses stipulates that there will have been no material changes in the business or financial status of Company X between the date of the execution of the contract and the date of the legal closing. There is thus the need for the accountant's "cold comfort letter" to cover this interim period. A deterioration in earnings picture of the bride may sufficiently discomfort the groom so that negotiations are terminated.

Tax Problems

There is always a chance—albeit a small one—that the IRS will render an unfavorable ruling as to the tax-free status of the merger. In addition, there are often insider tax problems, which may not be obvious but which may nevertheless sufficiently dishearten an insider about the deal so that a vote is cast against it.

Governmental Intervention

If applicable, the strongest threat is that of the Department of Justice. When the latter decides to prevent a merger, it usually gets its way. The risk is especially great because, as standard practice, the Department of Justice must request a temporary injunction to prevent the legal closing; and unfortunately for arbitrageurs, it usually chooses to do so at the "eleventh hour." The granting of the injunction is the death knell for the deal, as both parties are normally unwilling to fight lengthy and expensive court battles. The arbitrageur is indifferent to the fact that a merger may be attacked after its legal consummation. In fact, the eventuality of a court decision against a completed merger may provide additional business in the form of a divestiture, which may then become a spin-off.

The Federal Trade Commission (FTC) is another intervenor that has become more aggressive by virtue of being authorized on January 4, 1975, to represent themselves in court. In addition, FTC complaints often result in consent decrees, which are essentially out-of-court settlements.

Unusual Delays

There is always the chance that negotiations may become hopelessly bogged down, or that inexperienced officials may be handling the enormous quantities of paperwork involved, resulting in errors, legal tie-ups, and extended periods of SEC scrutiny.

Personalities

Personality clashes are always a possibility when two sets of officers, each accustomed to its own modus operandi, begin to realize that things may be done differently after the merger. Officers of the bride in particular have to be treated with just the right amount of respect, in order that they are not left with the feeling that they "had" to merge. Such respect is represented by proper jobs, appropriate titles, financial compensation, options, and so on.

AVERAGE EXPECTED RETURNS

Both a subjective and an objective element combine to formulate what to the arbitrageur is a satisfactory return, or an average expected or required return, in any given arbitrage situation.

The subjective element involves discounting the specific risks inherent in the deal. Those risks to which the arbitrageur ascribes the greatest importance are the price risk—both long and short—and the antitrust risk. The arbitrageur's discount for these two risks—and thus the required return—will be directly proportioned to his or her evaluation of the seriousness of said risks.

The objective element is the aggregate of the alternative risk arbitrage situations. Experience has shown that at a time when there is a great variety of situations in which to commit their risk capital, arbitrageurs are afforded the luxury of choosing among the available spreads, as there is less competition in the arbitrage community for a specific spread. Also, the amount of capital available to arbitrageurs as a group is fairly fixed in size over a given time span. Thus, when there are fewer attractive arbitrage deals, the same fixed capital is chasing the fewer spreads, often leading to a phenomenon referred to as "spread squeezing." This is an important factor to keep in mind, as popular brokerage clichés such as "the normal discount"—that is, spread, considered to be roughly 10 percent—will not be appropriate when referring to merger spreads in a risk arbitrage market characterized by a supply curve that has shifted upward.

Combining both the subjective and the objective element, then, what is a normal or average required rate of return?

In establishing their requirements, arbitrageurs will calculate, for a quick point of reference, the return on investment rather than on capital. The latter is normally determined only after the transaction has been consummated. Assuming then that we have a typical merger arbitrage transaction involving a standard set of risks, and furthermore that there is an ample number of attractive spreads available, arbitrageurs will require and will aim to take the long and short positions at prices that will yield a return on investment of 40 percent annum. In the final analysis, however, they are usually willing to settle for 30 percent as they will inevitably encounter unexpected delays in either the consummation of the merger or in the physical exchange of securities. Therefore, as a rule of thumb one aims at 40 percent but settles for 30 percent per annum. This does not necessarily imply that arbitrageurs will forgo a return of 20 percent. The 40 percent rate is after all only an average, and if they can obtain a rate of return of 20 percent in a transaction in which they visualize very little risk, then they will take a position so long as their financing cost is exceeded. It is, in fact, safe to say that when a spread is well below the normal rate of return for a "risk" arbitrage situation that the arbitrageurs, by collectively taking their positions, view it closer to the "riskless" variety. On the other hand, a return of 60 percent per annum may not warrant a position if it is thought that the Justice Department is lurking around the corner with an injunction request in hand, or if a stock selling at $40 is worth only $10 per share without the deal.

TAKING A POSITION

Having (1) studied the merger, (2) calculated the profit potential, (3) weighed the possible risks, and (4) compared these calculations with other arbitrage situations, an arbitrageur may decide to take a position in the subject deal. Let us assume that X is merging into Y, and that each X will get one Y in the exchange of securities, with X selling at $35 and Y at $40, and neither company will pay dividends prior to consummation. It is estimated that the merger will close four months hence, yielding a potential gross return on investment of 42.9 percent per annum before taxes, at the current prices.

$$\frac{\$40 - \$35}{\$35} \times 3 \text{ (four-month periods per year)}$$

$$= \frac{\$ 5}{\$35} \times 3 = 42.9\% \text{ per annum}$$

The size of the position which may now be taken will depend on (1) availability of capital, (2) degree of risk, (3) supply of X, (4) demand for Y, and (5) the availability of Y to be borrowed for delivery against the short sales of Y. With the Stock Exchange attentive to the "fail-to-deliver" problem, the ability to borrow stock has attained unparalleled importance, and often restricts the size of the position that may be taken when the Street supply is thin, or when Y has a small capitalization.

Selling Y short in merger arbitrage is an integral part of the position. In buying X at $35, one is also creating Y at $35, assuming that the merger is consummated. So, for all intents and purposes, one is long Y at $35 by virtue of the purchase of X. The actual price of Y—$40—is the price that must prevail at the closing of the transaction if the arbitrageur is to realize the projected profit. The only way to assure this profit is to sell Y short, thereby removing exposure to the vagaries of the marketplace. As a result of this short sale, the arbitrageur is strictly at risk of the deal, and not at the risk of the market.

A further reason for selling Y short is to realize potential tax benefits, which result in the creation of long-term capital gains, and also possibly short-term capital losses, which can offset short-term gains. This matter will be considered later in the chapter.

In actually taking a position in X long and Y short, one must carefully gauge the general market atmosphere as well as the liquidity of both X and Y. For example, if X is thin and there is a good demand for Y, it would be unwise to short Y prior to establishing the long position in X, particularly in a strong market. Similarly, in a weak market one would presumably have difficulty in shorting Y due to a need of an uptick, so that it would probably be better to short Y prior to going long X. As a general rule of thumb, it is better to short Y before buying X in a falling market, and better to buy X before shorting Y in a rising one. In a static market, the short sale should also precede the purchase.

Positioning small lots—300 to 500 shares at a time—is also a wiser course than attempting 3,000 to 5,000. The latter involves substantial market rise, unless the corresponding blocks of the "mate" are immediately available for positioning. To short 5,000 Y with only 300 X available at the desired spread would be sheer folly. And vice versa.

TURNING A POSITION

Let us again assume a share-for-share exchange of X for Y, with X at $30 and Y at $40. The merger is scheduled to be closed four months hence. An arbitrageur decides to take a position with this roughly 10-point spread, and let us say that one month later the spread has narrowed to four points. Having an unrealized profit of six points or 20 percent in one month, an arbitrageur will often turn the position, that is, close it out, rather than maintain it in order to make the remaining 13 percent, which would necessitate holding it for an additional three months.

A more delicate and precarious impetus for turning a position may develop when an arbitrageur has reason to believe that a deal will not be consummated, or that it may be delayed for a considerable period of time due to legal or antitrust complications. Arbitrageurs, if they wish to obtain the optimum prices for their long and short positions, must try to liquidate them in an unobtrusive manner. This often involves the use of "stooges," for were the arbitrage firm's name revealed on the floor of the Stock Exchange, it could well cause panic, price deterioration on the long position that is to be liquidated, and the disappearance of sellers in the case of the short position that must be covered. Bailing out of a listed stock simply involves utilizing a friendly "two-dollar broker" to execute the order. The latter is not obliged to give up the name of his or her sponsor until after the expiration of the day's trading, which is normally sufficient time to liquidate a major portion of the position. In a nonlisted stock, one must try to find a friendly over-the-counter firm that, for a commission, will try to liquidate a sponsor's position among the brethren of the arbitrage community. Every arbitrage firm has its established "stooge" to whom it can turn in such an emergency. This points out the very dangerous nature of risk arbitrage, for bad positions are often graciously turned over to one's competitors, who are presumably not aware of the problems in the deal until it too late to do anything about it. Arbitrageurs cheerfully contend that this is all part of their role; that all is fair in love, war—and arbitrage.

CONSUMMATION

In the normal course of events, after shareholder approval has been obtained, the only remaining requirement for the legal closing to occur is the receipt of a favorable tax ruling from the Internal Revenue Service. Once this has been received, the New York Stock Exchange will usually declare a "short exempt ruling" on the security, which has previously been the object of short sales.[3] This indicates that the Stock Exchange is itself satisfied that all conditions for merger between X and Y have been met and that there is practically no chance that any further complications will arise to prevent the merger. This short exempt ruling allows those investors who are long X and who wish to dispose of the shares to do so either as X, or if they prefer, in form of Y, even though in the strict legal sense X is not yet equal to Y. This ruling also permits the sale to be effected without the normally required uptick, and for private investors without a 50 percent "good faith" margin deposit. Those individual investors who henceforth buy X and simultaneously sell Y can hold both positions on margin of only 10 percent of the long position. Thus, from the time the ruling is rendered, the simultaneous purchase of X and sale of Y is recognized by the Stock Exchange as a bona fide arbitrage situation. For a member firm of the Exchange, long and short positions taken henceforth can be held in a "special arbitrage account" with a zero charge to the firm's capital.[4] In addition, the long X and short Y positions in the investment accounts no longer require a 30 percent capital charge once the short exempt ruling is delivered.

The short exempt ruling is a key factor of which few investors are aware. For if they wish to sell their X, they would often fare far better if they sell it as Y, as the X can only be sold to the discount (from parity) bid of the arbitrageur. The interesting fact is that the discount is somewhat greater than the normal commission that would be charged plus the carrying costs to be incurred pending exchange of securities. In fact, arbitrageurs do a huge volume of business after the closing of a merger by bidding over-the-counter for a newly delisted stock of the "just married" bride. The arbitrageur, by purchasing the public's X and immediately selling it as Y, cashes in on the public's indolence or ignorance.

The short exempt ruling has the additional effect of causing sudden pressure to be brought to bear on Y, as all sales of Y by arbitrageurs no longer require the uptick. Thus, often just as a merger is completed, there is an appreciable price erosion in Y. This pressure is strictly technical and usually abates once all the floating X is taken out of circulation. This artificial pressure is something that predictably coincides with merger closings, and may provide excellent buying opportunities for the shrewd investor.

TAX STRATEGY

An important reason for selling Y short is to derive certain tax benefits. The short sale gives the arbitrageur some strategic options in the qualitative, that is, after-tax returns of not only the department but of the firm as well. This potential benefit arises from the fact that the shares of two companies—X and Y—planning to merge are, as a rule of thumb, considered to be not substantially identical for tax purposes until the shareholders actually vote favorably on the merger proposal. Thus, if X and Y are respectively bought and sold in separate investment accounts prior to shareholder approvals, they are considered to be not substantially identical.

Between the date of the shareholders' meeting and the day when the New York Stock Exchange will declare Y "short exempt" (which signifies that there is no longer any risk involved and that holders of X may, if they wish, sell X in form of Y without the uptick and related margin requirements), there may exist a gray area as to whether or not securities are substantially identical. The Treasury Regulations say that this is to be judged on the basis of "the facts and circumstances in each case" and suggest as guidelines "the relative values, price changes and other circumstances." Even though shareholders have approved a merger, such approval does not necessarily render the securities substantially identical especially where there is still opposition to the merger by dissenting shareholders or government authority. Thus, if one wishes to continue building the position in X long and Y short, it should be done in a separate, or "number 2" investment account. Then, should the IRS take the position that X and Y were substantially identical during the latter period, it could be argued that the "number 2" account functioned as an "arbitrage account."

In the normal course of events, when there is little likelihood or further problems after shareholder approval has been obtained, so that X and Y are most assuredly substantially identical, any further positions should be placed in a "special arbitrage account" so as not to endanger the positions in the investment accounts of X and Y. Any gains or losses resulting from the special arbitrage accounts are naturally short-term. There exists the danger, however, that purchases in the special arbitrage account may contaminate short sales of Y in the investment account. This danger can be minimized by closing the positions in the special arbitrage accounts prior to closing those in the investment accounts. Also, care should be taken to leave no net short position in the arbitrage account at the close of any business day.

A long-term capital gain can be created in the X and Y investment accounts simply by establishing the requisite one-year holding period. When the merger is consummated, X is exchanged for securities of Y, so that the resulting positions in the two investment accounts are Y long and Y short. When the requisite holding period is attained, the arbitrageur is in the highly desirous position of having two alternatives. First, if Y is higher than $40 (recalling that we sold Y at that price)—let us say $45—then he or she can, on succeeding days, buy Y and sell Y until the Y long and Y short positions are completely closed out. In this manner, the Y long (formerly X) is sold for a long-term capital gain greater than the initial five-point spread. The covering of the Y short position results in the recognition of a short-term capital loss, which can be utilized to offset short-term capital gains of the arbitrage department and also for the firm. The net economic gain is still the initial five-point spread per share, but the character of the gain and loss is significantly different.

Second, if after the requisite holding period, Y is below $40, so that it would not be advantageous to reverse the positions as above (indeed, reversing would produce a long-term capital loss and a short-term capital gain), then the arbitrageur can record a long-term capital gain simply by pairing off the Y long and Y short positions with a journal entry.

The same general procedure as outlined above would be employed if, let us say, instead of an exchange of Y for X there would be a new issue of Y convertible preferred offered in exchange for X. In this case, the arbitrageur would, before the shareholders' meetings, go long X and short the amount of Y common represented by Y convertible preferred, so as to hedge the market risk in the new issue. After consummation and the exchange of securities, the accounts would show Y convertible preferred long and Y common short. The position is then held open for the requisite period, after which the arbitrageur simply converts and pairs off the positions or reverses them depending on market price relationships.

The closing out of positions in the marketplace for tax purposes thus produces increased activity in the securities for the former groom. Many arbitrage firms may be doing this during approximately the same time span as their respective positions attain long-term maturity. Their aggregate interaction in such cases will lend additional liquidity to the marketplace, particularly in a taxable year in which there are large arbitrage short-term gains to offset.

NOTES

[1]Reference to technical charts and knowledge of the probable size of the arbitrage community's positions are helpful indicators in determining the downside risk.

[2]A clue to the magnitude of this potential danger may be found in the monthly "short interest" figures published by both the New York and the American Stock Exchanges.

[3]New York Stock Exchange rules.

[4]Ibid.

Part 5

Finishing Touches

Chapter 22

Closing Services

Robert E. Shields

Partner, Drinker Biddle & Reath, Philadelphia, Pennsylvania

The negotiations were long and patience sometimes short. But, finally, the acquisition agreement is signed. Corks pop, bubbles flow, and off the parties go: the investment bankers to arrange another deal; the executives to explain the transaction to their key people; the managers to begin planning in earnest.

But some important tasks must be accomplished before the merger can close. The deal must be announced and reported to various agencies. The warranties in the merger agreement must be tested. Consents and approvals must be obtained. Shareholder meetings must be held. Various other conditions to closing the transaction must be satisfied.

REPORTING THE NEWS

Because of the possibility that a third party will try a hostile tender offer once it becomes known that the target is for sale, the negotiated acquisition normally proceeds to the executed agreement stage in complete secrecy. In some cases, however, disclosure requirements of securities law may, depending on the circumstances, have prompted an earlier announcement that negotiations were underway. But when the definitive agreement has been signed—possibly along with a "lock-up" option on a controlling block of stock or a crown jewel—the time for a public announcement has clearly arrived.

Good business practice, stock exchange requirements, and risks of legal liability all prompt timely and controlled dissemination of the news of the impending acquisition. There are frequently good business reasons for delaying a public announcement until key managers, union officials, customers, suppliers, and others can be informed. But once the news gets beyond the small group involved in the negotiations, it spreads like wildfire. The largely uncontrollable factor is the public securities market, which operates from 10 A.M. to at least 4 P.M. Eastern time. Securities exchanges do not look favorably upon requests for trading suspensions after a definitive agreement has been signed. Accordingly, it is important that any communications to key constituencies prior to public announcement be distributed on a carefully planned basis after the close of trading on the day the agreement is signed and before the market opens the next morning.

A carefully worded press release can explain the rationale for the transaction to securities analysts and reduce the risk of interference from outside interests. Thus, drafting of the announcement should not be left to the very last minute. Key executive, financial relations, and legal representatives of the buyer and seller should begin work on the press release when the definitive agreement reaches the final stages of negotiation. Although the rationale for the transaction can be explained to some extent in the press release, securities laws constraints on premature proxy solicitation and "gun jumping" (if securities are to be issued by the acquiring company) will prevent the parties from going too far.

DEALING WITH THE REGULATORS

The circumstances of each acquisition determine the reports that must be filed with various governmental agencies. Most sizable acquisitions must be reported to the Federal Trade Commission (FTC) and the Department of Justice under the Hart-Scott-Rodino Antitrust Improvements Act. The Hart-Scott-Rodino report must include extensive detailed information on both the acquirer and the target. This report gives the FTC or the Justice Department—depending on which agency assumes primary responsibility for assessing the combination—an opportunity to review antitrust aspects. The acquisition may not proceed for 30 days following submission of the report unless the time period is accelerated by the FTC or Justice. Moreover, a new 30-day period begins if the information is not complete and the agency requests additional data.

A lock-up option on a public company obtained in connection with the definitive agreement normally will necessitate the prompt filing by the acquirer of a Schedule 13D with the Securities and Exchange Commission (SEC). The target also may be required to file a report with the SEC because the grant of the option may constitute a change in control.

In regulated industries, governmental approvals of the acquisition may be required. In the case of a bank acquisition, for example, it normally is necessary to obtain the approval of the Federal Reserve Board under the Bank Holding

Company Act. Approval of the Comptroller of the Currency in the case of a national bank, or an appropriate state banking official in the case of a state-chartered bank, also is required. Following those approvals, the parties must wait for at least another 30 days for the transaction to be reviewed by the Justice Department under the Bank Merger Act. Acquisitions of other regulated businesses such as insurance companies will involve similar application and approval processes. If either party is an insurance holding company with significant operations in several states, it may be necessary to get approval from officials in each state.

Planning is the key, particularly when regulatory approvals are required. Attention to the regulatory requirements aspect in the early stages of the transaction can pay handsome rewards. Background briefings of key regulators promptly after the transaction is announced may uncover concern about a relatively minor aspect of the deal. Armed with insight into the thinking of regulators, the parties may well be able to make relatively modest changes in the structure of the transaction and thereby garner prompt regulatory approval that will expedite consummation.

TESTING THE WARRANTIES

The typical acquisition agreement contains a number of representations and warranties whose functions are twofold. First, a material breach of a warranty by one party will give the other party a justification not to proceed with closing the deal. Second, a breach by the seller that is discovered by the buyer after the closing may give the buyer a right to financial recompense.

Between the signing of the agreement and the closing, the major focus is on the first function of the warranties, namely, whether there is a material undisclosed problem that causes the buyer to change its mind about the acquisition. Once the transaction is closed, realistically it cannot be undone. Thus the last chance to avoid a terrible mistake may be diligent investigation between the signing and the closing. The usual emphasis is on the buyer's testing of the seller's warranties. When the seller's shareholders are receiving the acquirer's securities, testing of the buyer's warranties also can be important.

The extent of the investigation between signing and closing will depend on the amount of work done before the agreement is signed. If a privately held company is being acquired, the parties may have enjoyed the luxury of extensive investigation of the seller by the buyer before the agreement is signed. At the other extreme, the buyer may be a "white knight" brought in at the last moment to rescue the seller from an undesired takeover. The white knight's investigation may not begin until after the agreement is signed. Many transactions fall in between. What is important, however, is that the investigation be completed prior to the closing.

Financial and Business Investigations

The aspects of the target for which warranties should be obtained can be divided into financial, business, and legal segments. Investigation of the financial areas may be limited to testing warranties concerning previously reported operating results and statements of financial condition. Alternatively, the transaction may be structured so that the results of an audit conducted after signing of the agreement are critical to the pricing of the deal. Even if the financial and business investigations have been substantially completed before the agreement is signed, the figures can be updated and the buyer can obtain a more comprehensive understanding of the seller's business between signing and closing.

Legal Investigations

Exactly what aspects of the business are covered by the legal investigation will vary from transaction to transaction. In most cases, however, the investigation will begin with the organization of the corporation and its subsidiaries. Was there full compliance with the legal formalities in connection with organizing each of the corporations? Was all of the stock properly issued? Were any preemptive rights honored in connection with issuing additional shares? Does the seller own all of the stock of each of its subsidiaries? Investigation of these matters will necessitate review of the documents on file with the secretary of state in the jurisdiction in which the seller is incorporated and examination of the minute books and stock books of the target company and its subsidiaries. Review of the minute books may reveal references to other material matters that were not previously known to the buyer, thus necessitating further investigation.

The legal review also will entail examination of material papers relating to pending litigation against the target company, and it will include review of any consent orders or decrees by which prior litigation or governmental investigations were resolved. Agreements to adopt, or to refrain from, certain business practices that resolved prior litigation may have a disastrous impact if they become applicable to the acquiring company. The investigation of pending or threatened litigation against the company being acquired will extend into a review of law compliance programs. If the target company's attitude toward regulatory matters, such as environmental and OSHA requirements, is to attempt to control fires when they flare, significant further investigation may be warranted. But if the target company has an active legal compliance program, the buyer may feel less need to conduct a detailed investigation.

The legal investigation should extend to the various benefit plans of the target company. Failure to update benefit plans promptly so they comply with the frequent changes in applicable laws may have a significant financial impact.

The various instruments governing the indebtedness of the acquired company should be reviewed very carefully. If the indebtedness is to be kept in place after the acquisition, careful review of the instruments will be necessary to ensure that consent of the lender is not necessary or that the appropriate consent has been obtained. Important advantageous contracts also must be reviewed to determine that the transaction will not adversely affect contractual relationships. In most cases, investigation of these subjects will be made before signing of the agreement as a part of the process for deciding on the structure of the transaction.

Careful review must be given—particularly in acquisitions of privately owned companies—to relationships between the target company and interested managers or shareholders. Typical "boilerplate" warranties that there are no self-dealing transactions may have been given unthinkingly by the company being acquired. In a related area, it is extremely important for the acquirer to be certain that it is acquiring the totality of the business. If, for example, there is an important contract between the target and one of its shareholders that is terminable upon short notice, the situation will have to be resolved to the satisfaction of the acquiring company.

Depending on the circumstances, there are several other legal aspects that might be investigated, including title to properties, liens on real and personal property, and the nature and extent of insurance coverage, to name some.

Finding Surprises

The testing of the warranties frequently uncovers minor surprises. Fringe benefit programs may not have been amended to reflect the latest legislative changes. The lien structure on the target's assets may not be precisely as warranted. What the seller perceived as labor peace may be seen by the acquirer as serious rumblings. In rare circumstances, the surprise is major. The result is either abandonment of the acquisition or renegotiation of the financial terms.

Another major task is satisfaction of various conditions that must occur before the closing can take place. Generally the conditions that must be satisfied are that:

- The warranties be correct when made and continue to be correct at the closing.
- The target company has refrained from engaging in certain actions pending the closing.
- Various other specified events have occurred as prescribed in the agreement.

MONITORING THE COVENANTS

Many acquisitions involve a substantial delay between signing of the agreement and closing. The principal reasons for the delay are normally the need for stockholder, and perhaps regulatory, approval. The acquiring company usually wants to preserve the status quo during this interim period. Accordingly, the acquisition agreement normally restrains the ability of the target company to make changes in its capitalization or business between the signing and the closing.

The company to be acquired generally is prevented from issuing additional equity securities unless they are pursuant to existing commitments. Departures from current dividend policy are restrained. Significant business or asset acquisitions or dispositions normally are prohibited. Charter amendments are restricted. Changes in compensation or fringe benefits for key personnel often are restricted. Frequently the target company agrees to operate only in the ordinary course of business and in accordance with past practice. Capital expenditures or commitments often are restricted. The company to be acquired frequently agrees to continue its current insurance coverage. Many agreements prohibit the target from creating additional liens on assets.

Managers are not accustomed to operating under those types of restrictions. Accordingly, it is important that new procedures be implemented to ensure that the restrictions will be honored. Many of the prohibited transactions are so extraordinary that board approval would be required under normal circumstances. Restrictions on these activities easily can be implemented at the board level. Other restrictions—for example, a general prohibition against engaging in transactions outside the ordinary course of business—require implementation at lower levels in the organization. Because a prohibition on transactions not in the ordinary course of business can become a subjective issue, interpretation and explanation of the restrictions are necessary. Responsibility for instituting these control procedures falls on the officials of the target company.

The restrictions are normally subject to the proviso that any of the otherwise prohibited transactions may be permitted with the consent of the acquiring company. Therefore, it is important to designate an appropriate executive in the acquiring company who can deal with requests for approvals of restricted transactions. If there is doubt about whether a transaction requires approval, consent routinely should be sought from the buyer.

OBTAINING CONSENTS

Besides regulatory approval, many transactions also require consents of private third parties. To a large extent, the structure of the transaction will determine the number of third-party consents required. If the transaction involves a sale of assets and assumption of liabilities, it is likely that a number of third-party consents will be required. The need for such consents results largely because many contracts may not be assigned without the consent of another party to the contract.

In a sale of assets, the assets to be transferred often include rights under existing contracts. Many leases provide that they may not be assigned without the consent of the lessor. Similarly, equipment lease adjustments normally require the lessor's consent for assignment. Bank loan and other financing agreements require the lender's consent for substituting the acquiring company as the obligor on the indebtedness. Supply and sales contracts may require consents for assignments. In fact, the need for so many consents to assignment— and the possibility that important consents may not be given or that they may be given only if a price is paid—is a factor that causes many transactions to be structured as mergers rather than asset sales. Agreements for sales of assets frequently contain a provision that if a third-party consent is required but not obtained, the selling company will retain the asset and endeavor to make its benefits available to the acquiring firm.

Merger transactions frequently require fewer consents than sales-of-assets transactions. Although many contracts require the consent of another party for assignment of the contract, most do not require such consents in changes of ownership. In a merger, the contract remains in place. All that has changed is ownership of the stock of one contracting party. Some contracts, however, are written to require consent of the other party in the case of a change in ownership even if the change is accomplished by merger. Thus, it is important that contracts be reviewed and that appropriate consents be obtained.

The structuring of the transaction will be determined only after a review of all material factors. Tax ramifications, protection of the acquiring company against undisclosed liabilities, regulatory approval, and the need for third-party consents are all important. The merger structure frequently is chosen, however, principally because the need for third-party consents is minimized.

Although state laws usually require shareholders of both companies to approve a merger, approval by shareholders of the acquirer (if not required by controlling law or stock exchange policy) easily can be eliminated by the use of the subsidiary merger. In this structure, the acquiring company forms a subsidiary which is then merged with the company to be acquired. Approval of the shareholders of the target company still is required. But shareholder approval on the buyer's side will be sufficient if the parent corporation of the acquiring subsidiary delivers its endorsement.

COMPLETING FINANCING ARRANGEMENTS

If the purchase price is payable entirely or partially in cash, the acquiring company may borrow the money. A loan commitment obtained when the agreement was signed must be converted into a formal loan agreement by closing. Necessary consents or approvals for the borrowing must be obtained, and preparations must be made for closing the loan transaction concurrently with the closing of the acquisition.

If the stock of the target company is selling at a substantial discount from the merger price, or if the acquiring company wishes to reduce the dilution that will result from issuing its securities in the merger, the buyer will acquire target company stock in the open market. Care must be taken to give full consideration to the accounting, tax, and securities regulation aspects of such purchases. For example, pooling-of-interests accounting may be adversely affected by open-market purchases of target company stock. The partially tax-free nature of a combined stock and cash acquisition may be destroyed if too much target company common stock is purchased in the open market. Depending on the timing of the purchases and the formula (if any) in the merger agreement for pricing the transaction, open-market purchases of the target company stock by the acquiring company may violate the SEC's Rule 10b-6. That rule is designed to prevent issuers from supporting the price of their stock when a stock issuance is imminent.

The target company may have outstanding publicly held preferred stock or debt securities. If the merger agreement contemplates that these securities will remain outstanding, no action is required. On the other hand, particularly if the securities are convertible into the target's common stock, the agreement may require that they be called for redemption. If so, appropriate arrangements must be made for giving the requisite advance notice of the call and paying the redemption price of any unconverted securities. If the conversion provisions in the securities provide that after a merger the convertible securities will be exchanged for acquiring company stock based on the merger ratio, a call may not be required.

If the target's bank debt will remain outstanding after the acquisition, it frequently is necessary to deal with the target's lenders even if the transaction is structured as a merger. Financial convenants or change of control or other provisions in the loan agreement may require consent of the lenders in the target's sale. A simple written consent by lenders may suffice, but it may be necessary to make extensive revisions of the loan agreement. The documentation must be in place by the time of the closing.

THE PROXY STATEMENT

If the securities of the company being acquired are relatively widely held, it is necessary to prepare a proxy statement describing the proposed acquisition. When these securities are registered under the Securities Exchange Act, proxy materials must be filed with the SEC or, in the case of a bank, the appropriate banking regulator.

In an acquisition not requiring regulatory approval, the preparation of the proxy statement and the obtaining of shareholder approval are frequently the principal factors responsible for the delay between the signing of the agreement and the closing. If the parties wish to reduce the interim period, preparation of the proxy statement should commence at the earliest possible date. If both the acquiring and acquired companies file annual and other periodic reports with the SEC, much of the proxy statement may consist of material already contained in the most recent annual reports, although it must be updated in some respects to the date of the proxy statement. The principal additional information will be the description of the proposed merger and its background and, in many cases, pro forma financial statements reflecting the acquisition.

The proxy statement normally must contain extensive information about the proposed acquisition transaction and about the company being acquired. If securities are being issued by the acquirer, the proxy statement also will contain a description of the securities and of the acquiring company. Unless the securities being issued in the merger are exempt from registration under the Securities Act of 1933 (for example, because they are being issued by a bank or issued after a hearing on the fairness of the transaction by a state regulator), the acquiring company is required to file a registration statement registering the securities under the Securities Act. The proxy statement generally is the major part of any such registration statement.

Because preliminary proxy material is not publicly available, it is customary to file the documents with the SEC in the form of preliminary proxy material and to obtain the SEC staff's initial comments. The document then is revised and filed as a publicly available registration statement under the Securities Act. If the SEC staff comments have been responded to adequately, the registration statement is declared effective shortly after it is filed. The proxy statement, which comprises the bulk of the registration statement, then is mailed to the shareholders.

Approval by the acquirer's shareholders also may be required if mandated by state law or the policies of the securities exchange on which the acquiring company's securities are listed. However, directors of the acquiring company may wish to obtain shareholder approval even though it is not legally necessary.

When approval by both shareholder groups is sought, the custom is to prepare a joint proxy statement that will be used by both companies.

As noted earlier, if the acquiring company is issuing securities in connection with the acquisition, the proxy statement also must be filed with the SEC as a registration statement. Normally, the issuance of securities by the acquiring company—particularly if they are not listed on a national securities exchange—will require filings with various regulators under state securities or "blue sky" laws. These filings must be closely coordinated to ensure that the proxy materials can be mailed to all shareholders promptly upon the effectiveness of the SEC registration statement.

ARRANGING THE SHAREHOLDERS MEETING

When the schedule for receiving SEC staff comments on the proxy material becomes clear, shareholder meeting and record dates can be finalized. Normally, the proxy statement will be mailed approximately 30 days in advance of the meeting to permit as many shareholders as possible to vote.

Because of increasing institutionalization of the securities markets and use of securities depositories in recent years, large percentages of the shares of many companies are held for customers of banks and brokers in nominee names. Although nominees are entitled under state laws to vote shares held in their names, members of national securities exchanges are prohibited by exchange rules from voting on merger transactions without instructions from the beneficial owners. Thus, at the time this chapter is written, it is necessary for corporations to send proxy statements to the brokerage firms and for those firms to redistribute the materials to the beneficial owners and solicit their instructions. Pending regulatory changes could eliminate this bottleneck in most cases by giving the corporation the names and addresses of the beneficial owners, plus permitting direct mailing.

SMOOTHING THE EDGES

If the target company has a stock option plan, appropriate arrangements must be made to terminate the options or to convert them into options to purchase the acquiree's securities based on the merger ratio. Many option plans permit such substitutions or allow directors of the target to terminate the options if they are not exercised by the merger date.

When the acquisition involves the issuance of securities that are to be listed on a securities exchange, appropriate listing applications must be filed by the acquirer. Normally the listing application will consist essentially of the proxy statement for the merger. It is important, however, that the listing application be filed early to obtain exchange comments and allow sufficient time for formal exchange approval before closing.

If the parties wish a tax ruling from the Internal Revenue Service, it must be sought well in advance. As time for the closing approaches, they should contact the IRS for a formal ruling before the closing date.

Trading in the stock of the company being acquired usually continues until the time of closing. It is important that the appropriate securities exchanges, or the National Association of Securities Dealers (NASD) in the case of over-the-counter securities, be notified of the contemplated timetable for closing the transaction, particularly as the time for closing approaches. The exchange or the NASD will arrange for the necessary termination of trading in the target company securities.

Whether securities or cash are being issued, the target's shareholders are required to surrender their share certificates before receiving payment. A form of transmittal letter and accompanying instructions usually are mailed to shareholders of the acquired company immediately after closing. They must be prepared in advance and be ready for printing and mailing when the deal is finalized.

CLOSING ARRANGEMENTS

If no further regulatory approvals are required, the acquisition is accomplished by the delivery and filing of documents at a closing meeting held promptly after the shareholder approvals. Often the closing is held on the same day as the shareholders meeting. In many cases, all of the documents have been signed and packaged the day before the formal closing. This procedure is adopted to ensure that all goes smoothly at the closing and that it is over quickly.

The preclosing is the name given to the meeting—normally the day before closing—at which the closing documents are reviewed and signed, but not delivered. Typically, documents will have been agreed to by exchanges of drafts between representatives of the merger partners over an extended period before the preclosing.

Merger and Transfer Certificates

The closing documents will, of course, include the operative acquisition instruments. In the case of a merger, the key instrument is the articles or certificate of merger, put into a form that is appropriate for filing with the secretaries of state in the states where the merging companies are incorporated. Executed copies of the articles or certificates of merger frequently are signed at the preclosing and delivered to agents of the acquiring and acquired companies in the appropriate state capitals. They are filed upon receipt of telephone instructions after the closing has been completed.

In an assets transaction, the operative documents are the instruments under which the assets are transferred and the liabilities are assumed. Generally these instruments include a bill of sale, an assumption-of-liabilities agreement, and various collateral documents assigning other assets not included within the bill of sale. Such collateral documents could include deeds of real estate; assignments of leases; assignments of patents, trademarks, and copyrights; assignments of titles to motor vehicles; assignments of unemployment compensation and similar accounts; and transfers of deposits from the target's bank account to the buyer's.

Counsel's Opinions

Opinions of counsel for both companies always are among the collateral documents. Normally the contents of the opinions are specified in the acquisition agreement, but the acquisition agreement often calls for opinions from attorneys in several geographic areas on questions of local law. Timely delivery of these opinions is important to a smooth closing.

Comfort Letters

Most acquisition agreements call for the delivery of so-called comfort letters by the independent accountants for the company being acquired. Comfort letters usually state in substance that the accountants:

- Based on a recent review that does not constitute an audit, have no reason to believe that the financial statements of the acquired company are not presented in accordance with generally accepted accounting principles consistently applied;
- Have no reason to believe that specified financial or statistical information concerning the acquired company in the proxy statement is not in accordance with the company's books and records; and
- Have no reason to believe that there has been a decline in the earnings of the target (compared with the corresponding period in the prior year) or a decline in specified balance sheet items from those shown in the proxy statement.

If securities of the acquiring company are being issued, the acquisition agreement normally will provide for the issuance of a similar comfort letter by its independent accountants.

Collateral Documents

Other collateral documents typically are certificates of:

- Appropriate state officials, as to the good standing of the acquired company and its subsidiaries in their states of incorporation and states in which they do business;
- Corporate secretaries, as to the adoption of resolutions by their directors and shareholders approving the deal;
- Principal officers, that the representations and warranties continue to be true and correct and that all covenants have been complied with; and
- Corporate secretaries, concerning the incumbency, signatures, and authority of the officers executing the operative and collateral documents.

The closing documents also may include escrow agreements, employment contracts, resignations of the directors and officers, and, in asset sales, an amendment of the seller's certificate of incorporation to change its name.

When securities are used, individuals who may be deemed to be controlling persons of the target usually are required to deliver letters acknowledging that resale of the securities is subject to the limitations imposed by Rule 145 under the Securities Act of 1933—principally that stock sales not exceed approximately 1 percent of the total stock outstanding in any three-month period. If pooling-of-interest accounting is involved, the letters also contain a barrier to resale of the securities until publication of an interim earnings statement that includes operating results of the acquired company.

AT THE FINISH LINE

If all goes well at the preclosing, the documents are executed and packaged. This permits the closing to consist of simply a handshake and acknowledgment by both sides that the deal is done. In securities transactions, even arrangements for the issuance of the securities will be made at the preclosing. If the purchase price is payable in cash, however, the custom is to have the cash delivered by wire transfer on the day of closing. Unfortunately, wire transfers of funds often do not arrive as rapidly as desired. Corporate treasurers should monitor the transfer process to avoid situations in which many frustrated executives and professionals sit around a conference table awaiting confirmation of the receipt of wired funds.

With good planning and hard work, all necessary matters will be accomplished by the time of preclosing. All of the documents have been signed and packaged. The next morning the shareholders meet and approve the acquisition. Blessedly the funds arrive on time. The parties shake hands. The deal is closed. Corks pop, bubbles flow, and off they go.

Chapter 23

Forms and Paperwork

Alan H. Molod

Partner, Wolf, Block, Schorr & Solis-Cohen,
Philadelphia, Pennsylvania

When negotiations on a proposed acquisition reach the point of agreement, the lawyer faces an elaborate process of document drafting to reflect the terms of the transaction. Whether the acquisition takes the form of a merger, stock purchase, asset purchase, or some complex combination or variation, the fundamental document is the acquisition agreement itself, setting forth the terms and conditions of the agreement between the parties. Sometimes it is preceded by a brief and often rather general document known as a letter of intent, which describes the basic intention of the parties to accomplish an acquisition. The acquisition agreement often is accompanied or followed by a variety of documents required by federal and state laws regulating acquisitions, as well as a variety of documents pertaining to the acquisition agreement itself.

THE LETTER OF INTENT

The use of a letter of intent in an acquisition is optional. The typical letter of intent expresses the intention of the parties to accomplish the transaction. It states the agreed-upon or approximate purchase price, the nature of the consideration to be paid (cash, property, debt securities, or equity securities), employment arrangements, noncompetition covenants, the obligation of the potential buyer to hold in confidence certain matters learned during its investigation, and the various conditions to consummation of the transaction. Usually, the letter of intent will state that it is not a binding document. Typical language may state, "This letter is a letter of intent only and is not binding upon the parties. A purchase and sale of the business shall become binding only upon the execution and delivery by the parties of a formal acquisition agreement satisfactory in content and form to the parties." A general letter of intent might merely acknowledge the intent to enter into an acquisition transaction and state that the precise price, structure, and mode of payment are among the matters to be agreed to, after the buyer's further investigation of the business to be purchased.

Conversely, a letter of intent can be quite specific as to price, payment terms, and other important matters. A highly detailed letter may provide that the only condition to the transaction's becoming binding is the preparation of formal documents setting forth the terms in the letter of intent. These documents would contain the warranties, representations, and agreements customarily contained in such acquisition agreements. Indeed, a letter of intent may go as far as to provide that the transaction is binding, commiting both parties to proceed in good faith (often with a specific timetable) to create and execute formal acquisition documents containing customary representations, warranties, and agreements, and committing the seller not to negotiate with any other parties for the sale of the business. Letters of intent are often binding in certain limited respects only, such as commitments to maintain certain matters in confidence, to consult before issuing press releases, to refrain from negotiating with others, and so on.

Why a Letter of Intent Is Needed

Why have a letter of intent? For the party most anxious to have the transaction consummated, the letter of intent creates a certain moral obligation that many business people will respect. It also provides a sound basis for setting fundamental terms, thus acting to minimize friction and disagreement about such terms during negotiation of the formal acquisition documents. For the party that is least anxious for the transaction and is being "courted" by the other side, the letter offers an opportunity to gain concessions in writing that might be harder to get when the finer details are being worked out. The letter of intent also is a signal that an appropriate point has been reached for disclosing an agreement in principle to people beyond the direct negotiators. If a publicly held company is involved, the signing of the letter generally permits announcement of the news to the public to avoid problems of insider trading. Timing is an important matter in a public disclosure. Premature announcement of a proposed acquisition, especially if the transaction falls through, might be considered manipulative of a company's securities. But undue delay can result in improper insider trading and rumor-based trading of the securities. Thus, a written letter of intent is a convenient and appropriate device for triggering a public announcement. Even companies without publicly traded securities must be concerned with the impact on business from rumors that reach its employees, customers, suppliers, financing sources, and others.

However, if formal acquisition agreements can be prepared and entered into promptly after the agreement in principle, it often is desirable to forgo a letter of intent. Transactions still can be abandoned following execution of a letter of intent, and a deal that is aborted after public disclosure can be embarrassing and even harmful to one or both parties. Such embarrassment usually can be avoided if the parties make their announcement after entering into a formal acquisition agreement, as the likelihood that the transaction will be consummated is substantially higher than at the letter-of-intent stage. From a buyer's standpoint, although a public announcement creates pressure on a seller to consummate, it also announces to the world the availability of the seller and thus can trigger competitive offers.

THE ACQUISITION AGREEMENT

The acquisition agreement, to reiterate, is the basic document with respect to an acquisition. Generally, closing takes place days or months after execution of the acquisition agreement. This document spells out all of the conditions that must be met before a closing can take place, although some acquisitions close simultaneously with signing of the agreement.

Acquisition agreements customarily are drafted by counsel for the buyer. From a seller's standpoint, an acquisition agreement can be very simple, ideally a one-page bill of sale conveying the assets or corporate shares on an "as is" basis in return for a bank check representing the entire purchase price. The buyer, on the other hand, is not fully familiar with what it will receive in the form of assets, business relationships, personnel capabilities, and other facets of the acquired business. Consequently, when drafted by counsel for the buyer, an acquisition agreement often is quite extensive. The largest part of the agreement deals with various representations and warranties of the seller about the nature and condition of the business and assets being sold. The counsel doing the first draft of an acquisition agreement or any collateral document (such as an employment contract, lease of real estate not being acquired, etc.) has a strong psychological advantage over opposing counsel. Many changes that the opposing counsel might wish to make, and they often are numerous, might be dismissed by the drafting attorney as nitpicking even when they are justified. Thus, the side that is not doing the actual drafting may have to overcome considerable resistance in trying to insert legitimate terms favorable to its position.

Contents of the Agreement

The acquisition agreement generally contains:

- A statement of the purpose of the transaction
- A list of definitions of terms in the agreement
- A description of the assets or shares to be sold and the selling price
- Representations, warranties, and agreements of both the buyer and the seller

- Provisions on the conduct of the target business between the agreement and closing dates
- Conditions precedent to the obligation of each party to close
- Identification of the time and place of closing, along with an itemization of the documents and other material to be delivered by the parties at closing
- An indemnification provision often specifying procedures for resolving disputes, particularly breaches of seller's representations and warranties
- Covenants restricting postacquisition competition by the sellers or controlling stockholders of a corporate seller
- Miscellaneous matters such as escrow provisions, provision for payment of brokerage commissions, and conventional "boilerplate" provisions dealing with choice of law, notices, and other matters.

Representations and Warranties

In negotiating the terms of an acquisition agreement, the buyer must be concerned with the nature of the seller's representations and warranties. They generally are very broad and comprehensive. Even a seller that is very familiar with its own business inadvertently can overlook certain conditions and circumstances that actually exist but, on the basis of the warranties, are claimed to be nonexistent. If disclosed at the time of the signing, many of these matters might be accepted by the buyer without any effect on the purchase price. But if they are discovered after closing, they can constitute a breach of warranty and lead the buyer to demand a reduction in the price. Often, the seller may not be aware of any problems, such as a claim that was asserted only after the business changed hands. But the seller still is at risk if its representations and warranties are not limited strictly to circumstances within its knowledge.

Two matters almost always are subject to negotiation in the area of the seller's representations and warranties. They concern whether various representations are limited to the "knowledge of the seller" and whether the representations are limited to those that are "material." The honest seller that discloses everything it knows, except perhaps nonmaterial matters, wants to have no postclosing liability. Moreover, a seller can seek to minimize postclosing liability by negotiating a damages "basket" arrangement, under which the buyer agrees to absorb a certain amount of damages from breach of warranty before asserting claims against the seller. But, typically, a buyer will want to have the purchase price reduced if the business is not exactly as represented, regardless of whether the seller knew of any problems or whether such problems are material.

A buyer's draft acquisition agreement usually provides that all representations and warranties of the seller must be true at closing, or the buyer is not obligated to close. Taken literally, such an instrument can be little more than a buyer's option to purchase the business. For example, a multimillion dollar acquisition may contain a seller's representation that the business being sold is not a defendant in any litigation. If, on the morning scheduled for closing, a $1,000 nuisance suit is instituted, the acquisition agreement, if read literally, can permit the buyer to avoid closing. Sophisticated sellers therefore negotiate for materiality qualifications, for variations from the warranties and representations because of events that occur in the ordinary course of business, and, often, for a provision that closing must take place even in the case of certain material breaches, with a part of the price to be set aside pending resolution of the amount of damage created by such breaches.

The Disclosure Schedule

Practitioners often abandon conventional representations and warranties in favor of a separate disclosure schedule that is warranted by the seller for accuracy. Rather than build 20 to 30 pages of warranties and representations into the acquisition agreement and attach 15 to 20 supporting exhibits, the negotiators will settle on a warranty that the disclosure schedule initialed by the parties is true and correct. This disclosure schedule often is many pages longer than the acquisition agreement itself. It sets forth all of the representations and warranties desired by the buyer of the seller, and often provides for attachment of material documents such as leases, major contracts, and so on.

There are advantages to using a disclosure schedule. If the parties wish to move quickly, the purchaser's counsel can generate a discussion draft acquisition agreement much more promptly if the representations and warranties are omitted (although a first draft of an acquisition agreement can, of course, make provision for subsequent insertion of representations and warranties). And when public filing of an acquisition agreement is required, the voluminous materials that can be relegated to a disclosure schedule often can be excluded from the filing. This is generally desirable not only because it simplifies matters, but because the disclosure schedule has a great deal of information about the business being sold, and it often is not desirable to make all of that information public knowledge. Such a disclosure schedule might, for example, contain information about the status of certain litigation matters that the company would not like the other parties to the litigation to see.

Breach of Warranties

In most acquisition transactions the representations and warranties of the seller survive closing and, if breaches occur, give rise to a claim by the buyer for damages. Thus, a mechanism for the establishment of damages often is provided in the acquisition agreement. The buyer generally is required to give prompt notice to the seller of circumstances or third-party claims that might give rise to a claim against the seller. The seller often negotiates for the right to participate with its own counsel in the defense of any claims by third parties. Additionally, the seller frequently negotiates a damages "basket" to eliminate the nuisance of minor claims and seeks a cutoff date after which the buyer may not assert additional claims. The typical deadline is fixed at a point before the statute of limitations on the seller's liability expires. Often, there is a provision for arbitration of disputes.

The measure of damages for breach of warranty is frequently subject to difficult negotiation. If a buyer has calculated its purchase price as a multiple of the seller's earnings, a breach of warranty that can have a permanent, or even short-term, effect on earnings should reduce the purchase price by the same multiple, although as a practical matter sellers virtually never agree to such a formula. In situations where impact on earnings is not the issue, a breach in the nature of an undisclosed liability generally is accounted for in damages on a dollar-for-dollar basis. However, sellers often negotiate for an aftertax calculation of damages, as a breach can result in a deductible expense.

DEBT AND EQUITY INSTRUMENTS

The purchase price in an acquisition transaction often consists of debt and/or equity securities in addition to, or in lieu of, cash. In the case of equity securities that are not the fundamental common shares of the acquiring company, such as preferred stock, creation of the new security by amending the buyer's certificate of incorporation often involves a very elaborate and detailed description of the security being created. This description covers voting rights, dividends, redemption and liquidation features, call provisions, convertibility features, and complex antidilution provisions, among other characteristics.

When debt instruments are used, they often have many of the same complex features as equity securities, particularly if debenture holders are to have any voting rights, if the debenture is to be callable, or if it has any convertibility features or income rights other than a flat interest rate. In addition, the creation of a series of debentures often is accompanied by an indenture of trust, which contains a variety of provisions designed to protect the debenture holders.

SECURITIES AND EXCHANGE
COMMISSION FILINGS

When the acquiring company is issuing securities, the issuance of such securities constitutes a "sale" under the Securities Act of 1933. A registration statement must be filed with the Securities and Exchange Commission (SEC) unless an exemption, typically the "private placement" exemption, is available. Form S-4 is used for registration purposes and is designed to provide the shareholders of the target company with sufficient information about the acquiring company to make an informed judgment on the proposed transaction. It is often a lengthy and elaborate document, although in certain instances much of the information can be incorporated by reference to previously filed documents. If the target company has securities that are registered under the Securities Exchange Act of 1934, it must use a proxy statement or information statement that complies with the SEC's Regulation 14A governing the shareholders' meeting called to approve the acquisition. In that case, the Form S-4 registration statement is essentially a wraparound of the Exchange Act proxy statement. Even if the target company does not have securities registered under the Exchange Act and therefore does not have to comply with the proxy rules, the target company will have to make adequate disclosures to avoid violation of the antifraud provisions of the securities laws.

If the number and nature of the target company's shareholders render a registration statement unnecessary, counsel for the acquiring company must prepare all of the documents necessary to establish that a "private placement" exemption has been made under one of the "safe harbor" rules of the SEC's Regulation D. If Regulation D is not applicable and no other exemption (i.e., the exemption for purely intrastate offerings) is available, the buyer can try to bypass registration by asserting that the transaction otherwise meets the requirements of Section 4(2) of the Securities Act.

STATE SECURITIES LAWS FILINGS

When an acquisition transaction involves the "sale" of the acquiring company's securities, the buyer must comply with state securities laws ("blue sky" laws) in all states where its securities are being offered (namely, each state where the target company's shareholders reside). Although registration requirements are generally similar from state to state, each state statute has its own peculiarities. If a registration statement is being filed for the securities under the Securities Act of 1933, then in almost all states the securities can be registered by coordination, essentially by filing with the appropriate state agency a copy of the registration statement filed with the SEC. When a state does not allow coordination, the securities must be registered by qualification. This is a more complex process that is similar to registering under the federal Securities Act. Most states offer exemptions from registration for securities already listed on a national securities exchange or its equivalent. Exemptions frequently are allowed for limited offerings, such as offers to no more than 25 nonexcluded persons (generally financial institutions and other institutional buyers can be excluded in counting the number of offerees) in the state during any period of 12 consecutive months. But even offerings exempt from registration often require some type of filing with the state regulatory agency, and such a filing can be lengthy and complicated.

THE HART-SCOTT-RODINO ACT

The Hart-Scott-Rodino (HSR) Antitrust Improvements Act requires the parties to certain acquisition transactions to provide the Federal Trade Commission and the Antitrust Division of the Department of Justice with information about the businesses of the companies involved and the proposed deal. The law stays the consummation of covered acquisition transactions for at least 30 days. The purpose of this legislation is to help the government enforce antitrust laws relating to acquisitions, particularly Section 7 of the Clayton Act, by giving regulators time to evaluate a proposed acquisition and to determine if it should be challenged. The law is extremely complicated, and the filing is complex. In very general terms, a HSR filing is required when:

- The seller has annual sales or assets of at least $10 million and the buyer has sales or assets of at least $100 million, or vice versa; and
- After the acquisition the buyer holds 15 percent of the outstanding securities or

assets of the seller or the buyer's interest in the seller's securities or assets is valued at $15 million or more.

RULING REQUEST TO THE INTERNAL REVENUE SERVICE

A frequent condition to consummating an acquisition is the securing of a favorable ruling from the Internal Revenue Service (IRS) on tax treatment of the deal. The most typical request is that the IRS rule the transaction a tax-free reorganization. The ruling request is an extensive document that describes the acquisition in detail, formally asks for the ruling, and sets forth the applicant's supporting legal grounds. The service's response often takes several months.

ERISA FILINGS

The Employee Retirement Income Security Act of 1974 (ERISA) was enacted primarily to protect the interest of employee benefit plan participants and their beneficiaries. The law creates a number of "reportable events" related to acquisitions and requires the filing of reports with the Pension Benefit Guaranty Corp. in such cases. Reports must be filed when the acquisition changes the plan employer, leads to a complete or partial termination of a plan, or results in the merger of two or more plans. In certain circumstances, filings also must be made with the Internal Revenue Service.

LEGAL OPINIONS

Legal opinions, which are standard features of acquisition agreements, typically are rendered by counsel for both the buyer and seller on behalf of their respective clients. Besides stating that the parties are duly incorporated and in good standing, they affirm that the acquisition agreement:

- Has been duly authorized, executed, and delivered;
- Constitutes a binding obligation on the parties; and
- Does not violate the corporate client's charter, by-laws, or agreements of which the counsel has knowledge.

In addition to these typical opinions, there are a host of other matters on which the seller's counsel is asked to opine. These include the existence and status of litigation matters, and quality of title to securities being delivered, the quality of title to real and personal property of the business being sold, the validity and enforceability of various agreements to which the selling business is party, and qualification to do business in various jurisdictions.

Buyers often request from the seller's counsel extensive and unqualified opinions that may parallel many of the seller's representations and warranties. From the buyer's standpoint, such opinions provide two principal benefits. First, if the seller's counsel if responsible, it will not render opinions without being satisfied that such opinions are correct. Thus, the buyer is provided with the results of an independent investigation, and confirmation of the seller's representations and warranties. Second, responsible counsel provides an available deep pocket (from its own resources and/or malpractice insurance) in the event a representation or warranty that also is covered in the legal opinion is false.

Many opinions requested of the seller's counsel involve questions of fact or a mixture of fact and law, and are not strictly legal opinions (i.e., an opinion that the seller is not in default under any material contracts, or an opinion that the seller is not a defendant in any material litigation). The seller's counsel therefore must take care in its opinion to state the extent of the investigations on which the opinion is based, and the extent to which the factual portion of the opinion is limited to the counsel's knowledge.

MISCELLANEOUS AND REGULATORY FILINGS

When an acquisition takes the form of a statutory merger, documents (generally the plan or agreement of merger) must be filed in each state in which a corporate party to the transaction is incorporated. The merger documents must comply in form and content with the requirements of the business corporation law of each state in which they are filed. In many states the merger documents to be filed include state tax clearances, which can be time-consuming to obtain. When a corporation will, as a result of merger or acquisition, do business in a state where it had not previously operated, the company usually must obtain a certificate of authority to do business in the newly entered state before the effective date of the acquisition. When an acquisition is in a regulated business such as banking, transportation, or communications, filing with regulatory agencies such as the Federal Reserve Board, Interstate Commerce Commission, or Federal Communications Commission, often are required.

Chapter 24

Effective Due Diligence

H. Richard Grafer

Partner, Arthur Andersen & Co., New York, New York

P. Michael Baldasaro

Partner, Arthur Andersen & Co., New York, New York

Many acquirers operate under the theory that once the handshake has taken place, the deal is done. On the contrary, the work has just begun. It's time to determine whether the deal is as good as it looks on the surface. This requires further investigation, "due diligence" review, and verification of the seller's representations. A canny buyer should be conducting this "purchase investigation" even before the handshake.

Although a thorough investigation sounds like motherhood, it's amazing how often this basic principle is violated and buyers risk severe financial losses by proceeding on the basis of inadequate information and half-truths. When they are performed, purchase investigations frequently are handled ineffectively and don't obtain enough of the right information to evaluate the target and make a sound decision. This may stem from poor communication, misunderstandings, lack of careful planning, failure to fix responsibilities and coordinate the inquiry, and, perhaps most important, because the investigation often focuses on quantity rather than quality of the information. For example, with respect to marketing information, an acquirer should focus on how the target is different from others in the marketplace and whether its competitive strategy is working, not on how it resembles competitors. With respect to financial information, the acquirer should probe major exposure areas, trends, and unusual financial characteristics rather than every item in the financial statements.

NATURE AND SCOPE OF THE INVESTIGATION

A purchase investigation may be performed by company personnel, with or without help of outside consultants (e.g., accountants, investment bankers, lawyers, special industry consultants, actuaries, appraisers). The decision depends on the experience and availability of in-house personnel. We recommend that management play a major role in the investigation, because it will learn first-hand information that is important to both the decision to proceed with the deal and to successful operation of the target after the acquisition. Management, in fact, should be the prime mover, setting the scope and taking the lead. By delegating the entire investigation to subordinates or consultants, management frequently overlooks a lot of hard information, while missing the opportunity to get a "feel" for the target management and other qualitative concerns that are critical in the purchase decision.

The scope of an investigation may range from a minimum effort (reviewing available financial information, visiting the target's facilities, and talking to selling management) to a maximum effort that involves a comprehensive investigation and audit. Depth depends on the size and relative significance of the acquisition candidate, price, availability of audited financial information, degree of inherent risk, time allowed, and so on. In the case of an unfriendly tender offer, the ability to analyze internal information on the target company may be limited. Consequently, the acquirer and its professional advisers may not be able to do much more than gather, compile, and analyze available public information. But if the seller is a private company, the need for a full-scale investigation is much greater. Divestitures also require intense buyer scrutiny.

Frequently, it is advisable to perform more than one type of investigation on a candidate. A preliminary investigation may be conducted before the handshake or the signing of a letter of intent or preliminary agreement, with a purchase audit or limited examination following to verify the candidate's representations and help establish a final price.

The Businessman's Review

The businessman's review is a comprehensive review and analysis, usually without independent verification, of a target company's financial and accounting records and related information. The initial stage comes after preliminary interest is expressed, when the buyer needs to obtain additional information regarding the seller's operations to reach the handshake stage. It is designed to provide a broad understanding of all aspects of the company's business, including industry information; marketing, manufacturing, and distribution methods; financial reporting systems and controls; and industrial relations; as well as in-depth comprehension of the target's financial statements, accounting data, and tax position. At this stage, questions should be raised about research and development programs, regulatory reporting requirements, international factors, and legal matters.

Management is advised to prepare a checklist of questions it wants to raise with the target during a preliminary review so it gets the information it needs. Because this stage of the review does not usually involve verification procedures or detailed analysis of accounts, it easily can be performed by the buyer itself in cooperation with the target's personnel.

The second stage of the businessman's review typically begins after the handshake. It is a more detailed review of tax, financial, and accounting records with or without verification, and often is performed with the help of the acquirer's independent accountants. Usually, the accounting and tax principles and practices of the target are reviewed in depth, with special emphasis placed on whether they pose any problems to the specific transaction. It is important that the buyer and its accountants agree on the scope of this review and that the acquirer understands its objectives and limitations.

Purchase Audit and Other Verification Procedures

Independent verification or audit of the seller's financial statements and representations made by its management may be required, depending on the degree of assurance the buyer wants, the seller's past audit history, and the time permitted for premerger investigation. Verification procedures may involve a full-blown purchase audit or specially designed auditing procedures applied to specific accounts or exposure areas. For example, inventory is such a significant item to manufacturing and distribution enterprises that accountants frequently are asked to observe and test the physical inventories, audit their valuation, and determine any excess and obsolete inventory and valuation practices.

Verification procedures often disclose problems not previously known and are especially valuable in the current environment when integrity is not always considered a virtue. Although management frequently shuns the cost of an audit, the expense can buy an additional level of assurance that is hard to come by any other way.

When the target has a good audit history (i.e., a reputable accounting firm has examined the historical financial statements and prepared the tax returns), comprehensive verification procedures may not be necessary except in areas not normally covered by the annual audit and not previously verified. Quality of the target's products, its reputation with customers, and similar nonfinancial areas may be appropriate subjects for verification. However, as a minimum, workpapers of the target's auditors should be reviewed in detail to identify exposure areas, problems, and issues not fully disclosed in the financial statements.

AREAS OF INVESTIGATION

The businessman's review, with or without verification, should focus on a variety of matters.

Company Background and History

The general nature of the business, principal locations and facilities, history, and similar information should be collected in the early phase of this investigation. In addition, information should be obtained on the management, directors, and outside advisers. Whenever possible, information on the company's recent developments, plans for the future, and major problems—including lawsuits, government restrictions, environmental considerations, and sensitive transactions—should be covered. This information offers initial understanding of the prospective acquisition and identifies areas for further investigation.

Industry Information

When the target operates in an industry that is unfamiliar to the buyer, a detailed industry review, often with help from expert consultants, is prudent. It should precede the investigation of a specific candidate and include:

- Competition and competitive strategies, both within the industry and from other industries
- Industry growth rates in sales and profits (past and projected) and external factors affecting industry growth and profitability
- Mergers and acquisitions in the industry, to determine if a business combination is crucial for survival or growth in the industry
- Government regulations, decrees, and trends
- Patents, trademarks, copyrights, and so on, and their importance to competitors in the industry
- Essential elements of success and barriers to entry

Financial and Accounting Information

It is useful to compare financial ratios by major business segments for a period of years to determine important trends. These ratios usually include returns on assets and stockholders' investment, gross profits, profit margins, fixed charge coverage, current ratios, net quick ratios, and debt/equity ratios. Information concerning the impact of inflation or recession on operations, the company's ability to operate in the environment, current value and replacement cost data, and future capital requirements also should be obtained.

The buyer's sources can be balance sheets of prior fiscal years, statements of income, statements of changes in financial position, budgets, and forecasts for the future. In addition, it is important to understand any differences between buyer and seller in accounting principles and practices. Occasionally, such differences disclose questionable accounting practices.

A review of a manufacturer of electronic parts that was up for sale disclosed that its returned goods were accounted for differently than the buyer's returned goods. Further investigation determined that the seller's inventories were substantially overvalued. The prospective buyer called off the deal.

An investigation of a dealer in fertilizers revealed that, in accordance with industry practice, a dealer's purchase is binding, but a customer can back out because there is no legal requirement that he fulfill his side of the transaction. Because fertilizer prices were declining rapidly at the time of the proposed acquisition, this was important to the buyer because of the likelihood that fertilizer customers would refuse to take delivery. Because these "open" transactions should have been valued at current market values, instead of the higher contract prices, an inherent loss existed, and the deal was aborted.

Taxes

A review of the target's tax status serves a dual purpose. It satisfies the buyer that the tax liabilities of the target, as reflected in the purchase price, are properly stated on the target's books. It also focuses on the ability of the buyer to monetize a portion of the purchase price through proper tax planning strategies and tax attributes of the target.

The tax review essentially asks: "Has the target paid all of its tax liabilities on a current basis, and has a reasonable reserve been accrued for known and anticipated adjustments likely to arise on in-progress and future audits by various taxing authorities?" Generally this involves a review and analysis of the tax returns filed for a minimum of three prior years. Special emphasis should be placed on the reconciliation between financial statements and taxable incomes, on the most recent report of adjustments made by the various taxing authorities, and on adjustments in years still open for examination. The results of this review, when compared with the reserve for taxes, the so-called cushion, determine whether the target has provided adequately for past tax exposures.

Timing Items

Aside from absolute dollar liabilities, the audit should review so-called timing items, such as capitalization of repairs and other costs spread over a span of years. Any changes won't increase total taxes over time, but the Internal Revenue Service could dispute the capitalization schedule and claim that larger tax payments should have been made in prior years. The key expense here is interest costs, because interest assessments on past taxes have been escalated in recent years and applied on a compound basis. Sometimes, the ultimate interest cost could exceed the tax deficiency.

State Taxes

State taxes are a very important item for examination. Many states have become extremely aggressive in imposing and collecting taxes from multistate enterprises. And with the federal government adopting an accelerated depreciation schedule in 1980, state taxes are becoming an increasing share of the overall corporate tax bite. In the case of multinational corporations, country-by-country tax reviews may be warranted.

Gaining Tax Attributes

Because potential tax benefits and opportunities to recoup purchase prices through postacquisition assets sales are key elements in setting the price tag on a deal, the audit should determine which of the seller's tax attributes succeed to the buyer. Net operating loss carryforwards, unutilized investment tax credits, and other available credits should be identified and quantified. Quantification goes beyond merely pulling numbers off a tax return. It is necessary to get behind the target's numbers and adjust the attributes for any potential softness that may result from such things as an aggressive tax policy that is open to successful challenge by taxing authorities.

A buyer purchasing stock from an existing consolidated group should seek safeguards to protect against loss of tax benefits from postacquisition operating losses or from excess credits that can be carried back for tax purposes to the preacquisition period. This requires a tax-sharing agreement between the two parties that is tailored to the specific peculiarities of the transaction.

When a substantial premium is being paid over the target's asset tax basis or the buyer plans to sell off some of the target's assets after the acquisition, the audit should consider the opportunities for "step-up" or writing up the value of the acquired assets, and the tax consequences of this procedure. This should focus on "recapture" taxes and potential taxes due on the sale of the assets; the present tax basis for the assets, which often is lower than the book carrying value; and any other costs associated with the target's ability to step up asset values.

Essentially, the step-up analysis begins by allocating the purchase price to the target's various assets. Recapture costs associated with the allocation then are quantified and compared with the tax savings derived from stepping up the tax basis of the target's assets. Recapture taxes must be paid within a short period of time after the acquisition, but the step-up typically is realized over several years. Thus, a true comparison will discount future tax savings by using a reasonable interest rate. The buyer should be aware that tax changes during the early 1980s increased the potential for recapture tax liability and dimmed the luster of many deals that required significant up-front "recapture" tax payments.

Investment tax credits, depreciation, foreign and DISC earnings, and LIFO inventory reserves are some of the recaptures that could be triggered on a step-up. To combat these higher recapture costs, the buyer should seek intangible assets of the target that can be assigned value and for which a useful life can be developed. An allocation to intangibles may not generate as much recapture as fixed assets or LIFO inventory.

Management, Organization, and Industrial Relations

The buyer must appraise the capabilities of the seller's management, particularly when buying in an unrelated industry. The buyer should interview the senior officers and managers, review their prior business experiences, investigate their backgrounds, and compare compensation benefit levels and plans, because changes often will result from the transaction.

Union contracts, strike history, and related factors should be reviewed to determine any existing problems. Many planned personnel savings may not be possible because of labor agreements. Pension, profit-sharing, and other employee benefit plans must be studied to determine the effect on the future operations of the combined business. One target company had many valued, long-term employees, all in their late fifties, who would have caused a drain on the buyer's cash flow when the unfunded pension benefits had to be paid at their retirement. Consequently, the terms of the transaction were substantially lowered. On the other side of the equation, many pension funds have surpluses that serve to make the acquisition less expensive.

Marketing

Product and marketing factors to be analyzed include:

- Sales, profit, and backlog by product line
- Major products, new product developments, and obsolescece
- Annual and monthly sales histories (long-term trends and seasonal or cyclical fluctuations)
- Government sales
- Marketing and sales organization, including special compensation arrangements
- Sales planning and forecasting methods
- Advertising and promotion expenditures and methods
- Market shares of key competitors
- Product life cycles and technological
- Competitive strategies
- Key factors for success, including threats and barriers to entry
- Customer attitudes and buying power

The target's trends should be compared to industry averages to determine the company's relative performance. An example of how product obsolescence affects the transaction concerns the target company that manufactured a leading, long-established angina medication and demanded a high premium for its reputation. The acquirer discovered that, although the target's trend had been good, a new product, encompassing new technology and application, had just come on the market and would ultimately make the target's product obsolete. The buyer substantially reduced its offer. The marketing intelligence also should be compared to an analysis (aging and usage by item) of inventory to detect slow-moving, excess, and obsolete inventory. Some buyers who don't perform this inventory analysis frequently are forced into the costly scrapping of inventory after acquisition because they later find items that are components of discontinued or declining lines.

Manufacturing and Distribution

A review should include:

- Each production facility (name, location, owned or leased, book value, fair market value, capacity, employees, present condition, alternative uses)

- Manufacturing processes and efficiency
- Suppliers of major raw materials
- Physical distribution methods (purchase, intracompany transfers, final sales to customers)

Acquirers should also examine the following other areas.

Research and Development.   The buyer should analyze costs and benefits of the past, current, and planned R&D programs, personnel and facilities used in them, and methods of accounting for R&D.

Reporting Controls.   Understanding a seller's internal reporting and control systems is particularly important when the target is in a different industry than the buyer or has weak controls that can affect the business. Often, it is not possible to install identical systems in both companies because of operating or philosophical differences such as the degree of autonomy for subsidiaries. When such differences arise, any required changes should be made at reasonable cost after the acquisition.

Regulatory Reporting Requirements.   Reporting requirements promulgated by regulatory authorities should be given special attention. They can have a profound effect on the future of the combined business and lead to substantial fines and embarrassment if ignored. The buyer should satisfy itself that the target company's facilities are in compliance with requirements of the Environmental Protection Agency and the Occupational Safety and Health Administration.

International Factors.   Foreign operations of a target should be studied as to how they affect overall operation. Questions concerning the foreign country's investment climate, trade and investment restrictions, exchange controls, inflation rates, and reporting requirements should be addressed.

Discretionary Expenses.   Certain expenses, such as research and development costs and repair and maintenance costs, can be deferred for the short term by the seller with adverse long-term consequences to a potential buyer. A careful review will help avoid unanticipated future outlays of capital that effectively increase the cost of the acquisition.

COMMON PROBLEMS OR EXPOSURE AREAS

It is helpful to know some of the more common financial and accounting problems uncovered in purchase investigations.

Inventory Distortions.   Undervaluation of inventory by private companies minimizes taxes but can lead to distorted earnings trends and potential.

Overvaluation of Inventory.   A key source of overvalued inventory is unrecorded inventory obsolescence caused by product overruns, changing technology, new product development, and maturing or discontinued products. The undervaluation usually results from excessive obsolescence, write-downs, or failure to count inventory on hand accurately.

Litigation. Few firms are free of litigation, the most common resulting from product liability. This type of liability often surfaces well after the acquisition.

"Dressing up" of Financial Statements before Sale. "Dressing up" tactics can include deferral of R&D expenses and repairs and maintenance, "release" of inventory reserves, unduly low reserves or estimates for such things as bad debts, pension accounting, sales returns and allowances, warranties, slow-moving and excess inventories, and undisclosed changes in accounting principles or methods.

Receivables Not Collectible at Recorded Amounts. Doubtful accounts, cash and trade discounts, dated receivables, and sales returns and allowances may not be adequately reserved for.

Unrealizability of Certain Investments. Investments accounted for by the equity method and nonmarketable investments are required to be written down only for "permanent impairments" of value, not for temporary declines. Liberal judgments may have been applied to eliminate recognition of permanent impairment.

Credibility and Integrity of Management. A private investigation may be needed to obtain sufficient information and background on target management to determine if it is right for the job and trustworthy.

Personal Expenses in the Financial Statements of a Private Company. Personal expenses usually reduce reported net income. But such costs also can be used to affect trends and produce a favorable appearance that is misleading.

Tax Contingencies. Tax contingencies represent one of the biggest problem areas in an acquisition, because most companies tend to be very aggressive when preparing their tax returns.

Unrecorded Liabilities. Unrecorded liabilities may include vacation pay, sales returns, allowances and discounts (volume and cash), pension liabilities, claims items resulting from poor cutoffs, loss contracts, and warranties, among others.

Related-Party Transactions. Most often found in private companies, related party deals can have a material effect on the company under new ownership, or on the historical trends presented during negotiations.

Poor Financial Controls. Included in poor financial controls are poor pricing and costing policies, and deficient budgeting systems and controls.

Reliance on a Few Major Customers or Contracts.   Loss of a major customer can have a material effect on operations.

Need for Significant Future Expenditures.   Significant future expenditures needed might include plant relocation or expansion, replacement of aging property, plant, and equipment, or new product development requirements.

Foreign Operations.   Overseas units pose multiple problems, including labor, management, and operating difficulties, poor quality of accounting information, and differences in accounting principles and practices.

Unusual Transactions.   Extraordinary actions such as sales of assets often improve the trend presented by the target.

THE SELLER'S ACTIONS

The seller, of course, must respond to the many requests for information made by the buyer. If proper planning has gone into the sale process, the effort involved should be routine, thereby allowing the seller to concentrate on fine tuning the sale agreement and working out final details. Unfortunately, sale planning is frequently inadequate, making this period traumatic.

The seller should also consider making an investigation of the buyer to determine if that buyer is best able to capitalize on the seller's strengths, is compatible with the seller, and has no skeletons of its own. This is particularly important if the seller is continuing in management. The seller's investigation should focus on basically the same elements as the buyer's investigation. However, it need not be as comprehensive, unless the paper being accepted is subject to considerable risk.

Part 6

After
the
Merger

Chapter 25

Paying
the
Postmerger
Piper

James M. Needham

Partner, National Director of Mergers and Acquisitions,
Arthur Young & Co., New York, New York

Did I get what I planned for? Did I get what I paid for? For many acquirers the answers to these questions are in the negative as the euphoria of the honeymoon evaporates while unforeseen developments arise after the acquisition is completed. The seeds of these unforeseen developments may have predated the acquisition or the developments may have occurred subsequent to the acquisition as a result of the acquirer's actions or circumstances that the buyer could not control. How the acquirer can increase its chances of getting favorable responses to the opening questions will be addressed in this discussion.

The question "Did I get what I planned for?" assumes that the acquirer had realistic expectations against which it could measure postacquisition results, and that the plan and the results were measurable in a meaningful time period by objective criteria.

The acquirer's expectations may be based on preexisting beliefs about the target company and its industry, or derived from an acquisition staff's interpretation of its investigative results. An acquisition investigation will provide a basis for assessing the acquired company's resources (financial, tangible, and intangible), markets (for both its raw materials and end products), and personnel (operational and administrative), as well as the impact of the acquisition structure and any acquisition contingencies on the target's ability to perform.

Assumptions serve as putty in the piecing together of an analysis by the potential acquirer. Because both industry and market knowledge and the results of an investigation of the acquisition candidate are limited, assumptions must be used to fill in the gaps. Unfortunately, putty is easily molded to almost any shape, and is only a temporary measure at best. Too often, the expectations of the acquirer result from an analysis heavy with putty and molded to fit the expectations. This highlights the importance of a thorough investigation prior to the acquisition. Many of the problems that arise after an acquisition could have been foreseen and provided for—either in the purchase price or structure of the transaction—if an acquisition investigation was conducted to support clearly defined acquisition objectives and criteria, and identify and validate underlying assumptions.

Acquirers make a "buy" decision on the presumption that the sellers will provide certain attributes. Unless those desired attributes are clearly stated, it will be difficult for the acquirer's review team to address them, much less validate their existence or even recognize the need for validation. Similarly, downside risk often may be ignored as a result the acquirer's enthusiasm for the perceived upside potential of the acquisition. Basic strategic questions tend to go unanswered in the plethora of detail that is gathered—such questions as: What are the key factors for success in this business? Can we achieve them after this acquisition takes place?

To avoid paying the postmerger piper, a buyer should understand that the purpose of the acquisition investigation is both to validate assumptions on which the buy and price decisions will be made, and to provide an assessment of the risk and potential downside exposure. In addition, a postacquisition plan should be in place prior to consummation of an acquisition so as to ensure that the assets the buyer purchased—whether they be people, physical, or intangible—remain after the acquisition.

DEFINING ACQUISITION OBJECTIVES

Acquisition objectives often are regarded as either strategy- or financial-driven. What often is lost sight of is that acquisitions are, first of all, business-driven. Businesses are more than just amalgamations of assets and liabilities. They include people and know-how, reputation and market position, product quality and technology, which, in combination, produce more than the sum of the parts that may be easily measured and quantified. Some concepts that help explain a business are culture, people, style, values, and strategy—none of which can be easily transplanted from seller to buyer. These intangible and hard-to-measure characteristics may not guarantee the success of the business. But if they are lost, an ongoing business can be destroyed.

In setting both the acquisition objectives and acquisition criteria, it is important for the acquirer to state explicitly just what the acquisition is expected to provide, and what the buyer is expected to supply or is capable of supplying to the seller's business. Is the buyer seeking only an expanded product line? Production facilities? Technology? Market access? A proven management team? Or is the buyer seeking the synthesis of all these factors—a profitable ongoing business?

If the buyer is seeking only limited assets from an acquisition, such as a new product line to distribute through the buyer's distribution system, the chances of paying the piper after the acquisition are lessened. A review can be tailored to the explicit characteristics of the new product line and its anticipated benefits to the buyer. Some may argue that such an acquisition is really not an acquisition of a business, but an acquisition of a specific asset.

If the buyer is seeking an entity with all the intangible assets that make a business attractive, those elements must be identified and ranked in some order of priority. Candidates then can be screened not just on financial considerations and other quantifiable criteria, but on those substantial intangibles of business that indeed provide a competitive edge. Accordingly, a well-thought-out listing of needs that an acquisition candidate should supply, including those intangibles that make a business, is the first step on a hazardous journey toward a successful acquisition.

In our experience, acquisition searches often are limited and produce poor results because they rely exclusively on financial and product screens. Substantial data on industries and companies within those industries are publicly available. What is missing from all these data bases is a guide to the substance of the business. That search for substance forms the core of the acquisition search and review.

DEFINING THE SCOPE OF THE ACQUISITION REVIEW

With a clear set of acquisition objectives and criteria, the buyer has standards for measuring an acquisition candidate. In addition, a purchaser will have identified those assumptions on which a buy decision will be made and a price and structure determined.

But selection of the best target company to approach still is a most difficult decision. Unfortunately, no foolproof method of candidate selection exists. Certain steps taken at this stage can save much time, expense, and potential disaster. Depending on the nature of the acquisition and the closeness of its strategic fit with existing businesses, the selection process will vary from company to company and industry to industry.

A buyer that acquires a company in its own industry will have a greater chance of success because it already has a sense of those intangibles, such as management, culture, and values, that the seller may possess. Similarly, the buyer's organization will have a peer appraisal of counterparts in the target company. Much less quantification is required for such an acquisition, and the scope of the review can be directed at areas of potential downside risk, which prior knowledge of both the seller's industry and seller itself will help to identify. As the buyer moves away from its area of detailed knowledge of specific businesses and markets, it will have to rely on greater quantification of information, and the experiences and insight of industry experts who have direct knowledge of the candidates under review.

Companies often perform financial screens and limit their acquisition reviews to superficial financial analyses. It is in these cases that the greatest risk of postacquisition failure exists. For example, an understanding of the current and potential sources, uses, and timing of the acquisition candidate's cash flow is essential to valuing and structuring a transaction. How else can the buyer make an informed decision regarding an appropriate debt/equity structure and financing terms?

Superficial financial analysis will not provide the insight into a business or provide a prudent buyer with comfort concerning the reliability of internal financial statements and analyses. Internal financial information should provide the basis for a trend analysis of what products have produced the most profits over the last five to 10 years and point out the changes in product line mix, seasonality, geographic and customer concentration, and intercompany or affiliated company sales.

The tax area is another part of an acquisition that may be strewn with pitfalls for the haphazard investigator. For example, it is not uncommon for buyer and seller to reach an agreement and then find out that they ignored the matter of significant amounts of recapture taxes and just which side had the responsibility of paying for them. Indeed, the tax sector is so far-reaching that it requires a point-by-point examination of as many as three dozen different aspects of the deal, both before and after it is completed.

Gauging the Qualities of the Target

Corporate growth and management performance cannot be measured or reflected merely in terms of accounting measurements. The financial statements of a company for a given year may have little to do with the major decisions the company management took during that year. Actions by management to achieve corporate growth often take years to add value to the company. Management and personnel development, the building of a distribution system, research and development expenses, investments to expand market share, and customer relations programs are only some examples of areas where payoffs may be long in coming. It is the quality of these management decisions that one must assess in making judgments about a company's performance and growth prospects.

While the decisions of management ultimately are reflected at the bottom line, it is difficult to capture the true state of health of a corporation solely from its year-end financial statements. Often, financial statements don't provide investors and acquirers with much more than an indication of how the target performed in relation to a trend—such as a specific development that affected demand for its products or services—or within the context of the health of the general economy and its own industry. In fact, overreliance on "snapshots" of corporate performance may have provided public companies with disincentives for true overall growth by focusing too much attention on earnings per share growth as a way of rewarding both management and shareholders. Because corporate growth might be defined as adding value to the corporation, an acquisition analysis should pay more attention to the quality of the growth rather than arbitrary financial measurements. In fact, financial statements alone will not provide insight into many identified assets that a company or business may have, particularly if those assets are underutilized; it is basically those assets that may be the real prizes to be acquired. Identifying those elusive and underutilized assets requires disciplines other than straight financial analysis. It is for this reason that I often urge my clients planning acquisitions to consult with industry specialists, and people who have spent substantial parts of their lives in a particular industry, to gain insight into the target industry and its competitive dynamics. These industry insiders should be able to provide in-depth knowledge of the businesses and the corporate intangibles that exist within the seller, and pinpoint those attributes not defined in financial statements.

Accordingly, in determining the scope of a candidate review prior to the initial contract, one can make judgments about the intangible qualities of a business through personal experience, or through the retention of seasoned insiders who can provide information the acquirer may lack.

Not all acquisition review procedures can be easily segregated into prior-contact and post-contact procedures. In fact, they may overlap and will overlap.

CONDUCTING THE FINANCIAL REVIEW

In a financial review, the objective is to determine significant financial and accounting policies of the acquisition candidate and to compare them to the buyer's own policies for the purpose of putting together a pro forma consolidated set of financial statements. Adjustments generally are made to the seller's financial statements to bring them into conformity with the buyer's accounting policies. The impact of these changes and the cash impact of any tax effects from the acquisition should be well thought through prior to structuring the acquisition agreement. Other areas of investigation will be determined by the results of the nonfinancial review process. For example, the buyer, through its own experience or knowledge of the seller's industry, should be able to identify business areas that face the greatest tax exposure. And in reviewing the seller's projections of future performance, the buyer should determine whether forecasts made in previous years were achieved, in order to determine the reliability of the most recent projections.

Opinions of Outsiders

On the basis of my experience, an acquisition review always should include an assessment of the candidate by its industry peers. It is unlikely that negative aspects of a company will be highlighted by the seller during the selling process. But those negatives often are well known to competitors. One can, prior to an acquisition, and even prior to contact, interview a number of competitors, customers, and suppliers, synthesize their comments about various companies within that industry, and put together a matrix that will provide sufficient insight into not only the target company, but its competitors as well. My experience is that while competitors may not be anxious to talk about themselves, the various people in their organizations may be more than happy to give you opinions about other companies. Although these opinions might have to be treated with some degree of skepticism, they will form the closest thing to a peer review of the intangible aspects of the acquisition candidate that an acquirer will be able to obtain. Similarly, the buyer's own managers can identify their functional counterparts at the selling company and render a similar peer review. Such a review is not unlike the evaluation an executive search firm would perform when seeking qualified candidates for a management post. All of these reviews can be conducted by professionals who are retained by the buyer on a "no-name" basis.

Sources of Excessive Costs

The postmerger costs that exceed planned expenditures are the "piper's" payments. These costs can be divided into those that result from factors that are either internal or external to the combined organization. In both instances, the factors fall into controllable, impactible, and uncontrollable factors. Though the level of control in each factor may vary from one business to another, examples of typical factors that fit each category include the following.

Controllable Factors

Internal—Line of authority, compensation levels, staffing levels
External—Service to customers, payments to suppliers

Impactible Factors

Internal—Employee perception of the acquisition, the amount of time it takes to return to normality after the acquisition, the sense of common goals and shared values within the organization.
External—Customer perception, service and product quality, fixed versus variable interest rates to finance the acquisition

Uncontrollable Factors

Internal—Death or disability of key employees, regulatory changes affecting the company
External—Financial health of customers, interest rates, reaction of suppliers

The goal of the postmerger plan is to establish an orderly methodology for minimizing the payment to the postacquisition piper and maximizing the expected benefits. Specifically, this entails minimizing the costs of changing various aspects of the acquirer's organization and the costs of taking the steps necessary to meet the acquirer's expectations. The thorough investigation that took place in the acquisition review should have identified the factors important to achieving expectations as controllable, impactible, or uncontrollable. As with any business plan, a series of alternative scenarios should be examined to determine how sensitive operations are to each factor, or a combination of factors. Once the effects are identified, contingency measures can be planned to minimize the impact of various downside scenarios.

A critical factor at this phase of the planning process involves the acquirer's identification of where it must act to maximize benefits or cushion the blow from a reversal, and the determination of what actions must be taken in such circumstances. If this is not done, the buyer will deprive itself of a critical early warning signal that tips it to the best time for implementing a contingency plan. Precious time may be lost by waiting for financial information to pinpoint a problem, and corrective action may be applied too late. Above all, acquiring management must agree that all proposed actions are sound and can achieve desired results.

DEVELOPING THE POSTMERGER PLAN

The final state in any acquisition is the implementation of the postmerger plan to integrate the acquired company into the acquirer. The primary elements of this plan should revolve around what changes are necessary, how to implement those changes, and how to manage the fear of change. Many postmerger plans fail to recognize the basic problems of organizational changes—that the required changes rarely are perceived as beneficial by those people who are required to change. The absence of incentives to alter employee behavior may result in a number of adverse outcomes, ranging from a snail-paced integration process to outright sabotage of the integration effort.

The postmerger plan needs to address the fear of change—regardless of whether actual changes are planned—in each component of the business, including:

- Customers' fears of product or service changes
- Suppliers' fears of detrimental changes in the acquiree's financial strength or buying habits
- Labor's fears of major layoffs
- Managers' fears of staff redundancy
- Some executives' fears of additional administrative burdens
- Target management's fears of loss of resources, especially financial, as a subsidiary company
- The acquiree's fears of becoming a "stepchild" (the "we–they" syndrome) in the combined company

In many cases, operational integration will be avoided, in line with the axiom, "If it ain't broke, don't fix it." If so, only financial and operational monitoring will be required.

The postmerger plan should draw heavily on the information gained during the acquisition review, and focus especially on the particular attributes that comprise the substance of the business. The key managers—organizationally, operationally, and politically—need to be identified, addressed as to their futures, and provided with incentives to promote the desired changes. The overall level of operational autonomy needs to be decided with an eye to the perceptions of customers, suppliers, and employees, as well as the level of autonomy (or dependence) with which the buyer feels comfortable. Decisions regarding qualitative aspects of the business must be reached on such questions as:

- How does the proposed level of autonomy fit with the acquiree's corporate style and culture?
- How much internal competition is desirable?
- What steps will be taken to foster the level of cooperation and/or competition desired between the employees of the acquirer and target?
- What changes in accounting and clerical procedures should be made to provide better administrative contacts to the acquiree as well as the requisite information to the acquirer?

And, of course, difficult questions regarding the adjustment of compensation and benefits must be addressed.

In short, the postmerger plan for integration seeks to mold the working of the acquiree and acquirer to minimize the potential detriment to the substance of the acquiree's business. Central to this process is for the buyer to make it known to the seller's management that it is "they" who are the business, and that both parties are buying into the future business together, and that both will reap appropriate rewards. When this message is conveyed to the seller's management prior to the signing of the acquisition agreement, the chances of shortchanging the postmerger piper increase.

Chapter 26

The Postmerger Task Force

Andrew M. Rouse

Executive Vice President, CIGNA Corp.,
Philadelphia, Pennsylvania

Most premerger negotiations focus on financial, not organizational, arrangements. The key players are the chief executives and financial officers of the combining companies, assisted by their investment banking and legal advisers. If postmerger problems are considered in any depth at all, they tend to be those that concern only top executives involved in the deal: Who will have executive responsibility? How will power be divided? What titles, salaries, and other perquisites will be bestowed?

When merger talks are initiated, even the most experienced top corporate executives tend to be insensitive to the needs of their middle management and rank-and-file employees. Those directly involved in the negotiations tend to work out their own roles and relationships in the new company without dealing expressly with the merger's organizational and personal implications down the line. Further, despite the secrecy that normally surrounds the discussions, the merger frequently becomes a topic of corporate or even industrywide knowledge, if not of public record. This cloak-and-dagger atmosphere germinates rumor, insecurity, and frustration at the lower levels of the organization, weakening gravely the strength and stability of the newly merged entity.

Even when premerger negotiations involve several echelons of management, communication with a broad spectrum of interested parties, such as employees, labor unions, customers, vendors, the industry itself, and the financial community, often is restricted until after the deal is consummated. By that time, however, the realities of managing the new organization take precedence. Decisions and communications that should have been set in place carefully now have to be made ad hoc. Important individuals and groups, whose support could have strengthened the new entity from the outset, may now greet the merger with a wait-and-see attitude, if not outright hostility.

AN AGENT OF TRANSITION

There is an obvious solution to this typical premerger astigmatism. Top management should bring into being during the negotiation stage a representative executive group whose primary concern—from the moment of the initial agreement to some specified time in the future—should be to uncover, consider, and resolve postmerger problems involving the entire new organization. The postmerger task force is such a mechanism. It can minimize stress and poor communications, and bring to the surface those often-submerged tensions that accompany and plague any combination. To be fully effective, the postmerger task force must be organized and set in place during the preclosing period. The willingness of top managements to create such a joint unit and the attention they give to it may signal how effectively the constituent organizations will be able to work together after the merger "honeymoon" is over.

No set of instructions can form an effective guide to the operation of a task force unless there is a modicum of patience and goodwill among all parties, some determination from the outset to make the relationship work. If the top executives of the combining companies start with these attitudes, they can use the task force as a listening post, a sounding board, and a rumor control center. In any merger, the most divisive forces encountered at the start are divided loyalties and the recollection of the past. The existence of the task force from the inception of the merger is a barrier to divisiveness. It is a signal to all that top management is concerned about uniting the energies and loyalties of the merging organizations, as well as their assets.

The key characteristics of a joint task force are its responsibilities; the form it might take; the basic elements involved in its establishment, such as leadership, governance, and timing; the two key roles of the task force in communicating and monitoring change; and the self-liquidation of the task force when its counseling and communication functions have ended.

Two Approaches to Task Force Operation

The objectives of a postmerger task force can be accomplished through two different approaches. The task force can serve as the monitor of the bonding process—framing issues, assigning action to the relevant units of the new company, and following and critiquing progress. The task force also can play a more active role if it is empowered by the chief executive to develop and impose policy decisions, and if it is given the resources and the power to do that job. Of the two, the policy-making approach is the less frequently used. It diminishes the control of resources and the management responsibility of other executives. Sometimes it is fiercely opposed, thereby producing counterproductive results. The approach, while used occasionally, seems appropriate in those cases when the acquired company is to be completely integrated into the acquirer. Even in this instance, the need to retain talent suggests that the task force mandate should fall short of authority to act directly.

The chief executive who establishes a postmerger task force must be clear as to which approach is preferred. Failure to spell out formally both the mandate and the limitations of the task force can aggravate problems already latent in the merger. It can leave ambiguous the role of the task force in formulating and implementing solutions, and it can undermine the unit's ability to focus the disparate interests and agendas on a single goal, the success of the new organization.

The Monitoring Model

The monitoring model is clearly preferable to the direct action model for at least three reasons. First, the more people who can be involved officially in a controlled attack on the postmerger problems, the less sense of exclusion there is likely to be throughout both organizations. Second, managers performing their assigned roles are more likely to be forthright with their own subordinates, thereby widening the network of informed people.

Finally, many issues require expert help in their resolution. Professionals will perform more effectively when directed by senior executives who have expertise in the same areas of specialization.

Creating the Task Force

Once the desired approach has been established, there are several crucial elements that should be considered in creating the task force.

A Formal Mandate.   The memorandum establishing the task force should specify the areas in which the chief executive officer (CEO) expects the task force to operate, outline the approach it should take in working with others, and provide a preliminary statement of goals and objectives that the CEO wants to achieve. Setting forth both objectives and tone is important. Not only does the memo give direction to the members of the task force, it establishes a foundation of fact, not conjecture, concerning the intentions of the CEO, the mandate of the task force, and the manner in which the goals of management are to be accomplished.

The Role of the CEO.   The chief executive officer should resist the temptation to chair the task force or even to appoint as his proxy a member of top management that is too closely identified as his confidant. Likewise, he should avoid the temptation to attend its meetings or receive informal interim reports of its progress. In varying degrees, each of these practices subverts the delegation of authority and creates an imbalance among task force members, dividing them into home team and visitors, depending on their previous associations with the CEO of the merged enterprise. Because many CEOs rely more on some executives than others, the task force also should avoid inclusion of members of the CEO's "kitchen cabinet." This is not always possible, but when intimates must be used, the amount of informal conversation between the CEO and his close subordinates should be held to a minimum. The value of the task force can be seriously impaired if its members conclude that their effectiveness is measured by the amount of conversation with the chief executive, and not their less visible (or audible) exchanges with executives and employees of less exalted status.

The Reporting Function.   In the absence of informal feedback, the CEO should insist on frequent oral reports from the task force. These should be delivered in the presence of the general membership. Occasional written reports should be required. All task force proposals of actions to be taken should be in writing, reviewed by others before their transmittal, and modified where it seems advisable. The CEO who wants the task force to perform its job well needs to discipline himself rigorously, perhaps even more than do his subordinates. This is necessary for both the welfare of the task force and for the remainder of the organization. Too much involvement by the CEO will be interpreted either as a sign of a lack of confidence in the task force or a desire to make it a rubber-stamp instrument of control. On the other hand, a CEO has to make it clear that he is vitally interested in the work of the task force. If the task force is viewed as cosmetic, or irrelevant to the concerns of the chief executive, it will run out of steam. To avoid this, the chief executive should be punctilious about receiving timely oral and written reports. In addition, the way the chief executive seeks clarification and guides the task force conveys his ongoing interest. The balancing act between too much and too little involvement is difficult, and most CEOs receive average grades in handling it.

Membership.   The size of the task force should not be an issue. Large task forces may be somewhat unwieldy, but they are generally able to adopt a form and style of governance that fits their size. Breadth of experience and expertise are essential criteria for membership. In determining numbers, the most sensible approach is "the more the better," considering the range of issues and the sensitivity of matters to be covered. This will not make the self-important happy. It will, however, ensure a broader constituency for implementation.

Governance.   The CEO should appoint the task force leader, who should determine the method of operation, the number of subcommittees, leadership of those units, reporting requirements, frequency and timing of meetings, reports to the CEO, and procedures for involving corporate resources outside the task force.

The Executive Connection.   Throughout their tenure, task force members must understand the nature of their policy-making roles. To be most effective, and to be able to live with their management colleagues after the unit is disbanded, members must recognize that their functions are limited to communicating the facts about the merger, and to monitoring and ameliorating the effects of changes on concerned publics. The principal policy-making role remains with senior executives holding appropriate functional responsibilities, whether or not they are members of the task force. As new policies are being framed and implemented, task force members need to foster a cooperative spirit among their colleagues. They should encourage attendance at their meetings and expand the group to include other executives on a basis that seems most comfortable and productive. Nonmembers carrying out assignments for the group should be treated as fully participating colleagues. One effective method is to include nonmember executives on appropriate task force subcommittees.

The Role of the Consultant.   The postmerger task force usually finds considerable use for outside consultants. In areas such as personnel and compensation systems, pension plan changes, advertising, and public relations, consultants can be helpful because they can marshal problem-solving resources quickly, and offer recommendations that are more likely to be viewed as neutral or objective. In the postmerger environment, when everyone is looking anxiously for manifestations of power distribution, this kind of neutrality is as essential as it is rare. The task force leader should not interfere in the relationship of a consultant to a subcommittee, because this may dilute the subcommittee's authority.

Timing.   It is vital that the task force plan its own demise at the time its agenda is exhausted. Perpetuation of the task force to oversee complete implementation is a mistake. Day-to-day management of departments and divisions would be weakened seriously, and in time the company would become overpoliticized. In any area where the CEO has given his approval to proceed, the task force should relinquish control after assuring itself that the action assignment is in the right hands. From then on, the implementing executive should be accountable to the chief executive officer or his agent. This should be the case even if the work of the task force in other areas remains to be completed. There is no "right" tenure for a postmerger task force. Its duration will depend on the length and complexity of its agenda and its ability to resolve differences in approaches to getting things done. As a general rule, the more organizational integration required in a merger, the longer the life of the task force. Even then, a task force is likely to lose its bite if it remains in action for more than a year.

EXPLAINING THE MERGER

Any corporate merger is disruptive to the existing organizations. Each entity has spent years building organizational loyalty and esprit. Informal networks and chains of accountability have been created, and the security of every individual, from top to bottom, has been based on confidence in these networks of responsibility and control.

With the merger, the familiar landscape is thrown into turmoil. Unease is present in some degree at all levels of the merging organizations. Yet the tendency in premerger negotiations is to resolve only issues of responsibility at the highest level of management. This only magnifies the insecurity of those whose job stability and peace of mind depend on the confidence of those to whom they report.

The first role of the postmerger task force, then, is to do everything it can to neutralize these concerns, which can demoralize a formerly well-functioning organization. The task force must consider the nature and intensity of many concerns at different levels of the organization, including organization, compensation, range of responsibility, and postmerger procedures, attitudes, and values—those attributes known as "corporate culture."

Importance of Communications

There is no magic technique for dealing with these concerns, only the judicious use of written, oral, and visual communications. All too often, employees and middle managers learn about a merger through an announcement promising further details at a later date, or a brief item that has been leaked prematurely to the press. These are not adequate, because they create expectations that, as a practical matter, are rarely realized. Often, internal announcements resemble the public announcement, although they are intended to produce a different benefit. They are not responsive to any of the issues on the minds of employees. The disruptive effects may not occur immediately, but perceptions of what those disruptions might be are rife from the start.

The kind of communication that has the highest probability of success combines a timely general announcement (in writing, or more desirably, live or videotaped presentations) with small group sessions in which management personnel deal with those specific actions or policies that will directly affect individuals or groups. This should be followed by question-and-answer sessions that resolve problems or evaluate the progress toward their resolution.

Clearly, every echelon within both companies cannot be given the same degree of personal treatment. Although it may seem obvious, the key is to deal on an individual basis with at least middle and top management, and to discuss the merger with them in the context of their individual problems and concerns. Nevertheless, for some significant period of time after the merger, the task force must continue to assume responsibility for the form and content of communications through which employees are informed about changes that are likely to affect them.

Such matters as changes in benefits, for example, need to be thoroughly and carefully explained. These explanations should include a candid discussion of the reasons why the changes have taken place. Loss of credibility, as the new organization's leadership soon will discover, has even more lasting and potentially lethal effects than unpopular decisions presented candidly and openly. No matter what management does or how well it functions, there will be many in the organization who will not like the changes. But clear and open communication will remove one of the most serious roadblocks to adjustment—the sense employees often have that they must comply blindly with policies without being told why.

Assessment of Damage

Some mergers cause less disruption than others. There are few ripples when management mandates a minimum of organizational integration, or when the merged entity operates as a holding company. When something more sweeping is intended, there is a correlation between the extent of the proposed integration and the intensity of concern among employees in both predecessor organizations.

One of the first activities of the postmerger task force is to appraise realistically the extent of the potential damage created by the merger. This is often difficult to do. Just before and just after the merger, most managements do not want to be confronted with the kinds of problems that mergers generate. Thus the objectivity and self-discipline of the chief executive is vital in this time frame.

A good place to begin is with the members of the task force themselves. At the organizational meeting or immediately thereafter, the members should have a frank discussion of their own problems in accepting the merger and the problems they perceive in their organizations. This exchange can reveal both obvious and subtle differences in perspective among the members of the merging groups, based on the extent and the accuracy of the information each has received and the value system each uses to mold the data into a point of view. Once the task force has a clearer picture of the anticipated problems, members should meet with several of their non-task force colleagues to test their own perceptions.

Such pulse taking should result in a sense of how much direct communication will be necessary at each level of the organization and what the focus of that communication should be. The task force should come away from the interchanges with a more accurate sense of the problems on people's minds and the intensity with which the task force must work to allay employee concerns.

If unions and other employee organizations exist, it is important to communicate directly with their leaderships. In addition, the task force should present the facts about the merger to the corporation's human resources professionals and solicit their help in clarifying the issues and devising approaches for dealing with employee concerns. If it can be arranged, members of the task force should discuss the handling of merger issues with counterparts in other recently merged companies.

Organizing Information

Although mergers differ in the depth and intensity of effort needed to interpret them, there is a pattern as to the subjects that concern employees most. Recognizing this pattern will help the task force organize its work and focus on the issues that are of primary concern to the specific groups with whom they are communicating. Among these issues are: changes in organization and reporting; alterations in job description and responsibility; changes in grade, title, compensation, and benefits; and changes in physical location, working environment, and operating procedures and methods.

Dealing with so wide a range of matters is a daunting job. Therefore, the next task is to organize information in a way that makes the job more tractable. A good approach is to isolate the subject matter most relevant to each level of the organization and develop a communications program that is most appropriate. Individual programs may range from a single written bulletin to an intense series of interactions—written, oral, and visual—extending over a fairly long time period.

As satisfying as they may seem, it is not important that ringing declarations about the merger accompany its closing. If the merger is to work well within a reasonable time frame it is important that a series of personal communications accompany the events that follow the merger, when necessary. These events have a more direct effect on individuals and organizations than the fact of the merger itself. They are what employees need to know about if they are to re-commit themselves to the merged company.

COMMUNICATING MAJOR CHANGES

Beyond general information about the merger, the principal messages the task force communicates to employees should be about changes. These fall into three major categories:

Programs and systems affecting employees directly—modifications in job classification and grading systems; changes in compensation and benefits, such as pension and stock purchase plans; and changes in title structure and working locations

Practices and policies for presenting the organization to interested and essential publics—advertising, public relations, elements of corporate name and identity (such as logotypes and signage) and even such relatively minor matters as business cards and stationery

Changes that affect all employees as a group—modifications in procedures, practices, and individual and unit responsibilities.

The approach to each of these categories needs to be carefully thought through. There are differences among them in complexity and priority that will influence the number of people who will be involved, the level of expertise required, and the time and money needed to produce a resolution.

THE LAST WORD

After a merger is consummated, management, reasonably satisfied with the deal it has struck, will be anxious to achieve the benefits of the combination as rapidly as possible. Moderating this natural desire for quick results should be the understanding that making mergers operate smoothly is never easy. The tendency of top management is to assume that with the signing of agreements the necessary work is done. In this environment, suggestions for the creation of a postmerger task force often will be greeted with glazed eyes and mumbling about bureaucracy and impracticality.

For some mergers, this attitude may well be appropriate. But for most, it would be a mistake to succumb to this sort of impatience. At the very least, a postmerger task force provides an arena in which members of all parties to the merger can have practical experience in working together. At best, it establishes a forum in which known problems can be discussed openly.

A chief executive is free to reject the value of the postmerger task force and ignore the difficulties the merger creates for all parties. The CEO then can declare victory. But under those circumstances, the victory may not survive the disruption and deterioration of the merged organizations.

Chapter 27

Merging Benefit and Compensation Plans

Walter I. Jacobs
President, U.S. Consulting, Hay Group, Inc.,
Philadelphia, Pennsylvania

Kenneth P. Shapiro
President, Hay/Huggins Co., Inc., Philadelphia,
Pennsylvania

In an earlier and simpler time, few companies evaluated the implications of a merger on their employees' compensation and benefits. At best, consolidating the compensation and benefit programs of merged companies was an afterthought. But two factors have moved this afterthought to a prominent position in any proposed merger.

First, with the Employee Retirement Income Security Act (ERISA), the Pension Benefit Guaranty Corp. (PBGC), the Multiemployer Pension Plan Amendment Act (MPPAA), and other related legislation and regulation, pension liability "horror stories" have abounded. This elaborate structure has forced all parties in a merger or acquisition to evaluate early on the most important employee benefit considerations: the pension funds and their unfunded liabilities.

Second, research has shown that the cultural fit of companies is a major factor in their successful integration. Compensation always plays a very important role, either facilitating the cross-cultural understanding of two organizations or emphasizing key differences that underscore potential cultural barriers to business success.

Going into the process, the only certainty is that the two organizations will have different compensation and benefit programs. By the end of this planning process, however, a total remuneration program should emerge with a mix of compensation and benefit elements that best fits the combined organization. Thus, if the conclusion is that both companies should keep their existing programs intact because of the peculiarities of organization and business diversity, the determination will be the legitimate result of the planning process—not an accidental outgrowth of inaction.

Every issue in compensation and benefits need not be settled during negotiations. Because of the hectic nature of merger and acquisition activities, much of the strategy determination and plan analysis can be accomplished in the "quieter" postmerger atmosphere. So can consideration of the funding efficiencies of combining various benefits coverages. However, what to do with the pension plans, their assets, and their unfunded liabilities cannot be postponed until the deal is completed. Neglecting to address the important pension issue as a premerger activity can limit the options available after the fact. Sloppy or half-hearted work creates potential for loss of income, in addition to loss of opportunity.

The pension issue can involve known or hidden costs that are large enough to affect the price, or even the viability, of a deal. Before a deal is closed, this hurdle must be cleared. Addressing it early in the merger and acquisition process is essential. Similarly, the compensation component requires thorough analysis during the merger process and careful implementation during integration.

The chronology of an M&A deal highlights the compensation and benefits issues that should be considered at various stages along the way.

COMPENSATION AND BENEFITS ISSUES DURING NEGOTIATIONS

During negotiations, a group of senior managers from both companies should be assigned to analyze compensation and benefits issues. All too often, this has been left to the benefits and compensation specialists alone. A committee approach—using specialists as support people—should help ensure that the goals and strategies of the combined organizations are supported by an effective remuneration program. Indeed, this may be the first time either of the affected organizations ever addressed its own compensation and benefits issues through a top-down approach.

For defined-benefit pension plans, those pension programs that provide a definitely determinable benefit, generally based on level of compensation and length of service with the company, there are five alternatives. They include terminating the plan(s), freezing the benefit accruals, merging the plans, maintaining separate plans, and converting to an alternative pension vehicle.

Plan Termination Decisions

As a result of the Employee Retirement Income Security Act and subsequent creation of the Pension Benefit Guaranty Corp., companies have become liable for payment of any unfunded, vested liabilities in a benefit plan in the event of a plan termination. Currently, this reimbursement can equal up to 30 percent of a corporation's net worth. Thus, in considering the options for terminating a plan, this liability must be measured against these three factors: (1) the accelerated cash flow requirements (because the PBGC liability is an immediate claim), (2) the cost of continued fundings, and (3) the growth of the PBGC liability if the plan continues. (Nonfinancial factors, such as the existence of a plan at the acquiring company and its level of benefits, also are relevant factors.)

If the negotiating parties decide to terminate a target's plan, they should make sure that the plan is terminated before the company is acquired. Otherwise, the plan becomes a liability for the newly merged company. In addition, the termination date should be chosen carefully, and only after consideration of such factors as the market value of assets. Conversely, in some recent cases, significant amounts of overfunding have been returned to the company upon termination of a defined-benefit pension plan.

Freezing Benefits

An alternative to termination is freezing the benefits accrued up to the acquisition date. Although no additional benefits accrue under this option, service after the acquisition date must be counted toward vesting of the benefits already accrued.

This alternative serves two purposes. It honors the commitment made before the takeover, and it avoids the employee psychological trauma associated with a plan termination. In addition, because this approach allows for the future funding of liabilities, there is a potential cash flow advantage. However, it must be recognized that the PBGC liabilities will continue to grow (albeit slowly) as more participants near vesting service. Thus, anyone considering this option should weigh the cost of maintaining the frozen plan against the current and projected PBGC liability. Any funds produced from overfunding a frozen plan will not be returned to the employees, but remain plan assets that can be used to honor future liabilities.

Merging Plans

A third option is to merge the plans of the acquiring and acquired companies, which is especially attractive if the target's employees enjoy superior benefits. Even if the benefits for future service with the merged company are reduced, this option still is a better deal for the employees than freezing or terminating their plans. If the acquired company's plan is better funded, as Table 27.1 demon-

TABLE 27.1 Example of Pension Fund Comparisons: Premerger and Postmerger

	Before the merger		After the merger
	Acquiring company	Target company	Combined company
Covered payroll	$10,000,000	$4,000,000	$14,000,000
Pension expense:			
Dollar amount	700,000	250,000	870,000
Percent of payroll	7.00%	6.25%	6.21%
Present value of			
vested benefits	10,000,000	4,000,000	14,000,000
Assets	8,000,000	4,600,000	12,600,000
Funding ratio	80%	115%	90%
PBGC liability	2,000,000	-0-	1,400,000

strates, merging the assets and liabilities of the plans will reduce the overall PBGC liability and may trim the total pension expense as a percentage of payroll for the merged company's combined plan. (The pension expense of the combined plan is less than the sum of the two unmerged plans, because the merger reduces future service benefits for the acquired company's plan.)

Separate Plans

Another alternative is simply to maintain separate plans. This "wait-and-see" approach allows the acquiring company to keep its options for the future open.

Conversion

A final option is to convert the acquired pension plan into a defined-contribution vehicle such as thrift savings, profit sharing, or a 401(k) plan, a program that allows employee contributions from earnings in pretax dollars and provides for matching contributions from the employer. As in plan termination, conversion triggers PCBC liability. However, the conversion approach will maintain a plan for covering the employees of the acquired company.

MPPAA Implications

A final, although crucial, issue for the members of the merger and acquisition team regarding pension liabilities is the implication of the 1980 Multiemployer Pension Plan Amendment Act (MPPAA). Prior to this law, employers who participated in a multiemployer plan (set up under the Taft-Hartley Act so that several companies in one industry negotiate unified benefits with a union) were liable only for a "cents-per-hour" negotiated contribution and a potential liability if the plan terminated. Any one employer could leave the multiemployer plan and not be liable for any unfunded liability—as long as the plan survived for another five years. Under MPPAA, however, employers that withdraw from a multiemployer plan are liable for any unfunded liability they leave behind. These withdrawal liability payments can last as long as 20 years.

It is therefore crucial to analyze the extent to which a company being considered for acquisition or merger is involved in multiemployer plans, and then measure the potential withdrawal liabilities. If necessary, the purchase price should be adjusted accordingly.

INTEGRATING COMPENSATION AND BENEFITS

Another major issue that should be tackled during the negotiation period concerns the integration of compensation and benefit programs. This stage of analysis does not require resolution of any problems uncovered during the merger investigation, but does require the fact-finding and analysis necessary to make sure that these problems are, in fact, identified—and then estimating their potential severity.

The first variable in this analysis is the necessity for integrating plans. The degree of integration needed in compensation and benefits programs will be a direct function of the strategy, operating style, and organizational structure of the combined businesses. For instance, in a holding company environment, a newly acquired business that will be run with great operating autonomy and little or no interaction with other businesses, may very well retain entirely separate compensation and benefits plans. On the other hand, a horizontal merger of two companies in the same industry probably would require common compensation philosophy and programs. Figure 27.1 is a schematic representation of the relationships of operating style and business diversity with the need to have integrated compensation and benefit programs. The need for integrating programs intensifies as businesses become more centralized and more related.

A slight need generally would indicate that plans for most employees should be designed independently and adjusted to fit the needs of the business units, the industry, and the overall economic conditions. In almost all mergers, some executive compensation plans would be integrated, especially long-term incentives, but often short-term incentives and perquisites as well. Because the cost and difficulty of the integration process would be moderate, no further consideration usually needs to be given until after the close of the deal.

A moderate need calls for a well-articulated compensation philosophy and policy. All compensation and benefits programs should be tested within this rubric for two purposes: to determine proper fit, and to see if separateness or commonality between the business units best meets business goals. Although this process may be appropriate after closing a deal, management should at least consider it as early as the negotiating process.

A heavy integration need points toward a combined compensation and benefits program for the merging entities. At the very least, it indicates the necessity of further study to estimate feasibility and cost.

When the combining of programs is required, any evaluation should focus on two general indicators:

- Compensation and benefits philosophy
- Compensation and benefits cost

The greater the differences in compensation philosophy, the greater the risk

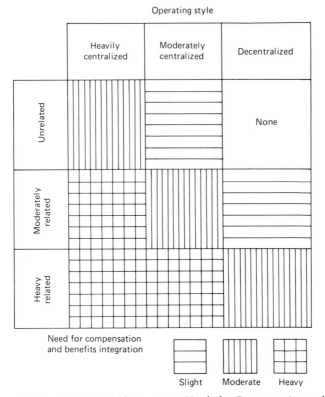

FIGURE 27.1 Model of Integration Needs for Compensation and Benefits

and difficulty in merging plans. How does one compare philosophies of pay and benefits? Perhaps the most revealing element is the risk-to-reward ratio or the leverage built into compensation plans. At one extreme is the security-oriented organization that generally pays only fixed base salaries and offers defined benefits. At the other end are the highly leveraged companies, with significant amounts of compensation at risk through various incentive plans.

Cost is an obvious factor. With rare exceptions, any joining of plans between merged companies tends to raise compensation and benefits to the highest program level offered by either company. Almost every company has internal data and external survey data available for a general analysis of pay levels and a quick estimate of the cost implications of moving to the higher level.

Figure 27.2 presents a matrix that is helpful in analyzing the difficulty and cost of integrating compensation and benefit plans. Each organization can take a place on the two-dimensional matrix based on its pay philosophy and cost. The degree of horizontal difference indicates the relative cost of integration (small for companies B and D, but great for companies A and C). The degree of vertical separation represents the difficulty in integrating differing pay philosophies (small for companies B and C, but great for companies D and A).

When done in a timely and thoughtful manner, analysis of these factors lends

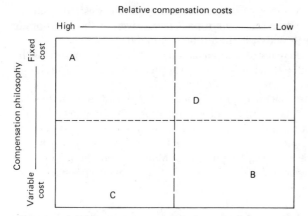

Relative compensation costs

FIGURE 27.2 Integration Analysis Model for Compensation and Benefits

important input to merger and acquisition negotiations. The data are important in pricing and can help eliminate honeymoon period surprises that may sour organizations at the critical point in their marriage.

INTEGRATION WORK AFTER CLOSING THE DEAL

Once a merger is finalized, the actual integration process begins. If the parties have done their preclosing homework, they already have a good feel for the difficulty of the task ahead. Fortunate are those who require little or no integration of their respective compensation and benefits programs. The challenge is far greater in those situations where heavy integration is required.

Setting the Objectives

First, to support the business strategies of the organizations, specific program objectives must be established. The architecture of the compensation programs not only must support business goals, it must foster the type of employee behavior necessary to reach those goals. Compensation plans can be designed to create individualistic, entrepreneurial, and high-risk behavior. Conversely, they can be designed to create team-oriented, low-risk behavior—or almost any combination desired. Business plans and strategy will dictate the appropriate employee behavior; the design of the compensation and benefits plans either will support or hinder achievement of those goals. Specific compensation/benefits objectives should address these issues:

- Competitive position
- Adequacy
- Funding
- Cost containment
- General plan design

Competitive Position. A primary objective is to identify the desired competitive level of the compensation and benefit package, as well as the appropriate external marketplace with which it should be compared.

Objectives regarding adequacy of compensation and benefits are addressed by answering such questions as: "What percentage of preretirement income should the pension plan replace?"

Although it is axiomatic that all employees desire effective funding, it does not necessarily follow that this should lead organizations to compensate at the lowest possible cost. For example, it may be easier administratively to place all insurance coverage with one carrier, even though the cost may be slightly higher than distributing coverage among two or more. Management should develop funding objectives that recognize the trade-offs between low cost and administrative convenience.

Cost Containment. Just as all companies want effective programs, they also desire cost containment. However, overall cost containment objectives should be set in addressing such issues as degree of employee involvement in cost sharing (through employer contributions toward health insurance premiums, for example). It is important to balance cost control with other objectives. For example, an objective that maximizes cost savings may conflict with a desire for a competitive program.

Plan Design. Finally, management must address general plan design objectives. For instance, should early retirement be encouraged or discouraged? Should the same plans be in effect for union and nonunion employees? What is the proper balance between short- and long-term incentives? How strong a performance orientation should the compensation programs have for various employee groups? These are but a few necessary questions.

Testing the Concepts

After the specific objectives have been set, the compensation and benefit programs of the merging organizations should be reviewed according to those objectives. Measurement of the competitiveness of the compensation and benefit packages of the merged companies against each other and the chosen external marketplace is a primary step. This is best accomplished by using an actuarial model of salary equivalent values for the benefit programs. Then, because the values of the benefit programs of the merged companies are stated in dollar value terms, they can be added directly to the competitive analysis of cash compensation.

A by-product of this analysis is the measurement of both the adequacy and the internal equity of the compensation and benefit programs of the merging companies.

When designing merged programs, decision makers will need information about the employee's perceived value of the compensation and benefit programs. These data are particularly useful when considering additional flexibility for a compensation and benefits program—such as providing employees with choices in trading one benefit for another, whether implemented before or after the merger.

A tailored questionnaire provides a tool to measure the perceived value of compensation and benefits as well as the return on the compensation and benefits investment. In this analysis, the perceptions of each employee about each compensation and benefits plan are quantified and expressed against a normative data base (see Figure 27.3). These perceived values, when related to actual costs, will uncover where company expenditures produce maximum and minimum perceived values—a measurement of the return on compensation and benefit investment.

With this overall set of objectives established and approved by management, the compensation and benefits professionals then can begin adding, deleting, and modifying programs to provide the integrated compensation package.

Obviously, when a large change in either philosophy or cost is required in the plans of one or both parties, design of the combined plan becomes more difficult. Two techniques can help alleviate the problems. When changes in cash compensation programs also require alterations in philosophy, a multiyear phasing of the new compensation schedule often is helpful. Behavioral change in an organization can be managed, but not overnight.

When integration of different benefit plans is required, the most common approach has been to adapt the plan that provides the most liberal benefits (and thus the most expensive) as the standard for the combined company. This is a

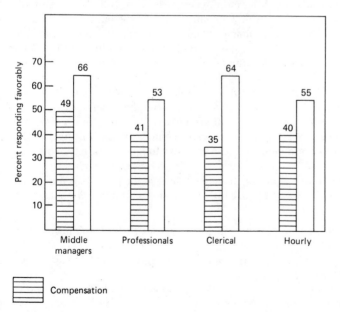

FIGURE 27.3 Satisfaction with Compensation and Benefits (*Source: Hay Employee Attitude Database 1984*)

potentially high-cost approach with marginal investment returns. Yet time after time, it occurs because these benefits have become an entitlement to employees, and companies have been loathe to make negative changes. One positive solution to this dilemma is a variable benefit program. While the best plans can be incorporated in the benefit package, costs still can be controlled. Under the variable benefits concept, the employee has a defined limit of credits to spend, and can use them to select a program from among several options. Cost is contained while the employee may select those benefits most appropriate to his or her individual circumstances.

IMPLEMENTATION OF THE PROGRAM

People in real estate are fond of saying that the most important factors in selling residential real estate are location, location, and location. In the context of following up the decisions to combine total compensation programs, the most important factors are communication, communication, and communication. Timely and informative communication is vital to address the concerns of employees during the merger process. Inevitably, many are skeptical, fearful, or angry. A strong message, delivered clearly and frequently, can help alleviate personnel unrest and maintain a productive environment.

Today, every company has professionals available to use a vast arsenal of media for communicating with its employees. Use them! But also make judicious use of the most effective employee communication system already intact at every company—the employees' managers and supervisors. Employee attitude studies consistently show that employees prefer to receive information from their supervisors, and that the information has higher credibility when it comes from the "boss."

Another adage of merit goes, "If it ain't broke, don't fix it." This does not, however, rule out preventive maintenance. New or modified compensation and benefit programs should be audited regularly to determine if they are meeting stated objectives. Some will require change or fine tuning. Do the necessary preventive maintenance before you have to replace the entire piece of equipment.

Dealing with compensation and benefits issues is an important and often neglected portion of the merger and acquisition process. Enhance the success of the business transaction by:

- Coping with critical pension and integration issues early in the negotiation phase
- Establishing specific compensation and benefit program objectives tied to business plans and goals
- Using quantifiable techniques in assuring the development of programs that meet the defined objectives
- Communicating the objectives and actual programs thoroughly and effectively
- Auditing continually the effectiveness of the compensation and benefits plans, and improving upon them where necessary

Chapter 28

The Right Way to Combine Managements

Ned Morse
Hay Group, Dallas, Texas

Mark Feldman
Hay Group, Walnut Creek, California

Ken Martin
Hay Group, Chicago, Illinois

The core issues of the human side of mergers and acquisitions are not losing key people and then getting those who are retained into the right jobs and the right frames of mind, once the deal has been completed. The flip side of this challenge is how to shed excess personnel in a timely and dignified manner that enhances the corporate culture.

How well the combined company handles these twin problems can have telling effects on the success of the combination, a success clearly measured by such criteria as sales, profits, or market share. But the hallmarks of proper integration of people into the merged organization also include its relatively smooth functioning throughout the transition period, its ability to compete effectively over time, and its proficiency in developing and pursuing a strategic program for future expansion and vitality. There is, of course, no quick and easy way to measure these characteristics. In truth, the criteria for differentiating the successful merger from the unsuccessful deal, as far as human perspective is concerned, are not yet empirically validated, statistically sound, or methodologically defensible. But the difficulties of evaluation should not serve as excuses for refusing to deal with the matter of integrating people into a productive organizational structure.

Management of the merged company at the very least should start by recognizing that integration is an issue it must address and then determining exactly how important it is to retain acquired personnel and their goodwill. Indeed, there are instances, such as when the target requires a drastic turnaround, in which the human side is of secondary importance, or even no importance. But if integration of personnel is determined to be a priority issue, management must proceed to work on it with dispatch and care, in line with the particular culture and characteristics that it has acquired or wishes to create in the future.

In preparing this chapter, we determined that it would be most appropriate to base our conclusions on what executives who actually have structured mergers and handled the integration process regard as successful experiences. We researched 28 companies of all sizes that collectively completed nearly 200 acquisitions. The ensuing material is based on their "real-life" experiences. It stresses guidelines for managing the human side of mergers and acquisitions that they have found workable or utilized with basic satisfaction.

AFTER THE WEDDING

The "wedding"—the actual combining of the two merger partners—usually takes place after months of courtship. When the mating period is harmonious, the key people from both sides have gotten to know each other. When it's acrimonious, as in the case of a hostile offer, knowledge of the other company's people is limited and strongly tinged by rumor-tainted perceptions. Regardless of the preliminaries, the marriage has taken place and the human side cannot be ignored. For our purposes, we will assume that decisions on how tightly to integrate the two concerns have been made and that product, market, and production policy decisions have been reached. There are at this point a number of key issues to be handled in implementing the plan.

Identifying People to Be Retained and Shed

Management of the acquiring company faces a stiff challenge in identifying who to keep and who to dismiss. Basically, it has taken on a pool of personnel and is not familiar with each person's talents. There is, furthermore, a problem in deciding which people from the acquired company it will listen to in reaching its decisions. And the buyer's management always must confront the knotty issue of whether a "good" employee in its own organization is better or worse than a "good" employee at the target. If management takes too long in reaching these important decisions, it risks the corrosive effects on performance and morale of prolonged periods of uncertainty. Thus, management is working against time to choose the winners. One executive, recounting a sobering postmerger experience, said, "It didn't take us long to identify the winners. They were the ones who left us after six months while we fretted with the inconsequentials."

Slotting People in the Right Jobs

An acquiring management may have to take some risks when putting some people into jobs in the combined organization. But a winner will perform well even if the job is outside the area of his or her previous experience.

Hanging on to the Winners

How do you hang on to the winners? How do you get them to stay during difficult postmerger periods of ambiguity, or even corporate dysfunction?

One tactic is to include them in some sort of transition or integration task force. Winners need and seek challenge. Putting them on a critical integration team will contribute to job satisfaction because they will be able to see an immediate impact on the merging organizations from their contributions. Of course, there are more direct ways, such as an appeal to the pocketbook. Alternatives that have worked include bonuses based on performance two or three years down the road, as well as an up-front stock position in the parent corporation with a rider that delays exercise of stock purchase options for two or three years.

Creating a Healthy Cultural Fabric while Reducing Staff

There are few areas in which management will be as closely scrutinized by the winners as in dealing with postmerger outplacement. One-on-one counseling will be appreciated not only by those who are released, but by those who stay. It is a bit of dignity that will be highly appreciated by everyone involved. Being "overly generous" when letting people go—such as allowing discretionary extras like the use of a company car for a few weeks, use of an office as a base for conducting a job search, and a generous pension settlement—will yield handsome returns in goodwill among the employees who remain.

PATTERNS OF SUCCESS

A successful integration begins with proper handling of people, and those companies that achieved the most satisfactory combinations were those that skillfully addressed the four people issues just described. The way in which these issues were addressed, in fact, set the pattern for the remaining integration issues. Through our work both as consultants to companies undergoing postmerger integration and as researchers to generate the material for this chapter, we identified a number of consistent themes that recurred in the integration programs that were deemed successful by their managers.

Creating a Vision

In many successful merger integrations, senior management went out of its way to stress the common good of the new organization and to create a vision of what the firm could become. Generally, this was a conscious action intended to instill pride in the new company—especially in the acquired management team, which may have seen its previous vision shattered by the corporate marriage. When the transactions were large, the buying company often created a vision that differed from its own previous self-image. One acquirer, which had viewed itself as being the "biggest and the best" in its field, shifted its emphasis to being "the biggest and the best—a leader in all respects." A diversified transportation company that regarded itself as a "leading transportation firm" transformed itself into a "totally integrated world-scale transportation company" after buying an international shipping operation to go with its trucking, rail, and pipeline businesses. Another company underscored the combination graphically by creating a new logo with elements and colors from each of the merger partners' previous logos.

The vision is developed not through simple sloganeering, but must be deeply thought through, and then purposefully woven into an orchestrated, deliberate communications program. Viable programs share these characteristics:

- There is an emphasis on senior management visibility—or actually getting executives in front of the "troops."
- A lengthy time frame, typically 18 months or so, is allotted.
- Consistent repetition of common themes is utilized.
- A variety of media are used to communicate the message.

Tending to Overcommunicate

Communication must be open, frequent, and fully presented. Virtually every company that was successful in integrating its acquisitions said that this was the most important element of its program. Conversely, unsuccessful companies said most often that if they could start their integration programs over, improved communications is what they would stress most.

The communications effort takes many forms in companies that successfully merge their people resources. Senior management frequently makes itself visible in both formal and informal settings to foster the program. One senior management team of a large, highly dispersed organization made extensive use of videotapings to get the message across. Initially, tapes were sent every other week to all company locations. At installations where company equipment was available, professional-sized tapes were sent. Most locations, however, received personal-sized tapes that employees could check out and take home. Another CEO increased his travel schedule sixfold, frequently holding breakfast, lunch, and dinner meetings in three different locations in order to talk personally about the company's merger. Before each meeting, he solicited anonymous written questions so that he could set straight current rumors or allay local fears.

Regular written updates devoted solely to the integration process also are used with frequency. The material may go either to the employee's home or to the workplace.

Recognizing Good People on Both Sides

Management of the surviving company often assumes that only "their" people are going to manage the concern. That's a truly naive assumption. There usually are good managers in both companies. The leader of the integration process must recognize this fact, and not assume ipso facto that only his or her people should manage the combined entity.

How has the judicious allotment of key posts been handled in successfully integrated organizations? In some cases, the CEO of the acquiring company sets a target for the percentage of surviving managers that will come from the target. The transition team thus has a mandate to take a serious look at the talent inherited with the acquisition.

Another approach is to use an objective outsider to evaluate the managerial talent on both sides, from the senior executive level down to the business segment director and manager level. The enlisted party does not have to be an independent consultant. A retired executive or a board member could fulfill the role. In many instances, these evaluators utilize both interviews and psychological testing to develop their recommendations while assessing candidates from both the acquiring company and the target. By using this approach, the acquiring CEO not only can obtain objective, third-party opinions but send a very strong message to the target's personnel that the new company is acting evenhandedly. Our research has found that a company can achieve an above-average management retention rate by using a third-party "umpire."

A third way to enhance the personnel evaluation process is to tap senior people from both companies, each of whom ideally is removed from the center of in-house political action, to develop assessment information. In one integration, two "elder statesmen" from each company were pulled together by the CEO, who explained that he wanted the "best people," regardless of prior affiliation. The CEO asked the designees to take the initiative in advising him—to be his eyes and ears within the organization. Because each man was highly regarded within his own company, the CEO, by basing his decisions on their advice, was able to make much sounder decisions than if he had relied solely on his traditional sources.

Is there a preferred way of doing this? No. The deciding factor is the personal operating style of the chief executive of the company employing the person in charge of the integration. The best results, however, have come from third-party appraisal, which tends to be more research-oriented, more expert, and more expeditious than other techniques. Additionally, the use of an outside party can ameliorate some of the paranoia that invariably exists within the acquired company. It may, however, heighten anxiety inside the parent company, because the managers who automatically assumed that "we are going to win," suddenly can't be so sure.

The major advantage of the third-party approach is that the process gets the period of uncertainty over quickly. Speed was one of the key traits that successful companies had in common. They were adept at making decisions quickly and putting the trauma of integration behind them as fast as possible. Less successful companies tended to let the process drag on, sometimes for a year-and-a-half to two years. When these companies finally made their decisions, they sometimes were surprised to find that they didn't have many good people to choose. Their "winners," disenchanted by the spell of ambiguity, had departed. A final side benefit of the third-party approach is that each side knows it is taking place and recognizes it as a presumably fair method of developing a company that had access to the talent of both companies.

The key point is to acknowledge first that there are good people in both organizations. After that the trick is to identify the winners and make sure they get positions commensurate with their abilities.

Putting the Company's Interests First

The most successful integrations were directed by people who placed the common good of the combined organization and its customers before all else. There are a number of ways to select the people with that motivation.

One approach is to form a transition task force composed of people drawn from the common functions of both organizations (such as electronic data processing, marketing, human resources, etc.). These people are reconciled to the reality that a reorganization is going to come about, and they are determined to make the transition as smooth and as high-quality as possible.

Successful companies, like a white blood cell fighting off an infection, tend to concentrate their resources around an issue in order to resolve it fast. Unlike unsuccessful companies, the successful integrators used as few as six and no more than 12 months from the announcement of the acquisition to reach the point at which management considered the new organization to be "up and running." Timing is especially critical because the new organization will be operating suboptimally throughout the entire transition period, when employees are suffering from a great deal of ambiguity and spend a lot of their time worrying and talking about what's going to happen. At the same time, the marketplace is unsure about how it will be affected by the change, leaving the competition free to exploit that uncertainty. Overall, the organization experiences reduced performance during the transition period. Obviously, if this period of impaired performance lasts only six months, the company is immeasurably better off.

The successful companies also shared a unique vision of the "common good." They communicated the necessity for not putting "our own" parochial interests first. The people involved in successful transitions recognized the chance to build a better organization than either constituent had enjoyed as a separate company. When that kind of thinking is introduced at the outset and maintained throughout the course of the transition, the resulting organization is far stronger than if the process is wracked by defensiveness, turf protection, and desires to retain the status quo.

The Task Force as an Asset.   At the successful companies we surveyed, task forces were effective in creating policies, crafting communications programs, and targeting the right people to "hang on to." The resulting corporate culture was stronger after the period of trauma than it was at either of the premerger companies. The effective task forces frequently were not granted formal decision-making power, but they enjoyed sufficient confidence with management that most of their key recommendations were accepted.

There are a number of reasons why the task force approach works. Recruitment is centered on people who know their fields—and their organizations—very thoroughly. Second, the team members realize that they are the ones who must live and work—every day—with what comes out of their deliberations. Third, because employees from throughout the organization can achieve considerable understanding about why certain decisions were made, they tend to have an appreciation of the trade-offs involved. As a result, they can persuade reluctant and defensive people that the right decisions were made.

Fourth, all organizations have two structures, the formal and the informal. The task force approach—reaching down into both companies—provides for the bridging of these organizations. In one integration, the task force became the communications conduit between both companies, with the result that the informal communications and power structures of the two organizations were understood more fully and meshed more quickly.

Finally, the senior management that uses task forces adroitly has a splendid opportunity to see good performers from both organizations in action. The task force process puts together the "best and the brightest" from each organization, providing further exposure to the winners and losers.

How long should a task force function? What should its "life span" be? Task forces typically go through two phases. Because the policy development or recommendation aspect of task forces appears to be good for everything but people issues, its life span usually is two to three months. Beyond this, the task force should be chartered to meet and report periodically—perhaps every other month—to the person overseeing the transition.

Establishing an Ombudsman. While task forces have proved highly efficient and successful, there are other ways to involve employees in the integration process. One alternative is to use an ombudsman, either an impartial outsider or someone who is known, perhaps even revered throughout the combined organization. The ombudsman can field ideas or complaints and allow employees to get them off their chests and into the pipeline for resolution. The ombudsman also serves as a communications center for rumors, ideas, problems, or anything that can create or dispel anxiety. The post must be filled carefully. It can become political and can be misused. Additionally, it's an "overload" position—one where it is impossible to do everything that could be done. So the new organization needs an ombudsman who has a lot of savvy, a sense of priorities, and a good deal of energy.

One organization named as its ombudsman a retired vice chairman of the acquiring company who also had done business with the target during his active career. The ombudsman sent a letter, also signed by both CEOs, to the employees outlining his role. He set up a post office box, and established a 24-hour telephone "hotline." He both published the hours he would be at the number and set up an answering machine to take calls in his absence. Considerable time was devoted to face-to-face meetings with employees—in the company lunchroom, at the bowling league, at their desks. He would drop in on meetings to "touch base" about the merger. The ombudsman would meet quickly with any business unit that had been stung with a key resignation or was suffering layoffs, to give people a chance to air frustrations and concerns. But the role worked two ways. The ombudsman had unlimited access to senior management, allowing him to communicate the true course of events at the lower levels and to influence the ultimate decisions at the top.

Decisive Action on Emotion-Charged Issues

In most successful integrations, management moved quickly to deal with the issues that were of the most concern to its personnel, both by eliminating unpopular or dubious policies and practices and by "enshrining" those that were well accepted and effective. Among the matters that should be given priority are the "turf issues,"such as titles, salaries, positions, and the pecking order that establishes who reports to whom. On one hand, the postmerger integration offers an opportunity to clean house of poor practices such as an ineffective budgeting process or a discriminatory compensation structure. On the other, "enshrining" the popular and effective practices, through direct action or notice that they indeed will be retained, gives employees assurances that some familiar elements will be kept. The emphasis in this area should be on action rather than passive or tacit approval. The employees should be informed clearly that a particularly favored element will be retained because it has been working well or enjoys wide acceptance. This practice will go a long way toward alleviating uncertainty, which, our research determined, was the prime reason that people left the organization following a merger. Although people have a certain degree of tolerance of ambiguity, it cannot be stretched indefinitely when there is an information vacuum.

A key sample of "enshrining the good" was when a major service firm that had just installed a 401(k) benefits program announced, immediately after being acquired by an overseas buyer, that the plan would be kept. The disclosure was reassuring news to employees, who recognized that future announcements might not be so reassuring. The move also brought the acquirer a measure of goodwill. The buyer in effect was serving notice that it would not tamper with the parts of the target that had been working well.

Another company that moved quickly to "enshrine the good" announced that it would not reduce a major commitment of the acquired firm's resources to a community relations program. The parent CEO not only clearly informed employees but made special efforts to reassure community leaders and local news media that the effort would be supported. In retrospect, the CEO said that the decision helped his company retain its winners and made people more tolerant of other changes that, while necessary, would not be so popular. "Enshrining the good," however, also can involve a lot of little things, such as retention of banquets or trips utilized as incentives for meeting sales goals.

There are less sensitive issues on which decisions can be put off for some time, provided they are not totally ignored and the integrating management acknowledges that it is giving attention to the situations and gathering information for making definite determinations. Faced with a choice of moving quickly on the basis of inadequate, biased, or politically tinted information, or waiting until a sufficient amount of quality data is in hand, the director of the transition probably is better off opting for some delay—although, to reiterate, some notice should be given that the matter is under objective consideration.

Management Visibility to Employees

If management is visible, it has the opportunity to squelch rumors and to give employees the opportunity to make first-hand assessments of the character of their new management. Visibility is required not only of the CEO, but of other top managers as well. And management accessibility should extend to employees of the acquiring company as well as the target's personnel. The management of a building materials company said that it experienced a minimum loss of its own personnel after a merger in part because the managers spent a good deal of time mixing with the "troops"—more time, in fact, than they had spent before the deal. This is a variation on the general's trip to the field to reassure the army.

On a second level, management of the acquiring company should make itself visible to personnel of the target as a means of letting the acquired people know who the buyers are and what they are really like. Invisibility often generates unhealthy speculation and perplexity about the individuals who lead the new organization. This element of visibility, however, must be handled with care. If parent management is too visible and makes too many visits to the target, this interest can be misinterpreted as a series of inspections for purposes of fashioning radical changes and drastic personnel cuts.

Through our research, we found that certain vehicles of visibility are used frequently. One generally effective method is the formal meeting at which a charismatic member of the acquirer's management team addresses a medium- to large-sized group. The presentation is followed by a question-and-answer period and, perhaps, a cocktail party or other type of less formal gathering that is structured to maximize contact between employees and their new management.

Challenges in the Turnaround.   A tricky situation is presented when the target is a poorly performing company in need of a major turnaround. The best approach is to depress the visibility of the inherited management ("They got us into this mess") and to stress accessibility of the buyer's top people. Emphasis should be on how the two groups can work together to restore the underperformer to health. Recommended approaches include frequent meetings at plants, offices, and other facilities with groups of all sizes in settings that are both formal and informal.

One company that has logged good success in several turnaround situations uses a "goal attainment strategy." It establishes a realistic performance goal for the newly owned operation—a target the management is certain it can attain. The parent then monitors the operation's progress until the goal is achieved. According to the company, the approach nets several benefits. It fosters faith in the parent management's ability to lead the operations back to health, and it helps wean employees from the old management. After the initial goals are met, the parent company gains easier acceptance for other changes it wants to introduce.

It was interesting that this company experienced a fairly small loss of talent, partly because top employees of the acquired firm sensed they were going to be part of a winning team and their careers would be commensurately enhanced.

Social Gatherings. Another approach begins with a series of social occasions at which the target managers meet the CEO, who moves through the crowd, spends a few minutes with each "guest," and gets a chance to size up each one. Subsequently, acquired managers are given a half hour or so to discuss their business privately with the CEO and/or the board of directors. The CEO can see how well each manager prepares by observing him or her in action before both a large group and a small one. Simultaneously, the manager should like the idea of getting a chance to talk about his or her part of the business.

Some companies have used a somewhat more formalized approach in which managers from both the acquirer and the target gather for a relatively lengthy conference—as long as two days—that focuses on a variety of business matters, including those dealing with the transition. The CEO and/or his chief lieutenants sit in on the meetings, using them as vantage points to make evaluations of the participating executives. An alternative is to have the head of the transition team attend the meetings and register observations in the role of ombudsman.

PATTERNS OF FAILURE

Just as common themes recurred among companies that believed they successfully integrated, there were recurring faults manifested by companies that believed they either mismanaged postmerger assimilation or, in hindsight, could have done better. If the miscues were to be summed up under a single heading, it would be that the acquiring companies concluded they had not reduced the air of uncertainty or ambiguity following completion of the deal.

Acquirers Believed They Had the Corner on Talent

Companies that admitted they mismanaged the integration process acted as if they monopolized all of the good managers, strategies, and business practices. They tended, either overtly or indirectly, to demonstrate a "so what" attitude toward acquired personnel in the belief that their own managers could handle the job if the target's people departed. No value was placed on retaining the right people or judiciously dismissing those who didn't fit in. The unsuccessful companies tended to believe in benign neglect and prolonged uncertainty. Their common belief was that the strong people who really wanted to stay would hang on.

The people who are truly winners are willing to take risks, but only if they see good reasons. The absence of information about the new company, about clarity of goals, and about a perceived advantage to staying obviously don't provide the winners with much incentive to hang on. Moreover, the winners have the easiest times marketing themselves outside the company, and will be the first ones to test their appeal in the open market. If that type of desertion occurs, the buyer is left with the dross and the people who are so scared of leaving that they will remain with a sinking ship. To the winners go the spoils.

"Corporate conceit" can be fatal to an integration. A management with a cavalierly superior attitude may find that the employee they most coveted will go stale or leave. Such an attitude is senseless from a business perspective, because in the quality- and service-oriented 1980s, an acquirer increasingly is buying talent, people initiative, and company culture. Admittedly, this talent and initiative will change over time, but unsuccessful acquirers told us that they did not care at first about the people they acquired and, as a result, forfeited their chances of retaining top-notch managers.

The typical scenario in less successful integrations has executives staying at their desks, refraining from visits to plant locations, and making no effort to maintain an ongoing stream of communications. There is no management by walking around. Usually, decisions on integrating the two companies are weighted heavily in favor of the acquiring firm. Virtual edicts are issued, and people from the buying company often are parachuted into senior positions at the acquired unit. The result is that people in the acquired company feel as if they have been in a war and lost. Good people leave that environment.

Fast Decisions Based on Shallow Perceptions

This was another characteristic of postmerger misfires. It is advantageous to make decisions quickly and decisively only if they are based on good data. In the absence of good data, take your time. The bad decisions, regardless of when they are made, can't be reversed. Delaying the decision-making process for a relatively short period of time to come up with a good decision is the best tactic. However, if such a delay heightens anxiety and uncertainty, there may be a need to act more quickly than a manager would like. The need to act may actually outweigh the need for more accurate information.

The companies with integration problems seemed to place someone at the head of the integration process who was not people-sensitive. On the basis of our own appraisal, or through a consensus of people involved in the integration, the director emerged as someone who lacked good intuition about people, the ability to empathize with the situation, and a knack for effective communications. Frequently, the integration "point man" had a brusque, cut-and-dried, no-nonsense personality and was neither liked nor respected. The mode of operation often perpetuated the belief that people were being steamrollered.

The integration ideally should be directed by someone who has exceptional people skills. If the CEO is not people-oriented or not highly charismatic, the integration post should go to someone who is. The "point person" should be someone that personnel of the acquired firm can look at, measure, regard as "good," and consider the personification of the combined company. In this instance, "good" doesn't mean "warm and fuzzy," but the ability to be respected as well as liked. The ideal is that rare person who combines intelligence and savvy with the ability to lead and can apply both qualities to the integration process. If there is no one in the acquiring company with this unique bundle of skills, that's a good reason to scour the acquired unit for promising talent.

Lack of an "Early Warning System"

An almost congenital weakness in many unsuccessful transitions was the lack of a systematic program for monitoring the integration process and determining if it was proceeding in desired fashion or going off the track. The heart of the system is establishment of a game plan for carrying out the integration, complete with "milestones" or specific deadlines for completing specified functions. For example, points in time may be set for consolidating the certain data bases or centralizing a sales force or allocating manufacturing functions between plants.

The successful companies not only had a game plan and monitored every action against the plan, but established "early warning signals" as well. An example is the identification of a personnel turnover rate that is considered acceptable. The acquiring company then monitors whether the actual turnover rate is within or exceeds the benchmark. Similarly, the acquirer might identify certain key people who are especially desirable. If these people started seeking work elsewhere, the acquiring company could react by launching a preset counterstrategy such as sending a member of its human resources team on "re-recruiting" trips to save the potential winners. One company built a warning signal into its employee assistance program by offering counseling in drug abuse, alcohol abuse, and other substance abuses, and tracking the number of people who participated. The number in the program quintupled in the four months following the merger announcement. This suggested that people were feeling significantly higher levels of stress than parent management regarded as acceptable. The signal was followed by an enhanced employee communication and involvement program that not only stayed personnel turnover but reduced participation in the counseling program.

Employee attitude surveys are used to generate early warning signals. A company that uses them routinely after acquisitions starts with a broad-based survey containing a cover letter that tells employees, "We care about what you think." The questions are tailored to elicit information on what the employees think should happen during the integration. Follow-up surveys are taken every four to six months to monitor changes in employee responses and to continue signaling employees that they, and their ideas, count. Another company in our survey uses exit interviews to find out what aspects of the acquisition played the greatest roles in the employee's decision to leave. If a repetitive pattern is found, the information immediately goes to the CEO, who acts to remove the offending "thorn."

Unilateral Imposition of Policies and Practices

Companies that admitted to less-than-successful integrations frequently conceded that they walked in and imposed their existing policies and procedures, virtually in toto, upon the target management. The attitude could be summed up as one of "You are now us, and this is how we do it!" This is the antithesis of the aforementioned approach of eliminating the bad and "enshrining the good" with some care and precision. Acquired personnel receive a symbolic message that the buyer cares little about their accumulated experience and expertise. When taken for granted, talented managers will tend to leave and offer their skills elsewhere, frequently to a competitor that is willing to show greater appreciation.

Some acquirers stubbed their toes when they adopted a somewhat less dictatorial approach but did not implement it with full commitment. They wanted things done their way but were willing to let the acquired personnel adjust. But they failed because they invested little time or resources in training and other transitional services and quickly lost patience when their procedures were not implemented with dispatch. People cannot be expected to switch gears overnight, and whether the buyer accepts the target's methods or generally imposes its own ways with little or no alteration, good communications, and some period of adjustment, are essential elements of working new people into the system.

"Heroes" of the Target Are Bypassed

Many unsuccessful buyers did not articulate from the beginning that they were seeking good people from the acquired company. Any notice that target personnel would be promoted into mainstream management was belated. By ignoring acquired talent, the buyer telegraphed its attitude that the target personnel had been vanquished. When the acquirer woke up to the presence of good managers at the target, the people they wanted most for promotions had left.

THE ENEMIES OF SUCCESSFUL INTEGRATION

Ambiguity and uncertainty undermine any integration effort. The more intense and prolonged the ambiguity, the greater the chance that key people will leave the organization. The best integration programs therefore attack the roots of ambiguity and uncertainty.

What is a company really buying? The definition has changed over the past 25 years. Today, many companies realize that they are largely buying people. Companies that care about the people element usually will be more efficient, more productive, and more profitable. The "winner gets the spoils" attitude is a short-sighted road to a crackup. Indeed, the companies that once fostered that demeanor now advise, "Don't do what we did."

Chapter 29

Stroh-Schlitz: A Successful Integration

Gary Wood

Partner, Touche Ross & Co., Detroit, Michigan

Acquisitions, often key elements of corporate strategic planning, are pursued to deepen penetration in existing lines of business, vertically integrate current operations, or enter entirely new lines of business. Unfortunately, many acquisitions do not achieve expected results because of the inability to integrate the acquired company into the buyer's operations. Especially disappointing is when the merger partners mishandle the opportunity for synergy that would have helped them forge a single operating entity with lower costs and higher revenues than the two independent companies enjoyed before the merger.

Translating merger benefits from concept to reality through actual integration of people, systems, policies, procedures, facilities, and other components is a tremendous challenge. But one major firm, Stroh Brewery Co., demonstrated how the challenge can be met successfully with proper planning and aggressive management.

A CHOICE FOR SURVIVAL

In the late 1970s, Stroh, a family-owned Detroit brewer, faced a difficult decision. The industry giants, Anheuser-Busch Cos. and Miller Brewing, commanded nearly 50 percent of industry sales with their national advertising and distribution, and were aggressively pursuing traditional Stroh markets in the Midwest. After more than 125 years of operating as a regional brewer, Stroh was faced with either further erosion of market share in its major territories or counterattacking by expanding operations to become a national company. The most direct path for Stroh to become a national company was through acquisition of other brewers with nationwide production, distribution, and advertising capabilities.

Stroh began to implement its plan to go national by acquiring F & M Schaefer Brewing Co. in June 1981. Schaefer was a regional brewer with a modern plant in southeastern Pennsylvania and a distribution network concentrated in the northeastern United States and Puerto Rico. The Schaefer acquisition was a positive action toward the achievement of Stroh's overall strategy, because it took Stroh into new markets, but it did not provide a nationwide distribution capability. Therefore, in June 1982, Stroh acquired the Milwaukee-headquartered Schlitz Brewing Co., a national brewer with substantially larger operations than the former Stroh/Schaefer business combined.

These acquisitions produced a fourfold expansion in the scope of Stroh, as shown in Table 29.1.

Three factors complicated Stroh's ability to integrate operations in June 1982. First, there was only a short interval between the Schaefer and Schlitz acquisitions. Second, shortly before the Schlitz acquisition was completed, the brewery workers' union at the Schaefer plant went on strike, and, within a month, they were followed by brewery workers at the five Schlitz plants. Finally, the Justice Department decree that was needed to complete the merger with Schlitz required that Stroh divest a key brewery in the southeastern United States.

STROH'S APPROACH TO
QUICK INTEGRATION

In this environment of labor unrest, tough competition, and regulation, Stroh management faced several difficult questions. How quickly should the integra-

TABLE 29.1   Evolution and Expansion of Stroh Brewing Co.

	Before acquisitions	After acquisitions
Brands	3	15
States served	22	50
Distributors	400	1,250
Breweries	1	7
Can manufacturing facilities	1	6
Malting operations	1	2
Annual barrelage	6,000,000	25,000,000
Annual net sales	$400,000,000	$1,600,000,000
Total employees	1,800	6,500+
National market share	$4\frac{1}{2}$%	13%

tion be completed? How should two large companies be put together? How could the risks be minimized? And most important, how could Stroh get maximum benefit from the potential synergies in the shortest possible time?

Stroh management concluded that the company's vulnerability to competition during integration, the need for a rapid national roll-out of Stroh brands, and the opportunity to reduce costs through a leaner corporate structure required that the integration be done quickly. Stroh established an aggressive timetable of three months for physically consolidating all corporate functions in its Detroit headquarters. This required development of a strong transition team to keep the integration moving smoothly.

One of Stroh's most immediate problems following the acquisition was to define the scope of the organization needed to operate the company over the long term. Stroh's desire to form a company that would be a low-cost producer demanded that Stroh put a lean organization in place and, where needed, supplement the permanent staff with temporary clerical employees, contract programmers, and outside consultants. This approach allowed Stroh to deal with the initial demands of the integration, and to fine-tune the organization as permanent organizational needs became clearer.

The actual integration at Stroh was coordinated by a full-time project team composed of members of Stroh's project planning and control department who were supplemented by outside consultants. However, the emphasis of the integration at Stroh was on assigning leaders within each functional area of the company to take responsibility for decisions and for getting things done in specific departments. The full-time integration team analyzed integration issues, monitored the status of critical activities, and helped assure that all departments' activities were coordinated. The role of the integration team, the problems encountered, and the reasons for success are described in more detail later.

A conceptual model of the integration process at Stroh is shown in Table 29.2 as a two-dimensional matrix of phases and functions. The phases included: (1) analysis and planning, (2) organization, (3) the actual integration, and (4) the development of the synergies made possible by the merger. For purposes of the table the integration is characterized by the three major functional areas of personnel, management and control, and systems/information integration. This focus on people, management, and systems throughout each phase of the integration allowed the merged businesses to converge quickly into a stable operation that could begin moving forward.

PERSONNEL AND ORGANIZATION

Planning

Because people represent a key element of a company's future, a priority was put on the development of the human resources and the organization necessary to support an integrated $1.6 billion company. Stroh quickly selected those top executives it believed should be retained from the Schlitz organization. Then the senior executives who were responsible for each functional area of the consolidated company worked with the integration team to define the needs of their

TABLE 29.2 An Integration Process for a Merger

Analyze and plan	Organize	Integrate	Pursue synergies
Personnel and Organization			
Select and recruit top executives	Select employees to be hired	Move to integrate personnel in a central site:	Reassess organizational effectiveness
Define new organization	Develop personnel policies:		Make changes as necessary:
Compare salary/benefits structure		Timetable	
	Severance	Real estate agent	Organization
	Move (incentives/pay scales)	Moving firm	Policy and process
	Contracts	New offices	
	Salary/benefits scales	Personnel	
	Make job offers to personnel in acquired company	Hire to fill voids	
		Train to assure continuity	
	Establish outplacement facility	Take action to enhance communication	
		Publish new organization charts	
Management and Control Process			
Define major policy and process issues:	Assign integration manager	Develop detailed departmental work plans	Review/update business plans
	Organize integration team:		Move quickly to take advantage of merger benefits:
Differences in corporate policy		Conduct frequent departmental project reviews	
Differences in management process	Incremental resources		Product expansion
	Leaders by department	Conduct interdepartment communication meetings	Geographic expansion
Develop integration approach:	Create management policy committee		Cost reduction

328

Issue/risk analysis	Analyze policy and process issues	Define and implement new policies and procedures
Utilize incremental resources management methods	Develop preliminary work plans	Monitor integration for stability:
Timetable		Projects succeeding/failing
		Meeting target dates
		Personnel turnover

Systems and Information

Analyze/compare existing systems	Define systems/integration strategy	Define systems activities required to support move	Develop new sysems strategy/plans to support business plans
	Assign responsibility for major systems support	Develop systems implementation sequence plans	
	Define simple combined management reports	Implement key systems	
		Provide added assistance to new system users	

organizations. The staffing requirements, as developed, included additional Schlitz personnel to be recruited, Stroh personnel who would continue in their existing capacities, and recruitment of more than 200 new people.

Organization and Integration

Before any Schlitz personnel were recruited, however, new compensation packages were prepared and personnel policies developed for severance, relocation, and management contracts. Attractive contracts were structured for up to nine months of extended employment for Schlitz personnel who did not want to move or were not asked to move yet who represented valuable talent and enjoyed knowledge that Stroh personnel needed time to absorb. Stroh then moved quickly to extend offers to the Schlitz personnel to be retained in order to dispel uncertainty within the acquired company. The integration team monitored each employee's status. This "position control" system assisted the integration process when Stroh moved to integrate all personnel in the Detroit headquarters.

The process of moving personnel to Detroit and integrating the two organizations required close coordination of leaders from personnel, administration, payroll, engineering, systems, and other functions to assure that people, offices, and systems were all available in time. To facilitate communication, the integration team developed and published new organization charts and held frequent meetings where the key middle managers were brought together. The top officers of Stroh also held meetings with groups of personnel to communicate plans and provide a forum for employees to voice concerns. Aggressive management of all of these activities provided Stroh with an essentially new organization in Detroit within four months of consummation of the transaction.

MANAGEMENT AND CONTROL PROCESS

Planning and Organization

Stroh's integration team initially consisted of the integration manager and one analyst, as well as outside consultants. Later people were assigned from each area to take responsibility for integration in specific departments. The team worked with the department leaders to evaluate each functional area, identify issues and risks, and review the major policy and process differences between the two companies. From this analysis the team developed an approach to integration, identified policy issues, and developed work plans with timetables that could be monitored. Recommendations for resolving major policy and process issues were developed by the integration team and reviewed by a policy committee of top executives. Timely decisions made by this group were instrumental in keeping the process moving. For example, major issues, such as differences in beer-age policy or in credit terms to customers, were defined, decisions were made by the policy committee, and new policies implemented in individual departments with interdepartment coordination fostered by the integration team.

Integration

The integration team, together with the department leaders, developed detailed work plans, which were reviewed and consolidated on an automated scheduling system controlled by the integration manager. The team also reviewed departmental projects frequently and conducted interdepartment communication meetings to monitor the status of the integration. Operating managers were under intense pressure to maintain control of day-to-day business functions and simultaneously integrate two major companies. Because this frequently resulted in a volume-of-work problem, temporary resources were used to assist departments that were falling behind the proposed integration timetable.

Many integration projects crossed organizational boundaries. The integration team was successful in dealing with projects or problems that crossed organizational boundaries because it was given complete independence from departments involved, and was charged with full authority by top management. Interdepartmental projects were handled by project teams led by a full-time integration team member and composed of systems personnel and users from each department affected.

SYSTEMS AND INFORMATION

Planning

Because systems and information comprise a key part of the management process at many large companies, the integration team carefully analyzed and compared the respective systems of the three companies and ultimately selected the Schlitz systems in Milwaukee because of their functional completeness and multiplant operational capability.

The systems integration was conducted in two phases: (1) support for the consolidation of headquarters in Detroit, and (2) integration of operational systems after the move. To support the rapid organizational consolidation in Detroit, all systems had to be made available to users in Detroit within three months. Because it was impractical to move the Schlitz computer center to Detroit or to attempt implementation of all systems at Stroh that rapidly, the system inputs, outputs, and reports had to be re-created in Detroit so that Schlitz effectively could be run from Detroit. Each systems analyst developed plans for equipment needs, rerouting of reports to Detroit, and training personnel in Detroit. The consolidation phase consumed all available systems resources during this period, but when it was completed, the systems group could turn its attention to systems integration.

The detailed comparison of systems that was performed previously by the integration team formed the basis for the systems integration plan. Groups of systems were identified that could be implemented independently with minimum disruption and maximum benefit. The integration team defined the sequence of systems implementation that generally followed the flow of information from the customers to the plants, and finally to the financial and marketing functions.

Stroh managed implementation of the Schlitz systems in Stroh and Schaefer plants and at corporate headquarters much like a normal "package" installation. The systems integration was difficult, however, because of tight deadlines and the loss of key user and systems personnel. As a result, Stroh signed contracts with Schlitz systems personnel in an effort to retain the necessary knowledge until it could be transferred to Stroh systems personnel.

Integration

Project teams were organized for each major effort, and formal project management and control mechanisms were utilized. Incremental resources were used extensively in the systems integration because of the massive effort required beyond day-to-day operational requirements of the business. In many cases, incremental resources were utilized to assist users in learning new systems or in improving their management process through controls, procedures, and increased data integrity. The sequential implementation plan generally was followed with exceptions made only for high-priority corporate projects. For example, a consolidated accounts receivable and electronic funds transfer system was developed early in the integration to satisfy the requirements of a new company-wide credit policy.

PURSUIT OF SYNERGIES

The competitive nature of the industry, coupled with the pressures of a large debt service requirement, forced Stroh to move quickly to take advantage of what it had acquired. Thus, both during and after the integration, there were extensive efforts to increase revenues and decrease costs.

During the planning phase, departments were evaluated carefully for staffing by function to define a combined organization that was substantially leaner than the two companies prior to the merger. During the integration phase the operations and purchasing functions moved quickly to standardize materials and reduce costs. Operations and marketing also moved rapidly to begin the expansion of the Stroh brands through the national distribution network acquired from Schlitz. Production was shifted to lower-cost plants, or to new plants, as demand evolved. As the integration progressed, Stroh took additional steps to expand aggressively into new markets and to cross-expand Stroh and Schlitz brands in existing markets. Stroh satisfied the Justice Department's decree by trading its brewery in Tampa, Florida, for Pabst Brewing Co.'s plant in St. Paul, Minnesota.

An added dimension of the integration phase was the successive review of key functional areas for organizational effectiveness. Operations reviews were conducted in each of the major departments to build increased effectiveness and further enhance the ability of the company to compete. This effectiveness is essential as consolidation continues in the industry and competition among the major brewers increases.

LESSONS LEARNED

Moving quickly with an integration can have substantial pay-back. It reduces uncertainty among employees about their status and reduces the length of time that they are inner-directed. Rapid integration shortens the period of vulnerability to competitive threat and allows a company to pursue synergies early, thereby gaining maximum financial advantage from an acquisition. The pressure to perform both day-to-day business functions and integration-related activities also causes good managers to stand out.

However, rapid integration also has inherent risks, particularly internal loss of control and loss of business. The potential for loss of control comes from the pressures of daily business on a possibly overworked staff, the snowball effect when something fails, and the loss of good people and knowledge. A company can face loss of business when employees become so busy with integration that their daily responsibilities for running the business suffer, or when competitors take advantage of the company's vulnerability.

There were several lessons learned from the systems integration activities at Stroh. First, because good systems personnel are in great demand, they may seek other employment rather than relocate even if the buying company asks them. Thus, it is important to have the acquiring company's systems group quickly learn as much as possible about the target company's systems. Second, because of the pressure of day-to-day business functions, the systems group cannot rely heavily on users for training or other involvement in systems implementation. Therefore, the systems group must be prepared to take the primary role in systems integration. Third, because policies and procedures may differ between merger partners, the integration team must develop a thorough understanding of exactly what is being replaced before integrating systems.

IMPLICATIONS FOR EXECUTIVES

Each merger or acquisition is unique in its combination of elements. A company purchasing another company in an unrelated business may choose to continue operating the acquired company as an independent entity without formal integration. But when synergies can be obtained by combining two independent companies, the effectiveness and completeness of the integration can have a substantial impact on a company's short- and long-term financial results. The key to achieving the desired results is an integration team composed of a core group that is independent of organizational boundaries, has full authority from top management, and includes leaders from various departments who are visibly assigned to the integration and take responsibility for their functional areas. The organization must also form a policy committee of senior executives who meet regularly, accept input from the integration team, make decisions, and provide guidance necessary to resolve disputes and provide direction.

Integration of two companies following an acquisition can be traumatic for the employees and potentially disruptive for the business. Approaches to integration, moreover, may vary. Stroh's successful approach was dictated by special circumstances—the need to combine organizations rapidly, stay competitive, expand from regional to nationwide operations, reduce costs, and absorb a company that was bigger than the buyer. Although the basic elements of the Stroh plan can be a prototype for many integration situations, every facet obviously may not be adaptable to other projects. The key messages of the Stroh experience are that the timeliness of decisions and integration must be tailored to fit the situation, key leaders from both companies must be assigned to the integration process, and incremental resources must be appropriate to assist in solving a one-time management problem such as integration.

Chapter 30

Pulling the Golden Parachute Ripcord

William L. White

*Principal, Towers Perrin Forster & Crosby, Los Angeles,
California*

"Pulling the ripcord" is what one does in taking advantage of a golden parachute to bail out of an acquired company on favorable terms. This means invoking the separation provisions of an employment contract under a change-of-control clause. This provision usually calls for payment of compensation at full or partial rates over a specified period, or a predetermined lump sum "in consideration for services rendered." In addition, certain perquisites and benefits often are provided, such as access to company facilities and general life and medical insurance during the remaining period of separation, which may run from one to five years or more.

The increasing use of golden parachutes has created a stir in the press and among the public. The general tenor of the complaint is that executives have been cushioned in their fall from grace—that, in fact, they have been *rewarded for failure*, which is the opposite of what enlightened capitalism is supposed to be about. The most "notorious" example of a golden parachute in recent memory is the case of William M. Agee, the youthful chairman of Bendix Corp., who was awarded a $4 million golden parachute package that he negotiated himself in the midst of a takeover battle gone sour!

To understand golden parachutes, we will examine the circumstances that have given rise to them, consider the ethics of these devices, and ponder the relationship of recent legislation (the Deficit Reduction Act of 1984) and sound business judgment to a corporate policy on golden parachutes.

RECENT HISTORY OF GOLDEN PARACHUTES

The rise in use of golden parachutes can be tied directly to the rise in acquisition and merger activity between the mid-1970s and mid-1980s (see Figure 30.1).

Data compiled by The Hay Group and other consulting firms showed that in the mid-1980s about 25 percent of the *Fortune* 500 firms had change-of-control or golden parachute features. Of note is the fact that 40 percent of these firms had employment contracts in effect that applied to normal working conditions and not specifically to takeovers. As one moves down the list of the top 1,000 industrial companies measured by revenues, golden parachute features become more pronounced. The implication of this is that smaller firms feel more vulnerable to takeovers than do larger firms.

The rationale for golden parachutes has been that they allow executives to engage in takeover negotiations that are in the shareholders' best interest without excessive concern for their own economic welfare. Curiously, however, golden

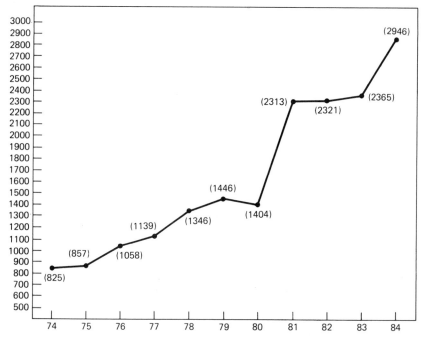

FIGURE 30.1 Merger and Acquisition Transactions 1974–1984, Including Reported Deals Valued at $1 Million or More (SOURCE: *M&A Data Base*).

parachutes are the ultimate—and fittingly ironic—expression of the short-term orientation and the uncertainty of the 1980s. The pressure on the top management of companies is to maximize return to shareholders, but there are perverse short-term constraints on what otherwise should be a long-term investment strategy. These constraints come in the form of:

- Pressure from money managers, mainly large institutional traders, and particularly those holding substantial pension assets, charged with producing investment results; and
- The necessity to take short-term tactical steps that are more "sure" than long-term strategic steps.

The first pressure—from money managers—stems from the increasingly short-term view they take on company performance. It used to be that institutional money managers handling large pension assets pursued a long-term investment strategy. They wanted to see evidence of capable, long-term-oriented management and predictable quantity and quality of growth, based on well-considered investment decisions. Now, however, with the increasingly competitive nature of the investment management business, these institutional money managers, who form the backbone of the investment community, are looking for strong short-term company results to elevate stock prices to favorable premiums. This induces an attitude of quick and sure profit at any cost among top management, which means cutting back on long-term investment decisions (if those decisions imply a lessening of short-term profit results) and maximizing the current portfolio through tactical pruning of relatively nonproductive assets, emphasis on cost reduction and revenue-generation activities, and prudent short-term investment decisions.

Adding to the combustible elements in this short-term profit-maximization mind-set is the availability of a new-found cache of buying power—the inflated value of company stock because of a bull market surge starting in August 1982. With this new-found "cheap" source of capital, companies had the buying power to acquire other concerns at relatively attractive prices—which is certainly better than making their own company success stories from the inside, because the cost of doing that is expensive (10 to 12 percent, at mid-1980s cost-of-capital rates, requiring returns of 22 to 26 percent pretax). This combination of short-term pressures, culminating in the attractive boost that acquisitions typically give to a company's stock immediately after consummation of the deal, makes top management more susceptible to the allure of acquisitions than ever before.

In the second case—that of the "uncertainty" in the economy, particularly regarding interest rates—managers are much more interested in "a bird in hand" rather than "two in the bush." If we look back over the sweep of American industry since World War II, there were great periods of relative inflation and interest rate stability (from the 1950s through the 1960s and into the 1970s). This predictable environment made long-range planning and major investment decision making more secure than it is today. With the dislocations in the economy, both domestically and internationally, the aura of uncertainty produces a gambler's mentality. As Professor Leonard Rapping of the University of Massachusetts wrote in a 1984 article in *The New York Times*:

This corporate ethics argument is mixed up with the question of uncertainty. I've been looking into why the gambling spirit ebbs and flows. Sometime in the mid-70s, with the oil crisis. . . , things changed and uncertainty and gambling expanded quite a bit.

The prior restraint was some kind of understanding that the System would take care of you. . . .

Now that's broken down. People are less sure of the future. A few years ago, Milton Friedman and Leo Savage, a statistician at the University of Chicago, wrote a paper on why people will buy insurance at one time and gamble at other times. Their argument was that within the same person both behavior patterns were there: it just depends on their situation when their expectations of rising income fall off, they're tempted to gamble.[1]

In the case of acquisitions, the gamble is that the deal consummated today will pay off more than an uncertain internal investment strategy that has an uncertain cost of capital attached to it. In most cases, it is a fairly safe short-term bet, because the acquisition *does* boost the stock price in the near term. So the stampede to gamble on corporate investment decisions—primarily through acquisition—has created its predictable defensive backlash: golden parachutes.

The more probing questions, given the nature of a truly uncertain operating environment and management's naturally defensive outlook, are: What's really fair? Are golden parachutes an unavoidable symptom of the times? Or is there a higher moral calling to which management should feel obligated?

THE ETHICS OF GOLDEN PARACHUTES

At heart, the golden parachutes issue touches the dichotomy between management's self-interest and the good of the shareholders. While the conventional wisdom is that golden parachutes assure peace of mind during a fierce struggle to promote the shareholders' interests, the truth is often quite different. The main threat is typically to entrenched management, not to the shareholders. Here, obviously, is a murky area. Talented management sometimes does fall prey to the stealthy corporate raider, and, perhaps in the long run, the shareholders would be served best by retaining current management. But the problem with golden parachutes, pure and simple, is that they create a protection device for the elite—the top handful of managers who are the key framers of corporate strategy and, therefore, most likely to be changed when a new management team takes over. No such protection is offered further down in the ranks to the middle manager, or to the blue-collar worker.

Not only are golden parachutes elitist, they insinuate that management is not willing to take the risk of betting its own performance on the same credo it subscribes to for the rest of the workforce: If you do well, you'll be retained and rewarded well.

Ever since the work of Adam Smith in *The Wealth of Nations* in 1776, students of management have been drawn to the conflicting interests of the manager and shareholder: "The directors of such [joint-stock] companies, however, being the managers of other people's money rather than of their own, it cannot well be expected that they would watch over it with the same anxious vigilance with which the partners in a copartnery frequently watch over their own."[2]

What we have today, however, is a near-panic condition in which the interests of managers and shareholders are becoming increasingly distant. Managers function with tremendous uncertainty about the long-term viability of their organizations, are increasingly driven to short-term gambling maneuvers to maximize their returns, and take steps to insure themselves against the worst, the loss of continued employment. Long-term shareholder-value creation seems to have fallen by the wayside in the process.

Patricia O'Toole, in her book, *The Corporate Messiah*,[3] points out how up-front signing bonuses, five-year contracts, and prearranged lucrative separation agreements in the event of failure are the hallmarks of today's executive who arrives in a troubled company to turn it around.

Although golden parachutes are used for management groups that are "in trouble" (i.e., they can't generate adequate returns above the cost of capital) or are vulnerable to takeover because of their companies' relatively small size, there is an increasing tendency to install golden parachutes at well-managed and large companies as well. This is a function of creative financing techniques that have made the acquisition of big, well-run companies both feasible and attractive, with returns on equity investments sometimes running in the range of 10 to 1. As a result, no executive, regardless of the characteristics or performance of the company, is immune from takeover, and managements of all types are seeking some buffer against adverse changes in corporate control.

The operative ethics of golden parachutes extend into many specific case situations, some of which are indicated by the following 10 questions:

1. Is there a legitimate need for golden parachutes in a well-managed company whose stock value is well priced because of favorable management strategies?
2. Don't employment contracts suffice to cover company obligations in most situations, including takeovers?
3. What is the value of covering just two to six executives when the entire management team is a valuable unit?
4. Aren't golden parachutes really excessive when management has asked for wage concessions from unions and has asked for a total pay-for-performance commitment over the longer term?
5. Might a board distinguish between golden parachutes for capable management that is threatened by industry-wide takeovers versus management that is clearly marginal?
6. If the industry situation appears threatening from a takeover standpoint (small banks, for example), and the directors agree that management is capable and should be protected, should the board suggest that golden parachutes be submitted to the shareholders for a vote of approval?
7. What are the limits to which compensation protection should be afforded to different levels of executives, and over what period of time?
8. Are golden parachutes irrelevant in a takeover battle, or do they impose a real impediment?
9. Is there a moral repugnance connected with golden parachutes from a public relations point of view (with unions, shareholders, and the public) that weighs against their adoption?
10. What is an appropriate alternative to golden parachutes?

TOWARD A MORE RATIONAL APPROACH

To answer these and other questions about golden parachutes in a rational way, it is important to examine the way that business judgment has developed around the use of golden parachutes, how the Deficit Reduction Act of 1984 set limits on the amounts that can be paid to executives without penalty, and the manner in which corporations may or may not be entitled to deductions for the expense.

It is important to understand that in the vast majority of cases, golden parachutes are approved by the board of directors without submission to the shareholders for a formal vote. This lack of shareholder approval and the often-staggering payoffs involved have led to some shareholder-initiated suits (i.e., Gulf Resources & Chemicals, Sunbeam, and Esmark). Nonetheless, these legal challenges to golden parachutes have been unsuccessful. Golden parachutes continue to operate under a business judgment rule, and these contracts have the impact of binding law if they're approved by a majority of a company's outside directors. This point of binding law is firm in premeditated golden parachutes, but not, apparently, in the case of golden parachutes hastily devised in the heat of takeover. The Securities and Exchange Commission, for example, has recommended that boards of directors not be permitted to adopt golden parachutes after a tender offer is announced.

Golden parachutes have evolved to address specific problems that are related to takeovers but are not covered by normal employment contracts. That is, normal employment contracts are silent on what happens to an executive's pay after a change of control, on what specifically constitutes a change of control, and on the terms and conditions affecting all elements of compensation for an executive after he or she is terminated or resigns following a change of control. Not only do golden parachutes address these issues, they are normally referred to in proxy statements as devices that will be triggered in the event of a change of control. They are, therefore, clearly special-situation contracts.

The law that has now imposed specific limits on the use of golden parachutes was a logical outcome of the groundswell of public reaction to these devices. The law restricts payments to an executive under a change of control (for the entire corporation or a significant portion of the corporation) to three times the base amount on a present-value basis. The base amount is identified as "includible gross compensation" on an annualized basis that considers five years of includible compensation prior to takeover. Moreover, an executive will have to pay an additional 20 percent income tax on any amount above the specified maximum, and the corporation will lose its deduction for this excess amount. There is also a provision that, to be legally binding, the golden parachutes have to be entered into at least one year prior to the date of change of control.

There is considerable fuzziness in the new law. While "earned but unpaid" compensation seems to be allowable, the items that constitute the base amount have not been fully identified. Succeeding legislation in the form of a technical correction will definitely be needed.

While these legal changes put new constraints on the use of golden parachutes, the ethical questions about the adoption of golden parachutes persist. Let us turn our attention, then, to a reasonable framework for addressing the issue of whether to adopt golden parachutes or not—and, if so, under what terms and conditions. Let us, in the process, answer the 10 questions about the need for golden parachutes under different conditions.

Legitimate need—There often is a legitimate need to install golden parachutes in a well-managed company, particularly if that company is vulnerable because of its small size or industry expertise that is complementary to the acquiring company. Even larger, well-managed companies have become acquisition targets. However, there is no need for blind, follow-the-leader practices—particularly if a company is a leader in its industry, and of substantial size.

Employment contracts—Employment contracts often are not specific enough to do the job of defining precisely what change-of-control circumstances are and defining what specific total compensation treatments (base salary, short-term and long-term incentive, perquisites and benefits) should be accorded to the executive after a change of control. Specific golden parachute contracts are necessary for this purpose.

Elitism—The elitist nature of golden parachutes—covering just the top two to six officers—is a problem, particularly if management previously has talked about team efforts or the efforts needed at key managerial levels down through the organization. Increasingly, as organizations flatten out, key managers are being defined at the unit or major functional levels. Thus, care should be taken to provide golden parachutes for all managers—at any level—who are key to the organization's success. (Obviously 10 to 20 is a better number than 100, because of the substantial costs involved with covering the larger group.)

Disparities—There are some sensitive situations in which golden parachutes will enrage critical groups—such as when a partnership plan has been worked out with the union, and part of the plan requires a prolonged period of union sacrifice on wages and benefits. In addition, management's promotion of a pay-for-performance ethic is significantly undermined by the introduction of golden parachutes, because it implies throwing in the towel and insurance for the few.

Management quality—Importantly, the board can be proactive in suggesting -that management does or does not deserve golden parachutes. The board should not be a rubber stamp for protection of failed management.

Shareholder approval—If the ethical implications of golden parachutes have been sorted out—and there is consensus that management is deserving and it would be in the best interests of shareholders to install parachutes—the additional step of submitting the adoption of parachutes to a formal shareholder vote lends added credibility to the plan.

Compensation limits—The limits to which compensation protection should be afforded to executives is now prescribed by law (three times the base compensation amount). However, this is only the upper limit. Lesser amounts can be afforded down through the ranks. The rule of three times the base amount also implies a three-year orientation to the separation agreement. However, shorter periods of six months to two years may be appropriate, particularly if management is talented and mobile.

Takeover deterrence—Golden parachutes can be costly (about 1.7 percent of the market value of equity and 12.1 percent of earnings prior to GP adoption, according to Professor David Larker of Northwestern University). However, they are usually not so costly that they actually deter takeovers, unless they are combined with antitakeover devices such as staggered board memberships or increasing the percentage of stockholders who must approve a tender offer.

Moral issue—There is an increasing moral repugnance associated with golden parachutes. In 1984 the chief executive officer of Allied Industries revealed that his company had decided not to adopt them, specifically because of adverse public reaction.

Alternatives—In essence, the most appropriate alternative to golden parachutes is a strong capital-accumulation program for top executives that is connected to performance. Even in the event of a change of management, for reasons outside the control of the executive, the capital accumulated from past performance (including the new premium value on stock after the takeover) will provide a suitable cushion for the displaced manager. His past successes, moreover, will stand him in good stead with his next employer.

Golden parachutes are certainly symptomatic of uncertain times, but they do require more stringent board review and control to make them appropriate to the situation. Over time, as the economy stabilizes and the gambler's mentality about acquisitions subsides, golden parachutes should become less and less of an issue.

NOTES

[1]Leonard Rapping, "An Era of Me-First Management: Losing Sight of Moral Standards," *The New York Times*, August 15, 1984.

[2]Adam Smith, *Wealth of Nations*, Oxford University Press, New York, 1976.

[3]Patricia O'Toole, *Corporate Messiah: The Hiring and Firing of Million-Dollar Managers*, edited by Pat Golbitz, William Morrow & Co., New York, 1983.

Part 7

LBOs,
Divestitures,
and Other
Modes

Chapter 31

Management Buy-outs and LBOs

J. Terrence Greve

Operating Partner, Wallner & Co., San Diego, California

The merger and acquisition process has proven to be an efficient method of reallocating corporate wealth. Traditionally, however, the primary benefactors of the reallocation process have been shareholders. Although management teams typically play key roles in merger or acquisition negotiations, their financial rewards usually are limited to their own shares or stock options in their company. Because this is often a relatively minor stake, managers have not been major beneficiaries of the wealth created by merger and acquisition transactions.

A restructuring of the buyout process that began in the late 1970s and continued into the 1980s has enabled corporate management teams to become significant equity participants in the companies they formerly operated for large bodies of stockholders. The mechanism that afforded this new breed of entrepreneur the opportunity to create its own wealth has been the leveraged buy-out.

A leveraged buy-out (LBO) entails the acquisition of an operating company with funds derived primarily from debt financing that is based on the assets and/or cash flow of the acquired (target) company. It differs from a typical corporate acquisition in that the ability to support and service acquisition debt is related primarily to the assets and/or cash flow of the target and, secondarily, on the equity contribution of investors, including management.

LBOs differ from the classic corporate acquisition not only in the financial structure of the transaction, but also in how the deal itself is initiated. In a typical corporate merger or acquisition, the proposed transaction usually is instigated by management of either the acquiring or the target company based on their respective corporate needs. In a buy-out, however, the deal initiator is often an outside third party called the "sponsor," who assumes a significant role in the financing and/or operation of the company.

THREE CLASSES OF LEVERAGED BUY-OUTS

Although all LBO transactions have common characteristics, there are many differences among deals, depending on the unique circumstances of the target. The commonly held belief that, to qualify for an LBO, a target company must meet a rigid set of criteria, is not completely accurate. In fact, there are three distinct classes of LBOs, two of which involve target companies that do not fit the classic LBO profile.

Class I: Premium Companies

The first class contains the ideal LBO target company, which meets all criteria demanded by the most discriminating lenders and investors. These include strong and proven management teams, a strong balance sheet with little long-term debt, dominant market shares, proprietary products, consistent cash flows, and undervalued assets.

Because they have all the characteristics of a "perfect" deal, companies in this class almost always command the highest prices. Price, of course, is a function of economic and market conditions. In 1980 and 1981, "premium companies" sold at close to book value. However, as the economic climate improved, these companies later sold at substantial premiums over book value, as buyers were willing to pay higher multiples for consistent earnings streams.

Management teams of "premium" companies are usually quite active and influential in sponsoring the deal or selecting the sponsoring party. They are largely responsible for the past success of the target company and, thus, are in a relatively strong position to negotiate with potential financing sources.

Class II: Second-Tier Companies

Firms in the second group differ from "premium" companies in that they lack one or more of the desirable traits of the ideal LBO. The target may compete in a cyclical industry or have a history of inconsistent earnings and cash flow. The company may have only a small share of the market or lack proprietary products, both of which render it more vulnerable to competition. The lack of a strong management team and inconsistent operating performance are other negative characteristics.

Many of these deficiencies can be corrected over time, but their mere existence places this type of company in a distinctly different class. Many lenders and investors will not be interested in financing such a company unless the sponsor has the operational expertise to correct the problems. The deficiencies usually are reflected in either marginal operating profits or overstated asset values. These factors, along with reduced interest among potential buyers and financing sources, result in more moderate valuations and diminish the seller's chances of receiving 100 percent cash. In fact, most buy-outs in this particular class rarely are sold for significant premiums over book value and often involve the seller's participation in the financing as a subordinated lender.

Management is generally in a weaker position to influence who is the ultimate buyer. In some cases, particularly corporate divestitures, management is the cause of the problem and the main reason for the decision to sell. Therefore, the seller does not perceive management as "the buyer" but looks rather to outside groups for prospective deals.

Class III: Troubled Companies

Companies with severe operating problems that are reflected in current and projected losses are the antithesis of a classic leveraged buy-out candidate. Therefore, "troubled companies" or "turnarounds" are not often LBO prospects. However, in the wake of the worst recession since the Great Depression, there emerged in the mid-1980s several buy-out sponsors that specialize in taking over troubled companies on a leveraged basis.

In contrast to the typical LBO, the leverage is already in place and, in most cases, very much in jeopardy. Usually, the operating performance and/or financial condition of the company has deteriorated to the extent that the lenders and investors are calling the shots. Controlling shareholders and management are at the mercy of these financing sources because they are dependent on them for future funding. The main objective of those who have invested in or loaned money to the company is to salvage their investments.

This represents an excellent opportunity for those buyers who have strong operational credentials and track records. They have the skills to take whatever corrective action is necessary. Moreover, their experience will influence those with money at risk in the company to transfer control of the company to stronger hands. The entire purchase price often is financed with existing debt or conversion of debt to equity at attractive rates and extended terms. In many cases the financing sources will agree to advance additional capital if they have confidence in the buyer's operating plan.

Managers usually are in a very weak position to influence the deal, mainly because they often are perceived as the source of the problem. In fact, many turnaround LBOs involve the immediate replacement of some or all of the management team.

HISTORICAL DEVELOPMENT OF THE LBO

Money Everywhere!

More than anything else, the proliferation of institutional financing sources has fueled the dramatic increase in LBO activity in the 1980s.

Prior to 1978, by contrast, LBOs were financed by a relatively small number of prominent insurance companies. Commercial banks, with their traditionally conservative credit policies, were relatively insignificant players in what were perceived as "inherently risky" leveraged transactions. Equity financing was provided by a small number of sophisticated private investors, as well as wealthy families, including the Rockefellers, Whitneys, and Hillmans.

In the mid-1970s, the confluence of several economic and political events created a fertile environment for capital formation, much of which was funneled into acquisition financing. Most prominent were persistently high inflation rates, which increased the disparity between the book and replacement values of corporate assets. This circumstance resulted in "hidden asset values" that became extremely attractive to lenders as collateral. Second, the tax rate on long-term capital gains was substantially reduced, resulting in dramatic increases in venture capital pools, some of which were earmarked for leveraged buy-outs. At the same time, the gradual deregulation of interest rate ceilings created intense competition for bank deposits, which in turn forced banks to seek higher-yielding loans. This led to the formation of many new "asset-based" lending groups, which quickly hit on aquisition financing as a fast way to book new loans.

Deals, Deals, Deals!

Along with greater access to money came an increase in available companies. Again, the timing of economic events was right. Public companies that went on "acquisition binges" in the late 1960s and early 1970s were suffering from acute "corporate indigestion." They reversed gears, creating large-scale divestitures of subsidiaries or divisions that no longer fit the parent's strategic plans. The "era of deconglomeration" continued into the 1980s and represents a significant portion of the targets acquired via leveraged buy-out.

At the same time, the stocks of many publicly held companies, especially "smokestack"-type concerns that lost favor to technology issues, remained very depressed. Some sold substantially below book value. Long-suffering shareholders became eager sellers when buy-out groups, including operating management teams, offered substantial premiums over market value. Because potential corporate acquirers were relatively inactive during much of the 1970s, management groups often were the only buyers. In addition, the owners of many private companies formed during and after World War II were nearing retirement age and seeking to sell out. The absence of corporate buyers created an unusual opportunity for managers and investors to acquire these businesses via LBOs.

FINANCIAL STRUCTURE OF AN LBO

The leveraged buy-out is not simply a transfer of ownership of the stock or assets of the target company from seller to buyer. It results in a simultaneous re-capitalization of the company in which a substantial amount of new debt is incurred. With a few strokes of the pen, the target is converted from a financially healthy condition (little or no debt) to a financially unhealthy condition (highly leveraged).

The postacquisition liability side of the target company's balance sheet may be broken into three horizontal financing layers, each representing a generic class of financing participant in the buy-out. The three layers of leveraged buy-out financing, the sources and their means of participation, are illustrated in Table 31.1.

Senior Debt Layer

The senior debt layer is the least risky position in the financial structure. The senior lenders have a first claim on some or all of the assets (secured transactions) or cash flow (unsecured transactions) in the event of liquidation. Their return is usually in the form of interest on loans or lines of credit. Because they have no participation in the equity of the acquired company, senior lenders must be assured that their loans can be repaid easily from the target company's cash flow, or the sale of secured assets if liquidation is necessary. The major sources of senior debt are commercial banks and asset-based lenders.

Although commercial banks have increased their roles in LBO projects, they remain the most conservative of all financing sources. Their investments are

TABLE 31.1   Sources and Types of LBO Financing

Layer	Lenders/investors	Loans/securities
Senior debt	Commercial banks Asset-based lenders Insurance companies Sellers	Revolving line of credit—unsecured Revolving lines of credit—secured by accounts receivable and inventory Fixed asset loans secured by machinery, equipment, and real estate Senior notes—unsecured
Subordinate debt	Insurance companies Pension funds Venture capital firms Sellers	Senior subordinate notes Junior subordinate notes
Equity	Insurance companies Venture capital firms Sellers Private investors Management	Preferred stock Common stock

in the form of unsecured or secured lines of credit that are amortized over three to seven years. They must be assured that there is sufficient risk capital below them to protect the financial integrity of the deal and provide adequate coverage of the total debt service. Because they are the most adverse to financial risk, banks offer the most competitive interest rates, usually no more than two points over prime.

Asset-based lenders (ABLs) are collateral-oriented lenders who require a first lien on the collateral against which they advance funds. Collateral preference increases with liquidity and marketability, with trade receivables the most preferred security and heavy equipment or real estate as the least desirable. ABLs often advance more money than commercial banks, but they also charge higher interest rates.

Subordinated Debt Layer

Subordinated lenders participate in LBOs by issuing securities with both debt and equity characteristics. These are usually unsecured notes that are subordinated to senior debt. Subordinated notes have lower, often fixed, interest rates with longer and more favorable terms. Inherently more risky than senior debt, the notes incorporate equity features that enable the lender to hold equity in the acquired company. These most often take the form of "cheap stock" acquired at the closing, or warrants to purchase stock at a favorable price in the future. To a lesser extent, subordinated notes that are convertible into common stock are used.

"Sandwiched" between the senior debt and equity layers, subordinated debt often is referred to as "mezzanine financing." In larger, more complex transactions, several institutions often participate as mezzanine lenders. Because these lenders may have different risk/reward criteria, multiple subordinated securities are structured so that some are "senior to" or "junior to" others. Generally, senior subordinated notes are amortized more quickly, have priority over junior notes in the event of liquidation, and enjoy less equity participation. The major participants in the subordinated debt (mezzanine) layer include insurance companies, venture capital firms, and pension funds.

Typically, mezzanine financing sources evaluate a prospective buy-out investment on the basis of the target company's ability to service the proposed acquisition debt while generating a premium return for the increased risk and lack of liquidity. Debt coverage is measured by the ratio of "free cash flow from operations" to the pro forma debt service of the target. A minimum debt coverage ratio of 125 percent is required, although it may be as low as 110 percent or as high as 175 percent, depending on the stability of the target company's cash flow. Mezzanine investors usually require minimum expected yields of 1.5 times the return that can be generated by BBB-rated bonds.

Insurance Company Financing

The larger life insurance companies have been the traditional subordinated lenders in leveraged buy-outs. Through their private debt placement activities, these institutions have gained extensive experience in corporate refinancing, and buy-out financing is a logical extension of this expertise. Insurance company participation in buy-out financing grew dramatically in the early 1980s when these firms diverted funds from real estate to corporate financing.

Venture Capital Firms

The proliferation of venture capital pools in recent years has created an abundance of risk capital, most of which is invested in high-technology companies. However, LBOs represent an attractive alternative to many venture capital firms seeking to balance the risk of high-technology start-ups with investments in established operating companies. An attractive feature offered by LBOs is the opportunity to generate a current yield on subordinated debt securities. This is particularly appealing to small business investment companies (SBICs), which seek to offset the cost of their borrowings from the U.S. Small Business Administration.

Pension Funds

Pension funds are recent entrants into LBO financing, which represents only a small fraction of their total assets. Only the largest funds have invested directly in LBOs as subordinated lenders. Because they lack the "in-house" expertise, most pension funds invest in LBOs through one or more of the mezzanine or equity funds formed in the early 1980s.

Equity Investors

Although equity financing is the riskiest of the three layers, it offers the highest return to investors. The line of demarcation between the equity and subordinated debt layers was at one time clearly defined. But as transactions became larger, more complex, and involved a greater number of financing participants, the distinction between subordinated lenders and equity investors became less clear. As noted above, the same investor often holds securities in both the subordinated debt and equity layers.

Equity investors, because they take the most risk, seek the highest return. Generally, venture firms will not invest in an LBO unless they believe the target can generate a 25 percent annually compounded rate of return over a five- to seven-year period. This return almost always comes in the form of capital gains when the target is sold or goes public. With the need for the target company's cash flow to service debt and provide working capital, dividends are rare in LBOs.

In most leveraged buy-outs, institutional financing sources require operating management to invest some equity. This need not be a significant percentage of the total capitalization, but usually represents a meaningful portion of management's personal net worth. The purpose is to ensure the commitment of a management that is personally at risk.

A notable development in LBO financing has been the formation of equity capital pools. The largest and most famous of these are funds created by

Kohlberg, Kravis & Roberts, a New York-based LBO specialist. Many institutions, such as insurance companies, pension funds, and endowment funds, have invested in these pools to utilize the expertise of the fund managers in sponsoring, financing, packaging, and negotiating deals.

THE LBO SPONSOR

The sponsor in an LBO, whether it be management or an outside group, brings together all the key players and resources to close the deal. Principal activities include structuring, financing, and negotiating the transaction. Sponsors with strong operating management backgrounds become extensively involved in monitoring the operations of the company after the closing.

Structuring and Financing. Experience in the LBO financing process and personal relationships with lenders and investors give sponsors the know-how to tailor the unique legal and financial structure needed for a proposed buyout. Relationships with lenders and investors in LBOs enable them to assemble quickly the necessary financing commitments.

Negotiating and Closing. Operating management is in a difficult position in negotiating the price and terms of a buy-out. As employees of the target, they are still responsible to the current owners. At the same time, they are integral parts of the ownership of the proposed buy-out. The outside sponsor's participation in the negotiations as a third party serves to minimize this conflict of interest.

Monitoring the Investment. Because the lenders and investors have substantial capital at risk in an LBO, it is necessary for a player with operating experience to monitor the company after closing. Corporate management teams are not accustomed to managing a highly leveraged business. A sponsor with managerial experience who serves on the board can be very helpful to management, especially during the early stages of the new ownership.

Types of LBO Sponsors

There are two major types of LBO sponsors: the financially oriented and the operationally oriented. The financially oriented sponsor specializes in the financial aspects of LBOs and usually manages a pool of capital available to back its own deals. The financial sponsor is very deal-oriented and takes an active role in orchestrating the entire transaction. Compensation for these services can take many different forms, including front-end financing or transaction fees, a carried interest, or free stock, in lieu of cash, in the new company. Sponsors also may be compensated by participation in the profits and the capital pool under management.

The operationally oriented sponsor emphasizes operating management skills. A successful track record of managing and monitoring businesses typically inspires major financing sources to have confidence in the sponsor's ability to succeed with the buy-out. The operational sponsor is more likely to buy out second-tier or troubled companies or firms that lack strong management skills or direction. They usually are compensated through equity participation in the target or continuing management service fees.

Changes in the Sponsorship Role

In the mid-1980s, the growth and maturity of LBOs led to subtle, but important, changes in the sponsor's role.

In the late 1970s and early 1980s, management teams lacking the necessary know-how and contracts to engineer an LBO selected an outside expert, usually an investment banker, to facilitate the buy-out. As LBOs grew in popularity and financing sources increased dramatically, the managers took a more active role in financing the transactions themselves. At the same time, many lenders and investors started to perform many sponsorship functions, presenting themselves to managements as "one-stop" deal packagers. The result was to diminish the role of the sponsor who was purely transaction-oriented and brought no capital or operational skills to the table.

Sponsorship Determination

Although some traditional sponsorship functions have been assumed by more sophisticated management teams, an outside third party usually is involved in some phase of sponsorship activities. In the new environment, the sponsor basically is selected on these factors:

- The controlling party in the deal
- The quality of the target company
- The extent of the skills in the management teams

Deal Control. In most buy-outs of privately held companies, or in corporate divestitures, the decision to sell is made by the controlling shareholder or parent company. Therefore, the owners or operating managements are the primary determinants of the outside investors who will finance and sponsor the transaction. The influence of operating management in these decisions depends on its relationship with the owner. If it is good, the owner may give management enough time to finance and close the deal itself. If the owner is not particularly loyal to the management, he or she may call all the shots and dictate the choice of outside groups to finance and acquire the target.

In some cases, particularly large buy-outs of public companies, the transaction is instigated by an LBO sponsor that makes a friendly tender offer with the full support of management. Without management cooperation and participation, most LBO sponsors and financing sources will not go forward.

Quality of the Target Company. A second determinant of sponsorship selection is the track record of the target company. An excellent company with consistent earnings and cash flow can obtain financing so easily that outside professionals may not be needed. Management can go directly to equity and mezzanine financing sources and even orchestrate the entire transaction. Many financing sources will avoid lower-quality operations, or require a strong, operationally oriented sponsor. A seller that lacks confidence in operating management also may want to control selection of prospective buying groups.

Management Skills and Experience. Operating a business, no matter how skillfully, seldom equips a manager with the temperament or the time to do an LBO. Management self-sponsorship also risks that the operation will be neglected at the expense of making the deal. Thus, most management buyers accept the need for outside sponsors to put the deal together.

In the final analysis, sponsorship selection depends largely on the strength and performance of operating management. A strong, capable team that has an excellent track record will be an integral part of the new ownership, and will have a significant voice in selecting its "partners." But if operating performance is questionable, management may not be the primary buyers and not have any say in choosing the sponsor.

Management Criteria for Sponsorship Selection

When management does have a voice in selecting sponsorship and financing sources, its criteria for evaluating prospective "partners" include compatibility of business philosophy, complementary skills and resources, operational control, equity split, and timetable for selling. The last three usually emerge as the most critical in the minds of managers.

Equity split is the division of ownership between management and investors. Much of this depends on how subordinated-debt and equity-financing sources perceive the future performance of the target company. The higher their expectations, the less ownership they will require. Management usually will seek partners that demand the smallest equity participation and reduce its interest the least.

Another major issue in selecting a sponsor is the differing objectives of sponsors when it comes to liquidating an investment in the target company. Institutionally backed sponsors and financing sources are under pressure to turn their LBO investments into cash or marketable securities within a five-year period. This may be in direct conflict with management's desire to retain its independence. These differences usually can be reconciled beforehand through future buy-out agreements.

Finally, there is the matter of operational control. Generally, proven management will team up only with investors who agree to some form of operational autonomy. Most investors don't have a problem with this as long as management performs. Mutually acceptable controls are established through sponsorship representation on the board of directors or provisions in the loan covenants. At the other end of the spectrum, sellers of companies with mediocre management teams, if they participate in the financing as subordinated lenders, will insist on strong operational sponsorship. In this case, management has little or no control in the ultimate disposition of the company.

LBO TRENDS IN THE 1980s

Leveraged buy-outs have been taking place for many years. Only in the 1980s, however, did they gain prominence in the U.S. financial press. This is due mainly to the number of large public companies taken private via LBOs in that period. Another factor was the phenomenal success stories of some companies that were taken public within a relatively short time after the buy-out, resulting in dramatic increases in wealth for sponsors and investors. Chief among these was the Gibson Greetings, Inc., deal sponsored by William Simon and his Wesray Corp., which turned an enormous profit for the sponsors following a modest equity investment. Wesray bought Gibson from RCA Corp. in 1982 for $58 million in cash and assumption of $22.6 million in liabilities and took the company public in May 1983 with a 3.5-million share offering at $27.50 a share. Simon and his partner, Raymond G. Chambers, retained more than 45 percent of Gibson stock. Simon's profit on just the sale of his shares in the public offering was reported at more than $14 million.

The factors that fueled the LBO boom are well documented: depressed stock prices, the pressure on public corporations to divest operating units, and the rapid increase in both the number and types of LBO financing sources.

But the mid-1980s LBO market is dramatically different than it was in the early 1980s. The improvement in economic conditions and higher stock values substantially increased the asking prices for potential buy-outs and, thus, the financial risk of leverage. At the same time, many new buyers appeared on the scene eager to play the game. Often these buyers were loaded with "hot" money but lacked buying experience. And lower interest rates lured both buyers and lenders into deals that would be marginal at best in a more hostile interest rate climate. LBO purchases spread to companies with questionable ability to generate sufficient cash flow or poor track records, and to divestitures designed by corporations strictly to get money-losing headaches off their books. In many cases, the results of "too much money chasing too few deals" were LBO purchases of targets with dubious prospects and the payment of prices that might have been considered excessive at earlier stages of the LBO movement.

If interest rates increase and economic conditions worsen, some of today's deals could be tomorrow's work-outs. Several prominent failures could cause much of the new-found LBO financing to disappear as quickly as it appeared. Many sponsors who lack the operational skills to steer a highly leveraged company through difficult times could vanish. But these same "problems" will create opportunities for those who are equipped to cope with them. In effect, leverage will always be available to those who use it prudently and manage it carefully.

Another recent development involves claims by an increasing number of critics that LBOs unfairly enrich operating management at the expense of public shareholders. Others complain that the LBO basically weakens the financial underpinning of corporate America. Although some of these claims certainly have merit, there are few issues in life that are all good or all bad. Both positive and negative characteristics are associated with any phenomenon such as the LBO. On balance, however, many experts maintain that LBOs have had a positive impact on the reallocation of capital in the private sector.

Chapter 32

Mergers of Equals

Geoffrey T. Boisi
Partner, Goldman, Sachs & Co., New York, New York

Terrence M. O'Toole
Associate, Goldman, Sachs & Co., New York, New York

The merger of equals is perhaps the most difficult type of corporate combination to bring to fruition. Not surprisingly, it is a transaction that has rarely been attempted in the merger market of the 1980s, which has emphasized strategic acquisitions of smaller firms by larger entities and purchases by entrepreneurial buyers who seek greater value by breaking up target companies' business portfolios. Of the 138 U.S. mergers and acquisitions involving prices of more than $100 million that were closed during 1983 or pending at year's end, we identified only four that possessed the characteristics of a merger of equals. And from 1979 to 1983, only 12 deals passed our qualifying screen. (See Table 32.1 for the complete list.) Although several additional transactions arguably might be included, it is nonetheless clear that mergers of equals comprise a very small component of contemporary M&A activity.

What qualities characterize the merger of equals? The transactions that em-

TABLE 32.1 Comparison of Selected Merger of Equals, 1979–1984

Closing date		Approximate market capitalization (before transaction announcement)		Approximate market capitalization (after transaction announcement)		Shares to be issued		
		$000s	Percent	$000s	Percent	New name	Exchange ratio	Perce voti powe
1/79	The Cross Company/	$ 66,406	49.1%	$ 64,813	49.1%	Cross &	2.00	52.0
	Kearney & Trecker Corporation	68,758	50.9	67,284	50.9	Trecker	1.00	48.0
		$ 135,164	100.0%	$ 132,097	100.0%			
8/80	Kraft, Inc./	$1,304.837	56.9%	$1,262.745	54.0%	Dart &	1.00	53.5
	Dart Industries, Inc.	988,362	43.1	1,073,776	46.0	Kraft	1.00	46.5
		$2,293,199	100.0%	$2,336,521	100.0%			
11/80	Chessie System, Inc./	$ 581,687	56.1	$ 549,780	58.2%	CSX Corp.	1.00	49.9
	Seaboard Coast Line Industries, Inc.	454,643	43.9	394,389	41.8		1.35	50.1
		$1,036,330	100.0%	$ 944,169	100.0%			
7/81	Nabisco, Inc./	$1,064,899	56.0	$ 991,738	55.7%	Nabisco	1.04	54.2
	Standard Brands, Inc.	836,755	44.0	790,268	44.3	Brands	1.00	45.8
		$1,901,654	100.0%	$1,782,006	100.0%			
4/82	Connecticut General Corporation/	$2,072,156	54.6%	$2,122,945	53.9%	CIGNA	1.00	51.3
	INA Corporation	1,720,700	45.4	1,819,025	46.1	Corp.	0.8534 and 0.158 convertible preferred shares convertible into 0.4221 CIGNA common shares	48.7
		$3,792,856	100.0%	$3,941,970	100.0%			
4/82	Norfolk and Western Railway Company/	$ 983,571	51.8%	$1,287,727	52.8%	Norfolk	1.00	51.9
	Southern Railway Company	916,629	48.2	1,151,564	47.2	Southern	1.90	48.1
		$1,900,200	100.0%	$2,439,291	100.0%			
9/82	Morton-Norwich Products, Inc./	$ 291,439	41.8%	$ 277,034	53.9%	Morton	1.00	53.0
	Thiokol Corporation[c]	406,150	58.2	237,245	46.1	Thiokol	1.3507	47.0
		$ 697,589	100.0%	$ 514,279	100.0%			
1/83	Pittsburgh National Corporation/	$ 351,644	58.8%	$ 305,171	61.2%	PNC	1.00	58.2
	Provident National Corporation	246,139	41.2	193,862	38.8	Financial	1.00	41.3
		$ 597,783	100.0%	$ 499,033	100.0%			
1/83	The Signal Companies, Inc./	$1,584,136	68.9%	$1,692,145	68.2%	Signal	1.00	67.9
	Wheelabrator-Frye, Inc.	715,728	31.1	787,938	31.8	Companies	2.00	32.1
		$2,299,864	100.0%	$2,480,083	100.0%			
1/84	Santa Fe/	$2,901,814	56.1%	$2,523,316	54.2%	Santa Fe	1.203	54.0
	Southern Pacific	2,267,127	43.9	2,132,517	45.8	Southern Pacific	1.543	46.0
		$5,168,941	100.0%	$4,655,833	100.0%			
1/84	First & Merchants Corp./	$ 178,819[e]	50.2%	$ 217,563	48.3%	Sovran	1.00	47.4
	Virginia National Bankshares, Inc.	177,158	49.8	233,053	51.7	Financial	1.15	52.6
		$ 355,977	100.0%	$ 450,616	100.0%			
Pending	Bank of New England Corp./	$ 266,083	46.7%	$ 325,685	46.3%	Bank of	1.75	47.5
	CBT Corp.	303,848	53.3	297,314	53.8	New	1.00	52.5
		569,931	100.0%	553,250	100.0%	England		

[a]Composition of Board of Directors of newly formed or proposed company.

[b]Assuming $51.00 preannouncement price for Connecticut General common as the price for CIGNA Corporation shares.

[c]Pursuant to the merger agreement, after announcement of the merger, Morton-Norwich commenced a tender offer for 5,700,000 Thiokol shares, or about 49.5% of the total outstanding, at $50 per share. Market capitalization of Thiokol after announcement excludes Thiokol shares purchased by Morton-Norwich. Transaction data concerning the resulting entity also give effect to the purchase.

[d]Earnings from continuing operations only.

[e]Includes 961,697 shares issuable upon conversion of convertible debentures and 400,130 shares issuable upon conversion of convertible preferred stock.

[f]Premiums over stated book value were (7.9%) for First & Merchants and (15.8%) for Virginia National. The change in book value was (2.8%) for First & Merchants and 2.2% for Virginia National.

[g]Headquarters of the holding company will be in Norfolk (Virginia National's location), and headquarters of the bank will be in Richmond (First & Merchant's location).

Price earnings ratio[d]		Premiums (before announcement)				
Before announcement	After announcement	Market before announcement	Tangible book value	Board members[a]	Source of new CEO	Location of headquarters
8.0x	7.4x	12.0%	36.6%	4	Kearney	Cross
8.4	8.2	0.0	30.6	4		
6.5x	6.3x	0.0%	4.1%	13	Kraft	Kraft
5.7	6.2	14.8	3.2	10		
11.1x	10.5x	0.0%	(50.5)%	12	Chessie	Seaboard
6.5	5.6	28.5	(51.7)	12		
7.8x	7.2x	0.0%	62.9%	13	Nabisco	New Jersey (compromise)
7.8	7.4	7.7	56.3	13		
6.4x	6.5x	0.0%[b]	(10.5)%	10	Both	New York (compromise)
6.1	6.4	8.5	(11.5)	10		
5.1x	6.6x	0.0%	(33.0)%	8	Norfolk	Norfolk (compromise)
5.3	6.7	(0.6)	(26.5)	8		
9.1x	8.7x	0.0%	(5.9)%	10	Morton	Morton
10.7	12.3	26.0	124.5	9		
5.5x	4.6x	0.0%	(13.6)%	18	Pittsburgh	Pittsburgh
6.9	5.1	0.4	0.2	7		
11.6x	12.4x	0.0%	(5.9)%	10	Signal	Signal
8.4	9.2	4.5	(6.6)	7		
15.8%	13.7x	0.0%	12.0%	15	Santa Fe	Santa Fe
17.9	16.9	10.6	(12.0)	15		
6.0%	7.2x	0.0%	(7.9)[f]	15	Virginia	Compromise[g]
5.2	6.8	11.9	41.6	15		
7.4x	7.1x	0.0%	(0.9)%	9	CBT	Bank of New England
6.6	6.5	(3.3)	0.8	10		

body the spirit of the merger of equals are those combinations or amalgamations of two business entities in which neither side "purchases" the other, entities of approximately equal "size" (defined primarily in terms of relative contribution to sales, earnings, book value, market value, and dividend yield) join to form a larger organization governed by a management team representative of the two firms' former managments, and neither side receives an acquisition premium. It is the last characteristic that most succinctly distinguishes a merger of equals from other forms of corporate combination. The absence of a premium signifies that both participants must believe that future benefits from a combination will be sufficient to justify their decisions to forgo a premium. True mergers of equals are effected at an exchange ratio that recognizes the relative pro forma contribution of each firm to the new entity and represents a relatively small (if any) premium to the market price of the company's common stock that prevailed before announcement of the merger.

The merger of equals entails a number of special considerations. Perhaps most difficult are the organizational factors, the efforts to blend management personalities and capabilities, and the corporate cultures. Many financial factors are unique to this type of transaction, including the absence of a premium and the interaction of the two participants' dividend policies—factors that combine to influence stock market reaction to the transaction. Special tactical considerations arise in a merger of equals. How does a board of directors deal with a competing offer at a premium to endorse a transaction with no premium? And what tactics can be used to prevent an interloper from interrupting the transaction?

Mergers of equals are rare, yet the transactions in Table 32.1 provide a reference group for examining the characteristics unique to this class of transaction. Using this group as a reference set, we will explore four broad considerations in greater detail: strategic, organizational, financial, and tactical.

STRATEGIC CONSIDERATIONS

The merger of equals, more than any other form of merger or acquisition, is consistent with the oft-cited but frequently elusive theory that a combination of two business entities with complementary strengths and weaknesses can create "added" value—a phenomenon called synergy. The motivation for the merger of equals almost always is a perception that substantially more value can be created by a union of the two entities than either entity could manifest as an independent firm. The increased value is regarded as so significant that both firms would forgo a "control" premium to produce a successful completion of the transaction.

Many corporations cite the existence of synergies in justifying payment of substantial premiums to market when acquiring another firm. But in the merger of equals, each company is contributing its assets, both financial and human, to create a new enterprise that will, in the longer term, benefit each firm's shareholders in a more assured manner and with greater return potential than each enjoys as an independent entity. Neither company is "selling" control: each is seeking to build on the other's strengths without losing its own identity.

The companies that joined in the mergers of equals cited in Table 32.1 all had some complementary factors. Cost efficiencies could be realized by eliminating redundant functions. Benefits could materialize by one company's use of facilities or capabilities previously possessed only by its merger partner. Markets could be expanded geographically, or by the introduction of new products to existing markets. Management skills could be shared and used to correct management weaknesses. Market share could be increased. In the final analysis, all of these factors present the same implication: maintenance or enhancement of profitability. All are consistent with a trend perceived by Wall Street research analysts that institutional investors will favor a transaction that has a "good story"—that is, a transaction where a strategic fit offers the possibility for significant enhancement of share value.

Banking and Railroads

Of the 12 completed transactions listed in Table 32.1, three involved railroads and three involved banks or bank holding companies. The Dart-Kraft transaction and the Nabisco-Standard Brands transaction resulted in two of the largest consumer food companies in the world. The concentration of mergers of equals in these three industries reflects the importance of strategic motivation.

The proxy statements issued in connection with these transactions offer some interesting insight into the rationale behind each transaction. In the three rail industry mergers (Chessie System-Seaboard Coast Line, Norfolk & Western-Southern Railway, and Santa Fe-Southern Pacific), a consistent theme can be found. The proxies express the desires to increase share by geographic expansion of the rail system, to increase operating efficiencies, and to take advantage of economies of scale. There also was a common assertion that the individual railroads' abilities to remain competitive would be, as the Southern Pacific-Santa Fe proxy said, "materially hindered absent their combination." The Norfolk & Western-Southern proxy, which specifically mentioned CSX in discussing the need for unification so that the two railroads could remain competitive, perhaps summarized the strategic rationale for the rail mergers best when it said:

> Railroads operate most efficiently and competitively over long distances, in part because costs and delays are greatest at origin, interchange and termination, and in part because shippers, given the alternative, prefer to deal with one system instead of two or more.

The Santa Fe-Southern Pacific proxy echoed that rationale by stating: "The combination provides the opportunity for substantial economies and efficiencies in the operation of geographically complementary railroads." The rail merger of equals, it is important to note, have occurred in an environment fostered by a relaxed Interstate Commerce Commission attitude toward such combinations. The formation of CSX created the second largest rail system in the nation, and the merger of the Santa Fe and Southern Pacific created the third largest. Given the considerable perceived benefits resulting from these amalgamations, carriers with complementary rail systems brought together companies of relatively similar market capitalizations and financial contributions, distributing ownership in the combined entity on bases relative to premerger values.

The banking industry mergers of equals emphasized strategic reasoning that was similar. Banks cited the desire to realize economies of scale and operating efficiencies, to increase flexibility in responding to the financial needs of customers, to position for regulatory changes, to press for market expansion, to strengthen their capital bases, and to diversify their asset/liability structures and revenue systems. These were discussed specifically in the Pittsburgh National-Provident National and First & Merchants-Virginia National proxy statements. Banking transactions also were influenced by the belief that the combinations were necessary to remain competitive in an industry that is both facing rapid change and already is characterized by a wave of mergers and acquisitions.

As in most well-designed mergers of equals, the banking and railroad transactions suggested that the merging managements were willing to forgo the "control" premium because they believed the combination would generate significant strategic benefits. Managements thereby took the position that by maintaining their proportionate interests in the combined company, shareholders gained the potential for significant increases in the values of their holdings. In addition, competitive changes in both the banking and railroad industries have spurred a general movement toward mergers and acquisitions, so that the large mergers of equals actually may have been fashioned as defensive measures to prevent loss of share value.

The Connecticut General-INA transaction joined two companies with complementary product lines. INA concentrated mostly on the property and casualty insurance business, whereas Connecticut General emphasized the group and individual life and health insurance and pension-related businesses. Of particular interest was the language in the proxy statement that referred specifically to the synergies derived from blending complementary interests:

> The combination will permit both companies to achieve the sought-after diversification and expansion without paying the acquisition premiums which might be required in independent acquisition programs.

Dependence on a Single Industry

The principal strategic disadvantage in a merger of equals is that the combined companies are concentrating their dependence on one industry. Management is, in essence, doubling the company's "bet" on its current business, or a business similar to its current operations. The merger of equals is predicated on the assumption that the anticipated synergies can be realized. If the partners guess wrong and fail to achieve the synergies, the targeted increase in shareholder value may not result. While complementary synergies potentially offer considerable benefits, the performance of the combined company is heavily dependent on the market environment in the industry to which it has hitched its star, no matter how successfully it integrates and how smoothly the merged operations function. The merger of equals rarely aims for or achieves strategic diversification. In addition, it should be remembered that the anticipated synergistic benefits do not become evident instantaneously. Often, the larger the combining organizations, the longer it may take to realize the strategic benefits of the combination. Years may pass before the "added" value of the combination takes hold.

ORGANIZATION CHANGES

Organization is a vital strategic element in securing the synergies promised by a merger of equals. Within the organizational framework come the blending of management skills, corporate cultures, and capabilities, the elimination of redundant positions, and the proper systems and techniques for governing an organization that doubles in size overnight. It is the area where people are most affected and, as a result, a merger of equals requires the complete support of both managements to cope with the organizational and social issues that have assumed paramount importance. Wall Street folklore abounds with stories of transactions that broke down when the personalities of the merging CEOs clashed or when the chairmen disagreed over such issues as headquarters location or use of the corporate jet. Although these ancillary questions have almost no effect on the supposedly central issue in any deal—shareholder value—in reality, organizational disputes (such as who will be in charge) are the most frequent deal busters.

Theoretically, correct attitudes on the part of top managements and the boards of the two concerns are the most critical elements in completing a successful merger of equals. Realistically, other factors, including special considerations, may be at work. For example, there may be an opportunity for a merger of equals when the CEO of one firm is nearing retirement and a sure-fire successor is not in-house. Thus, the merger is a way of recruiting management (in part because the head of an equal-sized firm in the same industry may be the only candidate capable of taking over). But whether these special conditions exist or the deal is structured purely on more clinical operational and financial lines, the correct attitude is for both sides to maintain a high regard for each other. Each must reject the notion that it is either "selling out" or "buying out" the other side and emphasize that it is seeking to build on the partner's strength without losing its own identity. Given the realities of human nature and the typical insecurities of any merger or acquisition, it is essential that both parties exude a form of corporate "self-confidence" built on the concrete benefits they can bring to the combination. Such elements would include:

- Strong management teams;
- Good historical performances in their respective areas of expertise; and
- Most important, committed and realistic CEOs who can work together in an atmosphere of mutual respect and dedicate themselves to developing a management structure that utilizes each company's strong points, compensates for their weaknesses, and creates opportunities for key people from both firms.

Accommodating the Partners

Although the organizational and social considerations in a merger of equals are complex, four easily observable indices of organizational integration can be used as proxies for measuring how well the two partners have accommodated each other. They are the name of the new corporation, the senior management structure, the composition of the board of directors and its committees (i.e., the balance of power), and the location of headquarters.

One overwhelming similarity among the deals in Table 32.1 is the adopted name of the new entity. In all but three cases, the choice was either a brand new name (CSX, PNC Financial) or a combination of the two former titles (Dart & Kraft, Nabisco Brands). While an equal contribution of members to the new board is desirable, there were four cases where one side had a one-to-three-person advantage, and in one instance the majority was considerable (Pittsburgh National gaining 18 of 25 seats on the PNC board). Generally, the slightly larger "partner" was the source of the corporate headquarters and the CEO of the combined company. But in four deals, a compromise arrangement was adopted for fixing the new headquarters site, usually by creation of a small corporate office to integrate merging operations. Only CIGNA formed a combined Office of the Chairman manned by the CEOs of both companies. But a more telling sign of whether the merger is equal in fact is the relative potency of the new power structures in the combined organization from the CEO down, a judgment that is almost impossible for the external observer to reach.

After successful consummation of a merger of equals, the combined company typically attempts to create an organization that distributes power and control equally among the two participants' managements. Immediately after the Dart & Kraft merger, for example, the new company's 12 senior corporate positions were filled by five Dart executives, five Kraft executives, and two outsiders, although the company said that there had been no conscious effort to keep the balance equal. Immediately after the CIGNA deal, former INA executives headed three of the four operating groups, with a Connecticut General executive heading the fourth unit. At Nabisco Brands (itself acquired by R. J. Reynolds in 1985) the merged company took only about a month to reorganize because, as F. Ross Johnson, president and chief operating officer of the new company, said, "We speak a very common language. We didn't go buy a coal company." Over time, however, the combined company will develop its own corporate culture, and efforts to maintain distribution of power and control will, in all likelihood, dissolve as the natural evolution of the new management structure unfolds.

Many companies express intentions to maintain separate identities when they announce the merger. Nabisco and Standard Brands, Connecticut General and INA, and Dart and Kraft explicitly stated desires to retain the autonomy and identity of individual business units. Yet some consolidation seems inevitable. Certainly, some corporate overhead is duplicative and could be pared, and some synergies would seem to exist among operating units. Indeed, if no operating synergies can be obtained from a consolidation of organization, the very wisdom of the merger may be called into question. Senior managers also must assess the correct methodology for fostering a unified corporate culture in the new company.

In summary, the merger of equals will work best when the transaction is structured in a manner that incorporates:

- Equal participation on the combined company's board to demonstrate a balance of power

- Location of headquarters at a neutral site, perhaps equidistant from each company's former head office
- A new corporate name for the holding company, with retention of the old corporate names at operating levels
- Positioning of the CEOs to reflect their status as co-engineers of a new strategic plan, a step that includes such elements as management contracts of equal duration and compensation
- A roughly equal contribution of senior management from each company
- Approximately equal voting power for each constituent stockholder group
- Frank and participatory discussion by senior managers from both firms in establishing the new corporate structure and operating philosophy

Adherence to these points should enable the newly formed company to communicate better its message of equality to both the investing public and its employees.

FINANCIAL CONSIDERATIONS

As its name implies, the merger of equals brings together two companies of approximately equal size. But what standard of size is indicative of equality? The answer emerges from an investigation of a combination of indices, principally each firm's contribution to the combined company's total assets, shareholders' equity, sales, net income, and market value (a value that is influenced by the market values of the two companies before the transaction, the interaction of the two participants' dividend policies, and investor reaction to the transaction). The interplay of these considerations, the correct balancing of inequalities, and the rationalization of financial strengths and weaknesses all must coalesce for the merger of equals to succeed from a financial perspective.

Table 32.2 presents an analysis of the contribution of participants to the pro forma combined company for 11 selected transactions. The financial information was extracted from proxy statements and represents the last full year's results before consummation of each transaction. No adjustments have been made for pro forma eliminations or adjustments to the financials. With few exceptions, the transactions demonstrate remarkable consistency. Only the Signal-Wheelabrator-Frye and Pittsburgh National-Provident National transactions offer instances in which one side contributed 60 percent or more to the combined company's total assets and shareholders' equity. The Santa Fe-Southern Pacific transaction shows a skewed earnings contribution, yet on total assets, shareholders' equity, and revenues the contributions were almost equal.

An examination of the market capitalization and price/earnings multiples displayed in Table 32.1 also shows consistency. With the exceptions of the Borg-Warner-Firestone proposal, the Chessie-Seaboard Coast Line transaction, and the Signal-Wheelabrator-Frye transaction, price/earnings multiples before announcement of the transaction were similar, as were market capitalizations.

The interaction of the two company's dividend policies bears upon the market reaction to the transaction. When the exchange-of-shares ratio was factored into the analysis, shareholders in only one transaction—Connecticut General-INA—faced dividend dilution. To overcome the disparity in dividend policy without

TABLE 32.2 Selected Mergers of Equals, 1979–1984: Contribution Analysis

	Total assets		Shareholders' equity		Revenues		Net income	
	$000s	Percent	$000s	Percent	$000s	Percent	$000s	Percent
The Cross Company/	109,291	56.5	54,111	50.7	139,895	59.0	8,893	52.0
Kearney & Trecker	84,048	43.5	52,613	49.3	97,150	41.0	8,198	48.0
	193,339[a]	100.0	106,724	100.0	237,045	100.0	17,091	100.0
Kraft, Inc./	2,530,700	56.4	1,368,600	55.8	6,432,900	72.8	188,100	52.3
Dart Industries, Inc.	1,952,400	43.6	1,082,800	44.2	2,403,300	27.2	171,700	47.7
	4,483,100	100.0	2,451,400	100.0	8,836,200[b]	100.0	359,800	100.0
Chessie System, Inc./	3,242,100	51.1	1,175,900	49.3	1,492,600	47.1	87,200	46.0
Seaboard Coast Line Industries	3,101,700[c]	48.9	1,209,700	50.7	1,678,700	52.9	102,400	54.0
	6,343,800	100.0	2,385,600	100.0	3,171,300[d]	100.0	189,600	100.0
Nabisco/	1,427,600	47.2	696,100	51.1	2,568,700	46.0	127,800	55.0
Standard Brands	1,597,200	52.8	665,500	48.9	3,018,500	54.0	104,400	45.0
	3,024,800	100.0	1,361,600[e]	100.0	5,587,200	100.0	232,200	100.0
Connecticut General/	17,962,246	61.3	2,375,075	51.9	5,279,438	52.8	329,813	53.0
INA	11,352,279	38.7	2,198,315	48.1	4,721,300	47.2	292,738	47.0
	29,314,525[f]	100.0	4,573,390[g]	100.0	10,000,738[h]	100.0	622,551[i]	100.00
Norfolk & Western Railway/	2,817,200	48.7	1,452,700	52.9	1,449,200	49.7	198,600	55.3
Southern Railway	2,971,600	51.3	1,291,900	47.1	1,467,300	50.3	160,600	44.7
	5,788,800	100.0	2,744,600[j]	100.0	2,916,500	100.0	359,200	100.0
Morton-Norwich/	746,935	61.2	383,887	59.3	804,818	50.4	48,499	55.8
Thiokol	473,134	38.8	263,637	40.7	793,373	49.6	38,392	44.2
	1,220,069[k]	100.0	647,524[l]	100.0	1,598,191[m]	100.0	86,891[n]	100.0
Pittsburgh National Corp./	6,991,893	67.5	407,181	61.7	—	—	57,397	59.2
Provident National Corp.	3,361,634	32.5	253,149	38.3	—	—	39,507	40.8
	10,353,527[o]	100.0	660,330[p]	100.0	—	—	96,904[q]	100.00

The Signal Companies/	3,607,500	68.2	1,683,000	68.7	5,487,600	78.0	214,000	70.4
Wheelabrator-Frye	1,678,700	31.8	766,400	31.3	1,548,300	22.0	90,100	29.6
	5,286,200[r]	100.0	2,449,400	100.0[s]	7,035,900[t]	100.0	304,100[u]	100.00
First & Merchants/	2,610,300	56.3	155,400	44.8	—	—	25,135	44.5
Virginia National	3,360,581	43.7	191,242	55.2	—	—	31,397	55.5
	5,970,881[v]	100.0	346,642[w]	100.0	—	—	56,532[x]	100.0
Santa Fe/	4,840,800	44.7	2,580,300	47.6	2,362,100	54.6	158,600	24.9
Southern Pacific	5,978,800	55.3	2,838,500	52.4	1,962,500	45.4	478,700	75.1
	10,819,600	100.0	5,418,800	100.0	4,324,600[y]	100.0	637,300	100.0

[a] Before elimination of $1.1 million.
[b] Before eliminating intracompany sales of $11.7 million in 1979.
[c] Before adjustments of $266.4 million of assets and $12.6 million in equity.
[d] Sum of revenues.
[e] Before additional $33.2 million.
[f] Before elimination of $389.5 million.
[g] Before elimination of $375.9 million.
[h] Before additional $17.4 million.
[i] Before additional $6.6 million.
[j] Before elimination of $54.8 million.
[k] Before addition of $10.0 million to total assets.
[l] Before elimination of $77.5 million.
[m] Before elimination of $12.6 million.
[n] Before elimination of $18.4 million.
[o] Before elimination of $13.3 million.
[p] Before elimination of $13.3 million.
[q] Before elimination of $0.9 million.
[r] Before additional $114.7 million.
[s] Before additional $122.7 million.
[t] Before additional $240.3 million.
[u] Before elimination of $3.6 million.
[v] Before elimination of $1.9 million.
[w] Before additional $17.2 million.
[x] Before additional $0.5 million.
[y] Before additional $63.4 million.

altering the distribution of voting control (as an alteration in the exchange ratio would do), the architects of the Connecticut General-INA transaction employed a new convertible preferred issue. Shareholders of INA common stock, which had paid an annualized dividend of $2.40 per share prior to the transaction, received 0.8534 share of CIGNA common stock and 0.158 share of a new CIGNA convertible preferred stock. The CIGNA common was anticipated to have an initial dividend of $2.30 per year and the CIGNA convertible preferred to have a dividend rate of $2.75. Thus, each share of INA common stock exchanged in the merger would receive securities initially paying dividends at an aggregate annual rate equal to INA's $2.40 premerger dividend. The postmerger components were approximately 43.5 cents attributable to 0.158 of a share of CIGNA convertible preferred and approximately $1.963 attributable to 0.8534 of a share of CIGNA common.

One company may bring an added feature to the combination if its stock is selling at a higher price/earnings multiple than its potential partner's stock. If this company were to act as the "acquirer" and utilize its common stock as the merger currency, the combined company may very likely trade at a higher multiple than the average of the two companies' multiples.

The importance of the interaction of these financial factors—that is, the relative contribution of each participant to the pro forma income statement, balance sheet, cash flow, and market valuation of the combined entity—is not unique to a merger of equals. All managements considering a merger or acquisition examine the financial impact the contemplated transaction will have. What distinguishes a merger of equals, however, is the relatively equal contribution each party brings to the transaction in a majority of the categories outlined. These transactions are truly amalgamations of similar-sized companies. Neither is truly acquiring the other.

No Control Premium

The most distinguishing characteristic of a merger of equals, however, is the absence of a "control premium" in the transaction. When the relative contributions of each participant in the financial categories are taken into account, it may be found that the balance of contribution falls more frequently to one side or the other. The firm bringing more to the transaction may achieve a premium to the former market price of its stock after the transaction is completed. However, in none of the transactions outlined in Table 32.1 do the premiums to market come close to the average premium of 51 percent over the target company's market price one month before announcement that was calculated by the Mergers & Acquisitions Data Base for 1985. The simple average of the transactions in Table 32.1 is 3.84 percent. An examination of premiums to book value also reveals a low premium. The average premium to book for the transactions in Table 32.1 is 6.5 percent. The average premium to tangible book is somewhat misleading, however, because individual premiums ranged from 124.5 percent of tangible book to a discount of 52.1 percent.

In a merger or acquisition transaction where one side is "selling out," the acquirer typically pays a premium over the financial contribution of the acquired company to compensate the sellers for relinquishing control. The absence of a premium to market, or a premium to tangible book, is an outgrowth of the basic rationale behind the merger of equals. In a merger of equals, to reiterate, each company is contributing its assets, both financial and human, to create a new enterprise that in the longer term will benefit each firm's shareholders in a more assured manner and with greater return potential than each has as an independent entity. Neither company is "selling" control. Each is seeking to build on the other's strengths without losing its own identity. For the merger of equals to succeed, shareholders of each participant must receive approximately equal shares in a new investment vehicle that, long term, has less downside risk and greater upside potential than the original investment security. Some small premium to market value may be paid to equity holders of one company if that company contributes a disproportionate share of assets or earnings power. Yet no control premium will be paid in the true merger of equals. In a sense, the merger of equals is the "essence of market efficiency."

One transaction seems to stand alone among our examples. In the Signal-Wheelabrator-Frye transaction, Signal contributed roughly two-thirds of the combined company's assets, equity, revenues, and net income, yet the transaction produced a relatively small premium to market for Wheelabrator shareholders. Why, then, have we included the transaction among our mergers of equals? As Wheelabrator chairman Michael D. Dingman said at the announcement of the transaction:

> It was treated like a merger. We're putting two companies together to make a new high-technology company for the 80's. So the sum, we think, is better than the parts individually. That's why there's no premium.

The combination appears to have been driven by two of the factors we discussed above: strategic considerations (as Dingman's comment demonstrates) and organizational considerations. Indeed, the latter factor was widely cited by observers of the merger as a prime motivation for the transaction. *The New York Times* quoted an unidentified source in its story on the merger as saying that the transaction was "a merger of equals, a friendly deal between people who have known each other for a long time."

TACTICAL CONSIDERATIONS

Once the two merger of equals candidates have agreed on the strategic, organizational, and financial aspects of the proposed amalgamation, one element remains—successful consummation of the transaction. In addition to the normal tactical considerations attending any merger or acquisition involving a publicly owned company, the merger of equals presents two unique problems. Because no control premium is being offered to either concern's shareholders, each company's board must be prepared to defend its endorsement of the contemplated transaction. And, in the absence of a control premium, the architects of the merger of equals must take steps to ensure that the transaction is not upset by an interloper, or that the combined company itself is not the target of an unfriendly bid. Thus, the board may be faced with a peculiar dilemma. How can directors justify not accepting a competing offer at a sizable premium? Doesn't the board have a moral and legal obligation to obtain the greatest value for its shareholders? An attractive firm entering into a publicly announced merger of equals is almost certain to draw, at a minimum, inquiries from potential suitors, if not a competing bid. How, then, can a board endorse a merger of equals at little or no premium over a competing offer at a sizable premium?

The answer is that the two proposals represent completely different types of transactions. Because neither company is desirous of "selling" control, the board need not approve a sale just because an offer has been made. In essence, each company's board is supporting its present management team in a strategic move that strengthens and expands the firm's present business and brings in a management team that has excelled in a different but complementary area of expertise. Furthermore, from the board's perspective, this is being accomplished in the most efficient way without paying an acquisition control premium. The merger of equals is not an acquisition or sale decision but an offensive strategic attempt to solidify and enhance the shareholders' investment by implementing a plan that favorably positions the respective companies. The sale-of-control decision is one that typically offers a shareholder a one-shot, two- or three-year acceleration in capital returns. The merger of equals, on the other hand, is an enhancement of an existing investment strategy by the individual investor that offers a longer-term, but potentially greater, return horizon. This rationalization is evidenced by the aforementioned "Reasons for the Combination" cited by Connecticut General and INA in their proxy. The notation stressed that the transaction "will permit both companies to achieve the sought-after diversification and expansion without paying . . . 'acquisition premiums'. . . ."

The second tactical consideration, preventing an unwanted suitor from queering the transaction with a higher bid, may be addressed through the use of cross-holdings, reciprocal options, and other devices designed to deter third parties. Simultaneous with the signing of their agreement, Connecticut General and INA each granted options to the other company to purchase up to approximately 16.5 percent of the grantor's stock outstanding at the market price prevailing before the merger announcement. Exercise of the options was conditioned on the formal commencement of a third-party tender or exchange offer to acquire the grantor's stock. Each participant's actual purchase of cross-holdings in the other is another tactic used to discourage potential interlopers. Morton-Norwich and Thiokol, for example, entered into agreements to purchase approximately 18 percent of each other's outstanding common stock when they executed their merger agreement. The Morton-Norwich-Thiokol transaction also was a two-step transaction. Morton-Norwich first tendered for 49.5 percent of Thiokol and then exchanged Morton-Norwich stock for the remaining 50.5 percent.

Confidentiality and Technology

The parties involved in the structuring of the transaction should take utmost care to ensure that confidentiality is maintained. Public announcement of the merger of equals should take place only after definitive agreements have been executed and the various lock-ups put in place. It is paramount that the public explanation of the transaction be put forth immediately upon announcement, carefully and logically detailing the strategic rationale behind the combination and the harmony of the management teams. A good "story" is critical in efforts to maximize positive reaction to the announcement.

The sheer size of many of the companies created in a merger of equals may discourage potential third parties from seeking to acquire the combined company. The Santa Fe-Southern Pacific combination, for example, had a pro forma shareholders' equity of $5.4 billion, and few companies are large enough to acquire an entity of that size. The company created in a merger of equals may, however, seek to include certain antitakeover provisions in its new corporate charter as an extra measure of protection.

In order to attempt to balance the ownership of the combined entity, the combined company may sometimes utilize a stock repurchase. The ancillary effect of the repurchase is often to place a floor on the stock price of the new entity.

Any companies contemplating a merger of equals also must consider the antitrust implications of the transaction. The most obvious examples of the importance of antitrust environment are the rail industry mergers that were direct outgrowths of a relaxed Interstate Commerce Commission attitude toward industry consolidation. Managements must solicit the opinions of counsel toward possible Federal Trade Commission and Justice Department objections to the transactions. Other legal considerations can play a role depending on the industry involved, such as the evolution in interstate and intrastate banking laws.

A PURE COMBINATION

The merger of equals is a rare occurrence. Yet the merger of equals is also theoretically the purest corporate combination from a strategic standpoint. No premium is paid by one participant to the other to compensate for a transfer of control. The two companies are combining to form an entity that can capitalize on perceived synergies to create incremental value for shareholders of each concern.

Only when the right combination of organizational, strategic, and financial factors come together, free from any significant negative exogenous influences, can the transaction culminate successfully in a new entity. To succeed, the transaction requires forward-looking and rational senior management teams guided by leaders who can overcome the human factors that often plague this type of transaction. When the right circumstances exist, however, the merger of equals can result in a new entity strategically positioned to increase value to both groups of shareholders.

Chapter 33

Restructuring by Divestiture

Robert F. Calman

Vice Chairman, IU International Corp.,
Philadelphia, Pennsylvania

Restructuring has been a priority at many American corporations and one of the most widely observed and examined trends of U.S. business during the 1980s. Although restructuring, also called redeployment and rationalization, includes acquisitions to add new businesses or expand existing ones, the movement more popularly is regarded in terms of shrinking or simplifying corporate structures. As a result, many corporate managements have not been hesitant to weed out businesses that have become mature or marginal, do not fit the present corporate mix or long-range strategic plans, require heavy investments of capital and other resources, or present other considerations that make divestiture advantageous.

Other than simply closing up an unwanted business, the principal avenues open to a restructuring management include straight sales of less desired operations or distributions to the corporation's shareholders. The restructuring lexicon of the 1980s is replete with transaction buzz-words such as:

- Divestments (sell-offs) and dispositions, or "straight" sales of corporate properties for a price, usually to third parties
- Leveraged buy-outs, often employed as a device for selling off businesses to

investment groups, which may include management of the divested units, who borrow heavily against the unit's assets
- Swaps, in which a business is disposed of through trading of stock that reduces the parent's outstanding shares
- Spin-offs, in which assets or income streams are distributed to stockholders as entirely new business entities

More recently, the lexicon has been expanded even further to include employee stock ownership plans (ESOP). There are now leveraged and unleveraged ESOP techiques available to the corporate restructurer.

IU International, a diversified $2 billion services company, has been at both ends of the restructuring spectrum—as an active acquirer during the 1960s, 1970s, and early 1980s, and subsequently, as a major practitioner of restructuring through various divestment modes. By 1970, IU's acquisitions had resulted in a globe-spanning company with 40 subsidiaries in 12 markets. By the end of 1985, restructuring had slimmed IU to a company with four major markets (transportation, environmental services, distribution, and agribusiness) and a clearer perspective and a better position for growth in each.

In the process, IU obtained considerable experience in utilizing each of several restructuring alternatives. A decision on the route to take in a specific transaction is not easy. It requires extensive consideration of the values and benefits in each technically complex approach. But each decision ultimately evolves from a very clear goal: increase the value for the IU shareholder.

PRACTICING THE
RESTRUCTURING ALTERNATIVES

The major restructuring moves by IU in 1979–1986 include:

Spin-offs—Gotaas-Larsen Shipping, a worldwide tanker fleet, and Echo Bay Mines, a Canadian-based gold mining concern.

Swap—A unique share-exchange project that shed IU's majority interest in Canadian Utilities Ltd.

Partial disposition—Sale of 50 percent of General Waterworks Corp.

Sell-offs—Sale of the Ryder/PIE trucking operations and divestiture of several industrial and distribution operations, including Unijax, a paper distributor.

Leveraged Buy-outs—In March 1986, IU agreed to sell most of its Hawaiian agribusiness assets to an investor group including management of the unit.

During this restructuring period (1979–1985), IU's revenues fell to $1.9 billion from $2.6 billion, and assets were reduced to $1.2 billion from $2.8 billion. However, there can be little doubt that the restructuring has increased shareholder value.

In mid-1979, before the announcement of the Gotaas-Larsen spin-off, IU was trading at between $10 and $11 per share. At the beginning of August 1985, IU common stock was trading at about $13. In addition, IU shareholders received the equivalent of $4.80 a share and $14 a share via the spin-offs of Gotaas-Larsen Shipping and Echo Bay Mines, respectively. The shareholder who continued to own these securities would have enjoyed combined current value of almost $32 per IU share, or approximately triple the prerestructuring value of 1979. In addition, the shareholder would have received a total of $6.58 per share in cash dividends on the IU and Echo Bay shares.

EXAMINING THE RESTRUCTURING CHOICES

Essential to any company's ability to evaluate restructuring alternatives successfully is the management's willingness to value realistically the parts of the overall company. Through realistic internal valuation, it is possible to compare aggregate internally estimated shareholder value against the actual market price per share of the company. Possibly even more important in terms of evaluating overall corporate restructuring prospects is the need for a realistic evaluation of the viability and estimated market value of the individual corporate components (subsidiaries, divisions, or product lines). A valuation of every individual unit provides a basis for estimating whether the component's standalone value is greater or less than if the unit remained a part of the parent company. Once realistic assessments are made of the viability and standalone values for individual units, the broad restructuring options can be evaluated against a variety of influencing factors.

The matrix in Table 33.1 rates the various broad types of restructuring alternative that are available for a given standalone component against certain critical or influencing factors. These factors include business viability, advantages and benefits, the availability of ready buyers or suitable partners, and the perceived relative per-share value of the parent company compared with the individual entity's estimated market value per share. Naturally, management's judgment about the availability of a "pure-play premium" for a component on a standalone basis is a very strong influencing factor, and, therefore, must be realistic in terms of viability and valuation.

According to the matrix, financial viability could be a restricting factor in considering a spin-off or a swap that would essentially create a new standalone

TABLE 33.1   Matrix of Corporate Divestment Alternatives

Factor	Spin-off	Swap	Sell-off 100%	Sell-off 50%
Business viability, advantages and benefits	R	R	NR	NR
Ready buyer			+	+
Pure-play premium	++	+		
Good partner available				++
Low parent company share price		++		
Low-tax basis	++	- -	- -	-
High-tax basis	-	++	++	+

R = restricting
NR = not restricting
++ = strongly positve
+ = positve
- = negative
- - = strongly negative
A blank indicates that the factor has little or no relevance to the alternative.

unit. The question posed by the restricting factor is whether the unit actually has the wherewithal to operate independently. Conversely, a sell-off, either complete or partial, would not be a restricting factor if a strong, qualified buyer was available to take it off the seller's hands, and, if necessary, resuscitate it, integrate it into other businesses owned by the buyer, or take advantage of synergies.

But the financial viability factor is not the only criterion used. While the restricting factor is evident, a spin-off also is favored by the prospect of a very strong pure-play premium and by a low-tax basis. And the restricting factor fades if the unit indeed can be cut loose as a financially sound entity. The "low-tax basis" utilized in the matrix involves a situation where the parent's tax basis in the subsidiary is low. If this unit is divested in a taxable transaction, the taxes paid by the divesting company relative to the proceeds would be substantial. The tax burden is essentially avoided in a spin-off. The stock received by the shareholders is generally free of taxes because, in compliance with federal tax laws and regulations, their tax basis in the shares of the parent is reduced by the spin-off. If the stockholder already is within a long-term capital gain holding period, taxes would be levied only on the proceeds of the shares received in the spin-off when and if they are sold.

In an outright sale, business viability is a nonrestricting factor, especially if the entity marked for divestment may not have to stand alone. The availability of a ready buyer is important, but tax considerations are even more critical. Thus, if the parent's tax basis in the entity is low, this becomes a very negative factor because relatively large taxes must be paid on the proceeds. But if the parent already has a high-tax basis in the unit, this is very positive because the taxes paid on the proceeds should be relatively low.

If an entity with a high market value but a low-tax basis is sold by the parent corporation in a taxable transaction, a corporate capital gains tax would become payable. If the proceeds are paid as dividends directly to the shareholders, the proceeds would be taxed again at ordinary rates to the shareholder. A spin-off avoids this "double tax" and defers the tax payable by the shareholder until the shareholder decides to sell.

One of the more important aspects of a spin-off is that the decision to hold or sell the spun-off assets ends up precisely where it should be—with the shareholder. The shareholder obtains the ability to determine, based on individual preferences, whether to continue to own the spun-off assets, or to sell at any time, consistent with the shareholder's individual investment and tax goals. Obviously, the shareholder also may elect to sell one security and use the proceeds to increase ownership of the other.

Aside from placement of investment and tax decisions directly with the shareholder, benefits derived from spinning off or swapping a valuable asset include:

- Increased value to shareholders from owning the independent entity as a pure play
- Greater opportunities for the spun-off unit as an independent company
- Improved relationships with customers, suppliers, vendors, and other outside agencies

- Unique tax incentives, financial grants, and financing capabilities for foreign-based components that may not be consistent with the parent company's U.S. corporate structure

The Echo Bay Mines Spin-off

It often is possible to achieve a double-pricing premium when the spun-off entity has its own unique market following and the former parent corporation itself becomes perceived as a pure play. In IU's 1983 spin-off of Echo Bay Mines (EBM), a Canadian gold producer, there appeared to be an opportunity for such a double-pricing premium.

Through a variety of internal and external valuations and analyses, including a small public offering of EBM shares, a standalone value of about $8 (U.S.) per IU share was determined to be realistic for a North American gold mining company with the ore reserves and production characteristics of Echo Bay. The aggregate value of this Canadian gold mining company was, therefore, estimated to be about $220 million. At the same time, however, EBM was expected to contribute only modest current earnings per share and cash dividends as part of IU.

If Echo Bay Mines had been sold for its estimated market value of $220 million, the aftertax proceeds would have been about $175 million. In order to be indifferent to the standalone, pure-play, spin-off premium that appeared to be available to the IU shareholders, the $175 million in aftertax proceeds would have had to be invested at a combined return on investment and price/earnings (P/E) ratio that would have yielded $8 per IU share.

Realistic investment alternatives were considered, including use of the proceeds to retire existing IU debt with an assumed 6 percent aftertax cost. However, the resultant IU savings of 40 cents per share would require a P/E ratio of 20 to be equivalent to the perceived $8 of spin-off value. Such a sale and reinvestment valuation scenario was not considered realistic. Echo Bay Mines is a gold mining company in Canada, where restrictions imposed on foreign investors would reduce the number of potential buyers available. Absent a single big buyer, it was considered probable that a sale of the whole company might require a discount from the estimated standalone market value, and the sale proceeds also would be subject to substantial taxes because of the relatively low Echo Bay Mines tax basis involved. With strong business viability, advantages, and benefits, a very strong pure-play premium available, and a low-tax basis, the matrix review suggested consideration of a spin-off or swap.

The spin-off of Echo Bay Mines took place in 1983 and provided that company with many of the other spin-off benefits in addition to the pure-play pricing for shareholders. EBM is a favorably positioned to attract equity capital, to take advantage of special incentives (tax and financial support), and to make acquisitions in Canada or the United States without nationalistic restrictions.

The Gotaas-Larsen Spin-off

In the earlier IU spin-off, Gotaas-Larsen Shipping (G-L) clearly received the benefit of improved relationships with its customers and a more favorable competitive environment when it became an offshore company. Prior to spin-off, G-L operated in worldwide shipping's oil and liquefied natural gas markets against foreign competitors who were not subject to U.S. income taxes, or to the public reporting requirements imposed by the Securities and Exchange Commission.

As a major international shipping company, G-L owned and operated its own fleet of ships, which it financed through a variety of loan agreements with major banks, international lending consortiums, and major shipbuilding companies. The company's capital expenditures, borrowings, and asset reinvestment requirements caused Gotaas-Larsen to be heavily leveraged, which was typical of companies in the shipping business. Operating in the international market, G-L was not required to provide U.S. taxes against current earnings, except to the extent that it paid dividends to IU. The contrasting dividend policies of IU and G-L thus appealed to very different types of investors.

The result was that the IU shareholders were confronted with a conflict that some have referred to as shareholder schizophrenia. For those shareholders attracted to IU primarily because of its relatively high dividend and its non-shipping businesses, the high debt levels, large reinvestment requirements, and low dividends from Gotaas-Larsen were inconsistent. The creation in 1979 of a new "offshore"Gotaas-Larsen, as a Liberian corporation headquartered in Bermuda, provided IU shareholders with the opportunity to cure their schizophrenia. The IU shareholders could make their own determinations whether to keep both IU and G-L or to sell one of them. At the time of the G-L spin-off in November 1979, IU was selling for about $13 to $14 a share. In the spin-off distribution, the IU shareholders were given one share of Gotaas-Larsen for every three shares of IU owned on the 1979 record date. Within a year, IU was selling for about $16 and G-L was trading for the equivalent of about $3 per IU share. Over time investors moved toward whichever company better suited their particular goals. IU and G-L each operate independently without the former inhibitions regarding capital structure, debt levels, and dividend payout. In mid-1985, Gotaas-Larsen was trading on an equivalent IU share basis for about $4.80, and IU was around $16.

The Canadian Utilities Swap

In June 1980, the IU shareholders were given a choice of owning IU or "swapping" their IU shares for shares in Canadian Utilities, Ltd. (CUL), a publicly traded gas and electric utility in Alberta, Canada, that was 58 percent owned by IU. This unique transaction was prompted by increasing concern about Canadian nationalism and several other circumstances, including:

- Relatively low IU share prices
- Low tax and book basis in CUL
- Relatively high CUL market value
- The interest of several large Canadian companies that were not concerned about future Canadian governmental policy in being owners of CUL

In this environment, IU previously had allowed its percentage ownership of CUL to be diluted by not subscribing to its pro rata portion of a series of CUL common equity offerings, and by a CUL swap in September 1973 under which Canadian shareholders of IU received CUL stock for 420,000 shares of IU. In 1980, IU announced plans to swap an additional 10 percent of CUL for IU stock. Two Canadian companies sought to capitalize on this situation, because they perceived that IU might not want to continue to be a 48 percent U.S. minority shareholder in CUL. Consequently, ATCO, Ltd., a Canadian corporation seeking control of CUL, agreed to tender for sufficient IU shares that could be traded for IU's entire 58 percent stake in CUL.

Just before the tender offer and swap, IU was selling for about $12 to $13 per share. ATCO acquired 16.2 million shares of IU at $17 per share, or an aggregate price of about $275 million. As part of a greatly expanded exchange offer, IU agreed to exchange all of its 12.1 million CUL shares, with a book value of about $170 million, for the 16.2 million shares of IU owned by ATCO. IU then retained the shares received from ATCO as treasury shares.

In general terms, IU redeemed 47 percent of its outstanding shares worth $275 million in exchange for giving up 22 percent of IU's earnings. About $290 million of consolidated CUL debt also was eliminated from IU's balance sheet, and the CUL earnings exchanged were capitalized for almost twice the book value of the utility, which resulted in a gross gain to IU of about $105 million before expenses and taxes. The IU shareholders who elected to sell their shares to ATCO for $17 received a premium of about 40 percent above the pre-tender price of $12. Furthermore, the CUL exchange was accomplished on a tax-free basis to the indirect benefit of the IU shareholders who elected not to sell to ATCO. (Subsequently, changes in U.S. tax law effectively precluded this type of swap-redemption transaction in which less than 80 percent ownership of a subsidiary is distributed to shareholders in exchange for the parent company's stock.)

COMPLETE AND PARTIAL DIVESTITURES

The partial disposition of General Waterworks Corporation (GWC) was another form of IU's restructuring techniques. In October 1982, IU sold about 42 percent of GWC, which had a net worth of $61 million, to a large French company, Societe Lyonnaise des Eaux et de l'Eclairage (SLEE), for $32.4 million. At the same time, GWC sold additional newly issued common shares to SLEE, reducing IU's ownership of GWC to exactly 50 percent. Following the GWC sale, IU deconsolidated the financial results, including the GWC consolidated debt, and reported the earnings of GWC on an equity basis after that. Prior to the sale, IU's consolidated balance sheet included about $90 million of GWC's debt, which was removed through the transactions. In 1985, IU sold its remaining 50 percent interest in GWC to SLEE for approximately $70 million.

Contemporaneous with the restructuring activities described previously, IU divested all 10 companies in its manufacturing operations and a dozen smaller distribution companies that were underperforming or were incompatible with IU's strategy of concentrating distribution operations in food service and paper-related products. In addition, many smaller "portfolio pruning" divestments were made to sharpen IU's focus on its four major markets. All of these operations were divested in separate straight-sale transactions to corporations, investment groups, or individuals. Given the presence of ready buyers, none of these smaller divested companies had sufficient other "influencing factors" to warrant spin-off or swap considerations.

By 1978, IU's distribution services segment was a highly diversified "collection" of companies distributing food, paper, pipe-valve fittings, dental supplies, and other industrial supplies. In the late 1970s, IU concluded that only its food and paper operations had long-term strategic importance. Starting in 1978, five distribution companies having aggregate sales and book value of approximately $290 million and $65 million, respectively, have been sold. The sell-offs resulted in the redeployment of capital from operations that no longer fit with IU's long-term goals to its food and paper distribution units, which offer greater potential.

IU's manufacturing segment included companies involved primarily in the manufacturing and production of equipment for the energy industry. Following the sharp increase in oil prices in the mid-1970s, the economics of a new energy industry emerged and prompted IU to reevaluate its investments in this area. The contraction of margins and the lack of growth in capital spending for energy production prompted the decision to redeploy capital from industrial units to IU's other major business segments. IU has divested five industrial-manufacturing companies with total sales approaching $110 million. IU has retained substantial industrial services businesses, in which it has invested almost $150 million.

THE NEW LOOK OF IU

IU thus restructured from a company with 40 subsidiaries in 12 markets in the mid-1970s to 15 operating units in five major markets by 1980. Further changes made it a diversified services company with major operations in just four markets by the mid-1980s.

Table 33.2 demonstrates a rough approximation of the impact that corporate restructuring has had on the composition of IU's invested capital since 1977. In 1977, 67 percent of IU's invested capital was in asset-intensive units such as ocean shipping, utilities, and industrial products and services. Today, all of IU's capital is invested in service-oriented units except for C. Brewer, which is an agribusiness company.

By 1984, IU's invested capital in its Transportation Services Group had increased to almost $500 million or approximately 54 percent of the company's total invested capital. This included about $300 million invested in Ryder/PIE, a nationwide, unionized trucking company that itself was the result of two mergers between four independently operated, unionized trucking companies owned by IU. The balance of IU's investment in Transportation Services in 1984 represented IU's investment in 10 other nonunion operations, including four companies acquired in 1983 and 1984.

Ryder/PIE was formed in 1983 from the combination of IU's two less-than-truckload carriers, Ryder Truck Lines and Pacific Intermountain Express. The "merged" Ryder/PIE had approximately 11,000 employees, including 7,500 members of the International Brotherhood of Teamsters. After deregulation of the trucking industry, IU concluded that neither company alone had the scope

TABLE 33.2   IU International Corp.: Changes in Proportions of Invested Capital as a Result of Corporate Restructuring (in percentages)

	1977	1979	1981	1983	1984
Transportation Services	7.4	13.3	23.8	40.0	54.5
Ocean Shipping	36.1	0.0	0.0	0.0	0.0
Water Services	6.8	8.9	17.0	4.8	4.2
Canadian Util.	25.7	46.1	0.0	0.0	0.0
Industrial Products & Services	5.6	11.4	19.3	16.3	15.3
Distribution Services	6.5	6.5	10.0	7.8	6.0
Agribusiness	9.8	11.8	23.0	25.5	19.5
Precious Metal Mining	.3	1.3	6.9	.2	0.0
Other	1.8	.7	0.0	5.4	0.5
Total IU:					
Percent	100.0	100.0	100.0	100.0	100.0
$ (millions)	2,159	1,574	917	772	916

of operations to compete effectively with the other three major nationwide-network carriers. Since Ryder/PIE, and two other IU companies were merged, significant operating and back-office problems had to be overcome, and they resulted in significant operating losses in 1985.

Exiting the Trucking Business

In 1985, IU got out of the waterworks business and divested the largest part of its trucking operations. The remaining 50 percent of General Waterworks was sold to IU's French partner in July 1985 for $70 million and a pretax gain of about $32 million. Subsequently IU cut its dividend by 50 percent, to a payout level that was more consistent with its new configuration.

As 1985 closed, the Ryder/PIE trucking business was sold to an investor group after the operation had experienced poor results because of the fierce competition imposed by trucking industry deregulation and other economic problems. IU took a book loss of $110 million on the sell-off. The straight divestiture replaced an original plan to sell a major interest in the trucking unit to an Employee Stock Option Plan (ESOP) in return for wage concessions by workers.

As 1986 unfolded, more restructuring was in progress.

Corporate restructuring is an ongoing process at IU. It will continue as long as there are possibilities to meet the constant goal of an increase in value for IU shareholders.

Chapter 34

International Acquisitions

Robert G. Kirk

Saatchi & Saatchi Co., PLC, London, United Kingdom

As a company evolves into a multinational enterprise, it typically passes through several stages of development. A company's operations at first will be limited to its home market. But the size of the home market and pressure from domestic competitors eventually will limit domestic growth opportunities. The next major phase, therefore, will occur when the company starts to export its goods and services to overseas markets, at first simply forming marketing links with locally based companies. Initially, the profitability of a company's overseas operations may be substantially lower than in the domestic market and, in order to increase market share and profitability, the company must become the "low-cost producer" in its market. The cost advantages obtainable from economies of scale in production, marketing, and distribution thus will increasingly necessitate the establishment of subsidiary companies within overseas markets. In the final phase of development the company will coordinate its production, marketing, and distribution across countries, and eventually across continents, as the concern develops into a multinational enterprise with a dominant share of the global market for its products.

The intermediate phase of successfully establishing subsidiaries within overseas markets is in many ways the most critical and complex facet of a company's development. The company's strategy during this stage must take on an international perspective, and the company must venture from the familiarity of the home market into relatively unknown territory, with all the attendant economic, legislative, administrative, and social differences.

A first step is for the company to identify the overseas markets that offers the greatest strategic benefits and growth prospects. This is a complicated task involving the interplay of a large number of factors. Strategy can be developed only within the context of, and with references to, a complex mix of restricting influences. The underlying economic conditions of the overseas market must be carefully appraised. The vast Latin American market, for example, may offer attractive long-term development prospects, but this must be balanced against the short-term detrimental influences of economic instability, rapid inflation, and severe currency fluctuations. Political risk often must be considered. Lebanon, off-limits because of violent upheavals in the mid-1980s, was once a most attractive investment proposition.

GOVERNMENT REGULATION
OF FOREIGN INVESTMENT

The most important initial consideration, however, is likely to be the variety of local government regulations and restrictions that surround direct foreign investment in the majority of overseas markets. In principle, overseas governments (even, to some extent, in the Eastern Bloc) welcome direct foreign investment. The principal benefits are generally accelerated economic development through the creation of jobs, infusion of external capital and new technology, and an improved balance of payments. In practice, such investment is permitted predominantly on a selective basis, and, the extent of government interference varies significantly among countries. Direct foreign investment in sectors judged to be of strategic importance, such as power and telecommunications, generally is severely restricted or prohibited. Many governments deliberately incorporate a degree of ambiguity into written regulations governing overseas investment in order to ensure themselves some level of discretion and the option of a selective case-by-case approach.

The Industrialized Nations

Restrictions generally are less severe in the industrialized, OECD group of countries, though here, too, there is a large degree of variation. In West Germany the regulations are the same as for national investors. There are no restrictions on the repatriation of dividends and no controls on foreign exchange. Taxation of foreign firms is governed by well-developed reciprocal exemptions, special investment incentives are available equally to foreign and domestic investors, and there are no performance requirements. In France, on the other hand, foreign investment above a specified sum requires government authorization. There are few established criteria for judging an investment, and the government proceeds on a case-by-case basis with a close watch on sectors regarded as being of strategic importance. The application process normally takes between two and four months, though it may take considerably longer. The government generally will seek a "French solution," which starts with finding a domestic suitor for the acquisition target. Government investment incentives are geared toward regional development, and performance requirements may be imposed for balance-of-trade effects, production plans, policies toward employees, and technology transfers.

In Australia and Canada, government investment regulations are administered in a particularly flexible manner and are subject to clarification and adjustment depending on particular circumstances. In Australia, for example, the Foreign Investment Review Board (FIRB) assists the government in meeting its stated goal of facilitating the efficient and practical administration of foreign investment policy. The board examines proposals and makes recommendations to the government, giving guidance where necessary to foreign investors so that their proposals may be in conformity with government policy. The board's functions are advisory only; responsibility for the administration of policy and decisions on investment proposals ultimately rests with the Treasury.

Japan: A Special Case

The situation in Japan is an exception among the industrialized countries. Government policy on direct foreign investment has been progressively liberalized in recent years, and though it remains an important consideration, it is ostensibly not a major impediment. It is principally the reluctance of Japanese companies to "sell out" to foreign investors that remains a strong barrier to entry. Acquisitions in general are very rare in Japan and are not regarded as a typical means of entering a particular market sector.

A prospective investor must first submit notice to the relevant Japanese ministry, using an appointed proxy if the party does not have a local office. The proposed transaction then is prohibited for a period of 30 days, though the period may be shortened or considerably extended depending on the character of the investment and whether the ministry decides that a detailed examination of the proposal is necessary. If certain Japanese companies are involved, an inquiry automatically will be made if the foreign investor's proportion of equity in the target exceeds a designated percentage. The purpose of the inquiry is to determine whether the intended foreign investment will have an adverse effect on national security, public order or safety, or the smooth running of the Japanese economy. The ministry also will judge whether the transaction will offend the principle of reciprocity by permitting the foreign investor to take advantage of favorable treatment in Japan that is not available to the Japanese investor in the home country of the foreign investor.

The Framework in Developing Nations

Government regulations on foreign investment in the developing regions of the world generally are more restrictive than elsewhere (though, paradoxically, it may be argued that it is here that the economic benefits of direct foreign investment tend to be greatest). This is often the result of a historical legacy of substantial foreign investment, with all the attendant suspicion of neo-colonialism, and a political climate that favors a high degree of government intervention in the workings of the economy, particularly in times of recession.

As in the industrialized countries, government policy in developing lands varies significantly, even within the same region. In Mexico, foreign equity participation generally is restricted to a maximum of 49 percent but to an even lower level in many business sectors, and may be prohibited altogether in still other sectors. Foreign investors must register with a regulatory commission that can, for example, approve or disapprove contracts governing the transfer of technology, such as patents and trademarks. Furthermore, generalized exchange control regulations restrict the right to remit profits. The Brazilian government, on the other hand, has a more liberal attitude toward foreign investors, who are treated in essentially the same way as domestic investors, and a range of fiscal and import incentives are available. As long as the investment is registered with the central bank, there are no restrictions on the repatriation of capital, and restrictions on the remittance of earnings are significantly less severe than those that apply in Mexico.

Korea offers a particularly severe investment climate. Foreign investment is allowed only in specially designated industrial subsectors. In a few areas, 100 percent equity ownership is permitted; but in the majority, ownership is restricted to 50 percent. Official policy announcements do not always translate into changes at the various working levels of government. Regulations sometimes are not even published, and investors learn of them only during the approval process. In some cases, potential investments permitted by the official guidelines actually have been disapproved.

In summary, then, government restrictions vary greatly among countries. In a number of countries, particularly in the developing regions, direct foreign investment is a sensitive political issue and government attitudes are in a state of continual change—particularly in times of economic recession.

IDENTIFYING OVERSEAS INVESTMENT OPPORTUNITIES

There may be a tendency for a company to consider strategy to be of unique and overriding importance, so that all financial and tactical considerations will be made to "fit," and the "right" investment in the chosen overseas market always will be sought. Alternatively, strategy may be determined within the constraints of, and even subordinated to, the nature of the market and its constituent companies. The ideal investment criteria, however, are very seldom met.

Direct foreign investment through the purchase of the assets of an already established indigenous firm, or an interest in its capital stock, is by no means the sole method by which an overseas market may be entered. A company usually will face three alternative forms of investing in the overseas market, including acquisitions. It also may enter into a joint venture with an indigenous firm, or it may establish a new business enterprise within the overseas market. The disadvantage of the joint venture is the consequent dilution of management control, whereas creation of a new business involves heavy start-up costs with a relatively lengthy initial period of low profitability.

The most immediate and most profitable route to an overseas market generally will be through the direct acquisition of an established local firm. This approach provides ready access to customers and product recognition as well as locally experienced technical and managerial personnel. For most companies, particularly in the services sector, where the "product" is principally a service provided by individuals (so that local familiarity with the firm is of vital importance), this will be the only viable investment alternative.

Given that the purchase of a going concern provides the least problematic basis for establishing a presence abroad, the goodwill payable by the direct foreign investor will be commensurate with the financial record of the acquisition target. The value of goodwill payable to a poorly performing company will be a function of an assessment of the managerial problems being purchased. The choice of the firm to acquire should be determined through a cost/benefit analysis of the available options, with reference to a wide variety of factors ranging from financial records to the less tangible aspects of compatibility between the mode of operation and personnel of the company and the prospective acquisition target.

Problems of Getting Information

The structure of ownership of target firms will be an important determinant of the amount of information available. Whereas publicly quoted firms legally are required to disclose information on their operations (principally financial detail), there is very little such requirement in the case of privately owned firms. Nevertheless, outside the United Kingdom and the United States, the absence of legal financial reporting requirements for (specifically private) companies means that the quality of information often is highly imperfect. Reliable financial information may not be available, and little will be obtainable to resolve the question of suitability. An assessment of the investment opportunities on the basis of available information may present the company with a number of less desirable options. Consequently, the "second-best" solution becomes all too easy to adopt.

Without prior knowledge of the target market, the solution to this impasse will be heavily dependent on the judgment of external advisors—either financial intermediaries or firms of accountants with local operations. With the help of these resources, the danger of adopting the second-best options may be avoided. In the final analysis, however, useful and detailed information on the prospective acquisition target frequently will not be available until the prospective target is approached directly.

THE INTERNATIONAL ACQUISITION PROCESS UNFOLDS

With particular reference to the cross-border acquisition, the initial meeting may be arranged through an intermediary, who usually in such a case will have identified the acquisition prospect in the first place. This method is generally preferable. The intermediary will have specialized local knowledge and normally will provide a wide "menu" of potential vendors. That offers the further advantage that the identity of the purchaser need not be disclosed. The use of intermediaries usually will be a function of the degree of development of capital markets in the country where the acquisition is to be made. In the developed countries, acquisitions through financial institutions are commonplace.

Developing a Rapport

A basic premise of the successful acquisition is that the whole will be greater than the parts—that the profitability of the combined operations of the acquiring company and the acquired firm will be greater than the sum of the profitabilities of the two entities operating separately. For this to be the case, there obviously needs to be a high level of mutuality of strategy, goals, and aspirations between the management of the company and that of the firm to be acquired. Additionally, however, the two parties will need to be able to communicate these common factors effectively and constructively. To establish a mutual rapport at the outset is thus a basic precondition to being able to identify a mutuality of interest between the two parties.

The importance of being able to develop a sound rapport is especially relevant in the service industries (such as the advertising industry), where the principal assets are the individuals and their client relationships. If the people are incompatible at the management level, this will reflect on a basic incompatibility throughout the two organizations and will indicate strongly that the acquisition may not be successful.

Publicly quoted firms represent a divorce of ownership from control, and an acquisition can be effected without ever having met the management. But this option often will depend on the nature of the industry in which the acquisition is made. Such a solution is more applicable, for example, in a manufacturing industry, where identifiable net tangible assets are a major part of the purchase price, than in a service industry, where the value of the company is principally its personnel. With privately owned firms there is an identity of ownership and control, and management has the incentive of direct financial gain when the firm is acquired. However, there often will be emotional factors to contend with, particularly where the business has been built from scratch, or is a historic family concern.

Negotiating the Deal

When a rapport is established, based on the belief that an essential compatibility of strategy and goals exists, detailed negotiations can begin. No detailed or systematic set of rules governing the method of negotiation will ever apply, because every acquisition presents its own complex and unique pattern. Though financial considerations will usually be of foremost concern, the longer-term issues of the role of the firm and its future development after it has been acquired will need to be further examined and agreed upon. In the long run, the deal must work for more than just money. There must be a strong mutual compatibility and understanding between the two organizations.

Again, at this stage the best available local advice will need to be used. The choice of good advisers with a sound knowledge of the specific problems of the local market often will be the "*sine qua non*" for completing the acquisition. Such advisers should be recommended by the company's consultants in the home market, or, ideally, by their overseas subsidiaries or affiliates. The company must ensure that its selected advisers thoroughly understand its strategy, goals, and mode of operation, as the company must be able to have a good deal of faith in its advisers' judgment and knowledge of local conditions.

COMPLETING THE AGREEMENT

Help from a Knowledgeable Lawyer

The lawyer is a key figure in the acquisition process. The company must develop a good relationship with the lawyer so that it may talk freely on all issues and trust the lawyer to negotiate on the company's behalf in its absence. The lawyer must be flexible: A basic problem with lawyers is that they tend to see the deal from a legal, not business, point of view. An unsuitable lawyer may kill a potentially successful deal by damaging the relationship between the company and the vendor. Equally, however, the lawyer may serve as a convenient scapegoat if relations sour.

In addition to the legal function, the lawyer may be an invaluable guide to local protocol, having first-hand knowledge of the method of approach and negotiating tactics of local businessmen. This is a particularly important function in a country such as Japan, where correct protocol is an especially sensitive issue. One must bring the right gifts, bow to the correct level, and even sit in the right part of the meeting room—away from the door!

The acquiring company will wish to be advised at the outset of any local legal issues or government regulations that may prohibit or materially delay the acquisition. It is therefore critical that the company's domestic and local lawyer be mutually aware of the legal and regulatory hurdles that need to be cleared, so that the company can take account of these in its negotiations with the vendors.

The local lawyer also will be responsible for advising the purchasing company on the best terms that a purchasing company can reasonably expect from local vendors, for example, in terms of the warranties that normally are given. These may be very different from the practices the company is accustomed to in its home country. Throughout the negotiations, the local lawyer also should be looking forward to the period following completion of the acquisition and advising the company on the effect of the whole range of local law on the company's business activities in the country. The attorney therefore will have to consider a very broad range of issues, from the impact of government restrictions to the observance of local labor laws. In the United States, for example, the potential impact of the regulations of the Securities and Exchange Commission and of antitrust legislation may cause a material delay in the timetable agreed to by the principal parties to the transaction unless they are advised in good time of the impact of those regulations.

While guiding the purchasing company through any regulatory pitfalls, the local lawyer will have two principal other responsibilities: first, the preparation, or at least negotiation, of the legal documentation required for the transaction; and second, the carrying out of a due diligence exercise. This amounts to an investigation of the target company's good standing, business, and contractual commitments. It is designed not only to identify problems—both legal and commercial—with the target's business (outstanding litigation or unusual contracts, for example), but also to inform the purchasing company about a whole variety of aspects of the target's business. These include the terms of the pension scheme, long-term service contracts with key executives, patents or trademarks owned or used by the target, and the terms of its real property leases, to name but a few matters.

At the closing of the transaction, particularly if the target company is based in the United States, formal written opinions will be delivered by the relevant U.S. law firms to the principal parties. Interestingly, the opinion delivered to the buyer—about, for example, the due issuance of the shares it is buying and the enforceability of the acquisition agreement—is given by the lawyers to the vendors and vice versa. The purchasing company therefore will seek assurance from its own lawyers that the vendor's lawyers are competent to give the opinion and have carried out the work necessary to enable the buyer to rely on the opinion.

Rationalization of Accounting Issues

Initially, the accountants will be concerned principally with an investigation into and confirmation of the financial state of the firm to be acquired. This usually will involve an examination of the financial record of the firm for its last five years, confirmation of its assets and liabilities according to the latest balance sheet, and an assessment of its future prospects with regard to profits and cash flow. Such an exercise requires a high degree of specialized knowledge of local accounting, tax, and legal practices, as these vary considerably among countries. Local financial statements frequently need to be restated for consistency of accounting treatment and to eliminate exceptional and nonrecurring items before the acquiring company can conduct a meaningful assessment of the financial state and potential of the acquisition target.

The accountants also will be required to report on the actual and potential tax position of the target company, particularly with regard to any tax advantages or disadvantages that are likely to flow from a change in ownership. Also requiring consideration is the potential impact on the tax position of the acquiring company in its home country because of the potential flow of dividends and other income from the target company. Tax advantages sometimes can accrue by acquiring overseas companies through one or more intermediate subsidiaries in one or more overseas countries that offer suitable tax benefits.

Major Financing Decisions

At an early stage, consideration must be given to the manner in which the purchase is to be financed. Cash, shares of the acquiring company, loan stock in the acquiring company, or a mixture of any or all of these three can be offered. If the consideration is to be in cash, is the cash to be borrowed, or is new money to be raised by the acquiring company by way of share issue? The country in which any borrowings are to be made must be identified, and terms, security, and interest rates negotiated. If loan stock is to be used, terms, interest rates, security, and repayment terms will have to be decided upon.

An alternative to a deal in which the consideration is agreed at the outset is "the structure earn-out" arrangement. Under such arrangements an initial capital payment will be made. Further payments will be made if profits following the acquisition exceed predetermined levels. The principal advantage to the purchaser is that it assures the continuing interest of the vendor in the performance of the company after control changes hands.

Integrating the Acquired Firm

After closing, the acquired company has to be integrated into the acquiring group. The management of the acquired company may be given varying degrees of autonomy in the future running of the concern, depending on the policy of the acquiring company and the quality of the acquired company's management. It is, however, vital that the acquired company follow and adhere to the financial control procedures of the new parent company. This may require considerable input from the financial staff of the new parent and substantial effort and cooperation from the financial staff in the acquired company.

THE DECISION ON GOING OVERSEAS

For the company with plans for international expansion, there are two central considerations: can target companies be identified clearly, and can the investing company get its money back? Government regulations, onerous as they often are, generally control only the extent of such investment rather then prohibit it altogether. Thus, they usually represent only a preliminary hurdle to the establishment of a base.

In trying to assess the full economic costs and benefits of any cross-border deal, however, the buyer must examine closely the secondary effects of operating in a foreign country. More specifically, these include the impact of broader regulations such as currency exchange controls and employment legislation. They are potentially damaging to the investment because they may put limitations on dividend repatriation or may add costs to plans for restructuring the acquired company. The postacquisition rules on how to operate ultimately determine whether the investing company indeed will get its money back.

Chapter 35

Asset-Based Financing

Michael R. Dabney

General Electric Credit Corp., Stamford, Connecticut

Since the early 1970s, asset-based financing techniques have been used increasingly in the acquisition of business enterprises. The technique is popularly referred to as a leveraged buy-out, or LBO. In a leveraged buy-out, a company is acquired in a transaction financed largely by borrowing that is supported by the assets and cash flow of the acquired company.

The increase in LBO activity in the 1970s and 1980s can be traced to several factors, including basic U.S. tax law, which allows deductibility of interest on acquisition debt; limitations on attractive major reinvestment opportunities in U.S. industry, which have resulted in an abundance of idle institutional capital; a "baby boom" generation of corporate executives who, now in their 40s, are looking for alternative career opportunities; and the evolution of LBO structures in the 1970s and their success as a corporate finance tool.

WHY A COMPANY CHOOSES AN LBO

A publicly traded enterprise (or corporate division) whose cash flow characteristics are relatively more attractive than its earnings per share and growth potential constitutes an ideal LBO candidate. Such companies generally will be valued higher in the private sector, with value increasing as a function of leverage, which reduces the weighted cost of capital on an aftertax basis. (Weighted cost of capital is the composite rate of return required for all layers of debt and equity that must be satisfied by the projected cash flow.)

Private companies with strong cash flow characteristics also may demand greater value in a private sale. By agreeing to accept LBO bids, the seller may expand the number of potential bidders to include management and/or other experienced operating groups that lack the resources to self-finance their bid. The inclusion of management in the purchase may be a public relations benefit to a public seller, a way to reward loyal employees, and a way to increase value by expanding the field of potential buyers.

The Players in an LBO Transaction

Investment banks are the traditional focal point for M&A activity and are often instrumental in bringing about an LBO. The process begins when the investment bank identifies a company that is being proposed for sale and begins discussions with its managers. It then proceeds to arrange for financing through various participating institutions, which may include the seller of the property, commercial finance companies, commercial banks, insurance companies, pension funds, and LBO partnerships. However, as the concept of merchant banking continues to evolve in U.S. financial markets, the role of each of the traditional groups of institutional participants mentioned above is becoming increasingly integrated and full-service in nature. For instance, the origination and structuring may be done by any one of the cited institutions and, conversely, many investment banking firms (traditionally agents) are investing in the equity layers of the transaction. On a contemporary note, the purchases of high-yield bonds represent the relatively new class of investor in LBO structures at the mezzanine layer.

THE STRUCTURE OF AN LBO

Constraints in terms of the amount of leverage that is created in an LBO transaction are determined by the rules generated by the various markets that are going to buy the securities and by the amount of risk that each descending layer of capital is willing to endure relative to its designated rate of return. In this context, leveraged buy-outs are generally structured from the top down.

Senior Debt

Traditionally, the most senior layer of debt is a percentage of the value of the target's working capital assets, net of cash and marketable securities. By definition, this layer of debt is useful as a source of proceeds only in asset-based secured structures, as opposed to cash flow structures. The value of this layer of debt is a function of the orderly liquidation value of accounts receivable and inventory that exists at closing and is projected to be retained throughout the life of the investment.

Typically, lenders will advance up to 85 percent of the accounts receivable and 50 percent of the value of inventory, excluding inventory that constitutes work in process. In practice, however, loan formulas can vary greatly, depending on the particular characteristics of a company's assets. For instance, accounts receivables that are billed due and payable in 30 days from the invoice date are more valuable than billing methodologies that allow extended terms. Accounts receivable that are generated from the sale of products pursuant to some continuing obligation (i.e., service and/or maintainance) are diminished in value. Accounts receivable that constitute a demand for a progress payment pursuant to delivery of products and services not yet completed are likely to have little or no value at all. Determining the value of inventory by some quick formula can be even trickier. As a rule, however, the more commodity in nature the inventory is, the greater the value it holds. If the inventory constitutes component parts of a total assembly or is highly specialized and has limited application, it may have little or no value.

The amount of capital to be supported by the value of these working capital assets may vary greatly with respect to the time of year and the particular point the company is at in its production cycle. Thus, it is critical in structuring an LBO to determine what the base layer of capital will be, relative to the lowest level of working capital assets that is likely to be available at any given time and to use no more than that amount as a portion of the payment for the acquisition price. This leaves the rest of the capital as cash available to finance the production cycle of the company.

Intermediate-Term Loan

The next layer of financing is traditionally the intermediate-term loan, secured by the property, plant, and equipment of the target company. The most common appraisal methodology used to determine the value of these assets is the orderly liquidation approach. This is generally defined as the value that would be received from the sale of such assets to a buyer for the same or some alternative use, given a reasonable length of time to solicit such a buyer.

The time frames most commonly used are six months to one year with respect to equipment sales and one to two years for real estate. The common loan formula used to determine how much capital will be provided as a function of these appraised values is 80 percent of the appraised value of the equipment and 50 percent of the appraised value of the real estate. Formulas, however, may be adjusted up or down, depending on the lender's perception as to the likely future value of such assets relative to the specific industry or location. It is important to keep in mind that these appraisals represent a "snapshot" of value at that specific point in time.

Mezzanine Layers

The next step is to determine the amount of capital and the form in which the capital will be invested by the principal buying group. In doing so, the lender can determine the differential between senior debt and buyer equity. This gap is commonly referred to as the mezzanine layer. It can be the most difficult of the transaction to structure, because it is not clearly debt or equity and often takes the form of some hybrid instrument(s), which has characteristics of both. If the target company will be a tax-paying entity, deductibility of interest (carrying cost) on the capital is important, and the capital provided will have the debt characteristics necessary to achieve this deductibility. But if the company is not likely to be a tax-paying entity following acquisition, the mezzanine layer will have more equity characteristics. In the event that the company will have no tax liability in the first few years but will be taxable in the later periods of the investment, exchangeable instruments can be used. Exchangeable instruments start out as debt and can be traded for equity instruments at some future date.

From an economic point of view, the target yield on mezzanine instruments is a function of the projected coverage available for principal and interest and/or dividend and sinking fund payments as required; the amount of underlying equity; and the ability of the company to normalize its capital structure over a five- to seven-year period, thus providing liquidity for the mezzanine holders of stock, options, warrants, etc., either through a public offering or a redemption triggered by "puts" and "calls."

Cash Flow-Based Structures

In a transaction structured primarily off its cash flow, the assets typically remain unencumbered, with the working capital financing being used exclusively to facilitate the ongoing operations of the company. The acquisition debt is created on a term basis. In this instance, the amount of capital available in each layer of the transaction is principally a function of the amount of projected cash flow available to service that layer (coverage), the underlying equity, and, as mentioned earlier, the institutional equity layers (mezzanine).

Cash flow structures tend to be less leveraged and provide higher coverage but correspondingly lower rates of return to the holders of equity capital.

FINANCIAL SOURCES FOR AN LBO

In secured transactions, the secured debt at both the working capital level and fixed asset level is traditionally provided by myriad commercial banks and commercial finance companies. The selection process is a function of the size of the transaction, the existence of banking relationships, and the comfort level of the institution for the LBO target's specific industry. Usually, transactions in excess of $20 million are financed at the secured level by money center banks and large independent finance companies, who , in turn, may sell participations to other financial institutions.

Mezzanine funds are provided directly by insurance companies, pension funds, and commercial finance companies and indirectly by LBO partnerships and participants in the high-yield bond market.

The seller of the target company is also frequently a source of mezzanine financing because its retention of a minor equity interest may serve as a purchase price hedge.

Industry preferences and knowledge, target yield, desired composition of yield (current versus total), willingness to purchase multiple layers in the capital structure, and desire to be proactive in management are among the major considerations in selection of mezzanine participants.

The common equity may be purchased exclusively by the operating management of the target company, functioning as purchasers, or by third-party purchasers with the operating experience and capital to attract institutional capital at the senior and mezzanine layers.

The foregoing provides largely a horizontal view of the LBO market. In fact, it is commonplace for all of the classes of lenders and investors to acquire vertical strips of financing within a single transaction. Such vertical strips represent all or part of each of the layers included in the investment package.

For example, we at General Electric Credit Corp. (GECC) commonly purchase all layers of financing above the common stock investment. At the other end of the spectrum, a third-party purchaser of the common stock may wish to structure a portion of this investment to include some mezzanine (debt/equity) and some common. In so doing, the buyer is afforded the current rate of return and greater leverage on the return to its common equity.

Underwriting Criteria

All institutional investors in the LBO marketplace share certain qualitative underwriting criteria, with each having selective standards unique to their respective companies. The underwriting of a transaction from an institutional perspective does not tend to start with the determination of structures relative to asset value and projected coverage ratios. In most cases, the underwriting process begins with a detailed understanding of the industry and markets in which the target company is a participant. The analysis includes an understanding of products being sold through those markets, their sensitivity to competition, and their potential for technical obsolescence.

This leads to a basic understanding of the company's competitive strategy, what it would take in economic terms to sustain that strategy and the formulation of projected cash flows that are consistent with the company's markets and continuing strategy. These cash flows, coupled with tax and legal considerations, become the basis for the determination of a particular LBO structure.

Other considerations that come into play are the perceived ability of management to execute, the quality of the financial systems in place, and the ability of the systems to provide reliable and timely information on the company's past acquisition performance relative to what was anticipated.

Postacquisition Surveillance

In the postacquisition phase, clear communication among all parties associated with the transaction is critical, particularly in the early stages when difficulties are most likely to arise. The process of using the LBO techniques to move a corporate enterprise out of an inefficient capital structure into one that is efficient should be viewed as an intermediate-term financial strategy of no more than five to seven years in duration. The first and best use of free cash flow in this defined period usually is to reduce debt. There is nothing wrong with doing a second transaction, but it is generally advisable initially to normalize the capital structure of the base transaction and create a firm foundation for future activity.

Getting It Done Right

Anyone contemplating corporate purchase through an LBO is advised to select the fewest intermediaries, advisers, lenders, and investors required to consummate the transaction, and to pick those who can handle a transaction of the required size. In so doing, the buyer is more likely to get both the needed attention and the required resources.

The LBO field is a specialized industry where industry-specific experience counts both in getting it done and doing it right. The inherent risk of extraordinary financial leverage in an operating company must not be underestimated. A careful and professional approach to structure and implementation is the critical element of success.

Part 8

The
Paper Chase:
Regulation,
Communication,
and Defenses

Chapter 36

Antitrust Guidelines

Douglas E. Rosenthal

Sutherland, Asbill & Brennan, Washington, D.C.

William Blumenthal

Sutherland, Asbill & Brennan, Washington, D.C.

In most proposed mergers, the antitrust laws present little more than a petty annoyance. After cursory reviews, most transactions raise no serious competitive issues, and antitrust compliance consists essentially of filing premerger notification report forms and sitting out any required statutory waiting period before closing the deal. However, the antitrust laws present serious obstacles in a significant minority of mergers. In those cases, the U.S. Department of Justice and the Federal Trade Commission (FTC), which share responsibility for antitrust enforcement, either may sue to block the deal or may call for major revision or restructuring. Private parties also may challenge mergers in the courts, although this rarely happens except in hostile tender offers.

LEGAL STANDARDS

The principal antitrust statute governing the legality of mergers is Section 7 of the Clayton Act, which prohibits any merger "where in any line of commerce in any section of the country, the effect of such acquisition may be substantially to lessen competition, or to tend to create a monopoly." The underlying goal of the statute is to prevent monopoly from developing. Other pertinent statutes include Section 1 of the Sherman Act, which prohibits contracts, combinations, and conspiracies that unreasonably restrain trade; and Section 2 of the Sherman Act, which prohibits monopolization, attempted monopolization, and conspiracies to monopolize. However, merger suits generally are brought under the Clayton Act because the government must satisfy a lower burden of proof than under the Sherman Act.

Evaluation of a proposed merger under Section 7 is a two-stage process: defining the markets that the merger will affect and then assessing the competitive impact on these markets. If the parties compete in the same market, the merger will be regarded as "horizontal." If they operate in markets that have purchaser-supplier relationships, the merger is "vertical." If the parties operate in unrelated markets, the merger is "conglomerate." Each of the classes is assessed under separate legal tests, with horizontal mergers facing the strictest scrutiny.

Market Definition

Market definition in many respects is the key stage in the merger evaluation process. Market definition often will determine whether a specific merger is viewed as horizontal, vertical, or conglomerate. Thus, a merger between a can manufacturer and a bottle maker might be viewed as horizontal if "packaging materials" is regarded as a single product, but conglomerate if "cans" and "bottles" are regarded as distinct products. In addition, market definition generally will determine the market shares of the parties to the merger—an important factor in the second stage of the evaluation process. Thus, in a merger between two bottle makers, the parties' market shares might be small if "packaging materials" is considered the product, but substantial if "bottles" is considered the product.

A relevant market consists of product ("line of commerce") and geographic ("section of the country") dimensions. Basically, the product market is defined by examining the functional interchangeability of use among products. Substitutes are regarded as falling within a single market, and especially close substitutes may be deemed a submarket within the broader market. Similarly, the geographic market is defined by the locations where purchasers of the relevant product may turn for sources of supply.

In both the product and geographic dimensions, the aim is to identify an insular grouping, relatively segregated from external competitive pressures. Case law provides little systematic guidance as to the necessary degree of interchangeability among products deemed to constitute a single market. The Justice Department tried to remedy this shortcoming by incorporating in its 1982 Merger Guidelines the so-called 5 percent test for identifying the competitors in a market. Under this yardstick, a market was deemed to exist if a price increase of 5 percent or more did not drive customers to a substitute product. The 1984 revision of the Guidelines replaced the 5 percent threshold with the more general concept of a "small but significant and nontransitory" price increase in gauging customer reactions.

As a practical matter, however, market definition largely is determined by the facts surrounding a specific merger. This can cause uncertainty in assessing the antitrust risk of a particular deal, but it also provides considerable latitude for the merger partners to develop the strongest case they can. The aforementioned bottle maker, for example, might marshal facts that suggest a narrow product market when it seeks to merge with a can manufacturer, but argue for a broad market when it wants to merge with another bottlemaker. However, the virtual case-by-case approach presents the danger that enforcement authorities will unduly emphasize facts that are of little competitive significance and that an improper market definition will result. In industries with government reporting requirements, for example, market boundaries sometimes have been set by reporting categories that may have little practical significance for actual competition in the marketplace. Enforcement authorities also can seize erroneously on stray remarks contained in internal documents. The FTC nearly sued to block a chemical industry merger several years ago because it believed wrongly that the northeastern United States was a relevant geographic market. (This had the effect of inflating the parties' apparent market shares.) The agency jumped to this conclusion because one of the parties had regional sales territories and its employees kept referring to the "northeast market," even though competition was on a nationwide basis.

Competitive Effects

Predicting a merger's competitive effects can be quite speculative. The courts have historically applied presumptive tests for analyzing horizontal mergers based on the market's structure and the merger parties' market shares, and the tests have resulted in relatively strict enforcement. However, the courts increasingly have shown a willingness to look behind horizontal merger presumptions, resulting in some relaxation from the stringency of the past. Enforcement efforts against nonhorizontal mergers have been infrequent since the mid-1970s and remain so.

Horizontal Merger Standards

The legality of a horizontal merger historically has depended principally on the market's concentration level and the parties' market shares, but other considerations may be taken into account. The government's enforcement standards since the 1982 Merger Guidelines have been based on the Herfindahl-Hirschman index (HHI). The HHI is calculated by determining the market share of each market participant, squaring the market shares, and adding the squares. Thus, in a market where the participants have shares of 30 percent, 25 percent, 20 percent, 15 percent, 5 percent, 3 percent, and 2 percent, the HHI would be 2,188, or the sum of $900 + 625 + 400 + 225 + 25 + 9 + 4$.

An HHI increase is twice the product of the market shares of the merging parties. Thus, a merger between firms with market shares of 8 percent and 6 percent would result in an HHI increase of 96, or 2 × 8 × 6. In markets with a postmerger HHI of less than 1,000, mergers generally will not be challenged. In markets with a postmerger HHI between 1,000 and 1,800, the government is unlikely to challenge mergers that increase the index by less than 100 points. In markets with a postmerger HHI over 1,800, the government is unlikely to challenge mergers that raise the HHI by less than 50 points.

Enforcement authorities have shown increased willingness in recent years to look beyond market shares. If past market shares do not accurately portray the future development of the market, it may be appropriate to adjust the shares for purposes of antitrust evaluation. Likewise, nonstatistical factors sometimes may be important, particularly if they indicate whether firms in the market could engage in tacit collusion. Such factors include ease of entry, product homogeneity, complexity of price structures, frequency and size of orders, and the antitrust history of the market.

Nonhorizontal Merger Standards

Concern over nonhorizontal mergers has waned in recent years, as the case law has discouraged challenges and as many economists have adopted the view that nonhorizontal mergers are unthreatening. The case law does, however, articulate several theories as to how nonhorizontal mergers may reduce competition. A vertical merger, for example, may prevent a supplier from doing business with a customer that has acquired a competing supplier, and a conglomerate merger may eliminate either buyer or seller as a potential competitor in a market. Over time, the courts have erected many preconditions to application of such theories.

Defenses

Certain defenses may be available to legitimize a merger that otherwise would be unlawful. Most important is the failing company defense, a judicially created doctrine suggesting that an otherwise unlawful merger is permissible if one of the parties is in grave danger of business failure, the prospects of reorganization are dim, and a less anticompetitive purchaser is unavailable. The third element often is the key, and merger partners usually must show that alternative purchasers have been solicited widely, but unsuccessfully.

The so-called failing division defense may apply when an otherwise healthy company threatens to shut down an unprofitable division or plant if it cannot sell the operation to a competitor. The critical question usually is whether the threat of shutdown is credible. If it is, the government normally will approve the transaction for both political and economic reasons—politically to prevent loss of jobs, economically to have the capacity operating, even if by a competitor.

Under the 1984 revision of the Merger Guidelines, the Justice Department will listen to the merger partners' pleas that an otherwise questionable transaction should be cleared if it creates efficiencies in a market or an industry. The Justice Department stopped short of saying that the argument alone will be persuasive, but it did acknowledge that efficiencies will be among the criteria it uses in determining whether to challenge a merger in the courts—which historically have rejected the efficiency defense. Another defense traditionally given short shrift has been the countervailing power argument, which maintains that an unlawful merger is needed for the two partners to compete with a larger company.

OBTAINING GOVERNMENT CLEARANCE

The formal process of obtaining government clearance for a merger begins with the filing of premerger notification report forms, when required, with the FTC and the Justice Department in compliance with the Hart-Scott-Rodino Act of 1976. The two agencies then decide which will review the proposed merger, based on their relative workloads and their expertise in a specific industry. The Justice Department tends to review mergers in steel, brewing, telecommunications, and financial services, for example, whereas the FTC usually handles the cement, food distribution, professional services, and chemicals industries. When both agencies are in conflict over a high-profile transaction raising serious antitrust questions, the one that gets the case usually is decided through bargaining. When Mobil Corp. launched a hostile tender offer for Conoco, Inc., in 1981, for example, both reviewing agencies asserted jurisdiction for several days, until the FTC yielded.

Under the Hart-Scott-Rodino Act, the transaction may not go forward for 30 calendar days (15 in the case of a cash tender offer) from the filing of premerger notification. If a merger presents no antitrust question, the parties may seek early termination of the waiting period. Otherwise, the reviewing agency will use the waiting period to conduct a preliminary investigation. If the agency concludes that the transaction is lawful, it will let the waiting period expire. But if the preliminary investigation has not satisfied the reviewing agency, it will ask for more information, a step that automatically extends the waiting period until 20 calendar days (10 in the case of a cash tender offer) after the parties have substantially complied with the request. It is generally possible to negotiate with the agency to limit the scope of the request, but compliance with even a narrowed request may be disruptive and costly. Files must be reviewed and copied by attorneys, and executive time must be diverted to respond to interrogatory-style specifications. Besides answering specific questions, executives of the merger partners also may have to help prepare position papers supporting the merger and make themselves available for meetings with agency staff members to explain competitive practices in their industry.

As the extended waiting period expires, the regulatory agency may let the merger proceed or take these other steps:

- Propose that the transaction be restructured or otherwise revised to lessen competitive concerns.
- File suit seeking a court injunction halting the transaction.
- Allow the deal to go forward, but file suit later to break up the merger or obtain other relief.
- Request that the parties "voluntarily" extend the waiting period (usually under threat of seeking an injunction if they do not).

The merger is not necessarily doomed if the partners cannot work out an accord with the government. Except in cases when the buyer previously has agreed to get government clearance before making an acquisition (such as in consent agreements or litigation settlements involving prior mergers) or when a deal needs clearance from an industry regulatory authority, *explicit federal approval is not required.* If the government does choose to fight the merger in the courts, it has the burden of proving that the transaction violates the antitrust laws. In recent years, the government has lost more than half the merger cases it has initiated.

Strategic Considerations

Because of the variety of options available to antitrust authorities, the merger partners should devise a strategy for obtaining government clearance, balancing what they really want out of the deal with what they might have to accept. Between allowing the deal to go forward and suing to block it, the spectrum of possible government decisions includes:

- Allowing the merger to proceed but continuing the investigation with an eye toward possible future divestitures.
- Filing suit after the deal has been completed to have it rescinded or reduced in scope.
- Permitting the deal to be closed, but requiring the buyer to hold the acquired business separate and unintegrated for a specified period of time.
- Requiring the buyer to agree to certain nonstructural conditions in return for having the deal cleared. Examples include adopting certain price policies or agreeing to supply smaller customers equally with larger customers in times of shortages.
- Requiring the buyer to divest certain assets after the deal goes through.
- Demanding a restructuring of the transaction so that fewer assets are acquired than originally proposed.

Many very large mergers go forward only after strings are attached. In the two giant oil mergers of 1984—Gulf Corp. into Chevron Corp. and Getty Oil Co. into Texaco, Inc.—the deals were cleared by the FTC only after the buyers agreed to divest a number of marketing, refining, and pipeline properties and to meet several nonstructural conditions.

The strategic interests of buyers and sellers may be quite different. In general, the seller, anxious to close the deal and pocket the proceeds, cares little about postconsummation investigations, decrees, or encumbrances. In contrast, the buyer's interests may fall anywhere along the spectrum, depending on its business objectives in undertaking the merger.

A second strategic decision facing merger parties concerns their degree of cooperation with the reviewing agency. The approach may range from effusively assisting the agency to acting belligerently and complying only with the bare letter of the Hart-Scott-Rodino Act so the agency is signaled that litigation would be trench warfare. The strategy selected should turn on an array of factors, including the antitrust merits of the transaction, the reputation of the reviewing agency staff, the personal style of the parties' lawyers and executives, and the willingness of the parties to suffer disruption in their regular operations. If a merger appears to be a close call, a strategy of cooperation generally will require senior executives to devote substantial time and effort to working with enforcement authorities.

The form and the timing of the advocacy campaign are also important strategic elements. Although a thorough presentation can be convincing, it also tips the advocate's hand and binds the parties, both at higher levels within the agency and before the courts. The parties also must decide whether to direct their primary efforts at the agency's investigating staff, its professional managers, or its political leadership. In most instances it is best to begin by focusing on the staff, which is usually the most enforcement-minded. If the staff can be convinced that the merger is lawful, its view seldom will be overruled by superiors in the agency.

Factors Other Than Antitrust Merits

Government clearance for a merger may depend on factors not related directly to the antitrust merits. Enforcement agencies have limited resources that must be allocated through prosecutorial discretion, and the resulting enforcement pattern sometimes seems arbitrary. The vigor and depth of an investigation may depend on the staff's workload and on the publicity surrounding the transaction. Some industries are more interesting than others and tend to attract greater attention; industries and companies with histories of antitrust problems often are monitored the closest. Among the industries that historically have attracted the government's attention are oil, steel, automobiles, paper, cement, and electrical equipment.

Antitrust enforcement also has a political side. This is not to say that the enforcement agencies are commonly susceptible to direct political pressure. Quite the contrary, such pressure often produces a counterproductive result. But a touch of politics always seems to be present, both because the antitrust laws have deep populist roots and because political considerations often are related to competitive effect. A merger is more likely to be cleared if it is necessary to prevent a plant shutdown or to allow an industry to cope more effectively with foreign competition. In contrast, a merger is more likely to draw a challenge if it strikes a populist nerve, especially by threatening to raise prices to consumers. Until the early 1980s, mergers in the relatively unconcentrated oil industry were vulnerable to challenge because of such concerns.

Perceptions, often unsupported, also can influence enforcement authorities. Documents submitted to the government may reflect typical management tendencies toward exuberant optimism and may distort the power and size of the merged concern. This would work against a merger, as would negative concerns among customers. In contrast, protests by competitors might persuade the government that the deal is procompetitive.

Nongovernment Threats

Even if the government clears the merger, private plaintiffs may sue to enjoin the transaction or to recover damages. Historically, private plaintiffs rarely have brought antimerger suits except in fighting hostile tender offers. A private plaintiff usually has standing—a sufficient interest to entitle it to assert legal rights—if it is a customer of the merger partners or a target of a hostile tender offer. There is some question, however, as to whether competitors generally have standing. A case pending before the U.S. Supreme Court in mid-1986 between Cargill, Inc., and Monfort of Colorado, Inc., may provide guidance.

STRUCTURING THE TRANSACTION

Merger partners often can structure the transaction both to reduce the likelihood of antitrust challenge and to protect against certain business risks if a challenge does materialize.

Transactions of Narrower Scope

If antitrust considerations preclude a merger (or a similarly broad transaction, such as the sale of an entire division), there are several vehicles available for structuring a narrower transaction. The simplest is to sell selected assets and retain a competitive presence in the market. Thus, a multiplant producer might sell several of the plants, portions of product lines, trademarks, and pieces of equipment. The crucial antitrust issue is whether the seller remains a viable competitive entity in the market after the transaction has been consummated. If the transaction sharply diminishes the seller's market share and either renders the seller noncompetitive or induces the seller ultimately to liquidate the assets it retains, the partial sale might well be viewed as if it were a complete sale.

An alternative approach is to divest selected assets of the target. This may be preferable if the likelihood of antitrust challenge appears slight or if the scope of divestiture is small relative to the entire deal. However, the approach carries at least three risks. First, it may delay the closing of the initial deal. In friendly deals, current government policy generally requires that a purchaser of the divested portion be lined up before the initial deal is closed. In hostile deals, the government generally will accept a consent decree in which the acquirer agrees to a postmerger divestiture. Second, the divestitures often must be made at fire-sale prices. Third, the divestitures often will be difficult to accomplish, especially when dealing with parts of product lines sold to consumers. For the divested portion to be viable, it may be necessary to devise some means of sharing goodwill, such as trademark licensing.

Another approach is for the parties to pool selected assets in a joint venture that could compete with the two parents. Although this is becoming increasingly fashionable, it, too, carries risks. First, joint ventures are notoriously difficult to control, and partners seldom are willing to have just one of them in control. Consequently, control is often split 50−50 (or 33−33−33 in a three-way venture), and the venture in effect answers to no one. Second, joint ventures raise many ancillary antitrust problems. For example, the venture must be designed so that it does not become a conduit for an impermissible exchange of information between the parents. Likewise, the venture agreement must not contain provisions that unreasonably restrain competition.

An example of complex, creative structuring is provided by the brewing industry, which was characterized by attempts of several regional producers to go national through merger during the early 1980s. In 1982 Heileman Brewing Co. proposed to acquire a majority interest in Pabst Brewing Co., a merger that had been rejected twice before by antitrust authorities. But a new structure was devised, the first step being a merger between Heileman, Pabst, and Olympia Brewing Co., 49 percent owned by Pabst. Pabst then was resurrected as an independent company owning all of Olympia. Heileman kept some Pabst and Olympia breweries, trademarks, and other assets in return for supplying Pabst with cash. Thus, Heileman expanded its operations and Pabst/Olympia remained as a brewing industy competitor.

In another deal that coincidentally touched on the Heileman-Pabst-Olympia arrangement, Stroh Brewery Co. bought Schlitz Brewing Co. after curing government objections that the deal would have lessened competition in the southeastern United States. Initially, Stroh promised to divest one of two Schlitz breweries in the Southeast; but after Pabst was re-created, Stroh worked out another arrangement. It traded a southeastern brewery for a Pabst brewery in the Great Lakes area. Pabst thereby shed excess capacity in the Great Lakes area and reentered the Southeast after it had ceded its former brewery there to Heileman.

Walkaway Point

In drafting the agreement embodying the terms of the transaction, the parties must decide how much heat they will take from the government or third parties before they will abandon their deal. The "walkaway point"—at which a party is entitled to withdraw from the deal without being in breach—normally is decided by careful bargaining.

The event triggering the right to withdraw can fall anywhere along a procedural spectrum. At one extreme, withdrawal would be permitted if the government issued a request for additional information. At the other extreme, withdrawal would be permitted only if a court issued an injunction against the transaction. Between these poles are various other possible triggering events—such as the passage of a fixed time period or a government announcement that it will challenge the merger.

In general, buyers seek the right to abandon the deal at the earliest possible stage because each successive step in the antitrust approval process imposes costs—in terms of out-of-pocket expenditures, executive time, organizational disruption, and diversion from pursuit of other opportunities. Sellers usually try to hold the buyer to the deal for as long as possible, preferring that the purchaser fight the government challenge and go forward with the deal unless enjoined.

One seldom-publicized factor in aborting a deal is the reluctance of the merger partners to expose antitrust skeletons lurking in their closets. They may be called on to produce documents that suggest they have engaged in price fixing or other acts, sometimes unrelated to the merger at issue, and such evidence could lead to a broader inquiry. Reportedly, an FTC monopoly investigation involving the titanium dioxide industry was triggered by information discovered in a merger review. (The investigation resulted in a complaint, which was eventually dismissed.)

SPECIAL ISSUES IN THE HOSTILE TAKEOVER SETTING

Hostile takeovers present both problems and opportunities. The usual Hart-Scott waiting periods are halved, the government usually is willing to permit the deal to go forward on the acquirer's promise that it will cure antitrust problems through future divestitures, and the buyer alone controls the terms on which it will abandon its tender offer.

But the target is certain to see that antitrust problems surface and usually will steer the government to facts that might not otherwise have been uncovered. This tactic may be risky, because it can limit the target's flexibility in finding a white knight or reaching acceptable terms with the would-be acquirer.

The target is also likely to begin private litigation. Under such circumstances, antitrust clearance must be obtained not only from the government, but also from a court, which may be less inclined to accept policy arguments and recent economic learning that favors mergers and may instead rely on precedents that are less hospitable to mergers.

Chapter 37

Finding Your Way around Washington

Martin Sikora

Editor, Mergers & Acquisitions, Philadelphia, Pennsylvania

Federal deregulation of industry—both by statute and by policy—has been a major force in facilitating the merger and acquisition process during the 1980s. The practical effects of the changes have allowed execution of many merger and acquisition transactions that would have been impermissable during much of the prior five decades, and either eliminated many time-consuming procedures needed for securing approval or markedly reduced the time and paperwork that are involved. Nevertheless, practically all M&A transactions must go through some type of federal government channels.

M&A involvement is most ubiquitous by the Antitrust Division of the Justice Department, the Federal Trade Commission (FTC), the Securities and Exchange Commission (SEC), and the Internal Revenue Service (IRS), whose jurisdictions cut across all industry areas. In addition, several agencies charged with regulation of specific industries or markets retain significant authority for approval of mergers, acquisitions, divestitures, and related transactions by companies in their domains. Aside from executive branch review, federal influence on merger and acquisition activity also is wielded by the legislative prerogatives of Congress and by federal court decisions in specific cases.

The roles of the Antitrust Division and the FTC in examining the competitive aspects of mergers and acquisitions have been detailed in Chapter 36. Therefore, this chapter will focus largely on the M&A powers of agencies that cover specific regulated industries, such as broadcasting, telephone, cable TV, railroads, trucking, bus transportation, airlines, banking, savings and loans, utilities, and foreign investment in the United States.

GENERAL REGULATION

Although the responsibilities of the IRS and the SEC have been covered in other chapters, as they relate to specific aspects of M&A, it is helpful to synopsize their principal duties in the field.

The SEC—The watchdog of the nation's securities industry is empowered to enforce the Tender Offer Act, more commonly known as the Williams Act. The SEC examines all registration statements by tender offering parties and documents distributed in connection with the offer to assure that full disclosure of material information is made to target shareholders. The SEC also reviews any proxy statements distributed to stockholders when they must approve mergers or acquisitions, again with an eye toward assuring full disclosure. In other merger-related matters, the commission enforces rules against insider trading of stocks and receives 13D registrations that disclose interests of 5 percent or more in publicly held companies by one party or group.

The IRS—The IRS usually appears at two major points in the merger and acquisition process. Prior to the closing, it frequently is asked to deliver an opinion on whether acquisition currencies paid to selling stockholders are subject to or exempt from federal taxes. Following the merger, the IRS requires the buying company to justify the price it paid by allocating the outlay among the assets it has acquired. If the IRS examination determines that there is a significant gap between the actual values of acquired assets and the purchase price, the difference is assigned to goodwill or going-concern value, two intangible assets that are not depreciable for tax purposes.

COMMUNICATIONS

The Federal Communications Commission (FCC) is the principal regulator in the communications field, with jurisdiction over broadcasters, telephone companies, and, to some extent, cable television operators. Strictly speaking, the FCC does not approve mergers and acquisitions directly but rules on the transfers of licenses and certificates that go from seller to buyer and are required for operating authority.

In the radio and television area, the FCC acts on sales of all stations, and its inquiry emphasizes the buyer's fitness to hold a broadcasting license. In addition, the agency has a number of significant rules concerning mergers, acquisitions, and diversifications by companies owning radio and television properties.

Some of the more important include the following:

- A single company or interest may own no more than 12 television stations, 12 AM radio outlets, and 12 FM radio stations. Additionally, a single company's TV stations may reach no more than 25 percent of the nation's TV households.
- Cross-media acquisitions in the same market are barred. Thus, a newspaper owner cannot purchase a TV station in the same market, and a TV station owner is prohibited from buying a newspaper or a radio station in the same market. Cross-media ownerships that existed before the rule was promulgated generally have been allowed to continue under a grandfather clause.
- Broadcasting networks are barred from owning syndicators of television programs and are limited in the amount of television programming they can produce directly. Conversely, syndicators cannot own networks.
- Networks cannot acquire or own cable television properties.
- A foreign company or citizen is limited to a 25 percent interest in any U.S. broadcasting property.
- A TV station owner cannot acquire another TV outlet in a separate market when the two stations have overlapping signals that serve the same geographic territory.

Mergers and acquisitions in the telephone industry are regulated if either of the parties operates interstate or the combined company will serve an interstate public. The FCC's rulings in this field cover the transfer of public convenience and necessity certificates that interstate telephone companies must hold. In the cellular telephone area, the agency rules on transfers of licenses that enable holders to use radio frequencies in their operations.

Acquisitions in cable television come under FCC scrutiny if the deal involves a transfer of a microwave license—which allows the holder to use microwave equipment to boost signal power. In all other cable TV ownership changes, the FCC must be notified within 30 days of the sale, although the commission has no specific authority to rule on the transaction.

BANKING

Federal regulation of commercial banking operates within a tripartite structure that includes the Federal Reserve Board; the Comptroller of the Currency, and the Federal Deposit Insurance Corp. (FDIC).

Although each agency has primary jurisdiction over specific types of bank mergers, acquisitions, and diversifications, the three agencies, as a practical matter, cooperate with each other through advisory opinions on competitive factors, financial wherewithal, and other key aspects of combining institutions. Additionally, the Antitrust Division usually presents an advisory opinion on the competitive aspects of a bank merger.

The Federal Reserve Board has primary authority when bank holding companies merge, when acquisitions involve holding companies as either acquirers or targets, and when a merger of banks creates a state-chartered institution that is a member of the Federal Reserve System. The Fed also has responsibility for holding company acquisitions of nonbank operations and regulatory say-so on certain acquisitions of bank stock or bank assets.

Diversification has been an important M&A issue for the Fed since the late 1960s. Through acquisitions, banking organizations have moved into a wide range of other financial services, such as mortgage banking, consumer finance, savings and loans, discount securities brokerage, and factoring, and also entered nonfinancial service businesses. As a result of banking deregulation, the only key financial service areas still off-limits to banks as of the mid-1980s were securities underwriting and most types of insurance.

As a practical matter, the Federal Reserve Board handles directly only about 6 percent (by board estimate) of the merger and acquisition situations that fall under its jurisdiction. It has delegated authority to the 12 Federal Reserve District banks to accept and review applications from banks in the geographic territories they serve and established guidelines for rulings by the district banks. Acting as the board's agents, the district banks may clear any deals covered by the guidelines, and typically approve more than 90 percent of the proposals put before them without involving the board. The district banks never reject a deal. But if they conclude that the merger proposals somehow go beyond the guidelines or present special problems or issues, the applications are forwarded to the board for ultimate action.

The Comptroller's Office, which is part of the Treasury Department, has authority when the survivor of a bank merger or consolidation is a federally chartered institution. The FDIC is the principal regulator in mergers that involve a state-chartered bank that carries FDIC insurance but is not a member of the Federal Reserve System, or when the resulting institution will be an insured nonmember bank.

SAVINGS AND LOANS

The Federal Home Loan Bank Board is the U.S. government agency that rules on mergers and acquisitions in the savings and loan (S&L) industry, and, in practice, it gets to act on substantially all M&A transactions involving S&Ls. The board has primary responsibility for combinations involving federally chartered S&Ls. But its effective jurisdiction is far wider because board members also serve as directors of the Federal Savings & Loan Insurance Corp. (FSLIC). The FSLIC must clear every deal involving an insured S&L (about 98 percent, according to a bank board estimate).

TRANSPORTATION

The Transportation Department considers mergers involving airlines, and the Interstate Commerce Commission (ICC) handles transactions covering land transportation—railroads, truckers, and buses.

The Transportation Department comes into play when the transaction is a merger of two airlines, acquisition of one airline by another, purchase of control of one airline by another, or acquisition of an airline by another aerospace concern, such as a manufacturer of aircraft. The department's review centers on competitive aspects of the transactions. It lacks authority if the target airline is being acquired by a company or an interest outside the airline or aerospace industries.

As for the railroad industry, the ICC generally has jurisdiction that is similar to the Transportation Department's authority over airlines—that is, rulings on deals in which both parties are railroads or have rail interests. The review also is based on competitive elements. Acquisition of a railroad by a nonrail concern does not come before the commission. The ICC has authority to rule on large-scale mergers involving interstate trucking and bus companies and issue decisions based on competitive factors. However, in the 1980s, such proceedings have not consumed significant amounts of time or effort.

A major policy change by the ICC during the 1980s has permitted cross-ownership, and acquisition, of different transportation modes—such as the coexistence of a railroad and a truck line in the same company. Prior to that shift, commission policy had barred a transportation company from owning more than one type or mode, unless an incidental unit was needed to service the core business. For example, a railroad could maintain a trucking operation that was tied directly to or serviced the rail unit. In the mid-1980s, the same railroad can own extensive and unrelated trucking businesses.

UTILITIES

The SEC, the Federal Energy Regulatory Commission (FERC), and the Nuclear Energy Regulatory Commission (NRC) share authority in the utility industry.

The SEC has direct responsibility for mergers, acquisitions, divestitures, and diversifications by interstate utility holding companies. The FERC is charged with jurisdiction over mergers involving all other electric utilities. In the natural gas area, the FERC rules on transactions in which gas companies purchase or divest physical facilities. The agency does not have jurisdiction in cases involving acquisition of gas company stock.

The NRC has limited jurisdiction in transactions involving nuclear energy facilities. Its authority principally covers situations in which partnerships or consortiums build and operate nuclear generating plants. The NRC must act when a partial interest in such a facility is being sold, when a new partner is enrolled in the ownership group, or when an existing partner wants to withdraw from the consortium.

FOREIGN INVESTMENT

Foreign investment in the United States is not generally regulated, and there is no specific agency with continuing responsibility for ruling on acquisitions of American companies by overseas concerns. However, there are a few hard-and-fast rules governing foreign investments, including statutes that mark certain industries off-limits to overseas-based interests.

The principal agency that is involved with mergers and acquisitions executed by non-U.S. companies is the Committee on Foreign Investment in the United States (CFIUS), an interdepartmental unit that studies and reviews foreign investments but lacks statutory authority. Principal members are representatives of the Treasury, Agriculture, State, Commerce, and Defense Departments, but personnel from other agencies may serve on it from time to time. As an oversight unit, the committee keeps track of trends and statistics and also screens specific transactions.

Despite its lack of enforcement authority, CFIUS can serve as the initiator of a formal regulatory process through its monitoring function. If it determines that questions exist about whether any particular deal is permissible under federal law or policy, it can refer the transaction for further study to the Council of Economic Advisers or the National Security Council. Such a case may, for example, arise if the American target is a supplier of a strategic material or service. The National Security Council has authority to block such acquisitions, although, to the best of anyone's knowledge, it never has taken formal action in that area.

However, federal laws specifically bar foreign companies or citizens from owning nuclear energy facilities, American-flag fishing boats, and vessels operating along inland waterways within the United States. In addition, alien companies or individuals are limited to 25 percent interest in broadcasting properties and airlines. Finally, there is a reciprocity requirement when a foreign interest or government buys an American concern holding drilling and mineral rights on federally owned lands. The buyer's home country must allow American interests to have similar rights on government-owned lands.

CONGRESS

Congressional influence on mergers and acquisitions is wielded principally through legislative prerogatives in three areas: antitrust, securities regulation, and taxes. As a result, most important M&A legislation is handled by three House committees and a like number in the Senate.

Antitrust—Responsibilities for antitrust legislation are held by the House and Senate Judiciary Committees. The Subcommittee on Monopolies and Commercial Law is the antitrust arm of the House committee.

Securities—Legislation affecting securities regulation is handled by the House Energy and Commerce Committee and the Senate Banking, Housing and Urban Affairs Committee. The House committee assigns securities matters to its Subcommittee on Telecommunications, Consumer Protection and Finance, whereas the Securities subcommittee is the comparable unit under the Senate committee.

Taxes—The House Ways and Means Committee and Senate Finance Committee deal with revenue-raising legislation. In the House, taxes related to mergers and acquisitions usually are handled by the Subcommittee on Select Revenue Measures.

Committees dealing with specific industries also may become involved in M&A-related legislation. These include the House Banking, Finance and Urban Affairs Committee (banking and financial services) and the Senate Commerce, Science and Transportation Committee (transportation). The aforementioned

House Energy and Senate Banking Committees also cover specific industries. Although they are not directly involved in M&A matters, several other committees may influence mergers and acquisitions. They include the Senate Small Business and Budget Committees, the House Small Business Committee, and the joint Taxation and Economic Committees.

JUDICIARY

The federal courts get into the M&A process when cases are brought to them for decisions under applicable laws. There are numerous instances that can lead to litigation, a few of which include:

- Requests by the SEC for decisions to support enforcement actions
- Requests by the Justice Department or the FTC to block allegedly anticompetitive mergers and acquisitions
- Appeals from decisions by federal agencies with primary powers to block or approve mergers and acquisitions in specific industries
- Private complaints under antitrust laws

When the IRS and an acquirer are unable to resolve a sharp difference in allocation of assets across a purchase price, the buyer may appeal an IRS ruling to the U.S. Tax Court. Tax Court rulings may be further appealed to the federal court system.

Chapter 38

Stock Exchange Disclosure Rules

Kenneth I. Rosenblum

President, Dimensional Fund Advisors, Inc.,
Santa Monica, California

Michael Wise

Associate Counsel, Midwest Stock Exchange, Inc.,
Chicago, Illinois

Merger and acquisition specialists must be aware of the roles played by securities self-regulatory organizations (SROs) in tender offers. The activities of SROs, which include stock exchanges, the National Association of Securities Dealers (NASD) and securities depositories, may affect a tender offer's conduct or defense. In addition to providing adequate disclosure to the SROs, the parties to a tender offer must recognize the advantage of maintaining communication with these organizations.

In particular, the stock exchanges must be informed when there is a tender offer for a listed company. Trading in a target company whose stock is listed on one or more of the nation's exchanges may be dramatically affected by news of a tender offer, whether hostile or friendly. The exchanges' rules provide mechanisms for communicating information on tender offers that should minimize unwanted consequences such as lengthy trading halts.

With regard to disclosure statements, exchanges generally must receive copies of the forms filed with the Securities and Exchange Commission (SEC). Individuals and companies subject to the disclosure provisions of the Securities Exchange Act of 1934 often are obligated to inform stock exchanges, as well as the SEC, of activities affecting listed companies. Although exchange notification is relatively simple, in the interest of expeditiously handling a tender offer, it should not be overlooked.

Under an SEC rule adopted in 1984, Rule 17Ad-14, bidders' agents must establish accounts at qualified securities depositories. This rule, to be discussed in detail later, is intended to facilitate the book-entry tender of a target company's securities, and avoid delays and inefficiencies associated with physical tendering.

TARGET COMPANY DISCLOSURE
TO STOCK EXCHANGES

Companies whose securities are listed on national stock exchanges are obligated to inform the exchanges of material developments. Obviously, a tender offer for a listed company's shares is the type of material development that must be relayed to the exchanges. The Midwest Stock Exchange (MSE) for example, warns listed companies that merger and acquisition negotiations carry the risk of untimely or inadvertent disclosure of information that has an impact on trading activity.

Because many players are involved in a tender offer, there is always a danger of information leaking prior to public announcement. The MSE and the New York Stock Exchange (NYSE) admonish corporate management to review trading in its securities. Unusual market activity in fact may compel public announcement of the company's intentions. Similarly, the MSE requires a listed company to "act promptly to dispel unfounded rumors which result in unusual market activity or price variations."[1]

Listed companies should inform the public of corporate news that would affect the market for their shares. Important information should be distributed to the press, either by telephone or press conference, or by written press release. Press releases normally should be circulated for "immediate release."

Direct communication with the exchanges also should be maintained, in order to minimize the occasions when market trading must be halted because of rumors or leaks. The exchanges recommend that they be informed of major press releases, preferably in advance of the announcement. Importantly, companies should inform the exchanges by telephone, because receipt of a written press release may take too long.

Trading Delays

After being informed of the company's announcement, the exchange may order a trading delay to provide time for public digestion of the disclosed information.

Although the exchanges attempt to keep trading halts to a minimum, longer delays may be necessary where there is an order imbalance.

A company also may request that the exchanges halt trading when there is significant news pending. The NYSE is implementing a new policy to reduce the length of trading halts.[2] The NYSE's new policy allows thirty minutes for a company requesting a trading halt to make its announcement, after which the exchange decides whether to reopen trading. This policy is grounded partly in the tactics of some target companies, which use a lengthy trading halt to exact a higher premium from an impatient bidder or to take steps to "defend" themselves.

Recently, increased attention has been focused on the role of the "third market" maintained by certain broker/dealers during a trading halt. Access to the third market generally is confined to institutional investors wishing to buy or sell large blocks of the halted issue. The exchanges, obliged to provide markets for both small and large investors, have suggested that this third market trading may be unfair to the investing public. It is anticipated that the SEC will address this matter. Until then the exchanges, holding a primary interest in maintaining an open and orderly market, can be expected to discourage frequent or lengthy trading halts in a target company's stock.

"EARLY WARNING" FILINGS UNDER THE EXCHANGE ACT

Through the Williams Act, enacted in 1968, Congress provided for an "early warning" mechanism in corporate acquisitions. Under Exchange Act Section 13(d), persons acquiring more than 5 percent of public companies' stock must disclose their ownership and investment intentions. This provision alerts target company management to possible "creeping acquisitions" of the corporation by outsiders.[3] In 1972, Congress supplemented the Williams Act with Section 13(g), which essentially requires all 5 percent beneficial owners to disclose their holdings regardless of when they were acquired. The net effect of Sections 13(d) and 13(g) is that a target company is alerted to the identity of its major shareholders. Exchange Act Regulation 13D-G delineates the disclosure duties of persons falling under these sections.

Exchange Act Section 13(d) and its regulations provide that any party that acquires ownership of more than 5 percent of an equity security of most publicly owned companies must file a Schedule 13D form disclosing the interest. Stock traded on a national securities exchange must be registered under Section 12(b), and its ownership would necessarily be subject to Section 13(d).

Schedule 13D requires the identification of the filing person or group acquiring the securities, and their relation to the target company. Importantly, the document must disclose the purpose of the securities acquisition. The reporting persons specifically must describe any plans to acquire additional securities, to take over the company, or to materially affect the issuer's business. As a practical matter, securities lawyers generally couch these sections in language that is broad enough to enable the filers to pursue a wide range of options for future acquisitions or control of the issuer's stock.

A Schedule 13D must be submitted within 10 days of the securities acquisition (although in 1985–1986, there was considerable support in Congress and the SEC for "closing the 10-day window"). In addition to filing the Schedule 13D with the SEC and the target, each exchange trading the security must receive a Schedule. If any material change occurs in the facts set forth in Schedule 13D, the filing person must promptly amend the Schedule and send it to the SEC, the issuer, and the exchanges.

Similar provisions apply to persons subject to Section 13(g). Certain beneficial owners, usually institutions such as registered investment companies or employee benefit plans, may use the "short form" provided by Schedule 13G. Additionally, the institution must have acquired its holdings in the ordinary course of its business and not with the purpose of affecting control of the issuer. Such "persons," in lieu of filing a Schedule 13D, may file a Schedule 13G within 45 days of the end of the calendar year in which they obtained their 5 percent holding.

The 13G document must be sent to the SEC, the target company, and the principal exchange where the security is traded. Additionally, persons acquiring more than 10 percent of an equity security must file a Schedule 13G within 10 days of the end of the first month after the transaction. As with the Schedule 13D, any material changes must be reported on a new Schedule 13G, and filed with the SEC, the target, and the exchange.

TENDER OFFER FILINGS UNDER THE EXCHANGE ACT

Section 14(d), which was enacted as part of the Williams Act, essentially makes it unlawful to initiate a tender offer unless a statement is filed with the SEC. Any party that makes a tender offer for a Section 12 equity security must file a Tender Offer Statement through a Schedule 14D-1 if such party will own more than 5 percent of a class of the security. The 14-D form requires the reporting party to identify itself, and to disclose its sources of funds and the number of shares subject to the offer. Other important disclosures include the bidder's purpose for the offer, business plans for the target, and present or future relationships between the bidder and the target or its executives. As with the Schedule 13D language, Schedule 14D filings usually are drafted in such a fashion as to keep the bidder's options open, pending completion of the tender offer.

Under Rule 14d-3, the Schedule must be filed "as soon as practicable on the date of the commencement of the tender offer." The schedule must be filed with the SEC, and hand delivered to the target and the competitive bidders. Additionally, the bidder must give telephonic notice to the exchanges where the target's securities are traded, followed by a mailing of the Schedule. The telephonic notice preferably should be given before the opening of the exchanges. For NASDAQ-listed stocks, similar notification must be given to the NASD. If any material change occurs in the information disclosed in the Schedule 14D-1, the reporting person promptly must amend the Schedule and file it with the SEC, the target company, and the exchanges.

Target management may respond to a bidder's offer by filing a "tender offer solicitation/recommendation statement" on Schedule 14D-9 with the SEC and the bidder. Similar notification provisions apply regarding the exchanges. The filing persons should give telephone notification prior to the opening of the target's stock, and follow up by mailing the Schedule 14D-9. Additionally, the exchange rules regarding communication obligations that were previously described would require notification from the listed company in response to a tender offer.

TENDER OFFER BIDDERS' AGENTS

In early 1984, the SEC adopted Exchange Act Rule 17Ad-14, requiring transfer agents acting on behalf of bidders in a tender or exchange offer to establish special accounts at qualified securities depositories. A depository acts as a custodian and operator of a centralized system for handling securities. Participants, such as broker-dealers or banks, deposit securities with a depository, which holds the securities in custody in a fungible mass with pro rata positions credited to the participants' accounts. The SEC promulgated the rule in response to problems experienced in certain offers due to the physical processing of a target company's shares. Physical processing of securities, as opposed to book-entry movement, leads to risks and inefficiencies in securities handling. In the past, some depositories often "exited" target companies' shares from their systems during a tender offer, forcing securities firms to tender their shares physically. In such situations, such as the competing offers for Conoco, Inc., in 1981, processing problems made it difficult to settle open stock and options transactions.

Rule 17Ad-14 is designed to remove these impediments to efficient securities processing. Under the rule, transfer agents that act as tender agents for a bidder must establish a special account at "qualified" depositories, such as the Midwest Securities Trust Co., Chicago, and Depository Trust Co., New York. The agent must open these accounts within two business days after the tender offer is commenced. Tendered shares then may be transferred by book-entry to the agent's account, reducing physical handling of securities. After the expiration of the tender offer, the depositories deliver all tendered shares to the agent, collect payment from the agent, and credit their tendering participants accordingly.

The SEC has emphasized that the qualified depositories must adopt relatively uniform procedures with regard to Rule 17Ad-14. The depositories have done so, in order to promote a standard method for handling tender offers. Acquisition specialists generally have adapted to this new procedure. Tender offer "tombstones," for example, now refer to tendering with qualified depositories. Practitioners should be aware of this securities processing aspect of mergers and acquisitions.

NOTES

[1]MSE Manual, par 1897, interpretation .01.

[2]*New York Stock Exchange.*

[3]Harold S. Bloomenthal, *Securities Law Handbook, 1979,* Clark, Boardman, New York, 1980.

Chapter 39

Fighting the Proxy Battle

Douglass M. Barnes

Vice President—Marketing, Lind Brothers, Inc.,
New York, New York

Proxies are the primary means for determining elections and deciding issues in the corporate sector. As the owners of a corporation, the stockholders comprise its electorate, which at least once a year chooses a board of directors and, if asked, passes on such propositions as by-law and charter changes, mergers, and recapitalizations. Because it is physically and logistically impossible for most shareholders of a publicly held corporation to attend the annual or special meeting required for tallying the ballots, the bulk votes through mailed-in proxies, each proxy equaling the number of votes to which a shareholder is entitled, based on share ownership. Proxies normally are solicited routinely by management, but when a nonmanagement element, such as dissident stockholders, decides to oppose the incumbents, the solicitation can become a contest for shareholder loyalty.

Proxy battles have been waged over many matters. In the 1940s, 1950s, and 1960s, they usually centered on control of corporate boards. But in the following decade, as tender offers became the preferred devices for seeking corporate control, social issues or noncontrol proposals put forth by stockholders became the focal points of proxy contests. By the 1980s, however, with restructurings

and break-up values surfacing as major considerations for investors and specula-
tors, battles for corporate control resumed prominence in the proxy-fight arena.

Since the railroad recapitalizations in the 1940s, a professional group of proxy
solicitors has grown in prominence. Not only do these organizations provide the
extensive manpower required for the shareholder solicitation, but they assist
the lawyers and publicists in framing issues and planning strategies. Proxy
solicitors normally work on a fixed-fee basis.

In general, proxy fights for corporate control were "rediscovered" in the 1980s
because they were often cheaper and faster than tender offers in taking over
companies during a period of high-priced mergers. But a proxy contest itself
can be costly in both time and money. A typical 1980s battle involves well-
orchestrated campaigns on both sides, employing expensive expertise from a
wide range of professional disciplines. One reason is the extensive use of print
and electronic media and increasingly sophisticated investor relations techniques to play to shareholder-voters. Another is the sweeping change in shareholder demographics that has occurred since the 1960s.

Whereas individuals continue to own the largest portions of stock in publicly
traded companies, many firms with large market capitalizations have institutional ownership approaching 70 percent of outstanding shares, and some even
higher. This is a two-edged sword in proxy fights. Institutions are under great
pressure to perform, and could be persuaded to side with opponents of management who promise to enhance the institutional commitments. Yet the very
sophistication of these heavyweight investors requires that they be approached
in a highly professional manner when their votes are solicited.

PREPARING FOR BATTLE

Together with the waning loyalties of individuals, a group once fiercely committed to incumbent managements, the presence of institutions frequently provides
dissidents with good chances to oust incumbent managements or win a duel over
noncontrol issues. But success obviously is not guaranteed under any circumstances. And because the decision on whether an ordinary proxy solicitation
becomes a full-blown battle rests with stock owners not aligned with management or "insider" groups, the rebels must carefully weigh such elements as their
goals, resources, and chances for success before even deciding to press the fight.

Stock Ownership: Key to Victory

Stock ownership is still the key to victory; the more the dissident or management
camp owns, the better the chances of winning. A traditional rule of thumb was
that dissidents needed at least 20 percent of the outstanding shares to stand a
chance of winning, but dissidents may not need that much in the 1980s.

Anytime they can fulfill the statutory minimum ownership requirements for
presenting a proposal at a routine or special meeting of shareholders, they have a
shot at winning. Although state securities laws vary and rarely affect proxies
rules, they should be reviewed. The Securities and Exchange Commission's
Regulation A, which was revised in 1984, sets forth the requirements for propos-

als of securities holders. Specifically, Rule 14a8 requires that an investor own at least 1 percent of the outstanding shares, or $1,000 in market value of the issuer's common stock, at least 120 days in advance of the date on the issuer's proxy statement. But the biggest advantage that either side can have is a big block of votes in its corner.

The company's most recent proxy statement discloses the holdings of management and other "insiders," and dissidents can compare the relative strengths with a quick look. Definitive information on the rest of the stockholdership must come from examination of the complete stockholder list, but the holdings of individuals and shares held by brokers in "street names" can be estimated by the target concern's average and current trading activity. The greater the activity, the larger the amount held by brokers is likely to be. Individuals who hold stock in their own names tend to be more loyal to management than those whose identities are shielded by "street names." Data on institutional holdings are contained in 13-F forms filed with the Securities and Exchange Commission (SEC). Standard & Poor's reports the total institutional holdings of individual publicly held companies, whereas the Vickers, Cortrac, and Spectrum services list the holdings of each institution and constantly update their data with the latest SEC filings. Because the massive holdings of institutions have the power to tip the balance in a proxy fight, contestants should analyze their types and voting characteristics to determine exactly how they should be approached.

Target Company Characteristics

Both management and dissident groups should undertake thorough analyses of the target company to fortify their positions. Management, which should be conducting this examination as an ongoing and integral part of its long-range strategy, can benefit by identifying strengths and weaknesses, anticipating impending fights for control, and taking precautionary measures. Dissidents gain ammunition for defining and fighting the key issues. Areas that should be reviewed include the following:

Earnings performance—Incumbent management's profit record of the last five years should be compared with such other financial measures as sales, equity, and assets to determine returns. The performances should be examined for cyclicality and contra-cyclicality characteristics and stacked against the showings of peer-group concerns such as competitors. Research reports by financial analysts are helpful not only in supplying aggregate numbers but in obtaining credible third-party assessments and determining the extent of investor support for management. Annual and quarterly reports, speeches to securities analysts, fact sheets and fact books, and other public statements should be reviewed for inconsistencies and any projections not met by actual performance. Annual meeting transcripts and newspaper clippings often report shareholder awareness of such inconsistencies and suggest a basis for discontent.

Stock performance—Because most investors buy stock for capital gains, an analysis of the target's stock performance, compared with those of its peers, is essential. Has the target's stock consistently enjoyed a high or a low

price/earnings ratio? Or has the target's stock led or lagged its competitors on
either the upside or downside?

Dividends—Dividend yield is often as important to investors as capital gains.
Analyses should determine if the dividend has been increased or reduced,
paid consistently or omitted at times, or is headed for increases, reductions,
or omissions in the future. Pay-out ratios and policies should be compared
with those of peer-group companies.

Management compensation—This can be a touchy subject if the company
isn't performing well or if the management of a relatively small company
pays itself high salaries. Comparisons should be made with peer-group
compensation systems.

Growth and redeployment—The well-prepared proxy contestant has information on successful new ventures as well as abandoned projects, divestitures
of prior acquisitions, and other failures. This knowledge helps measure
management's capability, foresight, prudence, and willingness to take or
avoid risks.

Other yardsticks to assess include unfunded pension liabilities or overfunding
of pension plans, and the company's litigation record, especially if there are
large case loads of long duration.

The Incumbent Board in the Crossfire

There are many characteristics of an incumbent board of directors that may help
or hinder either side in a proxy fight.

Stock ownership can be a sensitive issue. Usually a dissident slate will own
more stock than members of the target's board. Founding family members frequently have large positions, but if their positions were sufficiently substantive,
the company would not be faced with a proxy contest. Some companies have
attempted to remedy the small holdings of their boards by offering to pay some or
all of the directors' fees in stock and including directors in employee stock
ownership plans and similar stock purchase programs. One recommended solution is for management to request that new members purchase stock when
joining the board.

Shareholders have become increasingly skeptical of the independence of
so-called inside boards and vocally critical of these boards dominated by management members. If there is justification for the board's composition and a firm
policy relating to its composition, management should articulate them frequently, at least annually at the shareholders meeting and in the printed summary of the meeting that is mailed to shareholders and others.

Because guilt by association may be created in the minds of shareholders, the
performance of other companies where the target board members also serve
should be reviewed. A director's association with a poorly performing or questionable company can become embarrassing to an embattled management. The
personal business record of each director should be known. Boards facing a
proxy contest should inform members that damaging facts about their lives
could be revealed and urge them to come forward with potentially scandalous

information. A board member's involvement in bankruptcies, proxy fights, and litigation obviously is useful to dissidents, but if used properly by management, it can deflect the opposition's charges.

The issue is really bad versus good. Bad or negative images stir more emotions than good ones. An analogy is the nightly news, where the preponderance of news is negative and where negatives create more indelible impressions. Another analogy is politics. Perhaps expectations also affect the issues.

Insurgents' Strategy Plans

An opposition group must anticipate management's counterattacks. Incumbency provides management's slate with a built-in measure of credibility that dissidents lack, and management should be expected to probe the opposition's position for any signs of vulnerability. Performances of companies where the dissidents have served will be studied. Stock ownership by dissidents will be compared with the incumbent board's individual holdings. And both the business and personal records of the dissidents will be studied.

Legal Considerations

Legal considerations, including applicable laws and the target company's bylaws, often determine the permissible and most effective methods of mounting offensive and defensive strategies, and whether it is feasible to wage a proxy fight at all. Key provisions to be studied in consultation with legal counsel may include cumulative voting, classified or staggered boards, requirements for removing directors, possibilities of using written consents to bypass formal meetings, and steps needed to call special meetings.

Management's proclivity for litigation should be an important concern for opponents. As the incumbent leaders of the company, management has the financial resources and legal machinery of the company behind it, and can utilize the courts to stall proxy fights and hold up stockholders meetings, if necessary.

Likely Voting Patterns

After the legal requirements, the most important determinants in whether dissidents will proceed with a proxy fight are the possible voting patterns of stockholders. Both camps, of course, start with hard-core blocks of stock, but the outcome rests with the remainder of the shares. Clues to the result include the company's historical turnout for shareholder voting and the anticipated turnout of "free" stock—the shares not affiliated with either side. An experienced proxy solicitor can help by preparing a best-case/worst-case analysis of each stockholder segment. The analysis can't quantify the emotionalism of a proxy contest, but it can provide meaningful points of reference.

WAGING THE CAMPAIGN

Assembling the Team

Most members of a proxy-fight team usually are retained by management on an ongoing basis, but a dissident group often has to start from scratch. The first members of a dissidents' team—special legal counsel, a proxy solicitor, and, frequently, public relations counsel—normally are retained before the fight begins and actually help the rebel group decide if the battle should be started. If valuation of assets or operations is a likely issue in the fight, an investment banker is helpful.

The qualities desired in team members include experience in prior proxy fights, a reasonable record of success in these contests, and the depth of the organizations providing the requisite expertise. Experience in merger and acquisition work is not essential but can improve the effectiveness of the team.

Once the proxy fight starts, these additional professional practitioners will be required:

Public relations consultants—Public relations (PR) is an essential function, because communications with shareholders will be amplified by the media, which will be covering proxy fights as news events. The PR counsel should be an experienced firm with an understanding of all forms of news and advertising media, ability to write shareholder communications and follow-up news releases, and expertise in organizing presentations to investor groups.

Tabulators—Management normally will expect its transfer agent to count the proxies, but the opposition group must retain a firm to perform this function and to correlate the vote to the various segments of the shareholder list. Sizable computer processing capacity is a major requirement for this function.

Independent inspectors of election—In a routine election the company's accounting firm or transfer agent can serve in this capacity, but in a contested situation both sides frequently agree upon an independent trust company to ensure impartiality and professionalism in the election. Several corporate trust companies specialize in this activity.

Mailing services—A mailing firm and a telegram/mailgram capacity may be required and should be retained as soon as possible to guarantee their services for the contest.

Financial printers—The printer should have the capacity to quickly prepare and mail proxy statements and other communications to shareholders. Timing of these distributions may be critical. The printer will provide electronic typesetting, proofreading, and high-speed printing and distribution services, and will be equipped to handle rapid-fire copy changes to expedite dissemination.

Private investigators—They may be needed to develop information about the personal histories of the contestants that is not readily available. Major national or regional firms already may have established files on individual contestants or their affiliated organizations. Even if the data are not publicly revealed or used in written or oral communications, they may be helpful in developing strategies and tactics.

But the most important members of a team are the candidates for director. There are no hard-and-fast rules for these choices. But both sides should strive for people with national reputations for success, sufficient wealth to buy substantial amounts of the target's stock, willingness to endure an attack from the opposition, and loyalty to a chosen side. Most of the characteristics of the dissident slate could apply to the management slate as well. However, an important advantage for management exists: The investor already has purchased or inherited stock with the incumbent board in power and has been conditioned to some degree to appreciate its actions. Credibility must be gained by the aggressor. The investor must perceive some advantage to him or her to switch allegiance.

The criteria for directors are subjective. The best way to assemble a strong slate is to "see" it as the opposition would. What does each candidate bring to the collective strength of the board of directors? This question must be answered. Management experience in operating the company may be an advantage, particularly when the board candidate has a successful and lengthy service record. Management does not need to establish its expertise in the industry, assuming good company performance, whereas a dissident candidate must establish both professional and industry expertise. For management, however, the prospect of a fight may offer an opportunity to eliminate weak candidates, to increase the board's stock ownership, or to improve the credentials of the slate.

Obtaining the Shareholder List

One of the first critical steps for a rebel group is obtaining a complete shareholders' list from the corporation. Without it, the dissidents are flying blind. Although SEC regulations allow anyone with a "proper purpose," such as countering management's proxy solicitations, to get the list, management often may not release it without costly, time-consuming litigation designed to keep the dissidents off-balance and sap them of resources.

After dissidents obtain the list, they must convert it to a workable form so that they have the same information as management. That conversion includes breakdowns of shareholders by size, location, and type. Besides helping establish the magnitude and distribution of future print runs, the breakdowns determine the sizes of previously unknown positions for both individuals and "street name" accounts. Individual investors tend to be more loyal to management, whereas brokerage positions generally are represented by traders who are more sensitive to appeals that stress quick profits.

Proxy contests require voting instructions from beneficial holders, and a sizeable broker/nominee position demands attention. If the total broker position is large relative to the other segments, personal presentations should be scheduled with appropriate investment analysts and regional brokerage offices. Although most institutions should be identified during the preliminary analysis, the actual shareholders list may show significant changes and identify additional institutions that should be contacted.

The geographic breakdown is necessary for planning calling coverage by proxy solicitors, and the classification of owners by size determines cutoffs for coverage of round-lot holders by the solicitation firm, and for canvassing the largest holders by members of the dissident slate or its investment banker.

Normally, solicitation coverage of 90 percent of the shares outstanding is necessary to win a proxy contest. The remaining 10 percent probably will not vote.

Management's Position

Management's slate must stand on its record and its program for the future. Neither may be sufficiently clear to assure the successful reelection of the board. Consequently, management should utilize its territorial advantages. Because management has access to the corporate treasury, cost considerations are more favorable for management. Furthermore, only management (versus opposition) can increase the dividend, spin off operations, or create royalty trusts. On a less tangible but nonetheless important level, it should attempt to condition shareholders through routine correspondence, such as in annual and quarterly reports, and in special letters or mailgrams when they are appropriate and conform to proxy rules.

Management's record for the past 10 years, and more specifically the last three years, will be the primary measurement of management and board competence. Past reports to shareholders will demonstrate how successful they have been in delivering on past programs for the future. Successful actions, such as acquisitions or new product lines, are emphasized. Failures that require divestitures or changes in management must be explained carefully in recognition that these statements may become ammunition for the opposition.

Management's program for the future is inherently more subjective than its record of performance, yet its acceptance by shareholders is an essential element in reelection. Corporate values and direction are usually not well understood by shareholders, because management frequently fears it will suffer a competitive disadvantage by divulging its strategies and objectives to shareholders. Unfortunately, these deficiencies are primary causes of proxy contests. The prudent course of action would be to favor full disclosure while recognizing that some information could be detrimental. Because new investors are constantly being added to the list of shareholders and existing shareholders often have short memories, corporate values and programs should be explained frequently, especially to securities analysts, who often determine market values, but also to shareholders directly.

A management that has been explaining its actions routinely will be less likely to be involved in a proxy contest, and if it does become involved in one, its course of action should be easier. In a contest, management will have better credibility with full prior disclosure than if it must introduce new ideas under the trying conditions that exist in a contest. If prior disclosure has not occurred or has been inadequate, early disclosure is the most prudent course. Management also must develop issues against, and in response to, the opposition. The primary considerations are similar to the opposition's approach. If management has maintained an active investor relations program, it should have a distinct credibility advantage in attacking the dissidents.

Developing Issues

A dissident group usually will attack alleged failures of the incumbent board and company actions that were not in the best interests of all shareholders while mapping responses to management counterattacks. The preliminary analysis should provide an adequate basis for determining the direction of the campaign, and it can be supplemented by later information from private investigators and disclosures during litigation.

Failures of the board basically cover directors' actions specifically and management actions generally. The board is always accountable, because it selects management to carry out its policies and directions. Grounds for attacking the board and its management include contradictory actions and statements, inaccurate forecasts, an ill-defined outlook, bad judgment in acquisitions and divestitures, poor performance by other companies affiliated with board members, sparse attendance at board meetings, damaging articles in newspapers and business publications, bearish investment research reports, and most important, the withholding of important information from shareholders.

Among the board actions that shareholders might question as being in their best interests are golden parachutes, excessively high salaries, numerous and expensive perquisites, stock options not pegged to recent performance, wasteful litigation, and, perhaps the most egregious action, the issuance of voting securities to a friendly party without shareholder approval.

Surprise Disclosures

During every proxy contest there is invariably a "surprise" disclosure—by one side or the other. The key to winning is to avoid such situations by anticipating the other side's revelations. When potentially damaging information becomes known by the side it is most likely to hurt, the facts are best disclosed before the other side can develop them. Timely response or challenge often can neutralize a potentially harmful situation, although sometimes the best response is to ignore the surprise disclosure.

Samuel J. Heyman's ultimately successful takeover of GAF Corp. triggered such a surprise. In the 1982–1983 portion of the battle, the Heyman forces revealed that in a 1979 racketeering case, one of management's candidates admitted committing acts that constituted a federal crime because of a substantial cash payment to a union official. Subsequently, GAF uncovered a breach of fiduciary responsibility suit against the opposition leader by his sister. Neither revelation was a show stopper, but both were characteristic of surprise disclosures. The disclosures were designed to influence the shareholders' decision about the candidates' capacity to act responsibly as directors.

Delivering the Message

When the issues have defined the battle lines, the two sides are prepared to deliver their messages to the shareholder constituencies. The dissidents' scenario is to attack first so that management is on the defensive, anticipate an inevitable counterattack, break any bad or potentially damaging news first to weaken management's responses, and finish with a positive statement. The initial communication will attempt to establish identity and credibility for dissident director candidates, define objectives, and explain the reasons for the battle. Subsequent communications will try to discredit management and directors by explaining why and how they allegedly have failed. Succeeding communications will specify how the opposition believes its objectives and programs are better than the incumbents' and will seek to reinforce the outsiders' credibility. The opposition will wind up by presenting its "plan for progress," or explaining how it will perform better than existing management.

In roughly the same sequence, management will be presenting its case.

In every contest, each side always is looking for an issue or event that could be a show stopper, something so dramatic that the other side is forced to either capitulate or compromise.

Letters are the primary vehicles for reaching most shareholders. They should be printed on quality paper and in type large enough to attract and be understood by even the poorest reader. Telegrams and personal visits may be required to reach large individual and institutional holders. When time constraints are important, mailgrams can be used to send communications, deliver news releases, or even execute proxies.

Advertisements in newspapers, often repeating what is said in basic shareholder communications, can reach additional shareholders and deliver the message to people who are interested in the scrap, although not directly involved. Radio and television advertising featuring leading spokesmen for management and the dissidents is being increasingly utilized. Press releases should be used to update business reporters on the latest information and positions of the two sides. The contestants also should be prepared to supplement regular communications with fast-breaking bulletins triggered by any new information derived from analysis, investigation, and the discovery phase of litigation, or by responses to the opposition.

Soliciting Proxies

After the message is out, the proxy solicitor and other team members must systematically contact shareholders—primarily to obtain their proxies, but also to determine their inclinations to vote and gather any comments that might provide insight into the direction of the campaign. Assignments to team members should be made before the communications materials are distributed.

Because personal contact is an effective way to get votes, any team members who are personally acquainted with large individual or institutional investors should handle those presentations. If personal relationships don't exist, the job should be assigned to appropriate team members who can make presentations to analysts and brokerage offices. These designees could be either the proxy solicitor, investment banker, principals (management or opposition), or a combination of them.

The proxy solicitor is responsible for obtaining votes from the smaller individual holder. If necessary, the proxy solicitor should hire and train additional personnel to make the canvass. Often management's own personnel can be utilized, a distinct advantage. The solicitor's force receives cards listing names and addresses of the stockholders and is responsible for telephone calls to each of them, more than once if necessary.

Telephone manner is important. If the solicitor is too aggressive, the stockholder may be encouraged to go with the other side; if the solicitor is not aggressive enough, that also could translate into lost votes.

Mailgrams may be used if they are in accordance with the premeeting agreements between the opposing parties and their presumptions as to the validity of proxies. When the contest is close and time is running out, mailgrams may be the only vehicles for increasing the vote. Costs usually prohibit the use of mailgrams except for the final stages of a campaign. The basic mailgram procedure is to establish a toll-free phone number a shareholder can dial to record his or her vote by following a predetermined script; these proxies are delivered to the originator in the form of a mailgram.

Locking up Proxies

Normally the target company management uses its transfer agent to tabulate shareholder votes. The opposition, usually on the recommendation of the proxy solicitor, must retain a data processing or accounting firm to count votes. The tabulator maintains a running tally of the vote, records comments from the proxy cards, separates them from return envelopes, and files them in chronological order. The latest-dated proxy is the vote that counts, but often an undated proxy may be counted if the envelope's postmarked date can be substantiated.

If a returned proxy card is undated or lacks a signature, as in the case of joint tenants or if the signature is not the same as the record holder, the tabulator, on instructions from the proxy solicitor and upon review by counsel, must send a "curing letter" to the shareholder with a new proxy card. The curing letter asks the shareholder to correct the deficiency and return the new card. The defective card should be retained by the tabulator in case it can be substantiated.

Unfortunately, shareholders do not always pay adequate attention to what they are signing. Some automatically sign and return every proxy sent to them. After the second and subsequent mailings, the number of duplicate proxies, as a percentage of all proxy returns, will indicate the revocation rate. The revocation rate must be watched and analyzed. Because of revocations, each side must become increasingly concerned about shareholders receiving the last mailing with a proxy to be voted.

THE SHOWDOWN STAGE

Premeeting Considerations

Prior to the shareholders meeting, attorneys for the opposition should submit to management's counsel a proposed agreement on the conduct of the meeting. Management runs the meeting and usually wants to avoid anything that could make it vulnerable to a legal challenge on its conduct. The agreement also provides a degree of protection for dissident interests.

The agreement should set the agenda and establish basic rules. Those include whether and when dissidents may respond to shareholder questions during the meeting, when the polls for balloting open and close, and where proxy cards may be delivered, if different from the site of the meeting.

In addition to the basic agreement, certain presumptions on the validity of proxies should be decided by management and opposition. Often these presumptions are combined with the basic agreement.

Postmeeting Procedures

The inspectors should announce a preliminary tally as soon as possible after receiving all proxies held by the two sides and any ballots cast from the floor. But this is only a tentative count that is subject to often-extensive review after the polls have closed.

The extent of the review depends on such factors as the number of proxies cast, the closeness of the vote, and the possibility of further litigation. The review may involve just a double-check of the votes and rulings on the validity of the proxies in line with the premeeting agreement. Or it may become a "snake pit"—a laborious, time-consuming process in which each proxy is checked individually, largely because there has been no prior agreement.

After the review, a challenge period begins in which both sides have opportunities to attack the other's proxies. Experienced solicitors usually save their challenges until the very end of the challenge period, so as not to tip their hands. Only after the challenges are eliminated can a final vote be determined.

This is the climax of the battle. Either the incumbents have been returned or a new leadership has taken control of the company—assuming, of course, that the battle isn't prolonged by a new round of litigation.

Chapter 40

Public Relations Techniques in M&A

Richard E. Cheney

Vice Chairman, Hill and Knowlton, Inc., New York, New York

Robert W. Taft

Senior Vice President, Hill and Knowlton, Inc., New York, New York

In takeover situations, public relations often can make the difference between winning and losing. Many of the public relations skills needed in takeovers are similar to those required for general public relations. But the intensity of the conflict, the severe time pressures, the complexity of the transactions, and the sophisticated media coverage of takeovers all combine to make takeover work an increasingly more specialized area of public relations practice. The practitioner in takeover public relations should be skilled in organizing a campaign for either a raider or a target, developing constructive relationships with lawyers and investment bankers, effectively disseminating information, monitoring stock ownership, working with the media, and developing constituency support.

PREPARING IN ADVANCE FOR A TENDER OFFER

We are approached constantly by companies concerned about the possibility of a takeover. Sometimes, a known raider already has taken a position in the company's shares and has stated an intention to take control. More often, there is no raider and no offer to evaluate, but the company wants to "be ready" for a raid should it come.

A company's advisers, including public relations people, can help management plan a defense against a tender offer or other form of takeover attempt. Similarly, a raider's advisers will provide counsel on what to expect from the target. However, there is little a target can do to prevent an offer from being made. The arsenal of traditional takeover defense has become less potent in recent years as laws have changed and as raiders have developed counterstrategies to circumvent their targets' defenses.

Defensive changes in corporate by-laws, for example, pose a core communications problem. By proposing such ideas, management may give the impression that it fears a raid and, thereby, may draw unwanted attention. In the worst case, shareholders may reject antitakeover by-law proposals. A raider could interpret this action as an invitation by shareholders to make an offer. Therefore, many companies now test the waters before actually proposing by-law changes to determine shareholder reactions, and some are taking extra care to "presell" sensitive proposals to large institutional holders through face-to-face meetings between management and institutional personnel.

Aside from these overt defensive steps, many companies maintain a prealert status by educating board members on their responsibilities in a takeover, installing systems that allow rapid response to a sudden raid, developing a procedure for contacting key executives at any hour, and maintaining a communications program that highlights such management qualities as toughness, ability to make decisions fast, willingness to take risks, and the courage to reevaluate key businesses, including those once cherished. Occasionally, a company will go as far as to say it's "not for sale." In reality, directors have a legal obligation to consider any serious offer, although they also have wide discretion to reject it. So, "not for sale" may actually mean "not without a fight."

Even if these preparations don't spread a complete security blanket, they can give an embattled management a good start in its defense against an unwanted bid.

IMPORTANCE OF CONTINUING
PUBLIC RELATIONS

Takeover targets don't suddenly spring newborn to public attention like Venus from a clamshell. Their reputations and characteristics were established well before the battle. Most frustrating to a public relations practitioner is to work with a company that starts giving serious consideration to its public relations problems only after a takeover battle has broken out.

Companies with strong media connections can enjoy a leg up on a raider. Becton, Dickinson & Co. helped itself immensely in fighting an unwanted investment by Sun Co. in 1978 by placing several stories favorable to its cause, thanks to the media contacts of its public relations director. This controversy eventually was decided by a federal court decision forcing Sun to divest its Becton, Dickinson shares, which amounted to nearly a third of the medical products firm's stock.

Dictaphone Corp. also benefited from an established public relations program when Northern Electric Co. made a hostile bid in 1974. *The Wall Street Journal* suggested how well Dictaphone's program had succeeded when it published an article that alluded to insider trading before announcement of the offer: "Northern Electric stumbled off on the wrong foot yesterday in an offer for Dictaphone. . . ." The story highlighted Dictaphone's charges of questionable stock accumulations by Northern Electric rather than Northern Electric's offer itself. Dictaphone successfully fought off Northern Electric.

Unfortunately, concern about takeovers has made many companies reluctant to seek high public visibility. The theory is that a potential raider may overlook the company if it keeps a low profile. The fact is that raiders use an array of analytical tools and public information to identify potential targets, and there is no real correlation between recent publicity and a company's allure.

Of course, some topics sound alarm bells for raiders, and vulnerable companies should avoid them. Companies should not boast about large cash reserves and low debt, complain too loudly that their shares are selling well below book, or suggest that they have achieved their goals and intend to conduct business in a relatively static manner in the years ahead. Yet they should not hesitate to build a healthy and positive relationship with the media. A history of good media relations is a definite plus for a company entering a takeover fight.

THE ROLE OF PUBLIC RELATIONS AND THE PR PROFESSIONAL

When a company is involved in a takeover, public relations people should be at the planning table with the investment bankers and legal specialists. Public relations practitioners have experience, contacts, and familiarity with the most recent takeover strategies, as well as knowledge of the raider or target.

A public relations takeover specialist knows the rules, understands the roles of other professionals, knows what the media consider newsworthy, and has the resources to achieve results in any part of the country or world on short notice. The company public relations chief also should be involved because he or she knows local media contacts intimately and, as an insider, is sensitive to employee concerns and enjoys extensive knowledge of the industry involved. Most takeover situations leave a residue of damage that public relations must address, and in many cases, the in-house public relations person can suggest ways to mitigate serious injuries as the contest progresses.

The Fundamentals of Public Relations

In terms of public relations, the raider's message is quite simple. The raider seeks to tell holders of the shares in the company it is seeking that the offer is generous (or at least fair). When the offer is for stock rather than cash, or is for less than the whole company, the raider also argues that its ability to run the company is superior to that of present management or that it will liquidate portions of the company and benefit the shareholder either by reinvesting the proceeds or distributing them directly to shareholders.

The target company's public relations problems are more complex. It is best for a target company to have developed a complete defensive strategy, including the use of communications techniques, even before a battle begins. Extensive research and fact finding is a requisite activity. Thanks to electronic data bases and other reference materials, it is possible to retrieve almost everything written in the media about the company, its management, and even the raider in a matter of hours. Conversations with securities analysts, business writers, competitors, and previous targets of the raider also can provide valuable information. The idea is to identify strengths and weaknesses of both sides, including the personalities of board members and the raiding group.

Among the matters that concern public relations people are the reputations and public perceptions of the parties, the complexity of the offer or the defense, whether special issues can be developed, and whether and how to use advertising, direct mail, or other media to convey messages. Perhaps most important is the articulation of a central theme to keynote a campaign. It may be a simple theme ("The offer is too low because . . . ") or complex (Mr. X is not qualified to manage the company because . . . "). But a simple theme, consistently restated and carefully documented throughout the fight, generally has the best chance of success.

Coordination of Communications

Dozens of press releases must be prepared, cleared, and distributed in the course of a typical tender offer. Basic announcements would include the commencement of the offer, litigation, court decisions, Hart-Scott-Rodino developments, and charges and countercharges. It is not uncommon for a company to issue several releases a day. A well-organized, well-equipped, and well-coordinated communications operation to handle the effort is paramount. Often, the inside public relations department is good at disseminating routine corporate news. But in the high-pressure atmosphere of a tender offer, it generally lacks the resources or the experience to deal effectively with lawyers and investment bankers.

In a friendly tender situation, much of the public relations effort is directed to conveying the impression that the transaction is as good as done. There is always a possibility that a third party may seek to intervene. Lock-up provisions can effectively block intervention by a third party. Press releases about friendly tender offers will highlight the features of the transaction that make it difficult for a third party to intervene. They also will spell out clearly the timetables and approvals that will be required to complete the transactions.

It is our experience that in even the most carefully planned and cordial merger, some damage to employee morale and customer relations occurs. However, the objective of getting the deal done is superior to every other objective. Public relations efforts to repair the damage are normally deferred until the transaction is complete. An obvious exception is when employee or customer support is essential to the approval of the transaction.

It is important to seize the initiative in takeover communications, because the first announcements shape investors' perceptions. Whether the offer is friendly or hostile, the media must be provided promptly with complete information about the company. The first story will report the terms of the offer. On either the same day or the next, the media generally will have stories analyzing what the combined company will look like if the takeover is successful. These stories are assembled from previously published company materials, available research reports, and reporters' conversations with key analysts familiar with both companies. Public relations people should assist reporters by making company material available and by providing the names of analysts who are familiar with the target company. It is most beneficial if a company can identify analysts likely to anticipate and support management's position in a hostile offer. A company under attack will help itself by directing a reporter to an analyst who might describe an unsolicited offer as too low.

The public relations consultant also can help when the company chooses to say nothing. A seasoned public relations person knows how to say "no" or "no comment" to a reporter without compromising the company's expectations for fair reporting by that journalist.

Reworking Legal Material to Suit the Media

Public relations people must have enough clout and experience to stand up to articulate and vocal takeover lawyers and tell them that press releases prepared by attorneys very often must be rewritten to meet the requirements of the media.

Some lawyers in the takeover field have become sensitized to the communications demands of their work. Legal briefs often are written with an awareness of the need to provide quotable material for the media or to highlight the main charges so that they can be understood by the lay reader. On the other hand, many press releases may be difficult to understand for reasons that have nothing to do with the writer's command of English, but because they are crafted to conform to attorneys' perceptions of legal requirements. Because these releases must be distributed as written, it becomes the public relations person's role to help reporters understand what the release does and does not say.

A Monitoring System

In the early stages of a takeover, a system should be developed to rapidly monitor coverage of the contest and ensure that all interested reporters receive information promptly, that potentially damaging media coverage is identified quickly, and that the company responds as needed. It also is necessary to create a system to deliver the releases of one side back to the other side's hometown and, ideally, to areas of the country where the opposition has a large amount of shareholder support. There may be some advantage in "overreporting" developments by breaking them into several pieces or by issuing anticipatory releases ("The company plans to make an announcement later today . . . ") to build or sustain a sense of momentum and action.

The so-called "creeping tender" is an example of how news can be distributed in sequence to provoke emotional results. For example, when T. Boone Pickens, Jr., of Mesa Petroleum acquired about 2.6 million shares of Gulf Corp. stock late in 1983, it represented only about 1.3 percent of Gulf's outstanding shares. However, Pickens made five separate announcements of small purchases—on November 25, November 28, November 30, December 1, and December 5. Each announcement was reported separately by the media, and each noted that Mesa had increased its holdings. The cumulative impact may have suggested that Mesa's holdings in the company were large. In fact, Mesa held just 12.9 percent of Gulf's stock by early December.

Meeting Williams Act Requirements

The Williams Act, a principal statute in securities regulation, provides specific directives on communications, including the language corporate boards must use in telling stockholders their positions on takeover offers. Along with the Hart-Scott-Rodino Act, the Williams Act also establishes a series of timetables for conducting offers, but because bids are subject to revisions and intervening offers may be made, schedules in specific cases constantly may be changed. These legally established timetables and their alterations also govern much of the timing of communications issued in a takeover. The public relations practitioner must know the current status of the timetables at all times and also be apprised of the latest legal developments, such as when and where court hearings will be held, what issues will be decided, and what implications the client faces in potential court actions.

Timing Communications for Maximum Coverage

Timing is critical in getting news coverage. Often overlooked in takeover fights are that reporters like to go home at night and that they work against deadlines so that their publications can be printed and delivered on schedule. The public relations person must be able to explain to lawyers that filing a complaint at 5:00 P.M. and issuing a press release at 5:30 risks getting short shrift in the Eastern edition of *The Wall Street Journal*. In general, the earlier news is released, the more likely it is to be fully and accurately reported.

Keeping the Financial Community Informed

In addition to providing counsel on press relations, Hill and Knowlton serves as an information agent, providing "street name" holders with key information about the offer. As soon as a letter to stockholders has been drafted, it can be telecopied to New York from anywhere in the United States, printed on our client company's stationery over the signature of the CEO, and sent in appropriate quantities to "street names," often on the same day the letter is drafted. We also send key documents, such as complaints and court decisions, to the arbitrage community.

IMPACT OF FINANCIAL PUBLIC RELATIONS

A company that provides highly credible information on a when-needed basis tends to get some premium on its stock because of the reliability of its communications. This premium tends to force up a raider's offering price and makes analysts more critical of an inadequate offer.

In one recent friendly offer, the acquiring company was worried about the investment community's reaction to the proposed merger. Although the match looked good from both sides, the acquiring company feared that reporters would call analysts for off-the-cuff criticism of a merger they had not studied or even considered, and that this criticism would be incorporated in the reporters' stories. Thus, on the day the merger was announced, we had information packages on the desks of all 150 investment professionals who were following the acquiring company. The information packages included annual reports, quarterly reports, the 10-K and 10-Q forms filed with the Securities and Exchange Commission, a fact book on the company being acquired, and the client's offering circular. Within 24 hours, the same packet was delivered to another 100 professionals in other parts of the country. Our theory was that prompt delivery of this material would show that our client wasn't afraid to lay bare all of the particulars of the company being acquired. We also believed that the professionals would delay judgment on the merger until they had had a chance to study the material we sent them.

Case History: Tosco Corp. Proxy Fight

Tosco Corp.'s victory over dissident shareholders seeking control of the Los Angeles-based oil concern was an example of how careful planning and prompt execution of a communications program can help a besieged management. A central issue was the progress and prospects of the Colony oil shale project, a joint venture of Tosco and Exxon Co. to which Tosco had made a major commitment. Tosco got a head start by learning from financial community sources that a dissident group was being formed by investor Kenneth Good before his group made a formal announcement. Tosco's first step was to try to learn more about its stockholders, an important bank of information because a significant number of shares was held in "street names." One novel device Tosco used was to include with a quarterly earnings report an offer for a free oil shale paperweight. To order the paperweight, beneficial holders had to identify themselves; Tosco learned the names and addresses of more than 25 percent of its "street" holders in this way.

Tosco management also took the initiative in the mail campaign, firing off to stockholders the first information they received about the dissidents and actually completing two mailings before the rebels sent their first. Detailed plans for a stockholder solicitation campaign were set. Special training sessions were held nightly for phone solicitors to brief them on the most recent events. When Exxon canceled the Colony project just before the annual meeting, the solicitors were able to inform stockholders immediately of the consequences for Tosco. At the height of the battle, 70 phone solicitors were making up to 5,000 calls per night for Tosco. Management's victory was overwhelming, with 63 percent of the shares voted at the annual meeting for the incumbents.

The Audience for Takeover Communications

Individual investors are becoming more sophisticated about raids. Increasingly, they sell at or soon after the first announcement of an offer to capture a profit in the market and avoid the uncertainty of the outcome of a takeover. It is typical for volume in a target company's shares to soar the day a raid is announced. Within two or three days, huge amounts of the company's outstanding shares may be traded.

Many of the target company's shareholders may sell out before issues in a takeover are debated, and the audience may be reduced to a handful of professional arbitrageurs, judges, regulators, and reporters covering the story. Thus, the audience often can be segmented, and separate communications can be aimed at different segments. Similarly, companies frequently develop special communications for their employees, legislators, and other constituencies.

Influencing Public Opinion

Only a few takeovers lend themselves to public policy debate. But in the early 1980s, congressional concern rose when Canadian companies made a series of unrelated raids on American companies at about the same time. Congress also became involved on both sides of antitrust questions in some of the large takeovers of the early and mid-1980s. State legislatures have rallied to preserve businesses in their states. Such controversy adds a dimension and an urgency to takeover fights that normally benefit the target in its effort to prevent a takeover. Thus, it is to a target's advantage to publicize such issues, through advertising, press relations, briefings, and communications with elected officials to point out that their constituencies are, or soon will be, concerned.

MARATHON VERSUS MOBIL: PUBLIC
RELATIONS IN A TAKEOVER BATTLE

The Mobil Corp. attempt to take over Marathon Oil in 1981 was a fight in which public relations helped shape public opinion and made a clear difference. *The Wall Street Journal,* in a January 1982 article, put it this way:

> Marathon quickly buttressed its legal strengths with a highly effective public relations campaign. Like a jujitsu wrestler, Marathon used Mobil's weight against it by harping on Mobil's size, its well-known desire to obtain oil cheaply, its high public profile and its perceived "to-hell-with-them-all" attitude.
>
> Marathon's success in this endeavor may seem a bit surprising. Mobil's legions of experts may appear to have been splendidly equipped to fight a public relations battle, but Marathon's guerrilla campaign was highly effective.
>
> In fact, a careful reading of the judicial opinions in the court cases, combined with discussions with court officials, clearly indicate that Marathon's public relations campaign strongly influenced the court proceedings. To an unusual degree, social issues were incorporated in judicial decisions.
>
> The public relations battle clearly took its toll, a Mobil lawyer noted. "Obviously, certain policy considerations have got to affect the court," he says. "These policy arguments helped convince the appeals court that heard the case that a combination of Mobil and Marathon would somehow be 'morally wrong.'"

How did Marathon pull it off?

In October 1981, Mobil made an offer of $85 per share in cash and securities that was rejected by Marathon directors as "grossly inadequate." Marathon filed an antitrust suit against Mobil in federal court. U.S. Steel Corp. and Marathon then jointly announced a friendly merger valued at $125 a share for the first of two tiers. But the ensuing battle for control of Marathon was to last more than four months.

Marathon was a long-time client of Hill and Knowlton, and we took a two-pronged approach: creating a favorable public climate as a backdrop for Marathon's legal action, and persuasively presenting Marathon's case in support of the U.S. Steel offer to shareholders and other investors.

Initially, Marathon wanted to fight the Mobil offer simply on the basis that the price wasn't high enough. However, management was alerted that it had broad community and employee support and that it could use the public issues as well. Mobil was vulnerable because the case could be made that a Marathon acquisition was diverting money that should have been earmarked to search for oil. Mobil had been attacked on this basis before, when it acquired Marcor, a retailing and packaging company. Marathon drafted a very short statement asking whether an oil company should be spending money on an acquisition when it should be searching for oil. The statement was read by Harold Hoopman, chairman and chief executive officer, in the company cafeteria. Marathon mailgrammed the statement to editorial writers at every newspaper in the United States. To reach Marathon's installations around the country, the statement was broadcast via satellite after more than 200 television stations were told that it would be transmitted for taping at a specific time. The allegation that Mobil wanted to spend money on an acquisition during an oil shortage touched off a barrage of editorials.

Marathon also researched Mobil's series of public affairs advertisements on the op-ed page of *The New York Times* and incorporated them into ads of its own, asking, "How does this current offer reflect what Mobil says it should be doing?"

Feedback showed that the campaign helped mobilize public opinion on Marathon's side. Technically, the Marathon-Mobil fight was decided by the government and in the courts. The Federal Trade Commission blocked the Mobil bid on antitrust grounds, and the U.S. Supreme Court denied Mobil's request to delay U.S. Steel's ultimately successful effort to take control of Marathon. But Marathon's effective public relations effort clearly helped create a climate in which events unfolded in the company's favor.

Marathon was popular with its employees and the local townspeople. Some people have asked if the pro-Marathon rallies in Findlay, Ohio, where the company is headquartered, were a public relations stunt. On the contrary, Marathon was surprised at the extent of the community's support. When the battle was over, Marathon prepared a four-color "scrapbook" with pictures of all the community events to thank employees and the community for their support.

SOME KEY PR TOOLS FOR TAKEOVERS

Letters to Shareholders

Takeover communications normally are built around a series of "letters" addressed to shareholders by the company or the raider. Each side translates its message into letters mailed to shareholders, press releases, and, generally, paid advertisements. These documents are carefully crafted to present the company's case as clearly and persuasively as possible. When appropriate, the letters denigrate the opposition and its arguments. Letters to shareholders must be brief, readable, and easily understood. The public relations person must identify the most effective arguments for the side he or she represents and translate often complex issues into understandable prose. Each of the points in these letters becomes the grist for other public relations efforts to reinforce the main point or to elaborate on it with additional factual information or detail.

Tone and Quotable Quotes

The dialogue in takeover situations can become salty. Occasionally, it is desirable to reproduce a routine takeover letter for European audiences, which are not fed a daily diet of fight invective. Europeans often are shocked by the name calling and accusatory language of American fights. In the United States, however, it is becoming more difficult to gain attention for your side through strong language alone because it has become so common. Mere stridency is generally counterproductive and often serves to cover a weak argument.

Most players in fights, like it or not, convey some sort of a style. When the style can be directed in support of the objective, the odds of gaining the upper hand improve. When the style contradicts the assertions, the results can be damaging. Thus, a raider that claims that it can manage a company "better" than present management is vulnerable if it wages a sloppy campaign and is unprepared for the media or unresponsive to their questions.

Advertising

Advertising can be a powerful tool in takeover battles, but it is costly. In 1986, a full-page advertisement in the national edition of *The Wall Street Journal* cost $80,630.

Advertising can accomplish several things very effectively. It can reach "street name" beneficial owners and large numbers of employees and their families scattered across the country. It can reach into the other company's backyard—customers, employees and their families, communities—with an impact that no other medium can match. It can offer the opportunity for last-minute messages when there's no time to develop a full public relations campaign or, in a proxy fight, when the vote is close and a final push is needed. Because of delays necessitated by clearances, most fight advertisements replicate material that has been mailed directly to shareholders. Examples of fight ads developed as purely original advertisements are rare.

CAN PUBLIC RELATIONS
INFLUENCE THE OUTCOME?

The exact impact of public relations depends on the courage and resourcefulness of the management and its tender offer support team, along with their capacity for teamwork. And a lot depends on chance—in some instances, something as simple as the identity of the judge assigned to a case. Nevertheless, there are many examples where public relations played a significant role in determining the outcome of a battle.

Case History: Western Pacific versus Houghton Mifflin

When Western Pacific Industries took a position in Houghton Mifflin's stock, and suggested the possibility of a takeover, the publishing company encouraged its important authors, those who accounted for more than half of its revenues, to write Howard C. Newman, the Western Pacific CEO, and voice their determination not to work for a conglomerate. In essence, they told him that if Western Pacific proceeded with further stock purchases or a tender offer, they would switch to other publishers.

Houghton Mifflin provided *The Boston Globe*, its home-city newspaper, with copies of the authors' letters, resulting in an in-depth story that included interviews with some of the authors. Houghton Mifflin then sent the *Globe* story to *The New York Times'* Herbert Mitgang, a leader of a writers' league battling conglomerate takeovers of publishers. When Mitgang called Newman and asked about the revolt, Newman responded: "That's got all the spontaneity of a demonstration in Red Square."

Houghton's CEO, Harold T. Miller, responded by saying, "Does he think I can orchestrate Arthur Schlesinger or John Kenneth Galbraith?" Both were Houghton Mifflin authors. A story appeared with both quotes, and the results were devastating to Newman.

Miller sent the story to the authors, and they responded with indignation. They wrote to Newman again and asked him if he was really foolish enough to think they could be so easily manipulated. If he really wanted to know, they added, this was one big clue as to why they would never write for him. Eventually, Newman got the message: Western Pacific withdrew and sold its stock.

When Public Relations Cannot Help

There are, of course, instances when public relations can have little or no effect. Cash offers for 100 percent of a company generally offer few public relations defenses. It is common wisdom that "the offer speaks for itself." Similarly, fights involving complex businesses—the sale of tax shelters, for instance—may turn on issues that defy any brief analysis or popular interpretation. Unpopular businesses (such as the manufacture of toxic defoliants) or obscure businesses pose similar communications problems. Smaller companies and companies whose operations are limited to a remote area are also difficult to defend, although some hand-crafted local campaigns that created their own media, such as posters, handouts, and telephone campaigns, have had some success. In some cases these take on aspects of a local political campaign and rely on extensive personal contact with shareholders and the media.

Chapter 41

Selling Your Deal

Stephen M. Waters

Managing Director, Shearson Lehman Brothers,
New York, New York

Selling a transaction properly is among the most important, yet most overlooked, areas of acquisition planning. Successful presentation of the strategic rationale, financial effects, and personnel implications of a transaction significantly influence both the immediate and long-term performance of the acquired entity and the combined company. As much value can be lost through a poor selling and implementation program as can be created through effective negotiation of a transaction's terms.

Paradoxically, the task of explaining a transaction often is delegated to people who do not understand why it occurred or what its implications are. Many acquirers have no plan for talking to employees of the two companies involved, no coherent explanation for shareholders or funding sources, no media program, and only vague ideas about how to integrate the new organization. Frequently, the absence of such a sales plan reflects a lack of careful strategic thought itself.

This discussion will emphasize three key points:

1. How one sells a transaction is important.

2. Specific plans should be formulated for employees, shareholders, the investment community, rating agencies, and lenders, as well as for customers and suppliers.
3. Key members of management need to be involved.

WHY SELLING A TRANSACTION IS IMPORTANT

There is a simple answer to this question. An acquisition should create value, not destroy it. It is also axiomatic that managements and boards of directors want transactions to work, not fail.

A brief review of the past 10 years of acquisition activity vividly illustrates the difficulties that can be created when poor selling occurs and cultures are not meshed well. A consensus of deals that were unsuccessful in part because of poor selling might include:

- Exxon's acquisition of Reliance Electric for $1.1 billion
- Kennecott's acquisition of Carborundum for $567 million
- Inco's acquisition of ESB for $230 million
- Norton Simon's acquisition of Avis for $174 million
- Imperial Group's acquisition of Howard Johnson for $630 million
- General Electric's (U.K.) acquisition of A.B. Dick for $103 million

Without thoughtful postacquisition planning—which begins with a careful selling effort—key employees leave, those who stay are less productive, customers go elsewhere, financial results weaken, and the stock of the acquirer declines. The buyer's own operations may suffer because management must divert its attention to "fixing things." Senior officers lose credibility with employees, the board, and the investment community.

WHO MUST BE SOLD

The target groups that should be addressed in any selling campaign include:

- Managements of both companies, who must implement the strategy, run the business, and produce the financial results
- Other employees, who should take pride in their achievements and in their jobs, and who need to believe that they are being treated fairly
- The shareholders, who want to see their stock go up in price and/or desire a secure dividend
- The financial community, whose opinions can affect the stock price both in the short and long term
- Funding sources, which help provide debt and equity capital to implement the business plan
- Customers and suppliers, whose confidence is essential to continued sales

THE MESSAGES THAT MUST BE DELIVERED

Clearly, each group needs a message that answers its specific questions. Some buyers may find it productive to develop a series of criteria that can be matched against the specific group they are addressing. In doing so, four key areas deserve attention:

1. Strategic reasoning
2. Financial effects
3. Personnel implications
4. Uncertainty

The Strategy to Use

Virtually all of the groups affected by an acquisition would like to understand why the transaction occurred. Indeed, the only question that gets more attention is: "What does this mean for me?"

The significant points that involve strategy include why a specific target company makes sense, why the time to buy it is right, what benefits the transaction is expected to produce, what the risks are, and where the new company is heading. Almost always, each of these items is well understood by members of senior management, but almost never is their thought process understood by at least some of the affected groups.

The Numbers to Emphasize

Particularly for the financial community and lenders, *the numbers are important.* The effects on earnings, capital structure, cash flow, and asset values need to be explained, without management boasts about how great a deal it made. Management can describe its expectations for the new company's performance, and can voice its hopes for the stock price. Shareholders, in particular, deserve to hear about financial ramifications of a transaction.

The People to Address

Without doubt, the most important target group is the people who work in both the buying and selling companies. Prices of a stock can rise and fall, but without performance by management and employees, a company never will reach its potential, and shareholders never will experience both the satisfaction and the financial rewards of being involved with a "winning effort."

Alleviating Uncertainty

Too much uncertainty hurts employees, customers, suppliers, shareholders, lenders, and management itself. Alleviating uncertainty is critical to making an acquisition work.

SELLING THE KEY GROUPS

Detailed implementation of specific plans for specific groups is the heart of careful acquisition planning. Ironically, all one needs to answer well is the question: "What would I be concerned about if I were this person?"

Management and Employees

If a buyer does not begin with its own and the acquired employees, it is trusting to chance. Only the people can make an organization work effectively and, in turn, produce financial results. For the acquired organization, an acquisition is particularly upsetting, and a buyer needs to understand its concerns in order to create a new company that works.

In communicating to an acquired company's employees, the buyer should be prepared to explain:

The key precepts of its own organization—How it is run and what it considers important for success.

Its thoughts for the purchased company—Proposed management strategy, and importance of the new entity in the combined organization.

Incentive and compensation—These must be addressed in terms of both philosophy and fairness. It is critical that new employees understand how they will be judged and that they perceive a new system will be fair.

Advancement—Individuals, especially in management, want to understand what their "next steps" can be.

Although most acquirers tend to share their views only with top management, there is real benefit to addressing the concerns of other salaried employees and of the real "workers" in the new company. Each level of management should understand the messages that must be communicated to lower levels, and the sequence should not stop until the lowest level of the company has heard what is occurring and how it affects their lives. This clearly includes secretaries, clerical people, and factory workers. Discussions with union officials sometimes assume special importance.

It is helpful to note how to avoid some common pitfalls:

- Do not always act immediately to show who is boss and to change things. Unless an organization is in really bad shape, there is no need to act quickly, and you actually may learn something by watching what works and what does not.

- Avoid minor irritations, at least at first. Reductions in medical or dental coverage, holiday and overtime allowances, expense reimbursement practices, check cashing, and travel arrangements frequently assume too much importance in individuals' subjective reactions to a new organization.

- Do not prolong an individual's uncertainty. As noted earlier, there will always be uncertainty when an acquisition occurs. No buyer is likely to know how every individual will fit into the new company. All one can do is to understand and communicate directly or indirectly that each individual is important and will be treated fairly. This attitude tends to go a long way toward retaining employees and sustaining performance.

Shareholders

Because managements of public and private companies are ultimately responsible to their owners—the shareholders—this group deserves special attention. Many shareholders will be concerned about the strategic reasons for a transaction, but "the numbers" are also important. The key message to deliver is why shareholders will be better off in the long term and, hopefully, in the short term as well.

Shareholder concerns can be summarized in three catch phrases: "stock price," "earnings growth," and "dividends." Consequently, an effective presentation will include management's expectations for a company's future performance, the implications for dividends, and an implicit expectation that the stock price will respond positively. Countercyclicality, operating synergies, new technologies, and infusion of management are relevant points to raise. Obviously, the message must be delivered in a manner that does not raise unrealistic expectations.

For the most part, there are two ways to tell the story of the new company to shareholders—face-to-face, and in print. Major shareholders need direct contact with senior management, preferably in one-to-one discussions that emphasize strategy and expectations as well as numbers. It is impossible, however, to provide the same degree of contact to the shareholder population in general. Because annual meetings tend to emphasize form rather than substance, printed communications to most smaller shareholders are the best channels.

The Investment Community

There are many experts who are able to develop careful plans for selling a transaction to the investment community. The most important opinion leaders are key research analysts and major institutional holders. Wall Street is unfortunately subject to a herd instinct, in which a few groups pace public opinion. Consequently, this is where the sales effort should start, even when a convenient visit in connection with postacquisition financing is not contemplated.

Leading securities analysts will write the most accurate reports if they meet with key management to discuss both numbers and strategy, preferably one on one. These contacts need not be very frequent, but they at least should take place shortly after a transaction occurs. Periodic follow-up visits are appropriate. More general public discussions, such as at luncheons sponsored by security analysts in New York and other cities, can spread the news broadly, but rarely generate the long-term quality of support that face-to-face meetings provide.

Large institutional holders, or prospective holders, also merit special attention. The opinion-leading reference institutions, especially those that are cash-positive, repeat investors, deserve face-to-face meetings that have been carefully planned.

Brokerage houses, in particular those that sell large amounts of stock, are another group that deserves special attention, as do key market makers and/or specialists.

Financing Sources

Most chief financial officers, if not their chief executives, are especially concerned about their sources of debt capital. Commercial banks, rating agencies, and, to a lesser degree, insurance companies all need specific attention. In general, the discussion of strategy precedes a detailed analysis of numbers.

The financial institutions' primary concerns revolve around security of principal and coverage of interest and debt service. Avoiding problems rather than maximizing opportunity is key. Consequently, acquiring managements should visit their key lenders with exhaustive tables that analyze cash flow coverage, interest coverage, debt-to-capital ratios, covenant provisions, projected capital expenditures, working capital fluctuations, and expected dividends. The normal attitude of lenders is one of cautious acquiescence, because ongoing business is important. Waivers usually can be negotiated in return for rate or term concessions.

When borrowed capital is used to finance a transaction, discussions with lenders need to occur, confidentially, in advance. When debt funding is not needed, the talks can be scheduled after the transaction is completed. Rating agencies also can be contacted after consummation. Most chief financial officers and investment banks have sample presentations for rating agencies and key lenders.

Customers and Suppliers

Often overlooked are customers and suppliers, who seem to be expected to acquiesce to any transaction. In fact, a few well-chosen comments can alleviate their initial doubts, and ensure that these relationships will contribute to the continuing success of the business.

Customers are concerned that they will continue to receive quality products and service at competitive prices on a timely basis. Marketing officers, down to relatively low levels, should therefore initiate contact with major customers to answer their questions and to tell the new company's story. Many times the acquisition itself provides an opportunity for a very effective sales call.

Suppliers generally are concerned with continuing business on acceptable terms. Without limiting management's ability to achieve cost savings, contact with major suppliers can ensure that production continues unaffected during the period immediately following an acquisition.

TECHNIQUES OF SELLING A TRANSACTION

Who Should Be Used to Sell?

An effective sales process, to reiterate, matches the delivery of the message with the audience. For key employees, key customers, and key shareholders, senior management should be involved, particularly during the initial uncertainty following a transaction. Although each level of management in turn can carry a message to lower levels, selective joint appearances by senior management of both buyer and seller usually will reduce uncertainty. When management of the selling company will be involved in the new entity's management, its presence can be especially comforting.

The Media to Use

Although many managements enjoy reading about themselves and their acquisitions in the national media, relatively few transactions meet the media's criteria for "important" news. If an acquisition is very large, contested, or uniquely interesting, both newspapers and magazines probably will cover it extensively. Otherwise, the first several paragraphs of a press release are all that is likely to appear in *The Wall Street Journal* or *The New York Times*. Local papers will take more interest in transactions involving local companies, and they can be treated accordingly. National business magazines will write detailed follow-up stories about the reasons for an important or unusual transaction. Usually a longer article will require meetings with senior management.

Assigning Proper Importance

Selling a transaction is not particularly difficult, but it frequently receives inadequate attention from many acquirers. A poor "sales" program often is at fault when an acquired company does not perform up to its prior standards in the short term and, in the most disastrous cases, simply falls apart. Financial results decline, management is disappointed and shareholders suffer.

The key points to remember are:

- A proper plan must address the specific concerns of all groups that an acquisition affects, including management of both companies, employees of both companies, shareholders, the financial community, lenders, customers, and suppliers.
- Senior management must be involved, rather than just delegating the "sales" task to the staff.
- Key components of the sales plan must be developed *before* the deal is completed, so that it can be implemented quickly.

Chapter 42

Taking out Takeover Insurance

Charles M. Nathan

Managing Director, Merrill Lynch Capital Markets,
New York, New York

With the emergence in the late 1960s and the early 1970s of the hostile tender offer as a popular acquisition technique, potential target companies developed, with the aid of their legal and financial advisers, a diversified arsenal of defensive strategies. Among these strategies was the adoption of amendments to a company's charter and/or by-laws in order to deter unfriendly takeover bids. Commonly known as "shark repellents," the first generation generally fell into two categories:

- Impeding transfer of the control of the board of directors to a new shareholder
- Creating barriers to a second-step acquisition transaction following a successful hostile tender offer

Although it was never clear that such provisions were effective deterrents to unsolicited takeover bids, particularly 100 percent cash offers, many managements saw little harm in their adoption.

Yet, as such antitakeover charter provisions became more popular, their efficacy and advisability were questioned increasingly on both practical and philosophical grounds. In the 1970s the vast majority of hostile tenders were cash bids for all shares. Thus, provisions that focused on the second step of the acquisition transaction were largely ineffective as deterrents. And perhaps the most common type of antitakeover provision, that intended to delay the exercise of control by a new majority shareholder, was thought not to deter a tender offer at all. Once the offerer had acquired a majority of the target's outstanding shares, the directors, particularly outside directors, would have little reason to continue obviously futile resistance and had many reasons to surrender gracefully or resign.

Of virtually equal importance was that the increasing difficulty of obtaining shareholder approval became a crucial ingredient in management's consideration of whether to even put defensive charter provisions up to a shareholder vote. The defeat of such proposals at the hands of shareholders in several widely publicized instances made most managements increasingly cautious. It became clear that institutional shareholders, in particular, welcomed tender offers at substantial premiums over prevailing market prices, and many institutions adopted formal or informal policies of voting against antitakeover charter amendments. The defeat of antitakeover provisions would bring attention to the fact that the management considered the company a likely takeover prospect and that the shareholders likely would respond favorably to a tender offer. Thus, the risks of defeat no longer appeared worth what were widely regarded as the doubtful benefits of success. By the advent of the 1980s, defensive charter and by-law provisions appeared passé.

However, new acquisition strategies and tactics have become prominent in the 1980s, and shareholders apparently have displayed greater willingness to approve defensive proposals. These circumstances suggest that a reexamination of the merits of antitakeover provisions in corporate charters and by-laws is in order.

The most important change in takeover methods involves the proliferation of open-market purchase programs to establish "toeholds" or "beachheads" in target companies. Also worthy of note is the presence of two-tiered, front-end-loaded acquisitions under which the first step is a partial cash tender offer for approximately 50 percent of the target's stock and the second step is a merger involving the issuance of securities to the remaining shareholders. The securities issued in the merger phase sometimes unintentionally, but more often intentionally, have a market value substantially below the cash tender price. U.S. Steel's famed acquisition of Marathon Oil in 1982 is a prototype of such a two-tiered, front-end-loaded deal. U.S. Steel paid $125 a share in its first-step partial cash tender offer and $100 principal amount of its 12½ percent notes in the second-step merger. The notes were thought to have a market value of about $85 per Marathon share when the transaction was announced.

A final major psychological impetus for revising defensive charter provisions, even if they are not of importance in pragmatic terms for most companies, is the defensive strategy of a counter tender offer, or as the press has dubbed it so colorfully, the "Pac Man" defense.

OPEN-MARKET PURCHASE PROGRAMS AND THEIR RESPONSES

Large open-market purchase programs may serve a variety of goals. The purchaser may intend simply to make a passive investment constituting a substantial minority stake in the target company. That is rarely a reason to adopt defensive charter and by-law provisions. However, a different and more threatening type of minority investment program is intended to serve as a beachhead for the exercise of influence over the target company, a spearhead for a still larger investment, and, ultimately, a tool for control through a minority or bare-majority holding. That type of investment emerged as a common pattern in the 1980s. Implicit in this strategy is the acquisition of control without paying a "control premium" to the target's shareholders. The threat or actual waging of a proxy contest often is used as the lever for achieving such control.

"Greenmail" Situations

An even more common and voracious pattern develops when the sole goal of the minority investment is to gain short-term profit—so-called greenmail. In the common scenario, the new shareholder or shareholder group buys somewhere between 5 percent and 25 percent of a company's shares, and then seeks a quick profit through one of three basic alternatives:

- Persuading or coercing the target to buy back the shares at a premium by threatening a tender offer for majority control (by it or a third party) or a disruptive proxy contest for control
- Actually inducing a tender offer at a substantial premium by a third party, or selling the block to this third party prior to the commencement of such an offer
- Acquiring control of the target through a combination of share ownership and proxy contest in order to force a partial or complete liquidation of the company

The aggressive minority investor often is characterized by its emphasis on short-term results and an unwillingness or inability to stick it out for the long haul. Typically, though not always, the minority investor has smaller resources than a bidder for the entire company and cannot afford (absolutely or relatively) long-term carrying costs. When management resists such a shareholder's effort to stimulate a third-party acquisition of the company or a premium repurchase of its shares, the aggressive shareholder's best (and often only credible) alternative is to wage a proxy fight for control.

Staggererd Boards

Accordingly, charter or by-law provisions that delay seizure of control of the board may be effective deterrents to the very appearance of the aggressive minority shareholder. If the minority investor is seeking quick profits through the strategy outlined above and is choosing from among a number of potential targets, it presumably will stay away from those companies that present greater expenses and risks because of charter provisions that significantly delay the seizure of control. Such defensive charter provisions focus on the major opportunities for obtaining control of a corporate board: at the annual meeting where the directors are regularly elected, at special meetings between annual meetings, or by obtaining shareholder consents in writing.

Only one type of charter provision may actually lessen or eliminate the possibility of a proxy contest to gain control representation on, or control of, a company's board at the annual meeting. That is a classified (or staggered) board of directors. The typical classified board, which is permitted by the corporation law of all but about 10 states, is divided into three classes, with one-third of the board elected each year for three-year terms.

The staggered board serves as a deterrent to a proxy contest because it requires the minority shareholder to wage more than one proxy contest to obtain control of the board (assuming, of course, that the directors in classes not standing for election do not resign or are not removed during their terms in office). By reducing the credibility of the investor's threat to seize control, the staggered-board provision strengthens management's hand in dealing with a potentially disruptive investor.

Certain other charter provisions usually are considered necessary to render the classified board fully effective in delaying seizure of a board. These usually include provisions that require cause for the removal of directors, fix the number of directors to prevent an increase in the size of the board, provide that only the remaining directors may fill vacancies on the board, and mandate a super-majority vote to amend any shark repellent provisions, including creation of the classified board.

Special Meetings

If stockholders are able to call a special meeting, it may not be necessary for a minority shareholder to wait until the annual meeting to wage a proxy contest and attempt to seize control. Instead, at a special meeting called for that purpose at the insurgent's demand, a majority of shareholders could remove directors (assuming that the statute and charter do not require cause for such removal) and elect the minority shareholder's slate to take their place. Alternatively, the insurgent shareholder group might "pack" the board by expanding it and having its slate elected to the new directorships.

The special meeting typically is instigated by an insurgent when it files a formal demand with the target company's board asking for the meeting and setting forth the purposes. The key variable is the share-ownership percentage required to invoke this procedure. However, the availability of special meeting privileges largely is controlled by the corporation, and therefore it can be eliminated or severely constricted. For example, the charter could require a majority, or even a supermajority of shares, to be in favor of the special meeting before it can be scheduled.

Under the corporation law of many states, however, it is not possible to eliminate the right of the insurgent shareholder to call a special meeting or to increase the percentage requirement. Even in these states, it may be possible to prevent a change in board control at a special meeting by other means. The three key defensive charter provisions in this circumstance would be that directors may not be removed without cause, that the size of the board of directors may not be increased, and that only incumbent directors may fill vacancies, no matter how they are created. Moreover, there may be considerable flexibility under a statute with respect to how quickly the special meeting must be called once a demand is received by the corporation.

Written Consents

A small but significant minority of state corporation laws (including Delaware's) authorize a written-consent procedure for shareholder action. These statutes in effect allow stockholders, including insurgents, to by-pass annual and special meetings in pressing for action. Under applicable laws, the desired actions can be approved if the consents that are obtained at least equal the number of shares required to approve the same steps at a conventional stockholders' meeting. However, during the mid-1980s, many companies nullified application of the laws by eliminating written consent intitiatives—usually by requiring that actions needing shareholder votes be considered only at annual or special meetings.

The written-consent procedure and the shareholders' ability to call special meetings provide openings for changes in control between annual meetings. But the written-consent procedure poses special problems, primarily for solicitation and utilization of consents. Thus, there is at least the possibility that whenever the requisite number of consents is filed with the secretary of the corporation, the actions specified in them will be deemed to be in effect. Absent a by-law ban, management's defense against the consents is to try to persuade the shareholders who sided with the insurgents to sign documents revoking their consents, thus forestalling adoption of the desired actions by preventing the insurgents from mustering their written majority. The difficult part of using the management revocation procedure is the fear that the actions sought by the insurgents can become effective at any time that they can present a sufficient number of do-it-yourself unrevoked consents— even though management can move later to procure revocation. Thus, management may be temporarily saddled with procedures it opposes. The evil, in short, is that there is an election contest without a predetermined election day. The insurgent can declare whether and when the balloting ends. Management is at an obvious disadvantage because it may be continually off-balance. A response to the initial quick-strike campaign doesn't end the battle. The management may have to continue fighting in fear that the insurgents can sustain the battle and ultimately win.

The threat of forcing management into an endless solicitation of revocation of consents figured in the 1982 effort of Minneapolis investor Irwin Jacobs to take control of Pabst Brewing Co. through the written-consents tactic. But in litigation before the federal court in Delaware, the judge ruled that Delaware law set a finite period of 60 days for soliciting consents and revocations.

Supermajorities and Fair Price

Other antitakeover provisions also may help deter an aggressive minority investor seeking quick profits, but their effects are less direct and their efficacy more questionable. In particular, measures that are perceived as deterrents to any partial tender offer, such as the supermajority voting and fair-price provisions (discussed later), may weaken the ability of the toehold shareholder to trigger a tender offer. Similarly, a supermajority requirement for other structural transactions, such as a liquidation or sale of substantially all the corporation's assets, may make other minority-shareholder strategies less feasible. The potential investor, recognizing these possible barriers to short-term profit, should, at least in theory, eschew the target with such defensive charter provisions in favor of more vulnerable game.

PARTIAL TENDER OFFERS

Unlike the 1970s, which were characterized by the cash tender offer for any and all shares, the prevailing pattern of tender offers in the 1980s has involved partial cash offers for 40 to 60 percent of the target's outstanding shares, generally followed by a second-step merger. These bids are frequently "two-tier" tender offers in which the first-step cash tender offer price exceeds (often by a substantial amount) the value of the equity or the debt securities usually offered in the "back-end" or second-step merger.

It has long been recognized that defensive charter provisions intended to delay seizure of board control will not deter a bid for all the target's shares. Such provisions, moreover, generally are not effective deterrents to a partial bidder. Once a majority of shares has been acquired, or even a substantial minority, such as 40 percent, the incumbent board cannot win a proxy contest against the bidder; and as a practical matter, the battle will be over. Because the determined partial bidder, like a determined 100 percent bidder, will prevail in the end, it is unlikely (as experience repeatedly has confirmed) that holdover directors will stay on and fight for pyrrhic victories along the way. (On the other hand, the existence of the staggered board may encourage some directors to remain after the tender offer and, in fact, bargain on behalf of unaffiliated shareholders for a better deal in the second-step merger.) For this reason, the defensive charter provisions most likely to be effective deterrents against partial bids will be the ones that address directly the distinctive aspect of a partial offer, namely, the need for a second-step "freeze-out" merger to achieve a 100 percent acquisition. Such provisions may affect the ability of the successful hostile offerer to complete the second step by imposing voting barriers, by restricting the terms on which the second-step merger may be made, or both.

Supermajority Voting

The voting barrier generally takes the form of a supermajority voting requirement for certain transactions with so-called interested persons, typically defined to include successful hostile tender offerers, or others who have acquired a minority interest in excess of 5 to 10 percent without prior board approval. Although there is great variation in the mechanics of such provisions, they usually require the approval of 75 to 95 percent of the corporation's shareholders for a second-step merger or similar acquisition transaction with such an "interested person." An alternative and more stringent formulation requires a majority or supermajority vote of the unaffiliated public shareholders, no matter how great a percentage of the outstanding shares is held by the "interested" party.

The deterring value of a supermajority voting provision, standing alone, is open to some question. Unless there is a sufficiently large block of target stock in insider or other friendly hands that can be relied upon not to tender and not to vote in favor of a second-step merger, it is unlikely that a supermajority requirement will deter a 100 percent offer. It may not deter a partial tender offer either, although it may encourage a potential hostile bidder to negotiate first with the target. In general, a successful bidder will receive the requisite vote on the second-step merger, particularly from institutions and arbitrageurs, as long as the merger price exceeds the price that the stock likely would command in the market if no merger proposal existed. For these reasons, a supermajority voting provision seems at least as likely to affect the consideration offered in the second-step merger as to deter a hostile offer.

Fair-Price Requirements

So-called fair-price charter amendments more directly affect the consideration to be paid in the second-step merger. They require that the second-step price equal, or exceed by some percentage, the price paid in the tender offer or other initial purchases of the target's stock. Typically, however, transactions approved by a majority of the target's continuing directors are excepted from the fair-price requirement. A "continuing director" typically is defined as a member of the board of directors who is unaffiliated with the "interested person" and who became a member of the board prior to the time that the "interested person" became an "interested person." In the case of the hostile tender offer, this generally will encompass those directors who were in office prior to the purchase of shares pursuant to the tender offer.

In many instances, the fair-price provision also is drafted as an exception to the supermajority voting requirement, so that when a "fair" price is paid, the requirement for a supermajority vote is suspended.

It is difficult to say what effect, if any, fair-price provisions have on the calculus of potential partial bidders. The typical provision would, in most tender offer contexts, require only that the fair market value of the consideration paid in the second-step merger equal the cash price of the front-end tender offer. However, the practical reality is that a potential hostile offerer should be concerned with its ability to compete with other potential bidders, particularly "white knights." While all hostile bidders would be on the same footing in terms of pricing dynamics under a fair-price charter provision, a friendly bidder approved by the "continuing directors" would enjoy a possible advantage because it would be exempted from the fair-price provision. Thus the white knight could proceed with a front-end-loaded, two-tier offer free of charter constraints, whereas a hostile bidder could not plan on this advantage.

Assume, for example, that a hostile bidder makes a partial offer of $40 a share for a target company whose charter requires either board approval or a fair price for the back end. The bidder plans to offer securities valued at $40 a share for the back end as well. But if the target is willing to accept the same overall price from a white knight, the friendly bidder can structure the offer to pay $50 a share in cash up front and $30 a share in the back end—as long as the directors approve. Even though the overall price of both bidders is the same, the white knight would have a protected edge, because stockholders can be expected to prefer the $50-a-share front-end price.

THE PAC MAN

The counter-tender offer, or "Pac Man," was employed in at least five well-publicized takeover efforts in the early 1980s. These include the bitter 1982 battle between Bendix and Martin Marietta, which ended with Allied Corp.'s acquisition of Bendix and Martin Marietta's repurchase of its shares that had been tendered to Bendix. At the other extreme was the friendly 1982 deal involving joint investments by Pabst Brewing and Olympia Brewing in each other. Others include:

- American General Corp. and NLT Corp., which ended with American General's acquisition of NLT the following year
- Cities Service and Mesa Petroleum, which helped pave the way for the acquisition of Cities Service by Occidental Petroleum in 1982
- Coastal Corp. and Houston Natural Gas, a bitter 1984 contest that ended with the two companies buying back each other's interests and Coastal later adopting antitakeover provisions

Although the particular structure of the counter tender has been as varied as it has been bizarre in these cases, the basic strategy is simple. The target, in response to an actual or threatened tender offer, retaliates by initiating a tender offer for the original or potential offerer. In some cases this may be enough to cause the offerer to withdraw its offer or reach some compromise. However, when both companies go forward, differences in the timing or their respective abilities to exercise control of the other may determine which company comes out on top. Because of idiosyncracies of corporate structure and corporate law, this may depend not on which company is able to purchase shares of the other first, but rather on their relative abilities to be the first to seize control of the other's board.

Although the utility of the counter-tender offer as a defensive tactic is limited and will be available only in a few situations, no company can be sure that it might not wish to use the counter-tender in the future or, perhaps worse, that it might not be itself the subject of a Pac Man attack if it makes a bid. Thus, notwithstanding the statistical improbability of ever actually needing protection in the form of charter and by-law provisions, many companies will find such provisions worth considering. Mesa Petroleum, for example, after becoming embroiled in a counter-tender scenario with Cities Service in 1982, adopted additional antitakeover provisions before commencing its tender offer for General American Oil the following year. Mesa's panoply of defensive charter provisions may have played some role in General American's decision not to launch a counter-tender offer. General American, however, found a white knight buyer in Phillips Petroleum.

ADOPTING ANTITAKEOVER PROVISIONS

In a rare case, the corporate law of a company's state of incorporation and the corporation's charter may enable a board to enact significant antitakeover provisions as by-laws without obtaining shareholder approval. As a general rule, however, it will be necessary and, even if not necessary, advisable, to submit such provisions for shareholder approval.

If a company determines that antitakeover provisions are desirable, it must carefully evaluate the likelihood of shareholder approval. In this respect, Securities and Exchange Commission (SEC) requirements regarding proxy statement disclosure merit particular attention. Since 1978, the SEC has required that defensive charter proposals be accorded prominence in the proxy statement, and that the proxy statement emphasize both their purpose of deterring acquisition proposals and that these steps may have disadvantages for the corporation's shareholders. Any other actions taken by the corporation that also could be characterized as defensive also must be disclosed. Moreover, management also should try to ascertain whether the corporation's institutional holders have voting policies regarding defensive charter proposals.

Unequal Voting Common Stock

Probably the most effective of all antitakeover weapons is the structuring of the company's stock to concentrate voting power in the hands of relatively few stockholders. This may be done by creating two or more classes of voting stock with unequal voting privileges—such as one vote per share for one class and 10 votes per share for another—or depriving a particular class of any voting rights at all. This is an old feature of corporate equity capitalization, but it emerged as a significant factor in the antitakeover area during the mid-1980s when several companies got stockholder approval to erect new classes of supervoting or nonvoting stock strictly for defensive purposes. A variation in the takeover arena is to have the new nonvoting or supervoting stock spring to life only if there is a hostile bid for the company. Among companies that installed various types of unequal voting classes were Hershey Foods, General Cinema, Dow Jones, Kelly Service, and Coastal Corp.

Despite its effectiveness, many companies would consider unequal voting stock only as a last resort. Although most of those proposing the structure have sweetened it by distributing the new stock to all shareholders or permitting conversions into the new shares, there may be a potential problem in getting stockholder approval. Companies with the best chances of instituting multiple classes already enjoy large insider interests that have enough power to swing the vote on their own. In addition, multiple classes of common tend to turn off institutional investors, whose influence may be diluted by unequal voting.

Companies with more than one class of common stock traditionally have been barred from listing on the New York Stock Exchange, but the Big Board approved a proposal to change its rules. Firms such as Hershey, Dow Jones, and General Cinema were allowed to retain Big Board listings until a decision was made.

Another variation that surfaced with some regularity in the mid-1980s was the pegging of a common share's voting power to the length of time the holder had owned it. For example, a new investor would have only one vote per share, but if he or she held it for 48 months, the voting power would expand to four votes per share.

WEIGHING THE TRADE-OFFS

Antitakeover charter provisions have waxed and waned in popularity over the past decade and a half. New acquisition strategies and, in particular, the emerging importance of aggressive minority investment through open market purchase programs, whether as a prelude to greenmail or another destabilizing action, suggest that the time may be right for reconsideration of the desirability of proposing such provisions.

In general, it is hardly certain that such provisions will deter a strong bid for the acquisition of the entire equity interest in a company, whether such an acquisition is made through an any-or-all cash offer or a partial offer followed by a second-step merger. However, certain provisions may be effective deterrents to open-market purchase programs, particularly if the strategy of the investor is to realize profit through a relatively speedy disposition of its block.

Chapter 43

Defensive Tactics

Martin Sikora

Editor, Mergers & Acquisitions, Philadelphia, Pennsylvania

In addition to the corporate charter and by-law changes, recruitment of a "white knight" merger partner, and litigation that have been described in other chapters of *The Mergers and Acquisitions Handbook*, target companies have utilized a number of other defensive strategies and techniques to fend off unsolicited takeover bids. The goals range from making the target company unattractive to the suitor to making a hostile offer extremely difficult to accomplish.

One of the best-known techniques for dampening the ardor of an unwanted bidder is the "crown jewel" strategy. The target company sells off its most prized operation—its "crown jewel"—to diminish its value or worth. The crown jewel may be the most profitable or the fastest-growing arm of the target and often is the asset most coveted by the bidder. A variation of the crown jewel strategy is the "scorched earth" approach. Usually, "scorched earth" involves more radical surgery than "crown jewel." The target sells not only the crown jewel but other properties as well, in the most extreme cases substantially all of the operating assets. The remaining assets are not worth buying after the sell-offs have been completed.

Companies that don't want to tamper with their operations can supplement their capital structures with "poison pills"—securities designed to act as impediments to raiders. Terms and features that make the poison pill hard to swallow usually are prescribed by the target's directors. Most charters merely set quantitative limits on the amount of common and preferred shares that may be issued and are silent as to their terms and features. They are known as "blank check" shares. Thus, the directors are free to fill in the "blanks" by dressing them up with various conditions, as long as the board doesn't violate the quantitative ceilings.

Poison pills have been issued in several forms. In some cases, supervoting common and preferred shares have been issued, such as shares that may carry 10 votes each in contrast to a single vote for a regular common share. A variation involves a triggering device that is activated when certain conditions are present. For example, a board will distribute rights to purchase additional shares that become effective if a single party acquires, say, 20 percent of the company's stock, or makes a tender offer for, say, 30 percent of the shares. Many of the pills contain a "flipover" provision that is activated if the company is acquired. In that case, the target company shareholder can buy two shares of the acquirer for the then-prevailing price of one share. An innovative form of the flipover was proposed by Lenox, Inc., before it was acquired by Brown-Forman, Inc., in 1983. This was preferred stock that was convertible directly into shares of the acquirer.

"Flip-in" pills increase the number of shares a stockholder may purchase as the unwanted acquirer gets beyond the threshold level, also known as "kick-in" points. A "flip-out" permits stockholders to buy shares in subsidiaries when kicked in.

The capital structure can be used in other ways as a source of defensive weaponry. Short of seeking a white knight for an outright merger, the target can sell a substantial minority interest to a presumably friendly third party—a "white squire"—that would side with incumbent management. The third party may be another company, an outside individual or institution, or an employee stock ownership plan (ESOP). The target also can sell stock to its employee pension and benefit funds, although there are strict tests prescribed by federal statutes and rules concerning the propriety of pension and benefit fund investments.

Sale of stock in a defensive situation also allows many variations. For example, the target can sell a third party a special block of common or preferred shares that would either be superior in voting rights to regular common or would have to vote as a separate class in approving a merger.

If the company launches a stock repurchase program, it is engaging in a "self-tender." The aim is to keep large portions of publicly held shares away from the raider. If the raider's offer is conditioned on receiving a specified number or proportion of common shares, a successful self-tender could keep the bidder from obtaining its desired amount.

Other corporate moves that have been employed to dim the appeal of a target company include:

- Acquiring another company that could create an antitrust or regulatory conflict with the bidder
- Purchasing a poorly performing or money-losing company
- Sharply increasing debt
- Launching an expensive capital investment program
- Recapitalizing the company to raise shareholder value

Part 9

M&A Experiences in Three Industries

Chapter 44

High Technology: Special Challenges to Buyers

Donald C. Trauscht

Vice President, Borg-Warner Corp., Chicago, Illinois

High technology connotes a rather hybrid image to business, investors, and the public at large. Many people believe that they know what high technology is all about, but it frequently becomes a catch-phrase for things beyond normal understanding. High technology is actually an umbrella classification for a heterogenous family of industries and disciplines, a fragmentation which suggests that there are special guidelines for corporate acquirers who want to buy into the growth potential and technological innovation promised by the field. Some segments actually are closer to low- or medium-grade technologies and may be susceptible to orthodox managerial techniques. But others are so sophisticated that they require unique approaches to acquiring, integrating, and operating high-tech businesses.

The semiconductor industry, by way of illustration, symbolizes this diversity. Semiconductors usually are regarded as a high-tech industry, but the term semiconductors covers some very mundane products, such as semiconductors for digital watches, as well as some very exotic products, such as CMOS VLSI (composite metal oxide silicon very large scale integrated circuits) semiconductors used in microcomputers. CMOS VLSI circuits, which may contain as many as a million transistors per chip, have themselves given rise to still other high-technology industries, including a variety of computers, because great amounts of memory, logic, and arithmetic capabilities can be stored on a single chip at lower cost and with greater benefits than predecessor chips. These new end products include personal computers and programmable computers, as well as computers equipped with software to fit the general classifications of data-based systems, networks, and artificial intelligence.

Also at the "high" end of high-tech are such emerging industries as robotics, factory automation, genetic engineering, telecommunications, bioelectronics, and computer-assisted design and manufacturing (CAD/CAM). Companies at the so-called leading edge are expensive to acquire, difficult to evaluate, and, if personnel are not handled properly, troublesome to operate.

ADVANTAGES OF OWNING A HIGH-TECH BUSINESS

There are probably more reasons to acquire a high-tech business than businesses in more mundane or lower-technology areas. The principal motivation for owning a high-tech company is that it offers better growth and profit opportunities than a buyer's existing business. For example, the automotive industry in the United States generally grows at a rate of 2 to 3 percent per year. But solid state sensors, which are used in automobiles, tend to show a 20 percent annual growth rate. Hence, an investor in solid state sensors is able to get greater capital turnover, greater multiplication of the investment, and, because the industry is not as competitive as automobiles, a better profit margin.

Converting these obvious advantages to growth and value is, however, no simple task for the corporate acquirer. Because of their attributes, high-tech businesses sell at high price/earnings ratios, and the buyer who approaches the acquisition with the wrong attitude runs the risk of losing a substantial investment.

Most buyers used to less sophisticated businesses are not mentally prepared to deal with rapidly changing technology, continuing significant investment in research, and what they may view as the artistic "whims" of high-tech managers. Many buyers wind up treating high-tech managers the same way they treat the managers of their existing businesses, even though promises and vows are made to handle the new people differently. Because most buyers don't understand the high-tech business, it becomes very difficult for them to feed the business in terms of both investment and psychic values to the managers. Without proper understanding, or a dedication to understanding the high-tech businesses, investments that start with great promise ultimately can turn into investment disasters.

MANAGEMENT IS THE KEY TO SUCCESS

The mobility of high-tech personnel is great, and one way to spark a desertion of key people is to create a contentious relationship between the parent and its high-tech acquisition. It is essential for the parent to foster a creative environment and provide incentives to match the motivational factors of high-tech people. One company that acquired a producer of advanced semiconductors found out the hard way how it could be damaged by trying to impose its will on high-tech people. The parent instructed the high-tech subsidiary to use a new mainframe computer that it manufactured, a computer that the scientific personnel knew was not right for their work. Viewing the order as a portent of continual dictation by the parent and a dismal future for their unit, most of the scientific people left to form companies of their own. The subsidiary's management believed that their unit would die a slow death under the heavy hand of a parent that did not understand the intricacies of the business.

Another company that learned a grim lesson from management maltreatment was the large Midwestern controls producer that acquired a smaller West Coast semiconductor company and immediately began to spend money for plant expansion of its new unit. However, the controls company, insisting that its own people be in charge of the semiconductor business, moved aside the former owner and installed an executive who had run a valve factory. The new manager began to dictate decisions to the high-tech team, some of which were incorrect. As a result, the scientific team that had built the semiconductor company quit. The parent was forced not only to shut down the semiconductor operation, but to liquidate it at a cost estimated by some industry observers to be $250 million.

By contrast, a large diversified Midwestern company acquired a security business specializing in electronics and took a completely different tack. The parent retained the manager of the electronic security company and allowed him to operate it independently. A board of directors, consisting of executives of the parent, was set up to provide overview and liaison. The electronics security subsidiary has grown sixfold since the acquisition.

These widely divergent results stem from the way the new owners of the business treated the acquired personnel.

The Schlumberger Ltd. acquisition of Fairchild Semiconductor Co. in 1979 was another example of a high-tech acquisition that went poorly because of management misunderstanding. Executives of the parent company, which is headquartered overseas, attempted to treat Fairchild's Silicon Valley managers in the same manner as they treated their employees abroad, thereby ignoring the entrepreneurial instincts and special compensation schemes peculiar to the Northern California high-tech belt. Many of the Fairchild managers left to join other companies, and the performance of the semiconductor business deteriorated. Emerson Electric Co. had a far better experience when it acquired Rosemount Engineering, a solid state sensor company, in 1976. Emerson challenged the intellectual as well as management abilities of Rosemount managers and built the largest and most successful solid state sensor company in the United States. Emerson succeeded where Schlumberger failed because its executives understood that the motivational factors of the high-tech managers included more than just money and special compensation schemes.

UNIQUE ELEMENTS OF
HIGH-TECHNOLOGY BUSINESS

What differentiates high-technology industries from more conventional industries embraced by the buzz word, "Smokestack America?" The two industrial segments do not operate in totally separate spheres. Innovations generated by high technology may have dramatic impact on "smokestack" industries such as steel, automobiles, furniture, and home construction by furnishing the robots, programmable computers, networks, and advanced materials that make them more efficient. Yet there are vast differences. Unlike the smokestack industries, for example, high technology initially may require little capital investment. But large sums may be needed after start-up to finance a rapid rate of new product development and keep the company in step with exotic technologies that generate state-of-the-art developments with regularity.

Mobility of Personnel

Because high technology, generally speaking, is synonymous with brain power, the biggest difference is people. In contrast to smokestack industry personnel, people in high technology tend to be loyal not to individual companies, but to the industry in general. Hence, there is a great deal of movement from one concern to another. Silicon Valley, the high-tech pocket between San Francisco and San Jose in northern California, exemplifies this mobility. The region is home to many computer and semiconductor companies, including Fairchild Semiconductor, the company that had the original patents on the Planar transistor but proved such a headache for Schlumberger. The departures related to Schlumberger's acquisition were not unique. Fairchild has spawned or given rise to more than 100 new companies launched by people who left Fairchild to start their own businesses with their own ideas.

Why would people leave secure positions with a stable company to start their own businesses? The easy answers are to make money, build an estate, or reap capital gains. But monetary considerations only scratch the surface. High-tech scientists, like artists of other eras, want to express themselves in terms of their ideas. Indeed, they want to build something like a business, but most of all, they feel a need to exploit their talents and be recognized.

Many of these new-breed managers succumb to peer pressure. They see the successes of their former colleagues who struck out on their own, and they gain the courage to follow suit. High-tech industries tend to be concentrated in specific geographic areas such as Silicon Valley or Boston, rather than more broadly distributed throughout the United States, because of this peer influence.

Older high-tech companies also have difficulties taking care of the people aspects and the financial considerations that lead high-tech scientists to leave their employers and begin their own businesses. Some companies, such as Minnesota Mining & Manufacturing Co., Advanced Micro Devices, Inc., and Hewlett-Packard Co., have taken major steps to retain people by creating both personal and financial outlets for the more creative high-tech scientists. They have developed environments that not only encourage creativity but allow entrepreneurially minded technical people to establish their own businesses within the corporations and reap financial awards based on their successes. Under the 3M program, a new product idea, once it is beyond a certain point of development, is established as a new business and the person who spearheaded the initial work is assigned to manage the business, with responsibility for commercializing the opportunities. Such a program encourages other technical employees of the company to do likewise. Success feeds on success.

EVALUATING THE HIGH-TECH TARGET

A proper evaluation at the outset of a deal can make the difference between the success and failure of a high-tech acquisition. At this point, it is most imperative that the buyer discern the unique qualities of high tech as a business. As already noted, the purchaser is acquiring primarily brain power rather than brick and mortar. Thus, the evaluation should begin by focusing on the incentives, motives, personal drives, and character of the people being acquired, and then proceed to the unusual approaches that may be needed to retain and motivate this brain power.

Technology, Products, and Markets

A second phase of the evaluation should center on the technology, products, and markets of the high-tech business, areas that also may present special considerations for the buyer steeped in single-focus managerial techniques. Usually it is not one technology that needs to be evaluated, but a series of competing approaches for the same broad technology. For example, when the large-scale integrated (LSI) circuit industry began, there were several competing approaches to develop the circuit. In time, each of these approaches developed its own area of specialty. But unless a buyer carefully and properly evaluated the prospects and potential for each of these specific approaches, it could easily have made an incorrect decision on which way to go. If a company produced semiconductors for applications in the computer market that demanded lower cost and more bits of information, and its technology was unable to reduce costs and add storage capacity, an acquirer would have bought the wrong business.

Manufacturing and Processing

Although the premiums may be on people and technological advancement, the buyer cannot overlook the bread-and-butter aspects of high tech, notably the manufacturing and processing systems and facilities. No matter how advanced the product, its profit potential can be blunted if it cannot be made efficiently and at reasonable cost, especially in view of the intense competition that faces many products and technologies. The semiconductor industry, for example, requires a remarkable blend of processing technologies, including nuclear physics, chemical processing, vapor deposit metallurgy, and electronics, each of which must be as precise as, say, a high-tolerance metal cutting operation. Without a high level of manufacturing know-how, the best laboratory technology in the world cannot produce profits.

Growth Potential of People

Many high-tech companies are in their embryonic or developmental stages. Hence, decisions must be made as to whether incumbent personnel are capable of managing the business, and whether individual department heads can carry out successfully such important functions as marketing, accounting, and cost control as the company grows. The judgments in high tech are much different from those in a more mature business with a demonstrated track record. A high-tech business manager, for example, must make new product decisions in an industry that has rapid product turnover. A low-tech business manager is more concerned about cost reduction and normally enjoys much longer periods for new product turnover. In electronic instrumentation, a product life cycle might be two years or less. In specialty chemicals, by contrast, a product life cycle might be five or six years. The longer the product life cycle, the more time there is for market research. Often the business manager in electronic instrumentation simply does not have enough time for market research reports to be compiled and analyzed, and must rely on judgment to make decisions that he hopes will keep the company competitive.

Past the Start-up Stage

A situation that is almost unique to high technology is that many companies have been started with the aid of venture capitalists whose primary objectives are to provide seed money, help in a second or third round of financing, and then reap quick pay-offs by taking the company public or selling it out. Once the venture capitalists and their allies in management have reaped the harvest, the company is no longer a start-up situation, yet it is often ripe for an acquisition. At this point, a buyer finds that it must apply a different set of motivating factors to retain the management team than if the business had been acquired as a start-up. The managers already have achieved success and experience in running a growth business with certain techniques, and may not take kindly to a new parent's decision to impose its own controls and procedures on the high-tech unit. When the business has "won its spurs," the issue of dictating to a high-tech management is most sensitive, and the buyer must take the most care to encourage technical innovation and preclude a mass desertion.

Obtaining Outside Advice

Because of these special concerns, it would be wise for the buyer not to handle the total evaluation process by itself, but to retain an outside consultant to help. There is a problem in finding someone with the proper expertise and objectivity to help weigh such matters as alternative approaches to technology, manufacturing, processing, and people know-how. Most experts in technology follow one school of thought rather than a diversity of approaches, and may have predetermined biases even before looking at the facts involved in a specific high-tech target.

PRICES FOR HIGH-TECH BUSINESSES

Prices paid for high-technology companies tend to be very high. The risks also are very great, because failures or drop-outs are numerous. The personal computer industry of the early 1980s was a prime example of a high-tech industry with an astronomical casualty rate.

Nevertheless, if one is successful in selecting the right company to acquire, the rewards are significant. Conventional financial analysis programs, such as the present value method of cash flow, normally are not applicable in placing value on a high-technology company. Such approaches do not work because many high-technology companies tend to be capital-intensive in their growth phase, when they are cash users rather than cash providers. In practice, most buyers tend to set their prices in line with the public market's price/earnings ratios, high though they may be, because the multiples supposedly reflect future growth and earnings potential.

NEW STYLE OF BUSINESS FUNDAMENTALS

The buyer of a high-tech operation must cope with business fundamentals that may be entirely unfamiliar to executives of orthodox businesses. Research and development expenses are heavy—running to as high as 20 percent of the sales dollar compared with only about 5 percent for the typical mature business. But the financial ramifications of R&D reach far beyond initial funding and into such areas as new product introductions and capital investment. R&D is very tightly related to new product introductions in high tech, whereas the pipeline between the laboratory and the marketplace may be longer in the smokestack-type business. The result is that capital investment, although usually not as great as in standard businesses, may have to be allocated and timed more deftly. Capital spending may have to be allocated almost simultaneously to the laboratory and production floor, as both R&D and the manufacturing processes advance almost in lock-step. Given the shorter life cycle of high-tech products, these investments usually must be made more frequently than in mature businesses. And whereas smokestack industries can tolerate some length of time before booking pure returns, investments in high technology, given the risks and the short life cycles involved, require relatively short payback periods. Thus, the technical people's desire for as free a rein as possible notwithstanding, some judicious controls may be desirable to assure that the work in the laboratories is centered on economically feasible projects.

Heavy Cash Commitments

The buyer of a high-tech company in a rapid-growth area should not expect to take cash out of the business. Rather, the buyer should be prepared to invest in the business in order to maintain market share position and fuel growth. Whether the high-technology firm has put itself up for sale or is "discovered" by the buyer's search efforts, it's a good bet that it will need considerable financial support from the parent. R&D eats cash, and even some of the most successful high-tech operations, with high profit margins, lack the capital to fund their own continued growth. Even when capital investment requirements are not great, the buyer needs to have pockets of considerable depth to fund other expensive projects.

When Management Should Be Changed

Nevertheless, the buyer should expect a well-managed high-tech company to maintain its profit margins and its return on investment, and, with the right blending of technology, personnel, and growth opportunities, can earn a respectable return rather quickly. But the trade-off between financial goals and continuity of a creative environment can require the buyer to walk a managerial tightrope. Many high-tech managers were basically technical people who had enough managerial ability to start their companies and grow them to modest size before selling to larger organizations. The sale frequently coincides with a critical point in the evolution of the high-tech company when size requires a shift from an entrepreneurial to a professional management style. The adjustment can be difficult for both buyer and seller and requires considerable give on both sides if the acquisition is to succeed. The deal is in trouble if the high-tech manager cannot adapt in some degree to the new management style or the buyer is either too forceful or doesn't make a timely managerial change.

Creative Compensation Plans

Thoughtful and adequate compensation arrangements can help ease the adjustment of the high-tech manager, and several creative methods are available. One approach is to divide the equity capital of the acquired high-tech subsidiary into preferred and common stock. Preferred stock, which controls the company, is held by the parent, whereas the common stock is granted to management personnel on an earn-out or contingency basis. This allows the management team to earn capital gains on stock that is acquired at relatively low prices. If certain objectives are achieved, they can sell this stock at relatively high prices. In such arrangements, the common is awarded and subsequently cashed in by the management team over a five- to eight-year span. This structure provides time for the acquiring company to understand what it has bought, permits the business to be professionalized as it gets larger, and assures that the loss of any key people will not severely impair the functioning of the business. Normally, there is a "window" of time during which the common stockholders can sell their stock in a public offering. However, the acquiring company, which keeps control through the preemptive position of the preferred, usually has the option of cashing out the management team by buying the common stock.

CONVERTING GROWTH TO VALUE

The object of any acquisition is to create value for shareholders that a buyer would not be able to generate if it stuck to its existing businesses. If handled properly, high-tech acquisitions can be exceptional contributors to that goal. A mature business, with excess cash flow and the right attitude toward its new subsidiaries, can tap exceptional growth opportunities by playing the high-tech field.

Nevertheless, some companies without high-tech experience are forced in today's business environment to invest in high-tech areas simply to protect their existing businesses. At times this is rationalized on the basis of build-versus-buy decisions. Standard businesses are using increased numbers of high-tech products, and often it is cheaper to own a business that makes high-tech products than it is to purchase these products from the outside. The acquisition decision could be foolhardy if the high-tech business is not managed properly. The potential acquirer should very carefully ask itself whether it is equal to the challenge of a different business that employs different people, makes different products, and serves different markets. The answer will help determine if high tech is an appropriate territory to search for acquisitions.

Chapter 45

Retailing: Range of Acquisition Choices

Gilbert W. Harrison

Chairman, Financo, Inc., Philadelphia, Pennsylvania,
and Managing Director, Shearson Lehman Brothers,
New York, New York

Sheer magnitude makes retailing fertile ground for acquisitions. Nearly half the companies operating in the United States are retailers, and in 1985, they rang up combined sales of nearly $1.4 trillion, up 385 percent from the 1965 level of $285 billion—a whopping increase even with the high inflation rates of the late 1970s. Many retailers indeed have incorporated acquisitions into their growth strategies to meet newly emerging conditions and consumer demands, while older and smaller retailers, unable to keep pace, have decided to sell out.

Yet, aggressive buyers of retail businesses have been rare, and acquisitive companies within the retail ranks never have been plentiful. Unlike other industries, buyers of retail firms usually are established in some segment of retailing, or at least sufficiently cognizant of the industry's complexities to risk entrance. Even retailers with superior returns on sales and equity and strong cash flow have been bypassed by "merger booms." This shortage of buyers, however, has accentuated a surplus of sellers. Either by choice or by necessity, many retailers—particularly those with values of between $5 million and $75 million—traditionally have sought to become parts of larger operations.

The combination of reluctant buyers and eager sellers has, however, generated considerable acquisition activity. In 1985, retailing was one of the most active industries for mergers and acquisitions, with 136 completed deals compared with 115 in 1984, 73 in 1983, and 83 in 1982, according to the Mergers & Acquisitions Data Base.

SELLER PRESSURES AND OPPORTUNITIES

There are several reasons for the intensified buy–sell signals in the retail field in the 1980s. On the seller's side there was the slackening of consumer spending traceable to the 1981–1982 recession. In addition, there has been pressure on smaller retailers from a rise in competition, declining sales for independents, expansion of major chains, inroads of off-price retailers, the surplus cash generation of big retail companies, a slowdown in the construction of shopping centers, heavier markdowns, and the wishes of private or family-controlled public retailers to sell their businesses for a variety of personal reasons, including a desire to cash in on years of work.

But the biggest reason for selling a smaller or a growing retail business is that it lacks the depth of professional management and the additional capital needed to expand and compete. These retailers lack either the technical ability or the motivation required to build a large company. They have problems supplying expertise in real estate, marketing, merchandising, and other areas. Merging with a larger retailer, especially one that is cash-rich, may be the best way to solve their problems.

On the buyer's side, corporations with good cash positions or the willingness to use capital stock are seeing new opportunities to make acquisitions at fair prices. Real estate value is a common impetus; buying versus building, at a saving of time and money, is the primary motive behind most retail acquisition programs. Furthermore, the stock market has been treating retailers' shares more favorably through increased values and higher price/earnings multiples. The market was especially receptive to some specialty retailers that adjusted their companies' directions to meet the challenges of the 1980s through aggressive approaches to business, including expansion into areas such as the off-price field.

CATEGORIES OF ACQUIRERS

Six basic kinds of retail acquirers have emerged in the 1980s.

Conglomerate Buyers

Conglomerate retail buyers are comparatively rare, largely because they do not know the field. But conglomerates that have entered the retail field have tended to expand their initial interests. For example, General Mills, Inc., acquired the Wild West Chain of stores in May 1981, after previously buying Talbots, Inc., Eddie Bauer, Inc., Lee Wards Creative Crafts, and Wallpapers to Go. Similarly, INTERCO, Inc., originally a shoe manufacturer, expanded vertically into retailing, initially by purchasing footwear chains. INTERCO moved into general retail merchandising in 1964 with the acquisition of a junior department store chain located in the Midwest, and subsequently added other chains so that by the fiscal year ended February 28, 1983, general retail sales represented approximately 26.7 percent of the total sales of $2.6 billion. Quaker Oats Co. entered retailing through the acquisition of Brookstone Co., Inc., in 1980 and added Joseph A. Bank Clothiers, Inc., in 1981, and Eyelab in 1983.

Diversified Retail Buyers

Diversified retailers operate more than one retailing business. These include department store companies, which sell a wide variety of merchandise through large units, and specialty chains, which limit their stock to certain types of specialty goods and appeal to their customers on the basis of fashion or price. Most diversified retail buyers acquire companies that will be operated as separate entities. An apparel retailer may buy a footwear chain, or a department store chain may buy another department store company that will be run as a separate entity in a different market.

Diversified retailers have been major buyers in the 1980s. United States Shoe Corp., one of the most active acquirers, was founded as a footwear manufacturer in 1931. The company expanded vertically into shoe retailing in 1963 and became a diversified retailer through the 1970 acquisition of Casual Corner Co., a retailer of medium-priced fashions for young women. After years of inactivity, the company resumed its buying in 1981 and moved into off-price retailing with the acquisition of Sportique, Inc., which operates T. H. Mandy Stores. Subsequently, U.S. Shoe added Ups'N Downs, men's and women's apparel; United Linco, off-price linens; Little Folks Stores, children's apparel; and Winterbrook, mail order apparel, in 1982; and Petite Sophisticate, Inc., women's apparel, in 1983.

Melville Corp. is considered by many authorities to be the only true diversified "pure" specialty retailing chain, and is the most profitable, based on 1985 return on sales (4.6 percent) and return on average equity (20 percent). Founded in 1914 as a shoe wholesaler and retailer, it expanded vertically into shoe manufacturing in 1922. Thanks to acquisitions that began in 1969, the company's retail activities also include apparel, health and beauty aids, and toys and games. Melville bought a small women's apparel chain in 1969 that through subsequent expansion numbered more than 1,000 stores by 1984. In that same year, it entered health and beauty aids with the acquisition of the CVS chain. The Marshalls, Inc., off-price chain was added in 1976, Kay-Bee Toy & Hobby Shops in 1981, and Wilson's House of Suede, Inc., in 1982, whereas two 1983 deals augmented previous acquisitions—E. W. Kalkin, Inc., operator of the Linen'N Things off-price chain, and the Toy World division of Wickes Cos.

But "pure" single-line specialty chains also are using acquisitions to diversify. The Limited, Inc., best known for its acquistions of Lane Bryant, Inc., and Lerner Stores in 1985, and its run at the giant Carter Hawley Hale Cahin in 1984, also acquired Victoria's Secret, Inc., a lingerie chain, and Roamans, Inc., which is in the same market as Lane Bryant. Although these acquisitions played a major part in expanding The Limited to more than a thousand stores, they suggest how a diversification strategy has its risks. The Limited has had to work hard to reorganize Lane Bryant and widen its profit margins, and the postacquisition company found itself in need of an experienced in-depth management team capable of running a billion-dollar operation.

The experiences of two diversification-minded drug chains also point to the pitfalls that may be encountered in branching out. Rite Aid Corp., which became one of the nation's largest drug retailers through acquisitions, diversified into toy retailing by purchasing Circus World Stores, Inc., in August 1982, and it planned to use Circus World's real estate and hard goods background to expand into yet another retailing area. In mid-1985, however, Rite Aid agreed to sell Circus World to concentrate on its core businesses. Meanwhile, Jack Eckerd Corp.'s $83 million acquisition of American Home & Video Stores was a long-time headache, forcing divestituture in 1985; Jack Eckerd itself went private in a leveraged buy-out the following year.

Horizontal Buyers

Horizontal buyers, who purchase retail businesses for their basic lease and other asset values, have been the most active acquirers of other retailers in the 1980s, accounting for more than 50 percent of all retail deals. There have been major horizontal acquisitions of women's and men's specialty stores, discounters, catalog showrooms, supermarkets, drug stores and pharmacies, auto stores, and even department stores.

Petrie Stores Corp., a women's specialty chain, has been an especially active buyer and has concentrated its external expansion program in its basic segment by acquiring seven women's specialty store concerns between 1979 and 1984, taking a 53 percent stake in Winkelman Stores, Inc., and acquiring Miller-Wohl for $270 million in 1984. But Petrie also made a stab at future diversification by purchasing 25 percent of the Toys "R" Us, Inc., chain.

But the largest horizontal deals of the 1980s have been in the supermarket field, notably the Kroger Co.-Dillon Cos. merger, worth $607 million, in 1983 and the American Stores Co. acquisition of Jewel Cos. for more than a billion dollars the following year. Best Products Co., the largest catalog merchandiser, has spurred part of its growth through acquisitions, including the purchase of Modern Merchandising, Inc., for $150 million in September 1982. Service Merchandise Co. executed another major consolidation in catalog merchandising by acquiring H. J. Wilson Co. for $173.5 million in 1985.

Horizontal acquisitions, in reality, are asset transactions. They may be categorized as real estate transactions because the buyer acquires extremely valuable, low-rental leasehold interests along with their capital improvements, and, at times, inventory and other assets that have been significantly marked down. These "real estate"-type purchases are linked to a slowdown in shopping center construction that is expected to continue into the near future. As of December 31, 1984, there were 24,600 shopping centers, an increase of 2.5 percent from a year earlier. This is down sharply from the annual compounded construction growth rate of 5.8 percent for the 10 years ended in 1980.

Because of the slowdown in shopping center construction, the high cost of building of new centers, and the consequential high costs to the retailer for leases, the pattern of recycling real estate through acquisitions has emerged and is expected to continue for the foreseeable future. The use of asset values in valuing this type of transaction is important. Many specialty retailers find it more advantageous to acquire a smaller chain for its recycled real estate value than to open a unit in the same shopping center at a higher lease term, or even to open in a newly developed shopping center where high rentals may not be cost-effective. When a chain is acquired on a real estate basis, a buyer considers not only the cost of the lease, but the use clause, the volume on a store-by-store basis, and whether the buyer wants to be in a particular market or shopping center. The buyer then determines the feasibility of the acquisition by estimating the volume the acquired units can do under its method of operation, management, and merchandising.

Vertical Buyers

Vertical buyers seek either forward or backward integration. In recent years, vertical acquisitions in the retailing industry have not been significant, most being made by manufacturers to obtain retail outlets for their products. Two examples include the acquisition of Frigitronics, Inc., a major optical manufacturer, of House of Vision, Inc., an optical retailer; and the entry of Suave Shoe, a manufacturer, into shoe retailing through the purchase of Bari of Florida, Inc., The Limited, Inc., acquisition of Mast Industries, Inc., a clothing manufacturer, in the 1970s was a prime example of a retailer vertically integrating backward to ensure a source of supply.

LBOs and Private Transactions

The leveraged buy-out (LBO), venture capital investments, and private buyer purchases have been used fairly extensively as acquisition mechanisms. LBOs of retailers picked up in tempo in 1983 and 1984, with major deals including the buy-outs of Malone & Hyde and Cole National, but retailers were targets as early as 1981 when a Kohlberg, Kravis, Roberts group bought Fred Meyer, Inc., for $425 million. The LBO also has been a popular device for diversified companies to divest retailing properties that no longer fit their strategies. For example, Household International divested its retailing operations in a $700 million LBO in 1985.

It is interesting that many of the initial retailer LBOs were at prices that approximated or fell below book value, but as retailers increasingly became regarded as sizable cash flow generators, the prices rose significantly.

In 1981, AEA Investors ventured into the retail field with its buy-out of Loehmanns (later resold to Associated Department Stores), and in 1982 AEA acquired Shoe Town (which later went public). Unlike transactions in many other industries, the success of a retail merger is uniquely dependent on a talented management. Therefore, to ensure management continuity, management participation in the surviving company is requisite to its success. Because the initial LBOs of retail ventures have proven generally successful, others have followed this format. In the buy-out of Brooks Fashion Stores by Dylex, Ltd., the consideration was 4.1 times book value. Cole National was bought out by a Kohlberg, Kravis, Roberts & Co. group at 3.2 times book. In late 1984 and early

1985, the premium paid in a retail leveraged buy-out averaged two to three times book value.

Foreign Investors

Foreign investment, particularly by Europeans, has found its way into U.S. retailing with the stability of the American economy and political system serving as an attraction. B.A.T. Industries of Great Britain has purchased the Marshall Field department store chain; Imasco of Canada bought the Hardee's fast food network and Peoples Drug Stores; Anhold NV of the Netherlands acquired Giant Food, Inc., and Generale Occidentale of France owns the Grand Union supermarket chain. Vendex International, a Dutch retailer, has opted for partial acquisitions with interests in Dillard Department Stores, H. J. Wilson Co. (before its sale to Service Merchandise), and Mr. Goodbuys.

M&A ACTIVITY BY KEY SEGMENTS

Department Store Trends

Department store chains have pursued varied acquisition programs, some using them to diversify, others, such as R. H. Macy & Co., preferring to stay with standard-type chains. However, Macy itself was planning a going-private LBO. Federated Department Stores, Inc., the most active buyer among the major chains, not only has added department stores in new markets but has brought food and specialty retailing into its portfolio. Acquisitions also took Dayton-Hudson Co. into value-priced apparel (Mervyn's), Associated Dry Goods Corp. into discounting (Caldor) and off-price apparel (Loehmann's), May Department Stores into footwear (Volume Shoe), and Allied Stores Co. into specialty retailing (Garfinkel, Brooks Brothers, Miller & Rhodes). However, Carter Hawley Hale has concentrated on standard department store chains (John Wanamaker in Philadelphia; Thalhimer Brothers in Richmond, Va.).

K-Mart Corp., traditionally cautious on both acquisitions and diversifications outside its mainstream discount store business, broke the pattern in mid-1984. The deal, acquisition of the Walden book chain from Carter Hawley Hale, took an outlay of $295 million. K-Mart moved further afield in 1985 by acquiring Pay Less Drug Stores Northwest for $487.6 million. Before that, K-Mart had probed the acquisition field with purchases of restaurant firms in the early 1980s and an insurer in the 1970s.

But the boldest diversification has been staged by Sears, Roebuck & Co., which chose the financial services field for its biggest acquisitions. The program netted the Dean Witter Reynolds investment banking house and the Coldwell, Banker & Co. real estate organization in 1981, with smaller acquisitions of real estate brokerages supplementing the big deals. Joining the two major acquired operations with its Allstate Insurance Co., Sears has been aggressively opening a network of financial centers across the country to offer a full range of financial services. Sears, if successful, could be setting a pattern for other major retailers, especially as the financial services industry continues to be deregulated.

Off-Price Retailing

The explosion of off-price retailing not only has been one of the most significant trends in the retailing industry but has generated major implications for M&A activity. Once the ugly duckling of retailing, off-pricers—who buy brand-name close-outs, irregulars, and other hard-to-sell items at low prices and pass the savings on to buyers—have become among the most coveted acquisition targets in the retail field. As noted earlier, such giants as Melville Corp., Dayton-Hudson, U.S. Shoe, and Associated Dry Goods, in addition to F. W. Woolworth, Zayre Corp. and K-Mart, have substantial operations in the off-price field, mostly through acquisition.

M&A implications of the off-price expansion are twofold. One concerns the impact on the competition, with industry analysts noting that middle-range, middle-priced specialty stores—squeezed between the large department stores and the off-pricers—have been the most adversely affected. Depending on the buyer's perspective, many of these specialty units could become either bargain-priced acquisitions or properties to be shunned in the future. Although off-pricers have sufficient room for growth and should continue to provide numerous targets for larger acquirers, the second issue rides on fears that off-pricing will become oversaturated. The prevailing industry view is that saturation may well pervade the field in the late 1980s, touching off a shake-out similar to the one that hit the discounting segment in the 1970s. The larger and more profitable firms should survive, but the less profitable won't fare as well. This suggests that acquisition opportunities will continue in both classifications of the market.

Do-It-Yourself Retailing

The pricing of a retail company's stock is largely dependent on the company's growth outlook. Though management capabilities in both merchandising and operations are critical to long-term success, the market places a premium on new retail concepts that display a high growth potential. Even as the market rewards companies in new areas of retailing with significant premiums, it waits with baited breath for the least sign of failure, defined in many cases as growing at less than projected rates, and quickly metes out appropriate price/earnings (P/E) punishment.

The do-it-yourself (DIY) segment of specialty retailing is an excellent example of the life cycle of multiples in a new "high-growth" retail concept. The acknowledged leader and innovator in the DIY industry is The Home Depot. The company pioneered the concept of a large, well-stocked warehouse store that overwhelms the consumer with its breadth and depth of merchandise. The Home Depot made its initial public offering on September 21, 1981, at a P/E in excess of 50 times trailing 12 months' earnings and eventually commanded a P/E approaching 55. Wall Street's initial strong endorsement of The Home Depot reflected enthusiasm for the company, and for the DIY market in general.

The DIY industry has shown itself to be high-growth, resilient, and, in fact, expansionary in the face of a recessionary market. Total sales of hardware, building materials, lumber, and related products were $74 billion in 1985. Forecasts call for 1990 sales of $115.7 billion, a 140 percent increase over

1983 revenues. Studies predict that this business will outpace retailing in general through the 1990s.

Given the lofty multiple placed on businesses in this industry in conjunction with the inherent real opportunities presented to DIY retailers for continued growth throughout the 1990s, the inevitable onslaught of competition began. Once competition for market dominance occurs, Wall Street begins its process by lying in wait for the slightest hint of trouble with the industry leader. The Street was not disappointed. In the summer of 1984, The Home Depot announced increased second-quarter earnings, but not as large as analysts had expected. Within days, the company's stock fell by more than 40 percent, and its P/E contracted to around 26 to 28. Moreover, the entire industry was experiencing a shake-out by 1986, with only the strongest and most specialized likely to survive.

This pattern of reward and failure has been played out innumerable times within retailing. Prior to the DIY episode, it was the off-price phenomenon: and prior to that, discounters. By late 1984, DIY stocks in general had P/Es of between 10 and 15. The Home Depot still commanded a premium P/E, as did competitors such as Hechinger. In general, however, P/Es of DIY companies moved toward more traditional retailing P/E values, in the range of 8 to 12 times trailing 12 months' earnings. These multiples should remain the norm until the next innovative retailer catches Wall Street's fancy.

POSTACQUISITION TIPS FOR THE RETAIL FIELD

Aside from the "chemistry" between acquiring and target management, what makes for postacquisition success in retailing? Retailing companies that have made successful acquisitions have provided management of the acquired company with the ability to continue operating the retailing entity in the same manner as it was operated prior to the deal. Only the primary controls a large corporation needs in blending divisions into an entire entity were supplied.

The successful acquirer operates its acquired subsidiaries or divisions on an autonomous or quasi-autonomous basis. The parent company sets basic criteria and determines the capital budgets and expansion plans of the divisions, but it leaves the basic functions to the division manager. Many parent companies have operating boards on which divisional chief executives serve. These boards meet on a regular basis, usually monthly, to review the operations of both the divisions and the company as a whole.

Melville Corp., cited earlier as being among the most profitable retailers, exemplifies the system of blending divisional autonomy with oversight controls at the parent level. Melville's corporate house consists of 11 divisions or subsidiaries, all which are invested with the autonomy to operate in their specific markets. The headquarters, located in Westchester County near New York City, consists of the president, chairman, and about 40 other people who handle legal, financial, auditing, and real estate matters. Thus, the key decision making occurs at the divisional headquarters, while the lean headquarters staff provides the overview and the specialized services that support the division managers.

Chapter 46

Banking: Barriers to Expansion Crumble

Thomas L. Chrystie

Adviser on Strategy, Merrill Lynch & Co.,
New York, New York

The financial services industry is in a state of future shock. On every front—retail, wholesale, corporate, consumer, local, national—financial services are being redefined and conducted amid rapidly changing conditions.

Propelling the changes are fundamental economic forces. The cumulative toll of a 15-year period of high interest rates and unpredictable inflation trends had a profound effect on both users and providers of capital. As a consequence, banks and thrift institutions are being called upon to act as advisers, agents, underwriters, and providers of funds in a manner, and to an extent, that are unprecedented.

Since the mid-1970s, there have been occasional, important adjustments in the relationship between government and the providers of financial services. They have taken the form of rulings, fiats, and legislative initiatives, and they have had a common element: they lagged behind market changes. If this statement requires verification, one need only note that even as federal law technically places strong limits on interstate banking, New York-based Citicorp maintains 800 offices in more than 40 states, and San Francisco-based BankAmerica employs hundreds of people in Citicorp's backyard.

Economic forces, reflected in market conditions, have driven and will continue to drive change. Regulators and legislators will continue to play the role of rationalizing rather than authoring meaningful change. Even the concern generated by the plight of Continental Illinois Bank in 1984 has not slowed the loosening of restrictions on bank and thrift managements. Continental's turbulent decline will not have sufficient impact to retard the transformation of the financial industry that was well underway by the mid-1980s.

Thus, the managing executives of any depository institution who wait for a complete new regulatory framework to replace the old will be as successful in managing their institution as a driver heading down a freeway staring into the rear-view mirror.

Forward-looking planning is imperative.

This is not to say that the evolving regulatory framework has no relevance. Of course it has, especially in setting the rules for who may gain entry to which areas of financial services. But government regulations often control how, not whether, actions can be taken. Where de novo expansion of institutional capability is precluded, a far-seeing and imaginative management can diversify, proceed along strategically desirable lines, and gain its objectives through a skillfully implemented mergers and acquisitions program.

CONSOLIDATION OF THE FINANCIAL SERVICES INDUSTRY

The evolution of the financial services industry is likely to include a healthy furtherance of the consolidation process. The dollar volume of prices paid in major bank acquisitions rose from $2.4 billion in 1981 to $3.7 billion in 1982, $4.7 billion in 1983, $5.85 billion in 1984, and $7.1 billion in 1985. Another sign of structural change has been the declining number of thrift institutions and the increase in their average size. In the two decades after 1960, the number of savings and loans (S&Ls) and mutual savings banks fell from 6,800 to just over 5,000, while average total assets in the surviving institutions more than doubled to $500 million. Over this same period, the number of commercial banks actually increased—to 15,100 from 13,484, according to the Federal Deposit Insurance Corp.—but the growth has been remarkably slow considering the economic expansion over this span, and in more recent years the number has started to contract.

Technology, competition, and the erosion of interstate barriers to expansion should generate pressure for further consolidation in the future. Although no one can foretell the precise conformations of the financial services industry in 1990, consolidation is taking shape along these discernible lines:

Mergers of "equals"—The mergers of the mid-to-late 1980s are expected to encompass more "true" combinations of institutions of roughly similar size. This has important implications for the relative valuation of these transactions, because such mergers will likely be characterized by only normal market premiums.

Interstate banking—Reciprocal banking laws, which authorize acquisition of banks in one state by those with headquarters in another, are growing in importance. Larger, well-managed banks will have funding-cost advantages and greater fee-earning opportunities, as well as broader capital bases from which to diversify. With complete nationwide banking pending, there is a powerful force motivating regional managers to gain economies of size. Size, in turn, is expected to contribute to higher equity valuations for large institutions, which can gain earnings-per-share leverage through acquisitions. These acquirers may well attain market average multiples during the latter part of the 1980s.

Larger institutions—The merger process, staged in three acts (statewide, regional, and nationwide), will create many larger financial services institutions. Should disinflationary forces characterize the financial environment of the late 1980s, a key to superior performance in financial services could be the ability to generate strong growth in high-quality assets. Those institutions best positioned to excel would likely be large commercial banks with broad domestic and international market penetration, functional diversification, and the ability to engage in nontraditional activities. Asset generation—if it becomes a major theme during the late 1980s—could provide further rationale for extending the merger movement among financial institutions to create larger, more functionally and geographically balanced companies to achieve this objective.

National organization—The merger movement is expected to gain geographic as well as functional diversification. Although there inevitably will be institutions that operate profitably in traditional geographic or product niches, the ultimate reconfiguration of the financial system will likely create 25 to 35 national companies with multiple functions and technologically based systems. Once the full rationalization of the financial system takes place, surviving equity securities could equal or exceed average equity market price/earnings multiples in the late 1980s.

Given these environmental and market trends, the management of a bank must consider the types of healthy, viable institutions that could evolve in the late 1980s. The structure could include the following:

- There could be a handful of world-class financial firms—all large and global in reach but each with unique characteristics and strengths. These will provide most forms of financial services and will do so on a global basis.
- Other diversified firms will exist, but these will be limited geographically to country or region.
- Most other depository institutions will be forced to decide exactly what they are going to do, how they will specialize, and where they will compete. Their chances for prospering will improve as they become expert in a regional industry or specialty market and focus on narrowly defined functions that they can perform in superior fashion.
- A number of smaller financial firms, limited in geographic reach but blessed with a superior knowledge of local customers, also will have places in the future business landscape. Such firms can find niches in the industry. Whether they assume and exploit these niches, of course, depends on the soundness of their strategic plans and the abilities of their senior mangements.

The need, clearly, is for a strategy that calls for explicit choice—to build the type of institution that allows the shareholders and management to have competitive advantages (and to be able to minimize disadvantages). Recognizing the categories and finding the suitable one in which to compete are prerequisite to successful planning.

STRATEGIC ELEMENTS IN BANK ACQUISITIONS

For shareholders of depository institutions, the consolidation of the industry offers opportunities for significant capital gains. As interstate barriers to acquisition fall, it is conceivable that a single group of shareholders might see its stock acquired three times—first in a statewide merger, next in a regional acquisition, and finally in a nationwide takeover. However consolidation proceeds, and at whatever pace, shareholders stand a chance to take advantage of the expected competition for territory and takeover targets.

Determination to sell a financial institution entails consideration of a host of known and unknown factors.

The known (or perhaps, "knowable") factors include the institution's historical performance, its past stock-trading activity, the acquisition circumstances of comparable companies, and the comparable vital signs of similar depository institutions. A thorough analysis of these factors, undertaken by experienced investment bankers and other experts, should provide the foundation for any contemplated merger or acquisition.

Also among the knowable factors are the reasons that one depository institution buys another. Tactical and strategic advantages offered by acquisition include diversification of loan portfolios, access to more favorably priced funds that are available to larger institutions, and expansion of geographic reach.

When Midlantic Banks, Inc., announced in late 1984 that it had agreed to acquire Heritage Bancorp, New Jersey's sixth-largest bank holding company, Midlantic emphasized the complementary geographic reach of the newly created institution. "It's a unique fit," a spokesman said. "They have 95 branches, mostly in the southern part of the state, and we have 184, mostly in the north. We've overlaid this on the maps, and it fits us like a glove." The deal was completed in the spring of 1985 at a price of $202.4 million.

Other important inducements are the recruitment of new management expertise, penetration of important new markets, and exploitation of economies of scale. The bottom line, of course, should be enhancement of earnings.

Crossing Industry Segments

Although the reasons for purchasing a bank or thrift are knowable, the exact dimensions of the universe of potential buyers change with the regulatory tides. During 1983 the regulators' concerns for rescuing ailing banks and thrifts was expressed in liberal rulings on who might buy a depository institution. Such decisions broadened the camp of prospective buyers and enhanced the value of prospective targets.

The Federal Deposit Insurance Corp. (FDIC) provided a major potential outlet for nonfinancial companies to get into the market when it allowed Yankee Oil & Gas Co. to acquire Home Savings Bank, a financially troubled, federally chartered institution in Boston. This was the first time the FDIC had approved the acquisition of a thrift institution by a nonfinancial concern. It was followed by National Intergroup's purchase of an S&L and several similar transactions.

More significant for the valuation of thrift institutions is the possibility that an ailing S&L might be acquired by an out-of-state commercial bank. Within recent years Citicorp has laid the foundation for a nationwide branch system by purchasing troubled or failed thrifts in Florida and California. Once situated in these states, the giant bank holding company can purchase healthy institutions, merging them into its existing facilities. This was made possible by the Federal Home Loan Bank Board's policy of allowing an out-of-state institution with presence in a state as a result of a supervisory acquisition to expand as if it were an in-state institution.

Across State Lines

On another front, some larger institutions have acquired "stake-outs" in smaller institutions that they are barred by present law from controlling.

The "stake-outs" usually are 4.9 percent equity investments, though they may be nonvoting preferred, warrants, or convertible securities. Such investments give commercial banks footholds in similar banks in other states (that currently do not have reciprocal banking laws) or in thrift institutions. They establish the potential buyer's interest in the target and lay the groundwork for a merger when laws and regulations permit.

In 1983, for example, the Oregon bank holding company, U.S. Bancorp, proposed to purchase 4.9 percent of the outstanding voting shares of Old National Bankcorporation (ONBC) in the neighboring state of Washington. U.S. Bancorp's proposed investment was reviewed by the Federal Reserve Board, which acknowledged and tacitly approved of the underlying rationale—namely, that "U.S. Bancorp and ONBC have agreed to merge in the event that interstate banking becomes permissible." An allowable variation was the Bank of New York's proposal (also approved by the Fed in 1983) to acquire the shares of Northwest Bancorp of Stamford, Conn., "when legally permissible." The acquisition was set at a formula price, with a floor of approximately 1.85 times book value of Northeast Bancorp. In the meantime, the Bank of New York purchased 625,000 *warrants* convertible into 16.5 percent of Northwest Bancorp's outstanding voting stock.

As noted earlier, the legislative and regulatory tides react to the gravity of market forces, and a strategy must be implemented when the time is right. Legislation pending in Congress could affect the full range of interstate and cross-industry mergers and should be taken into account in the valuation of an institution by seller or buyer. In the meantime, however, inroads have been made on a regional basis, and cross-state transactions on a regional basis got a big boost from a 1985 U.S. Supreme Court decision that approved the concept of regional banking. The court's ruling approved reciprocal arrangements that allow a bank in one state to acquire a bank in another state if the laws of the two states permit acquisitions by out-of-state institutions. Statutes granting such reciprocity have been common in New England and the Southeast, and the Supreme Court decision paved the way for completion of several deals, including CBT Corp. (Connecticut) and Bank of New England (Massachusetts), Sun Banks (Florida) and Trust Co. of Georgia, and Wachovia Corp. (North Carolina) and First National of Atlanta (Georgia).

The clarification of the legality of the regionalized-reciprocal state merger process or the establishment of an appropriate legal format under which interstate mergers can take place is an important near-term variable affecting M&As in the financial services industry.

There is, to reiterate, no such thing as a viable *inactive* strategy. Waiting until options have been exhausted may permit competitor institutions to seize initiatives on behalf of *their* shareholders. In the environment of the 1980s, sitting tight and carrying on business as usual can invite trouble. The stand-patter risks an unfriendly takeover or the possibility of being a wallflower when pairing up is essential for survival.

EMERGENCE OF THE UNSOLICITED OFFER

One of the most conspicuous developments in the current bank M&A environment is the increased use of the publicly announced but unsolicited acquisition offer. A surprise, publicly announced intention to acquire can impose stiff demands on a target institution's directors. If they have no strategy in place, the directors can be severely strained by the clashing responsibilities to shareholders and management. Their dilemma is compounded if the offer incorporates a meaningful premium and no viable alternatives to selling out have been prepared.

In approaching the most attractive opportunities, prospective acquirers are adopting aggressive tactics, and there are strong indications that the number and frequency of unsolicited offers will rise. Acquiring a significant minority ownership in a financial institution or announcing a meaningful acquisition offer and pressuring the target's directors to capitulate by a certain date are tactics that will probably be repeated . . . and with success.

Defensive Maneuvering

Any likely target institution can, if it chooses, take steps to thwart takeover. Naturally, its management should publicize this feature of its strategy, openly identifying itself with its geographic and business markets and announcing its intention to remain independent.

Adopting a Strategy. Key members of management, the board of directors, and investment bankers expert in repelling unilateral offers should work together on a strategy. The bankers analyze the institution's vulnerability, prepare a comprehensive valuation study, identify potential "white knights," and provide ongoing counsel. The defense team should include lawyers skilled in responding to tender offers in the financial industry and public relations experts who can encourage shareholder loyalty and improve an institution's image within the investment community.

Shark Repellents. Corporate charters and by-laws can be amended to make acquisition difficult. In the financial area, these amendments must be in keeping with statutory and regulatory rules governing bank and thrift institutions, and they must be designed to satisfy the interests of the institution's shareholders.

"Shark repellents" that banks can use include a "supermajority clause" (requiring much more than a simple majority of outstanding shares to approve mergers), a "blank-check preferred" stock that could be issued to a friendly party, staggered terms for directors, and a requirement that the bidder's offering price match the highest price it has previously paid for shares. Other defensive tactics can include repurchase of stock, securing a line of credit for a counteroffer, and increasing dividends to strengthen shareholder loyalty.

Considering a Good Offer. But caution: If not already in place when a takeover offer has been made, such antitakeover tactics often are precluded.

Our discussion of resisting a takeover raises a central ethical question: At what point does a vigorous defensive strategy begin to violate management's fiduciary obligation to the shareholder? Regrettably, in some strategic plans—including some designed for an active defense against hostile acquisition—the shareholder is the neglected party.

This need not be the case. If takeover propositions are fairly and thoroughly examined by the full membership of the board of directors, the chances for misguided obsession with defense decline.

Furthermore, if every important strategy is examined in the light of this standard—"Does it serve the long-term interests of employees, customers, community, and shareholders?"—then a depository institution's management and board are likely to proceed in a reasonable manner.

IMPLEMENTING THE ACQUISITION STRATEGY

Once the senior executives of a bank or thrift accept the need for a corporate strategy, they will have to articulate their objectives and define who they are and where they want to go. They will have to iron out such problems as what share of precisely what market they wish to serve and how. And they should plan for what their competitors are capable of doing (and not become preoccupied with their competitors' stated intentions).

In sum, the successful depository institution of the late 1980s and beyond will be moving forward, guided by viable corporate strategy. Proposals that do not fit the strategy can be rejected with confidence. An acquisition or merger should be looked upon as a means to effect—and perhaps accelerate—the realization of the institution's long-term strategy.

Some final advice? Decide what you want to do—and have fun doing it well!

INTERMAC

Joe B. Leonard

International Association of Merger and Acquisition
Consultants, Dallas, Texas

The International Association of Merger and Acquisition Consultants (INTER-MAC) serves as a medium of exchange of information on merger and acquisition prospects and offers a wide variety of specialized services to professionals involved in buying, selling, or merging medium-sized businesses on a confidential basis. INTERMAC is the only independent, worldwide body of full-time professional merger and acquisition specialists who represent businesses in the $2- to $50-million sales range.

The association was founded in 1973 by seven M&A consultants and originally was named the National Association of Merger and Acquisition Consultants (NAMAC). The name was changed in March 1982 to International Association of Merger and Acquisition Consultants (INTERMAC), as membership and activities grew worldwide in scope. Approximately 50 member firms serve clients in principal cities in the United States, Europe, and South America.

M&A services provided by INTERMAC members include:

- Purchase or sale of private companies, including the critical "once in a lifetime" sale of the entrepreneur's family business

- Purchase or sale of product lines
- Divestitures of divisions or subsidiaries of diversified companies
- Acquisition search projects on behalf of national and international companies, under the regimen of highly disciplined requirements and confidentiality
- Arranging for financing packages

Principals in INTERMAC member firms have broad experience in retailing, manufacturing, aerospace, insurance, banking, broadcasting, publishing, and many other commercial and industrial fields in addition to M&A experience. All INTERMAC member firms adhere to these membership policies:

- A member firm shall exercise independent professional judgment on behalf of its clients and shall act only in their best interests.
- A member firm shall protect and preserve the confidences and secrets of its clients and will disclose them to others only with the prior consent of the client.
- Member firms subscribe to, and operate under, a code of ethics of the highest professional standards.
- INTERMAC members do not practice law or accounting but are available for consultation with the client's accountant and/or attorney in concluding agreements.
- Fees are normally contingent upon the successful completion of a transaction and are based on a percentage of the total consideration paid. Member firms that cooperate in introducing a buyer and seller are compensated by either the buyer or the seller.
- Fees may include retainers or may be based on a per-diem or hourly rate.
- Member firms must maintain a reputation of satisfactory client relationship.

INTERMAC's world headquarters in Dallas, Texas, provides key administrative functions for all members. Initial inquiries are directed to headquarters and then answered and/or referred to member firms as requirements dictate. World headquarters maintains a communications center, record center, data base, and library, and operates a computer center that stores information accessed worldwide by member firms through computer terminals.

INTERMAC membership is by invitation only. Admission is granted after a thorough investigation of qualifications, experience, and local reputation, and a personal interview by a principal of an incumbent member firm. After the initial approval, a candidate enjoys all advantages of membership on a conditional basis. Permanent membership is granted after the firm has served a minimum of six months, attended one semiannual meeting, and had its application formally approved by the board of directors. Initiation fees are $1,000 for firms in markets with more than 1 million population, and $700 for those in markets of less than 1 million population. Annual dues and assessments are $1,560. Some transactions are subject to referral and cooperation fees, which are used to support the central organization.

Individuals or firms interested in INTERMAC membership should write or call world headquarters. Some markets are limited to one member firm and are currently filled, but all inquiries will be welcomed. World headquarters are located at 9575 West Higgins Road, Rosemont, Illinois 60018. The telephone number is (312) 696—4330.

Association for Corporate Growth

William St. John

Executive Director, Association for Corporate Growth,
Glenview, Illinois

Founded in 1954 by a group of growth-oriented executives, the Association for Corporate Growth (ACG) provides a forum for ideas relating to both external and internal growth, including acquisitions and divestitures, joint ventures, and new or expanded products and services. The basic mission of the ACG is to foster sound corporate growth that is exemplified by high quality, rising earnings, and increasing value of a company.

Members are provided the opportunity to:

- Gain new ideas from speakers, seminars, and discussions with people working in the corporate growth field
- Develop additional skills and techniques in the corporate growth field to the benefit of their respective organizations
- Become acquainted with other corporate growth professionals who can help with professional counsel and contacts

Membership includes representatives of firms manufacturing a wide range of consumer and industrial products and firms supplying services closely related to the planning and growth of industrial companies. As a professional society, membership in the Association for Corporate Growth is granted on an individual basis only. There are no company memberships. The ACG's membership consists of 2,500 individuals representing 1,600 companies. Approximately two-thirds of the membership is drawn from the industrial and consumer products field and the balance from accounting firms, banks, investment houses, appraisers, consulting firms, financial intermediaries, and related service businesses.

Headquartered in Chicago, the ACG has 18 chapters within the continental United States. Chapters operate in Arizona, Atlanta, Boston, Chicago, Cleveland, Dallas/Fort Worth, Denver, Detroit, Houston, Los Angeles, Maryland, Minnesota, New York, Orange County, Philadelphia, San Diego, San Francisco, and Southern Florida. Foreign chapters exist in Calgary, Toronto, and London. Interested individuals who do not reside or work near an existing chapter location may join the association as members-at-large. Each chapter holds monthly meetings featuring guest speakers from the business world's most prestigious and successful organizations. ACG chapters continually emphasize the importance of growth, and award local companies for excellence in growth— both large companies and emerging companies that have shown outstanding growth records.

Intergrowth. Intergrowth is the registered name of the association's annual conference of its members. The conference is designed to provide an interchange of ideas between the members, and features speakers and programs on corporate growth and diversification.

Journal of Corporate Growth. The journal is a semiannual professional journal consisting of outstanding transcribed speeches from various meetings of ACG chapters. Each speech that appears in the journal has been screened by an editorial review board and relates to the implementation of corporate growth chiefly through mergers and acquisitions.

Growth Awards. Each year the ACG presents two awards to member organizations that exhibit outstanding growth records. The Peter Hilton Award is a tribute to the ACG's founder and first president. This award is for companies with annual sales of $250 million or more and is presented to a company that has demonstrated outstanding growth during the five years prior to the award date. The Emerging Company Award is presented to a company with annual sales of less than $250 million that has shown outstanding growth for at least three years.

Other activities include:

- Conferences and seminars for members
- Reports to members on new techniques of corporate acquisitions, new accounting practices and techniques for valuation and appraisal, new product screening and introduction, and current practices and experiences in international business development
- Liaison with other professional and trade associations that are developing information of interest to the members of the organization

- Advisory services to universities and other educational institutions seeking to develop courses of instruction on long-range planning for corporate growth
- Publication of reports of speakers contingent upon their approval

Criteria for Membership. Applications for membership in ACG are evaluated and processed by the individual chapters. Because each chapter offers various levels of activities, criteria for membership and annual dues vary among chapters. Information on specific programs and annual dues may be obtained from the chapter in your area. By joining a chapter of ACG, members automatically become members of ACG International.

Corporate growth professionals who are interested in joining the ACG should contact International Headquarters in Chicago or the nearest chapter for membership information. ACG headquarters are located at 1800 Pickwick Avenue, Glenview, Illinois 60025. The telephone number is (312) 724-2622.

North American Society for Corporate Planning

The membership of the North American Society for Corporate Planning is composed of business executives with strategic and corporate planning responsibilities. The objective of the organization is to provide a forum for exchange of experiences and ideas on planning among people in corporations, government, and academia throughout North America. Twenty-four chapters in major metropolitan areas in the United States and Canada offer regular meetings with speakers, study groups, and networking activities. Membership services include *Planning Review*, the society's bimonthly journal; *The Planner*, a newsletter; an annual membership directory; taped proceedings of the society's annual conference, and other special publications. The address is P.O. Box 2307, Dayton, Ohio 45401. The telephone number is (513) 223-4948.

Index

About the Author

Milton L. Rock, Ph.D., is publisher of *Mergers & Acquisitions* magazine, the authoritative journal of the mergers and acquisitions profession. He is the former chief executive of the Hay Group, a worldwide management consulting firm, and is chairman of Saatchi & Saatchi Consulting (UK) Ltd. Dr. Rock holds a master's degree from Temple University and a Ph.D. in psychology from the University of Rochester. He has written extensively for both professional and business publications and is also the editor of *The Handbook of Wage and Salary Administration*, published by McGraw-Hill.